Java™ Servlet and
JSP™ Cookbook™

Other Java™ resources from O'Reilly

Related titles
Enterprise JavaBeans™
Java™ & XML
Java™ Cookbook
Java™ Enterprise in a Nutshell
Java™ I/O
Java™ in a Nutshell
Java™ Performance Tuning

Java™ Programming with
   Oracle SQLJ
Java™ Security
JavaServer™ Pages
Java™ Swing
Learning Java™

Java Books Resource Center
java.oreilly.com is a complete catalog of O'Reilly's books on Java and related technologies, including sample chapters and code examples.

OnJava.com is a one-stop resource for enterprise Java developers, featuring news, code recipes, interviews, weblogs, and more.

Conferences
O'Reilly & Associates brings diverse innovators together to nurture the ideas that spark revolutionary industries. We specialize in documenting the latest tools and systems, translating the innovator's knowledge into useful skills for those in the trenches. Visit *conferences.oreilly.com* for our upcoming events.

Safari Bookshelf (*safari.oreilly.com*) is the premier online reference library for programmers and IT professionals. Conduct searches across more than 1,000 books. Subscribers can zero in on answers to time-critical questions in a matter of seconds. Read the books on your Bookshelf from cover to cover or simply flip to the page you need. Try it today with a free trial.

Java™ Servlet and JSP™ Cookbook™

Bruce W. Perry

O'REILLY®

Beijing · Cambridge · Farnham · Köln · Paris · Sebastopol · Taipei · Tokyo

Java™ Servlet and JSP™ Cookbook™
by Bruce W. Perry

Published by O'Reilly Media, Inc., 1005 Gravenstein Highway North, Sebastopol, CA 95472.

O'Reilly Media, Inc. books may be purchased for educational, business, or sales promotional use. Online editions are also available for most titles (*safari.oreilly.com*). For more information contact our corporate/institutional sales department: (800) 998-9938 or *corporate@oreilly.com*.

Editor:	Brett McLaughlin
Production Editor:	Philip Dangler
Cover Designer:	Emma Colby
Interior Designer:	Melanie Wang

Printing History:

January 2004:	First Edition.

RepKover™ This book uses RepKover™, a durable and flexible lay-flat binding.

ISBN: 0-596-00572-5
[M]   [11/04]

Table of Contents

Preface . . . . **xiii**

1. Writing Servlets and JSPs **1**

    1.1 Writing a Servlet   1

    1.2 Writing a JSP   7

    1.3 Compiling a Servlet   10

    1.4 Packaging Servlets and JSPs   11

    1.5 Creating the Deployment Descriptor   14

2. Deploying Servlets and JSPs **17**

    2.1 Deploying an Individual Servlet on Tomcat   17

    2.2 Using a Context Element in Tomcat's server.xml   22

    2.3 Deploying an Individual Servlet on WebLogic   24

    2.4 Deploying an Individual JSP on Tomcat   29

    2.5 Deploying an Individual JSP on WebLogic   30

    2.6 Deploying a Web Application on Tomcat   31

    2.7 Deploying a Web Application on WebLogic Using Ant   37

    2.8 Using the WebLogic Administration Console   39

    2.9 Using WebLogic Builder to Deploy a Web Application   43

    2.10 Using the weblogic.Deployer Command-Line Tool   46

3. Naming Your Servlets **49**

    3.1 Mapping a Servlet to a Name in web.xml   50

    3.2 Creating More Than One Mapping to a Servlet   52

    3.3 Creating a JSP-Type URL for a Servlet   54

    3.4 Mapping Static Content to a Servlet   55

    3.5 Invoking a Servlet Without a web.xml Mapping   57

    3.6 Mapping All Requests Within a Web Application to a Servlet   59

    3.7 Mapping Requests to a Controller and Preserving Servlet Mappings   61

    3.8 Creating Welcome Files for a Web Application   65

    3.9 Restricting Requests for Certain Servlets   66

    3.10 Giving Only the Controller Access to Certain Servlets   71

4. Using Apache Ant **74**

    4.1 Obtaining and Setting Up Ant   74

    4.2 Using Ant Targets   76

    4.3 Including Tomcat JAR files in the Build File Classpath   80

    4.4 Compiling a Servlet with an Ant Build File   83

    4.5 Creating a WAR File with Ant   86

    4.6 Creating a JAR File with Ant   89

    4.7 Starting a Tomcat Application with Ant   92

    4.8 Stopping a Tomcat Application with Ant   95

5. Altering the Format of JSPs **98**

    5.1 Precompiling a JSP in Tomcat   99

    5.2 Precompiling a JSP in WebLogic   102

    5.3 Precompiling JSPs with the Precompilation Protocol   104

    5.4 Mapping a JSP to Its Page Implementation Class   105

    5.5 Creating a JSP from Scratch as a JSP Document   106

    5.6 Generating an XML View from a JSP   110

6. Dynamically Including Content in Servlets and JSPs **119**

    6.1 Including a Resource Each Time a Servlet Handles a Request   120

    6.2 Using an External Configuration to Include a Resource in a Servlet   122

    6.3 Including Resources Nested at Multiple Levels in a Servlet   125

    6.4 Including a Resource that Seldom Changes into a JSP   130

    6.5 Including Content in a JSP Each Time the JSP Handles a Request   133

    6.6 Using an External Configuration File to Include a Resource in a JSP   137

    6.7 Including an XML Fragment in a JSP Document   141

    6.8 Including Content from Outside a Context in a JSP   144

7. Handling Web Form Data in Servlets and JSPs **148**

    7.1 Handling a POST HTTP Request in a Servlet   149

    7.2 Handling a POST HTTP Request in a JSP   153

    7.3 Setting the Properties of a JavaBean in a JSP   155

    7.4 Setting a Scoped Attribute in a JSP to the Value of a Form Parameter   158

    7.5 Posting Data from a Servlet   161

    7.6 Posting Data from a JSP   164

7.7	Using a Servlet to Add a Parameter to a Query String	168
7.8	Using a JSP to Add a Parameter to a Query String	170
7.9	Using a Filter to Read Parameter Values	171

8. Uploading Files **174**

8.1	Preparing the HTML Page for File Uploads	175
8.2	Using the com.oreilly.servlet Library	177
8.3	Uploading One File at a Time	178
8.4	Uploading Multiple Files	181
8.5	Renaming Files	185
8.6	Using a JSP to Handle a File Upload	187

9. Handling Exceptions in Web Applications **192**

9.1	Declaring Exception Handlers in web.xml	192
9.2	Creating an Exception-Handling Servlet	196
9.3	Sending an Error from a Servlet	199
9.4	Sending an Error from a JSP	201
9.5	Creating an Error-Handling JSP	202
9.6	Declaring a Special Exception-Handling JSP for Other JSPs	205

10. Reading and Setting Cookies **209**

10.1	Setting a Cookie with a Servlet	211
10.2	Creating an Array from All of the Request's Cookies	214
10.3	Setting a Cookie with a JSP	215
10.4	Reading Cookie Values with a Servlet	220
10.5	Reading Cookie Values with a JSP	222
10.6	Altering or Removing a Cookie That Has Already Been Set	225

11. Session Tracking **227**

11.1	Setting the Session Timeout in web.xml	228
11.2	Setting the Session Timeout in All Tomcat Web Applications	231
11.3	Setting the Session Timeout Programmatically	233
11.4	Checking if a Session Exists in an HttpServletRequest	235
11.5	Tracking Session Activity in Servlets	237
11.6	Tracking Session Activity in JSPs	240
11.7	Using URL Rewriting in a JSP	244
11.8	Using URL Rewriting in a Servlet	247
11.9	Using a Listener to Track the Session Lifecycle	251
11.10	Using a Listener to Monitor Session Attributes	254
11.11	Using a Filter to Monitor Session Attributes	258

12. Integrating JavaScript with Servlets and JSPs **263**

   12.1 Including JavaScript Modules in a Servlet   263

   12.2 Including JavaScript Modules in a JSP   267

   12.3 Creating a New Window with JavaScript in a Servlet   269

   12.4 Creating a New Window with JavaScript in a JSP   272

   12.5 Using JavaScript to Validate Form Values in a Servlet   274

   12.6 Using JavaScript to Validate Form Values in a JSP   277

13. Sending Non-HTML Content **279**

   13.1 Sending a PDF File   280

   13.2 Sending a Word Processing File   284

   13.3 Sending an XML file   286

   13.4 Sending an Audio File   289

   13.5 Viewing Internal Resources in a Servlet   292

14. Logging Messages from Servlets and JSPs **296**

   14.1 Logging Without Log4j   298

   14.2 Setting Up Log4j   300

   14.3 Using a Logger Without a Configuration File   301

   14.4 Adding an Appender to the Root Logger   304

   14.5 Using a Pattern with a Logger's Appender   306

   14.6 Using log4j in a JSP   310

   14.7 Logging Messages Using a Servlet Context Event Listener   316

   14.8 Logging Messages Using a Session Event Listener   320

15. Authenticating Clients **324**

   15.1 Creating Users and Passwords with Tomcat   324

   15.2 Setting Up SSL on Tomcat   325

   15.3 Using BASIC Authentication   328

   15.4 Using Form-Based Authentication   331

   15.5 Logging Out a User   335

   15.6 Using JAAS to Create a LoginModule   337

   15.7 Creating the JAAS Configuration File   344

   15.8 Using JAAS in a Servlet   346

   15.9 Using JAAS in a JSP   349

16. Binding, Accessing, and Removing Attributes in Web Applications **354**

   16.1 Setting ServletContext Attributes in Servlets   354

   16.2 Setting ServletContext Attributes in JSPs   357

   16.3 Accessing or Removing ServletContext Attributes in Servlets   360

16.4   Accessing or Removing ServletContext Attributes in JSPs   362

16.5   Setting Session Attributes in Servlets   364

16.6   Setting Session Attributes in JSPs   366

16.7   Accessing or Removing Session Attributes in Servlets   368

16.8   Accessing or Removing Session Attributes in JSPs   369

16.9   Setting Request Attributes in Servlets   371

16.10   Setting Request Attributes in JSPs   373

16.11   Accessing or Removing Request Attributes in Servlets   375

16.12   Accessing or Removing Request Attributes in JSPs   376

17.   Embedding Multimedia in JSPs **379**

17.1   Embedding an Applet in a JSP Using jsp:plugin   379

17.2   Embedding an Applet in a JSP Using the HTML Converter   382

17.3   Automatically Creating HTML Template for Including Flash Files   386

17.4   Writing HTML Template to Embed a Flash File   388

17.5   Embedding Flash in a Servlet   390

17.6   Embedding a QuickTime Movie in a JSP   392

17.7   Embedding an SVG File in a JSP   394

17.8   Embedding a Background Soundtrack in a JSP   396

18.   Working With the Client Request **398**

18.1   Examining HTTP Request Headers in a Servlet   398

18.2   Examining HTTP Request Headers in a JSP   400

18.3   Using a Filter to Alter Request Headers   402

18.4   Automatically Refreshing a Servlet   405

18.5   Automatically Refreshing a JSP   407

18.6   Counting the Number of Web Application Requests   408

19.   Filtering Requests and Responses **411**

19.1   Mapping a Filter to a Servlet   412

19.2   Mapping a Filter to a JSP   415

19.3   Mapping More Than One Filter to a Servlet   416

19.4   Changing the Order in Which Filters are Applied to Servlets   418

19.5   Configuring Initialization Parameters for a Filter   419

19.6   Optionally Blocking a Request with a Filter   422

19.7   Filtering the HTTP Response   424

19.8   Using Filters with RequestDispatcher Objects   427

19.9   Checking Form Parameters with a Filter   429

19.10   Blocking IP Addresses with a Filter   434

20. Managing Email in Servlets and JSPs **439**

   20.1 Placing the Email-Related Classes on your Classpath   439

   20.2 Sending Email from a Servlet   441

   20.3 Sending Email from a Servlet Using a JavaBean   444

   20.4 Accessing Email from a Servlet   449

   20.5 Accessing Email from a Servlet Using a JavaBean   454

   20.6 Handling Attachments from an Email Received in a Servlet   455

   20.7 Adding Attachments to an Email in a Servlet   461

   20.8 Reading a Received Email's Headers from a Servlet   466

21. Accessing Databases **471**

   21.1 Accessing a Database from a Servlet Without DataSource   472

   21.2 Configuring a DataSource in Tomcat   475

   21.3 Using a DataSource in a Servlet with Tomcat   478

   21.4 Creating a DataSource on WebLogic   481

   21.5 Using a JNDI Lookup to get a DataSource from WebLogic   484

   21.6 Using a DataSource from WebLogic in a JSP   488

   21.7 Calling a Stored Procedure from a Servlet   490

   21.8 Calling a Stored Procedure from a JSP   495

   21.9 Converting a ResultSet to a Result Object   500

   21.10 Executing Several SQL Statements Within a Single Transaction   505

   21.11 Using Transactions with JSPs   511

   21.12 Finding Information about a ResultSet   513

22. Using Custom Tag Libraries **519**

   22.1 Creating a Classic Tag Handler   520

   22.2 Creating a JSP 1.2 TLD for a Classic Tag Handler   524

   22.3 Creating a JSP 2.0 TLD for a Classic Tag Handler   526

   22.4 Packaging a Tag Library in a Web Application   529

   22.5 Packaging the Tag Library in a JAR File   530

   22.6 Using the Custom Tag in a JSP   532

   22.7 Handling Exceptions in a Custom Tag Class   533

   22.8 Creating a Simple Tag Handler   536

   22.9 Creating a TLD for a Simple Tag Handler   539

   22.10 Using a Simple Tag Handler in a JSP   541

   22.11 Creating a JSP Tag File   543

   22.12 Packaging the JSP Tag File in a Web Application   545

   22.13 Packaging the JSP Tag File in a JAR   546

| | 22.14 | Using a Custom Tag Associated with a Tag File | 547 |
| | 22.15 | Adding a Listener Class to a Tag Library | 548 |

23. Using the JSTL 551

	23.1	Downloading the JSTL 1.0 and Using the JSTL Tags in JSPs	552
	23.2	Downloading the Java Web Services Developer Pack	554
	23.3	Using the Core JSTL Tags	555
	23.4	Using the XML Core JSTL Tags	558
	23.5	Using the XML Transform Tags	561
	23.6	Using the Formatting JSTL Tags	564
	23.7	Using A SQL JSTL Tag with a DataSource Configuration	567
	23.8	Using A SQL JSTL Tag Without a DataSource Configuration	570
	23.9	Accessing Scoped Variables with the EL	572
	23.10	Accessing Request Parameters with the EL	574
	23.11	Using the EL to Access Request Headers	576
	23.12	Using the EL to Access One Request Header	577
	23.13	Accessing Cookies with the EL	579
	23.14	Using the EL to Access JavaBean Properties	580
	23.15	Using JSTL Functions	585

24. Internationalization 590

	24.1	Detecting the Client Locale in a Servlet	591
	24.2	Detecting the Client's Locales in a JSP	594
	24.3	Creating a ResourceBundle as a Properties File	596
	24.4	Creating a ResourceBundle as a Java Class	597
	24.5	Using the ResourceBundle in a Servlet	599
	24.6	Using the ResourceBundle in a JSP	602
	24.7	Formatting Dates in a Servlet	603
	24.8	Formatting Dates in a JSP	605
	24.9	Formatting Currencies in a Servlet	607
	24.10	Formatting Currencies in a JSP	609
	24.11	Formatting Percentages in a Servlet	610
	24.12	Formatting Percentages in a JSP	612
	24.13	Setting the Localization Context in the Deployment Descriptor	613

25. Using JNDI and Enterprise JavaBeans 615

	25.1	Configuring a JNDI Object in Tomcat	616
	25.2	Accessing the Tomcat JNDI Resource from a Servlet	619
	25.3	Accessing the Tomcat JNDI Resource from a JSP	625

25.4 Configuring a JNDI Resource in WebLogic   628

25.5 Viewing the JNDI Tree in WebLogic   630

25.6 Accessing the WebLogic JNDI Resource from a Servlet   631

25.7 Accessing the WebLogic JNDI Resource from a JSP   635

25.8 Accessing an EJB Using the WebLogic JNDI Tree   638

26. Harvesting Web Information **647**

26.1 Parsing an HTML Page Using the javax.swing.text Subpackages   648

26.2 Using a Servlet to Harvest Web Data   651

26.3 Creating a JavaBean as a Web Page Parser   656

26.4 Using the Web Page Parsing JavaBean in a Servlet   659

26.5 Using the Web Page Parsing JavaBean in a JSP   661

27. Using the Google and Amazon Web APIs **664**

27.1 Getting Set Up with Google's Web API   666

27.2 Creating a JavaBean to Connect with Google   667

27.3 Using a Servlet to Connect with Google   671

27.4 Using a JSP to Connect with Google   675

27.5 Getting Set Up with Amazon's Web Services API   677

27.6 Creating a JavaBean to Connect with Amazon   679

27.7 Using a Servlet to Connect with Amazon   684

27.8 Using a JSP to Connect with Amazon   688

Index **691**

Preface

On a historical timeline, the saga of Java as a server-side programmer's tool of choice began in early 1997 when Sun Microsystems released the "Java™ Web Server" beta and Java Servlet Developers Kit.* Servlets are a type of Java class that executes on a server. Servlets dynamically handle networked requests and responses, mostly using the Hypertext Transfer Protocol (HTTP). In June 1999, Sun introduced JavaServer Pages (JSPs), which intermingled Java code with JavaScript and HTML template text.

JSPs, as they are now evolving (with JSP Version 2.0), are designed to encapsulate domain logic in standard and custom tags, and separate this domain layer from the JSP component's presentation logic. The latter concept means "the stuff that people see" when they interact with a web application, such as HTML-related screen widgets. Ideally, a JSP uses tags to interact with databases and encapsulate domain rules, and static or dynamically generated template text, such as XML or XHTML, to create the visual page for the user.

During the late 1990s, I was a freelance, backend web developer using a number of different languages. When server-side Java appeared on the scene, I greeted the news with as much relief as joy. Designed from the bottom up as object-oriented and modular, Java represented a reassuring alternative to the ad hoc, ill-designed, albeit well-intentioned masses of web-related code I would often encounter when an organization brought me into the midst of a project.

Not only can you easily create your own reusable components for, say, sending email simply by designing and uploading to your web application one or more Java classes,† but you have the entire Java API at your disposal for dealing with essential, low-level items such as String-handling, file I/O, and Math calculations. What a deal!

---

* See Sun Microsystems Java milestones and history at: *http://java.sun.com/features/2000/06/time-line.html*.

† For example, the installation of a binary Active Server Pages (ASP) component often required the scrutiny and permission of the hosting Internet Service Provider (ISP), because a badly written or malicious ASP component could wreak havoc on the server machine.

The other big benefit Java provides is its cross-platform nature. Web developers can design their web applications, neatly package them in a special JAR file for web components called a Web Application Archive file, then install the WARs on various servers hosted by different operating systems (OSes). Java web components are not bound to a single OS or to a particular vendor's server software like other web-related software technologies.

Jump ahead to the present. By late 2003, Java has achieved status as the granddaddy of server-side development. Servlets and JSPs are included in the Java 2 Enterprise Edition (J2EE), a widely accepted enterprise technology for network-based and distributed computing. Hundreds of thousands of developers throughout the world work on the "web tier" of J2EE-based technologies, using servlets, JSPs, and sometimes special web frameworks such as Struts.

In fact, many web developers now spend a fair amount of time getting to know various "application servers"—like BEA WebLogic, JBoss, or IBM's WebSphere—that pull together the web tier, business or domain objects (such as components that handle weather data or a customer's financial accounts), and Enterprise Information Systems (EIS). These application servers represent the software host for servlets and JSPs. Many web developers, including myself, spend a lot of time working on web components that are hosted on Tomcat, a popular open source (*http:// www.opensource.org*) servlet engine and "reference implementation" for the new servlet and JSP APIs.*

The rapid maturation and well-established nature of Java has naturally led to a "cookbook" approach for our book. This cookbook focuses on how to initiate certain web-related tasks in Java, rather than tutoring the reader on how to use the Java language, or explaining the servlet and JSP APIs in finely grained detail. Countless tutorial-oriented Java books still exist, however, in new or reissued form, which attests to the popularity of Java as a web-development platform.

What's in the Book

In creating the recipes for this book, I tried to cover as many common and advanced web developer tasks as I could practically fit into one book. This amounts to about 230 different recipes. Each recipe shows how to implement a particular task using servlets, JSPs, and, in many cases, one or more supporting Java classes.

The recipes show how to:

- Authenticate web clients
- Interact with databases

---

* A reference implementation is software that is based on a commonly agreed upon specification, and is freely available to software developers and others as a demonstration of how the specified software system is designed to function.

- Send email
- Handle submitted data from a web form
- Read and set "cookies"
- Upload files from the client
- Integrate JavaScript with servlets and JSPs
- Embed multimedia files like digital movies and music in JSPs and servlets
- Handle web clients whose users speak different languages (internationalization)
- Log messages from servlets and JSPs
- Dynamically include chunks of content, as in traditional server-side include (SSI) code
- Interact with Enterprise JavaBeans (EJBs) from a JSP and servlet
- Use Amazon.com's and Google.com's Web Services APIs from a servlet or JSP

I have also included numerous technology-specific recipes, such as:

- Using "sessions" in your Java web applications (a concept that represents the tracking of a user's progress through a web site)
- Working with "filters"
- Using the open source ANT tool to build web applications
- Binding Java objects to a session or web application so they can be used as information or data containers
- Creating your own custom tags for JSPs
- Using the JavaServer Pages Standard Tag Library (JSTL), which is a large set of prebuilt tags you can use in JSPs

In short, the book is designed to help guide Java web developers in their everyday tasks, and to provide quick solutions to typical web-related problems.

BEA WebLogic Recipes

Because Java web developers tend to work with both Tomcat and a proprietary application server, I've included a number of different recipes to show how to implement common tasks with BEA WebLogic. As a practical matter, I could not cover the several other application servers that are available, such as IBM's WebSphere, JBoss, Jetty, Oracle 9*i* application server, or commercial servlet engines such as New Atlanta ServletExec and Caucho Resin. But I wanted to include recipes covering "how the other half lives" in terms of using various vendor tools for managing everyday web-application tasks. Solutions involving the deployment or revision of web components and deployment descriptors using visual interfaces such as WebLogic's Administration Console or WebLogic Builder can be quite different from those used with Tomcat.

As a result, this book includes a collection of basic WebLogic-related recipes, such as deploying web applications on WebLogic, and using a servlet to access a WebLogic DataSource. Chapter 25, *Using JNDI and Enterprise JavaBeans* shows how a servlet can interact with an EJB installed on WebLogic.

Audience

The recipes are mainly designed for experienced developers who design, build, deploy, and revise Java-based web applications. This includes JSP, servlet, and Java-Bean developers.

The book is also appropriate for experienced web developers who are just learning Java and migrating from another web programming platform, such as Active Server Pages, PHP, or Perl. These developers are usually knowledgable about the underlying mechanisms, such as sessions, cookies, file uploads, login authentication, and handling HTTP POST requests, but may not yet know how to implement these tasks in Java. The cookbook allows them to quickly look up a solution to a problem that they have probably already dealt with using another language.

Java developers who need to know how to implement new servlet API 2.4 and JSP 2.0 features (such as some of the new *web.xml* filter-mapping elements for request dispatchers and embedding the Expression Language [EL] in a JSP's template text) will also find the cookbook handy.

What You Need to Know

Readers should know the basics of the Java language or be learning how to program with Java.

Chapter 1, *Writing Servlets and JSPs*, includes brief introductions to servlets, JSPs, and deployment descriptors for readers who are not yet up to speed on these concepts. However, since the cookbook's focus is on concise solutions to specific problems, it does not include long tutorials on the servlet and JSP APIs. Each recipe includes an introduction that provides enough information to get started with the various technologies and code samples. The recipes also include numerous references to online information resources, such as Javadoc pages and tutorials, for readers who need to explore a topic in greater depth.

Readers will benefit from having already been introduced to various J2EE subject areas such as Java Database Connectivity (JDBC), the Java Naming and Directory Interface (JNDI), and Enterprise JavaBeans (I have included one recipe that involves connecting a web component with EJBs using JNDI).

Finally, a working knowledge of XML is also helpful, as Java web development involves XML-based deployment descriptors and configuration files.

Organization

The book begins with three chapters that cover the nuts and bolts of writing servlets and JSPs, deploying servlets and JSPs, naming or registering your servlets, and using the Ant tool.

I then explore several basic topics on web development, such as dynamically including content in web pages, uploading files, handling data that has been posted from an HTML form, reading and setting cookies, tracking sessions, and integrating JavaScript with JSPs and servlets.

Next, the book includes some more advanced recipes, such as logging messages, authenticating clients, binding attributes, working with the client request, and creating servlet filters. Chapter 20, *Managing Email in Servlets and JSPs*, and Chapter 21, *Accessing Databases*, cover two common and complex web-development tasks with 20 different recipes.

Chapter 22, *Using Custom Tag Libraries*, and Chapter 23, *Using the JSTL* describe custom tags and the JSTL. Chapter 24, *Internationalization*, discusses the crucial topic of internationalizing your web applications with servlets and JSPs.

For web developers whose web components must interact with EJBs using the Java JNDI, Chapter 25, *Using JNDI and Enterprise JavaBeans*, shows how to configure JNDI in both Tomcat and WebLogic, as well as how to access JNDI objects using both servers.

The book concludes with two chapters that describe different strategies for extracting data from web sites using Java web components. Chapter 26, *Harvesting Web Information*, has recipes on harvesting or "scraping" data from web pages. Chapter 27, *Using the Google and Amazon Web APIs*, describes how to use Google's and Amazon.com's web services APIs.

Conventions Used in This Book

The following typographical conventions are used in this book:

Italic

> Indicates new terms, URLs, email addresses, filenames, file extensions, pathnames, directories, and Unix utilities.

Constant width

> Indicates commands, options, switches, variables, attributes, keys, functions, types, classes, namespaces, methods, modules, properties, parameters, values, objects, events, event handlers, XML tags, HTML tags, macros, the contents of files, or the output from commands.

Constant width bold

Shows commands or other text that should be typed literally by the user, and is used to emphasize code in examples.

Constant width italic

Shows text that should be replaced with user-supplied values. In some cases where text is already italicized, user-supplied values are shown in angled brackets (< >)

This icon signifies a tip, suggestion, or general note.

This icon indicates a warning or caution.

Using Code Examples

This book is here to help you get your job done. In general, you may use the code in this book in your programs and documentation. You do not need to contact us for permission unless you're reproducing a significant portion of the code. For example, writing a program that uses several chunks of code from this book does not require permission. Selling or distributing a CD-ROM of examples from O'Reilly books *does* require permission. Answering a question by citing this book and quoting example code does not require permission. Incorporating a significant amount of example code from this book into your product's documentation *does* require permission.

O'Reilly & Associates and the author both appreciate, but do not require, attribution. An attribution usually includes the title, author, publisher, and ISBN. For example: "*Java Servlet and JSP Cookbook,* by Bruce Perry. Copyright 2004 O'Reilly & Associates, Inc., 0-596-00572-5."

If you feel your use of code examples falls outside fair use or the permission given above, feel free to contact us at *permissions@oreilly.com.*

Comments and Questions

Please address comments and questions concerning this book to the publisher:

O'Reilly & Associates, Inc.
1005 Gravenstein Highway North
Sebastopol, CA 95472
(800) 998-9938 (in the United States or Canada)
(707) 829-0515 (international or local)
(707) 829-0104 (fax)

O'Reilly has a web page for this book, where errata, examples, and any additional information is listed. You can access this page at:

http://www.oreilly.com/catalog/jsvltjspckbk

To comment or ask technical questions about this book, send email to:

bookquestions@oreilly.com

For more information about O'Reilly books, conferences, Resource Centers, and the O'Reilly Network, see our web site at:

http://www.oreilly.com

Acknowledgments

One night, more than a year ago, I dispatched an email to O'Reilly with an idea for a book. At that time, the likelihood that this casual email would eventually give rise to a published book seemed very remote. After numerous emailed "back and forths" between me and a couple of O'Reilly Java editors, and then several months of gentle nudging, solid editing, occasional reconceptualizations, and (of course) writing, writing, and more writing, the seed of the book idea germinated and reached fruition. Voilá, a cookbook is born!

The shaping of a book is always a collaboration among several people. This book probably would not have left the launching pad without my editor Brett McLaughlin's succinct and continuous reminders about what differentiates a cookbook from other book types. Brett is also a fine "word by word" copy editor, and having an editorial background myself, I appreciated his efforts from the writer's side. Also, Brett's knowledge of Java is deep, and his comments helped me avoid some awkward code design decisions.

I am very fortunate to have Jason Hunter and Sang Shin as technical editors. They are both well-known Java experts, and this is a much better book since they have read and commented on large chunks of it. Their review had a really short deadline, and this is a big book. I was amazed at the comprehensive coverage with such a short turnaround. As a technical writer, I am indebted to those who rescue me from embarrassing mistakes!

Some of us save our family members for last in acknowledging those who help us. Maybe that is because the last paragraph is the foundation on which the rest of the language sits, just as the family is every writer's foundation, giving them support and shielding them from distractions as they immerse themselves in prose and technology. This book would not have been created without the help from my wife Stacy, daughter Rachel, and even Scott, who inspires me from the tender vantage point of being less than one year old. I'll also repeat what I said in my AppleScript book; I thank my parents Robert and Anne Perry for installing in me a love of writing and books.

CHAPTER 1

Writing Servlets and JSPs

1.0   Introduction

The purpose of this chapter is to bring relative newcomers up to speed in writing, compiling, and packaging servlets and JSPs. If you have never developed a servlet or JSP before, or just need to brush up on the technology to jumpstart your development, then the upcoming recipes provide simple programming examples and an overview of the components that you require on the user classpath to compile servlets.

Recipes 1.1 and 1.2 provide a brief introduction to servlets and JSPs, respectively. A comprehensive description of a servlet or JSP's role in the Java 2 Platform, Enterprise Edition (J2EE), is beyond the scope of these recipes. However, information that relates directly to J2EE technology, such as databases and JDBC; using servlets with the Java Naming and Directory Interface (JNDI); and using servlets with JavaMail (or email) is distributed throughout the book (and index!).

The "See Also" sections concluding each recipe provide pointers to closely related chapters, an online tutorial managed by Sun Microsystems, and other O'Reilly books that cover these topics in depth.

1.1   Writing a Servlet

Problem

You want to write a servlet that is part of a web application.

Solution

Create a Java class that extends `javax.servlet.http.HttpServlet`. Make sure to import the classes from *servlet.jar* (or *servlet-api.jar*)—you'll need them to compile the servlet.

Discussion

A servlet is a Java class that is designed to respond with dynamic content to client requests over a network. If you are familiar with Common Gateway Interface (CGI) programs, then servlets are a Java technology that can replace CGI programs. Often called a *web component* (along with JSPs), a servlet is executed within a runtime environment provided by a *servlet container* or *web container* such as Jakarta Tomcat or BEA WebLogic.

A web container can be an add-on component to an HTTP server, or it can be a standalone server such as Tomcat, which is capable of managing HTTP requests for both static content (HTML files) as well as for servlets and JSPs.

Servlets are installed in web containers as part of *web applications*. These applications are collections of web resources such as HTML pages, images, multimedia content, servlets, JavaServer Pages, XML configuration files, Java support classes, and Java support libraries. When a web application is deployed in a web container, the container creates and loads instances of the Java servlet class into its Java Virtual Machine (JVM) to handle requests for the servlet.

A servlet handles each request as a separate thread. Therefore, servlet developers have to consider whether to synchronize access to instance variables, class variables, or shared resources such as a database connection, depending on how these resources are used.

All servlets implement the javax.servlet.Servlet interface. Web application developers typically write servlets that extend javax.servlet.http.HttpServlet, an abstract class that implements the Servlet interface and is specially designed to handle HTTP requests.

The following basic sequence occurs when the web container creates a servlet instance:

1. The servlet container calls the servlet's init( ) method, which is designed to initialize resources that the servlet might use, such as a logger (see Chapter 14). The init( ) method gets called only once during the servlet's lifetime.

2. The init( ) method initializes an object that implements the javax.servlet. ServletConfig interface. This object gives the servlet access to initialization parameters declared in the deployment descriptor (see Recipe 1.5). ServletConfig also gives the servlet access to a javax.servlet.ServletContext object, with which the servlet can log messages, dispatch requests to other web components, and get access to other web resources in the same application (see Recipe 13.5).

Servlet developers are not required to implement the init( ) method in their HttpServlet subclasses.

3. The servlet container calls the servlet's service( ) method in response to servlet requests. In terms of HttpServlets, service( ) automatically calls the appropriate HTTP method to handle the request by calling (generally) the servlet's doGet( ) or doPost( ) methods. For example, the servlet responds to a user sending a POST HTTP request with a doPost( ) method execution.

4. When calling the two principal HttpServlet methods, doGet( ) or doPost( ), the servlet container creates javax.servlet.http.HttpServletRequest and HttpServletResponse objects and passes them in as parameters to these request handler methods. HttpServletRequest represents the request; HttpServletResponse encapsulates the servlet's response to the request.

Example 1-1 shows the typical uses of the request and response objects. It is a good idea to read the servlet API documentation (at *http://java. sun.com/j2ee/1.4/docs/api/javax/servlet/http/package-summary.html*), as many of the method names (e.g., request.getContextPath( )) are self-explanatory.

5. The servlet or web container, not the developer, manages the servlet's lifecycle, or how long an instance of the servlet exists in the JVM to handle requests. When the servlet container is set to remove the servlet from service, it calls the servlet's destroy( ) method, in which the servlet can release any resources, such as a database connection.

Example 1-1 shows a typical servlet idiom for handling an HTML form. The doGet( ) method displays the form itself. The doPost( ) method handles the submitted form data, since in doGet( ), the HTML form tag specifies the servlet's own address as the target for the form data.

The servlet (named FirstServlet) specifies that the declared class is part of the com.jspservletcookbook package. It is important to create packages for your servlets and utility classes, and then to store your classes in a directory structure beneath *WEB-INF* that matches these package names.

The FirstServlet class imports the necessary classes for compiling a basic servlet, which are the emphasized import statements in Example 1-1. The Java class extends HttpServlet. The only defined methods are doGet( ), which displays the HTML form in response to a GET HTTP request, and doPost( ), which handles the posted data.

Example 1-1. A typical HttpServlet used for handling an HTML form

```java
package com.jspservletcookbook;

import java.io.IOException;
import java.io.PrintWriter;

import java.util.Enumeration;

import javax.servlet.ServletException;

import javax.servlet.http.HttpServlet;
import javax.servlet.http.HttpServletRequest;
import javax.servlet.http.HttpServletResponse;

public class FirstServlet extends HttpServlet {

  public void doGet(HttpServletRequest request,
    HttpServletResponse response) throws ServletException,
      java.io.IOException {

    //set the MIME type of the response, "text/html"
    response.setContentType("text/html");

    //use a PrintWriter to send text data to the client who has requested the
    //servlet
    java.io.PrintWriter out = response.getWriter( );

    //Begin assembling the HTML content
    out.println("<html><head>");

    out.println("<title>Help Page</title></head><body>");
    out.println("<h2>Please submit your information</h2>");

    //make sure method="post" so that the servlet service method
    //calls doPost in the response to this form submit
    out.println(
        "<form method=\"post\" action =\"" + request.getContextPath( ) +
            "/firstservlet\" >");

    out.println("<table border=\"0\"><tr><td valign=\"top\">");
    out.println("Your first name: </td>  <td valign=\"top\">");
    out.println("<input type=\"text\" name=\"firstname\" size=\"20\">");
    out.println("</td></tr><tr><td valign=\"top\">");
    out.println("Your last name: </td>  <td valign=\"top\">");
    out.println("<input type=\"text\" name=\"lastname\" size=\"20\">");
    out.println("</td></tr><tr><td valign=\"top\">");
    out.println("Your email: </td>  <td valign=\"top\">");
    out.println("<input type=\"text\" name=\"email\" size=\"20\">");
    out.println("</td></tr><tr><td valign=\"top\">");

    out.println("<input type=\"submit\" value=\"Submit Info\"></td></tr>");
    out.println("</table></form>");
    out.println("</body></html>");

    }//doGet
```

Example 1-1. A typical HttpServlet used for handling an HTML form (continued)

```java
public void doPost(HttpServletRequest request,
  HttpServletResponse response) throws ServletException,
  java.io.IOException {

  //display the parameter names and values
  Enumeration paramNames = request.getParameterNames();

  String parName;//this will hold the name of the parameter

  boolean emptyEnum = false;

  if (! paramNames.hasMoreElements())
      emptyEnum = true;


  //set the MIME type of the response, "text/html"
  response.setContentType("text/html");

  //use a PrintWriter to send text data to the client
  java.io.PrintWriter out = response.getWriter();

  //Begin assembling the HTML content
  out.println("<html><head>");
  out.println("<title>Submitted Parameters</title></head><body>");

  if (emptyEnum){
      out.println(
          "<h2>Sorry, the request does not contain any parameters</h2>");
  } else {
  out.println(
      "<h2>Here are the submitted parameter values</h2>");
  }

  while(paramNames.hasMoreElements()){

      parName = (String) paramNames.nextElement();

      out.println(
          "<strong>" + parName + "</strong> : " +
              request.getParameter(parName));

      out.println("<br />");

  }//while

  out.println("</body></html>");

}// doPost
}
```

You might have noticed that doGet( ) and doPost( ) each throw ServletException and IOException. The servlet throws IOException because the response.getWriter( ) (as well as PrintWriter.close( )) method call can throw an IOException. The doPost( ) and doGet( ) methods can throw a ServletException to indicate that a problem occurred when handling the request. For example, if the servlet detected a security violation or some other request problem, then it could include the following code within doGet( ) or doPost( ):

```
//detects a problem that prevents proper request handling...
throw new ServletException("The servlet cannot handle this request.");
```

Figure 1-1 shows the output displayed by the servlet's doGet( ) method in a browser.

Figure 1-1. The servlet's output for doGet( ) method

Figure 1-2 shows the servlet's output for the doPost( ) method.

See Also

Recipe 1.3 on compiling a servlet; Recipe 1.4 on packaging servlets and JSPs; Recipe 1.5 on creating the deployment descriptor; Chapter 2 on deploying servlets and JSPs; Chapter 3 on naming servlets; the javax.servlet.http package JavaDoc: *http://java.sun.com/j2ee/1.4/docs/api/javax/servlet/http/package-summary.html*; the J2EE tutorial from Sun Microsystems: *http://java.sun.com/j2ee/tutorial/1_3-fcs/doc/J2eeTutorialTOC.html*; Jason Hunter's *Java Servlet Programming* (O'Reilly).

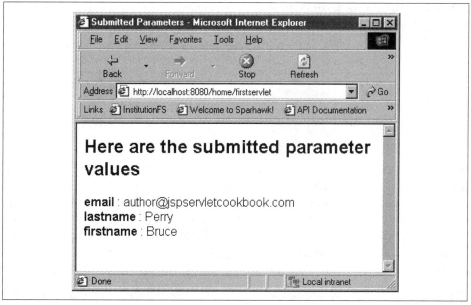

Figure 1-2. The servlet's output for the doPost() method

1.2 Writing a JSP

Problem

You want to create a JSP and include it in a web application.

Solution

Create the JSP as a text file using HTML template text as needed. Store the JSP file at the top level of the web application.

Discussion

A JavaServer Pages (JSP) component is a type of Java servlet that is designed to fulfill the role of a user interface for a Java web application. Web developers write JSPs as text files that combine HTML or XHTML code, XML elements, and embedded JSP actions and commands. JSPs were originally designed around the model of embedded server-side scripting tools such as Microsoft Corporation's ASP technology; however, JSPs have evolved to focus on XML elements, including custom-designed elements, or *custom tags*, as the principal method of generating dynamic web content.

JSP files typically have a *.jsp* extension, as in *mypage.jsp*. When a client requests the JSP page for the first time, or if the developer precompiles the JSP (see Chapter 5), the web container translates the textual document into a servlet.

> The JSP 2.0 specification refers to the conversion of a JSP into a serv-let as the *translation phase*. When the JSP (now a servlet class) responds to requests, the specification calls this stage the *request phase*. The resulting servlet instance is called the *page implementation object*.

A JSP compiler (such as Tomcat's Jasper component) automatically converts the text-based document into a servlet. The web container creates an instance of the servlet and makes the servlet available to handle requests. These tasks are transparent to the developer, who never has to handle the translated servlet source code (although they can examine the code to find out what's happening behind the scenes, which is always instructive).

The developer focuses on the JSP's dynamic behavior and which JSP elements or custom-designed tags she uses to generate the response. Developing the JSP as a text-based document rather than Java source code allows a professional designer to work on the graphics, HTML, or dynamic HTML, leaving the XML tags and dynamic content to programmers.

Example 1-2 shows a JSP that displays the current date and time. The example JSP shows how to import and use a custom tag library, which Chapter 23 describes in great detail. The code also uses the `jsp:useBean` standard action, a built-in XML element that you can use to create a new Java object for use in the JSP page. Here are the basic steps for writing a JSP:

1. Open up a text editor, or a programmer's editor that offers JSP syntax highlighting.
2. If you are developing a JSP for handling HTTP requests, then input the HTML code just as you would for an HTML file.
3. Include any necessary JSP directives, such as the `taglib` directive in Example 1-2, at the top of the file. A directive begins with the `<%@` symbols.
4. Type in the standard actions or custom tags wherever they are needed.
5. Save the file with a *.jsp* extension in the directory you have designated for JSPs. A typical location is the top-level directory of a web application that you are developing in your filesystem.

> Some JSPs are developed as XML files, or *JSP documents*, consisting solely of well-formed XML elements and their attributes. The JSP 2.0 specification recommends that you give these files a *.jspx* extension. See Recipe 5.5 for further details on JSP documents.

Example 1-2. A JSP file that displays the date

```
<%-- use the 'taglib' directive to make the JSTL 1.0 core tags available; use the uri
"http://java.sun.com/jsp/jstl/core" for JSTL 1.1 --%>
<%@ taglib uri="http://java.sun.com/jsp/jstl/core" prefix="c" %>

<%-- use the 'jsp:useBean' standard action to create the Date object;  the object is set
as an attribute in page scope
--%>
<jsp:useBean id="date" class="java.util.Date" />

<html>
<head><title>First JSP</title></head>
<body>
<h2>Here is today's date</h2>

<c:out value="${date}" />

</body>
</html>
```

To view the output of this file in a browser, request the file by typing the URL into the browser location field, as in: *http://localhost:8080/home/firstJ.jsp*. The name of the file is *firstJ.jsp*. If this is the first time that anyone has requested the JSP, then you will notice a delay as the JSP container converts your text file into Java source code, then compiles the source into a servlet.

> You can avoid delays by precompiling the JSP. If you request the JSP with a jsp_precompile=true parameter, Tomcat converts the JSP, but does not send back a response. An example is *http://localhost:8080/home/firstJ.jsp?jsp_precompile=true*.

Figure 1-3 shows the JSP output in a browser.

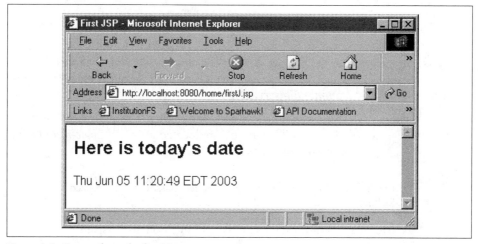

Figure 1-3. Output from the firstJ.jsp page

If you select "View Source" from the browser menu to view the page's source code, you won't see any of the special JSP syntax: the comment characters (<%-- --%>), the taglib directive, the jsp:useBean action, or the c:out tag. The servlet sends only the template text and the generated date string to the client.

See Also

Recipes 5.1–5.3 on precompiling JSPs; Chapter 2 on deploying servlets and JSPs; Recipes 1.1 and 1.3 on writing and compiling a servlet; Recipe 1.4 on packaging servlets and JSPs; Recipe 1.5 on creating the deployment descriptor; the J2EE tutorial from Sun Microsystems: *http://java.sun.com/j2ee/tutorial/1_3-fcs/doc/J2eeTutorialTOC.html*; Hans Bergsten's *JavaServer Pages* (O'Reilly).

1.3   Compiling a Servlet

Problem

You have written a servlet, and now you want to compile it into a class file.

Solution

Make sure that *servlet.jar* (for Tomcat 4.1.24) or *servlet-api.jar* (for Tomcat 5) is on your user classpath. Use javac as you would for any other Java source file.

Discussion

At a minimum, you have to place the servlet classes on your classpath in order to compile a servlet. These classes are located in these Java packages:

- javax.servlet
- javax.servlet.http

Tomcat 5 supports the servlet API 2.4; the JAR file that you need on the classpath is located at *<Tomcat-5-installation-directory>/common/lib/servlet-api.jar*. Tomcat 4.1.24 uses the servlet 2.3 API. The servlet classes are located at: *<Tomcat-4-installation-directory>/common/lib/servlet.jar*.

For BEA WebLogic 7.0, the servlet classes and many other subpackages of the javax package (e.g., *javax.ejb, javax.mail, javax.sql*) are located at: *<WebLogic-installation-directory>/weblogic700/server/lib/weblogic.jar*.

If you are using Ant to compile servlet classes, then proceed to Recipe 4.4, do not pass Go, do not collect $200. That recipe is devoted specifically to the topic of using Ant to compile a servlet. If you use an IDE, follow its instructions for placing a JAR file on the classpath.

The following command line compiles a servlet in the *src* directory and places the compiled class, nested within its package-related directories, in the *build* directory:

```
javac -classpath K:\tomcat5\jakarta-tomcat-5\dist\common\lib\servlet-api.jar
    -d ./build ./src/FirstServlet.java
```

For this command line to run successfully, you must change to the parent directory of the *src* directory.

 Recipe 1.4 explains the typical directory structure, including the *src* directory, for developing a web application.

If the servlet depends on any other libraries, you have to include those JAR files on your classpath as well. I have included only the *servlet-api.jar* JAR file in this command line.

You also have to substitute the directory path for your own installation of Tomcat for this line of the prior command-line sequence:

```
K:\tomcat5\jakarta-tomcat-5\dist\common\lib\servlet-api.jar
```

This command line uses the built-in `javac` compiler that comes with the Sun Microsystems Java Software Development Kit (JDK). For this command to work properly, you have to include the location of the Java SDK that you are using in the PATH environment variable. For example, on a Unix-based Mac OS X 10.2 system, the directory path */usr/bin* must be included in the PATH variable. On my Windows NT machine, the PATH includes *h:\j2sdk1.4.1_01\bin*.

See Also

Chapter 2 on deploying servlets and JSPs; Chapter 3 on naming servlets; Recipe 1.4 on packaging servlets and JSPs; Recipe 1.5 on creating the deployment descriptor; the J2EE tutorial from Sun Microsystems: *http://java.sun.com/j2ee/tutorial/1_3-fcs/doc/J2eeTutorialTOC.html*; Jason Hunter's *Java Servlet Programming* (O'Reilly).

1.4   Packaging Servlets and JSPs

Problem

You want to set up a directory structure for packaging and creating a Web ARchive (WAR) file for servlets and JSPs.

Solution

Set up a directory structure in your filesystem, then use the jar tool or Ant to create the WAR.

Discussion

Except in the rarest of circumstances, you'll usually develop a servlet or JSP as part of a web application. It is relatively easy to set up a directory structure on your filesystem to hold web-application components, which include HTML files, servlets, JSPs, graphics, JAR libraries, possibly movies and sound files, as well as XML configuration files (such as the deployment descriptor; see Recipe 1.5).

The simplest organization for this structure is to create the exact layout of a web application on your filesystem, then use the jar tool to create a WAR file.

 A WAR file is like a ZIP archive. You deploy your web application into a web container by deploying the WAR. See Chapter 2 for recipes about various deployment scenarios.

The web application structure involving the *WEB-INF* subdirectory is standard to all Java web applications and specified by the servlet API specification (in the section named *Web Applications*. Here is what this directory structure looks like, given a top-level directory name of *myapp*:

```
/myapp
    /images
    /WEB-INF
        /classes
        /lib
```

The servlet specification specifies a *WEB-INF* subdirectory and two child directories, *classes* and *lib*. The *WEB-INF* subdirectory contains the application's deployment descriptor, named *web.xml*. The JSP files and HTML live in the top-level directory (*myapp*). Servlet classes, JavaBean classes, and any other utility classes are located in the *WEB-INF/classes* directory, in a structure that matches their package name. If you have a fully qualified class name of com.myorg.MyServlet, then this servlet class must be located in *WEB-INF/classes/com/myorg/MyServlet.class*.

The *WEB-INF/lib* directory contains any JAR libraries that your web application requires, such as database drivers, the *log4j.jar*, and the required JARs for using the JavaServer Pages Standard Tag Library (see Chapter 23).

Once you are ready to test the application in WAR format, change to the top-level directory. Type the following command, naming the WAR file after the top-level directory of your application. These command-line phrases work on both Windows and Unix systems (I used them with Windows NT 4 and Mac OS X 10.2):

```
jar cvf myapp.war .
```

Don't forget the final dot (.) character, which specifies to the jar tool to include the current directory's contents and its subdirectories in the WAR file. This command creates the *myapp.war* file in the current directory.

The WAR name becomes the application name and context path for your web application. For example, *myapp.war* is typically associated with a context path of */myapp* when you deploy the application to a web container.

If you want to view the contents of the WAR at the command line, type this:

```
jar tvf alpine-final.war
```

If the WAR file is very large and you want to view its contents one page at a time, use this command:

```
jar tvf alpine-final.war |more
```

Here is example output from this command:

```
H:\classes\webservices\finalproj\dist>jar tvf alpine-final.war
     0 Mon Nov 18 14:10:36 EST 2002 META-INF/
    48 Mon Nov 18 14:10:36 EST 2002 META-INF/MANIFEST.MF
   555 Tue Nov 05 17:08:16 EST 2002 request.jsp
   914 Mon Nov 18 08:53:00 EST 2002 response.jsp
     0 Mon Nov 18 14:10:36 EST 2002 WEB-INF/
     0 Mon Nov 18 14:10:36 EST 2002 WEB-INF/classes/
     0 Tue Nov 05 11:09:34 EST 2002 WEB-INF/classes/com/
     0 Tue Nov 05 11:09:34 EST 2002 WEB-INF/classes/com/parkerriver/
   CONTINUED...
```

Many development teams are using Ant to compile and create WAR files for their servlets and JSPs. Recipe 2.6 describes using Ant for developing and updating web applications.

I jumpstart your progress toward that recipe by showing the kind of directory structure you might use for a comprehensive web application, one that contains numerous servlets, JSPs, static HTML files, as well as various graphics and multimedia components. When using Ant to build a WAR file from this kind of directory structure, you can filter out the directories that you do not want to include in the final WAR, such as the top-level *src*, *dist*, and *meta* directories.

```
myapp
    /build
    /dist
    /lib
    /meta
    /src
    /web
        /images
        /multimedia
    /WEB-INF
        /classes
        /lib
        /tlds
        /jspf
```

The *WEB-INF/tlds* and *WEB-INF/jspf* optional directories may contain Tag Library Descriptor files and JSP fragments (chunks of JSPs that are designed to be included in other JSPs, such as server-side includes), respectively.

See Also

Chapter 2 on deploying servlets and JSPs; Chapter 3 on naming servlets; The deployment sections of *Tomcat: The Definitive Guide*, by Brittain and Darwin (O'Reilly); the J2EE tutorial from Sun Microsystems: *http://java.sun.com/j2ee/tutorial/1_3-fcs/ doc/J2eeTutorialTOC.html.*

1.5   Creating the Deployment Descriptor

Problem

You want to create the deployment descriptor for your application.

Solution

Name the XML file *web.xml* and place it in the *WEB-INF* directory of your web application. If you do not have an existing example of *web.xml*, then cut and paste the examples given in the servlet v2.3 or 2.4 specifications and start from there.

Discussion

The deployment descriptor is a very important part of your web application. It conveys the requirements for your web application in a concise format that is readable by most XML editors. The *web.xml* file is where you:

- Register and create URL mappings for your servlets
- Register or specify any of the application's filters and listeners
- Specify context init parameter name/value pairs
- Configure error pages
- Specify your application's welcome files
- Configure session timeouts
- Specifiy security settings that control who can request which web components

This is just a subset of the configurations that you can use with *web.xml*. While a number of chapters in this book contain detailed examples of *web.xml* (refer to the "See Also" section), this recipe shows simplified versions of the servlet v2.3 and v2.4 deployment descriptors.

Example 1-3 shows a simple web application with a servlet, a filter, a listener, and a session-config element, as well as an error-page configuration. The *web.xml* in Example 1-3 uses the servlet v2.3 Document Type Definition (DTD). The main difference between the deployment descriptors of 2.3 and 2.4 is that 2.3 uses a DTD and 2.4 is based on an XML schema. You'll notice that the old version of *web.xml* has the DOCTYPE declaration at the top of the file, while the 2.4 version uses the namespace attributes of the web-app element to refer to the XML schema. The XML elements of Example 1-3 have to be in the same order as specified by the DTD.

Example 1-3. The deployment descriptor for servlet API 2.3

```
<?xml version="1.0" encoding="ISO-8859-1"?>
<!DOCTYPE web-app
    PUBLIC "-//Sun Microsystems, Inc.//DTD Web Application 2.3//EN"
           "http://java.sun.com/dtd/web-application_2_3.dtd"
>

<web-app>

  <display-name>Servlet 2.3 deployment descriptor</display-name>

  <filter>
    <filter-name>RequestFilter</filter-name>
    <filter-class>com.jspservletcookbook.RequestFilter</filter-class>
  </filter>

  <filter-mapping>
    <filter-name>RequestFilter</filter-name>
    <url-pattern>/*</url-pattern>
  </filter-mapping>


  <listener>
    <listener-class>com.jspservletcookbook.ReqListener</listener-class>
  </listener>

  <servlet>
    <servlet-name>MyServlet</servlet-name>
    <servlet-class>com.jspservletcookbook.MyServlet</servlet-class>
  </servlet>

  <servlet-mapping>
    <servlet-name> MyServlet </servlet-name>
    <url-pattern>/myservlet</url-pattern>
  </servlet-mapping>

  <session-config>
    <session-timeout>15</session-timeout>
  </session-config>
```

Example 1-3. The deployment descriptor for servlet API 2.3 (continued)

```
<error-page>
  <error-code>404</error-code>
  <location>/err404.jsp</location>
</error-page>
```

```
</web-app>
```

Example 1-3 shows the *web.xml* file for an application that has just one servlet, accessed at the path *<context path>/myservlet*. Sessions time out in 15 minutes with this application. If a client requests a URL that cannot be found, the web container forwards the request to the */err404.jsp* page, based on the error-page configuration. The filter named RequestFilter applies to all requests for static and dynamic content in this context. At startup, the web container creates an instance of the listener class com.jspservletcookbook.ReqListener.

Everything about Example 1-4 is the same as Example 1-3, except that the web-app element at the top of the file refers to an XML schema with its namespace attributes. In addition, elements can appear in arbitrary order with the servlet v2.4 deployment descriptor. For instance, if you were so inclined you could list your servlets and mappings before your listeners and filters.

Example 1-4. A servlet v2.4 deployment descriptor

```
<?xml version="1.0" encoding="ISO-8859-1"?>

<web-app xmlns="http://java.sun.com/xml/ns/j2ee"
  xmlns:xsi="http://www.w3.org/2001/XMLSchema-instance" xsi:schemaLocation=
    "http://java.sun.com/xml/ns/j2ee
      http://java.sun.com/xml/ns/j2ee/web-app_2_4.xsd" version="2.4">

<!-- the rest of the file is the same as Example 1-3 after the web-app opening tag -->

</web-app>
```

> The servlet 2.4 version of the deployment descriptor also contains definitions for various elements that are not included in the servlet 2.3 *web.xml* version: jsp-config, message-destination, message-destination-ref, and service-ref. The syntax for these elements appears in the specifications for JSP v2.0 and J2EE v1.4.

See Also

Chapter 2 on deploying servlets and JSPs; Chapter 3 on naming servlets; Chapter 9 on configuring the deployment descriptor for error handling; the J2EE tutorial from Sun Microsystems: *http://java.sun.com/j2ee/tutorial/1_3-fcs/doc/J2eeTutorialTOC.html*.

Deploying Servlets and JSPs

2.0   Introduction

This chapter describes how to take servlets or Java Server Pages (JSPs) and make them available to receive web requests on Tomcat's servlet container or BEA WebLogic Server 7.0. This discussion begins with deploying servlets and JSPs; in other words, getting them running on Tomcat or WebLogic, either alone or as part of a web application.

Developing and compiling a servlet or JSP within an integrated development environment (IDE) is one thing. Having the web component respond to HTTP requests is another. This is what *deployment* is all about with web-related software: placing the software into service within a web container like Tomcat or an application server such as BEA WebLogic Server 7.0. The following recipes detail deployment of servlets and JSPs on these web containers, first individually, and then as part of a web application.

The wonderful open source Jakarta Ant build and automation tool is commonly used for this purpose. It is mentioned wherever it is relevant in the following recipes, and Chapter 4 is completely devoted to installing and using Ant.

2.1   Deploying an Individual Servlet on Tomcat

Problem

You want to take a compiled servlet and install it in Tomcat to find out if it is working. You are doing a preliminary test and do not want to take the time to build a complete web application for the servlet.

Solution

Copy and paste the class file into Tomcat's default web application (or into a web application that you have already installed), then request it using the invoker servlet. Or use an Ant *build.xml* file to move the file temporarily into the Tomcat default web application.

Discussion

Sometimes you design a servlet and are anxious to see if the servlet works. Unless the servlet depends on other servlets or components in the application, you can test it on Tomcat by pasting the class file (including its package-related directories) into the default Tomcat web application. By default, this application is located at the path *<Tomcat-installation-directory>/webapps/ROOT*.

If the fully qualified class name of the servlet is jspservletcookbook.CookieServlet, then here is the entire process for manually getting a single servlet going on Tomcat:

- Shut down the Tomcat server by executing the shell script *<tomcat-installation-directory>/bin/shutdown* or by executing a shell script your server administrator has provided. An alternative is to "stop" the default application by requesting this URL in your browser: *http:// localhost:8080/manager/stop?path=/* .

- Create the *jspservletcookbook* directory in the *<Tomcat-installation-directory>/ webapps/ROOT/WEB-INF/classes* directory (make the classes directory if it does not already exist).

- Paste the CookieServlet class file into the *<Tomcat-installation-directory>/ webapps/ROOT/WEB-INF/classes/ jspservletcookbook* directory.

- Start up the Tomcat server by executing the shell script *<Tomcat-installation-directory>/bin/startup* or a shell script that your server administrator has provided. An alternative is to start the default application by requesting this URL in your browser: *http:// localhost:8080/manager/start?path=/* .

- Request the servlet in your browser with the URL *http://localhost:8080/servlet/ jspservletcookbook.CookieServlet*.

By now you are probably saying, "There must be a more elegant alternative to this slow, manual installation of a single servlet!" You are correct, and can use Jakarta Ant to convert this manual process to an automated one.

The *build.xml* file in Example 2-1 accomplishes the same testing process, assuming you have downloaded and installed Ant as described in Chapter 4. Place this build file in a convenient directory. Create in that directory a *global.properties* file that is customized according to your needs (see Example 2-2). Change to that directory in a command-line window and type ant. Ant takes care of the rest of the tasks, including starting and stopping Tomcat's default web application.

Example 2-1. Installing a servlet in the default web application

```
<project name="Cookbook" default="deploy-servlet" basedir=".">

    <taskdef name="start" classname="org.apache.catalina.ant.StartTask" />
    <taskdef name="stop" classname="org.apache.catalina.ant.StopTask" />

<!-- Load in some global properties -->

    <property file="global.properties" />
    <target name="init" description="Initializes some properties.">

        <echo message="Initializing properties."/>
        <property name="build" value=".\build" />
        <property name="src" value=".\src" />

        <!-- The context-path is just a slash character when it is the ROOT application;
        see the start and stop targets, which already include the slash as part of
        the URL pattern -->

        <property name="context-path" value="" />
    </target>

    <target name="prepare" depends="init">
        <echo message="Cleaning up the build directory."/>
        <delete dir="${build}"/>
        <mkdir dir="${build}"/>
    </target>

<!-- Set the CLASSPATH to various Tomcat .jar files -->

    <path id="classpath">
        <fileset dir="${tomcat.dir}/common/lib">
            <include name="*.jar" />
        </fileset>
        <fileset dir="${tomcat.dir}/common/endorsed">
            <include name="*.jar" />
        </fileset>
    </path>

<!-- start the default Tomcat web application -->

    <target name="start"
      description="Starts the default Web application">
        <echo message="Starting the default application...."/>
        <start
           url="${url}"
           username="${username}"
           password="${password}"
           path="/${context-path}"
        />
    </target>

<!-- stop the default Tomcat web application -->
```

Example 2-1. Installing a servlet in the default web application (continued)

```
    <target name="stop"
      description="Stops the default Web application">
        <echo message="Stopping the application...."/>
        <stop
           url="${url}"
           username="${username}"
           password="${password}"
           path="/${context-path}"
        />
    </target>

<!-- stop the default Tomcat web application, compile your servlet, add it to the default
Web application, then start the default web application -->

    <target name="deploy-servlet" depends="prepare"
       description=
       "Compile the specified servlet, then move it into Tomcat's default
       Web application.">

        <echo message="Stopping the default Tomcat application...."/>
        <antcall target="stop"/>
        <echo message="Compiling the servlet...."/>
        <javac srcdir="${src}" destdir="${build}">
            <include name="${compiled.servlet}.java" />
            <classpath refid="classpath"/>
        </javac>
        <echo message=
           "Copying the servlet to Tomcat ROOT web application..."/>

        <copy todir="${tomcat.webapps}/WEB-INF/classes">
            <fileset dir="${build}" />
        </copy>
        <echo message="Starting the default application...."/>
        <antcall target="start"/>
    </target>

</project>
```

The *global.properties* file that sits in the same directory as *build.xml* looks like
Example 2-2.

Example 2-2. global.properties file for Ant

```
tomcat.webapps=k:/jakarta-tomcat-4.1.12/webapps/ROOT
tomcat.dir=k:/jakarta-tomcat-4.1.12
url=http://localhost:8080/manager
compiled.servlet=CookieServlet
username=tomcat
password=tomcat
```

global.properties is just a list of *property-name=value* pairs. In other words, each line is composed of a string of characters that represents the property name (optionally including a period character), followed by an "=" sign and another bunch of characters that represents the value.

 Jakarta Ant's online manual is located at: *http://jakarta.apache.org/ant/manual/index.html.*

Here is what *build.xml* does:

1. Defines two tasks with a taskDef element, called start and stop. These tasks will be used by the targets start and stop later on in the *build.xml* file. These tasks allow you to use the Tomcat "manager" application-deployment tool from your Ant files.

2. Uses a property task to load in the set of properties that are defined in the *global.properties* file. This means that the property name tomcat.dir is now available for use later on in the *build.xml* file. The path element uses the tomcat. dir property by including its value (in the example, "k:/jakarta-tomcat-4.1.12") as part of a classpath definition. You get the value of these imported properties by using a reference like ${tomcat.dir}. Any time you want to give the property a different value before executing an Ant file, you can just change the properties file by typing in a new value in a text editor.

3. Creates an init target that echoes a message to the console and creates three properties (build, src, and context-path). The values of these properties are available only after the init target has been executed. For example, if the prepare target does not have "init" as the value of its depends attribute, the deploy-servlet target, which depends on prepare, cannot use the property values defined by init.

4. Defines a target called prepare.

5. Builds a reusable classpath (with the ID "classpath") out of all of the JAR files located in a couple of Tomcat directories.

6. Creates the start and stop targets. These targets echo a message to the console and then call the tasks (such as stop) that were defined with taskDef elements at the top of the *build.xml* file. The start and stop targets are actually invoked by the all-in-one target deploy-servlet.

7. Creates the deploy-servlet target. This target does all the major work inside the *build.xml* file. Notice that its depends attribute has the value "prepare." This means that prior to executing the instructions contained within the deploy-servlet target, Ant first executes the init and prepare targets. Since the prepare target depends on the init target, deploy-servlet calls prepare, which itself calls it own dependency, the init target. So just by launching the deploy-servlet

target, you have triggered a target chain that looks like init → prepare → deploy-servlet. Using an element called antcall with which a target may explicitly call another target, deploy-servlet calls both the stop and start targets. In this way it can:

   a. Stop the default Tomcat application.

   b. Compile the servlet using the javac task. The javac task includes the servlet that is specified by the compiled.servlet property, which is set inside the *global.properties* file.

8. Copies the compiled servlet to the *WEB-INF/classes* directory of Tomcat's default web application. The copy task creates this *classes* directory if it does not already exist.

9. Starts the default web application so that you can request your servlet in the browser.

See Also

The deployment sections of *Tomcat: The Definitive Guide*, by Brittain and Darwin (O'Reilly); Recipes 2.2, 2.4, and 2.6; the Jakarta Ant online manual at: *http://jakarta. apache.org/ant/manual/index.html*

2.2   Using a Context Element in Tomcat's server.xml

Problem

You want to deploy and redeploy a servlet on Tomcat 4.1.x without restarting the Tomcat web container.

Solution

Deploy the servlet as part of a Context element in Tomcat's *server.xml* file.

Discussion

You can paste a recompiled servlet class over an existing servlet class and invoke the servlet without restarting Tomcat:

1. Locate the Context element for your web application or create a new Context element in the *<tomcat-installation-directory>/conf/server.xml* file. Context elements must be nested within the Host element that represents the *virtual host* under which your web application is running.

2. Set the reloadable attribute of your Context element to true. This signals Tomcat to monitor the contents of *WEB-INF/classes* and *WEB-INF/lib* for any changes. If changes are detected, Tomcat automatically reloads the web application.

The Context element in *server.xml* looks like this:

```
<Context className="org.apache.catalina.core.StandardContext"
         crossContext="false" reloadable="true"
         mapperClass="org.apache.catalina.core.StandardContextMapper"
         useNaming="true" debug="0" swallowOutput="false"
         privileged="false" displayName="Home Web App"
         wrapperClass="org.apache.catalina.core.StandardWrapper"
         docBase="h:\home" cookies="true" path="/home"
         cachingAllowed="true"
         charsetMapperClass="org.apache.catalina.util.CharsetMapper"
>
```

The path attribute represents the context path for the application. The docBase attribute points to the directory that represents the top level of this web application. Most of the example's other attributes have values that are shared by other Contexts. For example, cookies="true" indicates that the Context will use cookies for the session identifier, and crossContext="false" prevents the servlets in this web application from obtaining request dispatchers for other web applications running in the virtual host.

 Setting the reloadable attribute to true incurs significant runtime overhead, so this configuration is recommended only for web applications in development mode.

Under this configuration, Tomcat 4.1.x displays a console message after a slight delay when you paste a new servlet class over the old one in the web application. Here is an example of a console message in response to a dynamic servlet reload:

```
WebappClassLoader:   Resource '/WEB-INF/classes/com/jspservletcookbook/OracleTest.
class' was modified;
Date is now: Sun Feb 02 22:17:41 EST 2003 Was: Sun Feb 02 21:38:52 EST 2003
```

See Also

The deployment sections of *Tomcat: The Definitive Guide*, by Brittain and Darwin (O'Reilly); Recipes 2.1, 2.4, and 2.6; Jakarta Tomcat documentation for the Context element: *http://jakarta.apache.org/tomcat/tomcat-4.1-doc/config/context.html*.

2.3 Deploying an Individual Servlet on WebLogic

Problem

You want to take your compiled servlet and install it in BEA WebLogic Server 7.0 to find out if it is working.

Solution

Copy and paste the class file into WebLogic's default web application (or into a web application that you have already installed). Use the WebLogic Administration Console to alter the *web.xml* file and give the servlet a sensible name with which to request it in a browser, or use an Ant build file to move the file temporarily into the WebLogic default web application.

Discussion

WebLogic 7.0's default web application is located on the following path: *<WebLogic-installation-directory>/user_projects/<mydomain>/applications/Default-WebApp*. In the default installation of the WebLogic 7.0 server, not much exists in the default web application but a *web.xml* deployment descriptor, and some image files. To add a servlet to the default application, paste your servlet class, including its package-related directories, into the *DefaultWebApp/WEB-INF/classes* directory. You might have to create a *classes* directory the first time you do this. Change the *web.xml* file to give the servlet a name (which is easier through the Administration Console) before redeploying the web application as described in Recipe 2.4.

Use the Administration Console to edit the *web.xml* file in order to give the new servlet a registered name and servlet-mapping element. You can also use another available tool, such as WebLogic Builder (Recipe 2.9) or a text editor. Figure 2-1 shows the DefaultWebApp in the Administration Console. Click on "Edit Web Application Deployment Descriptors…".

This displays the screen shown in Figure 2-2. This screen provides an easy graphical method of editing the *web.xml* file for any web application (in this case, the WebLogic default web application).

With this graphical editor, create the servlet and servlet-mapping elements for the servlet that you just added. Make sure to click on the "Web Descriptor" button in the left column of the Figure 2-2 window and then persist the changes that you made in the *web.xml* file. This action rewrites the *web.xml* file, adding the new servlet and servlet-mapping elements.

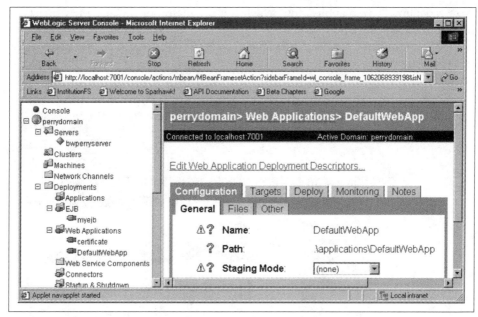

Figure 2-1. WebLogic Server Administration Console

Figure 2-2. Editing the web.xml file graphically

Now redeploy the web application, which is just a matter of clicking a few hypertext links in the Console. Choose the name of your web application in the left column of the Console, under the *mydomain* → Deployments → Web Applications node of the tree navigation structure in this lefthand column. Figure 2-3 shows the resulting window.

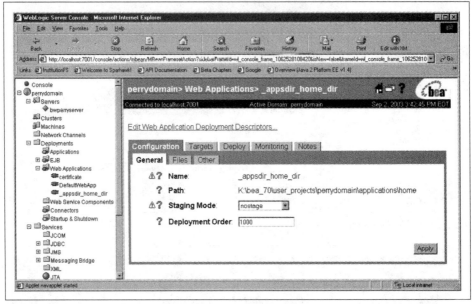

Figure 2-3. Using the Console to redeploy a web application

Click on the "Deploy" tab, then click the "Undeploy" button in the resulting HTML table. The web application is now unavailable for service.

To redeploy the application, click the "Deploy" tab, then select the "Deploy" button, as shown in Figure 2-4.

If the servlet that you are working on already exists in the web application, then you can also copy and paste a new servlet class over the old one in the *WEB-INF/classes* directory of the web application. The new servlet version becomes available immediately, without using the Console to redeploy the entire web application.

You can also use an Ant file to compile the servlet and copy it into WebLogic's default web application. The build file in Example 2-3 is very similar to the one used and described in Recipe 2.1; it's just revised for use with WebLogic's web container instead of Tomcat's.

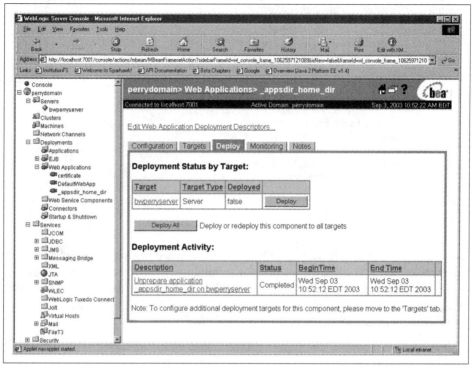

Figure 2-4. Graphically deploying a servlet

Example 2-3. Using an Ant file with a WebLogic servlet

```
<project name="Cookbook" default="deploy-servlet" basedir=".">

        <property file="wl.properties" />

  <target
        name="init"
        description="Initializes some properties.">
        <echo message="Initializing properties."/>
        <property name="build" value=".\build" />
        <property name="src" value=".\src" />
  </target>

  <target name="prepare" depends="init">
        <echo message="Cleaning up the build directory."/>
        <delete dir="${build}"/>
        <mkdir dir="${build}"/>
  </target>

  <path id="classpath">
        <fileset dir="${wl.dir}\server\lib">
              <include name="*.jar" />
        </fileset>
  </path>
```

Example 2-3. Using an Ant file with a WebLogic servlet (continued)

```
<target name="deploy-servlet" depends="prepare"
            description="Compile the specified servlet, then move it into
            WL's default Web application.">

        <echo message="Compiling the servlet ${compiled.servlet}...."/>
        <javac srcdir="${src}" destdir="${build}">
            <include name="${compiled.servlet}.java" />
            <classpath refid="classpath"/>
        </javac>
        <echo message="Copying the servlet to WL default web application..."/>
        <copy todir="${wl.webapp}/WEB-INF/classes">
        <fileset dir="${build}" />
    </copy>

</target>
</project>
```

This Ant build file first loads a set of properties contained in a file called *wl.properties,* which is located in the same directory as the build file. The build file typically has the name *build.xml*; however, you can call another build file in the same directory by using the -buildfile command-line option, as in ant -buildfile wl_build.xml. The *wl.properties* file for this example is shown in Example 2-4.

Example 2-4. wl.properties for WebLogic Ant build file

```
wl.webapp=k:/bea/user_projects/bwpdomain/applications/DefaultWebApp
wl.dir=k:/bea/weblogic700
compiled.servlet=test
```

The deploy-servlet target depends on a target named prepare that is also defined in this build file. The prepare target in turn has "init" as its depends attribute, which means that the init target executes prior to the prepare target. So calling the deploy-servlet target creates a chain of executing targets: init → prepare → deploy-servlet. In all, this is what the build file accomplishes:

1. init creates a couple of properties (build and source) that point to directories.

2. The prepare target deletes and then remakes the *build* directory, so that you start with a clean build.

3. deploy-servlet compiles the servlet into the *build* directory, then copies it into the directory specified by the wl.webapp property (which contains its value in the *wl.properties* file).

The path element creates a classpath out of the JAR files found in the *k:/bea/ weblogic700/server/lib* directory. This directory path is how Ant resolves the phrase "${wl.dir}\server\lib," which is parsed by attaching the value of the property wl.dir to the string "\server\lib."

See Also

Recipe 2.5, Recipes 2.7–2.10; the deployment sections of *WebLogic: The Definitive Guide*, by Mountjoy and Chugh (O'Reilly); WebLogic's Server 7.0 programmer documentation: *http://e-docs.bea.com/wls/docs70/programming.html*.

2.4   Deploying an Individual JSP on Tomcat

Problem

You want to place a JSP file into a web application.

Solution

Copy the new or revised JSP file into the top-level directory of the default Tomcat web application or of another deployed web application.

Discussion

The easiest way to test a new JSP file is to place it at the top level of Tomcat's default web application. This application is located in the *<Tomcat-installation-directory>/ webapps/ROOT/* directory. Tomcat 4.1.x compiles (or recompiles, if you are pasting a new JSP file over an old one) the JSP and display its response in a web page. You do not have to stop and start Tomcat using the Tomcat manager application for the new JSP file to be available to your web application.

> Placing a JSP file in a deployed web application will *not* work if the JSP depends on application-specific resources such as servlets, custom tags, or other Java classes, because there is no guarantee that the temporary host web application you are using for the JSP has access to those resources.

If you have to deploy a JSP separately from its web application, you can also place a JSP file in a deployed web application other than the Tomcat default application. This makes the JSP page available to application users without having to stop and restart Tomcat. Remember that the JSP files belong in the top level of the web application, which has the following directory structure:

```
index.html
default.jsp
anotherJsp.jsp
images/logo.jpeg
WEB-INF/classes/jspservletcookbook/myservlet.class
WEB-INF/lib/helperclasses.jar
WEB-INF/lib/utilities.jar
WEB-INF/web.xml
WEB-INF/mytags.tld
```

In other words, the top level of the directory contains the HTML and JSP files, as well as the *WEB-INF* directory. The *WEB-INF* directory contains:

- The *web.xml* deployment descriptor
- The *classes* directory, which contains package-related directories and servlet or support classes like JavaBeans
- The *lib* directory, which stores any Java Archive (JAR) files containing utility or helper classes that your web application uses
- Optionally, any Tag Library Descriptor files (files with *.tld* suffixes)
- Any optional directories for images, video files, XML files, or other web resources

See Also

The deployment sections of *Tomcat: The Definitive Guide* (O'Reilly); Recipes 2.1, 2.2, and 2.6.

2.5 Deploying an Individual JSP on WebLogic

Problem

You want to quickly test a JSP without deploying it as part of a new web application.

Solution

Copy and paste the JSP into the top-level directory of BEA WebLogic Server 7.0's default web application, then request the JSP in a browser.

Discussion

A JSP file can be "hot deployed" on WebLogic 7.0's default web application without having to redeploy the entire web application. This default web application is located at *<WebLogic-installation-directory>/user_projects/<name-of-your-domain>/applications/DefaultWebApp*. If you paste your JSP file into this directory (*DefaultWebApp*), it will be available to receive requests without redeploying the default web application. If your JSP file is named *newfile.jsp*, then the URL for requests to this page would be *http://localhost:7001/newfile.jsp*. Note the absence of a context path or application name in the URL. If the request is for the default web application, then the JSP files appear following the forward slash (/) after the *host:port* part of the URL (in other words, after the *localhost:7001/* part).

To repeat a prior caveat: placing a JSP file in a deployed web application in order to test it will *not* work if the JSP depends on application-specific resources such as servlets, custom tags, or other Java classes, because there is no guarantee that the temporary host web application you are using for the JSP has access to those resources.

In most cases, the JSP is already part of a web application, and several tools exist to redeploy a web application, including Ant, BEA WebLogic Builder, and the WebLogic Administration Console.

Finally, you can also copy and paste a JSP file into another WebLogic web application. However, that application must be deployed in exploded directory format, meaning that the application has not been deployed in archive form (as a WAR or EAR file). Therefore, place the JSP file in the application's top-level directory. If the application is named "newapp," this directory is named *<WebLogic-installation-directory>/user_projects/<name-of-your-domain>/applications/newapp*.

See Also

Recipe 2.3; Recipes 2.7–2.10; WebLogic's Server 7.0 programmer documentation: *http://e-docs.bea.com/wls/docs70/programming.html*.

2.6 Deploying a Web Application on Tomcat

Problem

You want to deploy an entire web application on Tomcat 4.1.x.

Solution

Create a Jakarta Ant build file. Ant can automatically compile your servlet classes, create a web application archive (*.war*) file, then deploy the WAR to the Tomcat 4.1.x server.

Discussion

The recommended method for the compilation and deployment of web applications is to use the Jakarta Ant automation tool. If you change anything in the application (such as altering a servlet or JSP), then all it takes is a single command-line execution of ant to compile, package, and redeploy the application on Tomcat. You do not have to go to the trouble of manually recompiling a changed servlet, creating a new WAR file, starting and stopping Tomcat, and redeploying the application.

Another method of deploying a web application on Tomcat is to place a directory containing a web application in the required directory structure in the Tomcat *webapps* folder. The name of the web application directory (such as *myapp*) then becomes the context path or name of the new web application. This deployment method is not guaranteed to work with other application servers, however, so it is an ineffective strategy for creating portable applications. In addition, since this manual method is not automated in any manner, it is awkward to replace and keep track of any changed servlet or JavaBean classes in these web application directories.

The end of this discussion describes how to configure Tomcat's *server.xml* configuration file so that a context path points to an unpacked web application directory elsewhere on the server. As an alternative to creating an archived application (a WAR file), Tomcat developers can use this method of deployment during development and testing.

Using Ant for deployment

Using Ant to compile and deploy an application involves the following steps:

1. Choose a directory to hold the Ant *build.xml* file, any *build.properties* files, and all of the contents of your web application.

2. Create the directories to hold the Java servlet source files, any JSP or HTML files, Java Archive (JAR) files for components (such as database drivers) and the web application archive file (WAR file). One way to create this directory structure is shown in Figure 2-5.

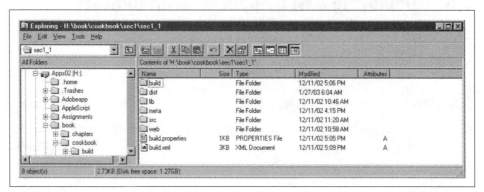

Figure 2-5. Web application directory structure

3. In this example, the *src* directory contains the Java source files for servlets and JavaBeans. The *web* directory contains the files that reside at the top level of the web application, such as JSP and HTML files. The *meta* directory holds XML deployment descriptors (at the very least, *web.xml*). The *build* directory is where Ant compiles the Java source files. These files will end up in the *WEB-INF/ classes* directory of the web application. The *lib* directory is for any JAR files that your web application uses, such as database drivers and/or tag libraries. Finally, the *dist* directory contains the WAR file.

4. Create the Java source code for the application and move any other related files (like JSPs and *web.xml*) into their specified directories.

5. Create any necessary property values in the *build.properties* file that *build.xml* will use during the compilation and deployment process. These properties will be described in more detail in the upcoming discussion.

6. Run the *build.xml* file on the command line by changing to the directory containing the *build.xml* file and typing ant.

Example 2-5 is the *build.properties* file that is referenced in step 5.

 The file does not have to be called *build.properties*; this name is used purely by convention. You could call it *global.props*, for instance.

Example 2-5. build.properties for web application deployment

```
tomcat.webapps=k:/jakarta-tomcat-4.1.12/webapps/
tomcat.dir=k:/jakarta-tomcat-4.1.12
url=http://localhost:8080/manager
username=tomcat
password=tomcat
manager.path=${tomcat.dir}/work/standalone/localhost/manager
```

Each of these properties is made available to or imported into the *build.xml* file by the following line within this file:

```
<property file="build.properties" />
```

This line represents a property task or XML element within the *build.xml* XML file. For example, the value of the tomcat.dir property inside the Ant XML file is "k:/jakarta-tomcat-4.1.12."

Example 2-6 is the entire *build.xml* file. It can be used to compile Java classes, create a WAR file, and deploy it to Tomcat—just by executing ant on the command line. The chief advantage of using Ant is that it automates an otherwise complicated process. If you have to change or add a servlet in the web application, for instance, you can recompile and redeploy the web application simply by running Ant. This *build.xml* file is fairly complex and introduces some advanced features of Ant.

Example 2-6. An Ant build file for deploying a web application

```
<project name="Deploy Project" default="deploy-application">

  <taskdef name="deploy" classname="org.apache.catalina.ant.DeployTask" />
  <taskdef name="undeploy" classname="org.apache.catalina.ant.UndeployTask" />
  <property file="build.properties" />

  <path id="classpath">
    <fileset dir="${tomcat.dir}/common/lib">
      <include name="*.jar" />
```

```
    </fileset>
    <fileset dir="${tomcat.dir}/common/endorsed">
      <include name="*.jar" />
    </fileset>
</path>

<target name="init"
  description="Initializes some properties.">
  <echo message="Initializing properties."/>
  <property name="build" value=".\build" />
  <property name="src" value=".\src" />
  <property name="dist" value=".\dist" />
  <property name="lib" value=".\lib" />
  <property name="web" value=".\web" />
  <property name="meta" value=".\meta" />
  <property name="context-path" value="myapp" />
</target>

<target name="prepare" depends="init">
    <echo message="Cleaning up the build and dist directories."/>
    <delete dir="${build}"/>
    <mkdir dir="${build}"/>
    <delete dir="${dist}"/>
    <mkdir dir="${dist}"/>
</target>

<target name="deploy"
    description="Deploys a Web application">
    <deploy url="${url}" username="${username}" password="${password}"
       path="/${context-path}" war="file:${dist}/${context-path}.war"
  />
</target>

<target name="undeploy"
    description="Undeploys a Web application" if="already.deployed">
    <undeploy url="${url}" username="${username}" password="${password}"
    path="/ ${context-path}" />
</target>

<target name="create-war" description="creates a web application archive file">
    <war destfile="${dist}/${context-path}.war" webxml="${meta}/web.xml">
        <classes dir="${build}"/>
        <lib dir="${lib}"/>
        <fileset dir="${web}"/>
    </war>
</target>

<target name="deploy-application" depends="prepare"
    description="Compile the web application....">
    <echo message="Undeploying the application only if it's deployed..."/>
    <available file="${manager.path}/${context-path}.war" property="already.deployed"/>
    <antcall target="undeploy"/>
```

```
    <echo message="Compiling the application files..."/>
    <javac srcdir="${src}" destdir="${build}">
        <include name="*.java" />
        <classpath refid="classpath"/>
     </javac>
    <echo message="creating the WAR file...."/>
    <antcall target="create-war"/>
    <antcall target="deploy"/>
  </target>
</project>
```

The `create-war` target uses the `war` Ant task to generate the WAR file, based on certain attribute values and nested elements. For example, the *web.xml* file that will be included in the WAR is specified as the value for the `war` task's `webxml` attribute. In addition, the classes that will be included in the WAR file's *WEB-INF/classes* directory are specified by this nested element of the war task:

```
    <classes dir="${build}"/>
```

The nice thing about this `classes` element, along with the `lib` and `fileset` nested elements, is that all of the nested directories inside the *build*, *lib*, and *web* directories are automatically included in the WAR. For example, the *web* directory includes an *images* directory containing the application's various GIF files. The *images* directory is included at the top level of the WAR file, along with any HTML or JSP files that are stored in the *web* directory, just by including this nested element:

```
    <fileset dir="${web}"/>
```

Also examine the `deploy-application` target, which embodies the meat of this *build. xml* file. As long as you properly set the PATH environment variable to point at the Ant component, the `deploy-application` target is called by default when you type ant at the command line.

First, the target finds out whether the web application has already been deployed on Tomcat. This function is included because this build file will presumably be run over and over again, not just the first time the web application is deployed. This line uses an `available` task, which sets a property to the value "true" only if the file specified in its `file` attribute exists:

```
    <available file="${manager.path}/${context-path}.war"
                property="already.deployed"/>
    <antcall target="undeploy"/>
```

If this particular file is found, it means that the Tomcat Manager application has already deployed the WAR file, and that the `already.deployed` property is set to true. This allows the *build.xml* file to conditionally undeploy the application, before the application is redeployed after any changes. In other words, it undeploys the application only if the web application is already deployed (otherwise, running the `undeploy` target raises an error and halts execution of the build file). The undeploy target runs only if the already.deployed property is set to true:

```
<target name="undeploy"
    description="Undeploys a Web application"
    if="already.deployed">
```

The handy antcall task calls another target in the file, similar to calling a method. Finally, the deploy-application target uses the javac task to compile the application's servlets into the *build* directory, then uses the antcall task to create the WAR file and deploy the new or changed application to Tomcat. The target echoes various messages to the console to help indicate to the developer what it is doing:

```
<target name="deploy-application" depends="prepare"
    description="Compile the web application....">
    ...
    <echo message="Compiling the application files..."/>
    <javac srcdir="${src}" destdir="${build}">
        <include name="*.java" />
        <classpath refid="classpath"/>
    </javac>
    <echo message="creating the WAR file...."/>
    <antcall target="create-war"/>
    <antcall target="deploy"/>
</target>
```

As an alternative to using the prior deployment method, you can configure Tomcat to point to an external directory that contains a valid web application. This strategy deploys the web application the next time Tomcat is restarted. It is an acceptable strategy when the application is under development, because you can configure Tomcat to automatically reload the application (Recipe 2.2) when a servlet is changed, or when a JAR file is added to *WEB-INF/lib*. However, developers should deploy applications as WAR files when the time comes to run the application on a production server.

Create a file that contains a Context element as this element would appear in *server.xml*. Give this file a *.xml* extension. It is sensible to call this file the same name as the context path or application name (for example, *myapp.xml*), but not required. Your file content might look like this:

```
<Context className="org.apache.catalina.core.StandardContext"
    crossContext="false" reloadable="true"
    mapperClass="org.apache.catalina.core.StandardContextMapper"
    useNaming="true" debug="0" swallowOutput="false"
    privileged="false"
    wrapperClass="org.apache.catalina.core.StandardWrapper"
    docBase="h:\book\cookbook\sec1\sec1_1\dist"
    cookies="true" path="/newapp" cachingAllowed="true"
    charsetMapperClass="org.apache.catalina.util.CharsetMapper">
</Context>
```

The reloadable attribute value of "true" configures Tomcat to monitor the classes in *WEB-INF/classes* and the components in *WEB-INF/lib* for any changes. Tomcat automatically reloads the web application if it detects any changes.

The value for the docBase attribute can be an absolute path to the directory that contains the web application, or the context root. It can also be the path to a WAR file. The docBase attribute can also be a path name relative to the *appBase* directory of the enclosing Host element in *server.xml*, such as relative to the *<Tomcat-installation-directory>/webapps* directory. The path attribute declares the context path for the new application, as in *http://localhost:8080/newapp/* (where */newapp* is the context path).

Place this file in the *<Tomcat-installation-directory>/webapps* directory (or whichever directory is configured as the appBase in the enclosing Host element in *conf/server.xml*) and restart Tomcat. This web application can now be invoked on Tomcat.

See Also

The deployment sections of *Tomcat: The Definitive Guide* by Brittain and Darwin (O'Reilly); Recipes 2.1, 2.2, and 2.4.

2.7   Deploying a Web Application on WebLogic Using Ant

Problem

You want to deploy a web application on WebLogic Server 7.0 using Jakarta Ant.

Solution

Create a Jakarta Ant build file. Ant can automatically compile your servlet classes, create a web-application archive (*.war*) file, and then deploy the WAR to WebLogic Server 7.0.

Discussion

You can either manually cut and paste web components into the WebLogic *applications* directory (as described in the sidebar), or use Ant to automate the process of compiling, generating a WAR file, and copying the WAR to this directory. An example directory path to *applications* is *k:\bea\user_projects\bwpdomain\applications*. This method would entail a minor edit of the *build.xml* and *build.properties* files described in Recipe 2.6.

Manually Deploying a Web Application

When BEA WebLogic Server 7.0 is running in development mode, if a WAR file, an enterprise archive application (EAR) file, or a directory that contains a valid web application is placed in the *applications* directory, then those applications are automatically deployed and become available on the server.

A valid web application contains a *WEB-INF/web.xml* deployment descriptor that does not generate any parsing exceptions. If the directory that you place in the *applications* folder does not contain a deployment descriptor, then WebLogic will *not* automatically deploy the application, even if the server is running in development mode. WebLogic raises an exception similar to this one in the console in which the server was started up:

```
<Unable to activate application, _appsdir_dist_dir, from source, K:\bea\user_
projects\bwpdomain\applications\dist. Reason: No J2EE deployment descriptor
found at "K:\bea\user_projects\bwpdomain\applications\dist".>
```

This deploy-application Ant target is edited in *build.xml* to deploy on WebLogic 7.0:

```
<target name="deploy-application" depends="prepare"
    description="Compile the web application....">
    <echo message="Compiling the application files..."/>
    <javac srcdir="${src}" destdir="${build}">
        <include name="*.java" />
        <classpath refid="classpath"/>
    </javac>
    <echo message="creating the WAR file...."/>
    <antcall target="create-war"/>
    <copy todir="${wl.applications}">
        <fileset dir="${dist}" />
    </copy>
</target>
```

In addition, the *build.properties* file could define the wl.applications property with a value such as "k:\bea\user_projects\bwpdomain\applications". Once the WAR file is copied to this special directory, a WebLogic server that is started in development mode will automatically deploy it.

 In the \user_project\bwpdomain directory (depending on your server domain name) the WebLogic start script is called *startWebLogic.cmd* on Windows and *startWebLogic.sh* on Unix. To start the server in development mode, the line in the start script should be set STARTMODE= (the value is an empty string here) or set STARTMODE=false. The server starts in production mode if it is set STARTMODE=true.

See Also

Recipe 2.3; Recipes 2.8–2.10; WebLogic's Server 7.0 programmer documentation: *http://e-docs.bea.com/wls/docs70/programming.html*.

2.8   Using the WebLogic Administration Console

Problem

You want to deploy a web application using WebLogic's Administration Console.

Solution

Bring up the Administration Console in your web browser and use its graphical interface to deploy either a WAR file or a web-application directory.

Discussion

The WebLogic Administration Console is a servlet- and browser-based tool for managing WebLogic server resources and Java 2 Enterprise Edition (J2EE) applications. To use the Console, WebLogic Server must be running. First, request the URL *http://localhost:7001/console* (or whichever your server address and port is, as in *http://<weblogic-server-address>:<port>/console*). Then enter your login name and password to gain entry to the browser-based tool. The resulting screen looks like Figure 2-6, with a hierarchical list of choices in the lefthand column and the current screen choice in the righthand column.

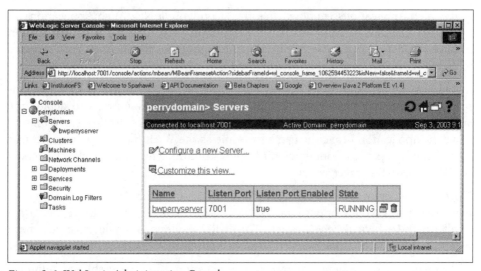

Figure 2-6. WebLogic Administration Console

In the left column, choose the name of your domain by clicking on the plus sign (+), which displays the domain's subnodes. The subnodes of the domain include Servers, Clusters, Machines, Network Channels, Deployments, Services, and Security.

Then choose the "Deployments" node, which gives you the choice of selecting its "Web Applications" subnode. Open up the "Web Applications" node by clicking on its plus sign. The resulting screen looks like Figure 2-7.

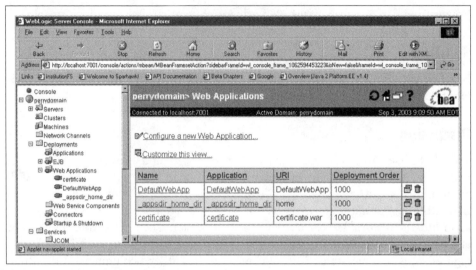

Figure 2-7. Web Applications node

In the Web Applications window, click the "Configure a New Web Application…" hyperlink. The next screen gives you the option of uploading the Web Application Archive (WAR) or Enterprise Application Archive (EAR) file through your browser to the server's filesystem, as shown in Figure 2-8.

Initiate this upload and then click on the "select" link next to the WAR file. Complete the three steps that Figure 2-9 shows: click the arrow buttons to deploy the application from the "Available Servers" column to the "Target Servers" column, name the application (leave the name the same as the WAR filename minus the *.war* suffix), then press the "Configure and Deploy" button. That is all it takes to deploy the WAR file to the target server.

Now test the deployment by requesting one of the servlets in the browser, using the name that you gave the application as the context path. An example URL is *http://localhost:7001/cookbook/cookieservlet*. This URL requests a servlet that has been mapped to the name "/cookieservlet." The web-application context path is */cookbook*.

Redeploying a previously undeployed web application using the WebLogic Administration Console involves the following steps:

1. Select the name of your application under the Web Applications node in the Console's lefthand column. This shows a screen similar to Figure 2-10.

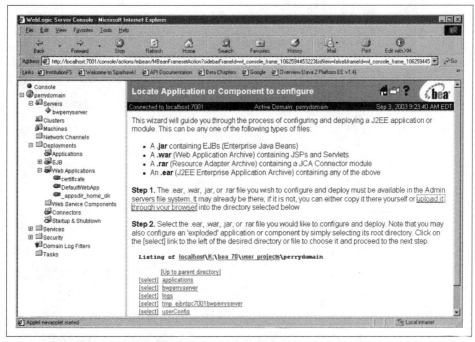

Figure 2-8. Deploying a web application as a WAR or EAR file

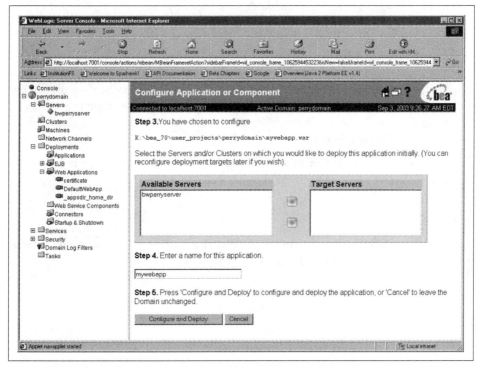

Figure 2-9. Final steps for deploying the WAR file

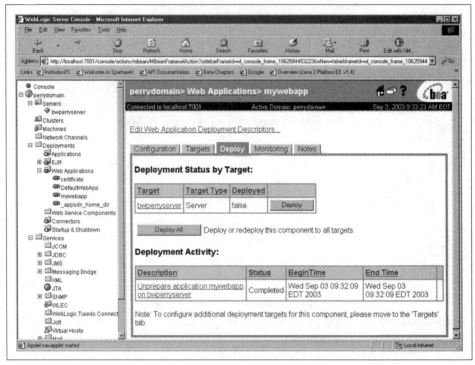

Figure 2-10. Selecting a web application in the Console

2. Click the "Deploy" button in the righthand screen. This reactivates the application, so that it can receive requests in the WebLogic web container.

If you want to delete a web application using the WebLogic Administration Console, click on the name of your domain in the lefthand column of the Console screen, then on the "Deployments" and "Web Applications" nodes. Clicking the trash can icon associated with the application, as shown in Figure 2-11, deletes the application from the WebLogic server.

Deleting a web application in this manner means that the application is no longer available to receive requests in the WebLogic web container.

See Also

Recipes 2.3 and 2.7; Recipes 2.9 and 2.10; WebLogic's Server 7.0 programmer documentation: *http://e-docs.bea.com/wls/docs70/programming.html.*

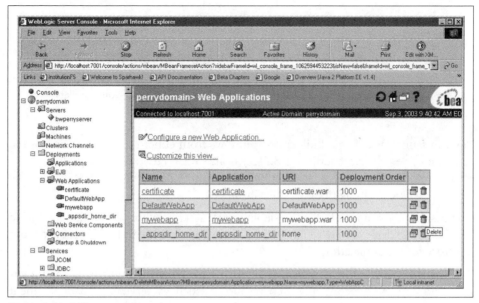

Figure 2-11. Deleting a web application

2.9   Using WebLogic Builder to Deploy a Web Application

Problem

You want to use WebLogic Builder to deploy a web application.

Solution

WebLogic Builder installs with the WebLogic 7.0 Server, so you can launch the Builder application and use its graphical tools to deploy the web application.

Discussion

WebLogic Builder is a graphical tool that installs with WebLogic Server 7. It can be used to edit deployment descriptor files such as *web.xml* and *weblogic.xml*, as well as for deploying web applications to a server. Using WebLogic Builder, you can open up, edit, and deploy web applications that exist as either WAR files or in exploded directory format.

Exploded directory format is a web-application directory structure as it would appear in your filesystem, but that is not in archived or in WAR form. To be deployed on WebLogic as a web application, the root directory must contain the *WEB-INF/web.xml* deployment descriptor and any other properly structured application components, such as a the *WEB-INF/classes* directory containing your servlets (including any package-related directories).

You can launch WebLogic Builder on Windows from either the "Start" menu or the command line. The start script for Buildcr is at: *<BEA_HOME>/weblogic700/server/ bin/startWLBuilder.cmd* (or *startWLBuilder.sh* on Unix). *<BEA_HOME>* is the directory where WebLogic Server 7.0 is installed.

It is easy to open up and edit the deployment descriptor for a web application in WebLogic Builder. Go to the File → Open menu and navigate to the WAR file or root directory for the application.

The result is the window depicted in Figure 2-12. The navigation tree in the upper-left window lets you configure web resources (such as servlets) and deployment descriptor elements (such as security constraints), then save the changes to *web.xml*.

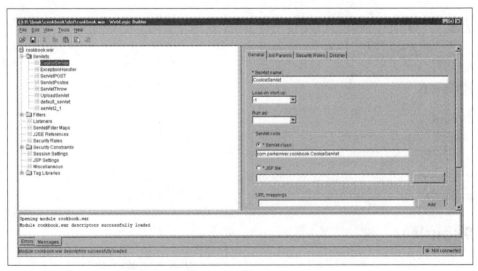

Figure 2-12. Opening a WAR file in WebLogic Builder

You can add or delete elements for servlets, servlet mappings, and filters, for instance. The changes are persisted to the deployment descriptor if you make *and* save changes to the application from within WebLogic Builder. You can then optionally connect to the server from the "Tools" menu, and deploy the application.

The "Deploy Module" window indicates whether the application is already deployed. Figure 2-13 shows this window. If you have already deployed the application, you can still make deployment-descriptor changes in Builder, then deploy the application again from the "Tools" menu. WebLogic Builder specifically undeploys the application, then redeploys it with the changes that you included in *web.xml*.

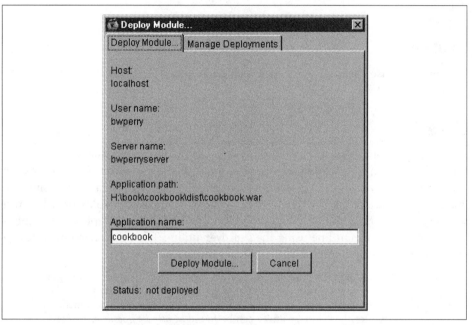

Figure 2-13. WebLogic Builder's Deploy Module window

WebLogic Builder does *not* show any JSP files that may be part of the web application. It will show any servlet mappings that are associated with JSP files.

See Also

Recipes 2.3, 2.7, 2.8, and 2.10; WebLogic's Server 7.0 programmer documentation: *http://e-docs.bea.com/wls/docs70/programming.html*; the local WebLogic Builder Help documentation: *<BEA_HOME>\weblogic700\server\builder\index.html*.

2.10 Using the weblogic.Deployer Command-Line Tool

Problem

You want to use the command line to deploy a web application on WebLogic Server 7.0.

Solution

Use the Java-based `weblogic.Deployer` command-line utility, which is installed with WebLogic Server 7.0.

Discussion

For developers or administrators who need to use the command line or shell scripts for deploying and redeploying web applications, WebLogic Server 7.0 provides the Java-based `Deployer` utility. This utility accomplishes the same tasks as using the graphical interface of the WebLogic Administration Console to deploy or redeploy a web application. First, this recipe describes how to deploy and redeploy a web application on the command line using the `Deployer` utility. Then the recipe provides an example of a Windows batch file that invokes the `Deployer` utility.

 The `Deployer` utility can initiate other tasks, such as redeploying individual web components in a web application. The online documentation for the `Deployer` utility can be found at *http://e-docs.bea.com/wls/ docs70/programming/deploying.html#1094693*.

The `Deployer` utility is a Java-based program that requires the following JAR file on your classpath before the program can run: *<BEA_HOME>\server\lib\weblogic.jar*. *<BEA_HOME>* represents the directory where WebLogic Server 7.0 was installed. The following command-line script on a Windows NT 4.0 machine redeploys the *cookbook.war* web application on a server named *bwpserver*:

```
java -cp k:\bea\weblogic700\server\lib\weblogic.jar;
    %CLASSPATH% weblogic.Deployer
    -adminurl http://localhost:7001
    -user bwperry -name cookbook -source .\dist\cookbook.war
    -targets bwpserver -activate
```

This command-line invocation deploys the web application represented by the archive file *cookbook.war*, so the application is now available to receive requests with the context path */cookbook*. When run on the command line, the program prompts the user for a password if you have not included it in the script with the -password option. The -source option specifies the location of the WAR file or web-application directory. The -targets option specifies one or more servers on which to deploy the web application. The final command for deploying the application is -activate.

This command-line invocation deactivates (makes unavailable) an existing web application on the server *bwpserver*. It prompts for the user password first, unless you add the -password option to the command line:

```
java -cp k:\bea\weblogic700\server\lib\weblogic.jar;
    %CLASSPATH% weblogic.Deployer
    -adminurl http://localhost:7001
    -user bwperry -name cookbook
    -targets bwpserver -deactivate
```

The -cp option specifies the classpath to use for running the Deployer Java utility, and must include the *weblogic.jar* JAR file. The -adminurl switch specifies the administration server (the default value is *http://localhost:7001*, so it does not have to be included here). The -name option specifies the name of the application to be deactivated, and the -targets option names the server where the application is running. The following command-line invocation redeploys the same "cookbook" application:

```
java -cp k:\bea\weblogic700\server\lib\weblogic.jar;
    %CLASSPATH% weblogic.Deployer
     -user bwperry -name cookbook -activate
```

This time, the -adminurl and -targets options were omitted. The default values for these switches are *http://localhost:7001* and all current targets (if the developer is redeploying an existing application), respectively. If the application is being deployed for the first time, the default target for the -targets option is the administration server.

It is easier to run shell commands from a batch file, because there is less typing for complicated command-line programs and the shell scripts can be permanently saved. Example 2-7 is the first example rewritten as a batch file on Windows NT 4.0.

Example 2-7. Deploying an application

```
@echo off
set WL_HOME=K:\bea\weblogic700

set BEA_CLASSPATH=%WL_HOME%\server\lib\weblogic.jar;%CLASSPATH%

java -cp %BEA_CLASSPATH% weblogic.Deployer -adminurl http://localhost:7001 -user bwperry
-name cookbook -source .\dist\cookbook.war -targets bwpserver -activate
```

This batch file sets two environment variables: WL_HOME and BEA_CLASSPATH. These are used to make sure that the classpath includes the *weblogic.jar* file, which contains the Deployer utility. If the script was saved as *deploy.bat*, this is how it would be run on the command line:

```
H:\book\cookbook>deploy
```

The resulting console output looks like this.

```
Enter a password for the user "bwperry":bwpserver_1968
Operation started, waiting for notifications...
....
#TaskID Action        Status  Target     Type    Application   Source
15      Activate      Success bwpserver  Server  cookbook      H:\book\
cookbook\.\dist\cook
```

See Also

Recipes 2.3 and 2.5; Recipes 2.7–2.9; WebLogic's Server 7.0 programmer documentation: *http://e-docs.bea.com/wls/docs70/programming.html*.

CHAPTER 3

Naming Your Servlets

3.0   Introduction

An important web application configuration task is to create the path by which your servlet is requested by web users. This is what the user types into the address field of his browser in order to make a request to the servlet. While this is sometimes the full name of the servlet, that convention often results in an awkward URI. For example, a web site might have a servlet that dynamically assembles a "Resources" page, instead of a static *resources.html* page. Using the full servlet name, the request URL might be *http://www.myorganization.com/servlet/com. organization.servlets.resources.ResourceServlet*. This is quite a path to type in; it makes much more sense to map this to a *servlet path*, which is an alias for the servlet. Using the servlet path, the (new) address for the dynamic page might be *http:// www.myorganization.com/resources*. The servlet path, in this case, is */resources*.

This servlet path is also the identifier used by other servlets or JSPs that forward requests to this particular servlet, as well as the address that an HTML form tag uses in its `action` attribute to launch parameter names and values toward the servlet. The servlet specification offers an intuitive and flexible way to map HTTP requests to servlets in the *web.xml* deployment descriptor.

This chapter describes how you can use the *web.xml* deployment descriptor to create one or more aliases (servlet paths) to your servlet. It also discusses how to invoke the servlet with other types of URLs, such as one that looks like a JSP page request (e.g., *info.jsp*) or one that looks like an HTML page request (*info.html*). Recipe 3.5 also describes how to access a servlet *without* a mapping in *web.xml*, for example, for the developer who wants to debug her servlet without modifying the *web.xml* file.

Finally, Recipes 3.7, 3.9, and 3.10 show how to map all requests to one "controller" servlet (3.7), restrict the requests for certain servlets to authenticated users (3.9), and block all requests to certain servlets except those forwarded from the controller (3.10).

3.1 Mapping a Servlet to a Name in web.xml

Problem

You want to create an alias, or servlet path, to your servlet.

Solution

Create servlet and servlet-mapping elements in *web.xml*.

Discussion

Creating an alias to the servlet takes place in the deployment descriptor's servlet-mapping element. All servlet elements must come before any of the servlet-mapping elements in the servlet 2.3 *web.xml* deployment descriptor. The servlet-mapping element refers to the name of the servlet that appears in the servlet-name element, such as:

```
<servlet><servlet-name>myservlet</servlet-name></servlet>
```

This is referred to as the servlet's *registered name*. The servlet-mapping then provides the name, or *URL pattern*, which web application users can type into their browsers to access the servlet. Example 3-1 shows a *web.xml* file with a servlet and servlet-mapping element. The registered name in this case is "CookieServlet".

Example 3-1. servlet and servlet-mapping elements

```
<?xml version="1.0" encoding="ISO-8859-1"?>
<!DOCTYPE web-app
    PUBLIC "-//Sun Microsystems, Inc.//DTD Web Application 2.3//EN"
          "http://java.sun.com/dtd/web-application_2_3.dtd"
>

<web-app>
  <servlet>
    <servlet-name>CookieServlet</servlet-name>
    <servlet-class>com.jspservletcookbook.CookieServlet</servlet-class>
  </servlet>

  <servlet-mapping>
    <servlet-name>CookieServlet</servlet-name>
    <url-pattern>/cookieservlet</url-pattern>
  </servlet-mapping>
</web-app>
```

In this example, the servlet element registers the name "CookieServlet" by using the servlet-name element. The class name is specified by the servlet-class element. The actual location of this servlet class may be *WEB-INF/classes/com/jspservletcookbook/*, or inside a JAR file that resides in *WEB-INF/lib*. "CookieServlet" becomes the

---

registered name by which the servlet `com.jspservletcookbook.CookieServlet` is referred to in the rest of the *web.xml* file.

Now create the servlet path by which the *web application users* will access this servlet in their web browsers. This aliasing is accomplished with the `servlet-mapping` element. `servlet-name` identifies the registered name by which the servlet is referred to in *web.xml*, and the `url-pattern` element creates the URL that is used to access this servlet. The / character inside the */cookieservlet* pattern means "begin at the web-application root." For example, if the context path for the site *http://www. mysite.org* is "cookbook," then the complete address for accessing the `CookieServlet` servlet is *http://www.mysite.org/cookbook/cookieservlet*. The */cookbook* part of the URL is the context path for your web application. The servlet is then identified with the */cookieservlet* pattern within that context.

Looking at this more generally, you have the following URL for any given servlet:

```
http://<host>:<port>/<context path>/<servlet-path>
```

 Most servlet containers allow for a *default context*, where the context path is /. In this case, the URL is in this form:
```
http://<host>:<port>/<servlet-path>
```

For example, if you are using Tomcat 4.1.x on your local machine and have created an application called "myapp" and a servlet URL pattern of */myservlet*, the entire web address for that servlet looks like *http://localhost:8080/myapp/myservlet*.

You can also access a servlet with a URL like this:

```
http://host:port/context path/servlet/registered-servlet-name
```

So if the registered servlet name was "MyServlet," then the request appears as *http://localhost:8080/myapp/servlet/MyServlet*.

Some servlet engines use a different servlet path than */servlet*, and others allow this path to be changed by an administrator. You should consult the documentation for your servlet container to ensure the correct path for your setup. What if the example servlet-mapping element appeared in the *web.xml* file for the server's default web application, in which the context path is /? In this case, users would access the `CookieServlet` servlet by using the address *http://www.mysite.org/cookieservlet*.

The url-pattern that you create for a servlet inside of a servlet-mapping element is case-sensitive in Tomcat and WebLogic. According to Chapter SRV.11.1 of the servlet v2.3 specification and v2.4 proposed final draft, "The container must use case-sensitive string comparisons for matching." If the user requests *http://www.mysite.org/cookbook/cookieSERVLET* instead of *http://www.mysite.org/cookbook/cookieservlet*, then the request is not directed to the mapped servlet (CookieServlet). In Tomcat 4.1.x and WebLogic 7.0, the request returns an HTTP 404 error code, which is the "File not found" type error returned by a web server.

The url-pattern inside the servlet-mapping element can take on different forms, which are discussed in the upcoming recipes.

See Also

Chapter 1 on *web.xml*; Recipes 3.2–3.8; Chapter 11 of the Servlet v2.3 and 2.4 specifications on mapping requests to servlets.

3.2 Creating More Than One Mapping to a Servlet

Problem

You want to create several names or URL patterns that web users can use to request a single servlet.

Solution

Associate the servlet element with more than one servlet-mapping element in the deployment descriptor.

Discussion

You can create a number of servlet-mapping elements for a single servlet, as shown in Example 3-2. A user can access this servlet by using one of two addresses: *http://www.mysite.org/cookbook/cookieservlet* or *http://www.mysite.org/cookbook/mycookie*.

Example 3-2. Two servlet-mapping tags

```
<?xml version="1.0" encoding="ISO-8859-1"?>
<!DOCTYPE web-app
    PUBLIC "-//Sun Microsystems, Inc.//DTD Web Application 2.3//EN"
        "http://java.sun.com/dtd/web-application_2_3.dtd"
>
```

Example 3-2. Two servlet-mapping tags (continued)

```
<web-app>
  <servlet>
    <servlet-name>CookieServlet</servlet-name>
    <servlet-class>com.parkerriver.cookbook.CookieServlet</servlet-class>
  </servlet>
  <servlet-mapping>
    <servlet-name>CookieServlet</servlet-name>
    <url-pattern>/cookieservlet</url-pattern>
  </servlet-mapping>
  <servlet-mapping>
    <servlet-name>CookieServlet</servlet-name>
    <url-pattern>/mycookie</url-pattern>
  </servlet-mapping>
</web-app>
```

Remember that the servlet-mapping elements have to appear after all of the servlet elements in the servlet 2.3 deployment descriptor.

 Only *exact* matches to the URL pattern will work. If a user requests */cookieservlet/* (note the final forward slash) instead of */cookieservlet*, she receives an HTTP error code instead of the servlet-generated page she was expecting.

You can use a wildcard character (*) to extend your mapping pattern. The mappings in Example 3-3 invoke the CookieServlet for all of the URLs that begin with */cookie/*, and then optionally include any names after the forward slash. For example, CookieServlet can be invoked with a URL of *http://www.mysite.org/cookbook/cookie/you* using this descriptor. This is because the url-pattern matches any HTTP requests ending with the "/cookie/" string.

Example 3-3. Using an asterisk in the URL pattern

```
<?xml version="1.0" encoding="ISO-8859-1"?>
<!DOCTYPE web-app
    PUBLIC "-//Sun Microsystems, Inc.//DTD Web Application 2.3//EN"
           "http://java.sun.com/dtd/web-application_2_3.dtd"
>
<servlet>
  <servlet-name>CookieServlet</servlet-name>
  <servlet-class>com.jspservletcookbook.CookieServlet</servlet-class>
</servlet>

<servlet-mapping>
  <servlet-name>CookieServlet</servlet-name>
  <url-pattern>/cookie/*</url-pattern>
</servlet-mapping>
```

You cannot use the asterisk character as a wildcard symbol inside the servlet-name element. The asterisk can be used only as a wildcard symbol in the url-pattern element (as in <url-pattern>/cookie/*</url-pattern>), or in patterns that point to all files with a certain extension or suffix (as in <url-pattern>*.jsp</url-pattern>). The latter pattern is called an *extension mapping*.

See Also

Chapter 1 on *web.xml*; Recipe 3.1; Recipes 3.3–3.8; Chapter 11 of the Servlet v2.3 and 2.4 specifications on mapping requests to servlets.

3.3   Creating a JSP-Type URL for a Servlet

Problem

You want to link a URL pattern that looks like a JSP file request to a servlet.

Solution

Create a servlet-mapping element that includes a JSP-style URL pattern.

Discussion

I mentioned in the previous recipes that you have a lot of latitude when creating aliases that point to servlets. For instance, a request that appears to access a JSP file can easily be mapped to a servlet. The deployment descriptor in Example 3-4 maps the URL pattern */info.jsp* to the JspInfo servlet.

Example 3-4. Deployment descriptor example of mapping a JSP-style URL to a servlet

```
<?xml version="1.0" encoding="ISO-8859-1"?>
<!DOCTYPE web-app
    PUBLIC "-//Sun Microsystems, Inc.//DTD Web Application 2.3//EN"
           "http://java.sun.com/dtd/web-application_2_3.dtd"
>
<web-app>
    <servlet>
        <servlet-name>JspInfo</servlet-name>
        <servlet-class>com.parkerriver.cookbook.JspInfo</servlet-class>
    </servlet>
    <servlet-mapping>
        <servlet-name>JspInfo</servlet-name>
        <url-pattern>/info.jsp</url-pattern>
    </servlet-mapping>
</web-app>
```

The forward slash that begins the URL pattern */info.jsp* means "begin at the root of the web application that uses this deployment descriptor." So the entire URL for the JspInfo servlet looks like this for the cookbook web application: *http://www.mysite.org/cookbook/info.jsp*.

You can also map *all* references to JSP pages to a single servlet, as shown in Example 3-5, which uses a *web.xml* entry with an extension mapping.

Example 3-5. Mapping all JSP URLs to a single servlet

```
<?xml version="1.0" encoding="ISO-8859-1"?>
<!DOCTYPE web-app
    PUBLIC "-//Sun Microsystems, Inc.//DTD Web Application 2.3//EN"
        "http://java.sun.com/dtd/web-application_2_3.dtd"
>

<web-app>
    <servlet>
        <servlet-name>JspInfo</servlet-name>
        <servlet-class>com.parkerriver.cookbook.JspInfo</servlet-class>
    </servlet>
    <servlet-mapping>
        <servlet-name>JspInfo</servlet-name>
        <url-pattern>*.jsp</url-pattern>
    </servlet-mapping>
</web-app>
```

Make sure to *exclude* the slash (/) in the URL pattern, as an extension mapping that uses a file extension suffix begins with an asterisk and ends with a period and the suffix itself, as in <url-pattern>*.jsp</url-pattern>. This type of mapping may be useful if you were migrating an application from one version that used a lot of JSP pages to a new version that relied entirely on servlets. This takes care of users who have bookmarked many URLs that involve JSP files.

 Tomcat 4.1.x includes an implicit mapping to its own JSP page compiler and execution servlet for any request ending in *.jsp*. If you include a mapping such as the one in the previous web-app fragment, then your mapping will override Tomcat's implicit mapping.

See Also

Chapter 1 on *web.xml*; Recipes 3.1 and 3.2; Recipes 3.4–3.8; Chapter 11 of the Servlet v2.3 and 2.4 specifications on mapping requests to servlets.

3.4   Mapping Static Content to a Servlet

Problem

You want requests for static content such as HTML-style URLs to request a servlet.

Solution

Use a `servlet-mapping` element in *web.xml* to map the servlet name to the static content.

Discussion

It often seems odd to the casual programmer, but you can have a servlet respond to a URL that appears to be static content, such as an HTML file. Example 3-6 maps the servlet HtmlServlet to all URLs ending in the *.html* suffix. Any request within the web application that contains this deployment descriptor and specifies a file ending with *.html* is directed to HtmlServlet.

Example 3-6. Mapping static content to a servlet in web.xml

```
<?xml version="1.0" encoding="ISO-8859-1"?>
<!DOCTYPE web-app
    PUBLIC "-//Sun Microsystems, Inc.//DTD Web Application 2.3//EN"
           "http://java.sun.com/dtd/web-application_2_3.dtd"
>

<web-app>
  <servlet>
    <servlet-name>HtmlServlet</servlet-name>
    <servlet-class>com.jspservletcookbook.HtmlServlet</servlet-class>
  </servlet>
  <servlet-mapping>
    <servlet-name>HtmlServlet</servlet-name>
    <url-pattern>*.html</url-pattern>
  </servlet-mapping>
</web-app>
```

The servlet-mapping element in this listing contains an extension-mapping URL pattern: it begins with an asterisk and ends with *.html*. If you want to map the servlet to just one HTML file, use XML that looks like this:

```
<url-pattern>myfile.html</url-pattern>.
```

Using this pattern, only requests for the *myfile.html* file are directed to HtmlServlet.

 Make sure that URL patterns never begin with a slash (/) when you are creating extension mappings.

See Also

Chapter 1 on *web.xml*; Recipe 3.3; Recipes 3.5–3.8; Chapter 11 of the Servlet v2.3 and 2.4 specifications on mapping requests to servlets.

3.5 Invoking a Servlet Without a web.xml Mapping

Problem

You want to request a servlet that does not have a `servlet-mapping` element in the *web.xml* deployment descriptor.

Solution

Use an invoker-style URL of the form *http://www.mysite.org/mywebapp/servlet/com.jspservletcookbook.MyServlet*.

Discussion

Some servlets may not have a path mapping in the web application's deployment descriptor. So how can a user request this servlet? What name and URL do they use?

Tomcat and other servlet containers provide a method for invoking servlets that are not mapped in *web.xml*. You can use a URL of the following form:

```
http://www.mysite.org/mywebapp/servlet/<fully qualified class name of servlet>
```

A servlet with the class and package name of `jspservletcookbook.MyServlet` is invoked as *http://www.mysite.org/mywebapp/servlet/jspservletcookbook.MyServlet*. Ensure that the path segment following the name of your web application is */servlet/* and not */servlets/*. If the servlet is stored in the default web application (generally at the top level of the servlet container), the URL for invoking it is *http:// www.mysite.org/ servlet/jspservletcookbook.MyServlet*.

The *web.xml* file located in *<Tomcat_install_directory>/conf* includes this definition and mapping for the invoker servlet:

```
<servlet>
  <servlet-name>invoker</servlet-name>
  <servlet-class>org.apache.catalina.servlets.InvokerServlet</servlet-class>
  <init-param>
    <param-name>debug</param-name>
    <param-value>0</param-value>
  </init-param>
  <load-on-startup>2</load-on-startup>
</servlet>

<servlet-mapping>
  <servlet-name>invoker</servlet-name>
  <url-pattern>/servlet/*</url-pattern>
</servlet-mapping>
```

The invoker servlet can also be used to invoke the servlets that *are* registered in *web.xml*. These URLs look like *http://www.mysite.org/cookbook/servlet/<Registered-ServletName>*. For instance, imagine you have a servlet element like this:

```
<servlet>
  <servlet-name>myservlet</servlet-name>
  <servlet-class>jspservletcookbook.MyServlet</servlet-class>
</servlet>
```

Consider that the web application context path is */cookbook*. If the Tomcat invoker servlet is enabled in this application, then this servlet can be invoked with its registered name at *http://www.mysite.org/cookbook/servlet/myservlet*.

 In Tomcat 4.1.x, the invoker servlet mapping may be commented out inside of the *<tomcat-installation-directory>/conf/web.xml* file. The purpose of thus disabling the invoker is to ensure that servlets can be invoked using only the paths specified by the servlet-mapping elements in *web.xml*.

If a servlet is requested using the form *http://www.mysite.org/myapp/servlet/<fully-qualified-classname>*, rather than using the servlet's registered name, any initialization parameters provided for that servlet in the *web.xml* file are *not* available. Example 3-7 shows a registered servlet with init parameters.

Example 3-7. A registered servlet with init parameters

```
<servlet>
  <servlet-name>Weather</servlet-name>
  <servlet-class>home.Weather</servlet-class>
  <init-param>
    <param-name>region</param-name>
    <param-value>New England</param-value>
  </init-param>
</servlet>
```

Because it is the registered name of the servlet that has the region parameter assigned to it, only a request for that registered name (or a servlet path mapped to that name) triggers the region parameters. Accessing the servlet through its fully qualified name will *not* result in the region parameter being passed to the Weather servlet.

See Also

Chapter 1 on *web.xml*; Recipes 3.1–3.4; Recipes 3.6–3.8; Chapter 11 of the Servlet v2.3 and 2.4 specifications on mapping requests to servlets.

3.6 Mapping All Requests Within a Web Application to a Servlet

Problem

You want to have all web application requests go to a single controller servlet.

Solution

Use a servlet-mapping element in your deployment descriptor, with a url-pattern element of <url-pattern>/*</url-pattern>.

Discussion

In some cases, you might want to have all requests related to the web application to go a single servlet. This servlet *controller* may log requests, implement security, or examine and optionally alter the request object before it forwards the request to another location (usually another servlet or JSP).

> For the Sun Microsystems description of the Front Controller design pattern, which is a method for using a servlet as a central processing point, see the Core J2EE Blueprints page at *http://java.sun.com/blueprints/corej2eepatterns/Patterns/FrontController.html*.

Once again, *web.xml* is the place to configure a servlet to receive all web application requests. Example 3-8 shows how to use a URL pattern to aim all requests at a controller servlet.

Example 3-8. Aiming all requests at a controller servlet

```xml
<?xml version="1.0" encoding="ISO-8859-1"?>
<!DOCTYPE web-app
    PUBLIC "-//Sun Microsystems, Inc.//DTD Web Application 2.3//EN"
        "http://java.sun.com/dtd/web-application_2_3.dtd"
>
<web-app>

    <servlet>
        <servlet-name>Interceptor</servlet-name>
        <servlet-class>com.jspservletcookbook.Interceptor</servlet-class>
    </servlet>

    <!-- The mappings for the Interceptor servlet -->
    <servlet-mapping>
        <servlet-name>Interceptor</servlet-name>
        <url-pattern>/*</url-pattern>
    </servlet-mapping>
```

Example 3-8. Aiming all requests at a controller servlet (continued)

```
<servlet-mapping>
    <servlet-name>Interceptor</servlet-name>
    <url-pattern>/servlet/*</url-pattern>
</servlet-mapping>
```

```
</web-app>
```

You may also have to override any default invoker servlet with your own mapping:

```
<url-pattern>/servlet/*</url-pattern>
```

Map the servlet that you want to receive all web application requests to this URL pattern as well. If you keep the invoker servlet the way it is, users could bypass the controller servlet by using a URL like *http://www.mysite.org/myapp/servlet/com. jspservletcookbook.CookieServlet.*

 In Tomcat, you can also disable the invoker servlet in the top-level *web.xml* file (in *<Tomcat_install_directory>/conf*) by commenting out the servlet-mapping element. This affects all other web applications running under that Tomcat instance, however, so this decision should be made collectively among administrators who deploy applications on that server.

You must also remove, alter, or comment out other servlet-mapping elements that allow servlet requests to bypass the controller servlet. If a more specific mapping (such as the one in Example 3-9) is included in *web.xml*, requests for the CookieServlet will bypass the Interceptor servlet.

Example 3-9. Specific mappings override mappings using wildcard symbols

```
<?xml version="1.0" encoding="ISO-8859-1"?>
<!DOCTYPE web-app
    PUBLIC "-//Sun Microsystems, Inc.//DTD Web Application 2.3//EN"
          "http://java.sun.com/dtd/web-application_2_3.dtd"
>

<web-app>

    <servlet>
    <servlet-name>Interceptor</servlet-name>
    <servlet-class>jspservletcookbook.Interceptor</servlet-class>
    </servlet>

    <servlet>
        <servlet-name>CookieServlet</servlet-name>
          <servlet-class>
            com.jspservletcookbook.CookieServlet
          </servlet-class>
    </servlet>
```

Example 3-9. Specific mappings override mappings using wildcard symbols (continued)

```
<servlet-mapping>
    <servlet-name>Interceptor</servlet-name>
    <url-pattern>/*</url-pattern>
</servlet-mapping>

<servlet-mapping>
 <servlet-name>CookieServlet</servlet-name>
 <url-pattern>/CookieServlet</url-pattern>
</servlet-mapping>
```

```
</web-app>
```

The servlet-mapping element for CookieServlet in this example would cause the servlet path of */CookieServlet* to bypass the Interceptor servlet, because the servlet path of */CookieServlet* (as part of a request that looks like *http://host:port/context-path/CookieServlet*) is a more exact match to the URL pattern of */CookieServlet* than it is to */**.

 The requests for static content such as welcome files (e.g., *index.html*) are also intercepted by the URL pattern */**. The requests for these static files will also go to the controller servlet.

See Also

Chapter 1 on *web.xml*; Recipes 3.1–3.4; Recipes 3.6–3.8; Chapter 11 of the Servlet v2.3 and 2.4 specifications on mapping requests to servlets; the Core J2EE Blueprints page: *http://java.sun.com/blueprints/corej2eepatterns/Patterns/FrontController.html*.

3.7 Mapping Requests to a Controller and Preserving Servlet Mappings

Problem

You want to map all requests to a single controller servlet, while preserving the servlet mappings for other servlets in a secure manner.

Solution

Use security-constraint elements in *web.xml* to prevent web users from making requests to the noncontroller servlets.

Discussion

What if the controller servlet that receives all requests wants to conditionally forward the request along to another servlet for specialized processing? If all of the other servlet mappings are removed from *web.xml* and the invoker-style URL pattern (*/servlet/**) is mapped to the controller servlet itself, even the controller servlet is prevented from forwarding a request to another servlet! How can you get around these restrictions?

A solution is to retain the individual servlet mappings in *web.xml*. Then you can use security-constraint elements to prevent web users from making requests to these noncontroller servlets. When the controller servlet wants to forward a request to another servlet, it uses an object that implements the javax.servlet. RequestDispatcher interface. RequestDispatchers are not restricted from forwarding requests (using the RequestDispatcher.forward(request, response) method) to URL patterns that are specified by security-constraint elements. Example 3-10 shows a servlet named Controller that uses a RequestDispatcher to forward a request to another servlet.

Recipe 3.9 describes how to protect servlets from receiving any web-user requests with the security-constraint element, so I won't repeat that information here.

Example 3-10. Using RequestDispatcher to forward a request

```
import javax.servlet.*;
import javax.servlet.http.*;

public class Controller extends HttpServlet {

  public void doGet(HttpServletRequest request, HttpServletResponse response)
    throws ServletException, java.io.IOException {

    RequestDispatcher dispatcher = null;
    String param = request.getParameter("go");

    if (param == null)
      throw new ServletException("Missing parameter in Controller.");
    else if (param.equals("weather"))
      dispatcher = request.getRequestDispatcher("/weather");
    else if (param.equals("maps"))
      dispatcher = request.getRequestDispatcher("/maps");
    else
      throw new ServletException(
        "Improper parameter passed to Controller.");

    //if we get this far, dispatch the request to the correct URL
    if (dispatcher != null)
      dispatcher.forward(request,response);
    else
      throw new ServletException(
        "Controller received a null dispatcher from request object.");
  }
}
```

The servlet checks the go parameter for its value. A request to this servlet might look like:

```
http://localhost:8080/home?go=weather
```

In this example, the `Controller` servlet is mapped to receive all web requests to the "home" web application. In other words, the controller's servlet-mapping in *web.xml* has a url-pattern of /*.

Based on the go parameter value, `Controller` creates a `RequestDispatcher` object with a different specified URL for forwarding. The servlet gets a `RequestDispatcher` object first by calling the request object's getRequestDispatcher(String path) method. The path parameter can be relative to the context root of the web application, as it is here, but it cannot extend beyond the current servlet context. Suppose the URL pattern */weather* is mapped to the registered servlet name "Weather":

```
<servlet-mapping>
    <servlet-name>Weather</servlet-name>
    <url-pattern>/weather</url-pattern>
</servlet-mapping>
```

In this case, the path passed to the getRequestDispatcher() method looks like getRequestDispatcher("/weather"). If the go parameter is either wrong or missing, the `Controller` throws a `ServletException` with an appropriate message. The `Weather` servlet, though, cannot be accessed by web users directly because it is restricted by a security-constraint element—but the `RequestDispatcher.` forward(request,response) method is not limited by these constraints.

You can also use the javax.servlet.ServletContext.getNamedDispatcher(String name) method to get a `RequestDispatcher` object for forwarding. Using this method, you do not have to include any servlet-mapping elements for the target servlet. The getNamedDispatcher() method takes as its parameter the registered name of the servlet in *web.xml*. Example 3-11 shows the prior servlet example altered to use getNamedDispatcher("Weather"), using the weather servlet's registered name instead.

Example 3-11. Using getNamedDispatcher() to forward a request

```
import javax.servlet.*;
import javax.servlet.http.*;

public class Controller extends HttpServlet {

    public void doGet(HttpServletRequest request,
        HttpServletResponse response)
         throws ServletException, java.io.IOException {

        RequestDispatcher dispatcher = null;
        String param = request.getParameter("go");

            if (param == null)
                throw new
```

Example 3-11. Using getNamedDispatcher( ) to forward a request (continued)

```
                    ServletException("Missing parameter in Controller.");
            else if (param.equals("weather"))
                dispatcher = getServletContext().
                    getNamedDispatcher("Weather");
            else if (param.equals("maps"))
                dispatcher = getServletContext().
                    getNamedDispatcher("Maps");
            else
                throw new ServletException(
                    "Improper parameter passed to Controller.");

         /*check for a null dispatcher, then
            dispatch the request to the correct URL*/
        if (dispatcher != null)
            dispatcher.forward(request,response);
        else
            throw new ServletException(
              "Controller received a null dispatcher.");
    }
}
```

The doGet( ) method has been changed to use a RequestDispatcher received from the ServletContext.getNamedDispatcher(String registered-servlet-name) method. Instead of a servlet path, the dispatcher object uses that servlet's registered name ("Weather") from *web.xml*, as in:

```
<servlet>
    <servlet-name>Weather</servlet-name>
    <servlet-class>com.jspservletcookbook.Weather
    </servlet-class>
</servlet>
```

If the ServletContext returns a null dispatcher because someone left out the necessary XML element in *web.xml*, then doGet( ) throws a ServletException explaining that the dispatcher object is null.

 An alternate strategy is to use a listener to check the request before it finds its way to a servlet. Chapter 19 describes how to use a listener to examine an HTTP request.

See Also

Chapter 1 on *web.xml*; Recipes 3.1–3.5; Recipe 3.8; Chapter 19 on using a listener to examine the request; Chapter 11 of the Servlet v2.3 and 2.4 specifications on mapping requests to servlets; the Core J2EE Blueprints page: *http://java.sun.com/ blueprints/corej2eepatterns/Patterns/FrontController.html*

3.8   Creating Welcome Files for a Web Application

Problem

You want to configure one or more welcome files for a web application.

Solution

Use a `welcome-file-list` element in your deployment descriptor.

Discussion

A welcome file is a tradition as old as the hypertextual Internet. Many sites have homepages or other welcome files that are designed to be the entry page or front door for their web sites. These pages usually have names like *index.html*, *welcome.html*, or *default.html*. You can configure your web application to direct requests toward these pages by adding a `welcome-file-list` element to your web application's deployment descriptor. Set up a welcome file list in *web.xml* in the manner demonstrated by Example 3-12. The `welcome-file-list` element must come after any `servlet` and `servlet-mapping` elements, and precede any `error-page` or `taglib` elements in the servlet 2.3 deployment descriptor.

Example 3-12. Setting up welcome files in web.xml

```
<?xml version="1.0" encoding="ISO-8859-1"?>
<!DOCTYPE web-app
    PUBLIC "-//Sun Microsystems, Inc.//DTD Web Application 2.3//EN"
        "http://java.sun.com/dtd/web-application_2_3.dtd"
>

<web-app>

<!-- Define servlets and servlet-mappings here -->

    <welcome-file-list>
        <welcome-file>index.html</welcome-file>
        <welcome-file>default.jsp</welcome-file>
    </welcome-file-list>

</web-app>
```

Whenever the servlet container encounters a URL for a web application that specifies only a directory, not a particular filename or servlet, then it looks for a `welcome-file-list` element in the application's deployment descriptor. The servlet v2.3 specification calls these kinds of URLs *valid partial requests*. The servlet container attaches any welcome filenames that it finds in *web.xml* to the request (in the order that they appear in *web.xml*) and returns those files to the client.

For example, let's say Tomcat receives a request for *http://www.mysite.org/cookbook/*. Also imagine that the *web.xml* file for the cookbook web application contains the welcome-file-list shown in Example 3-12. Tomcat then returns *http://www.mysite.org/cookbook/index.html* if that file exists; if it does not, Tomcat looks for the *default.jsp* file in the *cookbook* directory and returns that file instead.

The servlet container initiates this search in response to any directory-style URL that it receives (such as *http://www.mysite.org/cookbook/bookinfo/*). In other words, as long as an *index.html* or *default.jsp* (or whichever filenames you choose) exists in a web application's root directory, and the web developer has properly configured the welcome-file-list element, then those files are invoked by default in response to directory-style requests.

See Also

Chapter 1 on *web.xml*; Recipes 3.1–3.6; Recipe 3.9; Chapter 11 of the Servlet v2.3 and 2.4 specifications on mapping requests to servlets.

3.9   Restricting Requests for Certain Servlets

Problem

You want to allow only authenticated users to request certain servlets.

Solution

Use the security-constraint element in the *web.xml* deployment descriptor.

Discussion

Some web applications contain servlets that should not be invoked directly by web users, because they handle sensitive data and may have special jobs (such as administering the server or web application). For example, you could design a servlet that is accessed only by server administrators. How do you protect these servlets from being invoked improperly or by unauthorized users?

In the latter case, you can use *declarative security*, or *container-managed security*. This strategy involves configuring the *web.xml* deployment descriptor with your application's security information, thereby decoupling security information from your servlet's code. Any security changes for a web application can then be made in the XML configuration files (or via the WebLogic Server 7.0 Administration Console) without messing with the servlet's source code. The security configuration is then loaded and implemented by the servlet container.

You can also use *programmatic security*, which involves including security-related code within servlets, such as checking the HttpServletRequest object to see if a user is authorized to use a certain web resource.

For Tomcat, using the security-constraint element in *web.xml* requires creating a username and password in the XML file located at *<Tomcat-installation-directory>/conf/tomcat-users.xml*. This is an XML file in which you define internal users and passwords. It might look like Example 3-13.

Example 3-13. A tomcat-users.xml file

```
<?xml version='1.0' encoding='utf-8'?>
<tomcat-users>
  <role rolename="manager"/>
  <role rolename="tomcat"/>
  <role rolename="developer"/>
  <user username="tomcat" password="tomcat" roles="tomcat,manager"/>
  <user username="bruce" password="bruce1957"
    roles="tomcat,manager,developer"/>
  <user username="stacy" password="stacy1986" roles="tomcat"/>
</tomcat-users>
```

This XML fragment includes a tomcat-users root element containing one or more role and user elements, depending on how many users are defined for the web applications handled by that instance of Tomcat. This *tomcat-users.xml* configuration file is accessible by all of the contained web applications.

You then create security-constraint, login-config, and security-role elements inside of the web application's deployment descriptor, or *web.xml*.

If you are not using the servlet v2.4 deployment descriptor, the security-related elements have to appear in this order and follow most of the other elements that can appear in *web.xml*, or your deployment descriptor will not be a valid XML file. Specifically, the only elements that can come *after* security-role are env-entry, ejb-ref, and ejb-local-ref.

The security-constraint element looks like Example 3-14, given that the protected URL pattern in this case is <url-pattern>/CookieServlet</url-pattern>.

Example 3-14. The security-constraint element

```
<security-constraint>
    <web-resource-collection>
        <web-resource-name>CookieInfo</web-resource-name>
        <url-pattern>/CookieServlet</url-pattern>
        <http-method>GET</http-method>
        <http-method>POST</http-method>
    </web-resource-collection>
    <auth-constraint>
```

Example 3-14. The security-constraint element (continued)

```
            <description>This applies only to the
                        "developer" security role</description>
            <role-name>developer</role-name>
        </auth-constraint>
        <user-data-constraint>
            <transport-guarantee>NONE</transport-guarantee>
        </user-data-constraint>
</security-constraint>
```

The security-constraint element must contain one or more web-resource-collection elements. The web-resource-collection element describes which web resources in the web application are protected by the specified security constraint. In other words, a request over the Internet for a web resource, such as a servlet, triggers any security constraint that has been mapped to the resource. In this example, the security constraint protects any request that fits the URL pattern, *<web-application-root-directory>/CookieServlet*. The http-method elements specify the HTTP methods that this security constraint covers. In the example, a GET or POST request for */CookieServlet* triggers the configured security mechanism. If you do not include any http-method elements under the security-constraint element, the constraint will apply to any HTTP method (such as PUT or DELETE, in addition to GET and POST).

 The objects that implement the javax.servlet.RequestDispatcher interface may forward HTTP requests from one servlet to a protected servlet without triggering these security constraints.

The auth-constraint element is designed to describe the security roles that permit access to the web component. A security role is a name that represents the security privileges a user or group of users have in relation to a particular resource, such as a servlet. Examples of security roles are *admin*, *manager*, or *developer*. In the case of the *tomcat-users.xml* file, users are assigned to roles. Within the security-constraint element example, only users that are mapped to the *developer* role in the *tomcat-users.xml* file have access to CookieServlet.

How does a web application authenticate a user in the first place? For instance, how can the web application find out the requester's username and password, and thereby determine if he can be given access to the servlet? In container-managed security, this is what the login-config element is used for. This element appears after the security-constraint element in the *web.xml* file. Both elements might look like Example 3-15 in a web application's deployment descriptor.

Example 3-15. Using login-config with a security-constraint element

```
<security-constraint>
    <web-resource-collection>
        <web-resource-name>CookieInfo</web-resource-name>
        <url-pattern>/CookieServlet</url-pattern>
        <http-method>GET</http-method>
```

Example 3-15. Using login-config with a security-constraint element (continued)

```
            <http-method>POST</http-method>
        </web-resource-collection>
        <auth-constraint>
            <description>This applies only to the
                "developer" security role</description>
            <role-name>developer</role-name>
        </auth-constraint>
        <user-data-constraint>
            <transport-guarantee>NONE</transport-guarantee>
        </user-data-constraint>
</security-constraint>

<login-config>
        <auth-method>BASIC</auth-method>
</login-config>
<security-role>
        <role-name>developer</role-name>
</security-role>
```

The `login-config` element specifies the authentication method that is used to authenticate any user requests for protected web resources. Protected web resources are those specified by a `web-resource-collection` element, inside the `security-constraint` element. In the example, BASIC authentication is used for any requests that match the URL pattern */CookieServlet*. BASIC is a familiar form of web authentication in which the browser presents the user with a dialog window for entering the username and password. Tomcat compares the given name and password with the user information configured in the *tomcat-users.xml* file, and then uses the web application's `security-constraint` configuration to determine whether the user can access the protected servlet.

> The `auth-method` child element of `login-config` can also be given the values FORM, CLIENT-CERT, or DIGEST.

One more ingredient is necessary to complete this servlet security configuration: the `security-role` element. Example 3-15 creates a security role named *developer*. The *developer* value also appears in the `security-constraint` child element `auth-constraint`. This means that only users who are mapped to the security role *developer* are able to access web resources which are protected by the security constraint (i.e., that are identified by a `web-resource-collection` child element of `security-constraint`). In other words, this authentication method is actually a two-step process:

1. Check if the provided username and password are correct.

2. Determine if the user is mapped to the specified security role. For example, the user might provide a correct username and password, but she may not be mapped to the specified security role. In this case, she is prevented from accessing the specified web resource.

The users are mapped to security roles in Tomcat in the previously mentioned *tomcat-users.xml* file. Here is an example of what a user element might look like in the *tomcat-users.xml* file:

```
<username="bwperry" password="bruce2002"
    roles="developer,standard,manager" />
```

This user is assigned three different roles: *developer*, *standard*, and *manager*. The Tomcat servlet container uses these XML elements in the *tomcat-users.xml* file to determine whether certain username/password combinations have been assigned particular roles. Figure 3-1 is designed to unravel these confusing cross-references. Just think of a security role as a way to further refine a group of application users, or group them in terms of their user privileges.

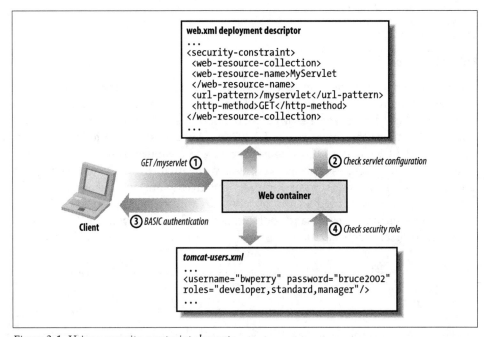

Figure 3-1. Using a security constraint element

The security configuration depicted by Example 3-15's XML text can be used with WebLogic 7.0, but the WebLogic-specific configuration file is called *weblogic.xml*.

 The *weblogic.xml* file accompanies the *web.xml* deployment descriptor inside your web application's *WEB-INF* directory.

Example 3-16 shows the XML within the *weblogic.xml* deployment descriptor.

Example 3-16. Security role in weblogic.xml

```
<!-- weblogic.xml security role mapping -->
<security-role-assignment>
    <role-name>developer</role-name>
    <principal-name>bwperry</principal-name>
</security-role-assignment>
```

In WebLogic 7.0, you can also establish users, groups, and security roles that are global to a particular WebLogic server through the Administrative Console.

This recipe described how to restrict the requests for certain servlets. The next recipe shows one way to prevent all requests except those forwarded from a controller servlet from reaching other servlets.

See Also

Chapter 1 on *web.xml*; Recipes 3.1–3.8; Chapter 11 of the Servlet v2.3 and 2.4 specifications on mapping requests to servlets; the Core J2EE Blueprints page: *http://java. sun.com/blueprints/corej2eepatterns/Patterns/FrontController.html*

3.10 Giving Only the Controller Access to Certain Servlets

Problem

You want to set up the web application so that only a controller servlet has access to certain servlets.

Solution

Create a `security-role` that does not have any users mapped to it, then specify in the `security-constraint` element the servlets that you want to preserve for the controller.

Discussion

This recipe shows how you can create a `security-constraint` element that forbids any requests from reaching specified URL patterns.

The servlets mapped to those URL patterns are forwarded requests only from one or more controller servlets that use an object that implements the `javax.servlet.RequestDispatcher` interface. Recipe 3.7 includes an example controller servlet that forwards a request to another servlet using a `RequestDispatcher`. Example 3-17 shows how you can set up the `security-constraint` element for an example servlet with the registered name "Weather".

Example 3-17. A security-constraint that allows only RequestDispatcher.forward-related requests

```xml
<?xml version="1.0" encoding="ISO-8859-1"?>
<!DOCTYPE web-app
    PUBLIC "-//Sun Microsystems, Inc.//DTD Web Application 2.3//EN"
          "http://java.sun.com/dtd/web-application_2_3.dtd">
<web-app>
<!-- configure the Weather servlet;
    it receives requests from a
      controller servlet -->
    <servlet>
        <servlet-name>Weather</servlet-name>
        <servlet-class>
          com.jspservletcookbook.Weather
        </servlet-class>
    </servlet>

    <servlet-mapping>
        <servlet-name>Weather</servlet-name>
        <url-pattern>/weatherurl-pattern></url-pattern>
    </servlet-mapping>

<!-- this element prevents the Weather servlet
    from directly receiving requests from users,
    because no users are mapped to the 'nullrole' role-->
    <security-constraint>
        <web-resource-collection>
            <web-resource-name>Weather
            </web-resource-name>
            <url-pattern>/weather</url-pattern>
            <http-method>GET</http-method>
            <http-method>POST</http-method>
        </web-resource-collection>
        <auth-constraint>
            <role-name>nullrole</role-name>
        </auth-constraint>
        <user-data-constraint>
            <transport-guarantee>NONE
            </transport-guarantee>
        </user-data-constraint>
    </security-constraint>
    <login-config>
        <auth-method>BASIC</auth-method>
    </login-config>
    <security-role>
        <role-name>nullrole</role-name>
    </security-role>
</web-app>
```

The next step in protecting the Weather servlet is to make sure that the *tomcat-users.xml* file does not map any users to the "nullrole" security role. The security-role element looks like this:

```
<security-role>
        <role-name>nullrole</role-name>
</security-role>
```

Here is what a typical *<Tomcat-installation-directory>/conf/tomcat-users.xml* file looks like:

```
<?xml version='1.0' encoding='utf-8'?>
<tomcat-users>
  <role rolename="manager"/>
  <role rolename="tomcat"/>
  <role rolename="developer"/>
  <user username="tomcat" password="tomcat" roles="tomcat,manager"/>
  <user username="bruce" password="bruce1957"
    roles="tomcat,manager,developer"/>
</tomcat-users>
```

In web applications configured in the manner of Example 3-17, any direct request to the URL pattern */weather* receives a response in the category of "HTTP Status 403—Access to the requested resource has been denied." However, a controller servlet can still use the RequestDispatcher.forward(request,response) method to forward a request to the */weather* URL for processing. Recipe 3.7 and Example 3-10 show a servlet that uses this forward method, so I won't repeat that code here.

 Make sure to configure friendly error pages for the users who make requests to restricted servlets. Chapter 9 describes how to designate error pages for certain HTTP response codes in the web application's deployment descriptor. You may want to provide automatic refreshes after a specified interval from the error page to the controller or any login pages.

See Also

Chapter 1 on *web.xml*; Recipes 3.1–3.9; Chapter 11 of the Servlet v2.3 and 2.4 specifications on mapping requests to servlets; the Core J2EE Blueprints page: *http://java.sun.com/blueprints/corej2eepatterns/Patterns/FrontController.html*.

CHAPTER 4

Using Apache Ant

4.0   Introduction

Apache Ant (*http://ant.apache.org/*) is a Java- and XML-based automation tool that is available as open source software from the Apache Software Foundation. Ant began its life as part of the Tomcat code base. The tool's first official release as a standalone software product was in July 2000, according to the Ant FAQ (*http://ant.apache.org/faq.html*). The original creator of both Ant and Tomcat is James Duncan Davidson.

Ant has evolved into the build tool of choice for automating Java software projects, which means building these projects from beginning to end. This includes compiling Java classes, creating JAR or WAR files, and initiating filesystem-related tasks such as creating directories and moving or copying files. All of these tasks are controlled by the Ant build file for a specific project.

An Ant *build file* is an XML file that is launched from the command line and executes Java classes behind the scenes. Ant is also extensible; you can customize this tool to suit your own purposes. In addition, Ant is cross-platform and very portable, since it is based on XML and Java. Once web developers become familiar with this handy and powerful tool, they find that it greatly eases the task of compiling, packaging, and inevitably altering and redeploying their web applications.

This chapter first describes how to download Ant and set it up on your system, and then explains Ant targets and tasks for those who are new to Ant. The rest of you can merrily move on to other recipes describing how to create a classpath that includes the necessary Tomcat JAR files, create WAR and JAR files, and use Ant to execute Tomcat's Manager application.

4.1   Obtaining and Setting Up Ant

Problem

You want to download and set up Apache Ant on your computer.

Solution

Point your browser to *http://ant.apache.org/*, download the binary or source distribution of Ant, then follow the instructions given in this recipe and on the Ant support site.

Discussion

The binary distribution of Apache Ant can be downloaded from *http://ant.apache.org/bindownload.cgi*. You can also download the source distribution, which contains the Java source files for Ant, from *http://ant.apache.org/srcdownload.cgi*. You must have the Java Software Development Kit (SDK) installed.

 Ant v1.5.3 will be the last release that supports JDK 1.1. Ant v1.5.1 can run with JDK 1.1, although some tasks work only on JDK 1.2.

To use Ant, you must have a Java API for XML Processing (JAXP)–compliant XML parser available on your classpath. The binary Ant distribution includes the Apache Xerces2 XML parser. If you opt for a different JAXP-compliant parser, you should remove *xercesImpl.jar* and *xmlParserAPIs.jar* from Ant's top-level */lib* directory (as in *jakarta-ant-1.5.1/lib*) and put the JAR file(s) for the alternative parser into Ant's */lib* directory. You can also add them directly to your user classpath.

 The *user classpath* is the classpath represented by the CLASSPATH environment variable on your machine. This classpath overrides the default value for the user classpath (., or the current directory). The java command-line tool's -cp or -classpath switches override the CLASSPATH environment variable. The user classpath can also be set by a JAR file specified by the java tool's -jar switch. This designation in turn overrides the other ways of specifying a classpath. The bottom line is that it is easier to place your parser of choice in the *jakarta-ant-1.5.1/lib* directory instead of fooling around with these classpath issues.

The complete installation directions for Ant and links to related Web pages are at *http://ant.apache.org/manual/index.html*.

Take the following steps to get Ant running on your machine:

1. Unpack the compressed file (in ZIP or TAR format) containing the Ant tool. With Ant v1.5.1, unpacking the distribution file creates a directory called *jakarta-ant-1.5.1*.

2. Set the ANT_HOME environment variable to the directory where you installed Ant. On Unix, this can be accomplished by typing a command-line phrase:

```
export ANT_HOME=/usr/local/jakarta-ant-1.5.1
```

On Windows type:

```
set ANT_HOME=h:\jakarta-ant-1.5.1
```

3. Add the *<Ant-installation-directory>/bin* directory to your PATH environment variable. This allows the developer to change to any working directory with a *build.xml* file and type ant to run this file (read the next recipe for a description of executing a *build.xml* file). The *<Ant-installation-directory>/bin* directory contains the scripts which launch the Java classes that form the basis of Ant.

4. Optionally, set the JAVA_HOME environment variable to the directory where your JDK is installed. You might as well set the JAVA_HOME environment variable, because the scripts that are provided with Ant in its */bin* directory can then automatically add the required JDK-related classes when you want to use the javac or rmic tasks. *Tasks* are XML elements that do certain jobs in Ant files, such as war (to create Web Archive files) and javac (to compile Java classes with Ant).

5. Test your installation by typing ant -version. If everything goes well, this command produces a return value like this:

```
K:\>ant -version
Apache Ant version 1.5.1 compiled on October 2 2002
```

See Also

Recipe 4.2 on using Ant targets; Recipe 4.3 on including Tomcat JAR files in the Ant classpath; Recipe 4.4 on compiling a servlet with Ant; Recipe 4.5 on creating a WAR file with Ant; Recipe 4.6 on using Ant to create JAR files; Recipes 4.7 and 4.8 on starting and stopping Tomcat with Ant; Recipes 2.1 and 2.6 on deploying web applications using Ant; the Apache Ant manual: *http://ant.apache.org/manual/index.html*; the Apache Ant Project: *http://ant.apache.org*.

4.2   Using Ant Targets

Problem

You want to create target elements for developing web applications with an Ant build file.

Solution

Create one or more target elements as child elements of a project element. Make sure the targets have the required name attribute and value.

Discussion

An Ant build file is an XML file—in other words, a plaintext file that includes elements and attributes. Example 4-1 shows an Ant file that echoes a message to the console. As mentioned in the introduction, Ant files execute Java code behind the scenes. The way you control the desired actions of your build file is by arranging one or more target elements inside the project root element.

Example 4-1. An Ant build file that echoes a console message

```
<project name="Cookbook" default="echo-message" basedir=".">
    <target name="echo-message"
        description="Echoing a message to the console">
        <echo message="Hello from the first Ant file"/>
    </target>
</project>
```

Ant files have one project root element, which must have a default attribute and value. The default attribute specifies the target that runs if no other targets are identified on the command line. The name and basedir attributes are optional. The name attribute, as you might have guessed, gives the project element a descriptive name. The basedir attribute specifies the directory by which paths that are referred to in the file are calculated. Its default value is the directory containing the build file.

What are targets? They are groups of tasks, represented in Ant by a target element. Targets group one or more tasks (which are in turn represented by a task element) into logical and named units of control, similar to Java methods.

Tasks include actions that compile Java files (the javac task), copy files from one location to another (copy), and create JAR or WAR files (aptly named jar and war). For instance, the echo-message target in Example 4-1 calls the echo task.

The target's name in Example 4-1 is echo-message, which is just a name that I created for it. A target's description attribute is optional, as are three other attributes: depends, if, and unless. I'll explain the purpose of depends shortly; the if and unless attributes allow the conditional execution of targets.

As long as Ant is properly set up on your computer, here is what the command-line sequence for executing this example *build.xml* file might look like:

```
H:\book\cookbook\sec1\sec1_3>ant
Buildfile: build.xml

echo-message:
     [echo] Hello from the first Ant file.

BUILD SUCCESSFUL
Total time: 3 seconds
```

First, the XML file with the project root element is saved with the filename *build.xml*. Then the user changes to the directory that contains this file and types ant, without any options. Ant then looks for a file called *build.xml* in the current directory and runs the project's default target (in Example 4-1, the echo-message target).

 You can give the build file a name other than *build.xml*, but then you need to run Ant with the -buildfile option:

```
ant -buildfile dev.xml
```

Most build files involve several targets that execute in a certain sequence to initiate Java development tasks. Example 4-2 demonstrates the depends attribute. This example shows how to execute several targets in a specified sequence.

Example 4-2. Using the depends target attribute to launch a sequence of targets

```
<project name="Cookbook" default="echo-message" basedir=".">

    <target name="init">
        <property name="name" value="Bruce Perry"/>
    </target>

    <target name="show-props" depends="init">
        <echo message=
          "The 'name' property value is: ${name}"/>
        <echo message=
          "OS name and version is: ${os.name} ${os.version} "/>
        <echo message=
          "Your Java home is: ${java.home} "/>
    </target>

    <target name="echo-message" depends="show-props">
        <echo message=
          "Hello from the first Ant file in directory: ${basedir}"/>
    </target>

</project>
```

This time, instead of just one target, the project element has several nested targets. The echo-message target is still the default target, but its behavior has changed due to the value of its depends attribute. This optional attribute specifies the name of one or more Ant targets that must be executed prior to the current target. In other words, the echo-message target specifies, "I depend on the show-props target, so execute it before me." The show-props target, however, also has a depends attribute that indicates a reliance on the init target. As a result, this build file establishes a sequence for executing its targets: init → show-props → echo-message.

The result of running the prior build file at the command line is shown here:

```
H:\book\cookbook\sec1\sec1_3>ant
Buildfile: build.xml

init:
```

```
show-props:
     [echo] The 'name' property value is: Bruce Perry
     [echo] OS name and version is: Windows NT 4.0
     [echo]  Your Java home is: h:\jdk1.3.1_02\jre

echo-message:
     [echo] Hello from the first Ant file in directory:
           H:\book\cookbook\sec1\sec1_3

BUILD SUCCESSFUL
Total time: 2 seconds
```

Here is what this build file accomplishes:

1. The init target first creates a name property that contains the value "Bruce Perry". The target uses the property task to accomplish this. Recall that tasks do the real work in Ant; targets are simply grouping elements that call one or more tasks.

2. The show-props target then echoes the values of the name property (created by the init target) and three built-in properties: os.name, os.version, and java.home.

3. The echo-message target issues its message to the console and returns the value of the basedir property. All of the targets use the echo task to deliver their messages.

Note that the name property would not be set if the init target was never executed. If the show-props target is defined as seen here, there will be problems:

```
<target name="show-props">
...</target>
```

However, it is properly defined as follows:

```
<target name="show-props" depends="init">
...</target>
```

Without the depends attribute, the init target would never be executed, because the build file's execution sequence would look like show-props → echo-message. The name property would never be given a value.

Ant build files are usually much more complex than these examples, which is more of a testament to Ant's power than evidence of poor design. Chapter 2 shows how to deploy individual servlets and web applications with more extensive Ant files.

See Also

Recipe 4.1 on downloading and setting up Ant; Recipe 4.3 on including Tomcat JAR files in the Ant classpath; Recipe 4.4 on compiling a servlet with Ant; Recipe 4.5 on creating a JAR file with Ant; Recipes 4.7 and 4.8 on starting and stopping Tomcat with Ant; Recipes 2.1 and 2.6 on deploying web applications using Ant; the Ant manual section on the property task: *http://ant.apache.org/manual/CoreTasks/ property.html*; the Ant manual segment on targets: *http://ant.apache.org/manual/ using.html#targets*; the Apache Ant manual index page: *http://ant.apache.org/ manual/index.html*; the Apache Ant Project: *http://ant.apache.org*.

4.3   Including Tomcat JAR files in the Build File Classpath

Problem

You want to establish an Ant classpath that includes various Tomcat JAR files.

Solution

Use a path-like structure to define the classpath, then refer to this classpath whenever you need it. Specify the directories where the necessary JAR files are located with an external properties file.

Discussion

Before you can compile a servlet using Ant, you must ensure that the servlet API classes are available on the classpath that the Ant build file is using for compilation. For example, the *<Tomcat-installation-directory>/common/lib* directory contains *servlet.jar*, which includes the necessary classes for compiling a servlet. In addition, you might want to include the *mail.jar* component from the same directory to compile a servlet that uses the JavaMail API. A different directory—*<Tomcat-installation-directory>/common/endorsed*—includes the *xmlParserAPIs.jar* file, which you might specify on the classpath to use the associated SAX and DOM XML programming classes.

Example 4-3 defines a classpath using a path XML element. A `compile-servlet` target further down in the XML file then uses the defined classpath to compile a servlet.

Example 4-3. Defining a classpath including Tomcat JAR files

```
<project name="Cookbook" default="compile-servlet" basedir=".">

  <!-- include compiled-servlet and tomcat-dir properties -->
  <property file="global.properties" />

<path id="servlet-classpath">
    <fileset dir="${tomcat.dir}/common/lib">
        <include name="*.jar" />
    </fileset>
    <fileset dir="${tomcat.dir}/common/endorsed">
        <include name="*.jar" />
    </fileset>
</path>

<target name="compile-servlet">
    <echo message="Compiling the servlet...."/>
    <javac srcdir="${src}" destdir="${build}">
        <include name="${compiled.servlet}.java" />
```

Example 4-3. Defining a classpath including Tomcat JAR files (continued)

```
        <classpath refid="servlet-classpath "/>
    </javac>
</target>

</project>
```

Using the path element, the classpath can be defined similarly to an instance variable of a Java class, and its value can then be used throughout the build file. The advantage of this approach is that the classpath may be very complex, but it has to be defined only once. Whenever there is a need for a classpath in an Ant file, the classpath element and its refid attribute can be used to pull in the defined classpath. In Example 4-3, the path element is given a unique ID, "servlet-classpath." The developer creates this name to uniquely identify the path-like structure.

Another core type of Ant task is a fileset. filesets are elements that represent groups of files. The two nested filesets in the example have dir attributes that specify two directories under the Tomcat installation directory: *./common/lib* and *./common/endorsed*. These are directories that contain many important Java libraries, such as *servlet.jar* and *mail.jar*. A fileset element's nested include element creates a pattern (with the name attribute) that specifies the types of files to include in each fileset. The example includes all files in the specified directories ending in ".jar".

If you wanted to further refine the types of JAR files that are included in a fileset, you could use the fileset's nested exclude element:

```
    <fileset dir="${tomcat.dir}/common/lib">
        <include name="*.jar" />
        <exclude name="commons*.jar"/>
    </fileset>
```

The pattern "commons*.jar" excludes all the JAR files from the classpath that begin with the word "commons," followed by zero or more characters and a ".jar" suffix.

The compile.servlet target in Example 4-3 echoes a message to the console, then uses the javac task to compile a servlet.

This code from Example 4-3 makes two properties that are defined in another file available to the Ant build file:

```
    <property file="global.properties" />
```

Here is what the *global.properties* file looks like:

```
    tomcat.dir=k:/jakarta-tomcat-4.1.12
    compiled.servlet=MyTask
    src=.\src
    build=.\build
```

The property compiled.servlet evaluates to the name of the Java source file that is being compiled. The *tomcat.dir* file is the file path to the Tomcat root directory.

In Example 4-3, the classpath element is nested inside the javac task, as in:

```
<javac srcdir="${src}" destdir="${build}">
        <include name="${compiled.servlet}.java" />
        <classpath refid="servlet-classpath"/>
</javac>
```

The classpath element's refid attribute pulls in the classpath that was defined earlier in the build file (including all the Tomcat JARs in *./common/lib* and *./common/endorsed*). The value of the refid attribute is the id of the path element ("servlet-classpath"). In other words, the path element in Example 4-3 represents a classpath; the element's id or name is "servlet-classpath."

If it is necessary to add more classes or JARs to the classpath that you are defining in an Ant file, then add another nested fileset to the path element. Example 4-4 adds all of the contents of the *build* directory to the classpath defined by Example 4-3 (along with the Tomcat-related JARs) by adding a third nested fileset.

Example 4-4. Nesting three filesets in a path structure

```
<path id="servlet-classpath">

    <fileset dir="${tomcat.dir}/common/lib">
      <include name="*.jar" />
    </fileset>

    <fileset dir="${tomcat.dir}/common/endorsed">
      <include name="*.jar" />
    </fileset>

    <fileset dir="./build"/>

</path>
```

> An idiom that often appears in path-related patterns is **, which means zero or more directories. For example, the following fileset tag includes all of the files contained in any nested *images* folders (src is a property name pointing to the source directory of this fileset), no matter how deeply they are nested:
>
> ```
> <fileset dir="${src}">
>     <include name="**/images/*"/>
> </fileset>
> ```

See Also

Recipe 4.1 on downloading and setting up Ant; Recipe 4.2 on writing Ant targets; Recipe 4.4 on compiling a servlet with Ant; Recipe 4.5 on creating a WAR file with Ant; Recipe 4.6 on using Ant to create JAR files; Recipes 4.7 and 4.8 on starting and stopping Tomcat with Ant; Recipes 2.1 and 2.6 on deploying web applications using

Ant; the Ant manual section on the property task: *http://ant.apache.org/manual/CoreTasks/property.html*; the Ant manual segment on targets: *http://ant.apache.org/manual/using.html#targets*; the Apache Ant manual index page: *http://ant.apache.org/manual/index.html*; the Apache Ant Project: *http://ant.apache.org*.

4.4   Compiling a Servlet with an Ant Build File

Problem

You want to set up a simple build file that you can use to compile individual servlets, without hardcoding servlet names.

Solution

Design a build file so that the name of the Java class to compile can be set from an external properties file or from the command line.

Discussion

If you are not using an IDE to develop and compile your servlets, an Ant build file can automate the compiling of your source files. In order to make this build file reusable, you should design it to get the name of the file from an external properties file or from the command line.

Ant's advantages come to the fore when it is used to automate all of the aspects of building, archiving, and deploying a web application. However, you can also use Ant as a kind of batch processor. In this recipe, I use Ant to dynamically choose a Java file to compile.

The *build.xml* file in Example 4-5 imports a couple of properties from a *build.properties* file, including the name of the servlet to be compiled. One way to choose a different Java file to compile is to change the value of the compiled.servlet property in this file, without touching the build file:

```
tomcat.dir=/users/bruceper/java/jakarta-tomcat-4.1.12
compiled.servlet=MyServlet
```

To run Example 4-5, change to the directory where the *build.xml* file is located and type ant without any options.

 If you are running an Ant build file with a different name, then launch it with this command line:

```
ant -buildfile ant_compiler.xml
```

First, this file imports the `tomcat.dir` and `compiled.servlet` properties from a *build. properties* file. This file is located in the same directory as the build file. The `tomcat. dir` property is used to create a classpath composed of the JAR files in two directories that are a part of Tomcat's directory tree (see Recipe 4.2).

Example 4-5. Compiling a servlet with an Ant build file

```
<project name="servlet compiler" default="compile" basedir=".">

    <property file="build.properties" />

    <path id="servlet-classpath">

        <fileset dir="${tomcat.dir}/common/lib">
            <include name="*.jar" />
        </fileset>

        <fileset dir="${tomcat.dir}/common/endorsed">
            <include name="*.jar" />
        </fileset>

    </path>

    <target name="init"
      description="Initializes some properties.">
        <echo message="Initializing properties."/>
        <property name="build" value="./build" />
        <property name="src" value="./src" />

    </target>

    <target name="prepare" depends="init">
        <echo message="Cleaning up the build directory."/>
        <delete dir="${build}"/>
        <mkdir dir="${build}"/>
    </target>

    <target name="compile" depends="prepare"
      description="Compile the servlet">
        <echo message="Compiling the Java file "/>
        <echo message="${compiled.servlet}.java..."/>
        <javac srcdir="${src}" destdir="${build}">
            <include name="${compiled.servlet}.java" />
            <classpath refid="servlet-classpath "/>
        </javac>
    </target>
</project>
```

The init target creates two properties representing the source (src) and destination (build) directories of the target servlet. The Java file waiting to be compiled is located in an *src* directory. A typical build file also has an init target that initializes several more properties. Since the compile target has a depends attribute that specifies the prepare target, and the prepare target depends on init, then the build sequence looks like init → prepare → compile.

The prepare target just cleans up the *build* directory to ensure that the *build* directory contains the latest compiled classes.

The compile target uses the javac task to actually compile the Java file. javac has attributes that specify the source and destination directories of the Java file(s) that it will attempt to compile. Example 4-5 uses the src and build properties to provide values for these attributes. Two nested elements of the javac task compile the specified servlet file and provide the classpath that the javac task uses (see Recipe 4.2).

Here is the console output after running this build file (with some editing for readability):

```
init:
     [echo] Initializing properties.

prepare:
     [echo] Cleaning up the build directory.
   [delete] Deleting directory
          /Users/bruceper/books/cookbook/sec1/sec1_3/build
    [mkdir] Created dir:
          /Users/bruceper/books/cookbook/sec1/sec1_3/build

compile:
     [echo] Compiling the Java file MyServlet.java...
    [javac] Compiling 1 source file to
          /Users/bruceper/books/cookbook/sec1/sec1_3/build

BUILD SUCCESSFUL
Total time: 6 seconds
```

Using the command line to declare the target servlet

What if you want to change the servlet that you are compiling, but are not inclined to type the new Java filename into the *build.properties* file? Running the *build.xml* Ant file from the command line in the following manner will override the imported compiled.servlet property:

```
ant -Dcompiled.servlet=AnotherServlet
```

AnotherServlet.java is the filename in this example of the Java file that awaits compilation in the *src* directory. This fragment of output shows that any properties passed in from the command line override properties of the same name created within or imported into the build file:

```
compile:
     [echo] Compiling the Java file AnotherServlet.java...
    [javac] Compiling 1 source file to
          /Users/bruceper/books/cookbook/sec1/sec1_3/build
```

The javac task compiles only only the java files in the *src* directory that do not have a corresponding class file, or in cases where the class file is older than its corresponding *.java* file. As always, check the Ant manual to find out about all the different variations and attributes of javac: *http://ant.apache.org/manual/CoreTasks/javac.html*.

 If you want to copy the compiled servlet class to a web application directory, you could add a deploy-servlet target that uses the copy Ant task:

```
<target name="deploy-servlet" depends="compile">
  <echo message=
    "Copying the servlet to Tomcat web app"/>
  <copy todir="${tomcat.webapps}/WEB-INF/classes">
    <fileset dir="${build}" />
  </copy>
</target>
```

The copy task takes its nested fileset, which represents the contents of the directory named by the build property value, and copies these class files to the *WEB-INF/classes* directory of Tomcat's default web application.

See Also

Recipe 4.1 on downloading and setting up Ant; Recipe 4.2 on writing Ant targets; Recipe 4.3 on creating a classpath for an Ant file; Recipe 4.5 on creating a WAR file with Ant; Recipe 4.6 on using Ant to create JAR files; Recipes 4.7 and 4.8 on starting and stopping Tomcat with Ant; Recipes 2.1 and 2.6 on deploying web applications using Ant; the Ant manual section on the property task: *http://ant.apache.org/manual/CoreTasks/property.html*; the Ant manual segment on targets: *http://ant.apache.org/manual/using.html#targets*; the Apache Ant manual index page: *http://ant.apache.org/manual/index.html*; the Apache Ant Project, *http://ant.apache.org*.

4.5   Creating a WAR File with Ant

Problem

You want to use Ant to create a Web ARchive (WAR) file.

Solution

Use the Ant war task.

Discussion

A WAR file is a web application archive that contains servlet classes, JSP files, HTML files, image directories, JAR files, XML configuration files, and other resources that a web application depends on. The WAR is deployed on a web container like Tomcat in order to make the web application available to the container's users. Ant includes a war task that makes it easy to generate a WAR from a directory structure that contains the necessary web application files.

Example 4-6 is a standalone build file that creates a WAR file. It could easily comprise one target in a complex build file that compiles Java files, creates the WAR, and deploys the application (see Recipe 2.6).

This example creates a build sequence of init → prepare → create-war. The init target creates several properties that refer to directories, such as the *build* directory containing the servlet class files. The context-path property provides the context path for the web application, and in this case, the name of the WAR file (*myapp.war*).

You execute this build file from a command prompt whose working directory is the web application's root or top-level directory.

Example 4-6. An Ant file using the war task

```
<project name="war-task" default="create-war" basedir=".">

    <target name="init"
        description="Initializes some properties.">

        <echo message="Initializing properties."/>

        <property name="build" value=".\build" />
        <property name="src" value=".\src" />
        <property name="dist" value=".\dist" />
        <property name="lib" value=".\lib" />
        <property name="web" value=".\web" />
        <property name="meta" value=".\meta" />
        <property name="context-path" value="myapp" />

    </target>

    <target name="prepare" depends="init">

        <echo message=
          "Cleaning up the build and dist directories."/>

        <delete dir="${build}"/>
        <mkdir dir="${build}"/>
        <delete dir="${dist}"/>
        <mkdir dir="${dist}"/>

    </target>

    <target name="create-war" description=
      "creates a web application archive file"
        depends="prepare">
```

Example 4-6. An Ant file using the war task (continued)

```
    <war destfile="${dist}/${context-path}.war"
      webxml="${meta}/web.xml">

        <classes dir="${build}"/>
        <lib dir="${lib}"/>
        <fileset dir="${web}"/>
    </war>
  </target>

</project>
```

If the build file was called *war-task.xml*, then the Ant file is executed with this command line:

```
ant -buildfile war-task.xml
```

The create-war target calls the war task.

The war task's destfile attribute is required; it specifies the location of the resulting WAR file. Example 4-6 creates the WAR in the *dist* directory. The webxml attribute specifies the location of the web application's deployment descriptor. This web application's *web.xml* file (in this example) is located in the *meta* directory.

The example war task has three nested elements: classes, lib, and fileset. The dir attribute of the classes element points to the directory that contains the Java classes that are located in the *WEB-INF/classes* directory. The war task automatically creates the *WEB-INF/classes* directory in the WAR file. This task also reproduces all the package-related directories in the *build* directory when it creates *WEB-INF/classes*. In other words, if the *build* directory includes a *com/jspservletcookbook* directory structure, then the WAR will have the same structure in *WEB-INF/classes*.

The lib element grabs and stores any JAR files that will be located in the WAR file's *WEB-INF/lib* directory. Finally, the fileset nested element, in this case, pulls in all the static files and any nested *image* directories that are contained in */web* and places them at the top level of the WAR's directory tree. Here is what the output of this build file looks like (with some editing for readability):

```
init:
    [echo] Initializing properties.

prepare:
    [echo] Cleaning up the build and dist directories.
  [delete] Deleting directory
        /Users/bruceper/books/cookbook/build
   [mkdir] Created dir:
        /Users/bruceper/books/cookbook/build
  [delete] Deleting directory
        /Users/bruceper/books/cookbook/dist
   [mkdir] Created dir:
        /Users/bruceper/books/cookbook/dist
```

```
create-war:
    [war] Building war:
        /Users/bruceper/books/cookbook/dist/myapp.war
```

The war task has numerous other optional attributes that are explained in the Ant manual at *http://ant.apache.org /ant/manual/CoreTasks/war.html*.

See Also

Recipe 4.1 on downloading and setting up Ant; Recipe 4.2 on writing Ant targets; Recipe 4.3 on creating a classpath for an Ant file; Recipe 4.4 on compiling a servlet with Ant; Recipe 4.6 on using Ant to create JAR files; Recipes 4.7 and 4.8 on starting and stopping Tomcat with Ant; Recipes 2.1 and 2.6 on deploying web applications using Ant; the Ant manual section on the property task: *http://ant.apache.org/ manual/CoreTasks/property.html*; the Ant manual segment on targets: *http://ant. apache.org/manual/using.html#targets*; the Apache Ant manual index page: *http:// ant.apache.org/manual/index.html*; the Apache Ant Project: *http://ant.apache.org*.

4.6   Creating a JAR File with Ant

Problem

You want to create a JAR file with Ant.

Solution

Use the built-in jar task.

Discussion

The jar task automates the creation of JAR files. Like the war task for WARs, the jar task allows you to automate the command-line phrases you would have to type in for creating JARs. In this way, build files using the jar task are somewhat like shell scripts or batch files for creating JARs. The Sun Microsystems JAR file specification can be found at *http://java.sun.com/j2se/1.4/docs/guide/jar/jar.html*.

In web applications, JAR files are used to contain separate code libraries that the web application depends on, such as a database driver. They are located in a web application's *WEB-INF/lib* directory. Example 4-7 shows an Ant target that uses the jar task to create a JAR, and then copies the JAR file to the *lib* directory of a web application. These actions precede the archiving of the web application into a WAR file, which can be included in the same build file to automate everything at once (see Recipe 4.5 on creating WAR files).

Example 4-7. Creating a JAR file with Ant

```
<project name="jar-task" default="create-jar" basedir=".">

    <target name="init"
      description="Initializes some properties.">

        <echo message="Initializing properties."/>

        <property name="dist" value="dist" />
        <property name="web" value="web" />
        <property name="meta" value="meta" />
        <property name="jar-name" value="myutils" />

    </target>

    <target name="prepare" depends="init">

    <echo message=
      "Cleaning up the build and dist directories."/>

    <delete dir="${dist}"/>
    <mkdir dir="${dist}"/>

    </target>

    <target name="create-jar"
      description="creates a JAR archive file"
        depends="prepare">

        <jar destfile="${dist}/${jar-name}.jar"
          basedir="../../"
            includes="**/*.class **/${web}/*.html">

            <fileset dir="../../images"/>

        </jar>

    </target>

</project>
```

This build file contains three targets in the build sequence init → prepare → create-jar. These targets create some properties and clean up a directory called *dist* that contains the resultant JAR file. The create-jar target calls the jar task, which looks like:

```
<jar destfile="${dist}/${jar-name}.jar" basedir="../../"
  includes="**/*.class **/${web}/*.html">

    <fileset dir="../../images"/>

</jar>
```

The destfile attribute of the jar element specifies the location and name of the JAR file after it is created. I used a property called jar-name here, so that the user can run this Ant file from the command line and feed a new JAR filename into the build file if need be, as in:

```
ant -Djar-name=mynewjar.jar
```

 Remember that any properties specified with the -D switch override the properties of the same name defined inside the build file.

The basedir attribute of the jar task identifies the top-level directory of files that will be included in the JAR. In the example, the pattern ../../ means "go up two directories from the basedir of this project"; in other words, go up two directories from where the Ant build file is located.

The includes attribute has two space-separated patterns (you can also separate them with a comma). The patterns further refine the types of files that will be included in the JAR file. The first pattern specifies the inclusion of all the files ending with the *.class* suffix that are located in zero or more directories beneath the basedir location. This JAR, as a result, contains all of the Java class files in all directories nested beneath the base directory; the JAR reproduces any nested directories that it finds with the class files. The other pattern (**/${web}/*.html) takes all directories nested beneath the base directory called *web* and includes any files that end with *.html* in the JAR. Once again, the nested directories will be included with the JAR and the HTML files.

Finally, a fileset element nested within the jar task grabs all the contents of the ../../ *images* folder and includes them in the JAR, *but it does not include the images folder itself.* A way to include the *images* folder and its contents at the top level of the JAR is to change the jar task to:

```
<jar destfile="${dist}/${jar-name}.jar" basedir="../../"
  includes="**/*.class **/${web}/*.html **/images/*.gif"/>
```

This task adds a third pattern to the includes attribute (**/images/*.gif), which grabs all the GIF files contained by any *images* directories that are nested in the base directory (the value of the jar element's basedir attribute). An *images* directory will be included in the JAR if one is found.

 The ** pattern is often used in Ant elements; it means "zero or more directories."

Manifest

The jar task creates a *META-INF/MANIFEST.MF* file for the JAR if the jar task's manifest attribute does not appear. The default manifest looks like this:

```
Manifest-Version: 1.0
Created-By: Apache Ant 1.5.1
```

If you want to specify the location of your own manifest file for reasons such as signing a JAR file or specifying the file that contains the main( ) method in an executable JAR, use the jar task's manifest attribute. This optional attribute can be either the file location of the manifest or the name of another JAR that has been added by using a nested fileset element. If it is a JAR, the task looks in that JAR for the *META-INF/MANIFEST.MF* manifest.

See Also

Recipe 4.1 on downloading and setting up Ant; Recipe 4.2 on writing Ant targets; Recipe 4.3 on creating a classpath for an Ant file; Recipe 4.4 on compiling a servlet with Ant; Recipes 4.7 and 4.8 on starting and stopping Tomcat with Ant; Recipes 2.1 and 2.6 on deploying web applications using Ant; the Ant manual section on the property task: *http://ant.apache.org/manual/CoreTasks/property.html*; the Ant manual segment on targets: *http://ant.apache.org/manual/using.html#targets*; the Apache Ant manual index page: *http://ant.apache.org/manual/index.html*; the Apache Ant Project: *http://ant.apache.org*.

4.7   Starting a Tomcat Application with Ant

Problem

You want to start a web application on Tomcat using an Ant file.

Solution

Use the Tomcat-supplied StartTask task so that Ant can manage Tomcat.

Discussion

The Tomcat servlet and JSP container includes a built-in web application called "Manager" that you can use to start, stop, deploy, and initiate other administrative tasks with web applications. Tomcat makes this application available from the */manager* context path.

Tomcat Version 4 (and later) includes Java classes that allow developers to use the Manager application from their Ant build files. The advantage of using the Manager application from Ant is that you do not have to configure the *conf/server.xml* file to make the web application dynamically reloadable (see Recipe 2.2). In addition, you can start or stop a single web application without disrupting other Tomcat applications.

 The Manager documentation is found online at *http://jakarta.apache. org/tomcat/tomcat-4.1-doc/printer/manager-howto.html*

Take these steps to start Tomcat from Ant:

1. Make sure you have the necessary JAR file required to use the Ant task for starting Tomcat: *<Ant-installation-directory>/lib/catalina-ant.jar*. Copy this JAR from the *<Tomcat-installation-directory>/server/lib* directory to your *<Ant-installation-directory>/lib* directory (otherwise known as *ANT_HOME/lib*).

2. Make sure the Tomcat user database includes a username that is linked to the *manager* role. Only administrative users should be authorized to start and stop web applications using the Manager tool. The *conf/tomcat-users.xml* file maps users and passwords to roles. A user has to be mapped to the *manager* role to be able to use the Manager tool. Here is an example of one of these user mappings in *tomcat-users.xml*:

```
<user username="doug" password= "_1968dgw" roles="manager,dbadmin"/>
```

3. Use the taskdef element in the Ant file to define the custom task and give it a name. Example 4-8 gives the task the name start, which is used by the target that is responsible for starting Tomcat.

4. Run the Ant file at the command line by changing to its directory and typing ant.

Example 4-8 shows the taskdef element that defines the start task, followed by the target that starts the specified Tomcat application.

Example 4-8. Starting Tomcat using an Ant file

```
<project name="My Project" default="start-tomcat" basedir=".">

<taskdef name="start" classname="org.apache.catalina.ant.StartTask" />

<!-- import properties specifying username, password, url, and context-path -->
<property file="global.properties" />

<target name="start-tomcat"
    description="Starts the Web application">
    <echo message="Starting the default application ${ context-path}..."/>

    <start
      url="${url}"
      username="${username}"
      password="${password}"
      path="/${context-path}" />
</target>

</project>
```

The start task has four attributes that Example 4-8 sets using a *global.properties* file. This is a text file containing four name/value pairs, which are imported into the Ant file using the property task:

```
<property file="global.properties" />
```

The *global.properties* file is located in the same directory as the Ant build file. Here are the contents of the *global.properties* file:

```
url=http://localhost:8080/manager
username=bruce
password=bruce1957
context-path=home
```

The url property specifies the Tomcat Manager URL, the username and password identify the user who is mapped in the Tomcat user database to the *manager* role, the context-path property specifies the context path of the web application you are starting, and the Ant file itself specifies the opening slash (/) character for the context path.

 Another way to pass properties to an Ant file is on the command line:

```
ant -Dusername=bruce -Dpassword=bruce1957
-Durl=http://localhost:8080/manager
-Dcontext-path=home
```

Properties added on the command line override those specified by the property task.

Launch this Ant file by changing to its directory at the command line and typing ant or ant -buildfile *buildfile-name*. Here is the command-line output:

```
H:\book\cookbook\code\chap4>ant -buildfile start.xml
Buildfile: start.xml

start-tomcat:
     [echo] Starting the default application home...
    [start] OK - Started application at context path /home


BUILD SUCCESSFUL
Total time: 4 seconds
```

If an application is stopped, it is unavailable to web users (see Recipe 4.8). When the application is started again, it can receive requests normally.

 The Tomcat manager application can initiate many other common administrative tasks such as deploying applications (see Recipe 2.6).

See Also

The Tomcat Manager application description: *http://jakarta.apache.org/tomcat/tomcat-4.1-doc/manager-howto.html*; Recipe 4.1 on downloading and setting up Ant; Recipe 4.2 on writing Ant targets; Recipe 4.3 on creating a classpath for an Ant file; Recipe 4.4 on compiling a servlet with Ant; Recipes 4.5 and 4.6 on creating WAR and JAR files; Recipe 4.8 on stopping Tomcat with Ant; Recipes 2.1 and 2.6 on deploying web applications using Ant; the Ant manual section on the property task: *http://ant.apache.org/manual/CoreTasks/property.html*; the Ant manual segment on targets: *http://ant.apache.org/manual/using.html#targets*; the Apache Ant manual index page: *http://ant.apache.org/manual/index.html*; the Apache Ant Project: *http://ant.apache.org*.

4.8   Stopping a Tomcat Application with Ant

Problem

You want to use Ant to stop a specific Tomcat web application.

Solution

Define a task in the Ant file using a `taskdef` element and the Java class `org.apache.catalina.ant.StopTask`.

Discussion

During development, you might need to stop a Tomcat web application so that you can add new servlets or deployment-descriptor entries, and then restart the application, allowing the changes to take effect. In the absence of a *conf/server.xml* configuration to make the application dynamically reloadable (see Recipe 2.2), you can use an Ant target to stop a particular web application without disrupting the other running web applications. This is the opposite of starting an application (Recipe 4.7); the application is taken out of service until you start it again.

The `org.apache.catalina.ant.StopTask` class provides a connection between Ant and the Tomcat Manager application. Manager is a built-in web application (at context path */manager*) that you can use to administer other Tomcat web applications.

Implement the same four steps discussed in Recipe 4.7 to use this `stop` task:

1. Make sure you have the necessary JAR file required to use the Ant task for stopping Tomcat: *<Ant-installation-directory>/lib/catalina-ant.jar*. Copy this JAR from the *<Tomcat-installation-directory>/server/lib* directory to your *<Ant-installation-directory>/lib* directory (otherwise known as *ANT_HOME/lib*).

2. Make sure the Tomcat user database includes a username that is linked to the *manager* role (see step 2 of Recipe 4.7 if you need more details).

3. Example 4-9 uses a `taskdef` element to give the task the name `stop`, which is used by the target that is responsible for stopping Tomcat.

4. Run the Ant file at the command line by changing to its directory and typing `ant` or `ant -buildfile` *buildfile-name*.

Example 4-9. Using Ant to stop a web application

```
<project name="My Project" default="stop-tomcat" basedir=".">

<taskdef name="stop" classname="org.apache.catalina.ant.StopTask" />

<!-- import properties specifying username, password, url, and context-path -->
<property file="global.properties" />

<target name="stop-tomcat"
    description="Stops the Web application">

    <echo message="Stopping the application ${context-path}..."/>

    <stop
        url="${url}"
        username="${username}"
        password="${password}"
        path="/${context-path}" />

</target>

</project>
```

The `taskdef` defines a task for this build file called `stop`. The defined task is then used in the build file:

```
<stop url="${url}" username="${username}" password="${password}"
        path="/${context-path}" />
```

Example 4-9 gets its property values from a property task that imports *global. properties* (the property file is located in the same directory as the Ant build file). The properties represent:

- The username and password of a user who is mapped to the *manager* role in *conf/tomcat-users.xml*
- The URL to the Manager application, as in *http://localhost:8080/manager*
- The context path for the web application that you are stopping

> The Tomcat manager application can initiate many other common administrative tasks such as deploying applications (see Recipe 2.6).

See Also

The Tomcat Manager application description: *http://jakarta.apache.org/tomcat/ tomcat-4.1-doc/manager-howto.html*; Recipe 4.1 on downloading and setting up Ant; Recipe 4.2 on writing Ant targets; Recipe 4.3 on creating a classpath for an Ant file; Recipe 4.4 on compiling a servlet with Ant; Recipes 4.5 and 4.6 on creating WAR and JAR files; Recipe 4.7 on starting Tomcat with Ant; Recipes 2.1 and 2.6 on deploying web applications using Ant; the Ant manual section on the property task: *http://ant.apache.org/manual/CoreTasks/property.html*; the Ant manual segment on targets: *http://ant.apache.org/manual/using.html#targets*; the Apache Ant manual index page: *http://ant.apache.org/manual/index.html*; the Apache Ant Project: *http:// ant.apache.org*.

CHAPTER 5
Altering the Format of JSPs

5.0 Introduction

This chapter covers two means of working with JSPs that fall slightly outside the norm. The first method precompiles JSPs and turns them into servlet source code. The second develops JSPs as XML documents.

Precompiling JSPs

Precompiling a JSP involves using a server-provided command-line tool to convert the JSP page into a servlet class file. A JSP is converted into a servlet, often called a *JavaServer Page implementation class*, before it handles any HTTP requests. The JSP specification refers to the stage by which the JSP container converts JSP page syntax into a servlet as the *translation phase*. In Tomcat, if you want to examine what the JSP page implementation class looks like after this conversion, go to this directory:

    Tomcat-install-directory/work/Standalone/name-of-host/name-of-web-app

name-of-host could be *localhost*, or any other hostname that refers to the server Tomcat is installed on. The name of the web application is also the name of the context; this is usually something like *examples*, *ROOT*, or *storefront*.

The indicated directory contains *.java* files, such as *default_jsp.java*. These are the Java source files that are compiled into class files, and then executed as servlets to respond to requests.

The reasons why a JSP developer may want to precompile a JSP page include:

1. Avoiding the perceptible delay caused when a JSP is first requested from the web container, during which the JSP compiler converts the JSP's source code into a servlet.

2. Allowing the developer to examine the Java source code for the JSP page implementation class, and optionally work on the code with their servlet IDE's source-code editor.

In both Tomcat and WebLogic, a command-line tool can be used to precompile a JSP. Recipe 5.4 covers the mapping in *web.xml* of a JSP page to its servlet implementation class.

JSPs as XML Documents

The later recipes in this chapter describe creating JSPs as XML files. Both the JSP specifications v1.2 and 2.0 describe the generation and use of JSPs as pure XML documents. This means that rather than create JSPs in typical JSP page syntax, they are instead coded as well-formed XML documents. According to the JSP specification, a *JSP document* is a namespace-aware XML document. The JSP container differentiates JSP documents from traditional JSP pages in at least one of three ways.

1. A `jsp-property-group` element in *web.xml* specifies a JSP document with the is-xml child element. (The `jsp-property-group` element is one of the JSP configuration elements that the JSP 2.0 specification has proposed adding to *web.xml*.)

2. The file has a *.jspx* extension.

3. The JSP page has a root element of `jsp:root`.

Recipe 5.5 shows what these files look like.

The JSP specification describes an XML view as a description of a JSP page in XML form. An *XML view* is generated by the JSP container during the translation phase. A subclass of `javax.servlet.jsp.tagext.TagLibraryValidator` can use the XML view to parse a JSP in order to validate that custom tags have been used correctly, before the container finally converts the JSP into its page implementation class (a servlet). Recipe 5.6 shows how to generate XML views for a JSP, and how to save the resulting XML files.

JSPs can be created as XML files for the following reasons, among others:

- Web containers can accept JSP documents in web applications, meaning that the web application can contain XML files instead of the pages in traditional JSP syntax. JSP documents can thus be integrated with other XML content, such as XHTML files, Scalable Vector Graphics (SVG), and the XML files that are part of web services transactions.

- You can use XML editors to work with JSP documents.

- You can use other XML technologies with JSP documents, such as XSLT, Simple Object Access Protocol (SOAP), SAX, and DOM.

5.1   Precompiling a JSP in Tomcat

Problem

You want to convert JSPs into servlets using Tomcat 4.1.x.

Solution

Use the *JspC* command-line tool found in *<Tomcat-installation>/bin*.

Discussion

Using the *JspC* command-line tool is the first step in precompiling Tomcat JSPs. This tool is offered in the form of a shell script—*jspc.sh* on Unix systems and *jspc.bat* on Windows—and creates the Java source files for the JSP page implementation classes with which it is supplied. The resultant *.java* files still have to be compiled into serv-let class files, using *javac* or another Java compiler. Since precompiling JSPs is a two-step process, I recommend a batch file for convenience. However, let's first examine how to use the *JspC* utility.

The Windows shell script for running *JspC* (*<Tomcat-install-directory>/bin/jspc.bat*) requires that a JASPER_HOME environment variable be set to the Tomcat installation directory. Set this environment variable with the following command line:

```
set JASPER_HOME=k:\jakarta-tomcat-4.1.12
```

Run the *JspC* utility by changing to the *%JASPER_HOME%\bin* directory and typing the following command (specify your own directory paths and issue the command on one line):

```
jspc -d H:\book\cookbook -webinc H:\book\cookbook\map.xml
   -webapp h:\book\cookbook\dist
```

The -d switch specifies the directory where you would like the source files to be gen-erated, and the -webinc switch specifies the name of an automatically generated file where *JspC* will create the servlet and servlet-mapping elements for the servlet files. If you compile a JSP page that is called *precomp.jsp*, the mappings would look like Example 5-1.

Example 5-1. Servlet mapping for a precompiled JSP

```
<servlet>
    <servlet-name>org.apache.jsp.precomp_jsp</servlet-name>
    <servlet-class>org.apache.jsp.precomp_jsp</servlet-class>
</servlet>
<servlet-mapping>
    <servlet-name>org.apache.jsp.precomp_jsp</servlet-name>
    <url-pattern>/precomp.jsp</url-pattern>
</servlet-mapping>
```

You can then cut and paste these servlet and servlet-mapping elements into the *web.xml* deployment descriptor for your web application.

The -webapp switch specifies a web-application directory, which must in turn have a */WEB-INF* subdirectory containing your application's *web.xml* file. *JspC* finds all of the *.jsp* files at the top level of this web-application directory and translates them into servlet source files, along with any JSPs in nested subdirectories. The resulting *.java* files are placed in the directory specified with the -d switch. Unlike -webinc, the -webxml switch creates an entire *web.xml* file that includes the new servlets and servlet mappings. Several other *JspC* options are described here: *http://cvs.apache. org/viewcvs/~checkout~/jakarta-tomcat-4.0/jasper/doc/jspc.html*.

You'll then need to compile the generated source files. I recommend using a batch file to take care of both steps at once. The Windows batch file in Example 5-2 generates the source files and uses the *javac* tool to compile the servlets.

Example 5-2. Using a batch file to precompile JSPs with Tomcat

```
@echo off
jspc -d H:\book\cookbook\classes -webinc H:\book\cookbook\map.xml -webapp h:\book\
cookbook\dist
set PRECLASSPATH=%CATALINA_HOME%\common\lib\servlet.jar;
    %CATALINA_HOME%\common\lib\jasper-runtime.jar;%CLASSPATH%

javac -classpath %PRECLASSPATH% -d ./classes *.java
```

Save this file in a text file with a name like *precomp.bat*. Change to the directory containing the batch file and type precomp. This batch file runs the *JspC* command on all *.jsp* files existing beneath the *h:\book\cookbook\dist* web-application directory. Using the -webinc switch, the command creates an XML fragment of servlet and servlet-mapping elements as shown earlier in this recipe. If there are no problems, the compiled files will be stored in the *h:\book\cookbook\classes* directory.

The code then creates a PRECLASSPATH environment variable that includes the *servlet. jar* and *jasper-runtime.jar* components, along with any directories or JARs that are part of the existing CLASSPATH environment variable. The *servlet.jar* component is necessary to import these Java packages during compilation:

- javax.servlet
- javax.servlet.http
- javax.servlet.jsp

Adding the *jasper-runtime.jar* is necessary to import the org.apache.jasper.runtime package. On Windows, you may have to set a JASPER_HOME environment variable to the Tomcat installation directory before this batch file runs properly.

Example 5-3 shows a Unix shell script that accomplishes the same task. This script executes the *jspc.sh* file in Tomcat's */bin* directory, precompiling all of the JSP files that the *JspC* tool finds in the current working directory. The script stores the resulting *.java* files in the *./classes* directory.

Example 5-3. A shell script for precompiling JSP files

```
#!/bin/sh
$CATALINA_HOME/bin/jspc.sh -d ./classes -webinc ./map.xml -webapp ./;
PRECLASSPATH=$CATALINA_HOME/common/lib/servlet.jar:$CATALINA_HOME/common/lib/jasper-
runtime.jar;
export PRECLASSPATH;
javac -classpath $PRECLASSPATH -d ./classes ./classes/*.java
```

See Also

Recipe 5.3 on the precompilation protocol; Recipe 5.4 on mapping the compiled JSP(s) in *web.xml*; the JSP precompilation section of *JavaServer Pages* by Hans Bergsten (O'Reilly); Chapter JSP.11.4 of the JSP 2.0 specification.

5.2   Precompiling a JSP in WebLogic

Problem

You want to precompile a JSP in WebLogic.

Solution

Use the *weblogic.jspc* Java utility that installs with WebLogic Server 7.0.

Discussion

WebLogic Server 7.0 installs with its own Java utility for precompiling JSPs: *weblogic.jspc*. This utility is part of the JAR file that can be found at this location: *<WebLogic-install-directory>/weblogic700/server/lib/weblogic.jar*. When you precompile JSPs using *weblogic.jspc*, it places the class files in the specified destination directory. Example 5-4 shows a simple batch file on Windows NT that precompiles an *example.jsp* JSP page into its servlet implementation class.

Example 5-4. Precompiling a JSP with weblogic.jspc

```
@echo off
set WLCLASSPATH=k:\bea\weblogic700\server\lib\weblogic.jar;%CLASSPATH%
java -cp %WLCLASSPATH% weblogic.jspc -d .\classes example.jsp
```

The second line of Example 5-4 sets an environment variable, WLCLASSPATH. This variable prepends a reference to *weblogic.jar* to the existing CLASSPATH variable. The next line of the example uses this combined classpath to run *weblogic.jspc*. The -d switch tells the program where to store the resulting class files, in this case, in the *classes* directory beneath the directory containing the batch file and *example.jsp*. This program generates a Java class file named *jsp_servlet.__example.class* (including the package name). If you do not specify a package for the compiled servlet, jsp_servlet is used as the default package name (see Example 5-6). Example 5-5 shows a shell script that is written on Mac OS X for precompiling a JSP with WebLogic.

Example 5-5. Precompiling JSPs with weblogic.jspc and a shell script

```
#!/bin/sh
WLCLASSPATH=/Users/bruceper/java/weblogic_jar/weblogic.jar:$CLASSPATH;
export WLCLASSPATH;
java -cp $WLCLASSPATH weblogic.jspc
  -d /Users/bruceper/books/cookbook/code/chap5/classes  newfile.jsp
```

 weblogic.jspc is different from Tomcat's *JspC* utility in that it compiles a file in JSP page syntax into the servlet class file in a single operation. Using Tomcat's *JspC* from the command line requires the use of a compiler, such as *javac*, to compile the *.java* files generated by *JspC* into class files. This second compilation step when using *JspC* is handled automatically when using *weblogic.jspc*.

The Windows batch file in Example 5-6 specifies a `jspservletcookbook` package for all the JSP pages found in the web application specified by the `-webapp` switch.

Example 5-6. Using weblogic.jspc to precompile all JSP pages in a web application

```
@echo off
set WLCLASSPATH=k:\bea\weblogic700\server\lib\weblogic.jar;%CLASSPATH%
java -cp %WLCLASSPATH% weblogic.jspc -d .\classes -package jspservletcookbook -compileAll
-webapp h:/home
```

Example 5-7 shows a Unix shell script that does the same thing.

Example 5-7. Precompiling all JSP pages in a web application with a shell script

```
#!/bin/sh
WLCLASSPATH=/Users/bruceper/java/weblogic_jar/weblogic.jar:$CLASSPATH;
export WLCLASSPATH;
java -cp $WLCLASSPATH weblogic.jspc -d /Users/bruceper/books/cookbook/code/chap5/classes
-package jspservletcookbook -compileAll -webapp /Users/bruceper/books/cookbook/code/chap5
```

Note this portion of the instruction in the example:

```
-compileAll -webapp h:/home
```

The `-compileAll` switch, along with an argument to `-webapp`, tells *weblogic.jspc* to precompile all the JSP files found in the web application configured in the *h:\home* directory, including any JSP files nested in subdirectories. This web application is in exploded directory format (not archived into a WAR file). In Example 5-6, the compiled classes are stored in the *\classes\jspservletcookbook* directory path.

See Also

Recipe 5.3 on the precompilation protocol; Recipe 5.4 on mapping the compiled JSP(s) in *web.xml*; the JSP precompilation section of *JavaServer Pages* by Hans Bergsten (O'Reilly); Chapter JSP.11.4 of the JSP 2.0 specification.

5.3 Precompiling JSPs with the Precompilation Protocol

Problem

You want to use the "precompilation protocol" that is part of the JSP specification to precompile one or more JSP files.

Solution

Send a request to the JSP container that includes a `jsp_precompile` parameter.

Discussion

The JSP 1.2 and 2.0 specifications require compliant JSP containers to support the use of the `jsp_precompile` request parameter. This parameter suggests that the container precompile the requested JSP. Here is how it works in Tomcat:

1. Request the JSP that you want precompiled with the `jsp_precompile` parameter added to the URL, as in *http://localhost:8080/home/url_rewrite.jsp?jsp_precompile=true*.

    The JSP container is not supposed to execute the JSP page; it just precompiles it. The result of the request, if you were making it in a web browser, is a blank page.

2. If the JSP file in JSP page syntax has not yet been compiled, or if the JSP file has been changed and has a later modification date than any existing page implementation class, Tomcat creates a new Java source and class file for the JSP in the *<Tomcat-install-directory>/work* directory. If the JSP file is named *url_rewrite.jsp*, Tomcat calls the Java source and class files *url_rewrite_jsp.java* and *url_rewrite_jsp.class*.

    Supplying the request parameter `jsp_precompile` (without the "=true" part) is the same as requesting `jsp_precompile =true` in the URL.

     The precompilation protocol in Tomcat will both create the *.java* file and compile that file into the JSP page implementation class. Using the *JspC* tool as described in Recipe 5.1 will generate only a *.java* file.

This protocol is best used with an automated tool that can make HTTP requests, such as the Jakarta Commons HttpClient component. Using such a tool allows you to automate the precompilation of dozens of JSPs by sending several HTTP requests from a single Java program.

See Also

Recipe 5.1 on using Tomcat's *JspC* utility; Recipe 5.2 on precompiling with WebLogic Server; Recipe 5.4 on mapping the compiled JSPs in *web.xml*; Chapter 7 on sending HTTP requests from a servlet or a JSP; the Jakarta Commons HttpClient homepage at *http://jakarta.apache.org/commons/httpclient/*; The JSP precompilation section of *JavaServer Pages* by Hans Bergsten (O'Reilly); Chapter JSP.11.4 of the JSP 2.0 specification.

5.4 Mapping a JSP to Its Page Implementation Class

Problem

You have already precompiled a JSP and want to specify a mapping to the JSP page implementation class in your deployment descriptor.

Solution

Cut and paste the servlet and servlet-mapping elements generated automatically by *JspC* into *web.xml*. Create the proper package-related directories in the *WEB-INF/classes* directory of your web application, then place the precompiled JSPs into that directory.

Discussion

Precompiling JSPs allows you to remove the JSP page syntax files from your web application and just use the resulting servlet class files. You can then use the servlet-mapping element in *web.xml* to map a JSP-style URL (e.g., *default.jsp*) to the compiled servlet class. Here is how to accomplish this task:

1. Precompile the JSP(s) as described in Recipes 5.1 or 5.2, including the compilation of Java source files into class files using *javac* or another compiler tool.

2. Cut and paste the servlet and servlet-mapping elements generated automatically by *JspC* into your deployment descriptor (if you are using Tomcat), or add those elements manually to *web.xml* (if you are using WebLogic or another container).

3. Make sure the servlet-mapping's url-pattern element points to a JSP-style file-name, such as *default.jsp*, or an extension mapping such as **.jsp*.

4. Place the class or classes, including the package-related directories, in *WEB-INF/classes*, or inside of a JAR file that is stored in *WEB-INF/lib*.

When the web users request the URL specified by the servlet-mapping for that JSP page implementation class, the web container will now direct that request to the mapped servlet class.

Example 5-8 shows a servlet configuration for a precompiled JSP.

Example 5-8. A web.xml entry for a precompiled JSP

```
<servlet>
    <servlet-name>org.apache.jsp.precomp_jsp</servlet-name>
    <servlet-class>org.apache.jsp.precomp_jsp</servlet-class>
</servlet>
<servlet-mapping>
    <servlet-name>org.apache.jsp.precomp_jsp</servlet-name>
    <url-pattern>/precomp.jsp</url-pattern>
</servlet-mapping>
```

The directory structure for this class in your web application should be something like: */WEB-INF/classes/org/apache/jsp/precomp_jsp.class*. If the context path for your web application is */home*, users can request this JSP's implementation class (a servlet, behind the scenes) with a URL similar to *http://localhost:8080/home/precomp.jsp*.

See Also

Recipes 5.1–5.3; Chapter JSP.11.4 of the JSP 2.0 specification.

5.5   Creating a JSP from Scratch as a JSP Document

Problem

You want to create a JSP document in an XML editor's tool.

Solution

Open up your XML editor of choice and create the JSP using only XML elements.

Discussion

A JSP document is a namespace-aware, well-formed XML file that contains JSP standard actions (such as jsp:include and jsp:useBean), custom actions (such as JSTL custom tags), and the XML equivalents of JSP directives. Table 5-1 specifies the XML equivalents for common JSP directives. Write the JSP document in an XML editor, preferably one where you can check its well-formedness. The JSP document has to be a well-formed XML document to be eligible for placement into a JSP container and execution.

Table 5-1. XML equivalents for JSP directives

Directive	Example	JSP document equivalent
page	<%@ page import="java.util.Date" %>	<jsp:directive.page import="java.util.Date" />
include	<%@ include file="footer.html" %>	<jsp:directive.include file="footer.html" />
taglib	<%@ taglib uri="WEB-INF/tlds/xml_gen.tld" prefix="t" %>	<jsp:root jsp:id="0" xmlns:jsp="http://java.sun.com/JSP/Page" version="2.0" xmlns:t="urn:jsptld:/WEB-INF/tlds/xml_gen.tld">

 In JSP 1.2, the only way to identify a JSP page as XML is by having a jsp:root element as the root. However, JSP 2.0 offers several new options—the JSP 2.0 specification states that a JSP document can also be distinguished from a JSP in non-XML syntax by a jsp-property-group element in the deployment descriptor, a *.jspx* file extension, or a jsp:root root element.

This recipe shows a simple JSP page and its XML equivalent, then repeats the comparison with the addition of a custom tag and a runtime expression for a JSP element attribute. Example 5-9 is a simple file in JSP page syntax showing the web server's local time.

Example 5-9. A simple JSP page-syntax file

```
<%@page contentType="text/html"%>
<%@page import="java.util.Date"%>
<html>
  <head><title>Welcome to the Web</title></head>
  <body>
    <h2>Welcome to the Web</h2>
    The server's local time is <%=new Date( ) %>.
  </body>
</html>
```

This JSP has two page directives and a JSP expression that displays a date and time string on the browser page. Figure 5-1 shows the execution of this page in a browser.

This page can be converted into a JSP document by cutting and pasting the code into an XML editor and replacing non-XML constructs with XML elements. Example 5-10 is the JSP document equivalent of Example 5-9.

Figure 5-1. Simple JSP before XML conversion

Example 5-10. A simple JSP document as well-formed XML

```
<jsp:root xmlns:jsp="http://java.sun.com/JSP/Page" version="2.0">
  <jsp:directive.page contentType="text/html"/>
  <jsp:directive.page import="java.util.Date"/>
  <html>
    <head><title>Welcome to the Web</title></head>
    <body>
      <h2>Welcome to the Web</h2>
      The server's local time is <jsp:expression>new Date( )</jsp:expression>.
    </body>
  </html>
</jsp:root>
```

Example 5-10 has `jsp:directive.page` elements instead of traditional JSP directives, which are not valid XML elements because of the <%@ syntax. Anything in a JSP page that uses <%-style delimiters cannot be used to distinguish JSP elements, because then the JSP document will not pass an XML well-formedness test.

Example 5-11 is a more complex JSP page with a `taglib` directive that specifies the core tag library from JSTL 1.0; the page also uses Expression Language (EL) code. Further, the page has a `jsp:useBean` element that sets a `java.util.Date` variable `dateString` to page scope.

Example 5-11. A JSP page presenting a complex XML conversion

```
<%@page contentType="text/html"%>
<%@ taglib uri="http://java.sun.com/jstl/core" prefix="c" %>
<html>
  <head><title>Welcome to the Web</title></head>
  <body>
    <h2>Welcome to the Web</h2>
    Hello, <c:out value="${param.firstName} ${param.lastName}"/><br><br>
    <jsp:useBean id="dateString" class="java.util.Date"/>
```

Example 5-11. A JSP page presenting a complex XML conversion (continued)

```
    The time is <c:out value="${dateString}" />.<br><br>
    The value of 10 + 24 + 35 = <c:out value="${10 + 24 + 35}" />
  </body>
</html>
```

Example 5-12 is the same JSP page converted to a JSP document.

Example 5-12. Referring to tag libraries (taglibs) in a JSP document

```
<jsp:root xmlns:jsp="http://java.sun.com/JSP/Page"
    xmlns:c="http://java.sun.com/jstl/core" version="2.0">
  <jsp:directive.page contentType="text/html"/>
  <html>
    <head><title>Welcome to the Web</title></head>
    <body>
      <h2>Welcome to the Web</h2>
      <jsp:text>Hello </jsp:text>
      <c:out value="${param.firstName} ${param.lastName}"/><br></br><br></br>
      <jsp:useBean id="dateString" class="java.util.Date"/>
      <jsp:text>The time is </jsp:text><c:out value="${dateString}" />.
      <br></br><br></br>
      <jsp:text>The value of 10 + 24 + 35 = </jsp:text>
      <c:out value="${10 + 24 + 35}" />
    </body>
  </html>
</jsp:root>
```

In a JSP document, any tag libraries can be included as namespace attributes, such as in the jsp:root element, as shown here:

```
<jsp:root xmlns:jsp="http://java.sun.com/JSP/Page"
    xmlns:c="http://java.sun.com/jstl/core" version="2.0">
```

The jsp:text element can be used to contain any template data in the JSP document. You can use the JSP standard actions such as jsp:useBean and custom tags like c:out with the same syntax used in a JSP page.

Figure 5-2 shows the browser output of the JSP document in Example 5-12. This page was requested by using this URL: *http://localhost:8080/home/example_xml2.jsp?firstName=Bruce&lastName=Perry.*

Here is what the HTML source code looks like, if you chose "View → Source" from the browser menu (with some carriage returns added for readability):

```
<html><head><title>Welcome to the Web</title></head>
<body>
<h2>Welcome to the Web</h2>
Hello Bruce Perry<br/><br/>
The time is Mon Feb 10 16:20:05 EST 2003.<br/><br/>
The value of 10 + 24 + 35 = 69
</body></html>
```

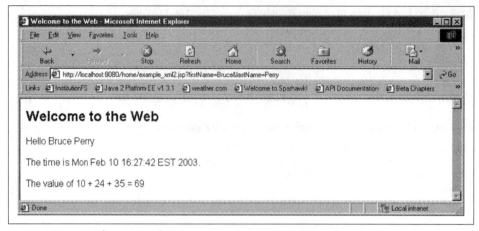

Figure 5-2. Output from Example 5-11

See Also

Recipe 5.6 on generating an XML view from a JSP; Chapter JSP.6 (JSP documents) of the JSP 2.0 specification; Chapter JSP.10 (XML views) of the JSP 2.0 specification.

5.6   Generating an XML View from a JSP

Problem

You want to automatically generate an XML view from a JSP page.

Solution

Create a custom tag and a TagLibraryValidator class, from which you can output the XML view of a JSP to a file.

Discussion

An XML view is an XML form of a JSP page that the JSP container generates during the translation phase, an intermediary stage before the container converts the JSP to its page implementation class (a servlet). A TagLibraryValidator class can use the XML view to validate the use of custom tags in the JSP prior to the JSP's conversion to a servlet. An XML view is very similar to a JSP document, which is an XML form of a JSP page that JSP developers can write and add to their web applications. The differences between the two XML files according to the JSP specification v2.0 are:

- An XML view expands any include directives that a JSP document contains into their corresponding JSP fragments.
- An XML view provides each XML element with a jsp:id attribute.

- An XML view adds a `jsp:root` element as the root element of the document if the document does not already have a `jsp:root` element.

- An XML view adds a `jsp:directive.page` element and `pageEncoding` attribute if they do not already exist, and sets the value of `pageEncoding` to "UTF-8".

- An XML view adds a `jsp:directive.page` element and `contentType` attribute if they do not already exist, and sets the value of `contentType` according to Chapter JSP.4.2, "Response Character Encoding," of the JSP 2.0 specification (e.g., "text/xml" for a JSP document).

Java developers can add subclasses of `javax.servlet.jsp.tagext.TagLibraryValidator` to their web applications as tools for validating the application's use of custom tags. The JSP container (Jasper is the name of the Tomcat JSP container) makes available to the `TagLibraryValidator` an XML view of a JSP page for the purpose of parsing XML elements in the page and validating whether or not they have been used correctly.

It is useful to examine the XML view of a JSP page in order to debug a `TagLibraryValidator` class that you are using in a custom tag library, or to open up your JSP in an XML editor and evaluate its syntax from an XML perspective. Here is a nice way (okay, a bit of a hack!) to automatically generate a file representing the XML view of a JSP page. This recipe uses a `javax.servlet.jsp.tagext.PageData` object, which automatically returns the XML view of a JSP page as a `java.io.InputStream`. Here is how it works:

1. Create a class that extends `javax.servlet.jsp.tagext.TagLibraryValidator`. These classes are used to validate the use of custom tags, and are explained in more detail in Chapter 23.

2. Override the `TagLibraryValidator.validate(String prefix, String uri, PageData page)` method to write the XML view information from the `PageData` parameter to a file.

3. Create a simple custom tag by extending `javax.servlet.jsp.tagext.TagSupport`. This tag "marks" a JSP page so that its XML view can be output to a file. The tag includes a "filename" attribute from which your validator class will get the filename for the XML view. The tag looks like this:

   ```
   <t:toxml filename="myxml_view" />
   ```

4. Create a Tag Library Descriptor (TLD) file for this tag library, specifying the `TagLibraryValidator` class you created as the validator for this library:

```
<validator>
    <validator-class>
      com.jspservletcookbook.ToXmlValidator
    </validator-class>
    <description>
    Saves XML views of JSP pages to the
    specified directory.
    </description>
</validator>
```

5. Place both the `TagLibraryValidator` and the `TagSupport` classes in the *WEB-INF/ classes* directory of the web application, or inside a JAR file that is stored in *WEB-INF/lib* (the examples in this recipe assume this format, rather than placing the classes in a JAR).

6. Place the TLD file in the *WEB-INF/tlds* directory.

7. Add a taglib element referring to your tags and TLD to the *WEB-INF/web.xml* deployment descriptor.

 The taglib element in *web.xml* is not needed with JSP Version 1.2 and 2.0, since the JSP container automatically searches *WEB-INF*, as well as the *META-INF* directory of your application's JAR files, for any file that ends with the extension *.tld*.

8. Create a properties file containing the directory path that you want to use for the automatically generated XML view. Store this properties file in *WEB-INF/classes* using the appropriate package names. This properties file is used to avoid the hardcoding of an absolute directory in the validator class's code.

9. Use the custom tag in the JSP file(s) for which you want the XML views generated as files.

First, Example 5-13 shows the XML view–related custom tag in a JSP file.

Example 5-13. Generating the XML view of a JSP page

```
<%@ taglib uri="/toxml_view" prefix="t" %>
<html>
<head>
    <title>Test tld</title>
</head>
<body bgcolor="#ffffff">

Hello, this page is using the toxml tag to look at its XML View.
<t:toxml filename="my_xmlview"/>

</body>
</html>
```

The `t:toxml` tag is an empty element that signals the validator class to generate a file containing an XML view. The file will be named *my_xmlview.xml* (the validator class adds the *.xml* extension). The tag otherwise has no effect on the appearance or behavior of this JSP. The following fragment of the deployment descriptor shows the taglib element specifying the URI that is used in Example 5-11's `taglib` directive. The `taglib` element in the deployment descriptor also specifies the location of the TLD file (*WEB-INF/tlds/xml_gen.tld*):

```
<taglib>
    <taglib-uri>/toxml_view</taglib-uri>
    <taglib-location>/WEB-INF/tlds/xml_gen.tld</taglib-location>
</taglib>
```

Example 5-14 shows the TLD file for this tag library, which specifies the validator class and the simple custom tag (a marker) used in Example 5-11. I am not going to show the code for the toxml tag, since it does not contain any code of interest, beyond the fact that it has one String member variable called filename. The sole purpose of the tag's use is to put the validator class to work. The JSP container creates one validator instance for each tag library that includes a validator class.

Example 5-14. The TLD file for the XML view custom tag

```xml
<?xml version="1.0" encoding="ISO-8859-1" ?>
<!DOCTYPE taglib
        PUBLIC "-//Sun Microsystems, Inc.//DTD JSP Tag Library 1.2//EN"
    "http://java.sun.com/dtd/web-jsptaglibrary_1_2.dtd">

<taglib>

    <tlib-version>1.0</tlib-version>
    <jsp-version>1.2</jsp-version>
    <short-name>Validator test</short-name>
    <description>Validator test</description>

    <validator>
        <validator-class>
           com.jspservletcookbook.ToXmlValidator
        </validator-class>
        <description>
        Saves XML views of JSP pages to the specified
        directory.
        </description>
    </validator>

    <tag>
        <name>toxml</name>
        <tag-class>com.jspservletcookbook.ToXml</tag-class>
        <body-content>EMPTY</body-content>
        <description>
        This tag demonstrates the production of JSP XML view files.
        </description>
        <attribute>
          <name>filename</name>
          <required>true</required>
          <rtexprvalue>false</rtexprvalue>
          <description>
           This attribute provides the filename.</description>
        </attribute>
    </tag>
</taglib>
```

The com.jspservletcookbook.ToXmlValidator class, the library's validator, executes its validate method when a JSP page using the toxml tag is loaded. How does the validator class know where to save the files representing the JSP's XML view? The com.jspservletcookbook.ToXmlValidator class derives the directory path for saving its generated files from the properties file shown below. This allows any deployer of the custom tag to change the directory for the saved XML views, without touching the validator class's source code. The properties file is located in the same directory as the validator class. The path to this properties file is *WEB-INF/classes/com/jspservlet-cookbook/validator.properties*:

```
directory=h:/home/xmlviews
```

The filename is provided by the tag itself, as in:

```
<t:toxml filename="my_xmlview" />
```

The entire file path for the XML view looks like: *h:/home/xmlviews/my_xmlview.xml*.

 The validator class adds the *.xml* extension when it creates the XML view file. The validator first extracts the filename from the toxml tag by using a SAX parser to parse the input stream from the javax.servlet. jsp.tagext.PageData object.

You now have all of the pieces together except for the all-important validator class, which is shown in Example 5-15. The validate method reads the directory property value using a java.util.ResourceBundle object. The validate method gets the filename by using the helper class that Example 5-16 shows. The validate method then generates the XML view of the JSP page by using the java.io.InputStream returned from PageData.getInputStream( ).

Example 5-15. A validator class for generating XML view files

```
package com.jspservletcookbook;

import javax.servlet.jsp.tagext.TagLibraryValidator;
import javax.servlet.jsp.tagext.ValidationMessage;
import javax.servlet.jsp.tagext.PageData;
import java.io.*;
import java.util.ResourceBundle;
import java.util.MissingResourceException;
import java.util.Date;

public class ToXmlValidator extends TagLibraryValidator {

    /** Creates new ToXmlValidator */
    public ToXmlValidator( ) {
    }

    public ValidationMessage[] validate(java.lang.String prefix,
      java.lang.String uri,PageData page){

        ValidationMessage[] vam = null;
        try{

        ResourceBundle bundle =
```

Example 5-15. A validator class for generating XML view files (continued)

```
      ResourceBundle.getBundle("com.jspservletcookbook.validator");
   String directory = bundle.getString("directory");
   String fileName = getFilename(page);

   //throw an Exception if the directory is invalid
   if (directory == null)
     throw new Exception(
       "Received a null directory for the XML view file.");
   //throw an Exception if the filename is invalid
   if (fileName == null)
      throw new IOException(
        "Received a null filename for the XML view file.");
   File file = new File(directory + "/" + fileName + ".xml");
   FileWriter writer = new FileWriter(file);
   BufferedReader in = new BufferedReader(
    new InputStreamReader(page.getInputStream( )));
    String line = "";
   //write the XML view to the specified file
   while ((line = in.readLine( )) != null ){
       writer.write(line);
    }

   in.close( );
   writer.close( );

   } catch (IOException io){

       //return a validation message
       ValidationMessage vmsg = new
         ValidationMessage(null,io.getMessage( ));
       vam = new ValidationMessage[1];
       vam[0] = vmsg;
       return vam;

   } catch (MissingResourceException mre){
       //return a validation message
       ValidationMessage vmsg = new
         ValidationMessage(null,mre.getMessage( ));
       vam = new ValidationMessage[1];
       vam[0] = vmsg;
       return vam;
   } catch (Exception e){
       //return a validation message
       ValidationMessage vmsg = new
         ValidationMessage(null,e.getMessage( ));
       vam = new ValidationMessage[1];
       vam[0] = vmsg;
       return vam;
   }

   //return empty array
   vam = new ValidationMessage[0];
```

Example 5-15. A validator class for generating XML view files (continued)

```
        return vam;
    }

    private String getFilename(PageData page) throws Exception {
        try{
          ValidateHandler handler = new ValidateHandler( );
          return handler.getFilename(page);
          } catch (Exception e){
           throw e; }
    }
}
```

Example 5-16 shows the ValidateHandler helper class that our validator uses to get the filename from the custom tag. The ValidateHandler makes a first pass through the XML view (before it is written to a file) to extract the filename that the user has added with the toxml element's filename attribute. The ValidateHandler does all the work behind the scenes to parse the XML so that the validator class can get the filename with a simple method call:

```
ValidateHandler handler = new ValidateHandler( );
return handler.getFilename(page);
```

The ValidateHandler uses the Java API for XML processing (JAXP) and the Simple API for XML (SAX) to parse the XML provided by javax.servlet.jsp.tagext. PageData.getInputStream( ). You have to place the ValidateHandler class inside of the *WEB-INF/classes* directory (or inside of a JAR file in *WEB-INF/lib*) so that your web application (the ToXmlValidator class) can find it. You can use any component you want to provide the SAX functionality that a web application needs. If you choose to use JAXP, and your web container is not yet bundled with the necessary JAXP components, then add the following JAR files to your *WEB-INF/lib* directory for a complete JAXP installation: *jaxp-api.jar, dom.jar, sax.jar, xalan.jar, xercesImpl.jar,* and *xsltc.jar*. You can download these components as part of the Java Web Services Developer Pack (*http://java.sun.com/webservices/webservicespack.html*), and the JAXP libraries are included as part of Java 1.4.x.

Example 5-16. A DefaultHandler that grabs the filename from the custom tag attribute

```
import org.xml.sax.Attributes;
import org.xml.sax.SAXParseException;
import org.xml.sax.SAXException;
import org.xml.sax.helpers.DefaultHandler;
import javax.xml.parsers.SAXParserFactory;
import javax.xml.parsers.FactoryConfigurationError;
import javax.xml.parsers.ParserConfigurationException;
import javax.xml.parsers.SAXParser;

import java.io.IOException;

import javax.servlet.jsp.tagext.PageData;
```

Example 5-16. A DefaultHandler that grabs the filename from the custom tag attribute (continued)

```
public class ValidateHandler extends DefaultHandler {

private String fileName = "";

public void startElement(String nameSpaceuri,
        String sname, String qname, Attributes attrs){

            for(int i=0; i<attrs.getLength();i++)
              if("filename".equals(attrs.getLocalName(i)))
                this.fileName=attrs.getValue(i);
}

public String getFilename(PageData page)
    throws FactoryConfigurationError, ParserConfigurationException,
      SAXException, IOException {
    try{
            SAXParserFactory factory = SAXParserFactory.newInstance();
            factory.setNamespaceAware(true);
            SAXParser saxparser = factory.newSAXParser();
            saxparser.parse(page.getInputStream(),this);
    } catch (FactoryConfigurationError fe){
            throw fe;
    } catch (ParserConfigurationException pce){
            throw pce;
    } catch( SAXException se){
            throw se;
    } catch( java.io.IOException io){
            throw io;
    } finally {
            return this.fileName; }
 }

public void error(SAXParseException e)
    throws SAXParseException
{
throw e;
}
}
```

Example 5-17 shows the XML view generated from the JSP page of Example 5-13 (with some carriage returns added). It might be ugly, but now you know what an XML view looks like! The HTML code is all treated as template data, enclosed in a jsp:text element and CDATA sections. The two XML elements, jsp:root and t:toxml, are given sequential ID numbers as part of their jsp:id attributes in the XML view. The TagLibraryValidator class can use these IDs to provide finely grained XML-related messages involving the validated JSP page.

Example 5-17. The XML view of Example 5-13

```
<jsp:root  jsp:id="0"  xmlns:jsp="http://java.sun.com/JSP/Page"  version="1.2"
xmlns:t="/toxml_view">
    <jsp:text><![CDATA[]]></jsp:text>
    <jsp:text><![CDATA[<html>]]></jsp:text>
    <jsp:text><![CDATA[<head>     ]]></jsp:text>
    <jsp:text><![CDATA[<title>Test tld]]></jsp:text>
    <jsp:text><![CDATA[</title>]]></jsp:text>
    <jsp:text><![CDATA[</head>]]></jsp:text>
    <jsp:text><![CDATA[<body bgcolor="#ffffff">Hello, this page is using the toxml tag to
       look at its XML View.]]></jsp:text>
    <t:toxml  jsp:id="1"  filename="my_xmlview"/>
    <jsp:text><![CDATA[]]></jsp:text>
    <jsp:text><![CDATA[</body>]]></jsp:text>
    <jsp:text><![CDATA[</html>]]></jsp:text>
</jsp:root>
```

See Also

Recipe 5.5 on creating a JSP from scratch as a JSP document; Chapter JSP.6 (JSP documents) of the JSP 2.0 specification; Chapter JSP.10 (XML views) of the JSP 2.0 specification.

CHAPTER 6

Dynamically Including Content in Servlets and JSPs

6.0 Introduction

Servlets and JSPs often include fragments of information that are common to an organization, such as logos, copyrights, trademarks, or navigation bars. The web application uses the include mechanisms to import the information wherever it is needed, since it is easier to change content in one place then to maintain it in every piece of code where it is used. Some of this information is static and either never or rarely changes, such as an organization's logo. In other cases, the information is more dynamic and changes often and unpredictably, such as a textual greeting that must be localized for each user. In both cases, you want to ensure that the servlet or JSP can evolve independently of its included content, and that the implementation of the servlet or JSP properly updates its included content as necessary.

This chapter recommends recipes for including content in both servlets and JSPs under several conditions:

- When the included information is refreshed every time a user makes a request.
- When the included information involves two or more nested levels—for example, when an included file in turn includes another piece of information, and so on.
- When you want to use the deployment descriptor to update the item that a servlet includes, which is a handy, less error-prone way of including content when the content is configurable and changes rather often.
- When you want to import resources into a JSP from outside the web application.

Recipe 6.1 describes how to import a resource each time the servlet handles a request.

6.1 Including a Resource Each Time a Servlet Handles a Request

Problem

You want to include information from an external file in a servlet each time the servlet handles a request.

Solution

Use the `javax.servlet.RequestDispatcher.include(request,response)` method in the `doGet( )` method of the servlet that includes the external file.

Discussion

Including the content in the `javax.servlet.http.HttpServlet`'s `doGet( )` method initiates the include mechanism whenever the web container receives a GET request for the servlet.

 When using this design, implement the servlet's `doPost( )` method to call `doGet(request,response)`.

Example 6-1 shows a servlet that imports a copyright template in the `doGet( )` method using the `javax.servlet.RequestDispatcher.include( )` method.

Example 6-1. Including content in the HttpServlet's init() method

```
package com.jspservletcookbook;

import javax.servlet.*;
import javax.servlet.http.*;

public class IncludeServlet extends HttpServlet {

 public void doGet(HttpServletRequest request,
   HttpServletResponse response) throws ServletException,
   java.io.IOException {

      response.setContentType("text/html");
      java.io.PrintWriter out = response.getWriter( );

      out.println("<html>");
      out.println("<head>");
      out.println("<title>Include Servlet</title>");
      out.println("</head>");
      out.println("<body>");
```

```
        out.println("<h1>Welcome To Our Universe</h1>");
        out.println("Imagine the rest of the page here.<br><br>");
        //Include the copyright information
        RequestDispatcher dispatcher = request.getRequestDispatcher(
        "/copyright");
        dispatcher.include(request, response);

        out.println("</body>");
        out.println("</html>");
    }//doGet
}
```

Example 6-1 gets a RequestDispatcher object by calling the javax.servlet. ServletRequest.getRequestDispatcher() method. The parameter to the getRequestDispatcher() method in this case is the servlet path to the resource that the include servlet imports: */copyright*. This path is mapped in *web.xml* to the Copyright servlet, which is shown in Example 6-2.

Example 6-2. The imported Copyright servlet

```
public class Copyright extends HttpServlet {

    public void doGet(HttpServletRequest request,
        HttpServletResponse response) throws ServletException,
        java.io.IOException {

        java.io.PrintWriter out = response.getWriter();
        out.println("Copyright&copy; 2003-2004 EmbraceAndExtend Corp.");

    }
}
```

The Copyright servlet outputs a line of text that includes the character entity code for the copyright symbol (©), so that the copyright symbol is displayed correctly in the resulting HTML. When the importing servlet calls the include() method, the copyright text is inserted in the method call's code location.

 A servlet can import an HTML page, as well as the output of a JSP page or servlet. If you are importing HTML fragments in this manner, make sure that the imported text does not break your HTML page, such as by repeating HTML tags or failing to close certain tags.

Figure 6-1 shows the page generated by the IncludeServlet in a browser.

Recipe 6.2 describes how to configure the imported resource in an external configuration file, such as *web.xml*.

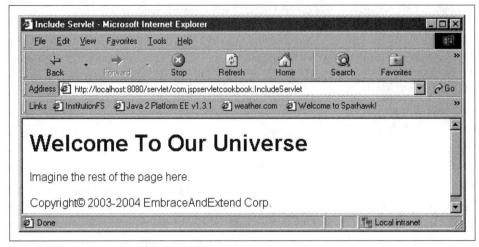

Figure 6-1. The IncludeServlet's page in a browser

 Jason Hunter, who provided a technical review of this book, points out that many people are using an offline build process to pregenerate static (e.g., HTML) files when a lot of the site's web content uses includes, such as importing headers and footers into most of the web site's pages. In most cases, the server can handle the requests for static files much more efficiently than requests for dynamic pages (such as a JSP that includes other resources). See Chapter 3, *Servlet Best Practices*, in the book *Java Enterprise Best Practices* (O'Reilly).

See Also

Recipes 6.2 and 6.3 on including resources in servlets; Recipes 6.4–6.7 on using jsp: include, the include directive, as well as including resources into JSP documents or XML files; Chapter SRV.14.2.5 of the Servlet 2.4 specification; Chapter JSP.5.4 on of the JSP 2.0 specification on jsp:include; Chapter JSP.1.10.3 of the JSP 2.0 specification on the include directive.

6.2 Using an External Configuration to Include a Resource in a Servlet

Problem

You want to use an external configuration file (such as *web.xml*) to configure the resource that is included in a servlet.

Solution

Use init parameters with the including servlet to allow the external configuration of the include mechanism, then include the resource with the `javax.servlet.RequestDispatcher.include(request,response)` method.

Discussion

You may want to periodically change the resource that a servlet includes, without changing and recompiling the servlet code. You can make these changes by altering the servlet's init parameters in *web.xml*. Using this strategy, either the included resource's file location itself or the method of retrieving the resource (such as from a database) can change. You can ensure that the servlet imports the correct resource by altering the content of the param-value element. Example 6-3 shows a servlet that is configured to include a file named *privacy.jspf*. This represents a standard privacy statement for the web application.

Example 6-3. Specifying an included resource by using the servlet's init-param element

```
<servlet>
    <servlet-name>PrivacyServlet</servlet-name>
    <servlet-class>com.jspservletcookbook.IncludeServlet</servlet-class>
    <init-param>
        <param-name>included-resource</param-name>
        <param-value>privacy.jspf</param-value>
    <init-param>
</servlet>
```

Example 6-4 shows the doGet( ) method of the PrivacyServlet. This method gets the value of the included-resource init parameter (*privacy.jspf*), then includes the JSP segment.

Example 6-4. Including a resource specified by an init parameter

```
public void doGet(HttpServletRequest request,
  HttpServletResponse response) throws ServletException,
   java.io.IOException {

        response.setContentType("text/html");
        java.io.PrintWriter out = response.getWriter( );

        out.println("<html>");
        out.println("<head>");
        out.println("<title>Include Servlet</title>");
        out.println("</head>");
        out.println("<body>");
        out.println("<h1>Welcome To Our Universe</h1>");
        out.println("Imagine the rest of the page here.<br><br>");
        //Include the privacy information based on an init-param value
```

Example 6-4. Including a resource specified by an init parameter (continued)

```
String includeRes = (String) getInitParameter(
  "included-resource");
//get a RequestDispatcher object based on the init-param value
RequestDispatcher dispatcher = request.
  getRequestDispatcher(includeRes);
dispatcher.include(request, response);
out.println("</body>");
out.println("</html>");



  }
```

Example 6-4 gets a `RequestDispatcher` representing the configured `init-param` value
with this code:

```
//the includeRes variable holds the init-param value "privacy.jspf"
RequestDispatcher dispatcher = request.getRequestDispatcher(includeRes);
```

Then the `dispatcher.include(request,response)` method is replaced by the output of
the *privacy.jspf* file. Example 6-5 shows the JSP segment that the `PrivacyServlet`
includes. The JSP's content has some HTML tags that fit into the HTML represented by the including page.

Example 6-5. A JSP segment included in a servlet with a RequestDispatcher

```
<%@page errorPage="/error.jsp"%>
<p><strong>Parker River Net Solutions Privacy Policy</strong></p>
<p>Any personal information you provide to us regarding Web- or software-development
services or shareware software, such as your name, address, telephone number, and e-mail
address, will not be released, sold, or rented to any entities or individuals outside
of Parker River Net Solutions.</p>
```

Included segments or pages cannot set or change response headers, so
any attempts to set the content type in an included servlet or JSP as in:

```
<%@ page contentType="text/xml" %>
```

are ignored.

All the included JSP does is specify an error page composed of some formatting-
related HTML tags and text. Figure 6-2 shows the browser page for the
`PrivacyServlet`.

You may also want to augment Example 6-4 to provide a default
resource for inclusion in the servlet, just in case the deployment
descriptor (*web.xml*) mistakenly omits an init parameter for the servlet. The method `getInitParameter` returns `null` in the event of this
omission. You could test for this `null` condition and then provide a
default value for the included statement.

Figure 6-2. A web page with an included JSP segment

See Also

Recipe 6.3 on including resources that have nested includes; Recipes 6.4–6.8 on including resources in JSPs; Chapter SRV.14.2.5 of the Servlet 2.4 specification; Chapter JSP.1.10.3 of the JSP 2.0 specification on including files in JSPs.

6.3   Including Resources Nested at Multiple Levels in a Servlet

Problem

You want to include resources in a servlet that already include servlets, JSPs, or HTML.

Solution

Use the `javax.servlet.RequestDispatcher.include(request,response)` method to include the top-level file. Make sure that error pages are properly configured in *web.xml*, just in case an exception is thrown in a deep-nested, imported file.

Discussion

Even though it does not represent the best architectural decision, it is possible for a servlet to include a resource that itself includes another resource, resulting in a number of inclusions taking place beneath the surface. Imagine the Russian dolls that fit inside each other. You unscrew the top half of the dolls, only to find smaller replicas of the dolls nested inside the outer ones. It is not outlandish to think of very complex web pages using HTML frame and table tags, containing headers and footers, with these segments of the page containing other specialized content using an include mechanism. One of the included files nested several levels deep could throw an exception or corrupt the chain of inclusions in some manner. Although there is no foolproof way to defend against this occurrence, for the purposes of debugging, make sure that the web application has an error page configured so that it can display information about the resource that ran into include problems.

This recipe provides an example of a servlet that has three levels of included resources. The outer servlet includes another servlet named Level2, which includes a JSP *level3.jsp*, which completes the picture by including the inner servlet, Level4. Figure 6-3 shows the browser display when a user requests the com.jspservletcookbook.MultipleInc servlet.

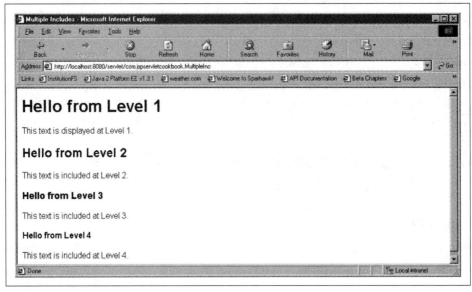

Figure 6-3. Three included files in one web page

Example 6-6 shows the servlet code. This servlet is responsible for the first level of text ("Hello from Level 1"), then each of the included resources contributes content to the response.

Example 6-6. The outer included servlet

```
package com.jspservletcookbook;

import javax.servlet.*;
import javax.servlet.http.*;

public class MultipleInc extends HttpServlet {

    public void doGet(HttpServletRequest request,
```

Example 6-6. The outer included servlet (continued)

```
    HttpServletResponse response) throws ServletException,
      java.io.IOException {

    response.setContentType("text/html");
    java.io.PrintWriter out = response.getWriter();

    out.println("<html>");
    out.println("<head>");
    out.println("<title>Multiple Includes</title>");
    out.println("</head>");
    out.println("<body>");
    out.println("<h1>Hello from Level 1</h1>");
    out.println("This text is displayed at Level 1.");
    RequestDispatcher dispatcher = request.
      getRequestDispatcher("/level2");
    dispatcher.include(request, response);
    out.println("</body>");
    out.println("</html>");

    }
}
```

The code:

```
    RequestDispatcher dispatcher = request.getRequestDispatcher("/level2");
      dispatcher.include(request, response);
```

includes the output of the servlet that is mapped to the servlet path */level2*, which Example 6-7 shows (just the doGet method).

Example 6-7. The first inner included servlet

```
public void doGet(HttpServletRequest request, HttpServletResponse response) throws
ServletException, IOException {

    java.io.PrintWriter out = response.getWriter();
    out.println("<h2>Hello from Level 2</h2>");
    out.println("This text is included at Level 2.");
    //Include the JSP file named "level3.jsp"
    try{

    RequestDispatcher dispatcher = request.getRequestDispatcher(
      "/level3.jsp");
    dispatcher.include(request, response);
    } catch (Exception se){

        String context_path = (String) request.getAttribute(
          "javax.servlet.include.context_path");

        String servlet_path = (String) request.getAttribute(
          "javax.servlet.include.servlet_path");

        String errMessage = new StringBuffer(
```

Example 6-7. The first inner included servlet (continued)

```
            "Exception raised during Level2 servlet include:<br>").
              append("Context path: "+context_path+"<br>").
                append("Servlet path: "+servlet_path).toString( );
          throw new ServletException(errMessage);
      }
      }
```

Example 6-7 writes more text to the response, then includes a *level3.jsp*, like the outer servlet, using a javax.servlet.RequestDispatcher object to initiate including the JSP. The Level2 servlet does some other stuff with a try/catch block and request attributes, in order to demonstrate the handling of exceptions that may be thrown during include operations.

According to the JSP API specification, included resources have access to five request attributes:

- javax.servlet.include.request_uri
- javax.servlet.include.context_path
- javax.servlet.include.servlet_path
- javax.servlet.include.path_info
- javax.servlet.include.query_string

In the catch block, the Level2 servlet gets the value of two of these request attributes with:

```
String context_path =
  (String) request.getAttribute("javax.servlet.include.context_path");

String servlet_path =
  (String) request.getAttribute("javax.servlet.include.servlet_path");
```

In the catch block, the Level2 servlet then throws a new ServletException with the attribute values as part of the exception message. An error page configured for the web application displays information about the exception that was generated by the include operation.

The error-page configuration in *web.xml* looks like:

```
<error-page>
    <exception-type>
        javax.servlet.ServletException
    </exception-type>
    <location>/error</location>
</error-page>
```

where "/error" is mapped to a servlet that displays exception-related information.

In Example 6-7, the context path was empty and the servlet path was /level2. Figure 6-4 shows a browser displaying the error page. The servlet generating the exception is specified as the top-level servlet (MultipleInc) because this was the code that originated the include mechanism which resulted in the ServletException.

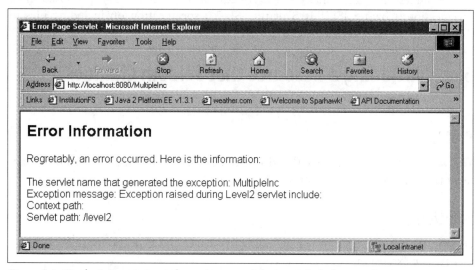

Figure 6-4. Displaying exception information caused during an include operation

Example 6-8 shows the JSP file (*level3.jsp*) that the first inner servlet imports. The *level3.jsp* file represents the second level of included content.

 The included servlets do not call the java.io.PrintWriter.close( ) method, because that action would prevent the response that follows the outer servlet's include code from being sent to the client. The outer servlet (MultipleInc in Example 6-6) finally calls PrintWriter.close( ) when it is finished including the nested resources.

Example 6-8. The included level3.jsp JSP file

```
<%@page errorPage="/error"%>
<h3>Hello from Level 3</h3>
This text is included at Level 3.
<jsp:include page="/level4"/>
```

Finally, the JSP file uses the jsp:include standard action to import the text returned from a servlet that is mapped to the /level4 path. The Level4 servlet does the same thing as the other of the recipe's servlets—it writes character data to the PrintWriter object—so I have not shown its source code. The reason I included was to demonstrate how several different resource types can be nested in a chain of included files. The outer servlet includes servlet two, which includes a JSP file, which in turn includes the text returned from a third servlet. The first included servlet enclosed its own include code in a try block to catch any exceptions raised by including a JSP file.

See Also

Recipe 6.1 on using the RequestDispatcher include mechanism; Recipe 6.2 on determining an included resource with an configuration file; Recipes 6.4–6.8 on including resources in JSPs; Chapter SRV.14.2.5 of the Servlet 2.4 proposed final specification; Chapter JSP.1.10.3 of the JSP 2.0 specification on including files in JSPs; Chapter 9 on specifying errors pages in web applications.

6.4   Including a Resource that Seldom Changes into a JSP

Problem

You want to include a resource that does not change very much (such as a page fragment that represents a header or footer) in a JSP.

Solution

Use the include directive in the including JSP page, and give the included JSP segment a *.jspf* extension.

Discussion

JSP pages are often composites of page fragments that represent navigation bars, headers (page elements that appear at the top of a web page), footers (elements that appear at the bottom of a web page), and the main body content. Since pages in a web application or a site may all use the same navigation bar, this file is maintained in one place and used by all of the web components that require it. If you are going to import a JSP segment that is a static or unchanging resource, use the include directive in the JSP, as in:

```
<%@ include file="/WEB-INF/jspf/navbar.jspf" %>
```

If you are using a JSP document (see Chapter 5) or XML syntax for the JSP, use this form of the include directive:

```
<jsp:directive.include file="/WEB-INF/jspf/navbar.jspf" />
```

If the value of the file attribute begins with a "/" character, then it is a *context-relative* path, meaning that it is relative to the web application containing the JSP that uses this directive. If the JSP includes the latter directive, then this file path means "begin at the web application root and include the */WEB-INF/jspf/navbar.jspf* file."

A file attribute value in include that does not begin with a "/" character is a *page-relative* path, which is relative to the JSP page that is using the include directive. The following `include` directive attempts to include a file inside of the *segments* directory, which has the same parent directory as the including JSP:

```
<%@ include file="segments/navbar.jspf" %>
```

The `include` directive includes the text or code of the included segment during the *translation phase*, when the JSP is converted into a servlet. The include mechanism is a more efficient way of importing the text or code that you would otherwise type into a JSP prior to its conversion to a servlet, such as HTML tags or `taglib` directives. Example 6-9 shows how to use the `include` directive to import a segment of `taglib` directives into a JSP.

 The difference between the `include` directive and the `jsp:include` standard action is that the `include` directive imports the actual text or bytes of the included segment, whereas the `jsp:include` standard action sends a request to the included page and then includes the dynamic response to that request. See Recipe 6.5.

Example 6-9. Including a JSP segment into a JSP page at translation time

```
<%@page contentType="text/html"%>
<%@ include file="/WEB-INF/jspf/taglib-inc.jspf" %>
<html>
<head>
<title>Main Content</title>
</head>
<body>
<h1>Here is the main content</h1>
This web application is using the following Servlet API:
<c:out value="${pageContext.servletContext.majorVersion}"/>.<c:out value=
    "${pageContext.servletContext.minorVersion}"/><br><br>

    <jsp:useBean id="timeValues" class="java.util.Date"/>
    <c:set target="${timeValues}" value=
        "${pageContext.session.creationTime}" property="time"/>

    The session creation time:
    <fmt:formatDate value="${timeValues}" type="both" dateStyle=
        "medium" /><br><br>

The toXml tag will create an XML view of this page.
<t:toXml filename="include-xmlview"/>
</body>
</html>
```

The second line of Example 6-9 includes a JSP segment named *taglib-inc.jspf*. This segment includes the `taglib` directives responsible for making available the JSTL and custom tag used in the page. Example 6-10 shows the *taglib-inc.jspf* page.

Example 6-10. A JSP segment containing taglib directives

```
<%@ taglib uri="http://java.sun.com/jstl/core" prefix="c" %>
<%@ taglib uri="http://java.sun.com/jstl/fmt" prefix="fmt" %>
<%@ taglib uri="/toxml_view" prefix="t" %>
```

The include directive includes these three taglib directives just as if you had typed them in yourself, then the JSP container converts the enclosing JSP into a servlet. The three taglib directives enable the use of the following tags in Example 6-9:

- c:out
- c:set
- fmt:formatDate
- t:toXml

> The JSP 2.0 specification recommends that you give incomplete JSP code that is designed to be included in other files a *.jspf* extension, which used to mean "JSP fragment." The 2.0 specification, however, now refers to these fragments as "JSP segments" in order to avoid confusing these files with the javax.servlet.jsp.tagext.JspFragment interface. This interface is part of the tag extension API.

Figure 6-5 shows what the JSP looks like in a browser window.

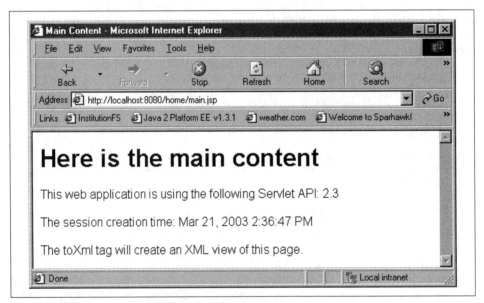

Figure 6-5. A JSP with an included JSP segment of taglib directives

This page displays the Servlet API used by the web container, the javax.servlet. http.HttpSession creation time (formatted using the fmt:formatDate JSTL tag), and the custom tag that is described in Recipe 5.6. This tag generates an XML view of the containing page and saves a new XML file named according to its `filename` attribute. It was included to show a method of including a few different types of `taglibs`.

See Also

Recipe 6.5 on using the `jsp:include` standard action; Recipe 6.8 on including JSP segments in XML files; Recipe 6.9 on including content from outside of a JSP's context; Chapter JSP.1.10.3 of the JSP 2.0 specification on including files in JSPs; Chapter 23 on the JSTL tags.

6.5   Including Content in a JSP Each Time the JSP Handles a Request

Problem

You want to include content in a JSP each time it receives a request, rather than when the JSP is converted to a servlet.

Solution

Use the `jsp:include` standard action.

Discussion

The `jsp:include` action includes a resource in a JSP each time it receives a request, which makes `jsp:include` more of a dynamic include mechanism than the `include` directive (see Recipe 6.4). Using `jsp:include`, the included JSP segments have access to the including page's `request`, `session`, and `application` implicit objects, and to any attributes these objects contain. Use the `jsp:include` action in each location of the file where you need to import resources such as JSP segments from the same web application.

 The `import` custom action, which is part of the core JSTL, can import resources from other web applications or from other locations on the Internet. See Recipe 6.8.

Example 6-10 shows a JSP page that receives submitted form information from another page in the web application. The receiving page uses `jsp:include` to include header and footer page segments at the top and bottom of the page.

Just to show that the included segments have access to the same request and session information as their parent page, the header segment displays the person's submitted name, which is stored in `fname` and `lname` request parameters, in the form of a greeting-related `title` HTML tag. The footer page element displays the session ID along with the user's submitted first and last name. First, Figure 6-6 shows an HTML page with a simple submission form for the user's first name, last name, and email address.

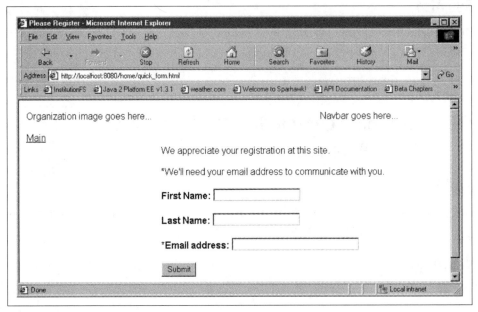

Figure 6-6. An HTML form

Assume that this form page includes embedded JavaScript to check the validity of the entered information. When the user clicks the Submit button, the form information is submitted with the following HTML tag to */solutions.jsp*:

```
<form method=post action="/solutions.jsp">
```

Example 6-11 shows the *solutions.jsp* page, which includes two JSP segments: *header.jspf* and *footer.jspf*. The *header.jspf* contains the contents of a head HTML tag, and places the user's submitted name in its nested `title` tag. The *footer.jspf* page— for the sake of demonstration—echoes the user's name and shows his session ID, which it obtains from the implicit `session` JSP object. The JSP 2.0 specification recommends that you keep these files in *WEB-INF/jspf*.

Example 6-11. Including two page segments and displaying submitted form values

```
<%@page contentType="text/html"%>
<html>

<jsp:include page="/WEB-INF/jspf/header.jspf" />

<body bgcolor="white">
<table width="660" border="0" summary="A two-column table in which resides a logo and
navigation bar">
```

Example 6-11. Including two page segments and displaying submitted form values (continued)

```
        <tr><td valign="top">
            Organization image goes here...<p>
        <u>Main</u>
        </td>
        <td align="right" valign="top">
        Navbar goes here...
        </td></tr><tr><td valign="top" align="center" colspan="2">

        <table border="0" summary=
          "A nested table for aligning body content">
         <tr><td><h2>Thanks for registering at this site</h2></td></tr>
         <tr><td>Here is the info you submitted:</td></tr>

         <tr><td>Name:

           <%= request.getParameter("fname") %>
           <%= request.getParameter("lname") %></td></tr>

          <tr><td>Email:

            <%= request.getParameter("eaddress") %>

</td></tr></table>

        </td></tr><tr><td></td></tr>
        </table>

<table width="660" border="0" summary=
    "A table containing a footer navigation bar.">

<tr><td valign="top" align="center">

<jsp:include page="/WEB-INF/jspf/footer.jsp" />

</td></tr>
</table>
</body>
</html>
```

Example 6-12 shows the *header.jspf* JSP segment.

Example 6-12. A JSP header segment included with jsp:include

```
<HEAD>
    <META name="author" content=
        "Bruce W. Perry, author@jspservletcookbook.com">
    <META name="keywords" content=
        "Java, JSP, servlets, databases, MySQL, Oracle, web development">
    <TITLE>Parker River: Thanks For Visiting
      <%= request.getParameter("fname") %>
      <%= request.getParameter("lname") %>
    </TITLE>
</HEAD>
```

All this segment does is include the user's name in the `title` tag. Example 6-13 shows the imported *footer.jspf* segment. This segment also writes the user's name to the displayed output and adds the session ID, after checking whether the `javax.servlet.http.HttpSession` object is `null`, and before it calls the `HttpSession.getId( )` method.

Example 6-13. A JSP footer segment included with jsp:include

```
Thanks for visiting
    <%= request.getParameter("fname") %>
    <%= request.getParameter("lname") %><br>
Session ID:
    <% if (request.getSession( ) != null)  {%>
        <%= request.getSession().getId( ) %>
    <% } else {%>
        Unknown
    <% } %> <br><br>
<a href="/index.html">Main</a> | <a href="/service.html">Services</a> |
  <a href="/sitemap.html">Site Map</a> |
    <a href="/resources.html">Resources</a> |
      <a href="/contacts.html">Contact Us</a>|
        <a href="/prns_privacy.html">Privacy</a>
```

Figure 6-7 shows the *solutions.jsp* page in a web browser.

Figure 6-7. The included header and footer segments displayed in a web browser

Using jsp:include, changes to included files are reflected immediately in the including pages. On the other hand, if you make changes to a page that is included using the include directive, those changes are not reflected in the including page until you modify that page and force the JSP container to recompile it.

See Also

Recipe 6.4 on the include directive; Recipe 6.7 on including JSP segments in XML files; Recipe 6.9 on including content from outside of a JSP's context; Chapter JSP.1.10.3 of the JSP 2.0 specification on including files in JSPs; Chapter 23 on the JSTL tags.

6.6   Using an External Configuration File to Include a Resource in a JSP

Problem

You want to include a file dynamically in a JSP, based on a value derived from a configuration file.

Solution

Use the jsp:include standard action. Provide the value in an external properties file or as a configuration parameter in the deployment descriptor.

Discussion

Using an external configuration to specify an include file for a JSP allows you to change the name and/or path to the included file without touching the JSP's code. In addition, when using jsp:include the JSP does not have to be recompiled to reflect any changes in the included file—the web resource is included by the JSP each time it handles a request. If you change the file pointed to by the configuration file, the response from the included resource is added to the including JSP's response during the next request.

The difference between a jsp:include standard action and include directive is that the include directive includes the bytes or contents of the imported file before the JSP is compiled (during the translation phase for the JSP). If the included segment changes, the updates will not be reflected in the JSP until the JSP itself is modified, which causes a JSP container (such as Tomcat's Jasper JSP container) to recompile the JSP.

Example 6-14 shows a JSP that uses an external properties file to specify the file to include.

Example 6-14. Using java.util.ResourceBundle.getBundle() to fetch an externally configured file

```
<%@page contentType="text/html"%>
<%@ taglib uri="http://java.sun.com/jstl/core" prefix="c" %>

<html>

<% java.util.ResourceBundle bundle =
    java.util.ResourceBundle.getBundle("com.jspservletcookbook.include");
     String segment = bundle.getString("external-include");%>

<jsp:include page="<%=segment %>"/>

<body>
<h2>Welcome to our Portal Home <c:out value="${param.fname}" /> <c:out value="${param.
lname}" /></h2>
<jsp:useBean id="dateString" class="java.util.Date"/>
The time is <c:out value="${dateString}" />.<br><br>
</body>
</html>
```

Example 6-14 includes a JSP segment that is found at the path specified by the external-include property. This property is written in a simple text file called *include.properties*, with content that looks like this:

```
external-include=WEB-INF/jspf/header_tag.jsp
```

The *include.properties* file is stored in *WEB-INF/classes/com/ jspservletcookbook*. When your servlet or JSP attempts to access a list of property values by calling the static method java.util. ReseourceBundle.getBundle("com.jspservletcookbook.include"), getBundle automatically replaces the period "." characters with "/" and appends ".properties" to the end of the String (making the search look like "com/jspservletcookbook/include.properties" in our example).

The example code saves the property value in a String variable segment with the following code:

```
String segment = bundle.getString("external-include");
```

Then the value of the segment variable, which is a filepath, specifies the file for the JSP to include: *WEB-INF/jspf/header_tag.jsp*. This is accomplished with the JSP expression—<%=segment %>—in the page attribute value for jsp:include:

```
<jsp:include page="<%=segment %>"/>
```

When the JSP page is executed, the included file's response is included in the part of the page where the jsp:include standard action occurs. Example 6-15 shows the content of the included file, *header_tag.jsp*.

Example 6-15. The content of the header_tag.jsp segment

```
<%@ taglib uri="http://java.sun.com/jstl/core" prefix="c" %>
<HEAD>
    <META name="author" content=
        "Bruce W. Perry, author@jspservletcookbook.com">
    <META name="keywords" content=
        "Java, JSP, servlets, databases, MySQL, Oracle, web development">
    <TITLE>Parker River: Thanks For Visiting
      <c:out value="${param.fname}"/>
      <c:out value="${param.lname}"/>
    </TITLE>
</HEAD>
```

This is a complete HEAD HTML tag, including two nested META tags and a TITLE tag. If you requested the including JSP page at *http://localhost:8080/home/externalInclude. jsp?fname=Mister&lname=Bean*, the returned content from this JSP segment—the actual text that the JSP container substitutes for the jsp:include tag in the output—looks like Example 6-16.

Example 6-16. The output when jsp:include is used

```
<HEAD>
    <META name="author" content=
        "Bruce W. Perry, author@jspservletcookbook.com">
    <META name="keywords" content=
        "Java, JSP, servlets, databases, MySQL, Oracle, web development">
    <TITLE>Parker River: Thanks For Visiting
      Mister
      Bean
    </TITLE>
</HEAD>
```

The included segment processes the request parameters fname and lname from the query string:

```
fname=Mister&lname=Bean
```

and includes their values in the TITLE tag. Figure 6-8 shows what the *externalInclude. jsp* page looks like in a browser.

> In this example, the included segment uses the proper taglib directive so that the c:out JSTL 1.0 tags can be used. If you are using JSTL 1.1, then the uri attribute value is http://java.sun.com/jsp/jstl/core:
>
> ```
> <%@ taglib
>     uri="http://java.sun.com/jstl/core"
>       prefix="c" %>
> ```
>
> You can also pass parameters for the included segment to process, in the manner of:
>
> ```
> <jsp:include page="<%=segment %>">
>   <jsp:param name="role" value="comedian"/>
> </jsp:include>
> ```

Figure 6-8. Browser view of JSP that uses jsp:include to include another JSP segment

If you want to use a context parameter in the web application's deployment descriptor instead to provide a path for the included file, add a `context-param` element to *web.xml* (as shown in Example 6-17).

Example 6-17. A context-param element provides an included file path

```
<context-param>
    <param-name>external-include</param-name>
    <param-value>WEB-INF/jspf/header_tag.jsp</param-value>
</context-param>
```

Then get the value of the context parameter in the including JSP:

```
<jsp:include page="<%=application.getInitParameter("external-include")%>"/>
```

The JSP then inserts the file path *WEB-INF/jspf/header_tag.jsp* as the value for the `jsp:include` page attribute.

See Also

Recipe 6.4 on the `include` directive; Recipe 6.7 on including JSP segments in XML files; Recipe 6.8 on including content from outside of a JSP's context; Chapter JSP.1.10.3 of the JSP 2.0 specification on including files in JSPs; Chapter 23 on the JSTL tags; this web page for how the `getBundle` method returns certain types of ResourceBundles: *http://java.sun.com/j2se/1.4.1/docs/api/java/util/ResourceBundle.html#getBundle(java.lang.String, java.util.Locale, java.lang.ClassLoader)*.

6.7 Including an XML Fragment in a JSP Document

Problem

You want to include a fragment of an XML file inside of a JSP document, or include a JSP page in XML syntax.

Solution

Use the `jsp:include` standard action for the includes that you want to occur with each request of the JSP. Use the `jsp:directive.include` element if the include action should occur during the translation phase.

Discussion

Because a JSP document is a well-formed XML file, both of the mechanisms that you can use to include JSP segments are XML elements: `jsp:include` and `jsp:directive.include`. A JSP document is a JSP page in XML syntax, in which all of the code is well-formed XML; in other words, the entire page consists of XML elements, attributes, and the body content of some XML elements. You then take the JSP document and place it in the root of your web application (or wherever you make your JSP pages available; the root is the usual place), and the JSP container translates the XML file into a servlet. One reason for using JSP documents is to integrate the JSPs with other XML technologies, such as XHTML, SVG, or SOAP. Recipe 5.5 describes JSP documents in more detail. Example 6-18 shows a JSP document version of Example 6-14, using `jsp:include` to include a file that is located at the path *WEB-INF/jspf/header_tag.jspf*.

Example 6-18. A JSP document using jsp:include to include a file

```
<jsp:root xmlns:jsp="http://java.sun.com/JSP/Page"
  xmlns:c="http://java.sun.com/jstl/core"
    xmlns="http://www.w3.org/1999/xhtml" version="2.0">

    <jsp:directive.page contentType="text/html"/>
    <html>

    <jsp:include page="WEB-INF/jspf/header_tag.jspf" />

    <body>
    <h2>Welcome to our Portal <c:out value="
        ${param.fname}" /><jsp:text> </jsp:text>
            <c:out value="${param.lname}" /></h2>
    <jsp:useBean id="dateString" class="java.util.Date"/>
    <jsp:text>The time is </jsp:text> <c:out value="${dateString}" />.
```

Example 6-18. A JSP document using jsp:include to include a file (continued)

```
    <br /><br />
    </body>
    </html>
</jsp:root>
```

In Example 6-18, the JSP page includes the text that is returned by *header_tag.jspf*. Using jsp:include, the included file does not have to be well-formed XML *itself*, as long as it returns text that is well-formed XML and fits correctly into the JSP document.

 The JSP 2.0 specification recommends that JSP segments that you include in JSP pages or JSP documents be given a *.jspf* extension. In addition, one way to differentiate JSP documents from conventional JSP pages is to give the JSP documents a *.jspx* extension (when using the Servlet 2.4 version of *web.xml*). Tomcat 4.1.x will compile and execute as JSP pages the files with these extensions if you add these servlet-mapping elements to *conf/web.xml*:

```
<servlet-mapping>
    <servlet-name>jsp</servlet-name>
    <url-pattern>*.jspf</url-pattern>
</servlet-mapping>
<servlet-mapping>
    <servlet-name>jsp</servlet-name>
    <url-pattern>*.jspx</url-pattern>
</servlet-mapping>
```

Example 6-19 shows the included file *header_tag.jspf*. It has its own taglib directive so that the JSTL-related tags inside the TITLE tags produce the proper output from the request parameters fname and lname. The comment at the bottom of Example 6-18 shows the text that is returned from this JSP segment, using jsp:include, when the enclosing JSP page is requested from *http://localhost:8080/home/x617.jspx?fname=Bruce&lname=Perry*.

Example 6-19. The included file header_tag.jspf

```
<%@ taglib uri="http://java.sun.com/jstl/core" prefix="c" %>
<HEAD>
    <META name="author" content=
        "Bruce W. Perry, author@jspservletcookbook.com"/>
    <META name="keywords" content=
        "Java, JSP, servlets, databases, MySQL, Oracle, web development"/>
    <TITLE>Parker River: Thanks For Visiting
      <c:out value="${param.fname}"/> <c:out value="${param.lname}"/>
    </TITLE>
</HEAD>
<!-- source text returned from header_tag.jspf

<HEAD>
    <META name="author" content=
        "Bruce W. Perry, author@jspservletcookbook.com"/>
```

Example 6-19. The included file header_tag.jspf (continued)

```
    <META name="keywords" content=
        "Java, JSP, servlets, databases, MySQL, Oracle, web development"/>
    <TITLE>Parker River: Thanks For Visiting
      Bruce Perry
    </TITLE>
</HEAD> -->
```

Figure 6-9 shows what the complete document looks like in a browser.

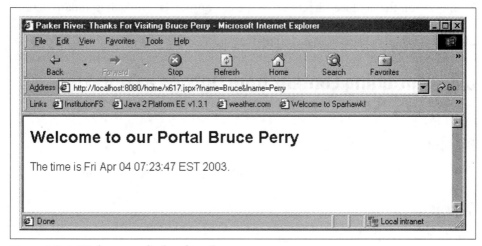

Figure 6-9. A JSP document displayed in a browser

You can also use the `jsp:directive.include` element, which includes the content before the JSP document is converted into a servlet, rather than at runtime as with `jsp:include`. To convert Example 6-17 to use an include directive, replace the `jsp:include` element with:

```
    <jsp:directive.include file="WEB-INF/jspf/header_tag.jspf" />
```

The included content cannot have any non-XML syntax forms, such as a JSP `taglib` directive, because the included code is included verbatim into the JSP document when it is converted into a servlet.

 An alternative approach is to use CDATA sections in the XML to attempt to preserve the words and symbols that would otherwise cause the XML file to fail the well-formed test. The CDATA sections look like <![CDATA[...]]>.

You would have to remove the `tag-lib` directive from the top of Example 6-19 for the JSP to compile correctly using `jsp:directive.include`. In addition, the `c:out` tags inside of the included segment would then be dependent on the inclusion in the enclosing JSP document of an `xmlns` attribute to make the core JSTL elements available, as in the top of Example 6-18.

A rule of thumb to use with the two include mechanisms is that if the included segment will change frequently and the enclosing JSP page must immediately reflect those changes, use `jsp:include`. If the included segment is relatively static and unchanging, use `jsp:directive.include`.

See Also

Recipe 6.4 on the `include` directive; Recipe 6.5 on the `jsp:include` standard action; Recipe 6.8 on including content from outside of a JSP's context; Chapter JSP.1.10.3 of the JSP 2.0 specification on including files in JSPs; Chapter 23 on the JSTL tags.

6.8 Including Content from Outside a Context in a JSP

Problem

You want to include a JSP segment from outside the including file's context.

Solution

Use the `c:import` JSTL core tag.

Discussion

The `c:import` tag gives JSP page authors much flexibility in pulling in resources from inside *and* outside their web application. The `c:import` tag allows a page to import web resources:

- From outside JSP's web container, using an absolute URL (such as *http://java.sun.com/api)*.

- From another context in the same web container. For example, your domain may include a central repository of included content at *http://www.mydomain.com/warehouse*. A JSP page that is installed in a context named */customer* could import a resource from the */warehouse* context by using: *<c:import url="/catalog_header.jspf" context="/warehouse" />*

- From the same context, similar to using `jsp:include`.

This recipe includes examples of importing resources from outside the importing JSP's context. Example 6-19 imports a JSP segment *header_tag.jsp* from the */dbproj* context. The url attribute specifies the resource to include; the context attribute declares the context from which the JSP imports the resource. To use the `c:import` tag, the JSP has to include a `taglib` directive such as:

```
<%@ taglib uri="http://java.sun.com/jstl/core" prefix="c" %>
```

Example 6-20 includes a group of taglibs by inserting the *taglib-inc.jspf* JSP segment in the second line.

Example 6-20. Using the c:import tag to import an external URL

```
<%@page contentType="text/html"%>
<%@ include file="/WEB-INF/jspf/taglib-inc.jspf" %>
   <html>

  <c:import url="/header_tag.jspf" context="/dbproj" />

   <body>
   <h2>Welcome to our Portal <c:out value="
       ${param.fname}" /> <c:out value="${param.lname}" />
   </h2>
   <jsp:useBean id="dateString" class="java.util.Date"/>
   The time is  <c:out value="${dateString}" />.
   <br /><br />
   </body>
   </html>
```

The c:import tag inserts the text generated by */dbproj/header_tag.jsp* in the part of the code where the c:import tag is located. The */dbproj* context path represents a different web application or context than the importing JSP. The top of the importing page now looks like the following text, since this is the HTML that the imported file produces:

```
   <html>
   <HEAD>
      <META name="author" content=
          "Bruce W. Perry, author@jspservletcookbook.com"/>
      <META name="keywords" content=
          "Java, JSP, servlets, databases, MySQL, Oracle, web development"/>
      <TITLE>Parker River: Thanks For Visiting
        Mister Bean
        </TITLE>
   </HEAD>
   <body>
   <!-- page continues from here... -->
```

 Using Tomcat, the context element in *conf/server.xml* has to include this attribute/value pair or the JSP that uses c:import will raise an exception if it attempts to import resources from another context:

```
       crossContext="true" <!--"false" by default-->
```

Example 6-21 imports a description of the HTTP/1.1 protocol, Request For Comments (RFC) 2068.

The example declares its content type as "text/plain," so that the browser does not try to display the text file as HTML, which can be unreadable with plaintext files. Then Example 6-21 uses a taglib directive so that the JSP can use the c:import tag.

The c:import tag specifies the location of the imported text file as an absolute URL: *http://www.ietf.org/rfc/rfc2068.txt*.

Example 6-21. Using c:import to import a text resource whose address is an absolute URL

```
<%@page contentType="text/plain"%>
<%@ taglib uri="http://java.sun.com/jstl/core" prefix="c" %>
   <c:import url="http://www.ietf.org/rfc/rfc2068.txt" />
```

 If a JSP uses c:import to access a forbidden resource (which will cause the receiving server to respond with a HTTP status code 403), the c:import tag throw ans exception and the JSP compilation will fail.

You can also include parameters with c:import using nested c:param tags. Example 6-22 imports a file *header_tag.jspf*, and makes available two request parameters for that file to process: fname and lname. The taglib directive at the top of Example 6-22 allows the use of the c:import and c:param tags later on in the code.

Example 6-22. Including parameter values using c:param

```
<%@ taglib uri="http://java.sun.com/jstl/core" prefix="c" %>
<html>
<c:import url="WEB-INF/jspf/header_tag.jspf" >
    <c:param name="fname" value="Mister"/>
    <c:param name="lname" value="Bean"/>
</c:import>
<body>
<h2>The rest of the page goes here ...</h2>
</body>
</html>
```

The *header_tag.jspf* file takes the values of the two parameters and adds them to the TITLE tag's greeting. Example 6-23 shows the HTML that results from this import action.

Example 6-23. Request parameter values are reflected in the HTML output

```
<html>
<HEAD>
    <META name="author" content=
        "Bruce W. Perry, author@jspservletcookbook.com"/>
    <META name="keywords" content=
        "Java, JSP, servlets, databases, MySQL, Oracle, web development"/>
    <TITLE>Parker River: Thanks For Visiting
    Mister Bean
    </TITLE>
</HEAD>
<body>
<h2>The rest of the page goes here ...</h2>
</body>
</html>
```

See Also

Recipes 6.1–6.3 on including resources in servlets; Recipes 6.4–6.7 on using jsp:include, the include directive, and including resources in JSP documents or XML files; Chapter 23 on Using the JSTL 1.0; Chapter JSP.5.4 of the JSP 2.0 specificationon jsp:include; Chapter JSP.1.10.3 of the JSP 2.0 specification on the include directive.

CHAPTER 7

Handling Web Form Data in Servlets and JSPs

7.0 Introduction

Every web developer is familiar with the scenario in which a client fills out an HTML form and then submits the inserted information to a server-side program for processing. Some of these programs use the HTTP request method POST to deliver the data to the server-side program. The POST method sends the data to the server in the body of the request, rather than as a query string appended to a URL (as in the GET method). For example, consider the HTML form tag in Example 7-1.

Example 7-1. HTML form tag set up for posting data

```
<form method=POST action="/project/controller">

<b>User Name:</b> <input type="text" name="username"
size="20">  <br><br>

<b>Department:</b> <input type="text" name="department"
size="15"><br><br>

<b>Email:</b> <input type="text" name="email"
size="15"><br><br>

<input type="submit" value="Submit">

</form>
```

When the client submits this form information, the top of the client's request text looks like this:

```
POST /project/controller HTTP/1.1
Accept: image/gif, image/x-xbitmap, image/jpeg, image/pjpeg, application/msword,
application/vnd.ms-powerpoint, application/vnd.ms-excel, application/pdf, */*
Referer: http://localhost:8080/project/login.jsp
Accept-Language: en-us
Content-Type: application/x-www-form-urlencoded
```

Beneath this text, after a few more headers, the body of the request carries the submitted data:

```
username=Bruce+W+Perry&password=bw_p1968
```

JSPs and servlets make parsing the POST data quite transparent for the developer. This is the topic of the next few recipes. We then discuss how to use servlets and JSPs to post data so that they essentially play the role of client, instead of acting as a server-side program.

7.1   Handling a POST HTTP Request in a Servlet

Problem

You want to process data that is part of a POST request.

Solution

Use the ServletRequest.getParameter(String name), getParameterMap( ), getParameterNames( ), or getParameterValues(String name) methods in the servlet's doPost method.

Discussion

The service method of a servlet calls the servlet's doPost method when a client sends a POST HTTP request. The servlet developer then has four different methods she can call to gain access to the posted data, which makes it pretty easy to process these requests. Just in case a client application uses a GET method to send the servlet its data as a query string, the servlet should also call:

```
doPost(request,response);
```

in the servlet's doGet( ) method. Example 7-2 demonstrates handling POST data with the oft-used getParameter(String name) method, as well as with the getParameterMap( ) method, which returns a java.util.Map. The map contains parameter keys and values. The getParameterNames( ) method returns a java.util. Enumeration of the parameter names. You can iterate through this Enumeration and pass the values to getParameter(String name). Another ServletRequest method, getParameterValues(String name), returns a String array of all the posted values for that parameter name (if there is only one value, the returned array contains one String). Figure 7-1 shows the browser display of the PostHandler servlet after a user has submitted the form in Example 7-1.

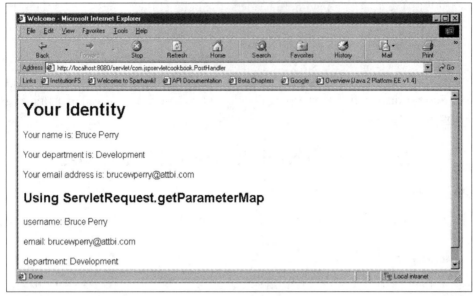

Figure 7-1. Servlet displays name/value pairs from posted form input

Example 7-2. Using the ServletRequest.getParameter and getParameterMap methods to handle posted data

```java
import javax.servlet.*;
import javax.servlet.http.*;
import java.util.Map;
import java.util.Iterator;
import java.util.Map.Entry;

public class PostHandler extends HttpServlet {

 public void doPost(HttpServletRequest request, HttpServletResponse response) throws
ServletException, java.io.IOException {

/* Use the ServletRequest.getParameter(String name), getParameterMap( ),
getParameterNames( ), or getParameterValues( ) methods in the servlet's doPost method*/

    String name = request.getParameter("username");
    String depart = request.getParameter("department");
    String email = request.getParameter("email");

    response.setContentType("text/html");
    java.io.PrintWriter out = response.getWriter( );

    out.println("<html>");
    out.println("<head>");
    out.println("<title>Welcome</title>");
    out.println("</head>");
    out.println("<body>");
    out.println("<h1>Your Identity</h1>");
```

```java
    out.println(
        "Your name is: " + ( (name == null ||  name.equals("")) ?
            "Unknown" : name));

    out.println("<br><br>");

    out.println(
        "Your department is: " + ( (depart == null ||  depart.equals("")) ?
            "Unknown" : depart));

        out.println("<br><br>");

    out.println(
        "Your email address is: " + ( (email == null ||
            email.equals("")) ? "Unknown" : email));

    out.println("<h2>Using ServletRequest.getParameterMap</h2>");

    Map param_map = request.getParameterMap();

    if (param_map == null)
        throw new ServletException(
            "getParameterMap returned null in: " +
                getClass().getName());

    //iterate through the java.util.Map and display posted parameter
    //values
    //the keys of the Map.Entry objects are type String; the values are
    //type String[],
    //or String array

    Iterator iterator = param_map.entrySet().iterator();
        while(iterator.hasNext()){
            Map.Entry me = (Map.Entry)iterator.next();
            out.println(me.getKey() + ": ");
            String[] arr = (String[]) me.getValue();

            for(int i=0;i<arr.length;i++){
                out.println(arr[i]);
                //print commas after multiple values,
                //except for the last one
                if (i > 0 && i != arr.length-1)
                out.println(", ");
            }//end for

            out.println("<br><br>");
        }//end while

    out.println("</body>");
    out.println("</html>");


}
```

Example 7-2. Using the ServletRequest.getParameter and getParameterMap methods to handle posted data (continued)

```
public void doGet(HttpServletRequest request, HttpServletResponse response)
  throws ServletException, java.io.IOException {

  doPost(request,response);
 }
}
```

Getting the value of a parameter is as simple as using request. getParameter(*parametername*). Then you can test for the failure to return a valid value with code from Example 7-2:

```
out.println("Your name is: " +
    ( (name == null ||  name.equals("")) ? "Unknown" : name));
```

If the name variable is an empty String or null, then the servlet prints "Unknown"; otherwise, it prints the name value. There are several design patterns you can use for validating form input, including client-side JavaScript and special validation Java-Beans.

Handling the java.util.Map type is more involved and entails more code. The servlet gets the parameter map by calling the ServletRequest method:

```
Map param_map = request.getParameterMap()
```

Then the code gets a java.util.Iterator from the java.util.Set returned from Map.entrySet(). The Set contains Map.Entry objects, which are key/value pairs representing the parameter name and value. The servlet uses the iterator to cycle through the parameter names and values:

```
Iterator iterator = param_map.entrySet().iterator();

while(iterator.hasNext()){

    Map.Entry me = (Map.Entry)iterator.next();
    out.println(me.getKey() + ": ");

    // The returned value is a String array
    String[] arr = (String[]) me.getValue();

    for(int i=0;i<arr.length;i++){

       out.println(arr[i]);

       //print commas after multiple values,
       //except for the last one
       if (i > 0 && i != arr.length-1)
          out.println(", ");

    }//end for

    out.println("<br><br>");
 }//end while
```

If this looks too elaborate for processing posted data, then reserve getParameterMap( ) for applications that are designed to deal with them, such as a validator bean that takes a Map as a constructor or method parameter. In addition, Recipe 7.2 shows a JSP that uses JSTL to conveniently process a parameter map.

See Also

Recipe 7.2 on handling a POST request in a JSP; Recipe 7.5 on posting data from a servlet; Recipe 7.7 on using a servlet to add a parameter to a query string; the ServletRequest API docs at *http://java.sun.com/j2ee/1.4/docs/api/index.html*.

7.2   Handling a POST HTTP Request in a JSP

Problem

You want to have a JSP handle the data posted from a form or client application.

Solution

Use the JSTL c:forEach tag to iterate over the parameter names and values.

Discussion

The JSTL makes it very easy to process input data from a POST method. The JSP in Example 7-3 uses only template text and JSTL tags to display posted information. The c:forEach tag iterates over the posted data using the implicit JSTL object param. The param object contains java.util.Map.Entry types, which each hold a key/value pair. The key and value correspond to the name of a submitted parameter and its value, such as "department=Development." Using the Expression Language (EL), the syntax "${map_entry.key}" or "${map_entry.value}" is the equivalent of calling the Map.Entry.getKey( ) and getValue( ) methods. The return values of these method calls are fed to the c:out JSTL tag for display in the HTML page. Figure 7-2 shows what the browser page looks like if the form submitted to the JSP is the one detailed in Example 7-1. With your taglib, use a uri value of http://java.sun.com/jsp/jstl/core for JSTL 1.1.

Example 7-3. Iterating posted data with the JSTL

```
<%@page contentType="text/html"%>
<%@ taglib uri="http://java.sun.com/jstl/core" prefix="c" %>
<html>
<head><title>Post Data Viewer</title></head>
<body>
<h2>Here is your posted data</h2>
```

Example 7-3. Iterating posted data with the JSTL (continued)

```
<c:forEach var="map_entry" items="${param}">
    <strong><c:out value="${map_entry.key}" /></strong>:
    <c:out value="${map_entry.value}" /><br><br>
</c:forEach>

</body>
</html>
```

Make sure to include the taglib directive when you are using the JSTL tags. The taglib in Example 7-3 takes care of any of the custom tags with the "c" prefix, as in c:forEach.

 Chapter 23 explains how to install the JSTL in your web application, make different custom tags, and use the EL.

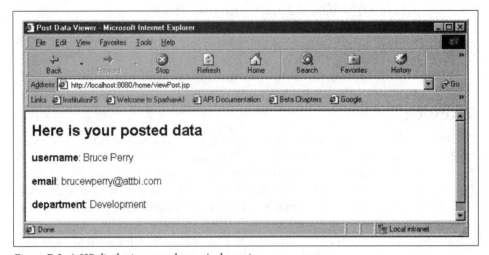

Figure 7-2. A JSP displaying posted name/value pairs

If you want to get the values of parameters without using a c:forEach tag, then use the code fragment in Example 7-4. This code displays the values of parameters when the parameter names are known by the developer (which is usually the case).

Example 7-4. Displaying individual parameter values using c:out

```
<h2>Here is your posted data</h2>
<strong>User name:</strong>: <c:out value="${param.username}"/>

<br><br>
<strong>Department:</strong>: <c:out value="${param.department}"/>
<strong>Email:</strong>: <c:out value="${param.email}"/>
```

Substituting this code into the JSP produces the same results as those shown Figure 7-2.

 The JSP 2.0 specification is designed to allow the use of the EL in template text—in other words, without the c:out JSTL tag.

See Also

Recipe 7.2 on handling a POST request in a JSP; Recipe 7.3 on setting the properties of a JavaBean to form input; Recipe 7.4 on setting a scoped attribute to the value of a parameter; Recipe 7.6 on posting data from a JSP; Chapter 23 on using the JSTL.

7.3 Setting the Properties of a JavaBean in a JSP

Problem

You want to set a JavaBean's properties to the values entered in a form.

Solution

Use the jsp:setProperty standard action, with its property attribute set to "*" and its class attribute set to the fully qualified class name of the JavaBean.

Discussion

The jsp:setProperty standard action has a built-in method for automatically mapping the values submitted in a form to a JavaBean's fields or variables. The names of the submitted parameters have to correspond to the names of the JavaBean's setter methods. Example 7-5 shows a *setBean.jsp* page that receives data from an HTML form:

```
<form method=post action="http://localhost:8080/home/setBean.jsp">
```

The JSP first instantiates an object of the type com.jspservletcookbook.UserBean using jsp:useBean. Then it sets the properties of the bean using jsp:setProperty. The name attribute of jsp:setProperty matches the id attribute of jsp:useBean. The property attribute of jsp:setProperty is simply set to "*".

Example 7-5. beanSet.jsp JSP that sets the UserBean's properties with form input

```
<%@page contentType="text/html"%>
<%@ taglib uri="http://java.sun.com/jstl/core" prefix="c" %>
```

Example 7-5. beanSet.jsp JSP that sets the UserBean's properties with form input (continued)

```
<jsp:useBean id="userB" class="com.jspservletcookbook.UserBean" >

<jsp:setProperty name="userB" property="*" />

</jsp:useBean>
<html>
<head><title>Post Data Viewer</title></head>
<body>
<h2>Here is your posted data</h2>

    <strong>User name</strong>:
    <c:out value="${userB.username}" /><br><br>

     <strong>Department</strong>:
    <c:out value="${userB.department}" /><br><br>

     <strong>Email</strong>:
    <c:out value="${userB.email}" />

</body>
</html>
```

Example 7-5 uses the c:out element of the JSTL to display the bean's various values in a browser page. The value attribute of c:out uses the EL to acquire a property value, as in "${userB.email}". This syntax is the equivalent of calling the UserBean's getEmail( ) method. Example 7-6 shows the UserBean, which uses the JavaBean naming conventions to ensure that its properties can be properly set and accessed. Figure 7-3 shows the browser display of the values.

Figure 7-3. Displaying form input via a JavaBean

The jsp:setProperty action, as used in this recipe, sets the JavaBean's properties by using introspection to line up parameter names with the bean's setter methods. If the bean has a field named "Username," then the parameter name must be exactly "Username" and the setter method must be exactly "setUsername(*String name*)" (if the bean's field is a String). Watch out, it's case-sensitive!

Example 7-6. Encapsulating the posted data in a JavaBean

```
package com.jspservletcookbook;

public class UserBean implements java.io.Serializable{

String username;
String email;
String department;

public UserBean( ){}

public void setUsername(String _username){

    if(_username != null && _username.length( ) > 0)
        username = _username;
    else
         username = "Unknown";
}

public String getUsername( ){

    if(username != null)
        return username;
    else
        return "Unknown";}

public void setEmail(String _email){

    if(_email != null && _email.length( ) > 0)
        email = _email;
    else
         email = "Unknown";
}

public String getEmail( ){

 if(_email != null)
        return email;
    else
        return "Unknown";}

public void setDepartment(String _department){

    if(_department != null && _department.length( ) > 0)
        department = _department;
```

Example 7-6. Encapsulating the posted data in a JavaBean (continued)

```
    else
        department = "Unknown";
}

public String getDepartment( ){

    if(department != null)
        return department;
    else
        return "Unknown";  }

}
```

Recipe 7.4 shows how to use a bean to validate form input, then set a scoped attribute to the input.

See Also

Recipe 7.2 on handling a POST request in a JSP; Recipe 7.4 on setting a scoped attribute to the value of a parameter; Recipe 7.6 on posting data from a JSP; Chapter 23 on using the JSTL.

7.4   Setting a Scoped Attribute in a JSP to the Value of a Form Parameter

Problem

You want to set a request-, session-, or application-scoped attribute to a value that a client has submitted as part of form input.

Solution

Use the jsp:useBean and jsp:setProperty standard actions to set a JavaBean's property to the submitted value. Then use the c:set JSTL custom tag to set the attribute to the validated value.

Discussion

Some web applications may validate form input such as an email/password combination, then set a request-, session-, or application-scoped attribute to the validated value. An efficient way to handle important data that a user submits is to use a Java-Bean whose purpose is to validate the submission against some business rule or external resource, such as a database. If the submission is valid, then the application creates a session attribute, for instance, with the value. If the submission is invalid, then a boolean variable in the JavaBean is set to false. The JSP to which the form input is sent can check this value before it handles the data as valid.

Example 7-7 shows a `ClientValidator` bean that has three fields: email, password, and valid. This bean is used by a JSP to validate form input before the JSP sets request-scoped attributes to the submitted values.

Example 7-7. The ClientValidator bean

```
package com.jspservletcookbook;

public class ClientValidator implements java.io.Serializable{

String email;
String password;
boolean valid;

public ClientValidator( ){

    this.valid=false;}

public boolean isValid( ){

    /* Use a Data Access Object to validate the email and password.
       If the validation does not fail, then set this.valid to true*/

    this.valid=true;
    return valid;

}

public void setEmail(String _email){

    if(_email != null && _email.length( ) > 0)
       email = _email;
    else
       email = "Unknown";
}

public String getEmail( ){

    return email;
}

public void setPassword(String _password){

    if(_password != null && _password.length( ) > 0)

       password = _password;

    else

       password = "Unknown";
```

Example 7-7. The ClientValidator bean (continued)

```
}

public String getPassword( ){

    return password; }

}
```

Example 7-8 is the JSP that uses `ClientValidator`. The JSP first uses `jsp:useBean` to create an instance of the bean. Then it sets the fields or properties of the bean to the values that have been posted to the JSP, which are "email" and "password". If the isValid bean property is true, which is tested with this JSTL code:

```
<c:if test="${isValid}">
```

then the JSP sets two request-scoped attributes. The attributes are now available to a page that is forwarded this request. Session attributes are accessible from servlets and JSPs that are associated with the same session (see Chapter 11). The application scope encompasses the context or web application.

> If you want to set session- or application-scoped attributes, change the code in Example 7-8 to:
>
> ```
> <c:set var="email" value="${chk.email}"
>     scope="session" />
> <c:set var="password" value="${chk.password}"
>     scope="session" />
> ```
>
> or:
>
> ```
> <c:set var="email" value="${chk.email}"
>     scope="application" />
> <c:set var="password" value="${chk.password}"
>     scope="application" />
> ```

Example 7-8. validChk.jsp page that uses a validator bean to check form input data

```
<%@page contentType="text/html"%>
<%@ taglib uri="http://java.sun.com/jstl/core" prefix="c" %>

<jsp:useBean id="chk" class="com.jspservletcookbook.ClientValidator" >

<jsp:setProperty name="chk" property="*" />

</jsp:useBean>
<%-- get valid property from ClientValidator bean --%>

<c:set var="isValid" value="${chk.valid}" />

<c:if test="${isValid}">

    <c:set var="email" value="${chk.email}" scope="request" />
    <c:set var="password" value="${chk.password}" scope="request" />
```

Example 7-8. validChk.jsp page that uses a validator bean to check form input data (continued)

```
</c:if>
<html>
<head><title>Client Checker</title></head>
<body>
<h2>Welcome</h2>

    <strong>Email</strong>:
    <c:out value="${email}" /><br><br>
     <strong>Password</strong>:
    <c:out value="${password}" />

</body>
</html>
```

See Also

Recipe 7.2 on handling a POST request in a JSP; Recipe 7.3 on setting the properties of a JavaBean to form input; Recipe 7.6 on posting data from a JSP; Chapter 23 on using the JSTL.

7.5   Posting Data from a Servlet

Problem

You want to send parameters and their values as a POST request from a servlet.

Solution

Use the Jakarta Commons HttpClient component and its PostMethod class to automate the posting of data to other programs.

Discussion

The Jakarta Commons HttpClient is a component that allows the developer to mimic the features of a web browser in his Java code, such as sending GET and POST HTTP requests, as well as using HTTPS for secure sockets. As the homepage describes this useful component, HttpClient "provides an efficient, up-to-date, and feature-rich package implementing the client side of the most recent HTTP standards and recommendations" (*http://jakarta.apache.org/commons/httpclient/*). HttpClient is offered under the Apache Software License.

This recipe describes using HttpClient to post data to another server-side program using the POST HTTP method. First, download the HttpClient distribution from the Jakarta site (*http://jakarta.apache.org/commons/httpclient/downloads.html*). Then unpack the distribution and place the JAR file that it contains in the *WEB-INF/lib* directory of your web application. At this writing, the JAR for Release 2.0 Alpha 3 was *commons-httpclient-2.0-alpha2.jar*. Once you have taken care of this installation, your servlets and beans can use the HttpClient classes.

Example 7-9 is a servlet that posts data to a JSP: *http://localhost:8080/home/viewPost. jsp*. Example 7-3 shows the *viewPost.jsp* file. Note the classes from the org.apache. commons.httpclient package that the servlet has to import at the top of the code.

Example 7-9. A servlet that posts data to a JSP using HttpClient

```
package com.jspservletcookbook;

import javax.servlet.*;
import javax.servlet.http.*;

import org.apache.commons.httpclient.HttpClient;
import org.apache.commons.httpclient.HttpStatus;
import org.apache.commons.httpclient.methods.PostMethod;
import org.apache.commons.httpclient.NameValuePair;

public class ClientPost extends HttpServlet {

 public void doPost(HttpServletRequest request, HttpServletResponse response)
    throws ServletException, java.io.IOException {

    HttpClient httpClient = new HttpClient();

    PostMethod postMethod = new PostMethod(
        "http://localhost:8080/home/viewPost.jsp");

    NameValuePair[] postData = {
        new NameValuePair("username", "devgal"),
        new NameValuePair("department", "development"),
        new NameValuePair("email", "devgal@yahoo.com")
    };

    //the 2.0 beta1 version has a
    //PostMethod.setRequestBody(NameValuePair[])
    //method, as addParameters is deprecated

    postMethod.addParameters(postData);

    httpClient.executeMethod(postMethod);

    //display the response to the POST method
    response.setContentType("text/html");
    java.io.PrintWriter out = response.getWriter();
    //A "200 OK" HTTP Status Code

    if (postMethod.getStatusCode() == HttpStatus.SC_OK) {

        out.println(postMethod.getResponseBodyAsString());
```

```
    } else {

        out.println("The POST action raised an error: " + postMethod.getStatusLine( ));

    }
    //release the connection used by the method
    postMethod.releaseConnection( );

}

public void doGet(HttpServletRequest request, HttpServletResponse response)
    throws ServletException, java.io.IOException {

    doPost(request,response);
}
}
```

The code sends three name/value pairs to the JSP (named username, department, and email), which will handle the posted data. HttpClient handles the returned text from the POST method so that you can display it in the same servlet. If you expect to receive large amounts of text as return values from the POST, then consider using the HttpMethodBase.getResponseBodyAsStream( ) method instead of getResponseBodyAsString( ). The getResponseBodyAsStream( ) method returns a java. io.InputStream. Example 7-9 is derived from sample code provided at the HttpClient web site.

Figure 7-4 shows the web browser display after requesting the ClientPost servlet.

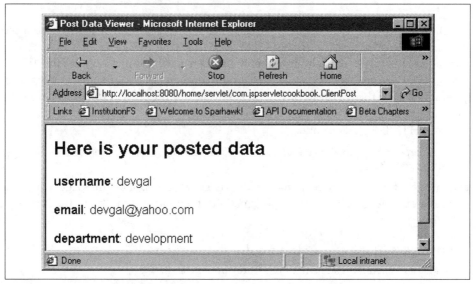

Figure 7-4. Displaying the returned text after posting data from a servlet

See Also

Recipe 7.1 on handling a POST request in a servlet; Recipe 7.7 on using a servlet to add a parameter to a query string; the Jakarta Commons HttpClient page: *http://jakarta.apache.org/commons/httpclient*.

7.6   Posting Data from a JSP

Problem

You want to send parameters and their values as an HTTP POST request from a JSP.

Solution

The easiest way to post data from a JSP is to do it the old fashioned way: use the HTML form tag and a Submit button. If you have to send the data dynamically (as in not relying on a user to press a form button), use a JavaBean that encapsulates the HttpClient code discussed in Recipe 7.5.

Discussion

The simplest way to initiate a POST method in a JSP is to set up the HTML template text as shown in Example 7-1: provide an HTML form tag that the user fills out and submits. Since Example 7-1 already shows a typical HTML form, I'll use this space to show a JavaBean that allows a JSP to dynamically post data to another server-side process.

Example 7-10 shows a *jspPost.jsp* page that uses a PostBean utility class to send a set of parameters/values to another JSP. The receiving JSP, *viewPost.jsp*, processes the parameters that the PostBean object sends it, then returns some text for the JSP in Example 7-10 to display. The JSP passes the parameters that it wants to post as a java.util.Map to the PostBean class. The PostBean url property is the destination for the posted data (the address that you would otherwise place in the action attribute of a form HTML tag). The code:

```
<jsp:setProperty name="postBean" property="parameters" value="<%= request.
getParameterMap( )%>" />
```

gets a Map of the parameters that were passed to the *jspPost.jsp* page with the HttpServletRequest.getParameterMap( ) method, then passes that Map to the PostBean class to be reposted.

Example 7-10. A JSP that posts parameters and values dynamically

```
<%@ taglib uri="http://java.sun.com/jstl/core" prefix="c" %>

<%-- create an instance of the PostBean class if once does not exist --%>
```

Example 7-10. A JSP that posts parameters and values dynamically (continued)

```
<jsp:useBean id="postBean" class="com.jspservletcookbook.PostBean" />

<%-- set the PostBean parameters property to a Map type --%>
<jsp:setProperty name="postBean" property="parameters" value="<%= request.
getParameterMap( )%>" />

<jsp:setProperty name="postBean" property="url" value="http://localhost:8080/home/
viewPost.jsp" />

<%-- Post the parameters and display the returned text --%>
<jsp:getProperty name="postBean" property="post"/>
```

Example 7-11 shows the PostBean class that the JSP page uses to post data. This bean uses the Jakarta Commons HttpClient component to send an HTTP POST request. The sending action happens in the PostBean.getPost( ) method, which sends off the parameters and returns the text result from the receiving servlet (in this example, it's *viewPost.jsp*). Because the bean method is called getPost( ), using the JavaBean naming conventions for methods that return property values, we can call the method in the JSP with:

```
<jsp:getProperty name="postBean" property="post"/>
```

The latter code is then replaced with the String return value.

Example 7-11. A data-posting JavaBean for use by a JSP or servlet

```
package com.jspservletcookbook;

import java.util.Map;
import java.util.Iterator;
import java.util.Map.Entry;

import org.apache.commons.httpclient.HttpClient;
import org.apache.commons.httpclient.HttpStatus;
import org.apache.commons.httpclient.methods.PostMethod;
import org.apache.commons.httpclient.NameValuePair;
import org.apache.commons.httpclient.HttpException;

public class PostBean implements java.io.Serializable {

private Map parameters;
private String url;

public PostBean( ){
}

public void setParameters(Map param){

  if (param != null)
      parameters = param;
}
```

Example 7-11. A data-posting JavaBean for use by a JSP or servlet (continued)

```java
public Map getParameters(){

    return parameters;
}

public void setUrl(String url){

  if (url != null && !(url.equals("")))
      this.url=url;
}

public String getUrl(){

    return url;
}


public String getPost() throws java.io.IOException,HttpException{

    if (url == null || url.equals("") || parameters == null)
        throw new IllegalStateException(
          "Invalid url or parameters in PostBean.getPost method.");

    String returnData = "";

    HttpClient httpClient = new HttpClient();

    PostMethod postMethod = new PostMethod(url);

    //convert the Map passed into the bean to a NameValuePair[] type
    NameValuePair[] postData = getParams(parameters);

    //the 2.0 beta1 version has a
    //PostMethod.setRequestBody(NameValuePair[])
    //method, as addParameters is deprecated

    postMethod.addParameters(postData);

    httpClient.executeMethod(postMethod);

    //A "200 OK" HTTP Status Code
    if (postMethod.getStatusCode() == HttpStatus.SC_OK) {

        returnData= postMethod.getResponseBodyAsString();

    } else {

        returnData= "The POST action raised an error: " +
            postMethod.getStatusLine();
    }

    //release the connection used by the method
```

```
    postMethod.releaseConnection( );

    return returnData;

}//end getPost

 private NameValuePair[] getParams(Map map){

        NameValuePair[] pairs = new NameValuePair[map.size( )];

        //Use an Iterator to put name/value pairs from the Map
        //into the array
        Iterator iter = map.entrySet().iterator( );

        int i = 0;

        while (iter.hasNext( )){

          Map.Entry me = (Map.Entry) iter.next( );

          //Map.Entry.getValue( ) returns a String[] array type
          pairs[i] = new NameValuePair(
                      (String)me.getKey(),((String[]) me.getValue( ))[0]);
          i++;
        }
        return pairs;
 }//end getParams

}
```

The displayed results looks exactly like Figure 7-5, which also uses *viewPost.jsp* to show the name/value pairs that were fed to the JSP. Again, if you have to use a JSP to dynamically mimic an HTML form, it is a good idea to delegate the mechanics of posting data to a JavaBean so that the JSP remains a presentation component and the bean can be reused elsewhere.

See Also

Recipe 7.2 on handling a POST request in a JSP; Recipe 7.3 on setting the properties of a JavaBean to form input; Recipe 7.8 on using a JSP to add a parameter to a query string.

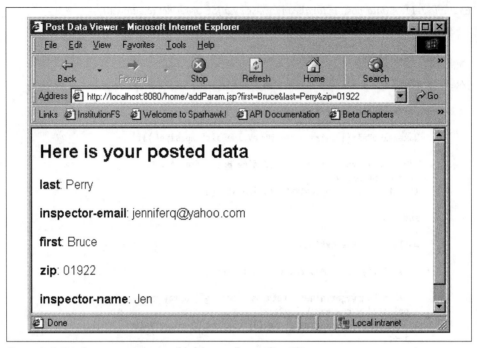

Figure 7-5. Displaying parameters added from a forwarding JSP

7.7 Using a Servlet to Add a Parameter to a Query String

Problem

You want to use a servlet to add one or more parameters to a query string, then forward the request to its final destination.

Solution

Use the HttpServletRequest API to get the existing query string. Then append any new parameters to the query string and use a javax.servlet.RequestDispatcher to forward the request.

Discussion

The servlet in Example 7-12 simply takes any existing query string and appends the parameters that it has to add to this String. Then it sends the now extended (or new) query string on its merry way with a call to RequestDispatcher.forward.

Example 7-12. Adding a parameter to a query string with a servlet

```
package com.jspservletcookbook;

import javax.servlet.*;
import javax.servlet.http.*;

public class QueryModifier extends HttpServlet {

 public void doGet(HttpServletRequest request, HttpServletResponse response)
    throws ServletException, java.io.IOException {

    //returns null if the URL does not contain a query string
    String querystr = request.getQueryString();

    if (querystr != null){

        querystr = querystr +
          "&inspector-name=Jen&inspector-email=Jenniferq@yahoo.com";

    } else {

        querystr = "inspector-name=Jen&inspector-email=Jenniferq@yahoo.com";}

        RequestDispatcher dispatcher =
           request.getRequestDispatcher("/viewPost.jsp?"+querystr);

        dispatcher.forward(request,response);
}
public void doPost(HttpServletRequest request, HttpServletResponse response)
    throws ServletException, java.io.IOException {

  doGet(request,response);

  }

}
```

The HttpServletRequest.getQueryString() method returns the query string without the opening "?", as in:

first=Bruce&last=Perry&zipcode=01922

If you want to get the request URL right up to the query string but not include the "?", use HttpServletRequest.getRequestURL(), which returns a java.lang.StringBuffer type.

See Also

Recipe 7.1 on handling a POST request in a servlet; Recipe 7.5 on posting data from a servlet.

7.8 Using a JSP to Add a Parameter to a Query String

Problem

You want to use a JSP to add one or more parameters to a query string, then forward the request to its destination.

Solution

Use the jsp:forward and jsp:param standard actions.

Discussion

Adding one or more parameters and forwarding to another component is as easy as four lines in a JSP. The jsp:forward action adds any jsp:params to existing parameters when it forwards this text to the processing component, as shown in Example 7-13.

Example 7-13. Adding parameters and forwarding in a JSP

```
<jsp:forward  page="/viewPost.jsp" >
    <jsp:param name="inspector-name" value="Jen"/>
<jsp:param name="inspector-email" value="jenniferq@yahoo.com"/>
</jsp:forward>
```

If this JSP is requested with the following URL:

```
http://localhost:8080/home/addParam.jsp?first=Bruce&last=Perry&zip=01922
```

then the three original parameters (first, last, and zip) are preserved when the jsp:forward action adds two additional parameters (inspector-name, inspector-email) and forwards the page. In the example, the page is processed by the *viewPost.jsp* page shown in Example 7-3. Requesting *addParam.jsp* in a browser forwards the request, and a total of five parameters to the *viewPost.jsp* page. Figure 7-5 shows the result in a browser.

See Also

Recipe 7.2 on handling a POST request in a JSP; Recipe 7.3 on setting the properties of a JavaBean to form input; Recipe 7.6 on posting data from a JSP.

7.9   Using a Filter to Read Parameter Values

Problem

You want to use a filter to intercept form input and read it.

Solution

Use the various getParameter methods of the ServletRequest API to take a look at parameter values in a filter.

Discussion

When you develop a filter for a servlet, your filter class has to implement the javax.servlet.Filter interface. This means that your Filter class has to implement the doFilter(request,response) and destroy() methods of that interface. The doFilter method contains the hook to the filtered servlet's parameter values. The doFilter's ServletRequest parameter has the getParameter, getParameterMap, getParameterNames, and getParameterValues methods which allow the filter to peek at a servlet's parameters and values.

First, you have to map the Filter you have designed to the servlet. This chunk of *web.xml* maps a Filter object to a servlet named Viewer.

```
<!-- any context-param elements go here -->
<filter>
    <filter-name>ParamSnoop</filter-name>
    <filter-class>com.jspservletcookbook.ParamSnoop</filter-class>
</filter>

<filter-mapping>
    <filter-name>ParamSnoop</filter-name>
    <servlet-name>Viewer</servlet-name>
</filter-mapping>
<!-- web.xml continues  -->
```

Place the filter class in the *WEB-INF/classes* directory of your web application, or inside a JAR file that is placed in *WEB-INF/lib*. The servlet container creates an instance when the container starts up of each filter that is declared in *web.xml*. The container then executes the filter (calls its doFilter method) when a user requests any of the servlets the filter is mapped to. So the ParamSnoop filter can inspect a request made to the Viewer servlet before the servlet processes the request.

 "Only one instance per filter declaration in the deployment descriptor is instantiated per Java virtual machine of the container," according to the Servlet v2.4 specification, Chapter SRV.6.2.1.

Example 7-14 gets access to the parameters in the intercepted request by calling ServletRequest.getParameterMap( ). However, you are free to use other ServletRequest API methods to look at parameters, such as getParameter*StringName*. The getParameterMap( ) method returns a java.util.Map of parameter names and values, which you extract from the Map using a java.util.Iterator and its next( ) method.

 The call Map.entrySet( ) returns a java.util.Set, from which you obtain an Iterator by calling Set.iterator( ). The objects returned from the Iterator.next( ) method in this case are Map.Entry objects that hold key/value pairs, relating to the parameter names and values.

Example 7-14 also shows how to pull the key/value pairs out of the map and log the values using the ServletContext.log( ) method.

Example 7-14. Snooping on parameter values with a servlet

```
package com.jspservletcookbook;

import javax.servlet.*;
import javax.servlet.http.*;

import java.util.Map;
import java.util.Iterator;
import java.util.Map.Entry;

public class ParamSnoop implements Filter {

    private FilterConfig config;

    /** Creates new ParamSnoop */
    public ParamSnoop( ) {
    }

    public void  init(FilterConfig filterConfig)  throws ServletException{

        this.config = filterConfig;
    }

    public void  doFilter(
      ServletRequest request, ServletResponse response, FilterChain chain)
        throws java.io.IOException, ServletException {

            Map paramMap = request.getParameterMap( );
            ServletContext context = config.getServletContext( );

            /* use the ServletContext.log method to log
            param names/values */
            context.log("doFilter called in: " + config.getFilterName( ) +
            " on " + (new java.util.Date( )));
```

Example 7-14. Snooping on parameter values with a servlet (continued)

```
            context.log("Snooping the parameters in request: " +
              ((HttpServletRequest) request).getRequestURI( ));

            Iterator iter = paramMap.entrySet().iterator( );
             while (iter.hasNext( )){

                Map.Entry me = (Map.Entry) iter.next( );
                context.log((String)me.getKey( ) + ": " +
                  ((String[]) me.getValue( ))[0]);
            }
        //continue the request, response to next filter or servlet
        //destination
        chain.doFilter(request,response);
    }

    public void destroy( ){
        /*called before the Filter instance is removed
        from service by the web container*/
    }
}
```

The only reason we used the ServletContext.log( ) method was to display the inspection of parameters by the filter. Here is an example of the Tomcat log in *<Tomcat-installation-directory>/logs* showing the two parameters that were stored in the servlet request (last, first). In other words, the web browser request was *http:// localhost:8080/home/viewer?first=Bruce&last=Perry*.

```
2003-04-13 17:13:33 doFilter called in: ParamSnoop on Sun Apr 13 17:13:33 EDT 2003
2003-04-13 17:13:33 Snooping the parameters in request: /home/viewer
2003-04-13 17:13:33 last: Perry
2003-04-13 17:13:33 first: Bruce
```

See Also

Recipe 7.1 on handling a POST request in a servlet; Recipe 7.7 on using a servlet to add a parameter to a query string; Chapter 19 on filtering requests and responses; Chapter SRV.6 on Filters in the Servlet 2.4 specification.

CHAPTER 8
Uploading Files

8.0 Introduction

Web sites use the HTML form tag to allow users to submit files from their own file-system for processing on the server. The form tag enables the uploading action with a nested input element that has a type attribute set to "file". The form and input tag is specified using the syntax described in Recipe 8.1.

The HTTP request for file uploading uses a content type of "multipart/form-data". The HTTP message that the user sends to the server by clicking the web page's Submit button contains descriptive headers and the body of each uploaded file. Each of the uploaded files is separated by a specified boundary pattern (see the Content-Type header value in Example 8-1). Example 8-1 shows an abbreviated view of a "multipart/form-data" type request including the uploading of three very small files. To make this example more compact, I have removed some of the values from the Accept request header.

Example 8-1. An HTTP request message with three uploaded files

```
POST /home/upload.jsp HTTP/1.1
Accept: image/gif, image/x-xbitmap, image/jpeg, image/pjpeg ...
Referer: http://localhost:8080/home/interact.html
Accept-Language: en-us
Content-Type: multipart/form-data; boundary=---------------------------7d33c11c6018e
Accept-Encoding: gzip, deflate
User-Agent: Mozilla/4.0 (compatible; MSIE 5.5; Windows NT 4.0)
Host: localhost:9000
Content-Length: 541
Connection: Keep-Alive
Cache-Control: no-cache
Cookie: JSESSIONID=7F6154184FFF3D1AE345E1F2FFF1A22E

-----------------------------7d33c11c6018e
Content-Disposition: form-data; name="file1"; filename="H:\home\file1.txt"
Content-Type: text/plain
```

Example 8-1. An HTTP request message with three uploaded files (continued)

```
This is file 1.
----------------------------7d33c11c6018e
Content-Disposition: form-data; name="file2"; filename="H:\home\file2.txt"
Content-Type: text/plain

This is file 2.
----------------------------7d33c11c6018e
Content-Disposition: form-data; name="file3"; filename="H:\home\file3.txt"
Content-Type: text/plain

This is file 3.
----------------------------7d33c11c6018e--
```

The HTTP request delineates each uploaded file with a boundary pattern:

```
----------------------------7d33c11c6018e.
```

Each of the files has a Content-Disposition and Content-Type header. The simple text files that Example 8-1 uploads to the server have only one line each to give you a clear snapshot of what this type of HTTP request looks like. For more details on the file-uploading mechanism itself, see RFC 1867: *http://www.ietf.org/rfc/rfc1867.txt*.

8.1 Preparing the HTML Page for File Uploads

Problem

You want to set up an HTML page to allow the user to specify a file from his filesystem to upload to the server.

Solution

Use the HTML form tag with its enctype attribute set to "multipart/form-data". Use an input tag nested in the form tag with a type attribute of "file".

Discussion

The HTML for file uploading involves a few "must haves." The form tag specifies the servlet (or other server-side component) that is handling the file upload in its action attribute. The method attribute must be POST (not GET) for the file upload action to work. The form tag's enctype attribute must be "multipart/form-data".

The widget with which the user enters the file to upload is an input tag with a type of "file", and looks like a text field. The name attribute uniquely names the particular input tag, which becomes important when the HTML specifies the uploading of more than one file (see the note at the end of this recipe). Without any additional intervention, the server saves the uploaded file with its original filename. The accept attribute is designed to limit the file types that the user can choose for uploading, such as to the "application/pdf" MIME type, but this attribute has poor support among browsers.

When displaying the HTML in Example 8-2, browsers automatically show a Browse button. When the form client selects the button, the browser displays a typical file-system navigation window with which the user can select the file.

Example 8-2. Simple HTML for file uploading

```
<!DOCTYPE HTML PUBLIC "-//W3C//DTD HTML 4.0 Transitional//EN">
<html>
<head>
    <title>Please Choose The File</title>
</head>
<body bgcolor="#ffffff">
<table border="0"><tr>

<form action="/home/servlet/com.jspservletcookbook.UploadServlet" method="post"
enctype="multipart/form-data">

<td valign="top"><strong>Please choose your document:</strong><br></td>

<td> <input type="file" name="file1">

<br><br>
</td></tr>

<tr><td><input type="submit" value="Upload File"></td></tr>
</form>

</table>
</body>
</html>
```

After selection, the text field displays the full path to the selected file. Figure 8-1 shows this HTML page in a web browser.

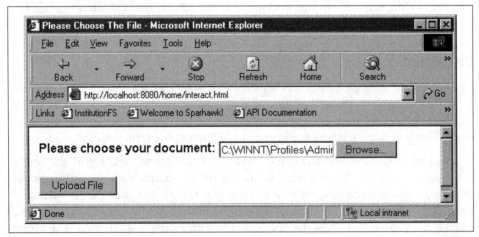

Figure 8-1. HTML page for uploading a file to a servlet

Figure 8-1 shows the input field after the user has already chosen the file. The browser then automatically fills in the text field with the complete file path.

 To allow the uploading of multiple files, include more than one input tag with different values for the name attribute. The browser associates a Browse button with each of them.

See Also

Recipe 8.4 on using the com.oreilly.servlet library for file uploading; Recipe 8.5 on handling a single file upload; Recipe 8.6 on handling multiple file uploads; Recipe 8.5 on controlling file naming; Recipe 8.6 on using a JSP to handle file uploads; the homepage for com.oreilly.servlet: *http://www.servlets.com/cos/index.html*; the RFC 1867 document on form-based file uploads: *http://www.ietf.org/rfc/rfc1867.txt*.

8.2   Using the com.oreilly.servlet Library

Problem

You want to use the com.oreilly.servlet classes that O'Reilly author Jason Hunter has developed to handle file uploads.

 Of course, this isn't much of a problem, as Jason's library takes most of the work out of uploading and accepting files. I use Jason's library here (with his permission, of course) because it handles file uploads nicely, and there's no good reason to reinvent a perfectly good wheel.

Solution

Download the distribution ZIP file from *http://www.servlets.com/cos/index.html*. Add the *cos.jar* file, which is part of the distribution to the *WEB-INF/lib* directory of your web application. Make sure that you adhere to the software license when using the library.

Discussion

A JAR file named *cos.jar* includes the com.oreilly.servlet and com.oreilly.servlet. multipart packages. These packages include several classes, such as all of the Java classes that begin with "Multipart," which can be used to handle file uploading in a servlet.

 The *cos.jar* archive also contains many other interesting and useful classes to use with servlets, but the following recipes focus on file uploads.

Download the latest ZIP file containing the distribution from *http://www.servlets. com/cos/index.html*. The contents of the ZIP file include *cos.jar*, which you need to add to the *WEB-INF/lib* directory of your web application. In your servlet, you then import the classes that you want to use:

```
import com.oreilly.servlet.MultipartRequest;
import com.oreilly.servlet.multipart.FileRenamePolicy;
```

Before you have integrated these classes into your code, make sure that you have read the accompanying software license for this code: *http://www.servlets.com/cos/ license.html*.

 The rest of the recipes in this chapter assume that you have *cos.jar* and the classes it contains available in your web application. If you don't take steps to make these classes available, none of the examples in this chapter will function properly.

See Also

Recipe 8.1 on preparing the HTML for a file upload; Recipe 8.5 on handling a single file upload; Recipe 8.6 on handling multiple file uploads in a servlet; Recipe 8.5 on controlling file naming; Recipe 8.6 on using a JSP to handle file uploads; the homepage for `com.oreilly.servlet`: *http://www.servlets.com/cos/index.html*; the RFC 1867 document on form-based file uploads: *http://www.ietf.org/rfc/rfc1867.txt*.

8.3   Uploading One File at a Time

Problem

You want to create a component that can receive a client file upload and store the file in a local directory.

Solution

Create a servlet that uses the `com.oreilly.servlet.MultipartRequest` class from Jason Hunter's *cos.jar* archive.

Discussion

The `MultipartRequest` class includes several overloaded constructors. The one used in Example 8-3 takes the `javax.servlet.http.HttpServletRequest` object, the path to the directory where you want to save uploaded files, and the size limit for the file as parameters. In Example 8-3, if the client uploads a file that exceeds 5 MB, then the `UploadServlet` throws a `java.io.IOException`. You can allow this exception to be managed by an error-page element in *web.xml* for `IOExceptions`, as Example 8-3 does, or use a try/catch block in the upload servlet to deal with errors.

See Chapter 9 for how to declare error pages for the web application.

With MultipartRequest, as soon as the code instantiates the object, the object is handling the file upload; in other words, you do not have to call a method to commence managing the upload.

The servlet in Example 8-3 initiates the file upload and then displays the name of the uploaded file(s).

Example 8-3. A servlet that uses the MultipartRequest class

```java
package com.jspservletcookbook;

import javax.servlet.*;
import javax.servlet.http.*;

import com.oreilly.servlet.MultipartRequest;
import java.util.Enumeration;

public class UploadServlet extends HttpServlet {

    private String webTempPath;

    public void init()
    webTempPath = getServletContext().getRealPath("/") + "data";
    }

    public void doPost(HttpServletRequest request,
                       HttpServletResponse response)
        throws ServletException, java.io.IOException {

        //file limit size of 5 MB
        MultipartRequest mpr = new MultipartRequest(
           request,webTempPath,5 * 1024 * 1024);
        Enumeration enum = mpr.getFileNames();

        response.setContentType("text/html");
        java.io.PrintWriter out = response.getWriter();

        out.println("<html>");
        out.println("<head>");
        out.println("<title>Servlet upload</title>");
        out.println("</head>");
        out.println("<body>");

        for (int i = 1; enum.hasMoreElements();i++)
            out.println("The name of uploaded file " + i +
              " is: " + mpr.getFilesystemName((String) enum.nextElement())
                + "<br><br>");
```

Example 8-3. A servlet that uses the MultipartRequest class (continued)

```
            out.println("</body>");
            out.println("</html>");


    }

    public void doGet(HttpServletRequest request,
                      HttpServletResponse response)
        throws ServletException, java.io.IOException {

        throw new ServletException("GET method used with " +
            getClass().getName()+": POST method required.");
    }
}
```

The code generates the path to the save directory by calling javax.servlet. ServletContext.getRealPath("/") to get an absolute pathname to the root of the web application (as in *h:\home*). Then the code adds the name of the directory where the file will be saved (*data*).

 This directory name could also be added using an external configuration such as a context-param element in *web.xml*. See Recipe 8.6 for details.

The method MultipartRequest.getFilesystemName(*StringName*) returns the filename from the client's filesystem. The file can be saved on the server end with its original filename, or you can use a different MultipartRequest constructor that takes as a parameter a FileRenamePolicy object. This constructor looks like:

```
MultipartRequest(javax.servlet.http.HttpServletRequest request,
                 java.lang.String saveDirectory, int maxPostSize,
                 FileRenamePolicy policy)
```

There are a few versions of the MultipartRequest constructor with the FileRenamePolicy parameter, which is used to rename uploaded files (see Recipe 8.5). Example 8-3 also throws a ServletException if the UploadServlet is requested with a GET method, which is not allowed with file uploads.

See Also

Recipe 8.1 on preparing the HTML for a file upload; Recipe 8.4 on downloading and using the com.oreilly.servlet library; Recipe 8.6 on handling multiple file uploads in a servlet; Recipe 8.5 on controlling file naming during file uploads; Recipe 8.6 on using a JSP to handle file uploads; the homepage for com.oreilly.servlet: *http://www.servlets.com/cos/index.html*; the RFC 1867 document on form-based file uploads: *http://www.ietf.org/rfc/rfc1867.txt*.

8.4   Uploading Multiple Files

Problem

You want to upload more than one file at a time from a client, and handle each file as it is uploaded.

Solution

Use the `MultipartParser` from Jason Hunter's *cos.jar* archive.

Discussion

The `MultipartParser` class allows the servlet to handle each file part sequentially as the server receives a multipart HTTP request.

> You can also use the `MultipartRequest` class to handle multiple files. However, the `MultipartParser` allows you to handle each part (such as by saving it to a database) during the parsing of a multiple-file upload.

In addition, the file's content type, size, and name can be read as the servlet handles the request. The servlet can also make basic checks using this class, such as counting how many files were uploaded and verifying whether the user uploaded a file for each of the available form `input` fields.

The HTML file from Recipe 8.5 has been altered to allow the upload of three different files from the user's filesystem, as shown in Figure 8-2.

This HTML form is created by including three input tags with `type="file"`, as in:

```
<input type="file" name="file1"><br><br>
<input type="file" name="file2"><br><br>
<input type="file" name="file3">
```

Example 8-4 handles the multiple file uploads by importing three classes from the *cos.jar* archive. The `MultipartParser` class restricts the size of file uploads to 5 MB in Example 8-4; however, you can set this constructor parameter to another value to allow smaller or larger file sizes, or leave the accepted file size at the 1 MB default.

> You can view the Javadoc for this class at *http://www.servlets.com/cos/javadoc/com/oreilly/servlet/multipart/MultipartParser.html*.

The `MultipartParser` object throws a `java.io.IOException` if any of the file uploads exceed the size limit. Calling the `MultipartParser.readNextPart( )` method returns a `Part` type, or `null` if the incoming stream does not contain any more parts. A `Part` can be either a `FilePart` or a `ParamPart`, depending on the content it includes. The

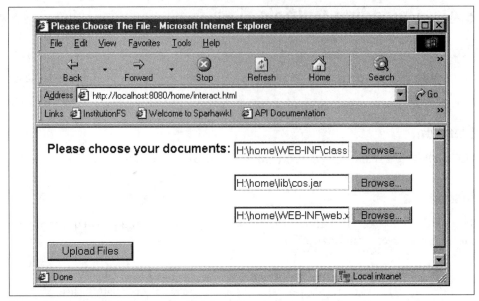

Figure 8-2. An HTML form for uploading three files

ParamPart covers the other parameters that an HTML form might include, such as
"username". The FilePart has several methods that provide information about the
uploaded file, such as its content type and the filename. The FilePart.writeTo(java.
io.File dir) method saves the file to the specified directory and returns the file size
as a long type. The FilePart can also write to an OutputStream, as in writeTo(java.
io.OutputStream out).

Example 8-4. A servlet handling multiple file uploads

```
package com.jspservletcookbook;

import javax.servlet.*;
import javax.servlet.http.*;

import com.oreilly.servlet.multipart.MultipartParser;
import com.oreilly.servlet.multipart.Part;
import com.oreilly.servlet.multipart.FilePart;

public class ParserServlet extends HttpServlet {

    private String fileSavePath;

  public void init(){

      // save uploaded files to a 'data' directory in the web app

      fileSavePath =   getServletContext().getRealPath("/") + "data";

  }
```

Example 8-4. A servlet handling multiple file uploads (continued)

```java
public void doPost(HttpServletRequest request,
  HttpServletResponse response) throws ServletException,
    java.io.IOException {

  response.setContentType("text/html");
  java.io.PrintWriter out = response.getWriter( );

  out.println("<html>");
  out.println("<head>");
  out.println("<title>File uploads</title>");
  out.println("</head>");
  out.println("<body>");

  out.println("<h2>Here is information about any uploaded files</h2>");

  try{

      // file limit size of 5 MB
      MultipartParser parser = new MultipartParser(
          request,5 * 1024 * 1024);

      Part _part = null;

      while ((_part = parser.readNextPart( )) != null) {

        if (_part.isFile( )) {

            // get some info about the file
            FilePart fPart = (FilePart) _part;
            String name = fPart.getFileName( );

            if (name != null) {

                long fileSize = fPart.writeTo(
                  new java.io.File(fileSavePath));

                out.println("The user's file path for the file: " +
                  fPart.getFilePath( ) + "<br>");

                out.println("The content type of the file: " +
                  fPart.getContentType( )+ "<br>");

                out.println("The file size: " +fileSize+ " bytes<br><br>");

                //commence with another file, if there is one

            } else {

            out.println(
              "The user did not upload a file for this part.");

            }

        }    else if (_part.isParam( )) {
```

Example 8-4. A servlet handling multiple file uploads (continued)

```
                // do something else if it is a non-file-type parameter,
                //such as a username
        }

    }// end while


    out.println("</body>");
    out.println("</html>");

} catch (java.io.IOException ioe){

    //an error-page in the deployment descriptor is
    //mapped to the java.io.IOException
    throw new java.io.IOException(
        "IOException occurred in: " + getClass().getName( ));
}
}//doPost

public void doGet(HttpServletRequest request,
  HttpServletResponse response) throws ServletException,
    java.io.IOException {

    throw new ServletException(
        "GET method used with " + getClass().getName( )+
            ": POST method required.");
}
}
```

Figure 8-3 shows the descriptive page that the servlet displays about each uploaded file.

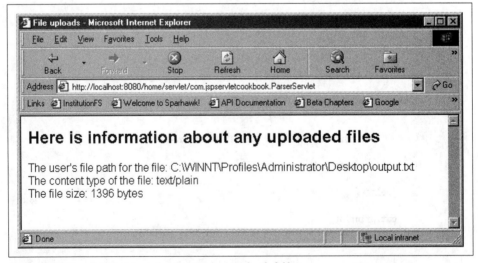

Figure 8-3. A servlet displays information about uploaded files

See Also

Recipe 8.1 on preparing the HTML for a file upload; Recipe 8.4 on downloading and using the com.oreilly.servlet library; Recipe 8.5 on handling a single file upload in a servlet; Recipe 8.5 on controlling file naming; Recipe 8.6 on using a JSP to handle file uploads; the homepage for com.oreilly.servlet: *http://www.servlets.com/cos/index.html*; the RFC 1867 document on form-based file uploads: *http://www.ietf.org/rfc/rfc1867.txt*.

8.5   Renaming Files

Problem

You want to rename the uploaded files according to a standard policy or to avoid conflicts with existing files that have the same name.

Solution

Create a class that implements the com.oreilly.servlet.multipart.FileRenamePolicy interface, or use the DefaultFileRenamePolicy class. Then use that class as a parameter in the constructor for the com.oreilly.servlet.MultipartRequest class.

Discussion

The com.oreilly.servlet.multipart package contains a FileRenamePolicy interface that can be used when you want to implement a particular file-renaming policy with file uploads.

The DefaultFileRenamePolicy class renames an uploaded file whose name conflicts with an existing file by adding a number to the uploaded filename. For example, if *index.txt* already exists, then the DefaultFileRenamePolicy class renames the uploaded file *index1.txt*; and if a second file is uploaded with the same name it will be renamed *index2.txt*, and so on.

If you want to implement your own renaming policy, then create your own class that implements the FileRenamePolicy interface, then implement the class's rename(java.io.File file) method to initiate the renaming action.

This code sample shows a MultipartRequest constructor from Example 8-3. This time, the constructor adds a DefaultFileRenamePolicy object as a constructor parameter:

```
MultipartRequest mpr = new MultipartRequest(
    request,webTempPath,(5 * 1024 * 1024),new DefaultFileRenamePolicy());
```

Make sure to include the following import statements in the servlet class:

```
import com.oreilly.servlet.MultipartRequest;
import com.oreilly.servlet.multipart.DefaultFileRenamePolicy;
```

As mentioned before, you can implement the FileRenamePolicy interface yourself and create a custom file-renaming mechanism. Example 8.5 shows a MyFileRenamePolicy class that renames each uploaded file by appending a timestamp to the end of its name. The simple timestamp is calculated as:

```
// seconds since Jan 1, 1970, 00:00:00
new java.util.Date().getTime( ) / 1000
```

The code renames the file by appending the String (representing a series of numbers) to the filename minus its extension, and then appending the extension at the end (if the filename originally had an extension).

Example 8-5. Renaming uploaded files with your own Java class

```java
package com.jspservletcookbook;

import java.io.File;
import java.util.Date;

import com.oreilly.servlet.multipart.FileRenamePolicy;

public class MyFileRenamePolicy implements FileRenamePolicy {

    //implement the rename(File f) method to satisfy the
    // FileRenamePolicy interface contract
    public File rename(File f){

        //Get the parent directory path as in h:/home/user or /home/user
        String parentDir = f.getParent( );

        //Get filename without its path location, such as 'index.txt'
        String fname = f.getName( );

        //Get the extension if the file has one
        String fileExt = "";
        int i = -1;
        if(( i = fname.indexOf(".")) != -1){

            fileExt = fname.substring(i);
            fname = fname.substring(0,i);
        }

        //add the timestamp
        fname = fname + (""+( new Date().getTime( ) / 1000));

        //piece together the filename
        fname = parentDir + System.getProperty(
            "file.separator") + fname + fileExt;

        File temp = new File(fname);

         return temp;
    }

}
```

Given that your new class is called com.jspservletcookbook.MyFileRenamePolicy and implements the FileRenamePolicy interface, the constructor for the MultipartRequest would now look like this:

```
MultipartRequest mpr = new MultipartRequest(
  request,webTempPath,(5 * 1024 * 1024),
    new com.jspservletcookbook.MyFileRenamePolicy());
```

Store your new class in the *WEB-INF/classes* directory of the web application using the same directory structure as the class's package name (as in *WEB-INF/classes/com/jspservletcookbook/MyFileRenamePolicy.class*).

 In general, the com.oreilly.servlet package also includes the MultipartFilter class. According to an article that Jason has written (*http://www.servlets.com/soapbox/filters.html*), "The MultipartFilter works by watching incoming requests and when it detects a file upload request (with the content type multipart/form-data), the filter wraps the request object with a special request wrapper that knows how to parse the special content type format."

See Also

Recipe 8.1 on preparing HTML for a file upload; Recipe 8.4 on downloading and using the com.oreilly.servlet library; Recipes 8.3 and 8.6 on handling single- and multiple-file uploads in a servlet; Recipe 8.6 on using a JSP to handle file uploads; the homepage for com.oreilly.servlet: *http://www.servlets.com/cos/index.html*; the RFC 1867 document on form-based file uploads: *http://www.ietf.org/rfc/rfc1867.txt*.

8.6   Using a JSP to Handle a File Upload

Problem

You want to use a JSP to handle a file upload.

Solution

Create a JavaBean that wraps the functionality of the com.oreilly.servlet. MultipartRequest class from Jason Hunter's *cos.jar* library. Then use the jsp:useBean standard action in a JSP to create an instance of this bean for handling the file uploads.

Discussion

This recipe describes a JavaBean that uses the com.oreilly.servlet.MultipartRequest class to manage file uploads. First, I'll show the bean that wraps the functionality of the MultipartRequest class, then the JSP that uses the bean to upload a file.

Example 8-6 shows the UploadBean used by the JSP in Example 8-7.

Example 8-6. A file-uploading JavaBean

```java
package com.jspservletcookbook;

import java.util.Enumeration;

import javax.servlet.http.HttpServletRequest;
import javax.servlet.ServletRequest;

import com.oreilly.servlet.MultipartRequest;
import com.oreilly.servlet.multipart.DefaultFileRenamePolicy;

public class UploadBean {

    private String webTempPath;
    private HttpServletRequest req;
    private String dir;

public UploadBean( ) {}

  public void setDir(String dirName) {

      if (dirName == null || dirName.equals(""))
        throw new IllegalArgumentException(
            "invalid value passed to " + getClass().getName( )+".setDir");

      webTempPath = dirName;

  }

  public void setReq(ServletRequest request) {

      if (request != null && request instanceof HttpServletRequest){

          req = (HttpServletRequest) request;

      } else {

          throw new IllegalArgumentException(
            "Invalid value passed to " + getClass().getName( )+".setReq");
      }

  }

  public String getUploadedFiles( ) throws java.io.IOException{

      //file limit size of 5 MB
      MultipartRequest mpr = new MultipartRequest(
        req,webTempPath,5 * 1024 * 1024,new DefaultFileRenamePolicy( ));

      Enumeration enum = mpr.getFileNames( );

      StringBuffer buff = new StringBuffer("");
```

Example 8-6. A file-uploading JavaBean (continued)

```
    for (int i = 1; enum.hasMoreElements( );i++){

        buff.append("The name of uploaded file ").append(i).
          append(" is: ").
            append(mpr.getFilesystemName((String)enum.nextElement( ))).
              append("<br><br>");
    }//for

    //return the String
    return buff.toString( );

  } // getUploadedFiles

}
```

This code imports the classes it needs to handle the uploaded files with the `MultipartRequest` class. The `DefaultFileRenamePolicy` class is used in the `MultipartRequest` constructor to handle conflicts between the names of uploaded files and any existing files with the same name. When these naming conflicts occur, the `DefaultFileRenamePolicy` class automatically adds a number to the end of the uploaded file, as in *index1.txt* if the uploaded file was named *index.txt*.

Example 8-6 uses the JavaBean naming conventions for its methods, as in `setDir( )` and `getUploadedFiles( )`, which allow the methods to be called using the `jsp:getProperty` and `jsp:setProperty` standard actions. Example 8-7 shows the use of both of these actions and the JSP that handles the file upload and display information about the uploaded files.

The JSP uses the `UploadBean`, the class I just defined. The JSP instantiates the bean using the `jsp:useBean` standard action, sets the directory name where the uploaded file will be saved with `jsp:setProperty`, then uses `jsp:getProperty` to save the file(s) to the specified directory.

Example 8-7. A JSP that uploads files and displays information about them

```
<jsp:useBean id="uploader" class="com.jspservletcookbook.UploadBean" />

<jsp:setProperty name="uploader" property="dir"
    value="<%=application.getInitParameter(\"save-dir\")%>" />

<jsp:setProperty name="uploader" property="req"  value="<%= request %>" />

<html>
<head><title>file uploads</title></head>
<body>
<h2>Here is information about the uploaded files</h2>

<jsp:getProperty name="uploader" property="uploadedFiles" />

</body>
</html>
```

The JSP in Example 8-7 creates an instance of the UploadBean with this code:

```
<jsp:useBean id="uploader" class="com.jspservletcookbook.UploadBean" />
```

The com.jspservletcookbook.UploadBean class must be placed in the web application's *WEB-INF/classes* directory (inside of *WEB-INF/classes/com/jspservlet/cookbook*), or in a JAR file inside of *WEB-INF/lib*.

The JSP then passes the HttpServletRequest object to the bean with this code:

```
<jsp:setProperty name="uploader" property="req" value="<%= request %>" />
```

Under JSP 2.0, you can pass along the request value with this code:

```
<jsp:setProperty name="uploader" property= "req"  value="${pageContext.request}" />
```

The JSP 2.0 specification allows the use of EL syntax in the jsp: setProperty value attribute.

The bean needs the request object to pass into the MultipartRequest constructor, which does all the file-uploading work. The JSP also specifies the directory where uploaded files are saved:

```
<jsp:setProperty name="uploader" property="dir"
    value="<%=application.getInitParameter(\"save-dir\")%>" />
```

The expression application.getInitParameter(\"save-dir\") returns the value of the context parameter save-dir, which is the path to the directory where the uploaded files are saved. Here is what this *web.xml* element looks like:

```
<!-- beginning of deployment descriptor -->
<context-param>
    <param-name>save-dir</param-name>
    <param-value>h:\home\data</param-value>
</context-param>
<!-- deployment descriptor continues -->
```

The final step is to call the bean's getUploadedFiles( ) method. The JSP accomplishes this task using the jsp:getProperty standard action, as in:

```
<jsp:getProperty name="uploader" property="uploadedFiles" />
```

The JSP can call the bean's method in this manner, as though the JSP was fetching a bean property, because I named the method with the standard "get" prefix: getUploadedFiles( ). Tricky!

Figure 8-4 shows the resulting web page after the user has submitted the HTML form.

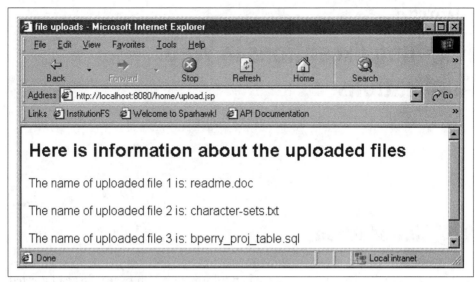

Figure 8-4. A JSP that handles file uploads

To use this JSP to handle a file upload, you have to specify it in an HTML form tag's action attribute, as in:

```
<form action="http://localhost:9000/home/upload.jsp" method="post"
enctype="multipart/form-data">
```

See Also

Recipe 8.1 on preparing the HTML for a file upload; Recipe 8.4 on downloading and using the com.oreilly.servlet library; Recipes 8.3 and 8.6 on handling single- and multiple-file uploads in a servlet; Recipe 8.5 on controlling file renaming as files are uploaded; the homepage for com.oreilly.servlet: *http://www.servlets.com/cos/index. html*; the RFC 1867 document on form-based file uploads: *http://www.ietf.org/rfc/ rfc1867.txt*.

CHAPTER 9

Handling Exceptions in Web Applications

9.0   Introduction

Web applications can sometimes show a number of errors that you don't want users to see. If a user who expects to be served an information-rich page is instead greeted with an ugly and incomprehensible announcement of an "HTTP Status 500" in her web browser, you can bet this visit to the site will be her last! All web sites handle unexpected HTTP status codes (such as the "404 Not Found" or "403 Forbidden") with a friendly and informative error message, but you'll want to hide these messages from your users. Tools to handle both Java runtime exceptions and these unanticipated HTTP status codes are available to developers, and the recipes in this chapter show you how to use them effectively.

9.1   Declaring Exception Handlers in web.xml

Problem

You want to display certain servlets or JSPs when a web component throws a Java exception or generates unexpected server response codes.

Solution

Use the error-page element in *web.xml* to specify the invocation of servlets or JSPs in response to certain exceptions or HTTP status codes.

Discussion

A Java web developer should handle these types of unexpected occurrences within his web application:

- The "404 Not Found" server response code, which indicates that the user has made a mistake when typing in the URL, or requested a page that no longer exists.

- The "500 Internal Server Error" that can be raised by a servlet when it calls sendError(500) on the HttpServletResponse object.

- Runtime exceptions that are thrown by the web application and not caught by the filter, servlet, or JSP.

You configure the handling of exceptions and server response codes with the error-page element in the deployment descriptor. The error-page element in *web.xml* comes after any servlet, servlet-mapping, session-config, mime-mapping, and welcome-file-list elements, as well as before any taglib, resource-env-ref, resource-ref, or security-constraint elements. The error-page element includes a mapping between the status code or exception type, as well as the path to a web resource. This resource, which should be a servlet, JSP, or HTML file, should inform the user about what happened and provide links to other parts of the web site, depending on the nature of the error.

Example 9-1 shows a deployment descriptor for servlet API 2.3 that configures error pages.

Example 9-1. Configuring error pages in web.xml

```
<?xml version="1.0" encoding="ISO-8859-1"?>
<!DOCTYPE web-app
    PUBLIC "-//Sun Microsystems, Inc.//DTD Web Application 2.3//EN"
           "http://java.sun.com/dtd/web-application_2_3.dtd"
>

<web-app>
<!-- top of deployment descriptor, such as filter, servlet, servlet-mapping, session-
config, welcome-file elements -->

<servlet>
    <servlet-name>Error404</servlet-name>
    <servlet-class>com.jspservletcookbook.Error404</servlet-class>
</servlet>

<servlet>
    <servlet-name>Error403</servlet-name>
    <servlet-class>com.jspservletcookbook.Error403</servlet-class>
</servlet>

<servlet>
    <servlet-name>ErrorIo</servlet-name>
    <servlet-class>com.jspservletcookbook.ErrorIo</servlet-class>
</servlet>

<servlet>
    <servlet-name>ErrorServlet</servlet-name>
```

Example 9-1. Configuring error pages in web.xml (continued)

```
      <servlet-class>com.jspservletcookbook.ErrorServlet</servlet-class>
</servlet>

<servlet>
      <servlet-name>ErrorGen</servlet-name>
      <servlet-class>com.jspservletcookbook.ErrorGen</servlet-class>
</servlet>

<!-- servlet mappings -->

<servlet-mapping>
      <servlet-name>Error404</servlet-name>
      <url-pattern>/err404</url-pattern>
</servlet-mapping>

<servlet-mapping>
      <servlet-name>Error403</servlet-name>
      <url-pattern>/err403</url-pattern>
</servlet-mapping>

<servlet-mapping>
      <servlet-name>ErrorIo</servlet-name>
      <url-pattern>/errIo</url-pattern>
</servlet-mapping>

<servlet-mapping>
      <servlet-name>ErrorServlet</servlet-name>
      <url-pattern>/errServ</url-pattern>
</servlet-mapping>

<servlet-mapping>
      <servlet-name>ErrorGen</servlet-name>
      <url-pattern>/errGen</url-pattern>
</servlet-mapping>

<!-- error-code related error pages -->
<!-- Not Found -->
<error-page>
      <error-code>404</error-code>
      <location>/err404</location>
</error-page>
<!-- Forbidden -->
<error-page>
      <error-code>403</error-code>
      <location>/err403</location>
</error-page>

<!-- exception-type related error pages -->

<error-page>
      <exception-type>javax.servlet.ServletException</exception-type >
      <location>/errServ</location>
```

Example 9-1. Configuring error pages in web.xml (continued)

```
</error-page>

<error-page>
    <exception-type>java.io.IOException</exception-type >
    <location>/errIo</location>
</error-page>

<! -- all other types -->
<error-page>
    <exception-type>java.lang.Throwable</exception-type >
    <location>/errGen</location>
</error-page>

<!-- web.xml continues; tag-lib, resource-ref, security-constraint elements, etc. -->

</web-app>
```

When a servlet throws an exception, the web container searches the configurations in *web.xml* that use the exception-type element for a match with the thrown exception type. In Example 9-1, if the web application throws a ServletException, then the web container invokes the */errServ* servlet. The web container invokes the closest match in the class hierarchy. For example, if a servlet throws an IOException, the container invokes the */errIo* servlet that is mapped to the thrown exception type, not the component mapped to java.lang.Throwable—even though IOException is in the same class hierarchy as Throwable. If this application throws an IllegalStateException, the container invokes the */errGen* servlet (which is mapped to Throwable), because there is no specific error page mapping for IllegalStateException.

In the event of an HTTP response code of 403 or 404, the container invokes the web components or HTML pages mapped with the location element to those exact numbers.

 The web container must return a response code of 500 if an exception occurs that is not handled by this error-page mechanism, according to the servlet API specification.

See Also

Recipe 9.2 on creating a servlet error handler; Recipe 9.3 on sending an error from a servlet; Recipe 9.4 on sending an error from a JSP; Recipe 9.5 on using JSPs to handle errors; Recipe 9.6 on declaring in a JSP that another JSP will handle its exceptions; Chapter 1 on the deployment descriptor; the Java servlet specification, which covers error handling in Chapter SRV.9.9: *http://java.sun.com/products/servlet/index.html*.

9.2 Creating an Exception-Handling Servlet

Problem

You want to create a servlet that generates an error page.

Solution

Create a servlet that displays some information about the error, then map `exception` types and/or error codes to the servlet in the deployment descriptor.

Discussion

An error-handling servlet has access to several request attributes that it can use to describe the error. The error page also has access to the `request` and `response` objects associated with the page that generated the error. For example, the `java.lang.Throwable` object associated with any exceptions can be accessed with the following code:

```
Throwable throwable = (Throwable)
    request.getAttribute("javax.servlet.error.exception");
```

You can access the server response code with this code:

```
String status_code = ((Integer)
    request.getAttribute("javax.servlet.error.status_code")).toString( );
```

Table 9-1 shows the request attributes that an error-handling servlet has access to.

Table 9-1. Request attributes available to servlet error pages

Request attribute	Java type
javax.servlet.error.status_code	java.lang.Integer
javax.servlet.error.exception_type	java.lang.Class
javax.servlet.error.message	java.lang.String
javax.servlet.error.exception	java.lang.Throwable
javax.servlet.error.request_uri	java.lang.String
javax.servlet.error.servlet_name	java.lang.String

Example 9-2 shows the ErrorGen servlet. The web container invokes this servlet when another servlet or JSP throws an unhandled `Throwable`, according to the configuration in Example 9-1.

Example 9-2. An error-handling servlet

```
package com.jspservletcookbook;

import javax.servlet.*;
import javax.servlet.http.*;
```

Example 9-2. An error-handling servlet (continued)

```
public class ErrorGen extends HttpServlet {

 public void doPost(HttpServletRequest request,
   HttpServletResponse response)
    throws ServletException, java.io.IOException {

    //check the servlet exception
    Throwable throwable = (Throwable)
      request.getAttribute("javax.servlet.error.exception");

    String servletName = (String)
      request.getAttribute("javax.servlet.error.servlet_name");
    if (servletName == null)
      servletName = "Unknown";

    String requestUri = (String)
      request.getAttribute("javax.servlet.error.request_uri");
    if (requestUri == null)
      requestUri = "Unknown";

    response.setContentType("text/html");
    java.io.PrintWriter out = response.getWriter( );
    out.println("<html>");
    out.println("<head>");
    out.println("<title>Error page</title>");
    out.println("</head>");
    out.println("<body>");

    if (throwable == null){
      out.println("<h2>The error information is not available</h2>");
      out.println("Please return to the <a href=\"" +
        response.encodeURL("http://localhost:8080/home") +
          "\">home page</a>.");
    } else{
         out.println("<h2>Here is the error information</h2>");

  out.println(
      "The servlet name associated with throwing the exception: "+
        servletName + "<br><br>");

  out.println("The type of exception: " +
       throwable.getClass().getName( ) + "<br><br>");

  out.println("The request URI: " + requestUri + "<br><br>");
  out.println("The exception message: " + throwable.getMessage( ));
   }
    out.println("</body>");
    out.println("</html>");

  }
```

Example 9-2. An error-handling servlet (continued)

```
public void doGet(HttpServletRequest request,
  HttpServletResponse response)
   throws ServletException, java.io.IOException {

  doPost(request,response);
 }
}
```

The servlet gets a reference to the thrown exception, then displays information such as the exception's class name and the exception message. The request URI represents a partial path (such as */home/errGen.jsp*) to the component that threw the exception, which can be very helpful for debugging and information purposes. Figure 9-1 shows what the browser displays when a servlet throws an exception using Tomcat's web container.

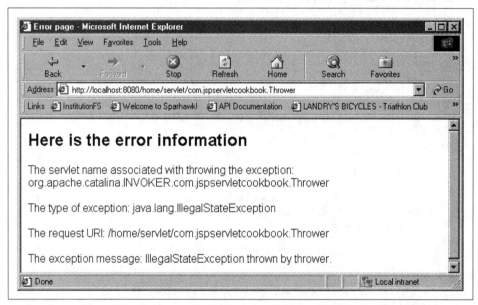

Figure 9-1. Error page HTML displayed by an error-handling servlet

Figure 9-2 shows the error page displayed by our example servlet when a JSP in the same web application throws a java.lang.ArithmeticException.

See Also

Recipe 9.1 on declaring exception handlers in the deployment descriptor; Recipe 9.3 on sending an error from a servlet; Recipe 9.4 on sending an error from a JSP; Recipe 9.5 on using JSPs to handle errors; Recipe 9.6 on declaring in a JSP that another JSP will handle its exceptions; Chapter 1 on the deployment descriptor; the

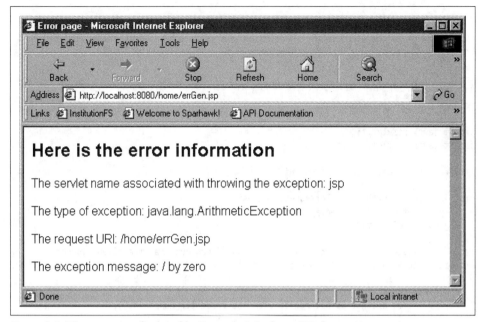

Figure 9-2. The error page displayed by Example 9-1 when a JSP throws an exception

Java servlet specification, which covers error handling in Chapter SRV.9.9: *http://java.sun.com/products/servlet/index.html*.

9.3   Sending an Error from a Servlet

Problem

You want to use a servlet to manually send a response error to the client.

Solution

Use the javax.servlet.HttpServletResponse.sendError() method.

Discussion

The javax.servlet.http.HttpServletResponse class has two versions of the sendError() method: one that takes an int parameter representing the HTTP response code (such as 500), and the other taking an int parameter and a String error message. The String parameter is used to display a message to the client if an error page is not configured for that particular response code. Example 9-3 shows the skeleton of a servlet whose commented sections describe various scenarios for sending response codes.

Use the two-parameter method version, so that a meaningful message is displayed in the event that the application has not configured an error page for a particular error code.

Example 9-3. Sending a response code from a servlet

```
package com.jspservletcookbook;

import javax.servlet.*;
import javax.servlet.http.*;

public class Sender extends HttpServlet {

 public void doPost(HttpServletRequest request,
   HttpServletResponse response) throws ServletException,
     java.io.IOException {

/* if the servlet tries to access a resource and finds out that the client is not
authorized to access it - "401 Unauthorized" */

        //response.sendError(401,
        //  "You are not authorized to view the requested component");

   /* if the servlet tries to access a resource that is forbidden for this client and there
is no further information on it - "403 Forbidden" */
        //response.sendError(403,
        //  "You are forbidden from viewing the requested component; no
        //further information");

/* if the servlet tries to access a resource that is not found given the client's provided
URL - "404 Not Found" */
        //response.sendError(404,
        //"The server could not find the requested component");
}

  public void doGet(HttpServletRequest request, HttpServletResponse response)
    throws ServletException, java.io.IOException {

    doPost(request,response);
  }
}
```

If an error page is configured for the error code that you specified in the sendError( ) method, the web container invokes the error page mapped to that error code. If the error code does not have an error page configured for it in *web.xml*, the web container generates a default HTML page containing the message you included as the String parameter to the sendError( ) method, as in Figure 9-3. The server leaves cookies and other response headers unmodified when it returns this HTML to the client.

If you call sendError( ) after already committing the response to the client (such as when the response buffer, a temporary storage location for the response data, is full and "auto-flushed"), sendError( ) throws a java.lang.IllegalStateException. You can set the buffer size with the javax.servlet.ServletResponse.setBufferSize( ) method.

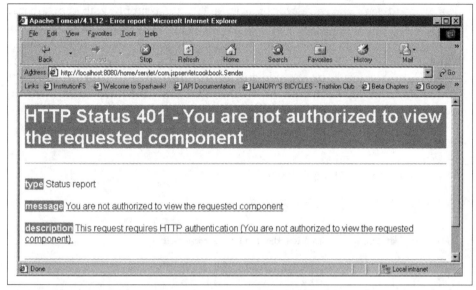

Figure 9-3. Server response to HttpServletResponse.sendError when there is no error page is configured for the error code

See Also

Recipe 9.1 on declaring exception handlers in the deployment descriptor; Recipe 9.2 on developing a servlet error handler; Recipe 9.4 on sending an error from a JSP; Recipe 9.5 on using JSPs to handle errors; Recipe 9.6 on declaring in a JSP that another JSP will handle its exceptions; Chapter 1 on the deployment descriptor; the Java servlet specification, which covers error handling in Chapter SRV.9.9: *http:// java.sun.com/products/servlet/index.html*.

9.4   Sending an Error from a JSP

Problem

You want to use a JSP to manually send a response error to a client.

Solution

Use the response implicit object and the sendError method inside a JSP scriptlet.

Discussion

If you want to send a response error from a JSP, then simply grab the response implicit object inside a scriptlet and call sendError() on it. Make sure not to call sendError() after already flushing or committing the response to the client, or the method will throw a java.lang.IllegalStateException. The JSP code in Example 9-4, which could be a standalone JSP or a fragment of a larger page, results in the display of Figure 9-3 when requested with the following query string: "?client-unauthorized=true".

Example 9-4. Using the response implicit object to send a response error from a JSP

```
<%@ taglib uri=
  "http://java.sun.com/jstl/core" prefix="c" %>

<c:if test="${param.client-unauthorized}" >

    <% response.sendError(401,
     "You are not authorized to view the requested component");
     %>

</c:if>
```

See Also

Recipe 9.1 on declaring exception handlers in the deployment descriptor; Recipe 9.2 on developing a servlet error handler; Recipe 9.3 on sending an error from a servlet; Recipe 9.5 on using JSPs to handle errors; Recipe 9.6 on declaring in a JSP that another JSP will handle its exceptions; Chapter 1 on the deployment descriptor; the Java servlet specification, which covers error handling in Chapter SRV.9.9: *http://java.sun.com/products/servlet/index.html*.

9.5   Creating an Error-Handling JSP

Problem

You want to use a JSP as your error page for both servlets and JSPs.

Solution

Create a JSP that displays information about the java.lang.Throwable reported by using the specified request attributes, such as javax.servlet.error.exception. Use the error-page attribute in *web.xml* to map certain exception types to the JSP.

Discussion

A JSP can display error information in the same manner as the servlet used in Recipe 9.2. Example 9-5 can be used as the error page for both JSPs and servlets. This sample JSP uses the JSTL and the EL to display the thrown exception's various characteristics, such as its fully qualified class name.

Example 9-5. Using a JSP as an error page

```
<%@page isErrorPage="true" %>
<%@ taglib uri="http://java.sun.com/jstl/core" prefix="c" %>
<html>
<head><title>Sorry about the error</title></head>
<body>
<h2>Sorry, We Erred Handling Your Request</h2>

<strong>Here is information about the error:</strong> <br><br>

The servlet name associated with throwing the exception:
<c:out value="${requestScope[\"javax.servlet.error.servlet_name\"]}" />
<br><br>

The type of exception:
  <c:out value=
    "${requestScope[\"javax.servlet.error.exception\"].class.name}" />
<br><br>

The request URI:
<c:out value="${requestScope[\"javax.servlet.error.request_uri\"]}" />
<br><br>

The exception message:
  <c:out value=
    "${requestScope[\"javax.servlet.error.exception\"].message}" />
</body>
</html>
```

The error page grabs the request Uniform Resource Indicator (URI), which is the servlet path beginning with the context path and not including any query string, with this code:

```
<c:out value="${requestScope[\"javax.servlet.error.request_uri\"]}" />
```

This passes the value of a request attribute named javax.servlet.error.request_uri to the c:out JSTL tag, which results in the attribute value displayed in the HTML. Make sure to escape the double quotes inside the EL phrase, as in:

```
"${requestScope[\"javax.servlet.error.request_uri\"]}"
```

The code gets information about the exception from the request attributes that are automatically created by the web container when the servlet or JSP throws an exception. For example, if you want to add the response status code to this information, then this number is available from the request attribute javax.servlet.error.status_code.

 See Table 9-1 for the complete list of these attributes.

In addition, the part of Example 9-5 that gets the class name of the exception calls getClass().getName() on the Throwable object. Figure 9-4 shows the browser display of this error page after a JSP named *errGen.jsp* generates an error.

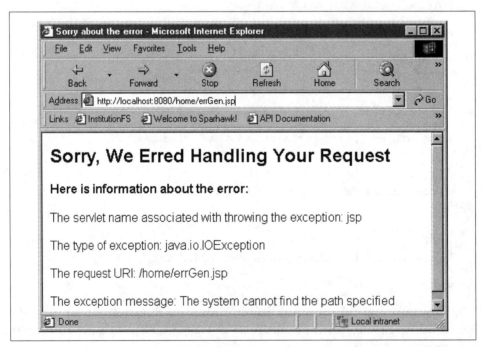

Figure 9-4. A JSP error page displays information about a thrown exception

The *web.xml* deployment descriptor uses the following element to specify that the error page of Example 9-5 should handle any `java.io.IOExceptions`:

```
<error-page>
    <exception-type>java.io.IOException</exception-type >
    <location>/errHandler.jsp</location>
</error-page>
```

Example 9-6 shows the JSP that throws the exception.

Example 9-6. A JSP that throws a java.io.IOException

```
<html>
<head><title>Exception Thrower</title></head>
<body>
<h2>Throw an IOException </h2>
 <% java.io.File file = new java.io.File(
    "z:" + System.getProperty("file.separator") + "temp");
 file.createNewFile( );%>
</body>
</html>
```

See Also

Recipe 9.1 on declaring error pages in *web.xml*; Recipe 9.2 on creating a special exception-handling servlet; Recipe 9.3 on sending an error from a servlet; Recipe 9.4 on sending an error from a JSP; Recipe 9.6 on declaring in a JSP that another JSP will handle its exceptions; Chapter 23 on using the JSTL; the JSP 2.0 specification and its Chapter JSP.1.4 on error handling: *http://java.sun.com/products/jsp/*.

9.6   Declaring a Special Exception-Handling JSP for Other JSPs

Problem

You want to declare inside of a JSP that another or external JSP will handle any thrown errors.

Solution

Set the page directive attribute `errorPage` to the special JSP error page's path in the web application. The JSP error page itself has its `page` directive attribute `isErrorPage` set to "true".

Discussion

The JSP specification allows a JSP author to declare at the top of the page that a special error-handling JSP will handle any exceptions thrown by the page that they are authoring. This design allows the encapsulation of error handling inside a specially designed JSP.

If you want to specifically target a JSP error page within JSP code, set the page directive's errorPage attribute to the target error page's location in the web application. Example 9-7 shows a JSP with a page directive declaring *errHandler.jsp* as its error page.

 This page directive declaration overrides any matching error-page configurations in *web.xml*. If this JSP throws an java.io.IOException and *web.xml* has an exception-type attribute for that exception, the web container invokes the error page specified by the page directive instead of any URI specified in the *web.xml* configuration.

Example 9-7. A JSP that specifies another JSP as its error page

```
<%@page errorPage="/errHandler.jsp" %>
<html>
<head><title>Exception Thrower</title></head>
<body>
<h2>Throw an IOException </h2>
 <%
 java.io.File file = new java.io.File("z:" + System.getProperty("file.separator") +
 "temp");
 file.createNewFile(); %>
</body>
</html>
```

The error page has access to an exception implicit object that represents the java.lang.Throwable object associated with the error.

Example 9-8 uses the JSTL and the EL to show information about the exception. See Chapter 23 if you have not yet been introduced to the JSTL or the EL.

Example 9-8. A JSP error page named errHandler.jsp

```
<%@page isErrorPage="true" %>
<%@ taglib uri="http://java.sun.com/jstl/core" prefix="c" %>
<html>
<head><title>Sorry about the error</title></head>
<body>
<h2>Sorry, We Erred Handling Your Request</h2>
<strong>Here is information about the error:</strong> <br><br>

The servlet name associated with throwing the exception:
<%-- JSP 2.0 usage only!
<c:out value="${pageContext.errorData.servletName}" />  --%>
<br><br>
The type of exception:
  <c:out value="${pageContext.exception.class.name}" />
<br><br>
The request URI:
```

Example 9-8. A JSP error page named errHandler.jsp (continued)

```
<%-- JSP 2.0 usage only!
<c:out value="${pageContext.errorData.requestURI}" /> --%>
<br><br>
The exception message:
  <c:out value="${pageContext.exception.message}" />
 </body>
</html>
```

Figure 9-5 shows the *errHandler.jsp* page displayed in a browser, after the JSP in Example 9-7 has thrown a java.io.IOException while trying to create a file on a phantom disk. The commented-out sections of Example 9-8 show the use of the javax.servlet.jsp.ErrorData class, which allows you to use the EL to get more information about the error. For example, you can get the request URI (as in */home/ errGen.jsp*) of the offending JSP with this syntax:

```
${pageContext.errorData.requestURI}
```

However, this usage fails in a JSP 1.2 container such as Tomcat 4.1.12, because it was introduced in JSP 2.0. This is why there is an empty space in the browser page after "The request URI:."

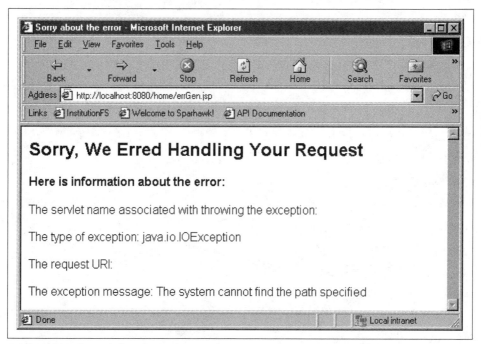

Figure 9-5. A JSP error page using the page directive attributes errorPage and isErrorPage

You can also use this syntax to get access to the java.lang.Throwable object in the error page:

```
<c:out value="${requestScope[
    \"javax.servlet.jsp.jspException\"]}" />
```

See Also

Recipe 9.1 on declaring error pages in *web.xml*; Recipe 9.2 on creating a special exception-handling servlet; Recipe 9.3 on sending an error from a servlet; Recipe 9.4 on sending an error from a JSP; Recipe 9.5 on using JSPs to handle errors; Chapter 23 on using the JSTL; Chapter JSP.1.4 of the JSP 2.0 specification on error handling: *http://java.sun.com/products/jsp/*.

CHAPTER 10

Reading and Setting Cookies

10.0 Introduction

In a typical visit to a web site, a user sends multiple requests for resources to a web server. If a web page contains many images (and most do!), then requesting the single web page involves one HTTP request for the HTML code and other template text (such as headlines and phrases), followed by separate requests for each image the web page contains. Future requests for the same page often return versions of these text and images that are cached on the client's computer for the sake of efficiency, depending on whether the fetched resources permit caching. At any rate, the server views each HTTP request for these web resources as separate and discrete from the other requests. Without the use of additional protocols, the server does not have a mechanism for managing *client state*, such as the progress of a web user through a questionnaire or storefront. Being able to logically relate one or more web requests as a single user session is where cookies come in.

A *cookie* is a small piece of information on a user's computer that a web server can use to identify that user the next time he visits the site. When a user initially visits the cookie-enabled site, the server responds with an extra response header that looks like:

```
Set-Cookie: mycookie=1051565332678; Domain=.myorg.com;
Expires=Tue, 29-Apr-2003 07:42:12 GMT
```

Consequently, when the user visits the same site, his browser sends an extra request header that contains the cookie associated with that web location. Here is what the request headers look like when the client returns to the site that previously set the cookie; since the servlet container is Tomcat 4.1.12, the Cookie request header also includes a name/value pair for the session-related cookie (JSESSIONID):

```
GET /home/cookie HTTP/1.1
Accept: image/gif, image/x-xbitmap, image/jpeg, image/pjpeg, application/msword,
application/vnd.ms-powerpoint, application/vnd.ms-excel, application/pdf, */*
Accept-Language: en-us
Accept-Encoding: gzip, deflate
```

```
User-Agent: Mozilla/4.0 (compatible; MSIE 5.5; Windows NT 4.0)
Host: localhost:9000
Connection: Keep-Alive
Cookie: JSESSIONID=F80F0F571FDE4873CFF3FF0B842D4938; mycookie=1051610231064
```

A cookie contains a name and a value; the cookie can also have several other optional attribute/value pairs, which are separated by semicolons:

Domain

> Specifies the domain to which this cookie will be sent in future requests, as in *Domain=.jspservletcookbook.com.* The default value of this optional attribute is the hostname of the domain that has sent the Set-Cookie header.

Path

> Further delineates the part of the web site that, when requested, is sent the cookie by the client. Most cookies give this attribute a value of /. For example, if only the *customer* context path should receive the cookie, then the Set-Cookie header would include the *path=/customer* attribute/value pair. The client would not send the cookie value when making any requests to the domain that do not include the */customer* context path.

Expires

> Specifies the maximum amount of time the user's browser should keep the cookie. This attribute is a date string representing a future date. If Expires specifies a past date, then the cookie is deleted. The Java Cookie API manages this attribute by calling the Cookie object's setMaxAge( ) method (see Recipe 10.1).

Version

> An optional value of 0 for Netscape's preliminary specification and 1 for the RFC 2109 document.

Secure

> True if the cookie can be sent only over a secure connection such as HTTPS.

Comment

> May have as a value a description of the cookie's purpose.

 A browser is expected to support 20 cookies for each web server, 300 cookies total, and may limit cookie size to 4 KB each, according to the javax.servlet.http.Cookie API documentation. The cookie name and value combine to represent the 4-KB limit, according to the Netscape preliminary specification. A typical cookie is far less than 4 KB in size.

The user can also disable cookies, so that his browser does not save any of the cookies in a web-server response. For example, in Netscape 7.1, the menu combination Edit → Preferences → Privacy & Security → Cookies allows you to prevent the acceptance of cookies by choosing the "Disable cookies" radio button. In this case, the web developer uses "URL rewriting" for any clients that have disabled cookies (see Recipes 11.7 and 11.8).

The Java servlet API abstracts a cookie as an object of type javax.servlet.http. Cookie. The recipes in this chapter show how to create new cookies, as well as read or alter existing cookies, with both servlets and JSPs.

10.1 Setting a Cookie with a Servlet

Problem

You want to set a cookie using a servlet.

Solution

Create the javax.servlet.http.Cookie object in a servlet, then set the cookie on a user's machine with the javax.servlet.http.HttpServletResponse.addCookie(Cookie cookie) method.

Discussion

Inside the servlet, create the Cookie by instantiating a new Cookie and calling its setter (or mutator) methods. The Cookie constructor includes the name and value for the cookie:

```
Cookie cookie = new Cookie("mycookie","the1cookie");
```

Example 10-1 creates a cookie and sets its path attribute (as in: cookie. setPath(*String path*)) to the name of the context path (as in */home*). With this path setting, the client will not send the cookie to the server unless the client requests resources within the specified context path. The code uses HttpServletRequest. getContextPath( ) to provide the value for the cookie's path attribute.

Example 10-1. A servlet that sets a cookie and displays some cookie information

```
package com.jspservletcookbook;

import javax.servlet.*;
import javax.servlet.http.*;

public class CookieServlet extends HttpServlet {

  public void doGet(HttpServletRequest request,
    HttpServletResponse response) throws ServletException,
    java.io.IOException {

      Cookie cookie = null;
      //Get an array of Cookies associated with this domain
      Cookie[] cookies = request.getCookies( );
      boolean newCookie = false;

      //Get the 'mycookie' Cookie if it exists
```

Example 10-1. A servlet that sets a cookie and displays some cookie information (continued)

```
    if (cookies != null){
        for (int i = 0; i < cookies.length; i++){
            if (cookies[i].getName( ).equals("mycookie")){
                cookie = cookies[i];
            }
        }//end for
    }//end if

    if (cookie == null){
        newCookie=true;

        //Get the cookie's Max-Age from a context-param element
        //If the 'cookie-age' param is not set properly
        //then set the cookie to a default of -1, 'never expires'
        int maxAge;
        try{
            maxAge = new Integer(
                getServletContext( ).getInitParameter(
                "cookie-age")).intValue( );
        } catch (Exception e) {

            maxAge = -1;
        }//try

        //Create the Cookie object

        cookie = new Cookie("mycookie",""+getNextCookieValue( ));
        cookie.setPath(request.getContextPath( ));
        cookie.setMaxAge(maxAge);
        response.addCookie(cookie);

    }//end if
    // get some info about the cookie
    response.setContentType("text/html");
    java.io.PrintWriter out = response.getWriter( );

    out.println("<html>");
    out.println("<head>");
    out.println("<title>Cookie info</title>");
    out.println("</head>");
    out.println("<body>");

    out.println(
    "<h2> Information about the cookie named \"mycookie\"</h2>");

    out.println("Cookie value: "+cookie.getValue( )+"<br>");
    if (newCookie){
        out.println("Cookie Max-Age: "+cookie.getMaxAge( )+"<br>");
        out.println("Cookie Path: "+cookie.getPath( )+"<br>");
    }

        out.println("</body>");
```

```
    out.println("</html>");
}
private long getNextCookieValue( ){

    //returns the number of milleseconds since Jan 1, 1970
    return new java.util.Date().getTime( );

}

public void doPost(HttpServletRequest request,
  HttpServletResponse response) throws ServletException,
    java.io.IOException {

    doGet(request,response);
}

}
```

Example 10-1 uses Cookie.setMaxAge(int age) to specify when the cookie will expire or be deleted by the browser. The method parameter represents the maximum number of seconds that the cookie will live on the user's machine after it is created. The example code gets the value for this method from a context-param element in *web. xml*, which allows a web developer to configure or optionally change this value in the deployment descriptor. Here is an example of a context-param element that provides a value for a cookie's age:

```
<context-param>
    <param-name>cookie-age</param-name>
    <param-value>31536000</param-value>
</context-param>
```

For example, if you wanted the cookie to linger for one year ($365 \times 24 \times 60 \times 60$ seconds), you could use this code:

```
cookie.setMaxAge(31536000);
```

Users can delete a cookie from their machine, regardless of the maximum age that you have created for it. Some browsers provide a window into a user's cookies, with features that allow the user to remove one or more cookies. Don't assume that because you set a maximum age, the cookie will always be available on users' machines.

Example 10-1 also checks for the existence of a cookie of the same name that the code plans to give the new cookie (*mycookie*). If the user has not already sent the *mycookie* cookie, then the servlet sets a new cookie and displays some of the cookie's values afterward.

Figure 10-1 shows the servlet output.

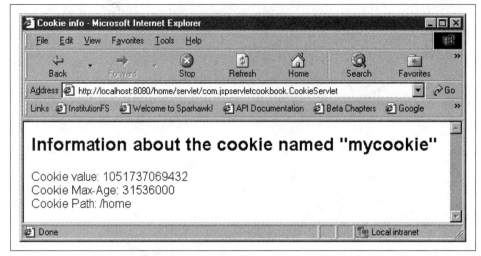

Figure 10-1. A servlet shows information about a new cookie

The cookie value is arbitrarily set to a String showing a large number, just to demonstrate how to provide the value for a cookie. As many cookies need unique values, you could use a method whereby the user's email address or unique database ID is encoded and then used as the cookie value.

See Also

Recipe 10.3 on setting a cookie with a JSP; Recipe 10.4 on using a servlet to read cookies; Recipe 10.5 on reading cookie values with a JSP; Recipe 10.6 on altering or removing an existing cookie; the RFC 2109 document dealing with cookies: *ftp://ftp. rfc-editor.org/in-notes/rfc2109.txt*; Netscape's preliminary specification for cookies: *http://wp.netscape.com/newsref/std/cookie_spec.html*; the Java Cookie API: *http://java. sun.com/j2ee/1.4/docs/api/javax/servlet/http/Cookie.html*.

10.2   Creating an Array from All of the Request's Cookies

Problem

You want to store all of the cookies contained by a client's request in a Cookie array.

Solution

Use the HttpServletRequest.getCookies( ) method, which returns an array of javax. servlet.http.Cookie objects.

Discussion

To create an array of Cookies representing all of the cookies included in a request, use the HttpServletRequest.getCookies( ) method. You can then access the name and value of a cookie by calling the Cookie class's getName( ) and getValue( ) methods.

The code for accessing an array of Cookies looks like Example 10-2.

Example 10-2. Creating a Cookie array

```
//servlet's doGet method

public void doGet(HttpServletRequest request,
  HttpServletResponse response) throws ServletException,
  java.io.IOException {

    Cookie cookie = null;

    //Get an array of Cookies associated with this domain
    Cookie[] cookies = request.getCookies( );

    //Check for a null value, then do something with any Cookies
    if (cookies != null){ //read each Cookie value
    }
//rest of the servlet
```

Once a cookie has already been created, the next time the user sends the cookie as a request header, the only information you can extract from the Cookie object is its name and value. You will not be able to derive the cookie's maximum age from the request header, because all the header will contain is the Cookie object: header name, then the name and value of the cookie.

See Also

Recipe 10.1 on setting a cookie with a servlet; Recipe 10.3 on setting a cookie with a JSP; Recipe 10.4 on using a servlet to read cookies; Recipe 10.5 on reading cookie values with a JSP; Recipe 10.6 on altering or removing an existing cookie; the RFC 2109 document dealing with cookies: *ftp://ftp.rfc-editor.org/in-notes/rfc2109.txt*; Netscape's preliminary specification for cookies: *http://wp.netscape.com/newsref/std/cookie_spec.html*; the Java Cookie API: *http://java.sun.com/j2ee/1.4/docs/api/javax/servlet/http/Cookie.html*.

10.3   Setting a Cookie with a JSP

Problem

You want to use a JSP to set a cookie on a client.

Solution

Wrap a JavaBean around the servlet API for creating cookies. Then use the bean in the JSP with the jsp:useBean standard action.

Discussion

A JSP can use a JavaBean to create the cookie and set the cookie on the client. Example 10-3 creates an instance of a JavaBean of type com.jspservletcookbook. CookieBean using the jsp:useBean standard action. Then the JSP sets a few bean properties. The bean will pass through the property values to the cookie that it is generating for the JSP. The JSP uses jsp:setProperty to set the following cookie properties:

- The cookie name (*bakedcookie* in the code).
- The maximum number of seconds the browser will hold on to the cookie (roughly one year in Example 10-2). This number is converted to a readable future date for the cookie's Expires attribute.
- The path on the server associated with this cookie. Once the JSP has sent this cookie to the client, the client will return the associated cookie only in the request headers for requests that contain the specified context path (such as */home*). For example, if the cookie is set by the JSP file to */home/cookieSet.jsp*, only requests for resources in */home* will include a Cookie header.

Example 10-3. A JSP that sends a cookie to a client

```
<jsp:useBean id="cookieBean" class="com.jspservletcookbook.CookieBean" />
<jsp:setProperty name="cookieBean" property="name"  value="bakedcookie" />
<%-- set 'Expires' attribute to about one year from now --%>
<jsp:setProperty name="cookieBean" property="maxAge"  value=
  "<%= (365*24*60*60) %>" />
<jsp:setProperty name="cookieBean" property="path"  value="<%= request.getContextPath( )
%>" />
<jsp:setProperty name="cookieBean" property="cookieHeader"  value="<%= response %>" />
<html>
<head><title>Cookie Maker</title></head>
<body>
<h2>Here is information about the new cookie</h2>
Name: <jsp:getProperty name="cookieBean" property="name" /><br>
Value: <jsp:getProperty name="cookieBean" property="value" /><br>
Path: <jsp:getProperty name="cookieBean" property="path" />
</body>
</html>
```

The JSP passes along the HttpServletResponse object to its wrapper bean, so that the bean can call response.addCookie(Cookie cookie) to send the client the new cookie.

The `response` object is passed to the bean using this code (see the `setCookieHeader( )` method in Example 10-4):

```
<jsp:setProperty name="cookieBean" property="cookieHeader"  value=
    "<%= response %>" />
```

The bottom of the JSP displays some of the new cookie's values. Figure 10-2 shows the JSP's output in a web browser. Repeatedly requesting the JSP will overwrite the existing cookie with a new one.

Figure 10-2. A JSP shows information about a new cookie

Example 10-4 shows the code for the `CookieBean` itself, which is rather lengthy due to all the getter and setter methods.

This JavaBean class must be placed in the *WEB-INF/classes* directory of the web application (including a directory structure that matches the bean's package name) so that the web container can load the class. The bean could also be archived in a JAR file that is placed in *WEB-INF/lib*; however, the JAR would still have to contain a directory structure that matches the bean's package name.

You can set the cookie value in the JSP (which is not done in Example 10-3) by calling the bean's `setValue(String value)` method via `jsp:setProperty`:

```
<jsp:setProperty name="cookieBean" property="value"  value="newvalue" />
```

The bean has to import the `Cookie` and `HttpServletResponse` classes, because it uses them to make the new cookie, then send the cookie to the client. Example 10-4 wraps its own methods around some of the `Cookie` class methods, such as `setValue( )` and `setMaxAge( )`.

Example 10-4. A JavaBean for making cookies

```java
package com.jspservletcookbook;

import javax.servlet.http.HttpServletResponse;
import javax.servlet.http.Cookie;

public class CookieBean {

  private Cookie cookie = null;

public CookieBean( ){}

//set the cookie name
public void setName(String name){

    if (name == null || (name.equals("")))
        throw new IllegalArgumentException(
          "Invalid cookie name set in: "+getClass().getName( ));

    cookie = new Cookie(name,""+new java.util.Date().getTime( ));
}

//set the cookie value
public void setValue(String value){

 if (value == null || (value.equals("")))
        throw new IllegalArgumentException(
          "Invalid cookie value set in: "+getClass().getName( ));

    if (cookie != null)
        cookie.setValue(value);
}

public void setMaxAge(int maxAge){

    if (cookie != null)
        cookie.setMaxAge(maxAge);
}

public void setPath(String path){

 if (path == null || (path.equals("")))
        throw new IllegalArgumentException(
          "Invalid cookie path set in: "+getClass().getName( ));

    if (cookie != null)
        cookie.setPath(path);
}

public void setCookieHeader(HttpServletResponse response){

    if (response == null )
        throw new IllegalArgumentException(
```

Example 10-4. A JavaBean for making cookies (continued)

```
            "Invalid HttpServletResponse set in: "+getClass().getName());
    if (cookie != null)
        response.addCookie(cookie);
}

public String getName(){

    if (cookie != null)
        return cookie.getName();
    else
        return "unavailable";

}

public String getValue(){

    if (cookie != null)
        return cookie.getValue();
    else
        return "unavailable";

}

public String getPath(){

    if (cookie != null)
        return cookie.getPath();
    else
        return "unavailable";

}
}
```

If the JSP fails to use jsp:setProperty to call the bean's setCookieHeader(HttpServletResponse response) method, then the cookie is created but never included in the response headers sent to the client. In this design, you allow the user to set some optional cookie attributes (such as Path) before she explicitly sends the cookie as part of the response.

See Also

Recipe 10.1 on setting a cookie with a servlet; Recipe 10.2 on creating an array from all of the request's cookies; Recipe 10.4 on using a servlet to read cookies; Recipe 10.5 on reading cookie values with a JSP; Recipe 10.6 on altering or removing an existing cookie; the RFC 2109 document dealing with cookies: *ftp://ftp.rfc-editor.org/in-notes/rfc2109.txt*; Netscape's preliminary specification for cookies: *http://wp.netscape.com/newsref/std/cookie_spec.html*; the Java Cookie API: *http://java.sun.com/j2ee/1.4/docs/api/javax/servlet/http/Cookie.html*.

10.4   Reading Cookie Values with a Servlet

Problem

You want to read cookie values from a client using a servlet.

Solution

Create a Java array of javax.servlet.http.Cookie objects by calling the HttpServletRequest.getCookies( ) method. Then cycle through the array, accessing each cookie and value as needed.

Discussion

The web user will send cookies to a web site only if the user originally received Set-Cookie headers from that domain. In addition, if the cookie was set with a Path attribute specifying a context path, then the servlet can access the cookie only if the servlet is also associated with the context path. As a result, always test the return value of the request.getCookies( ) method (which returns an array of Cookie objects) to see if it is null, indicating that the user has not sent any cookies, before operating upon it.

Example 10-5 displays the value of any found cookies in a web browser. The CookieReader class uses the javax.servlet.http.Cookie.getName( ) and getValue( ) methods in order to display this information.

Example 10-5. A cookie-reading servlet

```
package com.jspservletcookbook;

import javax.servlet.*;
import javax.servlet.http.*;

public class CookieReader extends HttpServlet {

  public void doGet(HttpServletRequest request,
    HttpServletResponse response) throws ServletException,
    java.io.IOException {

      Cookie cookie = null;
      //Get an array of Cookies associated with this domain
      Cookie[] cookies = request.getCookies();
      boolean hasCookies = false;

      //if cookies contains an array and not a null value,
      //then we can display information about the cookies.
       if (cookies != null)
          hasCookies = true;
```

Example 10-5. A cookie-reading servlet (continued)

```java
        // display the name/value of each cookie
        response.setContentType("text/html");
        java.io.PrintWriter out = response.getWriter( );

        out.println("<html>");
        out.println("<head>");
        out.println("<title>Cookie information</title>");
        out.println("</head>");
        out.println("<body>");
        if (hasCookies){
            out.println(
              "<h2> The name and value of each found cookie</h2>");

            for (int i = 0; i < cookies.length; i++){
                cookie = cookies[i];
                out.println(
                  "Name of cookie #"+(i + 1)+": "+cookie.getName( )+"<br>");
                out.println(
                  "Value of cookie #"+(i + 1)+": "+
                    cookie.getValue( )+"<br><br>");
        }//for

        } else {
            out.println(
              "<h2> This request did not include any cookies</h2>");
        }
        out.println("</body>");
        out.println("</html>");}

    public void doPost(HttpServletRequest request,
      HttpServletResponse response) throws ServletException,
        java.io.IOException {

        doGet(request,response);
    }
}
```

The javax.servlet.http.Cookie class is an abstraction of a cookie that has getter and setter methods for a cookie's attributes, such as its name, value, path, and secure attributes. However, when you retrieve a cookie, you can only get its name and value, because this is the only information that the client includes in the request header. The Cookie request header looks like:

```
Cookie: JSESSIONID=F80F0F571FDE4873CFF3FF0B842D4938; mycookie=1051610231064
```

For example, calling Cookie.getPath( ) on a retrieved cookie will return null, even if the cookie was originally set with a valid path attribute, such as */mypath*. You can only access these values in the servlet or JSP that creates the cookie object in the first place (see Recipes 10.1 and 10.3).

Figure 10-3 shows how a web browser displays this servlet's output.

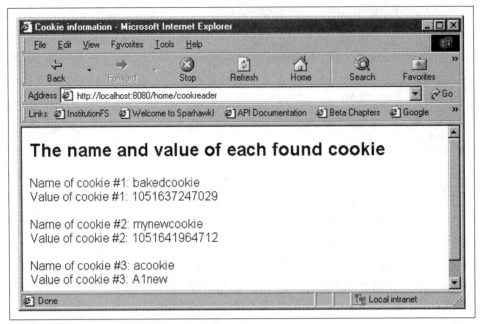

Figure 10-3. A servlet displays cookie information

See Also

Recipe 10.1 on setting a cookie with a servlet; Recipe 10.2 on creating an array from all of the request's cookies; Recipe 10.3 on setting a cookie with a JSP; Recipe 10.5 on reading cookie values with a JSP; Recipe 10.6 on altering or removing an existing cookie; the RFC 2109 document dealing with cookies: *ftp://ftp.rfc-editor.org/in-notes/ rfc2109.txt*; Netscape's preliminary specification for cookies: *http://wp.netscape.com/ newsref/std/cookie_spec.html*; the Java Cookie API: *http://java.sun.com/j2ee/1.4/docs/ api/javax/servlet/http/Cookie.html*.

10.5   Reading Cookie Values with a JSP

Problem

You want to read cookie values with a JSP.

Solution

Use the JSTL and its cookie implicit object to display the name and value of any cookies found in the request.

Discussion

The JSTL and its EL have a cookie implicit object (a variable that is automatically available to JSP or EL code) that you can use in JSPs to display any cookie names and values. For more information on the JSTL and EL, see Chapter 23.

You can access the cookie implicit object in JSP code this way:

```
${cookie}
```

This implicit object evaluates to a java.util.Map type whose values you can iterate over with the c:forEach JSTL tag. Each iteration of c:forEach returns a java.util. Map.Entry, which encapsulates a key/value pair. The key is the name of the cookie; the value is a javax.servlet.http.Cookie object.

Example 10-6 uses this code to retrieve a Cookie object from the Map of available cookies:

```
<c:forEach var="cookieVal" items="${cookie}">
```

The var attribute of c:forEach contains a Map.Entry object whose key is the cookie name; the value is the Cookie object. The code uses c:out tags to display the cookie names and values in the JSP. This odd syntax displays the value of each cookie:

```
<c:out value="${cookieVal.value.value}" />
```

The code cookieVal.value evaluates to the javax.servlet.http.Cookie object. The full phrase ${cookieVal.value.value} is the equivalent of calling Cookie.getValue( ).

Example 10-6. A JSP that reads cookie names and values

```
<%@ taglib uri="http://java.sun.com/jstl/core" prefix="c" %>
<html>
<body>
<%-- check whether the request contains any cookies --%>
<c:choose>
  <c:when test="${empty cookie}" >
  <h2>We did not find any cookies in the request</h2>
  </c:when>
<c:otherwise>

<h2>The name and value of each found cookie</h2>

<c:forEach var="cookieVal" items="${cookie}">
<strong>Cookie name:</strong> <c:out value="${cookieVal.key}" /><br>
<strong>Cookie value:</strong> <c:out value=
    "${cookieVal.value.value}" /><br><br>
</c:forEach>
</c:otherwise>
</c:choose>

</body>
</html>
```

Figure 10-4 shows the JSP displaying the available cookie information.

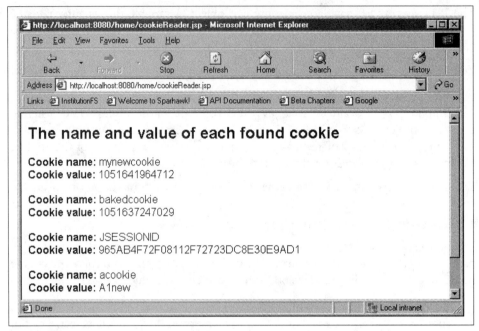

Figure 10-4. Output of the cookieReader.jsp page

 Make sure to include the taglib directive for the JSTL core library at the top of your JSP, so that you can use the JSTL tags to view any cookie values:

```
<%@ taglib uri=
"http://java.sun.com/jstl/core" prefix="c" %>
```

Use uri=http://java.sun.com/jsp/jstl/core when using JSTL 1.1

See Also

Recipe 10.1 on setting a cookie with a servlet; Recipe 10.2 on creating an array from all of the request's cookies; Recipe 10.3 on setting a cookie with a JSP; Recipe 10.4 on using a servlet to read cookies; Recipe 10.6 on altering or removing an existing cookie; the RFC 2109 document dealing with cookies: *ftp://ftp.rfc-editor.org/in-notes/rfc2109.txt*; Netscape's preliminary specification for cookies: *http://wp.netscape.com/newsref/std/cookie_spec.html*; The Java Cookie API: *http://java.sun.com/j2ee/1.4/docs/api/javax/servlet/http/Cookie.html*.

10.6   Altering or Removing a Cookie That Has Already Been Set

Problem

You want to overwrite or remove an existing cookie.

Solution

Send a cookie with the same name and path as an existing cookie to overwrite the existing cookie. To delete a cookie, send a cookie with the same name and path but set the Expires attribute to a date in the past.

Discussion

You can overwrite a cookie and optionally provide different values for its attributes (such as the cookie value) by including a cookie in a response header that has the same name and path as an existing cookie. For example, imagine a servlet has set a cookie on the client with the following response header:

```
Set-Cookie: newcookie=1051642031398; Expires=Wed, 28-Apr-2004 18:47:11 GMT; Path=/home
```

This cookie can be overwritten on the client by changing its cookie value, but not the name and path:

```
Set-Cookie: newcookie=A1lnew; Expires=Wed, 28-Apr-2004 18:52:50 GMT; Path=/home
```

This response header will replace *newcookie* with a cookie of the same name. The new version has a new value (A1lnew) and an Expires attribute value.

Deleting a Cookie

You can delete a cookie by sending a response header to the client with the same cookie name and Path value, but with an Expires attribute value that represents a date in the past. With Java's Cookie API, you simply call the javax.servlet.http. Cookie.setMaxAge( ) method with an argument value of 0. Example 10-7 is the JSP of Recipe 10.2. This time the JSP is deleting *mycookie* by setting the maxAge property to 0 using jsp:setProperty.

Example 10-7. Deleting an existing cookie

```
<jsp:useBean id="cookieBean" class="com.jspservletcookbook.CookieBean" />
<jsp:setProperty name="cookieBean" property="name"  value="mycookie" />
<%-- delete the cookie by calling Cookie.setMaxAge(0) --%>
<jsp:setProperty name="cookieBean" property="maxAge"  value="0" />
<jsp:setProperty name="cookieBean" property="value"  value="finished" />
<jsp:setProperty name="cookieBean" property="path"  value=
    "<%= request.getContextPath( ) %>" />
```

Example 10-7. Deleting an existing cookie (continued)

```
<jsp:setProperty name="cookieBean" property="cookieHeader" value=
    "<%= response %>" />
<%-- rest of JSP continues --%>
```

Cookies can be deleted only by a Set-Cookie response header emanating from the same domain that created the cookie, with the same cookie name and Path attribute. Here is what the response header from the deleting JSP looks like:

```
HTTP/1.1 200 OK
Content-Type: text/html;charset=ISO-8859-1
Set-Cookie: mycookie=finished; Expires=Thu, 01-Jan-1970 00:00:10 GMT; Path=/home
Transfer-Encoding: chunked
Date: Tue, 29 Apr 2003 19:18:59 GMT
Server: Apache Coyote/1.0
```

Note that the Expires attribute value is a date in the past. As a result, the client will no longer send the *mycookie* cookie in its request headers when it makes a request to the same domain at the */home* context path. However, it may send other cookies (with different names) that were created during prior visits to the same domain and context path.

> The browser user can delete a cookie from his machine anytime he wants, so always plan accordingly.

See Also

Recipe 10.1 on setting a cookie with a servlet; Recipe 10.2 on creating an array from all of the request's cookies; Recipe 10.3 on setting a cookie with a JSP; Recipe 10.4 on using a servlet to read cookies; Recipe 10.5 on reading cookie values with a JSP; the RFC 2109 document dealing with cookies: *ftp://ftp.rfc-editor.org/in-notes/ rfc2109.txt*; Netscape's preliminary specification for cookies: *http://wp.netscape.com/ newsref/std/cookie_spec.html*; the Java Cookie API: *http://java.sun.com/j2ee/1.4/docs/ api/javax/servlet/http/Cookie.html*.

CHAPTER 11

Session Tracking

11.0 Introduction

This chapter describes how to monitor sessions in servlets and JSPs. A *session* represents an interaction between a web user and a web application. The Hypertext Transfer Protocol (HTTP) is a stateless protocol, meaning that it is not designed to maintain state, or the progress of a single user as she interacts with a web server by exchanging HTTP requests and responses. Each request for a JSP or servlet, at least from the HTTP server's point of view, is considered separate from other requests and not associated with the same user. Many web applications, however, need to follow a user's progress step by step throughout the application, to keep track of her purchased items and/or preferences.

For example, when a user buys books at Amazon.com, the web site monitors what is added to or removed from the customer's shopping cart and uses this information during the checkout and payment process. In addition, Amazon.com shows users which books they have looked at during their current session. Sequential visits by a single user to an e-commerce site like this are considered parts of one session.

Web applications commonly use cookies in order to implement sessions. All servlet containers have to support the use of cookies to track sessions, according to the Servlet v2.3 and 2.4 specifications. A *cookie* is a small piece of information that is stored by the client web browser in response to a response header issued by the web server. Cookies are described in more detail in Chapter 10, but since they are central to the session concept, I include a brief overview of their use in session tracking here.

When a user requests a page from a web server, the server responds with a collection of name/value pairs called *response headers*, along with the HTML response. These headers may include one labeled Set-Cookie, which requests that the client store some state information locally. The only required element of the Set-Cookie HTTP response header is the cookie name and value. The cookie may include other pieces of information separated by semicolons. The cookie that Java web containers set in order to implement session tracking looks like jsessionid=*cookie-value*, where *cookie-value* is usually a long numeric string of bytes using hexadecimal notation. According to the servlet specification v2.3, this cookie's name must be JSESSIONID. Some web containers generate the name in lowercase, however, like Tomcat. A typical session-related cookie looks like the following:

    jsessionid=3CAF7CD0A0BFF5076B390CCD24FD8F0D

The cookie value represents the session ID. This ID uniquely identifies the user for the period when he is making requests to the web server. For example, if 10 users are interacting with the web application at the same time, the web server assigns them 10 unique session IDs. Additionally, if a person sits down at his PC and connects with the web application using Internet Explorer, then moves over to a connected laptop and opens up Safari to the same web application, those browsers will be associated with two different session IDs. The web server does not have any way of knowing that the same person is interacting with the web application from two different browsers at the same time, particularly if he is connecting from behind a proxy server. However, as long as the user works with a single browser and that user's session has not yet timed out, a web server can track that user's actions, and associate them as one session.

Disabled Cookies

What if the user blocks cookies? Web browsers typically allow the disabling of cookies in the user preferences. Servers may also use the Secure Sockets Layer (SSL), which has a built-in session-tracking mechanism. In addition, URL rewriting is a common fallback method of session tracking. URL rewriting involves adding the session ID as a path parameter to the URL when linking from one page to the next, so that the next page has access (without cookies) to the session ID. These URLs look like this:

    /home/default.jsp;jsessionid=3CAF7CD0A0BFF5076B390CCD24FD8F0D

As most page requests in everyday web use are not made using SSL, you should code your session tracking–related web components to accommodate URL rewriting.

11.1 Setting the Session Timeout in web.xml

Problem

You want to configure a timeout period for the web application in the deployment descriptor.

Solution

Create a session-config element in *web.xml*.

Discussion

The length of time that a session lasts before the server invalidates the session and unbinds any of its objects is an important component of your web application. In Tomcat 4.1.x, the default timeout period for a session is 30 minutes. If any requests that are associated with the session have been inactive for that period, the session times out. If the user decides to return to the web application after 30 minutes, using the same browser, then a new session is created for him. Example 11-1 shows how to set your own timeout period for sessions.

Example 11-1. Configuring the session timeout

```
<?xml version="1.0" encoding="ISO-8859-1"?>
<!DOCTYPE web-app
    PUBLIC "-//Sun Microsystems, Inc.//DTD Web Application 2.3//EN"
            "http://java.sun.com/dtd/web-application_2_3.dtd"
>

<web-app>

<!-- filter, listener, servlet, and servlet-mapping elements precede session-config -->

  <session-config>
    <session-timeout>15</session-timeout>
  </session-config>

</web-app>
```

Place one nested session-timeout element within the session-config. The timeout is expressed as minutes, and overrides the default timeout (which is 30 minutes in Tomcat, for example). However, the HttpSession.getMaxInactiveInterval( ) method in a servlet returns the timeout period for that session in *seconds*; if your session is configured in *web.xml* for 15 minutes, getMaxInactiveInterval( ) returns 900.

Another way to configure a timeout value for a servlet is to use the init-param element in *web.xml*, as shown in Example 11-2.

Example 11-2. Adding an init-param to a servlet to set a session timeout interval

```
<servlet>
  <servlet-name>Cart</servlet-name>
  <servlet-class>com.jspservletcookbook.TimeoutSession</servlet-class>
  <init-param>
    <param-name>timeout</param-name>
    <param-value>600</param-value>
  </init-param>
</servlet>
```

The servlet element in this web application's *web.xml* file has a nested init-param, which creates a parameter called timeout. The Cart servlet takes the parameter value

(600 seconds, equivalent to 10 minutes) and passes it to the session.
setMaxInactiveInterval(int seconds) method. Example 11-3 shows the doGet()
method of the servlet, which sets the session timeout variable to the configured
parameter value.

Example 11-3. Using init parameters to set a servlet's session timeout

```java
public void doGet(HttpServletRequest request,
  HttpServletResponse response)
    throws ServletException, java.io.IOException {

      response.setContentType("text/html");
      java.io.PrintWriter out = response.getWriter();

      HttpSession session = request.getSession();

      //initially set to default timeout interval
      int _default = session.getMaxInactiveInterval();

      int timeout = _default;

      try{

          timeout = new Integer(getInitParameter("timeout")).intValue();

      } catch(NumberFormatException nfe){

          //report any problems with the configured value in web.xml
          log("Problem with configuring session timeout in: " +
              getClass().getName()) ;
      }//try

      //now set the session to the configured timeout period
      if(timeout != _default && timeout > -2)
          session.setMaxInactiveInterval(timeout);

      out.println("<html>");
      out.println("<head>");
      out.println("<title>Cart Servlet</title>");
      out.println("</head>");
      out.println("<body>");

      out.println("The timeout interval is: " +
          session.getMaxInactiveInterval());

      out.println("</body>");
      out.println("</html>");

}
```

Figure 11-1 shows the result of running this servlet in a browser window.

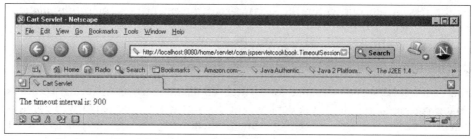

Figure 11-1. Dynamically changing the session timeout

The session timeout is changed only if the configured value is different than the initial value, and if the value is greater than −2:

```
if(timeout != _default && timeout > -2)
                session.setMaxInactiveInterval(timeout);
```

A timeout interval can be set to −1, which is defined by the Servlet v2.4 specification as a session that never expires.

 This behavior may not be implemented consistently from server to server.

As mentioned before, sessions are implemented the majority of the time as cookies. Chapter 10 includes recipes describing the handling of cookies in JSPs and servlets.

See Also

Recipes 11.2 and 11.3 on configuring the session timeout in Tomcat web applications; Chapter 1 on *web.xml*; Chapter 7 of the Servlet v2.3 and 2.4 specifications on sessions; the session-tracking sections of *Java Servlet Programming* by Jason Hunter (O'Reilly) and *JavaServer Pages* by Hans Bergsten (O'Reilly).

11.2   Setting the Session Timeout in All Tomcat Web Applications

Problem

You want to configure a session timeout period for all of the web applications that are running within an instance of Tomcat.

Solution

Set the session timeout within the session-config element in *<Tomcat-installation-directory>/conf/web.xml*.

Discussion

You can set the session timeout for all web applications by configuring Tomcat's default *conf/web.xml* file. If the deployment descriptor for a particular web application does not have a session-config element, then the application uses the value set in *conf/web.xml* as the default session timeout. The content of the session-timeout element (nested within session-config) represents the time in minutes until an inactive session expires.

Example 11-4 shows the session-config element in the default *web.xml* file for Tomcat 4.1.x, with the accompanying XML comment.

Example 11-4. The session-config element inside of the default Tomcat web.xml file

```
<!--==================== Default Session Configuration =================-->
<!-- You can set the default session timeout (in minutes) for all newly-->
<!-- created sessions by modifying the value below.-->

    <session-config>
        <session-timeout>30</session-timeout>
    </session-config>
```

On application deployment, Tomcat processes its default *web.xml* file, followed by the deployment descriptors for each web application. Your own session-config element overrides the one specified in *conf/web.xml*. It is usually a better idea to configure sessions for each web application individually, particularly if they are designed to be portable.

See Also

Recipe 11.1 on configuring the session timeout; Recipe 11.3 on setting the session timeout programmatically; Recipe 11.4 on checking the validity of a session; Chapter 1 on *web.xml*; Chapter 7 of the Servlet v2.3 and 2.4 specifications on sessions; the session-tracking sections of *Java Servlet Programming* by Jason Hunter (O'Reilly) and *JavaServer Pages* by Hans Bergsten (O'Reilly).

11.3   Setting the Session Timeout Programmatically

Problem

You want to set a session timeout in your servlet code.

Solution

Use the HttpServletRequest object's getSession( ) method to get a reference to the HttpSession object. Then change the timeout period programmatically by using the HttpSession.setMaxInactiveInterval(int *seconds*) method.

Discussion

The HttpSession.setMaxInactiveInterval(int *seconds*) method sets the timeout for a session *individually*, so that only the particular session object being operated upon is affected. Other servlets that do session tracking in the web application still use the session-timeout value in *web.xml* or, in the absence of this element, the server's default session-timeout value. Example 11-5 checks the timeout period for a session, then resets that timeout period to 20 minutes.

Example 11-5. Resetting a default timeout period

```
package com.jspservletcookbook;

import java.util.Date;
import java.text.DateFormat;

import javax.servlet.*;
import javax.servlet.http.*;

public class SimpleSession extends HttpServlet {

 public void doGet(HttpServletRequest request,
   HttpServletResponse response)
    throws ServletException, java.io.IOException {

        response.setContentType("text/html");
        java.io.PrintWriter out = response.getWriter( );

        HttpSession session = request.getSession( );

        out.println("<html>");
        out.println("<head>");
        out.println("<title>Simple Session Tracker</title>");
        out.println("</head>");
        out.println("<body>");
```

Example 11-5. Resetting a default timeout period (continued)

```
        out.println("<h2>Session Info</h2>");

        out.println("session ID: " + session.getId( ) + "<br><br>");

        out.println( "The SESSION TIMEOUT period is " +
            session.getMaxInactiveInterval( ) + " seconds.<br><br>");

        out.println( "Now changing it to 20 minutes.<br><br>");

        session.setMaxInactiveInterval(20 * 60);

        out.println("The SESSION TIMEOUT period is now " +
            session.getMaxInactiveInterval( )  + " seconds.");

        out.println("</body>");
        out.println("</html>");

    }
}
```

Figure 11-2 shows the result of requesting this servlet in a web browser.

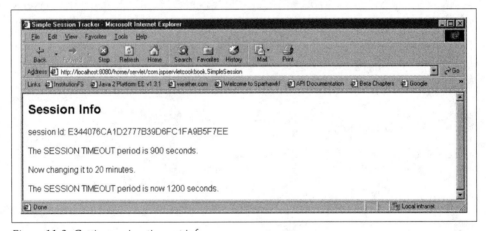

Figure 11-2. Getting session-timeout info

This servlet gets the HttpSession object with the HttpServletRequest class's getSession( ) method.

Whatever the servlet's default timeout period is, say, 30 minutes, Example 11-5 changes the accessed session's timeout to 20 minutes:

```
    session.setMaxInactiveInterval(20 * 60);
```

Remember, this method alters the default session-timeout interval only for the session associated with the users who request this servlet. Why would some users get a different timeout interval than others? Perhaps web-user testing at your organization has indicated that a session timeout of five minutes is more appropriate for your shopping cart–related servlets, whereas some chart- or map-creation servlets require the default timeout of 30 minutes or more, since their users might linger over the complex images in their browsers for a long period.

In most web applications, the session timeout is set (or altered) in the deployment descriptor, and you will not have to dynamically change the timeout in the servlet code.

See Also

Recipe 11.1 on configuring the session timeout; Recipe 11.2 on setting the session timeout in all Tomcat applications; Recipe 11.4 on checking the validity of a session; Chapter 1 on *web.xml*; Chapter 7 of the Servlet v2.3 and v2.4 specifications on sessions; the session-tracking sections of *Java Servlet Programming* by Jason Hunter (O'Reilly) and *JavaServer Pages* by Hans Bergsten (O'Reilly).

11.4 Checking if a Session Exists in an HttpServletRequest

Problem

You want to check if a web application user has a valid session.

Solution

Use the HttpServletRequest object's getSession(false) method to find out whether the HttpSession object is null.

Discussion

Some web components are designed to monitor if a session is valid, then optionally redirect or forward the user to another web component based on the validity of the session. For example, imagine that a user makes a request to a component that expects to find a custom object stored in the session object, such as a "shopping cart." You want to check if the session is valid; however, you do not want to create a new session for the request if the session is not valid, because another web component farther back in the chain of application components is responsible for creating new sessions and populating them with shopping cart items. The user may have entered the web application at Step 3 instead of Step 1. In this case, if the session is invalid, the request is forwarded to another access point in the application (such as a login screen).

If you call the HttpServletRequest object's getSession(false) method and the method returns false, then the user does not have a valid session and the request object has not created a new session for her.

 Either HttpServletRequest.getSession(true) or getSession( ) will attempt to create a new session.

Example 11-6 is a servlet that checks a user's session, then redirects the user to another web component if the session object is null.

Example 11-6. Checking if a session is valid or not

```
import javax.servlet.*;
import javax.servlet.http.*;

public class SessionCheck extends HttpServlet {

 public void doGet(HttpServletRequest request, HttpServletResponse response)
    throws ServletException, java.io.IOException {

        HttpSession session = request.getSession(false);

        if (session == null){
            response.sendRedirect("/myproj/login.jsp");
        } else {
            response.sendRedirect("/myproj/menu.jsp");
        }
 }
}
```

If the session in Example 11-6 is null, the servlet redirects the request to the *login.jsp* page at the context path */myproj*. If the session object is valid, the request is redirected to the */myproj/menu.jsp* component.

 The HttpServletResponse.sendRedirect(String location) method sends the client an HTTP response that looks like this:
```
HTTP/1.1 302 Moved Temporarily
Location:
http://localhost:9000/dbproj/login.jsp
Content-Type: text/html;charset=ISO-8859-1
...
```
The client then sends another request for the URL specified in the location header of the HTTP response.

See Also

Recipes 11.1 and 11.3 on configuring the session timeout; Chapter 1 on *web.xml*; Chapter 7 of the Servlet v2.3 and 2.4 specifications on sessions; the session-tracking sections of *Java Servlet Programming* by Jason Hunter (O'Reilly) and *JavaServer Pages* by Hans Bergsten (O'Reilly).

11.5   Tracking Session Activity in Servlets

Problem

You want to use a servlet to track the creation time and last-accessed time for a session.

Solution

Use the `HttpServletRequest` object's `getSession( )` method to get a reference to the `HttpSession` object. Then call the `HttpSession.getCreationTime( )` and `HttpSession.getLastAccessedTime( )` methods on that object.

Discussion

This recipe describes how to use the `HttpSession` API to find out the creation time and the last-accessed time for a session. How would a web application use this information? For one, you might want to monitor the pattern of request activity in a web application by comparing the session creation time, the last-accessed time, and the current time. For example, the difference between the creation time and the current time (measured in seconds) would indicate how long the web application had been tracking a particular user's session.

The method `HttpSession.getLastAccessedTime( )` returns the time (as a long datatype) of the last time the user made a request associated with a particular session.

 A servlet that calls getLastAccessedTime( ) represents the most current request associated with the session. In other words, the time at which the user requests the servlet that calls getLastAccessedTime( ) becomes the last accessed time.

Example 11-7 displays the current time, as well as the session's creation and last-accessed times.

The HttpServletRequest.getSession( ) method associates a new session with the request if one does not already exist. The HttpServletRequest.getSession(false) method returns null if a session is not associated with the request and it will not create a new HttpSession for the user. See Recipe 11.4.

Example 11-7. Calling HttpSession methods in a servlet

```java
package com.jspservletcookbook;

import javax.servlet.*;
import javax.servlet.http.*;

import java.util.Date;
import java.text.DateFormat;
import java.util.Enumeration;

public class SessionDisplay extends HttpServlet {

 public void doGet(HttpServletRequest request,
   HttpServletResponse response)
     throws ServletException, java.io.IOException {

     response.setContentType("text/html");
     java.io.PrintWriter out = response.getWriter();

     HttpSession session = request.getSession();

     Date creationTime = new Date(session.getCreationTime( ));

     Date lastAccessed = new Date(session.getLastAccessedTime( ));

     Date now = new Date( );

     DateFormat formatter =
       DateFormat.getDateTimeInstance(DateFormat.MEDIUM,
       DateFormat.MEDIUM);

     out.println("<html>");
     out.println("<head>");

     out.println(
       "<title>Displaying the Session Creation and "+
       "Last-Accessed Time</title>");

     out.println("</head>");
     out.println("<body>");
     out.println("<h2>Session Creation and Last-Accessed Time</h2>");
     out.println(
       "The time and date now is: " + formatter.format(now) +
       "<br><br>");
```

Example 11-7. Calling HttpSession methods in a servlet (continued)

```
    out.println("The session creation time: "+
      "HttpSession.getCreationTime( ): " +
      formatter.format(creationTime) + "<br><br>");

    out.println("The last time the session was accessed:  " +
      HttpSession.getLastAccessedTime( ): " +
      formatter.format(lastAccessed) );

    out.println("</body>");
    out.println("</html>");
 }//doGet

 public void doPost(HttpServletRequest request,
   HttpServletResponse response)
     throws ServletException, java.io.IOException {

      doGet(request,response);
   }//doPost
}
```

An example of a browser display for this servlet is shown in Figure 11-3.

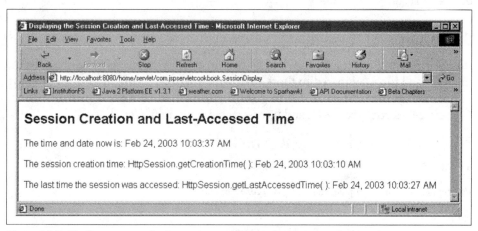

Figure 11-3. Finding out a session's creation and last-accessed times

As in the prior recipe, this example uses a `java.text.DateFormat` object to format Date Strings for browser display. The date-related `HttpSession` methods `getCreationTime( )` and `getLastAccessedTime( )` return `long` datatypes, from which `java.util.Date` objects can be created:

```
    Date creationTime = new Date( session.getCreationTime( ) );
```

The session's creation time can then be displayed using the `DateFormat`'s `format(Date _date)` method.

The next recipe shows how a JSP can track session activity.

See Also

Recipes 11.5 and 11.8; Chapter 1 on *web.xml*; Chapter 7 of the Servlet v2.3 and 2.4 specifications on sessions; the javax.servlet.http.HttpSession API at *http://java.sun. com/j2ee/sdk_1.3/techdocs/api/javax/servlet/http/HttpSession.html*; the session-tracking sections of *Java Servlet Programming* by Jason Hunter (O'Reilly) and *JavaServer Pages* by Hans Bergsten (O'Reilly).

11.6   Tracking Session Activity in JSPs

Problem

You want to find out a session's creation time and last-accessed time using JSPs.

Solution

Use the JSTL to get access to the JSP's associated HttpSession object. Then call the HttpSession.getCreationTime() and HttpSession.getLastAccessedTime() methods on that object.

Discussion

It is very easy to keep track of session activity in a JSP; you just use slightly different methods and tools compared to those used with a servlet. Example 11-8 uses the out custom action from the JSTL 1.0 to display information about the current session. Chapter 24 describes the JSTL and its associated EL in more detail.

Example 11-8. Tracking sessions using the JSTL

```
<%@page contentType="text/html"%>

<%@ taglib uri="http://java.sun.com/jstl/core" prefix="c" %>

<html>
  <head><title>View Session JSP </title></head>
  <body>
    <h2>Session Info From A JSP</h2>

    The session id: <c:out value="${pageContext.session.id}"/><br><br>

    The session creation time as a long value:
      <c:out value="${pageContext.session.creationTime}"/><br><br>

    The last accessed time as a long value:
      <c:out value="${pageContext.session.lastAccessedTime}"/><br><br>

  </body>
</html>
```

This JSP uses a `taglib` directive to make the custom actions that are part of the core tag library available. By convention, the `uri` attribute for the core tags is *http://java. sun.com/jstl/core*, and the prefix is c (you can create your own prefix in the `taglib` directive). With JSTL 1.1, the `uri` value is *http://java.sun.com/jsp/jstl/core*. The JSP then uses the out tag from the JSTL's core tag library to display the current session ID (the return value of `HttpSession.getId( )`), the session's creation time as a `long` type, and the session's last-accessed time. Figure 11-4 shows a browser display of these values.

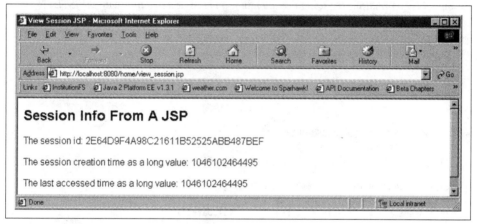

Figure 11-4. Showing session info in a JSP

The out element writes the value of its `value` attribute to the JSP's response stream. However, it is the EL that does the fetching of the value. For example, the following EL expression gets the value of the session's creation time:

```
${pageContext.session.creationTime}
```

 The `pageContext` reference is one of the implicit objects that can be accessed from the EL. This is equivalent to the implicit JSP scripting object of the same name.

The way the creation time is accessed is different than a method call; you use the dot (.) operator to get the `pageContext`'s session property, then in turn use the dot operator to access the `session` object's `creationTime` property. So the whole phrase looks like this:

```
pageContext.session.creationTime.
```

Finally, in the EL, all variable and property values are dereferenced (to get their values) by bracketing them in `${ }` characters.

The JSP gets the other session values in the same way. For example, the session's last-accessed time (the long type return value from the method HttpSession.getLastAccessedTime( )) is returned using this syntax:

```
${pageContext.session.lastAccessedTime}
```

Example 11-8 displays the last-accessed time for a session as a large, unfriendly number. Naturally, this value is more understandable displayed as a date. Example 11-9 shows how to use the JSTL's custom formatting actions to format a date string.

Example 11-9. Formatting the session creation time and last-accessed time with the JSTL

```
<%@page contentType="text/html"%>
<%@ taglib uri="http://java.sun.com/jstl/core" prefix="c" %>
<%@ taglib uri="http://java.sun.com/jstl/fmt" prefix="fmt" %>

<html>
  <head><title>View Session JSP </title></head>
  <body>

    <h2>Session Info From A JSP</h2>

    The session ID: <c:out value="${pageContext.session.id}"/>

    <h3>Session date values formatted as Dates</h3>

    <jsp:useBean id="timeValues" class="java.util.Date"/>

    <c:set target="${timeValues}" value=
      "${pageContext.session.creationTime}" property="time"/>

    The creation time: <fmt:formatDate value="${timeValues}" type="both"
        dateStyle="medium" /><br><br>

    <c:set target="${timeValues}" value=
    "${pageContext.session.lastAccessedTime}" property="time"/>

    The last accessed time:  <fmt:formatDate value="${timeValues}" type=
      "both" dateStyle="short" />

  </body>
</html>
```

Figure 11-5 shows the browser display for this JSP.

This JSP takes two date-related session values: the date/time when the session was created and the last date/time when a request associated with this session was made to the web application. It displays their values in the browser. As mentioned previously, these values are returned from the HttpSession object as long Java types. You have to create a Date object with its time property set to these long values. Then use

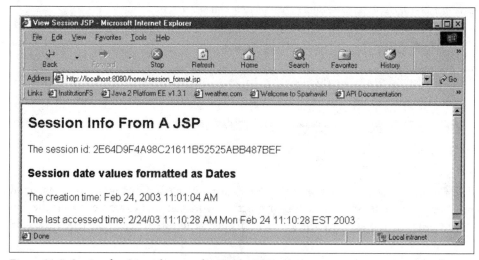

Figure 11-5. Session date/times formatted using the JSTL

the JSTL formatting custom actions to create readable Strings from the dates. First, make the formatting tag library available to the JSP with this taglib directive:

```
<%@ taglib uri="http://java.sun.com/jstl/fmt" prefix="fmt" %>
```

The java.util.Date object that will be used to create dates out of long values is generated using a JSP standard action called jsp:useBean. Here is the example's syntax:

```
<jsp:useBean id="timeValues" class="java.util.Date"/>
```

This line creates a new Date object and stores the object in a variable called timeValues, making it available through the EL with the syntax ${timeValues}. The JSP then uses the set custom action to set a time property in the Date object:

```
<c:set target="${timeValues}" value="${pageContext.session.creationTime}"
       property="time"/>
```

The value of set's target attribute is the JavaBean whose property you are setting. The property name is specified by the set element's property attribute. The value this expression sets the time property to is the long type returned from this JSTL expression:

```
${pageContext.session.creationTime}
```

In other words, using the custom action this way is the equivalent of calling the java.util.Date.setTime(long secs) method on the timeValues Date object. This time value is actually set and displayed twice, to represent the creation time and last-accessed time of the session. Example 11-10 is the code chunk that does the setting and displaying, including the fmt:formatDate custom action.

Example 11-10. Displaying a session's creation time and last-accessed time

```
<c:set target="${timeValues}" value="${pageContext.session.creationTime}"
    property="time"/>

The creation time: <fmt:formatDate value="${timeValues}" type="both"
    dateStyle="medium" /><br><br>

<c:set target="${timeValues}"value=
  "${pageContext.session.lastAccessedTime}" property="time"/>

The last accessed time:  <fmt:formatDate value="${timeValues}" type="both"
    dateStyle="short" />
```

The `formatDate` element is one of the JSTL's formatting actions, which are described in Chapter 24. The way the `formatDate` action works in this example is that the following code is replaced by the formatted date value, as in "Jan 21, 2003 1:57:39 PM":

```
<fmt:formatDate value="${timeValues}" type="both" dateStyle="short" />
```

In order to display their differences, Example 11-10 gives two different values (`medium` and `short`) for the `dateStyle` attribute.

See Also

Recipe 11.4 on checking the validity of a session; Chapter 1 on *web.xml*; Chapter 7 of the Servlet v2.3 and 2.4 specifications on sessions; the `javax.servlet.http.HttpSession` API at *http://java.sun.com/j2ee/sdk_1.3/techdocs/api/javax/servlet/http/HttpSession.html*; the session-tracking sections of *Java Servlet Programming* by Jason Hunter (O'Reilly) and *JavaServer Pages* by Hans Bergsten (O'Reilly).

11.7   Using URL Rewriting in a JSP

Problem

You want to make sure that URL rewriting is used in a JSP, in case any users disable cookies in their browsers.

Solution

Use the `url` custom action in the JSTL to create URLs that automatically include the session ID as a parameter.

Discussion

It is possible that some users of a web application will configure their browsers to disable cookies. Since cookies are the default basis for session tracking with JSPs, how will disabling cookies affect these users' experience with the web application? I recommend designing all session-tracking JSPs to accommodate URL rewriting, so that the cookie-averse users do not crash and burn in your web application.

One solution to this problem is to use the url custom action that is part of the JSTL.

The url element automatically inserts the session ID as a parameter with URLs that will be used in href, form, and frameset tags, for instance. This allows the pages that these links point to, such as servlets or JSPs, to track sessions without using cookies.

One of the nice things about using the url element like this is that it adds the session ID as a parameter to the URL when necessary, without the JSP author's intervention. Example 11-11 shows how to use url.

Example 11-11. Using the url core tag to rewrite URLs

```
<%@page contentType="text/html"%>
<%@ taglib uri="http://java.sun.com/jstl/core" prefix="c" %>

<html>
  <head><title>URL Rewriter</title></head>
  <body>
    <h1>This page will use URL rewriting if necessary</h2>

    <c:url value="/default.jsp" var="goToDefault" escapeXml="false"/>

    Go to the default.jsp page <a href="<c:out value="${goToDefault}"/>">here</a>.

  </body>
</html>
```

This example uses a taglib directive to make the JSTL's core tag library available. This directive looks like this:

```
<%@ taglib uri="http://java.sun.com/jstl/core" prefix="c" %>
```

The url element of this tag library creates a URL representing the web component *default.jsp* located on the top level of the web application. The URL is stored in a goToDefault variable using the url element's var attribute. The escapeXml attribute is set to false (it is true by default) to prevent characters such as ampersands and angle brackets from being converted to their character entity codes in the URL. The url element looks like this:

```
<c:url value="/default.jsp" var="goToDefault" escapeXml="false"/>
```

The URL created by the custom action is then used as the value for an href attribute in the following manner:

```
<a href="<c:out value="${goToDefault}"/>">here</a>
```

This code uses the out custom action and an EL expression (${goToDefault}) to create the hyperlink. After the page is requested, the returned HTML looks like this if cookies are disabled in the browser:

```
<a href="/home/default.jsp;jsessionid=3CAF7CD0A0BFF5076B390CCD24FD8F0D">here</a>
```

You may notice two differences between the URL that was created here:

```
<c:url value="/default.jsp" var="goToDefault" escapeXml="false"/>
```

and the URL that was generated from the out custom action:

```
/home/default.jsp;jsessionid=3CAF7CD0A0BFF5076B390CCD24FD8F0D
```

First, the url custom action has automatically added the context path (*/home* in the example) as a prefix to */default.jsp*. Second, the session ID was added to the URL as a path parameter named jsessionid, so that the link destination can access the session ID associated with this user and undertake session tracking.

 A *path parameter* begins with a semicolon and a name/value pair, as in *;jsessionid=3CAF7CD0A0B*.

The URL that the JSP creates by using the out element may also have additional parameters. Example 11-12 is the same as the first recipe example, except that parameters have been added to the URL inside the url custom action.

Example 11-12. Adding parameters using the url custom action

```
<%@page contentType="text/html"%>
<%@ taglib uri="http://java.sun.com/jstl/core" prefix="c" %>

<html>
  <head><title>JSP Page</title></head>
  <body>
    <h1>This page will use URL rewriting if necessary</h2>

    <c:url value="/default.jsp?n=${param.first}&l=${param.last}"
           var="goToDefault" />

    Go to the default.jsp page <a href="<c:out value="${goToDefault}"
        escapeXml="false" />">here</a>.

  </body>
</html>
```

The URL now looks like this:

```
/default.jsp?n=${param.first}&l=${param.last}
```

This URL uses embedded EL syntax to access two request parameters, called first and last. If code uses the EL to access a parameter named first, for instance, then it uses the param EL implicit object, followed by the dot operator, and the name of the parameter, as in ${param.first}. Suppose the example JSP is requested in the following manner:

```
http://localhost:8080/home/url_rewrite.jsp?first=Bruce&last=Perry
```

The url element's value attribute resolves to this code:

```
<c:url value="/default.jsp?n=Bruce&l=Perry" var="goToDefault" />
```

The out custom action further along in the example JSP has its escapeXml attribute set to false. If escapeXml is left with its default value (true) and the ampersand character (&) is replaced with its character entity code (&), the query string in the URL looks like this when the JSP is executed:

```
<a href="/home/default.jsp;jsessionid=D37AF592DACABD?n=Bruce&amp;l=Perry">
here</a>
```

To prevent this outcome when generating linked URLs with the out element, make sure to set out's escapeXml attribute to false.

Table 11-1. Special characters and entity codes

Character	Entity code
<	&lt;
>	&gt;
&	&amp;
'	&#039;
"	&#034;

 Make sure to use relative URLs of the form */default.jsp* when using URL rewriting with the url element. URL rewriting will not take place if an absolute URL is used in url's value attribute, as in *http://www. mysite.com/home/default.jsp*.

See Also

Recipe 11.6 on tracking session activity in JSPs; Recipe 11.8 on using URL rewriting in a servlet; the JSP Configuration section of the JSP v2.0 specification; Chapter 23 on the JSTL; the session-tracking sections of *JavaServer Pages* by Hans Bergsten (O'Reilly).

11.8   Using URL Rewriting in a Servlet

Problem

You want to create a servlet that uses URL rewriting if the user has disabled cookies in his browser.

Solution

Use the `HttpServletResponse.encodeURL(String url)` method to encode all URLs that are used to link with other pages.

Discussion

The `javax.servlet.HttpServletResponse` class includes a nifty method that will encode a URL with the current session ID, in the event that the user making the servlet request has disabled cookies.

In fact, if you use the `HttpServletResponse.encodeURL(String url)` method to encode the URLs that are used in a servlet, this method takes care of URL rewriting if necessary, and you won't have to worry about whether cookies are enabled in users' browsers. You must conscientiously encode every URL link involved with the servlet when using this method. Example 11-13 is a servlet version of the example used in Recipe 11.6.

Example 11-13. Using URL rewriting in a servlet

```
import javax.servlet.*;
import javax.servlet.http.*;

public class UrlRewrite extends HttpServlet {

  public void doGet(HttpServletRequest request,
    HttpServletResponse response)
     throws ServletException, java.io.IOException {

        response.setContentType("text/html");
        java.io.PrintWriter out = response.getWriter( );

        String contextPath = request.getContextPath( );

        String encodedUrl =  response.encodeURL(contextPath +
        "/default.jsp");

        out.println("<html>");
        out.println("<head>");
        out.println("<title>URL Rewriter</title>");
        out.println("</head>");
        out.println("<body>");
        out.println(
        "<h1>This page will use URL rewriting if necessary</h2>");

        out.println("Go to the default.jsp page <a href=\"" + encodedUrl +
            "\">here</a>.");

        out.println("</body>");
        out.println("</html>");
  }
```

Example 11-13. Using URL rewriting in a servlet (continued)

```
public void doPost(HttpServletRequest request,
   HttpServletResponse response)
    throws ServletException, java.io.IOException {

    doGet(request,response);
  }
}
```

In the page that is sent to the browser with cookies disabled, the URL looks like:
/home/default.jsp;jsessionid=3CAF7CD0A0BFF5076B390CCD24FD8F0D.

One of the differences between using encodeURL and the JSP solution in Recipe 11.7 (which used the url custom action from the JSTL) is that the custom action in JSTL 1.0 will automatically prepend the context path to the URL. If the context path was */home*, and the URL was */default.jsp*, then the rewritten URL would look like */home/default.jsp;jsessionid=3CAF7CD0A0BFF5076B390CCD24FD8F0D.* Automatically adding the context path in this manner to the URL is a separate operation compared with URL rewriting; it is not performed by the encodeURL method. If you want to duplicate this operation with a servlet, add the context path to the URL before calling the encodeURL method, as in:

```
String contextPath =request.getContextPath( );
         String encodedUrl = response.encodeURL(contextPath +
 "/default.jsp")
```

You can also use the related HttpServletResponse.encodeRedirectURL(*String url*) method to initiate URL rewriting with calls to HttpServletResponse. sendRedirect(*String url*). The servlet doGet( ) method in Example 11-14 uses encodeRedirectURL to ensure that the destination URLs have access to the session ID of the redirected user.

Example 11-14. Using encodeRedirectURL in a servlet doGet method

```
public void doGet(HttpServletRequest request, HttpServletResponse response) throws
ServletException, java.io.IOException {

     //redirect the user depending on the value of the go param
      String destination = request.getParameter("go");
      String contextPath = request.getContextPath( );

     if(destination == null || destination.equals(""))
        throw new ServletException(
         "Missing or invalid 'go' parameter in " +
         getClass().getName( ));

     if(destination.equals("weather")){
     //ensure URL rewriting
        response.sendRedirect(
          response.encodeRedirectURL(
```

Example 11-14. Using encodeRedirectURL in a servlet doGet method (continued)

```
            contextPath + "/weather") );}

    if(destination.equals("maps")){
    //ensure URL rewriting
        response.sendRedirect(
          response.encodeRedirectURL(
            contextPath + "/maps") );}
  }
```

The `response.sendRedirect(`*`String url`*`)` method redirects the request to the destination represented by its `url` parameter. The server sends an HTTP status message to the client:

```
HTTP/1.1 302 Moved Temporarily
```

Additionally, a `Location` response header is sent along that provides the client with the new URL for the requested file. If necessary, the response. `encodeRedirectURL(`*`String url`*`)` method adds the session ID to the redirect destination of this URL. The example gets the name of a servlet from the value of the request's go parameter:

```
String destination = request.getParameter("go");
```

The servlet throws a `ServletException` if the parameter is either missing or is an empty `String`. If the go parameter is valid, the servlet redirects the request to one of two servlets, with paths of */weather* or */maps* (the context path in the example is */home*). If implemented properly on the server, the following code adds the session ID to the URL if the requester's cookies are disabled, so the destination servlet can initiate session tracking:

```
response.sendRedirect( response.encodeRedirectURL(contextPath + "/weather") );
```

See Also

Recipe 11.4 on checking the validity of a session; Recipe 11.7 on using URL rewriting in a JSP; Chapter 1 on *web.xml*; Chapter 7 of the Servlet v2.3 and 2.4 specifications on sessions; the javax.servlet.http.HttpSession API at *http://java.sun.com/ j2ee/sdk_1.3/techdocs/api/javax/servlet/http/HttpSession.html*; the session-tracking sections of *Java Servlet Programming* by Jason Hunter (O'Reilly) and *JavaServer Pages* by Hans Bergsten (O'Reilly).

11.9 Using a Listener to Track the Session Lifecycle

Problem

You want an object that implements the HttpSessionListener interface to respond when a session is created or destroyed.

Solution

Create a listener class that implements the HttpSessionListener interface, and register the class in your deployment descriptor.

Discussion

The servlet API provides the javax.servlet.http.HttpSessionListener interface for use in responding to session creation or destruction. A class that implements this interface can perform custom behavior on either (or both) of these two events. Here is the process for creating and declaring a session listener for your web application:

1. Create a class that implements the HttpSessionListener interface. This interface defines two methods: sessionCreated( ) and sessionDestroyed( ), each of which accept a single HttpSessionEvent parameter.

2. Make sure the implementing class has a zero-argument constructor.

3. Place the compiled class in the *WEB-INF/classes* directory of your web application (including any of its package-related directories); or store the class in a JAR located in the *WEB-INF/lib* directory.

4. Declare the listener in the *web.xml* deployment descriptor.

5. Restart the web container (if necessary), which will instantiate your listener class and register it as a listener for all new sessions and session invalidations in the web application.

> Objects that are bound to sessions should implement the HttpSessionBindingListener interface. This listener does not have to be configured in the deployment descriptor, but the bound objects must implement HttpSessionBindingListener, as well as the valueBound( ), valueUnbound( ), and init( ) methods. The HttpSessionActivationListener is designed for sessions that migrate between Java Virtual Machines (JVMs). Objects that are bound to these sessions must implement HttpSessionActivationListener and its two methods: sessionDidActivate( ) and sessionWillActivate( ).

Here is the *web.xml* entry for our example listener class:

```
<listener>
    <listener-class>com.jspservletcookbook.SessionListen</listener-class>
</listener>
```

The HttpSessionListener class in Example 11-15 keeps a count of live sessions in the web application and writes a message to the console whenever a session is created or destroyed. It would be better to log messages using a component such as log4j, which I'll discuss in Chapter 14.

Example 11-15. Keeping track of session activity with a listener class

```
package com.jspservletcookbook;

import java.util.Date;
import javax.servlet.*;
import javax.servlet.http.*;

public class SessionListen implements HttpSessionListener {

    private int sessionCount;

    public SessionListen() {
        this.sessionCount = 0;
    }

    public void sessionCreated(HttpSessionEvent se){

        HttpSession session = se.getSession( );

        session.setMaxInactiveInterval(60);

        //increment the session count
        sessionCount++;


        String id = session.getId( );

        Date now = new Date( );

        String message = new StringBuffer(
          "New Session created on ").
            append(now.toString( )).append("\nID: ").
              append(id).append("\n").append("There are now ").
                append(""+sessionCount).append(
                  " live sessions in the application."). toString( );

        System.out.println(message);
    }

    public void sessionDestroyed(HttpSessionEvent se){

        HttpSession session = se.getSession( );
```

Example 11-15. Keeping track of session activity with a listener class (continued)

```
        String id = session.getId( );

    --sessionCount;//decrement the session count variable

        String message = new StringBuffer("Session destroyed" +
          "\nValue of destroyed session ID is").
            append(""+id).append("\n").append(
              "There are now ").append(""+sessionCount).append(
                " live sessions in the application.").toString( );

        System.out.println(message);
    }
}
```

Each listener must have a zero-argument constructor. The SessionListen class has one instance variable, an int that keeps track of the number of sessions. In the sessionCreated( ) method, the code gets access to the new session by calling the HttpSessionEvent.getSession( ) method. The session's timeout is then reset to 60 seconds, so the creating and destroying can be observed in the console without a lot of delay.

 An HttpSessionListener class is notified only of requests to pages that create *new* sessions, such as with the request.getSession( ) method. This listener is also notified if a servlet or JSP invalidates an existing session, an event that will trigger the class's sessionDestroyed( ) method. If a servlet or JSP is accessed, but does not do session tracking, then the listener is *not* notified of those activities; the same is true when the session is further accessed through the web application after it is created, unless it is explicitly invalidated.

Similar messaging and access to the HttpSession object takes place in the sessionDestroyed( ) method. The resulting console in Figure 11-6 shows that you can get information about the HttpSession object in both of the listener's methods.

Using the HttpSessionListener interface, it is possible to create classes that monitor how many sessions are created during a certain period of time, and how long it takes before they are left idle and timeout.

See Also

Chapter 14 on using listeners to log messages; Recipe 11.4 on checking the validity of a session; Chapter 1 on *web.xml*; Chapter 7 of the Servlet v2.3 and 2.4 specifications on sessions; the javax.servlet.http.HttpSession API at *http://java.sun.com/ j2ee/sdk_1.3/techdocs/api/javax/servlet/http/HttpSession.html*.

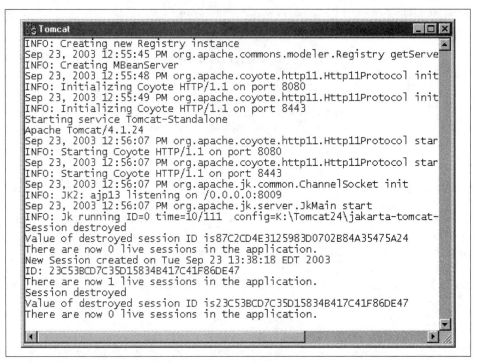

```
Tomcat                                                    _ □ X
INFO: Creating new Registry instance
Sep 23, 2003 12:55:45 PM org.apache.commons.modeler.Registry getServe
INFO: Creating MBeanServer
Sep 23, 2003 12:55:48 PM org.apache.coyote.http11.Http11Protocol init
INFO: Initializing Coyote HTTP/1.1 on port 8080
Sep 23, 2003 12:55:49 PM org.apache.coyote.http11.Http11Protocol init
INFO: Initializing Coyote HTTP/1.1 on port 8443
Starting service Tomcat-Standalone
Apache Tomcat/4.1.24
Sep 23, 2003 12:56:07 PM org.apache.coyote.http11.Http11Protocol star
INFO: Starting Coyote HTTP/1.1 on port 8080
Sep 23, 2003 12:56:07 PM org.apache.coyote.http11.Http11Protocol star
INFO: Starting Coyote HTTP/1.1 on port 8443
Sep 23, 2003 12:56:07 PM org.apache.jk.common.ChannelSocket init
INFO: JK2: ajp13 listening on /0.0.0.0:8009
Sep 23, 2003 12:56:07 PM org.apache.jk.server.JkMain start
INFO: Jk running ID=0 time=10/111  config=K:\Tomcat24\jakarta-tomcat-
Session destroyed
Value of destroyed session ID is87C2CD4E3125983D0702B84A35475A24
There are now 0 live sessions in the application.
New Session created on Tue Sep 23 13:38:18 EDT 2003
ID: 23C53BCD7C35D15834B417C41F86DE47
There are now 1 live sessions in the application.
Session destroyed
Value of destroyed session ID is23C53BCD7C35D15834B417C41F86DE47
There are now 0 live sessions in the application.
```

Figure 11-6. Notifications of session creation and invalidation

11.10 Using a Listener to Monitor Session Attributes

Problem

You want a listener class to be notified when a session attribute is added, removed, or replaced.

Solution

Create a Java class that implements the HttpSessionAttributeListener interface. Register this class using the web application's deployment descriptor.

Discussion

The HttpSessionAttributeListener interface has three methods: attributeAdded( ), attributeRemoved( ), and attributeReplaced( ); all have a parameter of the type HttpSessionBindingEvent. This listener is notified when the session sets, removes, or changes an attribute. Therefore, the method calls in the web application that cause an HttpSessionAttributeListener notification are:

- HttpSession.setAttribute(*String name,Object value*).
- HttpSession.removeAttribute(*String name*).
- A call to HttpSession.setAttribute( ) when an attribute of the same name is already bound to the session. The original attribute is replaced, triggering a call to the attributeReplaced(HttpSessionBindingEvent event) method.

Example 11-16 displays a message to the console when a session object is bound, including the value of the object (which is a String in this simple example). Messages are also displayed when the attribute is removed or replaced. To make this listener available to the application:

1. Give the class a zero-argument constructor.
2. Add the class to the web application's *WEB-INF/classes* or *lib* directory (when it's in a JAR).
3. Declare the listener in the deployment descriptor.
4. Restart the web container (if necessary) so it can instantiate the listener.

Example 11-16. Listening for session object binding or unbinding

```
package com.jspservletcookbook;

import javax.servlet.*;
import javax.servlet.http.*;

public class SessionAttribListen implements HttpSessionAttributeListener {

    //Creates new SessionAttribListen
    public SessionAttribListen( ) {

        System.out.println(getClass().getName( ));
    }

  public void attributeAdded(HttpSessionBindingEvent se) {

        HttpSession session = se.getSession( );

        String id = session.getId( );

        String name = se.getName( );

        String value = (String) se.getValue( );

        String source = se.getSource().getClass().getName( );

        String message = new StringBuffer(
          "Attribute bound to session in ").append(source).
            append("\nThe attribute name: ").append(name).
```

```
                append("\n").append("The attribute value:").
                  append(value).append("\n").
                    append("The session ID: ").
                      append(id).toString( );

        System.out.println(message);
    }

    public void attributeRemoved(HttpSessionBindingEvent se) {

        HttpSession session = se.getSession( );

        String id = session.getId( );

        String name = se.getName( );

        if(name == null)
            name = "Unknown";

        String value = (String) se.getValue( );

        String source = se.getSource().getClass().getName( );

        String message = new StringBuffer(
          "Attribute unbound from session in ").append(source).
            append("\nThe attribute name: ").append(name).
              append("\n").append("The attribute value: ").
                append(value).append("\n").append(
                  "The session ID: ").append(id).toString( );

        System.out.println(message);
    }

    public void attributeReplaced(HttpSessionBindingEvent se) {

        String source = se.getSource().getClass().getName( );

        String message = new StringBuffer(
          "Attribute replaced in session   ").
            append(source).toString( );

        System.out.println(message);
    }
}
```

When attributes are added, replaced, and removed from a session in the web application, this class prints information about the attribute and the session to the web container's console. The HttpSession type that binds the attribute can be accessed by
calling the HttpSessionBindingEvent class's getSession( ) method. In all three of the
listener's methods, you can get the ID of the session associated with the attribute, as

well as the attribute's name and value. Inside the listener class's constructor is a line of code that prints the listener class name to the console when it is instantiated:

```
System.out.println(getClass().getName());
```

This message indicates to the developer that the listener is properly referenced in *web.xml*, and that the web container has created an instance of the listener. Finally, this listener class prints a message to the console about the session class that is the source of the event. The listener uses the `java.util.EventObject.getSource()` method (which is inherited by the `HttpSessionBindingEvent` object) to get a reference to the source of the session-binding event:

```
String source = se.getSource().getClass().getName();
```

The se variable is the `HttpSessionBindingEvent` object. Here is the information that is printed to the Tomcat console:

```
Attribute bound to session in org.apache.catalina.session.StandardSession
The attribute name: session-attribute
The attribute value: Hello
The session ID: 9ED2C34964778265A34F7AB0DEA4B884
Attribute replaced in session  org.apache.catalina.session.StandardSession
Attribute unbound from session in org.apache.catalina.session.StandardSession
The attribute name: session-attribute
The attribute value: Hello there.
The session ID: 9ED2C34964778265A34F7AB0DEA4B884
```

The listener allows you to get the session ID, as well as the name and value of the session attribute, during the attribute's removal from the session. The `HttpSessionBindingEvent.getValue()` method returns the value of the attribute as a `java.lang.Object`. Therefore, if you want access to the attribute in the listener, then you would have to cast the `Object` type to its appropriate type during its addition, removal, or replacement. For example, imagine that you have stored a `java.util.Map` in a session. You want to check the `Map` contents in the listener's `attributeRemoved` method. If the variable be is of type `HttpSessionBindingEvent`, then this code checks the return type of `be.getValue()`:

```
java.util.Map map = null;

Object value = null;

if((value = be.getValue()) instanceof java.util.Map){

    map = (java.util.Map) value;
    System.out.println("HashMap value: " + map.get("key"));

}
```

This method returns the value of the session-bound object that's being removed. If the return type is a `Map`, the local variable value is cast to a `java.util.Map`, then the `get()` method is called on that `Map` (given that the `Map` instance contains a key called "key").

See Also

Chapter 14 on using listeners to log messages; Recipe 11.4 on checking the validity of a session; Recipe 11.9 on using a listener to track session lifecycle; Chapter 1 on *web.xml*; Chapter 7 of the Servlet v2.3 and 2.4 specifications on sessions; the javax.servlet.http.HttpSession API at *http://java.sun.com/j2ee/sdk_1.3/techdocs/api/javax/servlet/http/HttpSession.html*.

11.11 Using a Filter to Monitor Session Attributes

Problem

You want to use a filter to check a session attribute prior to the request reaching a servlet.

Solution

Create a Java class that implements javax.servlet.Filter, write session-related code in the class's doFilter( ) method, then configure the filter in your deployment descriptor.

Discussion

Filters, as their name suggests, are semipermeable barriers through which requests to your web application must pass before they reach servlets, JSPs, or even static content. Filters are technically Java classes that implement the javax.servlet.Filter interface. A filter can have a look at the ServletRequest and ServletResponse objects before these objects find their way to a servlet's service methods (which include service( ), doGet( ), and doPost( )). Filters can initiate authentication, logging, encryption, database actions, caching, and just about any other task that passes through request and response objects.

Filters are configured in *web.xml*. In Example 11-18, a filter checks a logged-in HttpSession attribute, and logs its activities by calling the ServletContext object's log( ) method. This filter is mapped to a servlet registered in *web.xml* as MyServlet. Any requests to the MyServlet servlet cause the SessionFilter.doFilter( ) method to be called. Example 11-17 shows the relevant entries in *web.xml*.

Example 11-17. Configuring a filter in web.xml

```
<!-- the beginning of web.xml goes here -->

<filter>
    <filter-name>SessionFilter</filter-name>
    <filter-class>com.jspservletcookbook.SessionFilter</filter-class>
</filter>
```

Example 11-17. Configuring a filter in web.xml (continued)

```
<filter-mapping>
    <filter-name>SessionFilter</filter-name>
    <servlet-name>MyServlet</servlet-name>
</filter-mapping>
<!-- more filters or listener classes added here -->

<servlet>
    <servlet-name>MyServlet</servlet-name>
    <servlet-class>com.jspservletcookbook.MyServlet</servlet-class>
</servlet>

<!-- deployment descriptor continues ...-->
```

The filter element specifies the filter's registered name and its fully qualified Java class. You package the filter class with the rest of the web application by placing the class in *WEB-INF/classes* or in a JAR file in *WEB-INF/lib*. The filter-mapping element maps the filter to the servlet registered in the deployment descriptor as MyServlet. Filters can also be mapped to URL patterns (Chapter 20 explains this syntax in detail). Example 11-18 is the source code for com.jspservletcookbook. SessionFilter.

Example 11-18. A filter that snoops on session information

```
package com.jspservletcookbook;

import javax.servlet.*;
import javax.servlet.http.*;

public class SessionFilter implements Filter {

    private FilterConfig config;

    //Creates new SessionFilter
    public SessionFilter( ) {}

    public void  init(FilterConfig filterConfig)  throws ServletException{

        System.out.println("Instance created of "+getClass().getName( ));
        this.config = filterConfig;
    }

    public void  doFilter(ServletRequest request, ServletResponse response,
        FilterChain chain) throws java.io.IOException, ServletException {

        HttpSession session = ((HttpServletRequest) request).getSession( );

        ServletContext context = config.getServletContext( );

        /* use the ServletContext.log method to log
           filter messages */
        context.log("doFilter called in: " + config.getFilterName( ) +
           " on " + (new java.util.Date( )));
```

Example 11-18. A filter that snoops on session information (continued)

```
        // log the session ID
        context.log("session ID: " + session.getId( ));

        // Find out whether the logged-in session attribute is set
        String logged = (String) session.getAttribute("logged-in");
        if (logged == null)
            session.setAttribute("logged-in","no");

        //log a message about the log-in status
        context.log("log-in status: "+
            (String)session.getAttribute("logged-in"));

        context.log("");

        chain.doFilter(request,response);
    }

  public void destroy( ){
        /*called before the Filter instance is removed
        from service by the web container*/
    }
}
```

 Every filter has to have a zero-argument constructor, just like listener classes.

The init( ) method displays a console message when its instance is created by the web container. The javax.servlet.FilterConfig object is used to get the ServletContext object for this filter (by calling FilterConfig.getServletContext( )). The ServletContext.log( ) method is used to log messages from the filter. These messages can then be read in the server logs. In Tomcat, look in the *<Tomcat-install-directory>/logs* directory for log files with names such as *localhost_home_log.2003-01-24.txt*. Here is an example of the log entries for this filter:

```
2003-01-24 11:56:09 doFilter called in: SessionFilter on Fri Jan 24 11:56:09 EST 2003
2003-01-24 11:56:09 session ID: E04DE93D9B88A974ED2350BCF7945F34
2003-01-24 11:56:09 log-in status: no
```

The filter gets access to the session with this code:

```
HttpSession session = ((HttpServletRequest) request).getSession( );
```

Since the doFilter( ) method has a ServletRequest parameter type, and not a HttpServletRequest type, the request parameter has to be cast to the latter type so that the code can call the request.getSession( ) method.

 Beware of doing this blindly in environments where you are not *positive* that all servlets are HttpServlets. If you aren't sure, a simple class check before casting can solve this problem.

Once the filter has access to the session object, it looks for a certain session attribute (logged-in). If session.getAttribute("logged-in") returns null, this attribute is added to the session with the value "no". The code then calls chain. doFilter(*request*,*response*) inside of the filter's doFilter( ) method.

This method call on the FilterChain object ensures that the request and response are passed along to the next filter on the chain, or, in the absence of any more mapped filters, to the targeted web resource. Example 11-19 shows the doGet( ) method of the MyServlet servlet that the filter in Example 11-18 is mapped to.

Example 11-19. doGet method of a servlet to which a filter is mapped

```
public void doGet(HttpServletRequest request,
  HttpServletResponse response)
    throws ServletException, java.io.IOException {

        response.setContentType("text/html");
        java.io.PrintWriter out = response.getWriter( );

        HttpSession session = request.getSession( );

        String logged = (String) session.getAttribute("logged-in");

        out.println("<html>");
        out.println("<head>");
        out.println("<title>Filter Servlet</title>");
        out.println("</head>");
        out.println("<body>");

        out.println("<h2>Session Logged in Info</h2>");

        out.println("logged in : " + logged+ "<br><br>");

        out.println("</body>");
        out.println("</html>");

    }
```

This servlet checks the logged-in session attribute and displays its value, as shown in Figure 11-7.

A filter is mapped to a servlet's registered name like this:

```
<filter-mapping>
  <filter-name>SessionFilter</filter-name>
  <servlet-name>MyServlet</servlet-name>
</filter-mapping>
```

The requests for this servlet will not pass through the mapped filter first, however, if the servlet is requested with an "invoker"-style URL of the form *http://localhost:8080/servlet/com.jspservletcookbook.MyServlet*. If this causes problems for the web application, consider disabling or overriding the URL mapping of */servlet/** in your web application. Recipe 3.6 describes how to do this.

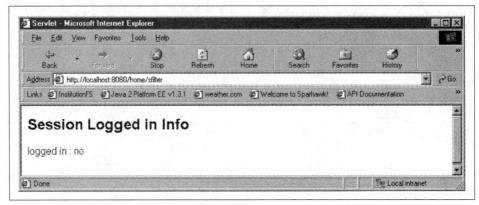

Figure 11-7. Checking a session object after a filter has altered it

A filter can take a number of actions with a session object before it reaches a servlet or JSP that does session tracking, such as add, remove, or change session attributes. It can also alter the session's timeout period (with the HttpSession. setMaxInactiveInterval(int *seconds*) method) based on an attribute of the session or request.

See Also

Chapter 19 on using filters; Recipe 11.4 on checking the validity of a session; Chapter 1 on *web.xml*; Chapter 7 of the Servlet v2.3 and 2.4 specifications on sessions; the javax.servlet.http.HttpSession API at *http://java.sun.com/j2ee/sdk_1.3/ techdocs/api/javax/servlet/http/HttpSession.html*; Chapter 1 on *web.xml*; Chapter 6 of the Servlet v 2.3 and 2.4 specifications on filtering.

CHAPTER 12

Integrating JavaScript with Servlets and JSPs

12.0 Introduction

JavaScript is a scripting system for web pages, standalone applications, and servers. Netscape Corporation invented JavaScript, which has become such a popular and useful programming tool that all major browsers now support it. Unlike the Java code shown in this book, JavaScript is mainly executed in the web browser as a client-side scripting system, rather than on the server.

Most busy web sites use JavaScript for dynamic behavior, such as validating form input or creating new browser windows (much to the chagrin of users, who are often overwhelmed by irresponsible and dynamically generated pop ups!). Just choose "View Source" from the browser menu bar for a typical web page, and often the first text items you'll see displayed are endless lines of JavaScript. JavaScript is used for advanced tasks such as controlling or animating browser shapes (dynamic HTML), creating flying objects, and initializing the behavior of embedded videos.

Developers converting static web pages to JSPs or servlets may have to integrate existing JavaScript code into their Java source code. This is what the upcoming recipes are all about.

 JavaScript guides are available from *http://devedge.netscape.com/*.

12.1 Including JavaScript Modules in a Servlet

Problem

You want to import a module or file containing JavaScript code so that the JavaScript can be included in the servlet's HTML output.

Solution

Use the `javax.servlet.RequestDispatch.include()` method to import the needed JavaScript into your page.

Discussion

An efficient method for handling JavaScript throughout a web project is to store the JavaScript code in separate files or modules. Servlets that require the JavaScript functions can then import the JavaScript modules. You would not store your Java class files willy-nilly all over the computer's filesystem without an organization that mirrors the code's purpose. Nor should you organize your JavaScript in anything but well-defined modules.

The JavaScript is included in the servlet's HTML output with `script` tags and executed in the browser when needed. Example 12-1 shows a module of JavaScript code named *functions.js*. This module is stored in the web application's *WEB-INF/ javascript* directory.

 A sensible place to store JavaScript modules is in their own directory, so that they are easy to locate and do not clutter up the top-level directory of the web application. The JavaScript directory can be a subdirectory of *WEB-INF*, as in this recipe.

Example 12-1. A JavaScript module

```
<script language="JavaScript">

function CheckEmail(email)
{
    var firstchunk,indx,secondchunk

    if (email == ""){
        alert("Please make sure you have entered a valid " +
            "email before submitting the info.")

        return false
    }

    //get the zero-based index of the "@" character
    indx = email.indexOf("@")

    //if the string does not contain an @, then return false
    if (indx == -1 ){

        alert("Please make sure you have entered a valid " +
            "email before submitting the info.")

        return false
    }
```

Example 12-1. A JavaScript module (continued)

```
    //if the first part of email is < two chars and thye second part is < seven chars
    //(arbitrary but workable criteria), reject the input address

    firstchunk = email.substr(0,indx) //up to but not including the "@"

    //start at char following the "@" and include up to end of email addr
    secondchunk = email.substr(indx + 1)

    //if the part  following the "@" does not include a period "." then
    //also return false

    if ((firstchunk.length < 2 ) || (secondchunk.length < 7) ||
        (secondchunk.indexOf(".") == -1)){

        alert("Please make sure you have entered a valid " +
            "email before submitting the info.")

        return false
}

    //the email was okay; at least it had a @, more than one username chars,
    //more than six chars after the "@", and the substring after the "@"
    // contained a "." char

    return true

}//CheckEmail

function CreateWindow(uri) {

    var newWin =
        window.open(uri,'newwin1',
            'width=500,height=400,resizable,' +
            'scrollable,scrollbars=yes');
    newWin.focus( );

}

</script>
```

The module in Example 12-1 contains a script block with two JavaScript function definitions. The function CheckEmail ensures that the email address a user has typed into an HTML form contains at least an @ character, two characters preceding the @ and seven characters after that character, and that the characters after the @ contain a period character (.). The CreateWindow function creates a new browser window with the supplied URI.

Example 12-2 shows a servlet that imports this JavaScript file using the javax. servlet.RequestDispatcher.include( ) method.

Example 12-2. A servlet includes a JavaScript file

```java
package com.jspservletcookbook;

import javax.servlet.*;
import javax.servlet.http.*;

public class ModuleServlet extends HttpServlet {

    public void doGet(HttpServletRequest request, HttpServletResponse response) throws
    ServletException, java.io.IOException {

        response.setContentType("text/html");
        java.io.PrintWriter out = response.getWriter( );
        out.println("<html><head>");

        RequestDispatcher dispatcher = request.getRequestDispatcher(
            "/WEB-INF/javascript/functions.js");

        dispatcher.include(request, response);

        out.println("<title>Client Forms</title></head><body>");
        out.println("<h2>Enter Your Name and Email</h2>");

        out.println("<form action=
            \"/home/displayHeaders.jsp\" name=\"entryForm\" onSubmit=
            \" return CheckEmail(this.email.value)\">");

        out.println("<table border=\"0\"><tr><td valign=\"top\">");
        out.println(
            "First and last name: </td>  <td valign=\"top\"><input type=
            \"text\" name=\"name\" size=\"20\"></td></tr>");

        out.println("<tr><td valign=\"top\">");
        out.println("Email: </td>
        <td valign=\"top\"><input type=\"text\" name=
            \"email\" size=\"20\"></td>");
        out.println("<tr><td valign=\"top\"><input type=
        \"submit\" value=\"Submit\" ></td>");
        out.println("</tr></table></form>");

        out.println("</body></html>");

    } //doGet
}
```

The servlet in Example 12-2 uses a RequestDispatcher to include the code contained in *functions.js* within the HTML head tag generated by the servlet. The generated page includes an HTML form tag. When the page user clicks the Submit button, the form tag's onSubmit event handler checks the email address that the user typed into the form using the imported JavaScript CheckEmail function. This function returns false, which cancels the form submission if the email address does not meet the simple criteria specified by the function.

Figure 12-1 shows what the web page looks like when the user has entered an email address into the form.

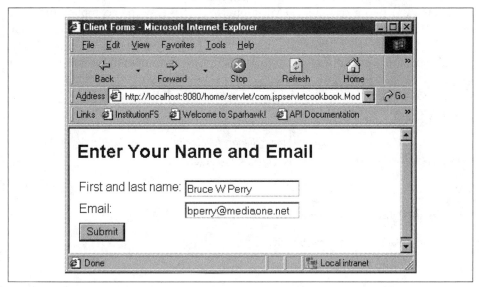

Figure 12-1. A servlet generates a web page containing JavaScript

Users can also use the built-in src attribute of the HTML script tag to import a JavaScript module, as in:

```
<script src="functions.js">
```

See Also

The Netscape DevEdge site at *http://devedge.netscape.com/*; Recipes 12.2, 12.4, and 12.6 on using JavaScript with JSPs; Recipe 12.3 on using JavaScript with servlets for creating new browser windows; Recipe 12.5 on validating form values with a servlet and JavaScript; Recipe 18.3 on using a filter with HTTP requests.

12.2   Including JavaScript Modules in a JSP

Problem

You want to include a module or file containing JavaScript code within a JSP page's output.

Solution

Use the c:import JSTL core tag.

Discussion

The previous recipe described how to include a file containing JavaScript (Example 12-1) into a servlet's HTML input. It is very easy to accomplish the same task in a JSP, such as by using the *importMod.jsp* file shown in Example 12-3. This JSP uses the JSTL core tag c:import to include a file named *functions.js*. The *functions.js* module contains a script tag with two JavaScript function definitions (Example 12-1 in Recipe 12.1). The HTML generated by the JSP shows that the c:import action positioned the script tag within the JSP's head tag. The JSP generates the HTML form shown previously in Figure 12-1.

Example 12-3. Using the JSTL c:import tag to import JavaScript

```
<%@ taglib uri="http://java.sun.com/jstl/core" prefix="c" %>
<html>
<head>

<c:import url="/WEB-INF/javascript/functions.js" />

<title>Client Forms</title></head><body>

<h2>Enter Your Name and Email</h2>

<form action="/home/displayHeaders.jsp" name="entryForm"
      onSubmit="return CheckEmail(this.email.value)">

<table border="0"><tr><td valign="top">

First and last name: </td>  <td valign="top"><input type="text" name="name" size="20"></
td></tr>

<tr><td valign="top">
Email: </td>  <td valign="top"><input type="text" name="email" size="20"></td></tr>

<tr><td valign="top"><input type="submit" value="Submit"></td>
</tr></table>

</form>
</body></html>
```

When the user submits the HTML form, her action is intercepted by the form tag's onSubmit event handler, which does a basic syntax check on the email address the user typed into the form. The form submit, targeted to a */home/ displayHeaders.jsp* page, is cancelled if the submitted email address has the wrong syntax.

> The JavaScript code this.email.value returns the String that the user typed into the text field named email. The keyword this refers to the form object, which contains the event handler onSubmit. The JavaScript code is a parameter of this event handler.

See Also

The Netscape DevEdge site at *http://devedge.netscape.com/*; Recipe 12.4 on using JavaScript to create a new window in a JSP; Recipe 12.6 on using JavaScript to validate form input in a JSP; Recipe 12.3 on using JavaScript with servlets for creating new browser windows; Recipe 12.5 on validating form values with a servlet and JavaScript; Recipe 18.3 on using a filter with HTTP requests.

12.3   Creating a New Window with JavaScript in a Servlet

Problem

You want a servlet to contain JavaScript that can generate a new browser window.

Solution

Use a `javax.servlet.RequestDispatcher` to include the JavaScript function in the servlet. The JavaScript function calls the JavaScript window object's open method.

Discussion

This recipe uses the same imported module as the first two recipes, but this time the servlet uses the second function definition (`CreateWindow`) rather than the first. Example 12-4 generates an HTML button widget. When the user clicks the button, JavaScript generates a small window (sometimes referred to as a *windoid*, or pop up). The servlet dynamically retrieves the URL for loading into the new window from a servlet init parameter, which is something you cannot do with a static HTML page.

Example 12-4. A servlet that loads JavaScript for creating a window

```
package com.jspservletcookbook;

import javax.servlet.*;
import javax.servlet.http.*;

public class WindowServlet extends HttpServlet {

  public void doGet(HttpServletRequest request, HttpServletResponse response) throws
  ServletException, java.io.IOException {

    //URL for the pop-up window is configured
    String url = getInitParameter("popup-url");

    //just in case the initParameter is misconfigured

    if (url == null || url.equals(""))
        url = "/displayHeaders.jsp";
```

Example 12-4. A servlet that loads JavaScript for creating a window (continued)

```
        //add the context path as a prefix to the URL, as in /home
        url = request.getContextPath( ) + url;

        response.setContentType("text/html");
        java.io.PrintWriter out = response.getWriter( );
        out.println("<html><head>");

        RequestDispatcher dispatcher = request.getRequestDispatcher(
            "/WEB-INF/javascript/functions.js");

        dispatcher.include(request, response);

        out.println("<title>Help Page</title></head><body>");
        out.println("<h2>Cookie Info</h2>");

        out.println("<form action =\"\" onSubmit=\" return false\">");
        out.println("<table border=\"0\"><tr><td valign=\"top\">");

        out.println(
            "Click on the button to get more info on cookies: </td>");

        out.println("<td valign=\"top\">");

        out.println("<input type=\"button\" name=\"button1\" " +
            "value=\"More Info\" onClick=\"CreateWindow('" + url +
            "')\"></td></tr>");

        out.println("</table></form>");

        out.println("</body></html>");
    } //end doGet
}
```

This servlet assumes some configuration steps have been taken in the application's deployment descriptor. This configuration includes an init-param that specifies the URL for loading into the new window. The url variable is the CreateWindow function's parameter (see Example 12-1 for a definition of the JavaScript functions). The servlet generates the HTML and dynamically provides the URL for loading into the new window. Here is the HTML button definition in the servlet's output:

```
<input type="button" name="button1" value="More Info"
    onClick="CreateWindow('/home/cookieReader.jsp')">
```

> If the application is dynamically reloadable (the web container monitors the deployment descriptor for any changes and reloads the context if the file is altered), then the developer can change the value of the servlet init-param in the deployment descriptor. The servlet pop-up window then loads the new URL without recompiling the servlet or stopping the server.

Here is the configuration for this servlet in *web.xml*:

```
<servlet>
    <servlet-name>windowservlet</servlet-name>
    <servlet-class>com.jspservletcookbook.WindowServlet</servlet-class>
    <init-param>
        <param-name>popup-url</param-name>
        <param-value>/cookieReader.jsp</param-value>
    </init-param>
</servlet>
```

The servlet loads the definition for the JavaScript function `CreateWindow` with this code:

```
RequestDispatcher dispatcher = request.getRequestDispatcher(
        "/WEB-INF/javascript/functions.js");
```

In the HTML code the servlet generates, the `script` tag containing the JavaScript code appears within the HTML head tag. When the user clicks the form button on the servlet-generated web page, a new window is created and the URL specified by the `init-param` element in *web.xml* (*cookieReader.jsp*) is loaded. Figure 12-2 shows the servlet output. Figure 12-3 shows the pop-up window.

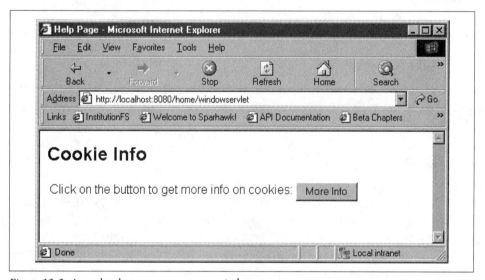

Figure 12-2. A servlet that creates a pop-up window

See Also

The Netscape DevEdge site at *http://devedge.netscape.com/*; Recipes 12.2, 12.4, and 12.6 on using JavaScript with JSPs; Recipe 12.5 on validating form values with a servlet and JavaScript; Recipe 18.3 on using a filter with HTTP requests.

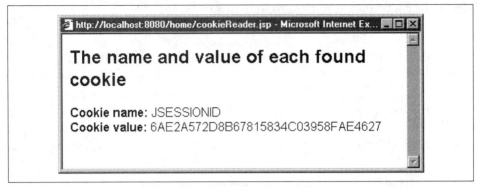

Figure 12-3. The new window loads a URL value from a servlet init-param

12.4 Creating a New Window with JavaScript in a JSP

Problem

You want to use JavaScript in a JSP to create a new browser window.

Solution

Use the c:import JSTL tag to import the JavaScript code into the JSP. Then use the initParam JSTL implicit object to dynamically provide the URL for a JavaScript-generated window.

Discussion

The JSP in Example 12-5 (*windowJ.jsp*) uses the JSTL's c:import core tag to import the JavaScript function definition for creating a new window. The JSP then calls the JavaScript function (CreateWindow) in the onClick event handler for a web page button. The CreateWindow function loads the URL specified in its parameter into the new browser window. Example 12-5 uses the c:out core tag and EL syntax to dynamically acquire the URL for the JavaScript window from a context parameter. The c:out tag looks like this:

```
<c:out value=
"${pageContext.request.contextPath}${initParam[\"jsp-url\"]}"/>
```

The value attribute specifies two EL expressions. The first one provides the JSP's context path, while the second gives the value of the context-param element jsp-url. The full URL specified by these concatenated EL expressions is */home/cookieReader.jsp*.

Example 12-5. Using the JSTL to import JavaScript into a JSP

```
<%@ taglib uri="http://java.sun.com/jstl/core" prefix="c" %>
<html>
<head>

<c:import url="/WEB-INF/javascript/functions.js" />

<title>Help Page</title></head><body>
<h2>Cookie Info</h2>

<form action ="" onSubmit=" return false">
<table border="0"><tr><td valign="top">
Click on the button to get more info on cookies: </td>
<td valign="top">

<input type="button" name="button1" value=
    "More Info" onClick=
"CreateWindow('<c:out value=
    "${pageContext.request.contextPath}${initParam[\"jsp-url\"]}"/>')">

</td></tr>
</table></form>
</body></html>
```

This JSP uses the following context-param element in *web.xml*:

```
<context-param>
    <param-name>jsp-url</param-name>
    <param-value>/cookieReader.jsp</param-value>
</context-param>
```

The EL implicit object `initParam` evaluates to a `java.util.Map` containing the names and values of any `context-param` elements configured for the web application. An *implicit object* is a variable that the JSTL automatically makes available to your JSP code.

 Example 12-5 uses the EL syntax `initParam[\"jsp-url\"]`, as opposed to `initParam.jsp-url`, in order to return the intended value in Tomcat 5 (alpha version as of this writing). The code's purpose is to escape the hyphen character (-) in "jsp-url."

See Also

The Netscape DevEdge site at *http://devedge.netscape.com/*; Recipes 12.2 and 12.6 on using JavaScript with JSPs to import JavaScript and validate form input; Recipe 12.3 on creating new browser windows with servlets and JavaScript; Recipe 12.5 on validating form values with a servlet and JavaScript; Recipe 18.3 on using a filter with HTTP requests.

12.5   Using JavaScript to Validate Form Values in a Servlet

Problem

You want to validate form input values using JavaScript in a JSP.

Solution

Use a `javax.servlet.RequestDispatcher` to include the validating JavaScript in the servlet. Then call the validating JavaScript function in the form's `onSubmit` event handler.

Discussion

Example 12-6 is a JavaScript module named *validate.js*. This file should be located in *WEB-INF/javascript/validate.js*. The file contains a `script` tag that contains one function definition: `validate`. This JavaScript function iterates through the form elements (such as `input` tags whose `type` attribute is `text`—in other words, text form fields) to determine if any of them have been left blank. The parameter for the `validate` function is a `form` object.

If the user has left the fields empty, this function displays an alert window and then cancels the form submit. A more realistic validation function might involve a greater degree of complex business logic, but I am keeping this example simple in order to demonstrate the mechanics of including the function in a servlet.

Example 12-6. A JavaScript module named validate.js for validating form input

```
<script language="JavaScript">
function validate(form1)
{
    for (i = 0; i < form1.length; i++){
      if( (form1.elements[i].value == "")){
          alert("You must provide a value for the field named: " +
              form1.elements[i].name)
          return false

      }
    }
    return true
}
</script>
```

The servlet in Example 12-7 includes the *validate.js* file using a `RequestDispatcher`. The `RequestDispatcher` positions the JavaScript `script` tag within an HTML `head` tag in the servlet's output. The servlet page's `form` tag has an attribute that is composed of the context path (the return value of `request.getContextPath( )`) concatenated with the */displayHeaders.jsp* JSP file. If the form fields are filled out properly, the browser submits the form to the JSP page (*/home/displayHeaders.jsp*).

Finally, the form's onSubmit event handler calls the included JavaScript function validate, passing in the this JavaScript keyword. The this parameter evaluates to the form object. If the user fails to fill out the name and email fields, the validate function cancels the browser's submission of the form by returning false.

Example 12-7. Importing JavaScript in a servlet to validate form values

```
package com.jspservletcookbook;

import javax.servlet.*;
import javax.servlet.http.*;

public class FormServlet extends HttpServlet {

  public void doGet(HttpServletRequest request,
    HttpServletResponse response) throws ServletException,
      java.io.IOException {


      response.setContentType("text/html");
      java.io.PrintWriter out = response.getWriter( );
      out.println("<html><head>");

      RequestDispatcher dispatcher = request.getRequestDispatcher(
        "/WEB-INF/javascript/validate.js");

      dispatcher.include(request, response);

      out.println("<title>Help Page</title></head><body>");
      out.println("<h2>Please submit your information</h2>");

      out.println(
        "<form action =\"" + request.getContextPath( ) +
          "/displayHeaders.jsp\" onSubmit=\" return validate(this)\">");

      out.println("<table border=\"0\"><tr><td valign=\"top\">");
      out.println("Your name: </td>  <td valign=\"top\">");
      out.println("<input type=\"text\" name=\"username\" size=\"20\">");
      out.println("</td></tr><tr><td valign=\"top\">");
      out.println("Your email: </td>  <td valign=\"top\">");
      out.println("<input type=\"text\" name=\"email\" size=\"20\">");
      out.println("</td></tr><tr><td valign=\"top\">");

      out.println(
        "<input type=\"submit\" value=\"Submit Info\"></td></tr>");

      out.println("</table></form>");
      out.println("</body></html>");

    } //doGet
}
```

Figure 12-4 shows the browser page containing the form. Figure 12-5 shows the alert window generated by the JavaScript function.

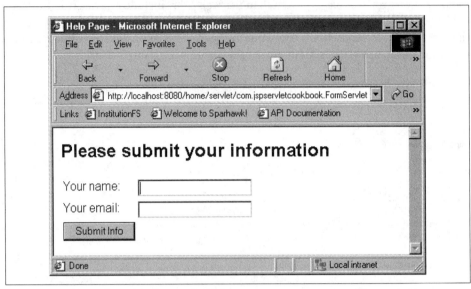

Figure 12-4. The servlet output for an HTML form

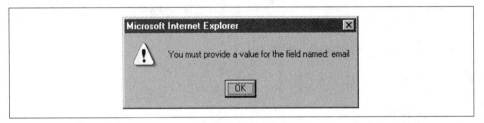

Figure 12-5. The included JavaScript validate function produces an alert window

Another option for validating form input is to use a filter to check parameter values, and then return the user to the form page or a new page if the input contains an error. Developers might prefer this option because a filter allows you to use Java code to parse the parameter values and gives you a great deal of control over the customization of the response page, in the case of a form input error. Recipe 18.3 describes how to use a filter with a servlet to deal with client requests.

See Also

The Netscape DevEdge site at *http://devedge.netscape.com/*; Recipes 12.2 and 12.6 on using JavaScript with JSPs to import JavaScript and validate form input; Recipe 12.3 on creating new browser windows with servlets and JavaScript; Recipe 12.5 on validating form values with a servlet and JavaScript; Recipe 18.3 on using a filter with HTTP requests.

12.6 Using JavaScript to Validate Form Values in a JSP

Problem

You want to import JavaScript into a JSP to validate HTML form values.

Solution

Use the `c:import` JSTL core tag to import the JavaScript function definitions. Then validate the HTML form input by using the `form` tag's onSubmit event handler.

Discussion

The JSP in Example 12-8 uses the JSTL core tag `c:import` to include the contents of the */WEB-INF/javascript/validate.js* file. See Example 12-6 for the contents of *validate.js*, which is a definition for the function `validate`. This function determines whether the user has left any form fields blank.

The rest of the JSP is straightforward: the onSubmit event handler calls the validate function and passes in the `form` object (represented by the JavaScript keyword this) as a parameter. By returning `false`, the validate function cancels the form submit if it finds any blank fields.

Example 12-8. A JSP uses JavaScript to validate HTML form input

```
<%@ taglib uri="http://java.sun.com/jstl/core" prefix="c" %>

<html>
<head>

<c:import url="/WEB-INF/javascript/validate.js" />

<title>Help Page</title></head><body>
<h2>Please submit your information</h2>

<form action ="/home/displayHeaders.jsp" onSubmit=" return validate(this)">

<table border="0"><tr><td valign="top">

Your name: </td>  <td valign="top">
<input type="text" name="username" size="20">
</td></tr><tr><td valign="top">
Your email: </td>  <td valign="top">
<input type="text" name="email" size="20">
</td></tr>
```

Example 12-8. A JSP uses JavaScript to validate HTML form input (continued)

```
<tr><td valign="top">
<input type="submit" value="Submit Info"></td></tr>

</table></form>
</body></html>
```

Figure 12-4 shows the web page containing the form. Figure 12-5 depicts the alert window that would be displayed if the user leaves one or more text fields blank when submitting the form.

See Also

The Netscape DevEdge site at *http://devedge.netscape.com/*; Recipes 12.2 and 12.4 on using JavaScript with JSPs to import JavaScript function definitions and create new browser windows; Recipe 12.3 on creating new browser windows with servlets and JavaScript; Recipe 12.5 on validating form values with a servlet and JavaScript; Recipe 18.3 on using a filter with HTTP requests.

CHAPTER 13

Sending Non-HTML Content

13.0 Introduction

Most web sites offer a smorgasbord of media types to their users. Typical web content these days includes Portable Document Format (PDF) files, word-processing documents, audio files, movies, and Extensible Markup Language (XML). In some cases, these alternative file types are stored in databases as *binary data*, or streams of unencoded bytes. Web developers cannot always provide their users with straightforward hyperlinks to these files for downloading. The user chooses a link or enters a URL in the browser's location field, and a servlet or some other web component downloads the binary data to the client. The client in most cases saves the data as a file, for use later in document viewers and other applications.

The following recipes describe how to initiate this download method. In a typical scenario, the servlet sets up a download whereby the browser prompts the user with a "Save As" dialog allowing him to save the files on his own filesystem. These strategies, however, do not guarantee 100-percent consistent behavior among web browsers. Some browsers allow the user to precisely configure how he wants to handle handle certain file types (such as a PDF document). For example, Opera 5 gives the user all kinds of options for dealing with downloads, such as opening up an external helper application, displaying a file using a plug-in, or immediately downloading a file to a specified folder without first opening up a "Save As" window.

 Test how your web application works in various browsers, in response to different browser configurations, as well as on different platforms, so that you are aware of the different browser responses elicited by the servlet.

The alternative to these strategies is simply providing a link to a PDF file—for instance—if the data exists as a file. This method, however, also places a great deal of the responsibility on the client browser, and the user who configures the browser, for managing the media type. While advanced users may like this approach, it is rarely sufficient for less-experienced users.

13.1 Sending a PDF File

Problem

You want to send binary data representing a PDF file to a user.

Solution

Use a servlet and a `java.io.BufferedInputStream` to read the bytes from the file. Send the file content to the user with a `javax.servlet.ServletOutputStream` retrieved from the `javax.servlet.http.HttpServletResponse` object.

Discussion

PDF files are ubiquitous on the Web, as most users are equipped with the Adobe Reader application that reads them. Example 13-1 takes a filename from a query string that is part of the request to the servlet, and responds with binary data that represents the PDF file. The servlet identifies the file that it sends to the client as the MIME type *application/pdf* by using the `Content-Type` response header.

 Multipurpose Internet Mail Extensions (MIME) designate the media types of various data that are sent as email or as part of HTTP responses on the Web. A MIME type has a top-level type and a subtype separated by a forward-slash character, as in *text/html*, *application/pdf*, or *audio/mpeg*. The `Content-Type` response header is the method the server response uses to convey the intended type and format of the data that the server sends to a network client such as a web browser. See the following Request For Comments (RFC) technical documents on MIME for more information: *ftp://ftp.rfc-editor.org/in-notes/rfc2045.txt* and *ftp://ftp.rfc-editor.org/in-notes/rfc2046.txt*.

Table 13-1 shows several MIME types that web developers may encounter.

Table 13-1. Some common MIME types

File	MIME type	Extension
XML	*text/xml*	.xml
HTML	*text/html*	.html
Plaintext file	*text/plain*	.txt
PDF	*application/pdf*	.pdf
Graphics Interchange Format (GIF) image	*image/gif*	.gif
JPEG image	*image/jpeg*	.jpeg
PNG image	*image/x-png*	.png

Table 13-1. Some common MIME types (continued)

File	MIME type	Extension
MP3 music file	*audio/mpeg*	*.mp3*
Shockwave Flash animation	*application/futuresplash or application/x-shockwave-flash*	*.swf*
Microsoft Word document	*application/msword*	*.doc*
Excel worksheet	*application/vnd.ms-excel*	*.xls*
PowerPoint document	*application/vnd.ms-powerpoint*	*.ppt*

The request to the servlet looks like this:

```
http://localhost:8080/home/sendpdf?file=chapter5
```

Example 13-1 checks to see if the request parameter file is valid and then adds the file extension *.pdf* to the filename if it does not already have that suffix. This is the filename the HTTP response recommends to the browser (it will appear as the default filename in any displayed "Save As" windows).

 Jason Hunter in *Java Enterprise Best Practices* (O'Reilly) points out that it is often useful to include the intended filename (for the "Save As" dialog box the browser produces) directly in the URL as extra path info. The browser detects that name as the requested resource and may specify the name in the "Save As" dialog window. An example URL in this case looks like:

```
http://localhost:8080/home/chapter5.pdf?file=ch5
```

Example 13-1. Sending a PDF file as binary data

```java
package com.jspservletcookbook;

import java.io.FileInputStream;
import java.io.BufferedInputStream;
import java.io.File;
import java.io.IOException;

import javax.servlet.*;
import javax.servlet.http.*;

public class SendPdf extends HttpServlet {

  public void doGet(HttpServletRequest request,
    HttpServletResponse response) throws ServletException,
      IOException {

      //get the filename from the "file" parameter
      String fileName = (String) request.getParameter("file");
      if (fileName == null || fileName.equals(""))
          throw new ServletException(
            "Invalid or non-existent file parameter in SendPdf servlet.");

      // add the .pdf suffix if it doesn't already exist
      if (fileName.indexOf(".pdf") == -1)
```

Example 13-1. Sending a PDF file as binary data (continued)

```
        fileName = fileName + ".pdf";

    //where are PDFs kept?
    String pdfDir = getServletContext( ).getInitParameter("pdf-dir");
    if (pdfDir == null || pdfDir.equals(""))
        throw new ServletException(
            "Invalid or non-existent 'pdfDir' context-param.");

    ServletOutputStream stream = null;
    BufferedInputStream buf = null;
    try{

    stream = response.getOutputStream( );
    File pdf = new File(pdfDir + "/" + fileName);

    //set response headers
    response.setContentType("application/pdf");

    response.addHeader(
        "Content-Disposition","attachment; filename="+fileName );

    response.setContentLength( (int) pdf.length( ) );

    FileInputStream input = new FileInputStream(pdf);
    buf = new BufferedInputStream(input);
    int readBytes = 0;

    //read from the file; write to the ServletOutputStream
    while((readBytes = buf.read( )) != -1)
        stream.write(readBytes);

    } catch (IOException ioe){

        throw new ServletException(ioe.getMessage( ));

    } finally {

    //close the input/output streams
    if (stream != null)
        stream.close( );
    if (buf != null)
        buf.close( );
    }

    } //end doGet

public void doPost(HttpServletRequest request,
   HttpServletResponse response)
     throws ServletException, IOException {

     doGet(request,response);
  }
}
```

Example 13-1 gets the directory where the PDF files are stored from a `context-param` element in the deployment descriptor:

```
<context-param>
    <param-name>pdf-dir</param-name>
    <param-value>h:/book/distribute</param-value>
</context-param>
```

 Remember that the `context-param` elements appear before the `filter`, `filter-mapping`, `listener`, and `servlet` elements in the *web.xml* version for servlet API 2.3.

The code then gets the `ServletOutputStream` from the `HttpServletResponse` object. The binary data representing the PDF is written to this stream:

```
stream = response.getOutputStream( );
```

The servlet does not use a `java.io.PrintWriter` as in `response.getWriter( )`, because a `PrintWriter` is designed for returning character data, such as HTML, that the browser displays on the computer screen. Example 13-1 adds the response headers that help prevent the browsers from trying to display the bytes as content in the browser window:

```
response.setContentType("application/pdf");
response.addHeader(
        "Content-Disposition","attachment; filename="+fileName );
response.setContentLength( (int) pdf.length( ) );
```

The `Content-Disposition` header field signals the client to treat the received content as an attachment, not as characters to be displayed in the browser. This optional response header also provides a recommended filename, which the browser may include as the default filename in any "Save As" windows.

 See RFC 2183 at *ftp://ftp.rfc-editor.org/in-notes/rfc2183.txt* for background information on the `Content-Disposition` header.

The client browser can use the `Content-Length` header value (provided with `response.setContentLength( )`) to indicate to the user the download progress with a widget that shows a horizontal bar steadily filling with color. The servlet also uses a `java.io.BufferedInputStream` to buffer the input from the file in a `byte[ ]` array, which speeds up the transfer of data from the server to the client.

 See Recipe 13.5 for an example of using a `java.net.URLConnection` (as opposed to a `FileInputStream`) to get an input stream associated with a web resource. A `URLConnection` is useful when you want to obtain binary data from a PDF file that is available only as a web address beginning with "http://".

The code closes the ServletOutputStream and the BufferedInputStream in a finally block to release any system resources used by these objects. The code within the finally block executes regardless of whether the code throws an exception.

 Internet Explorer 5.5 usually raises an exception that is displayed in the Tomcat log file when a request is made to this recipe's servlet. The logged exception does not disrupt the application, nor does it appear when the servlet is requested by Opera 5, or by Internet Explorer 5.2 and the Safari Macintosh browsers. The exception message includes the text "Connection reset by peer: socket write error." This message has raised speculation on various servlet-related mailing lists that the IE client browser on Windows has caused the exception by severing the connection with Tomcat after the data transfer. Nobody has yet devised a definitive solution to this apparently harmless exception, beyond suggesting that the servlet container's logging mechanism be configured to ignore exceptions of this type.

See Also

Recipes 13.2–13.4 on sending Word, XML, and MP3 files as binary data; Recipe 13. 5 on getting an input stream representing a web resource such as *web.xml*; RFC technical documents on MIME: *ftp://ftp.rfc-editor.org/in-notes/rfc2045.txt* and *ftp://ftp. rfc-editor.org/in-notes/rfc2046.txt.*; RFC 2183 at *ftp://ftp.rfc-editor.org/in-notes/ rfc2183.txt* for background information on the Content-Disposition header; the Media Types section of the *HTTP Pocket Reference* by Clinton Long (O'Reilly).

13.2 Sending a Word Processing File

Problem

You want to send a Microsoft Word file as binary data.

Solution

Use the same servlet setup as described in Recipe 13.1, but include a different file extension and a Content-Type of *application/msword*.

Discussion

You might have some Microsoft Word documents that you want to distribute as binary data from a servlet. Example 13-2 uses the same basic structure as Example 13-1, with a few changes to adapt the servlet for sending Microsoft Word documents. These include accessing a different context-param element (you *could* keep all files for download in the same directory, however), and using a different MIME type as the parameter for the setContentType( ) method, as in response. setContentType("application/msword").

Example 13-2. Sending a Word file as binary data

```java
package com.jspservletcookbook;

import java.io.FileInputStream;
import java.io.BufferedInputStream;
import java.io.File;
import java.io.IOException;

import javax.servlet.*;
import javax.servlet.http.*;

public class SendWord extends HttpServlet {

 public void doGet(HttpServletRequest request,
   HttpServletResponse response) throws ServletException,
    IOException {

     //get the filename from the "file" parameter
     String fileName = (String) request.getParameter("file");
     if (fileName == null || fileName.equals(""))
         throw new ServletException(
           "Invalid or non-existent file parameter in SendWord.");

     // add the .doc suffix if it doesn't already exist
     if (fileName.indexOf(".doc") == -1)
         fileName = fileName + ".doc";

     //where are Word files kept?
     String wordDir = getServletContext().getInitParameter("word-dir");
     if (wordDir == null || wordDir.equals(""))
         throw new ServletException(
            "Invalid or non-existent wordDir context-param.");

     ServletOutputStream stream = null;
     BufferedInputStream buf = null;
     try{

     stream = response.getOutputStream();
     File doc = new File(wordDir + "/" + fileName);

     //set response headers
     response.setContentType("application/msword");

     response.addHeader(
        "Content-Disposition","attachment; filename="+fileName );

     response.setContentLength( (int) doc.length() );

     FileInputStream input = new FileInputStream(doc);
     buf = new BufferedInputStream(input);
     int readBytes = 0;

     //read from the file; write to the ServletOutputStream
```

Example 13-2. Sending a Word file as binary data (continued)

```
    while((readBytes = buf.read( )) != -1)
        stream.write(readBytes);

    } catch (IOException ioe){

        throw new ServletException(ioe.getMessage( ));

    } finally {

        //close the input/output streams
    if(stream != null)
        stream.close( );
    if(buf != null)
        buf.close( );
    }

} //end doGet

public void doPost(HttpServletRequest request,
    HttpServletResponse response) throws ServletException,
        IOException {

    doGet(request,response);
    }
}
```

The `ServletOutputStream` (the information sent as the servlet response) and the `BufferedInputStream` (from which the servlet gets the file to send) are both closed in the `finally` block to make sure any system resources they use are released. See the end of the discussion in Recipe 13.1 for a further description of this code, including the warning at the end of that recipe about the Internet Explorer–related exception.

See Also

Recipe 13.1 on sending a PDF file; Recipes 13.3 and 13.4 on sending XML and MP3 files as binary data; Recipe 13.5 on getting an input stream representing a web resource such as *web.xml*; RFC technical documents on MIME: *ftp://ftp.rfc-editor.org/in-notes/rfc2045.txt* and *ftp://ftp.rfc-editor.org/in-notes/rfc2046.txt*; RFC 2183 at *ftp://ftp.rfc-editor.org/in-notes/rfc2183.txt* for background information on the `Content-Disposition` header; the Media Types section of the *HTTP Pocket Reference* by Clinton Wong (O'Reilly); Chapter 1 introducing the development of a servlet.

13.3 Sending an XML file

Problem

You want to send an XML file as binary data from a servlet.

Solution

Use the javax.servlet.ServletOutputStream obtained from the javax.servlet.http.HttpServletResponse object to send the XML file as binary data to the client.

Discussion

This recipe describes how to send an XML file as binary data from a ServletOutputStream, so that the user can handle the file as downloaded XML. Example 13-3 obtains the bytes that represent the XML as a BufferedInputStream wrapped around a FileInputStream. The code is very similar to Example 13-1 in Recipe 13.1, except that it uses a MIME type of *text/XML*.

 In a popular form of converting XML into a readable format, you could convert the XML content to HTML or another form using Extensible Stylesheet Language Transformations (XSLT). If the intent is to use XSLT for generating the content in a browser, leave out the Content-Disposition response header, because this header is designed to handle the XML as a downloaded file that will be saved in the user's filesystem. See Chapter 23 on using the x:transform JSTL tag.

Example 13-3. Sending an XML file with a servlet

```
package com.jspservletcookbook;

import java.io.FileInputStream;
import java.io.BufferedInputStream;
import java.io.File;
import java.io.IOException;

import javax.servlet.*;
import javax.servlet.http.*;

public class SendXml extends HttpServlet {

  public void doGet(HttpServletRequest request,
    HttpServletResponse response) throws ServletException,
     IOException {

    //get the filename from the "file" parameter
    String fileName = (String) request.getParameter("file");
    if (fileName == null || fileName.equals(""))
        throw new ServletException(
          "Invalid or non-existent file parameter in SendXml servlet.");

    // add the .xml suffix if it doesn't already exist
    if (fileName.indexOf(".xml") == -1)
        fileName = fileName + ".xml";

    //where are XML files kept?
```

Example 13-3. Sending an XML file with a servlet (continued)

```
    String xmlDir = getServletContext( ).getInitParameter("xml-dir");
    if (xmlDir == null || xmlDir.equals(""))
        throw new ServletException(
            "Invalid or non-existent xmlDir context-param.");

    ServletOutputStream stream = null;
    BufferedInputStream buf = null;

    try{

        stream = response.getOutputStream( );
        File xml = new File(xmlDir + "/" + fileName);

        //set response headers
        response.setContentType("text/xml");

        response.addHeader(
            "Content-Disposition","attachment; filename="+fileName );

        response.setContentLength( (int) xml.length( ) );

        FileInputStream input = new FileInputStream(xml);
        buf = new BufferedInputStream(input);
        int readBytes = 0;

        //read from the file; write to the ServletOutputStream
        while((readBytes = buf.read( )) != -1)
            stream.write(readBytes);

    } catch (IOException ioe){

        throw new ServletException(ioe.getMessage( ));

    } finally {

        //close the input/output streams
        if(stream != null)
            stream.close( );

        if(buf != null)
            buf.close( );

    }//finally

} //end doGet

public void doPost(HttpServletRequest request,
    HttpServletResponse response)
        throws ServletException, IOException {

        doGet(request,response);
    }
}
```

For the context-param to work correctly in this code, you have to include in *web.xml* an element that looks like:

```
<context-param>
    <param-name>xml-dir</param-name>
    <param-value>h:/home/xml</param-value>
</context-param>
```

 See Chapter 1 if you need an introduction or refresher for the deployment descriptor *web.xml*.

The discussion in Recipe 13.1 describes the basic mechanics of this code, so I don't repeat that information here. See the note at the end of Recipe 13.1 about the Internet Explorer–related exception that you may experience with servlets of this type.

See Also

Recipe 13.1 on sending a PDF file; Recipe 13.2 on sending a Microsoft Word file as binary data; Recipe 13.4 on sending MP3 files as binary data; Recipe 13.5 on getting an input stream representing a web resource such as *web.xml*; the RFC technical documents on MIME: *ftp://ftp.rfc-editor.org/in-notes/rfc2045.txt* and *ftp://ftp.rfc-editor. org/in-notes/rfc2046.txt*; RFC 2183 at *ftp://ftp.rfc-editor.org/in-notes/rfc2183.txt* for background information on the Content-Disposition header; the Media Types section of the *HTTP Pocket Reference* by Clinton Wong (O'Reilly); Chapter 1 introducing the development of a servlet; a tutorial on *java.sun.com* on XSLT: *http://java.sun. com/webservices/docs/1.1/tutorial/doc/JAXPXSLT.html#wp68287*.

13.4   Sending an Audio File

Problem

You want to send an audio file such as an MPEG layer 3 (MP3) media type.

Solution

Use a java.io.BufferedInputStream to fetch the audio data, and the javax.servlet. ServletOutputStream from the javax.servlet.http.HttpServletResponse object to send the data to the client.

Discussion

The code in Example 13-4 uses the same approach as the prior recipes, except for the MIME type, which is specified as *audio/mpeg*.

Web browsers associate a number of other MIME types for MP3 files, including *audio/x-mpeg*, *audio/mp3*, and *audio/x-mp3*.

The user requests a filename in the URL, as in:

```
http://localhost:8080/home/sendmp3?file=song_name
```

The deployment descriptor (*web.xml*) maps the servlet path */sendmp3* to the servlet class of Example 13-4: com.jspservletcookbook.SendMp3. If the requested file does not already have the *.mp3* suffix, then the code adds that file extension. A context-param element in the deployment descriptor specifies the directory where the audio files are kept:

```
<context-param>
    <param-name>mp3-dir</param-name>
    <param-value>h:/home/mp3s</param-value>
</context-param>
```

Example 13-4 uses this directory name, plus the filename, as the constructor parameter to create a new java.io.File object, which is the source for a java.io. FileInputStream. A BufferedInputStream buffers the bytes from the song file, which the ServletOutputStream response reads.

Example 13-4. Sending an MP3 file

```
package com.jspservletcookbook;

import java.io.FileInputStream;
import java.io.BufferedInputStream;
import java.io.File;
import java.io.IOException;

import javax.servlet.*;
import javax.servlet.http.*;

public class SendMp3 extends HttpServlet {

  public void doGet(HttpServletRequest request,
    HttpServletResponse response) throws ServletException, IOException {

      //get the filename from the "file" parameter
      String fileName = (String) request.getParameter("file");
      if (fileName == null || fileName.equals(""))
          throw new ServletException(
          "Invalid or non-existent file parameter in SendMp3 servlet.");

      // add the .mp3 suffix if it doesn't already exist
      if (fileName.indexOf(".mp3") == -1)
          fileName = fileName + ".mp3";

      //where are MP3 files kept?
```

Example 13-4. Sending an MP3 file (continued)

```java
        String mp3Dir = getServletContext( ).getInitParameter("mp3-dir");

        if (mp3Dir == null || mp3Dir.equals(""))
            throw new ServletException(
            "Invalid or non-existent mp3-Dir context-param.");

        ServletOutputStream stream = null;
        BufferedInputStream buf = null;
        try{

            stream = response.getOutputStream( );
            File mp3 = new File(mp3Dir + "/" + fileName);

            //set response headers
            response.setContentType("audio/mpeg");

            response.addHeader(
            "Content-Disposition","attachment; filename="+fileName );

            response.setContentLength( (int) mp3.length( ) );

            FileInputStream input = new FileInputStream(mp3);
            buf = new BufferedInputStream(input);
            int readBytes = 0;

            //read from the file; write to the ServletOutputStream
            while((readBytes = buf.read( )) != -1)
                stream.write(readBytes);

        } catch (IOException ioe){

            throw new ServletException(ioe.getMessage( ));

        } finally {

            //close the input/output streams
            if(stream != null)
                stream.close( );

            if(buf != null)
                buf.close( );

        }

    } //doGet

    public void doPost(HttpServletRequest request,
      HttpServletResponse response) throws ServletException, IOException {

        doGet(request,response);
    }
}
```

Review Recipe 13.1 for a further explanation of this code, including the warning at the end of the "Discussion" section about logged exceptions that may occur with Internet Explorer.

See Also

Recipe 13.1 on MIME types and sending a PDF file as binary data; Recipes 13.2 and 13.3 on sending Word and XML files, respectively, as binary data; Recipe 13.5 on receiving an input stream representing a web resource such as *web.xml*; the RFC technical documents on MIME: *ftp://ftp.rfc-editor.org/in-notes/rfc2045.txt* and *ftp:// ftp.rfc-editor.org/in-notes/rfc2046.txt*; RFC 2183 at *ftp://ftp.rfc-editor.org/in-notes/ rfc2183.txt* for background information on the Content-Disposition header; the Media Types section of the *HTTP Pocket Reference* by Clinton Wong (O'Reilly); Chapter 1 introducing the development of a servlet.

13.5   Viewing Internal Resources in a Servlet

Problem

You want to use a servlet to fetch internal resources from a web application for viewing by authenticated users.

Solution

Use the javax.servlet.ServletContext.getResource(String path) method to generate the input stream from the web resource.

Discussion

A servlet could be used while a web application is in development to provide a view of the deployment descriptor. Web developers often have to double-check *web.xml* for the values of context-param elements, a servlet's registered name, and other information. Wouldn't it be nice to just request a servlet in the browser to view *web.xml*?

Example 13-5 opens up *web.xml* using the ServletContext.getResource( ) method, which returns a java.net.URL object representing the deployment descriptor at the path *WEB-INF/web.xml*.

The code opens a connection to the XML file by calling the URL object's openConnection( ) method, which returns a java.net.URLConnection object. Then the code buffers the input stream to the resource by wrapping it in a BufferedInputStream:

```
buf = new BufferedInputStream(urlConn.getInputStream( ));
```

The urlConn variable refers to a URLConnection.

If the browser is not savvy about displaying XML files in a readable fashion (Netscape 7.1 and Internet Explorer can display these files properly), you can use XSLT to convert the XML into HTML before it is sent to the browser.

Example 13-5. Displaying the deployment descriptor via a servlet

```java
package com.jspservletcookbook;

import java.io.BufferedInputStream;
import java.io.PrintWriter;
import java.io.IOException;

import java.net.URL;
import java.net.URLConnection;
import java.net.MalformedURLException;

import javax.servlet.*;
import javax.servlet.http.*;

public class ResourceServlet extends HttpServlet {

 public void doGet(HttpServletRequest request,
   HttpServletResponse response) throws ServletException,
    IOException {

     //get web.xml for display by a servlet
     String file = "/WEB-INF/web.xml";

     URL url = null;
     URLConnection urlConn = null;
     PrintWriter out = null;
     BufferedInputStream buf = null;

     try{

         out = response.getWriter( );

         //access a web resource within the same web application
         // as a URL object
         url = getServletContext( ).getResource(file);

         //set response header
         response.setContentType("text/xml");

         urlConn = url.openConnection( );

         //establish connection with URL representing web.xml
         urlConn.connect( );

         buf = new BufferedInputStream(urlConn.getInputStream( ));
         int readBytes = 0;
```

Example 13-5. Displaying the deployment descriptor via a servlet (continued)

```
        //read from the file; write to the PrintWriter
        while((readBytes = buf.read( )) != -1)
            out.write(readBytes);

    } catch (MalformedURLException mue){

        throw new ServletException(mue.getMessage( ));

    } catch (IOException ioe){

        throw new ServletException(ioe.getMessage( ));

    } finally {

        //close the input/output streams
        if(out != null)
            out.close( );

        if(buf != null)
            buf.close( );

    }

} //doGet

public void doPost(HttpServletRequest request,
  HttpServletResponse response)
    throws ServletException, IOException {

    doGet(request,response);
}
}
```

 This servlet is designed for developers; if just anyone has a chance to study the deployment descriptor, it will compromise the web application's security. Therefore, you should remove the servlet from production versions of the web application, or use authentication to allow only authorized users to view the servlet's output (see Chapter 15 for details).

The code uses a PrintWriter to write the bytes received from the input stream, because the servlet intends to display the response as characters (instead of offering the response to the client as a downloaded resource). The ServletContext. getResource(*String path*) method takes a path that beings with the / character. The path is interpreted as beginning at the context root, or top-level directory, of the web application. Therefore, the servlet obtains *web.xml* with the following code:

```
String file = "/WEB-INF/web.xml";
...
url = getServletContext( ).getResource(file);
```

The ServletContext.getResouce( ) method returns null if it is unable to return a valid resource representing the path parameter.

See Also

Recipes 13.1–13.4 on sending PDF, Word, XML, and audio files, respectively, as binary data; the RFC technical documents on MIME: *ftp://ftp.rfc-editor.org/in-notes/ rfc2045.txt* and *ftp://ftp.rfc-editor.org/in-notes/rfc2046.txt*; RFC 2183 at *ftp://ftp.rfc-editor.org/in-notes/rfc2183.txt* for background information on the Content-Disposition header; the Media Types section of the *HTTP Pocket Reference* by Clinton Wong (O'Reilly); Chapter 1 introducing the development of a servlet.

CHAPTER 14

Logging Messages from Servlets and JSPs

14.0 Introduction

Logging involves sending messages from your application and displaying this information in a variety of ways for web developers and administrators. The messages can be delivered to a console, or they can be stored persistently in files or databases. Logging may be used only for sending debug-related information while a web application is being developed, or these messages may provide information from an application in production, including data about warnings and fatal errors.

This chapter describes a very powerful open source logging tool called *log4j*. This is a Java ARchive (JAR) file (*log4j-1.2.8.jar*) that you can add to your web application by placing it in your *WEB-INF/lib* directory. This makes it available for use in any servlets or beans that you want to send logging messages from. This section provides only a brief introduction to *log4j*, because its power does entail some complexity.

log4j involves three main concepts: *loggers*, *appenders*, and *layouts*. *log4j* uses an external configuration file, similar to a deployment descriptor, to configure these three logging elements. The upcoming recipes provide some examples of these configuration files, which are mostly simple text files involving a list of name/value pairs. The power of using external files is that you can change the properties in these text files to alter a logger (for instance, modify the format of its messages) instead of recompiling the servlet code.

 For the changes to take effect, you may require a reload of the servlet or other component that initializes the logging system for the application.

Loggers

A logger is the entity that a servlet uses to log messages. To use one, import the *log4j* classes into the servlet, create an instance of a logger (specifically an org.apache.

log4j.Logger), then call the logger's methods. The methods are named after the logging level of the message. For example, to log an informational message (an INFO level) you would call:

```
logger.info("HttpServlet init method called.");
```

log4j has five different levels of log categories: DEBUG, INFO, WARN, ERROR, and FATAL. The log categories are organized in ascending order beginning with DEBUG—a logger configured for INFO-level logging logs only INFO, WARN, ERROR, and FATAL messages (but not DEBUG-level messages, because in this hierarchy DEBUG is beneath INFO and the other levels). Here is a brief description of the purpose of each level:

- DEBUG involves logging messages while initially developing and debugging an application.
- INFO helps you monitor the progress of an application.
- WARN designates potentially harmful situations.
- ERROR represents an error that the application can likely recover from.
- FATAL suggests errors that will cause an application to abort.

Every logger is configured with a level (such as DEBUG) in the *log4j* properties or configuration file (see Recipe 14.4). *log4j* also associates the messages that you log with a specified level, which makes it easy to use because the method names are the same as the level names. The logger does not send these messages unless the logger's level is equal to or greater than the level represented by the method call (as in logger.debug(*Object message*)).

For example, let's say you configure the logger with a level of DEBUG, then develop a servlet with a number of logger.debug(*Object message*) calls.

Later, you can change the configuration file and give the logger an INFO level. Changing the configuration in this manner "turns off" DEBUG-level logging in that servlet, so that these logging messages no longer show up in the log files, database, or other logging repository. This is because DEBUG is not equal to or greater than INFO in the hierarchy of logging categories.

Similarly, you can turn back on DEBUG-level logging in the prior example by simply switching the logger's configuration back from INFO to DEBUG. As a result, the debug-level messages will no longer be filtered out.

Programmers writing software with several DEBUG-level method calls can easily switch into WARN- or ERROR-level debugging once the application moves into its next stage of development, or goes into production.

Appenders

log4j is also very powerful in terms of the different ways you can log messages. You can use *log4j* to log messages to a console, a file, a *rolling file* (which automatically creates a backup file when a log file reaches a specified size), a database, an email server, and several other types of log repositories. *log4j* calls each of these logging mechanisms an appender. Recipe 14.4 introduces the configuration file in which you can describe appenders.

Layouts

What does the actual logged message look like? What information does it include? *log4j* shines in this area too. You can specify numerous different layouts for the messages using the *log4j* configuration file. *log4j* lets you specify very complex (or simple) layouts using *conversion patterns*, which are somewhat similar to regular expressions. To achieve the most basic layout, you can specify an org.apache.log4j. SimpleLayout. With this format, the log contains the level name, followed by a dash (-) and the actual message:

```
INFO - HttpServlet init method called.
```

Using an org.apache.log4j.PatternLayout is more powerful, and Recipe 14.5 provides some examples of different layouts for logging messages.

14.1 Logging Without Log4j

Problem

You want to put a message in the server logs.

Solution

Call the ServletContext.log( ) method inside the servlet.

Discussion

If you just want to log a message in the servlet container's log file and do not need the power of *log4j*, use the ServletContext.log( ) method. Example 14-1 shows the two versions of the log( ) method. One takes the String message as a parameter, and the other has two parameters: a String message and a Throwable. The servlet log will contain the stack trace of the Throwable if you use this log( ) form.

Example 14-1. A servlet uses the ServletContext.log() method

```
package com.jspservletcookbook;

import javax.servlet.*;
import javax.servlet.http.*;

public class ContextLog extends HttpServlet {


  public void doGet(HttpServletRequest request,
      HttpServletResponse response) throws ServletException,
```

Example 14-1. A servlet uses the ServletContext.log() method (continued)

```
        java.io.IOException {

    String yourMessage = request.getParameter("mine");
    //Call the two ServletContext.log methods
    ServletContext context = getServletContext();

    if (yourMessage == null || yourMessage.equals(""))
    //log version with Throwable parameter
    context.log("No message received:",
        new IllegalStateException("Missing parameter"));
    else
        context.log("Here is the visitor's message: " + yourMessage);

    response.setContentType("text/html");
    java.io.PrintWriter out = response.getWriter();
    //logging servlets probably want to display more HTML
    out.println(
        "<html><head><title>ServletContext logging</title></head><body>");
    out.println("<h2>Messages sent</h2>");
    out.println("</body></html>");
    } //doGet
}
```

The ServletContext logs its text messages to the servlet container's log file. With Tomcat these logs are found in *<Tomcat-installation-directory>/logs*. Below is the output of Example 14-1 and the second form of ServletContext.log( ), which prints the message and the Throwable's stack trace (only the first two levels of the method stack are shown). You can see that the log includes the date and time of the logging activity, and the message text:

```
2003-05-08 14:42:43 No message received:
java.lang.IllegalStateException: Missing parameter
    at com.jspservletcookbook.ContextLog.doGet(Unknown Source)
    at javax.servlet.http.HttpServlet.service(HttpServlet.java:740)
...
```

The single-parameter form of the log( ) method simply displays the date, time, and text of the message, as in the first line of the prior log sample. Each log( ) method call places the message on a new line in the server log file.

See Also

Recipes 14.2–14.8 on using *log4j* to design your own custom logging mechanism; Chapter SRV.3 of the servlet API on the servlet context; links to the latest servlet specification: *http://java.sun.com/products/servlet/index.html*.

14.2 Setting Up Log4j

Problem

You want to set up *log4j* for use in your web application.

Solution

Download the *log4j* distribution from the Apache Jakarta project and place the accompanying *log4j-1.2.8.jar* file (the name will be different for different *log4j* versions) in the *WEB-INF/lib* directory of your web application.

Discussion

The *log4j* package is available for use under the Apache Software License, which is included with the distribution. Here are the steps for setting up *log4j* for your web application:

1. Go to the *log4j* web site and download the distribution in ZIP (Windows) or gzipped (Unix-based systems) format: *http://jakarta.apache.org/log4j/docs/download.html*. The downloaded file will be named something like *jakarta-log4j-1.2.8.zip* or *jakarta-log4j-1.2.8.tar.gz*.

2. Unpack the distribution, which creates a directory *jakarta-log4j-1.2.8* (for Version 1.2.8 of *log4j*). Inside the *dist* directory of this top-level directory is the *log4j-1.2.8.jar* file. Copy this JAR file into the *WEB-INF/lib* directory of your web application(s).

3. Create a *log4j* properties file and place it in the web application's *WEB-INF/classes* directory. This is typically a text file with name/value pairs for configuring *log4j* elements such as loggers, appenders, and layouts. Recipe 14.4 includes an example of this file.

4. In the servlets or beans where you will use a logger, include the proper `import` statements. Example 14-2 is a skeletal servlet showing the classes that you might typically use.

Example 14-2. Importing log4j-related packages

```
import org.apache.log4j.Logger;
import org.apache.log4j.PropertyConfigurator;

import javax.servlet.*;
import javax.servlet.http.*;

public class LoggerSkel extends HttpServlet {

  private Logger log;
```

Example 14-2. Importing log4j-related packages (continued)

```
public void init(){

    //log4j will find the log4j.properties file
    //in WEB-INF/classes
    log = Logger.getLogger(LoggerSkel.class);

    //Just an example of using the logger
    log.debug("Instance created of: " + getClass().getName());

}

public void doGet(HttpServletRequest request,
  HttpServletResponse response) throws ServletException,
    java.io.IOException {

  //do logging here if necessary

  } //doGet

}
```

As long as *log4j-1.2.8.jar* is located in *WEB-INF/lib*, your servlet can use the necessary classes from the org.apache.log4j.* packages.

See Also

Recipes 14.3–14.8 on using *log4j* to design your own custom logging mechanism; the *log4j* download site: *http://jakarta.apache.org/log4j/docs/download.html*; the *log4j* project documentation page: *http://jakarta.apache.org/log4j/docs/documentation.html*.

14.3   Using a Logger Without a Configuration File

Problem

You want to use a logger in a servlet without setting up your own configuration file.

Solution

Create the logger in the servlet and use the org.apache.log4j.BasicConfigurator class to configure the logger.

Discussion

log4j allows the configuration of a logger without a provided configuration or properties file. Example 14-3 is a servlet that instantiates a logger in its init() method, which the servlet container calls when the servlet instance is created. The static BasicConfigurator.configure( ) method creates a ConsoleAppender; in other words, the logger will log its messages to the console using a default format.

Example 14-3. A servlet uses BasicConfigurator to configure a logger

```
package com.jspservletcookbook;

import org.apache.log4j.Logger;
import org.apache.log4j.BasicConfigurator;

import javax.servlet.*;
import javax.servlet.http.*;

public class LoggerNconfig extends HttpServlet {

private Logger log = null;

  public void init( ){

      //use the root logger
      log = Logger.getRootLogger( );

      //this logger will log to the console with a default message format
      BasicConfigurator.configure( );


  }

  public void doGet(HttpServletRequest request,
    HttpServletResponse response)
      throws ServletException, java.io.IOException {

      //display a DEBUG level message
      log.debug("Sending a DEBUG message");

      // display an INFO level message
      log.info("Sending an INFO message");

      //better display some HTML
      response.setContentType("text/html");

      java.io.PrintWriter out = response.getWriter( );
      out.println(
        "<html><head><title>Servlet logging</title></head><body>");
      out.println("<h2>Hello from a Logger with no Config file</h2>");

      //This logger's parent is the root logger
      out.println(
          "Your logger name is: " + log.getName( )+"<br>");
      out.println(
        "Your logger parent is: " + log.getParent().getName( )+"<br>");
```

Example 14-3. A servlet uses BasicConfigurator to configure a logger (continued)

```
        out.println("</body></html>");

    } //doGet

    public void doPost(HttpServletRequest request,
      HttpServletResponse response) throws ServletException,
        java.io.IOException {

        doGet(request,response);
    }
}
```

Example 14-4 shows an example message from the servlet. The message is based on a default format that includes the thread name (Thread-5), the level name (DEBUG), the logger name (com.jspservletcookbook.LoggerNconfig), and the actual message ("Sending a DEBUG message"). Recipe 14.5 shows how to create a format pattern for logging messages, so that you can customize the type of information that the logger sends.

Example 14-4. Example of a logged message using BasicConfigurator

```
4061660 [Thread-5] DEBUG com.jspservletcookbook.LoggerNconfig  - Sending a DEBUG message
4061660 [Thread-5] INFO com.jspservletcookbook.LoggerNconfig  - Sending an INFO message
```

Here is the pattern used for the layout associated with BasicConfigurator:

```
    %-4r [%t] %-5p %c %x - %m%n
```

See Recipe 14.5 for details on the org.apache.log4j.PatternLayout class.

See Also

Recipe 14.2 on downloading and setting up *log4j*; Recipes 14.4–14.8 on using *log4j* to design your own custom logging mechanism; the *log4j* download site: *http://jakarta.apache.org/log4j/docs/download.html*; the *log4j* Javadoc page: *http://jakarta.apache.org/log4j/docs/api/index.html*; the *log4j* project documentation page: *http://jakarta.apache.org/log4j/docs/documentation.html*.

14.4   Adding an Appender to the Root Logger

Problem

You want to configure an appender or logging destination for the root logger.

Solution

Create a configuration file called *log4j.properties* and place it in the *WEB-INF/classes* directory of your web application.

Discussion

Now our discussion moves on to the *log4j* configuration file, where developers can customize loggers, appenders, and layouts. Here are the steps for using this recipe's examples:

1. Create a properties file named *log4j.properties* (its contents look like Example 14-5).
2. Place the properties file in the *WEB-INF/classes* directory of the web application.
3. Import this class into your servlet: `org.apache.log4j.Logger`.
4. In the servlet, get a reference to the root logger with the static `Logger.getRootLogger( )` method, and start logging.

Example 14-5 configures the root logger, a kind of "super logger" for your application, with a `DEBUG` level. The root logger uses an appender named *cons*. This appender is of a type `org.apache.log4j.ConsoleAppender`, meaning that it sends its log messages to the console.

Example 14-5. The log4j.properties file for creating a root logger appender

```
log4j.rootLogger=DEBUG, cons

log4j.appender.cons=org.apache.log4j.ConsoleAppender

log4j.appender.cons.layout=org.apache.log4j.SimpleLayout
```

The third line of the *log4j.properties* file states that the logger will use a `SimpleLayout`, which logs the level name (`DEBUG`), a dash (-), and the message itself. Example 14-6 shows the servlet that is using the logger. *log4j* will find the *log4j.properties* file automatically in *WEB-INF/classes* because the servlet has not otherwise configured the logger with a call to `BasicConfigurator.configure( )`, as shown in Recipe 14.3.

Example 14-6. Using the root logger configured with the log4j.properties file

```
package com.jspservletcookbook;

import org.apache.log4j.Logger;

import javax.servlet.*;
import javax.servlet.http.*;

public class LoggerWconfig extends HttpServlet {

  private Logger log = null;
```

```
public void init( ){

    //The root logger will get its configuration from
    //WEB-INF/classes/log4j.properties
    log = Logger.getRootLogger( );

    log.info("LoggerWconfig started.");
}

public void doGet(HttpServletRequest request,
  HttpServletResponse response)
    throws ServletException, java.io.IOException {

    //display a DEBUG-level message
    log.debug("Sending a DEBUG message");

    // display an INFO-level message
    log.info("Sending an INFO message");

    //better display some HTML
    response.setContentType("text/html");
    java.io.PrintWriter out = response.getWriter( );
    out.println(
      "<html><head><title>Servlet logging</title></head><body>");

    out.println(
      "<h2>Hello from a Logger with a log4j.properties file</h2>");

    out.println("Your logger name is: " + log.getName( )+"<br>");

    out.println("</body></html>");
    } //end doGet

}
```

Example 14-6 logs an INFO message in the servlet's init( ) method, then logs two messages in the servlet's doGet( ) service method. The logger logs all of these messages to the console because this is how the *log4j.properties* file configures the root logger's appender. This is what the console output looks like:

```
INFO - LoggerWconfig started.
DEBUG - Sending a DEBUG message
INFO - Sending an INFO message
```

Figure 14-1 shows the servlet's output in a web browser.

See Also

Recipe 14.2 on downloading and setting up *log4j*; Recipe 14.3 on using a *log4j* logger without a properties file; Recipes 14.5–14.8 on using *log4j* to design your own

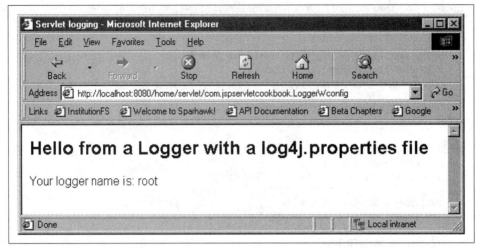

Figure 14-1. The logger displays its name in a servlet

custom logging mechanism; the *log4j* download site: *http://jakarta.apache.org/log4j/docs/download.html*; the *log4j* Javadoc page: *http://jakarta.apache.org/log4j/docs/api/index.html*; the *log4j* project documentation page: *http://jakarta.apache.org/log4j/docs/documentation.html*.

14.5   Using a Pattern with a Logger's Appender

Problem

You want to create your own logger for a servlet and give the logger an appender.

Solution

Include the appender configuration in the *log4j.properties* file.

Discussion

This recipe creates a new logger, which brings us to the discussion of *log4j*'s inheritance structure. The root logger is the "super logger" that all logger's inherit from, similar to java.lang.Object in Java's object oriented programming setup. Example 14-7 creates a new logger named com.jspservletcookbook, which inherits the root logger's level (DEBUG) and console appender (named *cons*). Example 14-7 also creates an appender for the com.jspservletcookbook logger. Place this *log4j.properties* file in the *WEB-INF/classes* directory.

Example 14-7. The configuration for a logger named com.jspservletcookbook

```
log4j.rootLogger=DEBUG, cons
log4j.logger.com.jspservletcookbook=, myAppender

#the root logger's appender
log4j.appender.cons=org.apache.log4j.ConsoleAppender

#the com.jspservletcookbook logger's appender
log4j.appender.myAppender=org.apache.log4j.RollingFileAppender

log4j.appender.myAppender.File=h:/home/example.log

log4j.appender.myAppender.MaxBackupIndex=1

log4j.appender.myAppender.MaxFileSize=1MB

#the root logger's layout
log4j.appender.cons.layout=org.apache.log4j.SimpleLayout

#the com.jspservletcookbook logger's layout
log4j.appender.myAppender.layout=org.apache.log4j.PatternLayout

log4j.appender.myAppender.layout.ConversionPattern=%-5p Logger:%c{1}
Date: %d{ISO8601} - %m%n
```

You probably noticed the similarity between package names and the name of the new logger in Example 14-7: com.jspservletcookbook. *log4j* uses a naming scheme based on Java's. Here's the basic rundown on this scheme:

- All loggers inherit from the root logger.
- All loggers whose name contains a prefix that matches a configured logger's name (such as com.jspservletcookbook) also inherit from that configured logger. Therefore, a logger named com.jspservletcookbook.LoggerWconfig derives its characteristics from the com.jspservletcookbook logger.

In Example 14-7, the com.jspservletcookbook logger specifies that it will use an appender named myAppender. The myAppender appender is a *rolling file appender*, which is a log file that automatically creates a backup file when the original log reaches a certain size. The appender is based on the Java class org.apache.log4j. RollingFileAppender, which is among the set of classes that *log4j* uses.

If you look at the Javadoc for that class, then you see that it has a bunch of methods that look like get*XXX*( ), where *XXX* is one of the logger's properties. You set these properties of the appender in the configuration file by giving each property a value. To set the myAppender appender's File property, the syntax is:

```
log4j.appender.myAppender.File=h:/home/example.log
```

This configuration element specifies the file location where the appender will log its messages. When this file reaches its MaxFileSize of 1 MB, *log4j* renames the file *example.log.1* and creates a new *example.log* to receive log messages. The `MaxBackupIndex` means that *log4j* will create only one backup file.

 The Javadoc for `RollingFileAppender` can be found at: *http://jakarta. apache.org/log4j/docs/api/org/apache/log4j/RollingFileAppender.html*.

Example 14-7 also specifies a layout for the `com.jspservletcookbook` logger, and a rather elaborate one at that:

```
log4j.appender.myAppender.layout=org.apache.log4j.PatternLayout
```

```
log4j.appender.myAppender.layout.ConversionPattern=%-5p Logger:%c{1} Date:
%d{ISO8601} - %m%n
```

The first line specifies that the `myAppender` layout will use an `org.apache.log4j. PatternLayout`, which is based on the conversion pattern of the `printf` function in C, according to the `PatternLayout` Javadoc. This pattern language combines literal text and *conversion specifiers* to generate a formatted log message. The conversion specifiers are letters (like c) that have special meanings as placeholders. For example, the letters may represent dates or logger names.

The `%` character precedes the conversion pattern symbols. For example, consider the following pattern:

```
Logger:%c{1}
```

This translates to "the literal text 'Logger:' followed by the logger's name." The number 1 in curly braces (`{1}`) following the `%c` characters is a precision specifier, which means "display just one segment of the name beginning from the righthand side." If the logger is `com.jspservletcookbook.LoggerServlet`, then the `%c{1}` pattern displays "LoggerServlet" in the log text. This is because the c conversion specifier is a placeholder for the logger name.

The letter m displays the log message itself, the letter n produces the platform-specific line separator, and the letter d represents the date. The entire string `%d{ISO8601}` is a *log4j* date formatter, which displays the date in detailed form. See *http://jakarta. apache.org/log4j/docs/api/org/apache/log4j/helpers/ISO8601DateFormat.html*.

Example 14.8 shows a servlet that uses a logger that inherits its characteristics from two configured loggers: the root logger and the `com.jspservletcookbook` logger.

Example 14-8. A servlet uses a descendant logger

```
package com.jspservletcookbook;

import org.apache.log4j.Logger;

import javax.servlet.*;
import javax.servlet.http.*;
```

Example 14-8. A servlet uses a descendant logger (continued)

```
public class LoggerNewConfig extends HttpServlet {

private Logger log = null;

  public void init(){

      //the logger's name is the same as the class name:
      //com.jspservletcookbook.LoggerNewConfig
      log = Logger.getLogger(LoggerNewConfig.class);

      log.info("LoggerNewConfig started.");
  }

  public void doGet(HttpServletRequest request,
    HttpServletResponse response)
      throws ServletException, java.io.IOException {

      //display a DEBUG-level message
      log.debug("Sending a DEBUG message");

      // display an INFO-level message
      log.info("Sending an INFO message");

      //better display some HTML
      response.setContentType("text/html");
      java.io.PrintWriter out = response.getWriter();
      out.println(
        "<html><head><title>Servlet logging</title></head><body>");

      out.println(
      "<h2>Hello from a Logger with its own configuration in the "+
      log4j.properties file</h2>");

      out.println("Your logger name is: " + log.getName()+"<br>");

      out.println(
        "Your logger parent is: " + log.getParent().getName()+"<br>");

      out.println("</body></html>");
  } //end doGet
}
```

The static org.apache.log4j.Logger.getLogger(*Class className*) method creates a logger named after the class in Example 14.8 (com.jspservletcookbook. LoggerNewConfig). Therefore, this new logger inherits the appender that the properties file in Example 14-7 set up for the logger com.jspservletcookbook, because the new logger's name has com.jspservletcookbook as a prefix. In fact, any other logger created in classes that are part of the com.jspservletcookbook package inherits these properties, as long as the developer keeps naming her loggers after the Java class in which they are created.

Here is an example of what the entire pattern the configuration file of Example 14-7 created generates in the log file:

```
INFO   Logger:LoggerNewConfig Date: 2003-07-10 17:16:22,713 - LoggerNewConfig started
DEBUG Logger:LoggerNewConfig Date: 2003-07-10 17:16:34,530 - Sending a DEBUG message
INFO   Logger:LoggerNewConfig Date: 2003-07-10 17:16:34,530 - Sending an INFO message
```

Visit *http://jakarta.apache.org/log4j/docs/api/org/apache/log4j/PatternLayout.html* for more details on pattern layouts.

 Because of the inheritance structure established by the log4j configuration file, the servlet in Example 14-8 also logs its messages to the console.

See Also

Recipe 14.2 on downloading and setting up *log4j*; Recipe 14.3 on using a *log4j* logger without a properties file; Recipe 14.4 on adding an appender to the root logger; Recipe 14.6 on using loggers in JSPs; Recipes 14.7 and 14.8 on using *log4j* with application event listeners; the *log4j* download site: *http://jakarta.apache.org/log4j/docs/download.html*; the *log4j* Javadoc page: *http://jakarta.apache.org/log4j/docs/api/index.html*; the *log4j* project documentation page: *http://jakarta.apache.org/log4j/docs/documentation.html*.

14.6   Using log4j in a JSP

Problem

You want to include logging statements in a JSP.

Solution

Design a custom tag that uses *log4j* to initiate logging messages.

Discussion

A custom tag is an XML element that you invent or design for use in a JSP. In other words, the JSP container does not provide the custom actions; the web developer himself designs the Java classes that provide the tag functionality. A custom tag or action can be used to implement *log4j* logging functionality in JSPs.

In this recipe, I show:

- A Java class that provides the tag handler for a custom tag named cbck:log.
- A Tag Library Descriptor (TLD) that provides the web application with information about the tag.
- A JSP page that uses the cbck:log tag.

Example 14-9 shows the Java class LoggerTag on which the cbck:log tag is based. Each custom action is actually driven behind the scenes by one or more Java classes. In this case, LoggerTag is like a JavaBean that wraps the *log4j* classes, which we import at the top of the tag class.

Custom JSP actions are a complex topic, so I explain this tag by focusing mainly on its *log4j* features. See Chapter 22 to help fill in the missing spaces in your own knowledge about custom tag development.

Example 14-9. A custom tag that uses log4j

```java
package com.jspservletcookbook;

import org.apache.log4j.Logger;
import org.apache.log4j.PropertyConfigurator;

import java.lang.reflect.Method;

import javax.servlet.jsp.*;
import javax.servlet.jsp.tagext.*;

public class LoggerTag extends BodyTagSupport {

    private Logger log = null;
    private String configFile = null;
    private String level = null;
    private static final String[] LEVELS =
        { "debug","info","warn","error","fatal"};

    public void setConfigFile(String fileName){

        this.configFile = fileName;

    }

    public void setLevel(String level){

        this.level = level;

    }

    public int doEndTag( ) throws JspException {

        String realPath = pageContext.getServletContext( ).getRealPath("/");
        String fileSep = System.getProperty("file.separator");
```

Example 14-9. A custom tag that uses log4j (continued)

```
    if (realPath != null && (!realPath.endsWith(fileSep))){
        realPath = realPath + fileSep;}

    //configure the logger if the user provides this optional attribute
    if (configFile != null)
        PropertyConfigurator.configure(realPath +
            "WEB-INF/classes/" + configFile);

    //throw an exception if the tag user provides an invalid level,
    //something other than DEBUG, INFO, WARN, ERROR, or FATAL

    level = level.toLowerCase( );

    if (! contains(level))
      throw new JspException(
        "The value given for the level attribute is invalid.");

    //The logger has the same name as the class:
    //com.jspservletcookbook.LoggerTag. Therefore, it inherits its
    //appenders from a logger defined in the config file:
    //com.jspservletcookbook
    log = Logger.getLogger(LoggerTag.class);

    String message = getBodyContent().getString().trim( );
    Method method = null;

    try{

        method = log.getClass( ).
          getMethod(level,new Class[]{ Object.class });

        method.invoke(log,new String[]{message});

  } catch (Exception e){}

  return EVAL_PAGE;
} // doEndTag

public void release( ){

    //release resources used by instance variables
    log = null;
    configFile = null;
    level = null;

}// release

private boolean contains(String str){

    for (int i = 0; i < LEVELS.length; i++){

        if(LEVELS[i].equals(str))
```

Example 14-9. A custom tag that uses log4j (continued)

```
            return true;
    }
    return false;
  }// contains
}
```

The LoggerTag extends the javax.servlet.jsp.tagext.BodyTagSupport class, which is designed for custom actions that process body content, or the text that may appear between opening and closing tags.

The tag attributes, a required attribute named level and the configFile optional attribute, are handled like JavaBean properties: with "setter" methods (e.g., public void setLevel(*String level*)). The doEndTag( ) method does most of the important work for the tag:

1. It attempts to configure the logger if the user has provided a configuration file-name in the configFile attribute.

2. It checks if the level is valid (one of DEBUG, INFO, WARN, ERROR, or FATAL).

3. It logs the message.

Example 14-10 shows the TLD, which conveys tag specifics to the JSP container, such as whether an attribute is required or optional. The tag library associated with this TLD describes only the cbck:log tag. The TLD files must be located in *WEB-INF* or a subdirectory thereof, or inside of the *META-INF* directory of a JAR that is placed in *WEB-INF/lib*.

Example 14-10. The TLD for the custom logger tag

```xml
<?xml version="1.0" encoding="ISO-8859-1" ?>

<!DOCTYPE taglib
        PUBLIC "-//Sun Microsystems, Inc.//DTD JSP Tag Library 1.2//EN"
    "http://java.sun.com/dtd/web-jsptaglibrary_1_2.dtd">
<taglib>

    <tlib-version>1.0</tlib-version>
    <jsp-version>1.2</jsp-version>
    <short-name>cbck</short-name>
    <uri>jspservletcookbook.com.tags</uri>
    <description>Cookbook custom tags</description>

    <tag>
        <name>log</name>
        <tag-class>com.jspservletcookbook.LoggerTag</tag-class>
        <body-content>JSP</body-content>
        <description>This tag uses log4j to log a message.</description>

        <attribute>
            <name>configFile</name>
```

Example 14-10. The TLD for the custom logger tag (continued)

```
        <required>false</required>
        <rtexprvalue>false</rtexprvalue>
        <description>
         This attribute provides any configuration filename for the
         logger. The file must be located in
         WEB-INF/classes.
        </description>
    </attribute>

    <attribute>
        <name>level</name>
        <required>true</required>
        <rtexprvalue>false</rtexprvalue>
        <description>This attribute provides the level for the log request.
        </description>
    </attribute>

  </tag>
</taglib>
```

Example 14-11 shows the *logger.jsp* page and how the custom action can be used.

Example 14-11. A JSP uses a log custom action to access log4j

```
<%@page contentType="text/html"%>
<%@ taglib uri="jspservletcookbook.com.tags" prefix="cbck" %>
<html>
<head><title>A logging JSP</title></head>
<body>
<h2>Here is the logging statement</h2>

<cbck:log level="debug">
Debug message from logger.jsp
</cbck:log>

Debug message from logger.jsp
</body>
</html>
```

First, the page uses the `taglib` directive to declare the tag library that contains our custom action. Example 14-10 shows the TLD file, an XML file that describes the properties of a tag library's various tags. Chapter 22 describes TLDs in more detail.

The `cbck:log` custom action allows a developer to log a message from the JSP by nesting the message text within the `cbck:log` tag (i.e., the body content of the tag is the log message). The `cbck` part of the tag is the prefix that the `taglib` directive declared. The `log` part is the name of the tag. The tag allows the developer to declare the logging level with the custom action's `level` attribute.

Typically, a component such as an initialization servlet initializes the *log4j* logging system when the web application starts up. The custom action described here does not have to initialize *log4j* itself. However, I've included an optional configFile attribute that permits me to specify the name of a *log4j* configuration file, which will configure the logger's level, appender(s), and layout.

For this tag, assume that you want to decide which logging level to use, and thus pass in a value for the level attribute. The tag class does not know whether the message will request a logging level of DEBUG, INFO, WARN, ERROR, or FATAL. Since the logger's methods in *log4j* use the same name as the levels, we can dynamically call the proper method based on the value of the level attribute. This is the purpose of the code:

```
method = log.getClass().
    getMethod(level,new Class[]{ Object.class });

method.invoke(log,new String[]{message});
```

We get a java.lang.reflect.Method object that is named either DEBUG, INFO, WARN, ERROR, or FATAL, and then invoke that method calling method.invoke, passing in the log message from the JSP page.

A configuration filename is not required for this tag, so how does *log4j* know how and where to log the message? This tag assumes that a servlet has already initialized the *log4j* system for the web application, which is typical for the use of *log4j* in a web environment. The configuration file is the one described by Recipe 14.4 and shown in Example 14-5.

You can also use a servlet as an *log4j*-initialization servlet, similar to Example 14-6.

That configuration file created a logging mechanism that sends messages to the console and a file, so that is where the custom tag's messages go. For example, running *logger.jsp* displays a message on the console:

```
DEBUG - Debug message from logger.jsp
```

The tag's logger writes the following message in the file *example.log*:

```
DEBUG Logger:LoggerTag Date: 2003-05-12 12:53:13,750 - Debug message from logger.jsp
```

If you want to include your own configuration file, you can include a configFile attribute when using the custom tag. The tag will configure the logger using that file instead of any previously initialized one:

```
if (configFile != null)
    PropertyConfigurator.configure(
      pageContext.getServletContext().getRealPath("/") +
        "WEB-INF/classes/" + configFile);
```

The `PropertyConfigurator.configure( )` method allows you to specify the name of a *log4j* properties file when you initialize the logging system, if the filename is different than *log4j.properties*. The `PropertyConfigurator.configure( )` method (in *log4j* Version 1.2.8) does not throw an exception that can be caught in the tag class. You could check for the existence of the `configFile` value (representing the path to a file in the web application) explicitly in the code using the `java.io` API, and then throw an exception if the `configFile` attribute declares an invalid filename.

See Also

Recipe 14.2 on downloading and setting up *log4j*; Recipe 14.3 on using a *log4j* logger without a properties file; Recipe 14.4 on adding an appender to the root logger; Recipe 14.5 on using a pattern layout with a logger's appender; Recipes 14.7 and 14.8 on using *log4j* with application event listeners; the *log4j* download site: *http://jakarta. apache.org/log4j/docs/download.html*; the *log4j* Javadoc page: *http://jakarta.apache. org/log4j/docs/api/index.html*; the *log4j* project documentation page: *http://jakarta. apache.org/log4j/docs/documentation.html*.

14.7   Logging Messages Using a Servlet Context Event Listener

Problem

You want to log messages using *log4j* when a servlet context is created and shut down.

Solution

Use *log4j* and a servlet context event listener.

Discussion

The servlet API includes a listener interface named `javax.servlet. ServletContextListener` that you can use to notify a specific Java class when a servlet context is created or shut down. This notified class may want to log the servlet context creation or shut down or store an object attribute in the servlet context, actions that the Java class (the listener) takes when it receives its notification.

The servlet context listener is an application event listener, a category that also includes session event listeners (see Chapter 11 or Recipe 14.8) and request event listeners. For example, the session event listener receives notifications when the servlet container creates new HTTP session objects in order to track a user's progress through a web application. The servlet container notifies the request event listener when a user makes a web application request, so that a listener can take some kind of action—such as logging the user's IP address.

A `javax.servlet.ServletContext` is used to store attributes or access context parameters that are common to a web application, get `RequestDispatcher` objects for forwarding or including files (see Chapter 6), or get information such as an absolute pathname associated with a web resource. Every web application has one associated servlet context.

 There is one servlet context instance per web application (per Java Virtual Machine (JVM), in the case of distributed web applications) according to the ServletContext Javadoc: *http://java.sun.com/j2ee/1.4/ docs/api/javax/servlet/ServletContext.html*.

log4j is a good choice for generating custom-designed log messages from a class that implements the `ServletContextListener` interface. Example 14-12 shows the `ContextLogger` class, which uses *log4j* to send messages in its two methods.

Example 14-12. A servlet context event listener that sends log messages

```
package com.jspservletcookbook;

import org.apache.log4j.Logger;
import org.apache.log4j.PropertyConfigurator;

import javax.servlet.*;
import javax.servlet.http.*;

public class ContextLogger implements ServletContextListener {


  private Logger log;

  public ContextLogger( ){}

  public void contextDestroyed(ServletContextEvent sce)  {

    String name = sce.getServletContext().getServletContextName( );

    //log request of the INFO level
    log.info("ServletContext shut down: " + (name == null ? "" : name ));

    //do other necessary work, like clean up any left-over resources
    //used by the web app
  }

  public void contextInitialized(ServletContextEvent sce) {

    ServletContext context = sce.getServletContext( );
```

```
    String realPath = context.getRealPath("/");
    String fileSep = System.getProperty("file.separator");

    //Make sure the real path ends with a file separator character ('/')
    if (realPath != null && (! realPath.endsWith(fileSep))){
        realPath = realPath + fileSep;}


    //Initialize logger here; the log4j properties filename is specified
    //by a context parameter named "logger-config"

    PropertyConfigurator.configure(realPath +
      "WEB-INF/classes/" + context.getInitParameter("logger-config"));

    log = Logger.getLogger(ContextLogger.class);

    String name = context.getServletContextName();

    //log request about servlet context being initialized
    log.info("ServletContext ready: " + (name == null ? "" : name ));

  }
}
```

Give this class a no-args constructor, place it in *WEB-INF/classes* or in a JAR located in *WEB-INF/lib*, and register it in *web.xml*:

```
<listener>
    <listener-class>
    com.jspservletcookbook.ContextLogger
    </listener-class>
</listener>
```

The ServletContextListener tracks the lifecycle of a servlet context with two methods: contextInitialized( ) and contextDestroyed( ). The servlet container calls the first method when the servlet context is created and the web application is ready to receive its first request. The container notifies the listener class and calls the contextDestroyed( ) method when the servlet context is about to be shut down, such as when a web application is stopped prior to being reloaded.

Tomcat 4.1.24 initializes the servlet context listener prior to creating servlet instances, even if the application configures the servlet to be preloaded. Example 14-12 initializes the *log4j* system in the contextInitialized( ) method.

The deployment descriptor can instruct the servlet container to load a servlet instance and call its init( ) method at startup by including a load-on-startup element nested in the servlet element, as in:

```
<servlet>
    <servlet-name>logger</servlet-name>
    <servlet-class>
    com.jspservletcookbook.LoggerServlet
    </servlet-class>
    <load-on-startup>1</load-on-startup>
</servlet>
```

The value of load-on-startup is an integer indicating the order in which the container loads the servlet.

In the contextInitialized( ) method, the listener configures *log4j* using the file specified by a context-param element in *web.xml*:

```
<context-param>
    <param-name>logger-config</param-name>
    <param-value>servletLog.properties</param-value>
</context-param>
```

This *log4j* configuration file (*servletLog.properties*) is located in the *WEB-INF/classes* directory. The listener then logs its messages to the console and to a file when the web application starts up or is shut down. Example 14-13 shows the configuration file the listener uses for *log4j*.

Example 14-13. Log4j configuration file used by the servlet context listener

```
log4j.rootLogger=DEBUG, cons
log4j.logger.com.jspservletcookbook=, myAppender

log4j.appender.cons=org.apache.log4j.ConsoleAppender

#configure the 'myAppender' appender

log4j.appender.myAppender=org.apache.log4j.RollingFileAppender
log4j.appender.myAppender.File=h:/home/example.log
log4j.appender.myAppender.MaxBackupIndex=1
log4j.appender.myAppender.MaxFileSize=1MB

log4j.appender.cons.layout=org.apache.log4j.SimpleLayout
log4j.appender.myAppender.layout=org.apache.log4j.PatternLayout
log4j.appender.myAppender.layout.ConversionPattern=
%-5p Logger:%c{1} Date: %d{ISO8601} - %m%n
```

The listener gets a logger with this code:

```
log = Logger.getLogger(ContextLogger.class);
```

This names the logger after the class com.jspservletcookbook.ContextLogger. Therefore, in the *log4j* naming scheme, the listener's logger inherits the appender that

Example 14-13 defines for the logger com.jspservletcokbook. This is because the configuration does not define a logger for com.jspservletcookbook.ContextLogger; consequently, the listener's logger inherits the next defined logger available: com.jspservletcookbook. The com.jspservletcookbook logger has a console appender and a file appender.

As a result, the servlet context listener sends its log messages to the console and the *h:/home/example.log* file. Example 14-13 has different layouts for the console and file appenders. The listener's console messages look like this:

```
INFO - ServletContext shut down: The home web application
INFO - ServletContext ready: The home web application
```

The log file messages have a different format:

```
INFO  Logger:ContextLogger Date: 2003-05-12 16:45:20,398 - ServletContext shut down:
The home web application
INFO  Logger:ContextLogger Date: 2003-05-12 16:45:20,999 - ServletContext ready: The
home web application
```

The format of these messages consists of the name of the logging level (e.g., INFO), the logger name, the date of the log request, and the message itself.

See Also

Recipe 14.2 on downloading and setting up *log4j*; Recipe 14.3 on using a *log4j* logger without a properties file; Recipe 14.4 on adding an appender to the root logger; Recipe 14.5 on using a pattern layout with a logger's appender; Recipe 14.6 on using a logger with a JSP; Recipe 14.8 on using *log4j* with session event listeners; the *log4j* download site: *http://jakarta.apache.org/log4j/docs/download.html*; the *log4j* Javadoc page: *http://jakarta.apache.org/log4j/docs/api/index.html*; the *log4j* project documentation page: *http://jakarta.apache.org/log4j/docs/documentation.html*.

14.8   Logging Messages Using a Session Event Listener

Problem

You want to log messages in a custom-designed manner from a session event listener.

Solution

Design a session event listener that uses a *log4j* logging mechanism.

Discussion

The servlet container notifies a session event listener class when it creates a new HttpSession, as well as when it is about to invalidate or expire a session. Web applications use sessions to track a user's progress through the web application, typically by identifying him with a cookie named JSESSIONID. See Chapter 10 for more information on cookies, and Chapter 11 for detailed coverage of sessions.

Example 14-14 implements the javax.servlet.http.HttpSessionListener interface and the interface's two methods: sessionCreated( ) and sessionDestroyed( ). The code logs messages relating to new sessions in sessionCreated( ) and relating to invalidated sessions in sessionDestroyed( ).

Example 14-14. Using log4j in a session event listener

```
package com.jspservletcookbook;

import org.apache.log4j.Logger;
import org.apache.log4j.PropertyConfigurator;

import javax.servlet.*;
import javax.servlet.http.*;

public class SessionLogger implements HttpSessionListener
{

  private Logger log;

  public SessionLogger( ){

  /*
    The loggers are typically initialized by a special initialization
    listener or servlet.  If this is not the case, then initialize the
    logger here:

    java.util.ResourceBundle bundle =
      java.util.ResourceBundle.getBundle(
      "com.jspservletcookbook.global");

    PropertyConfigurator.configure(bundle.getString(
      "log-configure-path"));
  */

  log = Logger.getLogger(SessionLogger.class);

  }

  public void sessionCreated(HttpSessionEvent se)    {

    //log request of the INFO level
    log.info("HttpSession created: " + se.getSession().getId( ));

  }
```

Example 14-14. Using log4j in a session event listener (continued)

```
public void sessionDestroyed(HttpSessionEvent se) {

  //log request about sessions that are invalidated
  log.info("HttpSession invalidated: " + se.getSession().getId( ));

 }
}
```

Give this class a no-args constructor, place it in *WEB-INF/classes* or in a JAR located in *WEB-INF/lib*, and register it in *web.xml*:

```
<listener>
    <listener-class>
    com.jspservletcookbook.SessionLogger
    </listener-class>
</listener>
```

The `SessionLogger` class gets a logger in its constructor; it depends on the application already having initialized the *log4j* logging mechanism in a servlet or in the servlet context listener (as in Recipe 14.4).

> A web application can configure its *log4j* mechanism using a special initialization servlet or listener, so the other classes or beans that do logging do not have to handle the *log4j* configuration stage. You can initialize the *log4j* logging mechanism using a servlet such as the one shown in Recipe 14.6.

The commented-out code in the constructor shows another way that this listener class could configure its own logger in the event that the application has not yet configured the logging mechanism.

Here is the message logged to the Tomcat console after the first request to a servlet or JSP that participates in session tracking:

```
INFO - HttpSession created: A65481C53B92F869BD18961D635BBF52
```

When the session is invalidated, the console text is:

```
INFO - HttpSession invalidated: A65481C53B92F869BD18961D635BBF52
```

Like the listener described in Recipe 14.7, the session listener's logger inherits the logging destinations or appenders from the `com.jspservletcookbook` logger. The configuration file of Example 14-13 shows how this logger is set up to send messages to both the console and an *example.log* file. The log file's appender layout is specified using a `PatternLayout`, which is a different layout than the one used with the console appender. Here is example text from this log when the servlet container invalidates a session:

```
INFO  Logger:SessionLogger Date: 2003-05-12 20:41:05,367 - HttpSession invalidated:
A65481C53B92F869BD18961D635BBF52
```

See Also

Recipe 14.2 on downloading and setting up *log4j*; Recipe 14.3 on using a *log4j* logger without a properties file; Recipe 14.4 on adding an appender to the root logger; Recipe 14.5 on using a pattern layout with a logger's appender; Recipe 14.6 on using a logger with a JSP; Recipe 14.8 on using *log4j* with session event listeners; the *log4j* download site: *http://jakarta.apache.org/log4j/docs/download.html*; the *log4j* Javadoc page: *http://jakarta.apache.org/log4j/docs/api/index.html*; the *log4j* project documentation page: *http://jakarta.apache.org/log4j/docs/documentation.html*.

CHAPTER 15

Authenticating Clients

15.0 Introduction

Because of the increase in digital commerce and a corresponding rise in the need to transfer and store sensitive data (such as credit card numbers and financial accounts), security is of paramount importance to Java web applications.

This chapter's recipes cover tasks that involve authentication, which is designed to answer the question "are you who you say you are?" Authentication usually involves an interaction between a client or user and server-side code for the purpose of checking a username and password (and sometimes a digital certificate, biometric data, or other evidence) against stored information, such as a user database.

The recipes describe how to set up Secure Sockets Layer (SSL), as well as use BASIC- and form-based authentication with Apache Tomcat. The later recipes describe how to use a powerful security framework called Java Authentication and Authorization Service (JAAS) with servlets and JSPs.

15.1 Creating Users and Passwords with Tomcat

Problem

You want to create usernames and passwords for authenticating requests for certain web components.

Solution

Add the usernames, passwords, and roles to the *tomcat-users.xml* file.

Discussion

A very easy method of authenticating users with Tomcat involves creating usernames, passwords, and roles in the *tomcat-users.xml* file. This file is stored in *<Tomcat-installation-directory>/conf*.

Everyone is familiar with usernames and passwords, but what are roles? Roles are logical ways to describe groups of users who have similar responsibilities, such as *manager* or *databaseAdmin*. Example 15-1 shows a *tomcat-users.xml* file that creates two roles and two users with two aptly named XML elements: role and user.

Example 15-1. The tomcat-users XML file

```
<?xml version='1.0' encoding='utf-8'?>

<tomcat-users>
  <role rolename="dbadmin"/>
  <role rolename="manager"/>
  <user username="BruceP" password="bwperry" roles="dbadmin,manager"/>
  <user username="JillH" password="jhayward" roles="manager"/>
</tomcat-users>
```

In Example 15-1, the user BruceP is associated with two roles (*dbadmin* and *manager*), while user JillH is associated only with the *manager* role. Tomcat uses this file when authenticating users with BASIC and form-based authentication, as described in Recipes 15.3 and 15.4.

See Also

The Tomcat documentation and Recipe 15.2 on setting up SSL for use with authentication: *http://jakarta.apache.org/tomcat/tomcat-4.1-doc/ssl-howto.html*; Recipe 3.9 on restricting requests for certain servlets; Recipe 15.3 on using BASIC authentication; Recipe 15.4 on using form-based authentication; Recipe 15.5 on logging out a user; Recipes 15.6–15.9 on using JAAS.

15.2   Setting Up SSL on Tomcat

Problem

You want to set up SSL on Tomcat so that you can transmit usernames and passwords in encrypted form.

Solution

Create a digital certificate for the Tomcat server using the *$JAVA_HOME\bin\keytool* utility, then uncomment the SSL Connector element in *conf/server.xml*.

Discussion

When transferring usernames and passwords over HTTP, you should set up SSL on Tomcat or whichever application server you are using. This protocol ensures that the names and passwords are in encrypted form as they travel across the network, and thus protected from theft and malicious use by hackers and other intruders.

Setting up SSL on Tomcat 4 is a two-step process:

1. Use the keytool utility to create a *keystore* file encapsulating a digital certificate used by the server for secure connections.

2. Uncomment the SSL Connector element in Tomcat's *conf/server.xml* file, and alter its attributes if necessary.

The keytool utility is located in the *bin* subdirectory of the directory where you have installed the JSDK. The following command line creates a single self-signed digital certificate for the Tomcat server within a *keystore* file named *.keystore*. This file is created in the home directory of the user running the command.

```
%JAVA_HOME%\bin\keytool -genkey -alias tomcat -keyalg RSA
```

The Unix version of this command is:

```
$JAVA_HOME\bin\keytool -genkey -alias tomcat -keyalg RSA
```

 For this command to succeed, the JAVA_HOME environment variable must be set to the directory where the Java 2 SDK is installed, such as *h:\j2sdk1.4.1_01*.

Example 15-2 shows the console output resulting from executing the keytool command. The keytool will request some information about you and your organization, but you can accept the default values by pressing Enter. This information is incorporated into the server's certificate and presented to the user (via her web browser) when she requests any components with a URL that starts with *https://*.

In setting up SSL for Tomcat, you must use the same password for both the *keystore* and the certificate that is stored in the *keystore*.

 The default password used in Tomcat is "changeit": *http://jakarta. apache.org/tomcat/tomcat-4.1-doc/ssl-howto.html*.

Example 15-2. The console output resulting from using the keytool utility

```
Enter keystore password:  changeit
What is your first and last name?
  [Unknown]:  Bruce Perry
What is the name of your organizational unit?
  [Unknown]:
What is the name of your organization?
  [Unknown]:
```

```
What is the name of your City or Locality?
  [Unknown]:
What is the name of your State or Province?
  [Unknown]:
What is the two-letter country code for this unit?
  [Unknown]:
Is CN=Bruce Perry, OU=Unknown, O=Unknown, L=Unknown, ST=Unknown, C=Unknown correct?
  [no]:  yes

Enter key password for <tomcat>
        (RETURN if same as keystore password):
```

Finally, uncomment the SSL Connector element in the *conf/server.xml* file (shown in Figure 15-3) by removing the comment characters around it (`<!-- -->`). Then restart Tomcat.

Example 15-3. The Connector element inside server.xml

```
<!-- Define a SSL Coyote HTTP/1.1 Connector on port 8443 -->

<Connector className=
  "org.apache.coyote.tomcat4.CoyoteConnector" port=
  "8443" minProcessors="5" maxProcessors="75" enableLookups=
  "true" acceptCount="100" debug="0" scheme="https" secure="true"
  useURIValidationHack="false" disableUploadTimeout="true">

    <Factory className=
    "org.apache.coyote.tomcat4.CoyoteServerSocketFactory" clientAuth=
    "false" protocol="TLS" />

</Connector>
```

The Connector uses a different port number (8443) than that used by insecure HTTP connections (in Tomcat, it's usually 8080). After you have restarted Tomcat, you can now make a secure connection to a web component in the *home* application with a URL that looks like this:

```
https://localhost:8443/home/sqlJsp.jsp
```

 Don't forget the `https` (as opposed to `http`) part in setting up these web links!

See Also

The Tomcat documentation on setting up SSL for use with authentication: *http://jakarta.apache.org/tomcat/tomcat-4.1-doc/ssl-howto.html*; Recipe 15.1 on creating usernames and passwords in Tomcat; Recipe 15.3 on using BASIC authentication; Recipe 15.4 on using form-based authentication; Recipe 15.5 on logging out a user; Recipes 15.6–15.9 on using the JAAS.

15.3   Using BASIC Authentication

Problem

You want to use BASIC authentication with web components in a Tomcat web application.

Solution

Use the `security-constraint`, `login-config`, and `security-role` elements in the deployment descriptor to protect one or more URLs.

Discussion

BASIC authentication is a security method that has been used with web resources for several years, and all popular browsers support it. This method of authentication involves the transfer of usernames and passwords over a network encoded with the Base64 content-encoding mechanism. Base64 is easy to decode and therefore not very secure. The solution is to combine BASIC authentication with SSL, which will further encrypt the data as it is transferred across the network (see Recipe 15.2).

Here is how setting up BASIC authentication works with web applications that you have installed on Tomcat:

1. Set up usernames, passwords, and roles in the *conf/tomcat-users.xml* file described in Recipe 15.1.

2. Create a `security-constraint` element in the deployment descriptor (*web.xml*), specifying the web resources for which you are requiring authentication.

3. Include a `login-config` in *web.xml*; this element has a nested `auth-method` element that contains the text "BASIC".

When the user requests any of the protected resources, the server sends along a response header that looks like this:
```
WWW-Authenticate: BASIC Realm="MyRealm"
```

You are probably familiar with what happens next: the browser displays a standard dialog window requesting the client to provide a username and password (Figure 15-1). If the username and password are incorrect, the browser will either give the user another chance to log in by redisplaying the dialog window, or simply send back a server status code "401: Unauthorized" type of response.

The usernames and passwords in the *conf/tomcat-users.xml* file are case-sensitive. The user has to type them into the dialog window using upper- and lowercase letters exactly as they appear in *conf/tomcat-users.xml*.

Example 15-4 shows the *web.xml* elements that are designed to initiate BASIC authentication for the URL pattern */sqlJsp.jsp*.

Example 15-4. A security-constraint initiates authentication with a JSP file

```
<!-- Beginning of web.xml deployment descriptor -->

<security-constraint>

    <web-resource-collection>

        <web-resource-name>JSP database component</web-resource-name>

        <url-pattern>/sqlJsp.jsp</url-pattern>

        <http-method>GET</http-method>
        <http-method>POST</http-method>

    </web-resource-collection>


    <auth-constraint>
        <role-name>dbadmin</role-name>
    </auth-constraint>

    <user-data-constraint>
        <transport-guarantee>CONFIDENTIAL</transport-guarantee>
    </user-data-constraint>

</security-constraint>

<login-config>
        <auth-method>BASIC</auth-method>
</login-config>

<security-role>
    <role-name>dbadmin</role-name>
</security-role>

<!-- Rest of web.xml deployment descriptor -->
```

The security-constraint element in Example 15-4 contains a web-resource-collection element. This element specifies the following constraints that apply to any requests for */sqlJsp.jsp*:

- The constraints apply to any GET or POST requests (as specified by the http-method elements).

- The auth-constraint element nested inside security-constraint contains the role-name *dbadmin*. Therefore, the requestor must enter the proper username and password (as specified in the *tomcat-users.xml* file) *and* be associated with the *dbadmin* role. Only those who have the *dbadmin* role can gain access to the protected web resource, even if they enter a proper username and password.

Figure 15-1 shows the dialog box that Netscape 7.1 produces when Tomcat is using BASIC authentication. The URL is used is *https://localhost:8443/home/sqlJsp.jsp*.

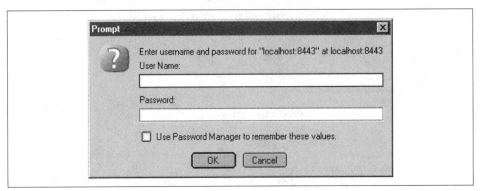

Figure 15-1. A browser dialog window requests a name and password

Notice that the URL uses a secure connection to request the JSP: an HTTPS protocol and port 8443 on Tomcat.

Figure 15-2 shows a browser window after a client has failed authentication.

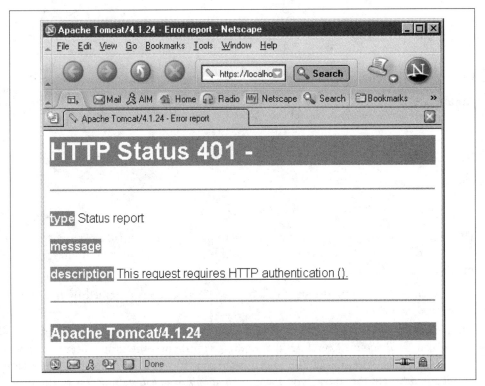

Figure 15-2. A server status code 401 page as viewed in the web browser

See Also

The Tomcat documentation and Recipe 15.2 on setting up SSL for use with authentication: *http://jakarta.apache.org/tomcat/tomcat-4.1-doc/ssl-howto.html*; Recipe 3.9 on restricting requests for certain servlets; Recipe 15.5 on logging out a user; Recipes 15.6–15.9 on using JAAS.

15.4   Using Form-Based Authentication

Problem

You want to design your own form to receive the user's name and password during BASIC authentication.

Solution

Use the `login-config` element in the deployment descriptor and give its nested auth-method element a value of "FORM".

Discussion

The servlet API offers an alternative to using plain-vanilla BASIC authentication: *form-based authentication*. This method allows you to design your own form for receiving the user's name and password, as well as specifying the informative page that the servers send to the client if the user's authentication fails. This gives you the ability to provide a much more friendly and customized user interface for applications involving BASIC authentication.

> The form-based method should still be combined with SSL and the HTTPS protocol so that the names and passwords are encrypted as they travel through the network.

Example 15-5 shows the form-based setup for the web application's deployment descriptor. It differs from Recipe 15.3's setup in one area: the `login-config` element, which is emphasized in the following code sample.

Example 15-5. The web.xml elements designed for form-based authentication

```
<!-- Beginning of web.xml deployment descriptor -->

<security-constraint>
    <web-resource-collection>
        <web-resource-name>JSP database component</web-resource-name>
        <url-pattern>/sqlJsp.jsp</url-pattern>
        <http-method>GET</http-method>
        <http-method>POST</http-method>
```

Example 15-5. The web.xml elements designed for form-based authentication

```
    </web-resource-collection>

    <auth-constraint>
        <role-name>dbadmin</role-name>
    </auth-constraint>

    <user-data-constraint>
        <transport-guarantee>CONFIDENTIAL</transport-guarantee>
    </user-data-constraint>

</security-constraint>

<login-config>

    <auth-method>FORM</auth-method>

    <form-login-config>

        <form-login-page>/login.html</form-login-page>
        <form-error-page>/loginError.jsp</form-error-page>

    </form-login-config>

</login-config>

<security-role>
    <role-name>dbadmin</role-name>
</security-role>

<!-- Rest of web.xml deployment descriptor -->
```

The auth-method element includes the text "FORM". The form-login-config element specifies the login (*/login.html*) and authentication failure page (*/loginError.html*) that your application uses. The forward slash (/) preceding the filenames means to navigate to the page from the web application's root directory.

Almost by magic, if a user requests a protected resource in your application, the server sends him the *login.html* page (in this example) instead of initiating the typical behavior in which the browser displays its own dialog window. If the name and password the user enters turns out to be incorrect, the server routes his request to the *loginError.html* page.

Example 15-6 shows the *login.html* page, for reference.

Example 15-6. The login form

```
<!DOCTYPE HTML PUBLIC "-//W3C//DTD HTML 4.0 Transitional//EN">

<html>
<head>
    <title>Welcome</title>
</head>
```

Example 15-6. The login form (continued)

```
<body bgcolor="#ffffff">
<h2>Please Login to the Application</h2>

<form method="POST"  action="j_security_check">

<table border="0"><tr>
<td>Enter the username: </td><td>

<input type="text" name="j_username" size="15">

</td>
</tr>
<tr>
<td>Enter the password: </td><td>

<input type="password" name="j_password" size="15">

</td>
</tr>
<tr>
<td> <input type="submit" value="Submit"> </td>
</tr>
</table>

</form>

</body>
</html>
```

Figure 15-3 shows what this form looks like in a web browser.

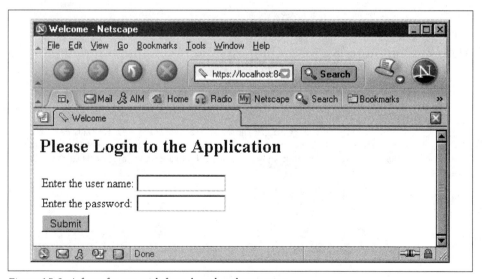

Figure 15-3. A form for use with form-based authentication

With form-based authentication, the `form` tag's action attribute must have the value "j_security_check". The input elements for the username and password must specify the values "j_user_name" and "j_password", respectively, for their `name` attributes.

Figure 15-4 shows the HTML page that the server sends the user if her authentication fails.

Figure 15-4. Form-based authentication allows the inclusion of your own login-failure page

Example 15-7 shows the source for this page. The form-based approach is more predictable and friendlier than the various browsers' methods for dealing with BASIC authentication.

Example 15-7. The server displays the loginError.jsp page when authentication fails

```
<html>
<head>
    <title>Login Error</title>
</head>
<body bgcolor="#ffffff">
<h2>We Apologize, A Login Error Occurred</h2>
Please click <a href="http://localhost:8080/home/sqlJsp.jsp">here</a> for another try.
<%-- Or, dynamically list hyperlinks to your protected resources here,  perhaps by getting
them from a database or configuration file, instead of hard-coding a link into the error
page. --%>

</body>
</html>
```

See Also

The Tomcat documentation and Recipe 15.2 on setting up SSL for use with authentication: *http://jakarta.apache.org/tomcat/tomcat-4.1-doc/ssl-howto.html*; Recipe 3.9 on restricting requests for certain servlets; Recipe 15.5 on logging out a user; Recipes 15.6–15.9 on using JAAS.

15.5   Logging Out a User

Problem

You want to log out a user in a system that uses form-based authentication.

Solution

Call `invalidate( )` on the user's `HttpSession` object.

Discussion

Invalidating a user's `HttpSession` object will log the user out in an application that uses form-based authentication. Naturally, this code involves calling `HttpSession.invalidate( )`. Example 15-8 displays some information about a logged-in user, then logs him out by invalidating his session. The next time this user requests a protected resource, the web application will send him to the configured login page, because he has been logged out of the application.

Example 15-8. Logging out a user

```
package com.jspservletcookbook;

import javax.servlet.*;
import javax.servlet.http.*;

public class LogoutServlet extends HttpServlet {

  public void doGet(HttpServletRequest request,
    HttpServletResponse response)throws ServletException,
      java.io.IOException {

      HttpSession session = request.getSession( );
      response.setContentType("text/html");
      java.io.PrintWriter out = response.getWriter( );
      out.println(
      "<html><head><title>Authenticated User Info</title></head><body>");
      out.println("<h2>Logging out a user</h2>");
      out.println("request.getRemoteUser( ) returns: ");
      //get the logged-in user's name
      String remUser = request.getRemoteUser( );
```

Example 15-8. Logging out a user (continued)

```
        //Is the request.getRemoteUser() return value null? If
        //so, then the user is not authenticated
        out.println(remUser == null ? "Not authenticated." : remUser );
        out.println("<br>");
        out.println("request.isUserInRole(\"dbadmin\")  returns: ");
        //Find out whether the user is in the dbadmin role
        boolean isInRole = request.isUserInRole("dbadmin");
        out.println(isInRole);
        out.println("<br>");
        //log out the user by invalidating the HttpSession
        session.invalidate();
        out.println("</body></html>");

  } //doGet

public void doPost(HttpServletRequest request,
    HttpServletResponse response) throws ServletException,
      java.io.IOException {

    doGet(request,response);

  } //doPost

} //LogoutServlet
```

A logged-in user who requests this servlet sees the output in Figure 15-5. The servlet displays the return values of HttpServletRequest.getRemoteUser() (the username) and HttpServletRequest.isUserInRole(). The latter method returns a boolean value indicating whether the user is associated with the role specified by the method's String parameter.

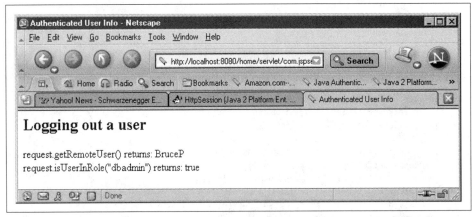

Figure 15-5. A servlet shows some user-related information before logging out the user

The servlet then invalidates the user's session to log her out. Rerequesting the servlet produces the output shown in Figure 15-6.

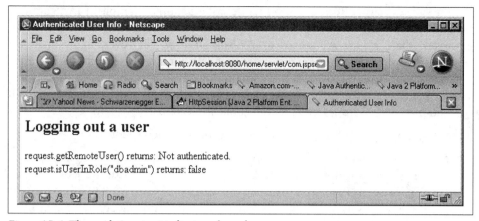

Figure 15-6. The servlet's output indicates a logged-out user

See Also

The Tomcat documentation and Recipe 15.2 on setting up SSL for use with authentication: *http://jakarta.apache.org/tomcat/tomcat-4.1-doc/ssl-howto.html*; Recipe 3.9 on restricting requests for certain servlets; Recipes 15.6–15.9 on using JAAS.

15.6   Using JAAS to Create a LoginModule

Problem

You want to use the Java Authentication and Authorization Service (JAAS) to create an authentication module that a servlet or JSP can use.

Solution

Create a javax.security.auth.spi.LoginModule class for your application, then store the class under *WEB-INF/classes* or *WEB-INF/lib* (in a JAR file).

Discussion

The JAAS is a security API that can be used to create standalone, pluggable authentication or authorization tools for Java applications. *Pluggable* means that the JAAS security code is not bound to a particular application; it is stored in a JAR file and can be dropped or plugged into web applications and other types of Java programs.

 JAAS is a Java version of a framework named Pluggable Authentication Module (PAM). Here's a link to a paper on that very topic: *http:// java.sun.com/security/jaas/doc/pam.html*.

For the sake of clarity, Recipes 15.5–15.7 describe a simple example of JAAS authentication that requires two classes, and one servlet that uses the JAAS API. In our examples, these classes are stored in *WEB-INF/classes*. However, many organizations have a complex security architecture that calls for a more extensive authentication and authorization model, and thus more Java code and objects. In these cases, you'll want to create a separate package name for your JAAS code, archive it in a JAR file, and place it in *WEB-INF/lib* for web applications to use.

Take the following steps to use JAAS for authenticating web clients:

1. Make sure you have installed the JAAS packages for use with a web application. JAAS has been integrated into the Java 2 1.4 SDK, so you can use JAAS if Tomcat or your application server is using this version of Java. See the following web site if you are using Java 1.3, which requires you to download and install JAAS as a Java extension: *http://java.sun.com/products/jaas/index-10.html*.

2. Create a `LoginModule` class to handle the authentication. This class must be stored in *WEB-INF/classes* or in a JAR file placed in *WEB-INF/lib*.

3. Create a `CallbackHandler` class that deals with interaction with the client to get its username and password. Store this class with your `LoginModule`.

4. Create a JAAS configuration file that specifies which `LoginModule`(s) you are using for authentication. Place the configuration file in a location where the JAAS-related code can read it (see the description of the configuration file in Recipe 15.7).

5. Include a `LoginContext` object in servlet code and call its `login( )` method.

 Authentication checks whether a user or client has a particular identity, which is typically one of a set of usernames and passwords. JAAS can also be used for *authorization*, which specifies the extent of access to data a user has once she is successfully authenticated. This recipe focuses solely on authentication.

In order to make clearer a rather complex matter, I have broken these steps up into three recipes:

- This recipe describes steps 1–3.
- Recipe 15.6 shows how to create the JAAS configuration file.
- Recipe 15.7 uses the JAAS authentication classes in a servlet.

Example 15-9 shows a class that implements the `javax.security.auth.spi.LoginModule` interface. It performs most of the work in identifying clients, and uses packages that are part of the JAAS API (emphasized with bold in the code sample). You have to make this class available to the servlet engine by placing it in *WEB-INF/classes* or in a JAR file stored in *WEB-INF/lib*.

Example 15-9. The LoginModule for web authentication

```
package com.jspservletcookbook;

import java.util.Map;
import java.sql.*;

import javax.naming.Context;
import javax.naming.InitialContext;
import javax.naming.NamingException;

import javax.security.auth.spi.LoginModule;
import javax.security.auth.*;
import javax.security.auth.callback.*;
import javax.security.auth.login.*;

import javax.sql.*;

public class DataSourceLoginModule implements LoginModule {

    //These instance variables will be initialized by the
    //initialize( ) method
    CallbackHandler handler;
    Subject   subject;
    Map       sharedState;
    Map       options;

    private boolean loginPassed = false;

  public DataSourceLoginModule( ){}//no-arguments constructor

  public void initialize(Subject subject, CallbackHandler handler,
    Map sharedState, Map options){

      this.subject = subject;
      this.handler = handler;
      this.sharedState = sharedState;
      this.options = options;

  }

  public boolean login( ) throws LoginException {

      String name = "";
      String pass = "";

      Context env = null;
      Connection conn = null;
      Statement stmt = null;
      ResultSet rs = null;
      DataSource pool = null;

      boolean passed = false;
```

Example 15-9. The LoginModule for web authentication (continued)

```
try{

    //Create the CallBack array to pass to the
    //CallbackHandler.handle() method
    Callback[] callbacks = new Callback[2];

    //Don't use null arguments with the NameCallback constructor!
    callbacks[0] = new NameCallback("Username:");

    //Don't use null arguments with PasswordCallback!
    callbacks[1] = new PasswordCallback("Password:", false);

    handler.handle(callbacks);

    //Get the username and password from the CallBacks
    NameCallback nameCall = (NameCallback) callbacks[0];

    name = nameCall.getName();

    PasswordCallback passCall = (PasswordCallback) callbacks[1];

    pass = new String ( passCall.getPassword() );

    //Look up our DataSource so that we can check the username and
    //password
    env = (Context) new InitialContext().lookup("java:comp/env");

    pool  = (DataSource) env.lookup("jdbc/oracle-8i-athletes");

    if (pool == null)
        throw new LoginException(
        "Initializing the DataSource failed.");

    //The SQL for checking a name and password in a table named
    //athlete
    String sql = "select * from athlete where name='"+name+"'";

    String sqlpass = "select * from athlete where passwrd='"+pass+"'";

    //Get a Connection from the connection pool
    conn = pool.getConnection();

    stmt = conn.createStatement();

      //Check the username
      rs = stmt.executeQuery(sql);

    //If the ResultSet has rows, then the username was
    //correct and next() returns true
    passed = rs.next();

    rs.close();
```

Example 15-9. The LoginModule for web authentication (continued)

```
        if (! passed){

            loginPassed = false;
            throw new FailedLoginException(
                "The username was not successfully authenticated");

        }

         //Check the password
        rs = stmt.executeQuery(sqlpass);

        passed = rs.next( );

        if (! passed){

            loginPassed = false;
            throw new FailedLoginException(
            "The password was not successfully authenticated");

         } else {

            loginPassed = true;
            return true;

        }

    } catch (Exception e){

        throw new LoginException(e.getMessage( ));

    } finally {

        try{

            //close the Statement
            stmt.close( );

            //Return the Connection to the pool
            conn.close( );

        } catch (SQLException sqle){ }

    } //finally

} //login

public boolean commit( ) throws LoginException {

    //We're not doing anything special here, since this class
    //represents a simple example of login authentication with JAAS.
    //Just return what login( ) returned.
    return loginPassed;
```

Example 15-9. The LoginModule for web authentication (continued)

```
    }

    public boolean abort( ) throws LoginException {

        //Reset state
        boolean bool = loginPassed;
        loginPassed = false;

        return bool;
    }

    public boolean logout( ) throws LoginException {

        //Reset state
        loginPassed = false;
        return true;

    } //logout

} //DataSourceLoginModule
```

A class that implements LoginModule has to implement the interface's five declared methods: initialize( ), login( ), commit( ), abort( ), and logout( ). login( ) initiates the main task of checking the username and password and determining whether to successfully authenticate the client. Since this is a simple example, the DataSourceLoginModule focuses on the login( ) method. The other methods in Example 15-9 simply reset the object's state so that it can perform another authentication, although a more complex login process involves other tasks, such as setting up authorization-related objects for the authenticated user.

 JAAS is a quite comprehensive framework. Refer to Sun Microsystems' documentation (*http://java.sun.com/products/jaas/index-14.html*) for guidance in developing more advanced JAAS programs than those described in this recipe.

JAAS separates the responsibility for interacting with the client (such as getting the username and password) and performing authentication into CallbackHandlers and LoginModules, respectively. The LoginModule in Example 15-9 uses a CallbackHandler to get the username and password, then checks this information by accessing a table from an Oracle 8i database. The module uses a JNDI lookup to get access to the database, which Chapter 21 explains in detail.

Basically, the LoginModule borrows a Connection from a database-connection pool, uses SQL SELECT statements to check the client's name and password, then returns the Connection to the shared pool by closing it.

The CallbackHandler in Example 15-10 gets the client's username and password from HTTP request parameters. The class's constructor includes a ServletRequest argument, from which the class can derive request parameters by calling ServletRequest's getParameter( ) method. This process will become much clearer when you see how the servlet (see Example 15-11 in Recipe 15.7) uses these classes to perform the authentication.

Example 15-10. A CallbackHandler for use in web authentication

```java
package com.jspservletcookbook;

import javax.security.auth.callback.*;
import javax.servlet.ServletRequest;

public class WebCallbackHandler implements CallbackHandler {

    private String userName;
    private String password;

  public WebCallbackHandler(ServletRequest request){

      userName = request.getParameter("userName");
      password = request.getParameter("password");

  }

  public void handle(Callback[] callbacks) throws java.io.IOException,
    UnsupportedCallbackException {

      //Add the username and password from the request parameters to
      //the Callbacks
      for (int i = 0; i < callbacks.length; i++){

          if (callbacks[i] instanceof NameCallback){

              NameCallback nameCall = (NameCallback) callbacks[i];

              nameCall.setName(userName);

          } else if (callbacks[i] instanceof PasswordCallback){

              PasswordCallback passCall = (PasswordCallback) callbacks[i];

              passCall.setPassword(password.toCharArray( ));

          } else{

              throw new UnsupportedCallbackException (callbacks[i],
                "The CallBacks are unrecognized in class: "+getClass( ).
                getName( ));

          }

      } //for
  } //handle

}
```

Just to summarize how the `LoginModule` and `CallbackHandler` fit together before you move on to the next two recipes, one of the `LoginContext`'s constructors takes a `CallbackHandler` as its second parameter, as in the following code:

```
WebCallbackHandler webcallback = new WebCallbackHandler(request);
LoginContext lcontext = null;

    try{

        lcontext = new LoginContext( "WebLogin",webcallback );
    } catch (LoginException le) { //respond to exception...}
```

Recipe 15.7 shows how to create a JAAS configuration file, which specifies the `LoginModule`(s) that certain applications will use during authentication.

See Also

Sun Microsystems' JAAS developer's guide: *http://java.sun.com/j2se/1.4.2/docs/guide/security/jaas/JAASLMDevGuide.html*; a list of JAAS tutorials and sample programs: *http://java.sun.com/j2se/1.4.2/docs/guide/security/jaas/JAASRefGuide.html*; the Javadoc relating to JAAS configuration files: *http://java.sun.com/j2se/1.4.1/docs/api/javax/security/auth/login/Configuration.html*; Recipe 15.9 on using JAAS with a JSP.

15.7   Creating the JAAS Configuration File

Problem

You want to create the JAAS configuration file.

Solution

Create the configuration file, then specify the configuration's location on your file-system in the *${java.home}/jre/lib/security/java.security* file.

Discussion

Using JAAS also involves writing a configuration file to identify the `LoginModule`(s) that a particular application will use. The configuration file in Example 15-11 specifies an application named "WebLogin."

Example 15-11. A JAAS configuration file

```
WebLogin {
   com.jspservletcookbook.DataSourceLoginModule requisite;
};
```

Although only one module is specified in this recipe, one of the powerful features of the JAAS security design is to use multiple `LoginModules` or layers in order to authenticate users. A user might have to be authenticated in several ways before she gains access to web components and data (e.g., first her irises are scanned, then she must specify a username and password).

The configuration file specifies:

- The fully qualified class name of the `LoginModule`(s).
- A "Flag" value, which is just a constant expression such as "required" or "requisite." The example uses "requisite." Table 15-1 describes the different Flag values.
- One or more "options" (Example 15-11 does not identify any options). The options represent a space-separated list of name/value pairs, such as debug="true" (you can use any name/value pairing you want). The options allow the configuration file to pass properties and values to the underlying `LoginModule`.

Table 15-1. Flag values for JAAS configuration files

Flag name	Description
Required	The `LoginModule` is required to succeed, and overall authentication fails if a `LoginModule` marked "required" fails. However, if a failure occurs, authentication still continues down the `LoginModule` list.
Requisite	The `LoginModule` is required to succeed, and runtime control returns to the application (rather than continuing with any other listed `LoginModules`) if authentication failure occurs.
Sufficient	If the `LoginModule` succeeds, control returns to the application and does *not* continue with any other listed `LoginModules`. If an authentication failure occurs, authentication continues with any other `LoginModule`. In other words, the failure of this `LoginModule` does not automatically lead to the failure of overall authentication, as in "required" or "requisite."
Optional	Success is not required with this `LoginModule`. If authentication success or failure occurs, authentication continues with any other listed `LoginModules`.

The basic structure of the configuration file looks like this:

```
ApplicationName{

    ModuleName Flag Options;
    ModuleName Flag Options;
    ModuleName Flag Options;
};

AnotherApplication{

    ModuleName Flag Options;
    ModuleName Flag Options;
};
```

Again, you do not have to use multiple `LoginModules`.

See this Javadoc page for more details on configuration: *http://java.sun.com/j2se/1.4.1/docs/api/javax/security/auth/login/Configuration.html*.

How does the JAAS implementation find the configuration file? The directory *${java.home}/jre/lib/security* contains a file named *java.security*. This is a "properties" or "policy" file in Java security parlance—a text file containing name/value pairs. The following line of text provides the location of the JAAS configuration file for the authentication servlet of Example 15-11:

```
login.config.url.1=file:h:/home/.java.login.config
```

If you have other JAAS configuration files that you want to combine with this one, use syntax similar to `login.config.url.2=file:h:/home/.my.config` (note the incremented number 2), placed within the *java.security* file.

You can use any filenaming convention; the configuration filename does not have to begin with a period.

A single JAAS configuration file can specify the `LoginModule(s)` for multiple application names. Recipe 15.8 shows a servlet that uses the `LoginModule` described in Recipe 15.5.

See Also

Sun Microsystems' JAAS developer's guide: *http://java.sun.com/j2se/1.4.2/docs/guide/security/jaas/JAASLMDevGuide.html*; a list of JAAS tutorials and sample programs: *http://java.sun.com/j2se/1.4.2/docs/guide/security/jaas/JAASRefGuide.html*; the Javadoc relating to JAAS configuration files: *http://java.sun.com/j2se/1.4.1/docs/api/javax/security/auth/login/Configuration.html*; Recipe 15.8 on using JAAS with a servlet; Recipe 15.9 on using JAAS with a JSP.

15.8   Using JAAS in a Servlet

Problem

You want to authenticate servlet clients with JAAS.

Solution

Create a JavaBean that wraps the functionality of the JAAS API classes that you have included in your web application.

Discussion

Using JAAS in a servlet requires that you have a `LoginModule` installed in your web application, either in *WEB-INF/classes* or stored in a JAR file in *WEB-INF/lib*.

Example 15-12 shows a servlet named `LoginServlet` that implements JAAS authentication. This servlet uses the `CallbackHandler` described in Recipe 15.5. This `CallbackHandler` must also be placed in *WEB-INF/classes* or included in a JAR stored in *WEB-INF/lib*. A browser request for this servlet looks like:

> *http://localhost:8080/home/servlet/com.*
> *jspservletcookbookLoginServlet?userName=Bruce%20W%20Perry&password=bw*
> *p1968*

Use a `POST` request from an HTML form in conjunction with SSL (Recipe 15.2) if you want to use the much more secure strategy of keeping usernames and passwords out of visible URLs.

Example 15-12. A servlet for authenticating and logging in clients

```
package com.jspservletcookbook;

import javax.servlet.*;
import javax.servlet.http.*;

import javax.security.auth.login.LoginContext;
import javax.security.auth.login.LoginException;
import javax.security.auth.callback.CallbackHandler;

public class LoginServlet extends HttpServlet {

  public void doGet(HttpServletRequest request,
    HttpServletResponse response)
      throws ServletException, java.io.IOException {

      //The CallbackHandler gets the username and password from
      //request parameters in the URL; therefore, the ServletRequest is
      //passed to the CallbackHandler constructor
      WebCallbackHandler webcallback = new WebCallbackHandler(request);

      LoginContext lcontext = null;

      boolean loginSuccess = true;


      try{

          lcontext = new LoginContext( "WebLogin",webcallback );

          //this method throws a LoginException
          //if authentication is unsuccessful
          lcontext.login( );
```

Example 15-12. A servlet for authenticating and logging in clients (continued)

```
    } catch (LoginException lge){

        loginSuccess = false;

    }

        response.setContentType("text/html");

        java.io.PrintWriter out = response.getWriter( );

        out.println(
        "<html><head><title>Thanks for logging in</title>"+
        "</head><body>");

        out.println("<h2>Your logged in status</h2>");

        out.println(""+ ( loginSuccess ? "Logged in" :
          "Failed Login" ));

        out.println("</body></html>");

    } //doGet

    public void doPost(HttpServletRequest request,
        HttpServletResponse response) throws ServletException,
        java.io.IOException {

        doGet(request,response);

    } //doPost

} //LoginServlet
```

This servlet:

1. Creates a WebCallbackHandler (Example 15-10) and passes the ServletRequest into the constructor (from where the CallbackHandler gets the client's name and password).

2. Creates a LoginContext object with two constructor parameters: the name of the login application (from our configuration file in Recipe 15.6, "WebLogin") and the WebCallbackHandler object.

3. Calls the LoginContext's login( ) method, which beneath the surface calls the DataSourceLoginModule's login( ) method (from Example 15-9), in order to perform authentication.

Figure 15-7 shows the web browser output when an attempted login using this servlet succeeds.

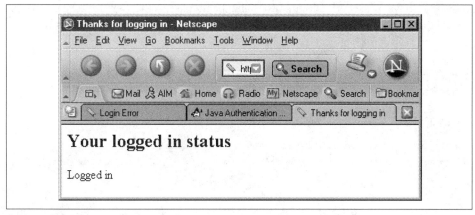

Figure 15-7. The LoginServlet signals success

See Also

Recipe 15.6 on creating a JAAS `LoginModule`; Recipe 15.7 on creating the JAAS configuration file; Chapter 21 on accessing databases with servlets; Sun Microsystems' JAAS developer's guide: *http://java.sun.com/j2se/1.4.2/docs/guide/security/jaas/ JAASLMDevGuide.html*; a list of JAAS tutorials and sample programs: *http://java. sun.com/j2se/1.4.2/docs/guide/security/jaas/JAASRefGuide.html*; the Javadoc relating to JAAS configuration files: *http://java.sun.com/j2se/1.4.1/docs/api/javax/security/ auth/login/Configuration.html*; Recipe 15.9 on using JAAS with a JSP.

15.9   Using JAAS in a JSP

Problem

You want to use a JSP and JAAS to authenticate clients.

Solution

Create a JavaBean that wraps the functionality of the JAAS API classes that you have included in your web application.

Discussion

Recipes 15.5–15.7 cover the JAAS basics, so this recipe focuses on adapting a JSP to the JAAS security API.

The JSP in this recipe uses a JavaBean to perform the login.

The JavaBean in Example 15-13 has two properties (in the form of instance variables): a `ServletRequest` and a `boolean` value indicating whether the name and password have passed the login test. The bean passes the ServletRequest to the WebCallbackHandler constructor; the WebCallbackHandler ultimately extracts the username and password from request parameters.

Example 15-13. A JavaBean uses the JAAS API to perform authentication

```
package com.jspservletcookbook;

import javax.servlet.ServletRequest;

import javax.security.auth.login.LoginContext;
import javax.security.auth.login.LoginException;

public class LoginBean {

    //private bean instance variables or properties
    private ServletRequest req;
    boolean loginSuccess;


  public LoginBean(){ }//bean's no-args constructor

  public boolean getLoginSuccess() throws LoginException {

    //the ServletRequest property has to be set before this
    //method is called, because that's where we get the
    //username and password from

    if (req == null)
        throw new IllegalStateException(
        "The ServletRequest cannot be null in getLogin()");

    WebCallbackHandler webcallback = new WebCallbackHandler(req);

    try{

        LoginContext lcontext = new LoginContext(
        "WebLogin",webcallback);

        //Call the LoginContext's login() method; if it doesn't
        //throw an exception, the method returns true
        lcontext.login();

        return true;

    } catch (LoginException lge){

        //login failed because the LoginContext.login() method
        //threw a LoginException
        return false;

    }
```

```
    } //getLoginSuccess

    public void setReq(ServletRequest request) {

        if (request == null)
            throw new IllegalArgumentException(
            "ServletRequest argument was null in: "+
            getClass().getName());

        this.req = request;

    } //setReq

} // LoginBean
```

The bean depends on its ServletRequest property being set properly before the getLoginSuccess( ) method is called. This method performs the login by using the familiar LoginContext class and its login( ) method (that is, familiar if you read Recipe 15.5!).

The Java object using the bean knows that the login succeeded or failed based on the boolean return value of the getLoginSuccess( ) method. The object using the bean in this case is a servlet instance originating from the JSP in Example 15-14.

The JSP includes the jsp:useBean standard action to create an instance of the LoginBean (in a variable named jaasBean). Then the code uses JSTL tags to:

1. Set the bean's ServletRequest property (named req) to the current request (using c:set).

2. Find out whether the login succeeded by using the EL syntax to call the bean's getLoginSuccess( ) method.

This recipe combines many Java-related technologies. See Chapter 23 for a description of the JSTL and its associated EL syntax.

Example 15-14. A JSP that logs in users using the JAAS API and a JavaBean

```
<%@ taglib uri="http://java.sun.com/jstl/core" prefix="c" %>

<html>
<head><title>Authenticating JSP</title></head>
<body>
<h2>Here is your login status...</h2>

<jsp:useBean id="jaasBean" class="com.jspservletcookbook.LoginBean" />

<%-- The bean's 'req' property is set using the 'request' property of the Expression
Language's pageContext implicit object --%>
```

Example 15-14. A JSP that logs in users using the JAAS API and a JavaBean (continued)

```
<c:set target="${jaasBean}" value="${pageContext.request}"
property="req"/>

<c:choose>

    <c:when test="${jaasBean.loginSuccess}">
    Logged in successfully.
    </c:when>

    <c:otherwise>
    Login failed.
    </c:otherwise>

</c:choose>

</body>
</html>
```

The LoginBean has a getLoginSuccess( ) method that returns false if the login fails, and true if it succeeds. With the EL, you can call any of a bean's accessor methods with the terminology:

> bean name.bean property name

The *bean property name* part represents the actual property name, not the name of the method, even though the end result of using this syntax is that the accessor method associated with that property gets called. Therefore, Example 15-14 gets the return value of the getLoginSuccess( ) method by using:

> ${jaasBean.loginSuccess}

If this expression returns true, the JSP displays the text "Logged in successfully." Otherwise, it shows "Login failed."

Figure 15-8 shows the JSP's browser display when a login fails.

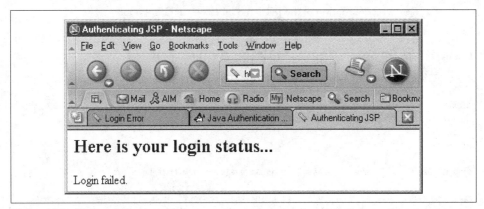

Figure 15-8. A JSP signals a login failure

See Also

Recipe 15.6 on creating a JAAS `LoginModule`; Recipe 15.7 on creating the JAAS configuration file; Recipe 15.8 on using JAAS with a servlet; Chapter 23 on the JSTL; Sun Microsystems' JAAS developer's guide: *http://java.sun.com/j2se/1.4.2/docs/guide/ security/jaas/JAASLMDevGuide.html*; a list of JAAS tutorials and sample programs: *http://java.sun.com/j2se/1.4.2/docs/guide/security/jaas/JAASRefGuide.html*; the Javadoc relating to JAAS configuration files: *http://java.sun.com/j2se/1.4.1/docs/api/javax/ security/auth/login/Configuration.html*.

CHAPTER 16

Binding, Accessing, and Removing Attributes in Web Applications

16.0 Introduction

An *attribute* is a Java object that servlet code can *bind*, or store, in a certain scope, such as a ServletContext, a session, or a request. The object can temporarily store and share a small piece of data in a way that is not otherwise available to servlet developers. Then, when the application no longer has use for the object, your code can remove, or *unbind* it, and the web container makes the object available for garbage collection.

This chapter describes how to work with attributes in all three scopes: ServletContext, session, and request. If you need to make an object available to all of the servlets and JSPs in a context, then you can bind the object to a ServletContext. If the application calls for an object such as a "shopping cart" to be bound to a session (see Chapter 11), you can set the object as a session attribute. Finally, if the application requires two servlets that communicate via a RequestDispatcher to share an object, then the servlets can use an object attribute bound to a request scope.

 Since sessions and requests are associated with numerous users in a busy web application, developers have to pay attention to the size and resource use of any objects that are bound as attributes to requests or sessions.

16.1 Setting ServletContext Attributes in Servlets

Problem

You want to make an object available to all servlets in a context or web application.

Solution

Bind an object to the ServletContext using the javax.servlet.ServletContext. setAttribute( ) method.

Discussion

A ServletContext attribute is available to all servlets and JSPs in a context or web application. Here are the steps to bind an object to a ServletContext:

1. Create the Java class that you want to bind to a ServletContext.
2. Place the class in the *WEB-INF/classes* directory, including the necessary package-related directories. You can also store the class in a JAR file in *WEB-INF/lib*.
3. Create a servlet that binds the object to the ServletContext using the javax. servlet.ServletContext.setAttribute( ) method.
4. Access the object using ServletContext.getAttribute( ) in (other) servlets whenever it is needed.

I'll first show the object that this recipe binds to the ServletContext. The recipe then demonstrates a servlet that stores the object attribute in the ServletContext. Example 16-1 shows a simple object wrapped around a java.util.Map type. Use the Map to store a characteristic of each request made to the web application. In this example, each Map key is the IP address of the client making the request. Each Map value is the date it requested the servlet.

Example 16-1. The object that a servlet binds to the ServletContext

```
package com.jspservletcookbook;

import java.util.Collections;
import java.util.HashMap;
import java.util.Iterator;
import java.util.Map;
import java.util.Set;

public class ContextObject  {

    private Map map;

  public ContextObject(){

     map = Collections.synchronizedMap(new HashMap( ));
  }

  public void put(Object key, Object value){

     if (key == null || value == null)
       throw new IllegalArgumentException(
```

```
                "Invalid parameters passed to ContextObject.put");

        map.put(key,value);
    }

    public String getValues(){

        StringBuffer buf = new StringBuffer("");
        Set set = map.keySet();

        //you have to explicitly synchronize when an Iterator is used
        synchronized(map) {

            Iterator i = set.iterator();

            while (i.hasNext())
                buf.append((String) i.next() + "<br>");
        }//synchronized

        return buf.toString();

    }

    public String toString(){

        return getClass().getName() + "[ " +map+ " ]";

    }//toString

}
```

The ContextObject class has methods to add keys and values to the Map (put(*Object key*, *Object value*)) as well as to output the Map's current key values (getValues()). The Map is synchronized, which is essentially thread-safe; it is created in the ContextObject's constructor in the following manner:

```
map = Collections.synchronizedMap(new HashMap());
```

 When you generate a Map using the static java.util.Collections. synchronizedMap() method, only one thread at a time can call the Map's methods. This is important with ServletContext attributes that may be accessed by several servlets and/or multiple threads at the same time.

Example 16-2 shows the skeleton of the ContextBinder servlet that binds an instance of the ContextObject class in Example 16-1 to the ServletContext.

Example 16-2. A servlet binds an object to the ServletContext

```
package com.jspservletcookbook;

import javax.servlet.*;
import javax.servlet.http.*;

public class ContextBinder extends HttpServlet {

  public void doGet(HttpServletRequest request, HttpServletResponse response) throws
  ServletException, java.io.IOException {

    //bind an object to the ServletContext
    getServletContext( ).setAttribute(
        "com.jspservletcookbook.ContextObject", new ContextObject( ));

    //display some HTML
    ...
  } //end doGet
}
```

The servlet method getServletContext( ) returns a javax.servlet.ServletContext instance. You then call that instance's setAttribute( ) method with the String attribute name and the bound object as parameters. As a convention, you should consider naming attributes after their fully qualified class name—in this case, "com. jspservletcookbook.ContextObject."

See Also

Recipe 16.2 on setting ServletContext attributes in JSPs; Recipe 16.3 on accessing or removing a ServletContext attribute; Recipes 16.5–16.8 on handling session attributes in servlets and JSPs; Recipes 16.9–16.12 on handling request attributes in servlets and JSPs; Recipe 14.5 on using a ServletContext event listener; the Javadoc for javax.servlet.ServletContextAttributeListener: *http://java.sun.com/j2ee/1.4/ docs/api/javax/servlet/ServletContextAttributeListener.html.*

16.2   Setting ServletContext Attributes in JSPs

Problem

You want to store an object attribute in the ServletContext using a JSP.

Solution

Use the JSTL c:set tag to bind an object to application scope. The JSTL uses the application implicit object to represent the ServletContext, which is also the scope used for the object attributes discussed in the previous recipe.

Discussion

JSP developers can use the JSTL core tags and the `jsp:useBean` standard action to implement the same functionality as the servlet in Recipe 16.1. Like the program in that recipe, the upcoming JSP stores in the `ServletContext` an object attribute that contains a `java.util.Map` type. The `Map` stores key/value pairs that are accessed by other servlets or JSPs in the same context.

Here are the steps to bind an attribute to the `ServletContext` using a JSP:

1. Create the Java class that you will instantiate and bind to the `ServletContext`.

2. Place the Java class in the *WEB-INF/classes* directory, including any package-related directories (if the class is named `com.jspservletcookbook.ContextObject` then place the class in *WEB-INF/classes/com/jspservletcookbook*), or in *WEB-INF/lib* if the class is stored in a JAR file.

3. Create the JSP that will bind the object attribute to the `ServletContext`. Store the JSP in the web application's top-level directory.

4. If the web container does not already provide the JSTL-related components, include them in *WEB-INF/lib* (see Chapter 23) so that the JSP can use these tag libraries.

First I show the object attribute that the JSP binds to the `ServletContext`. Example 16-3 is the same Java class as Example 16-1, except for the `getMap()` method, which returns the `Map` type that this object uses to store information. I added this method to make the `Map` available to the `c:set` core tag (see Example 16-4). Because the two code samples are exactly the same except for the `getMap()` method, Example 16-3 has been abbreviated to show just the creation of the synchronized map and its getter method (see Example 16-1 for the other parts of the class).

Example 16-3. The object attribute bound to the ServletContext by a JSP

```
package com.jspservletcookbook;

import java.util.Collections;
import java.util.HashMap;
import java.util.Iterator;
import java.util.Map;
import java.util.Set;


public class ContextObject  {

    private Map map;

  public ContextObject( ){

      map = Collections.synchronizedMap(new HashMap( ));
```

```
    }

  public Map getMap( ){

      return map;

  }
// see Example 16-1 for the other parts of the class
}
```

Example 16-4 does the work of creating an instance of the object attribute and then binding the attribute to the ServletContext. The code creates the ContextObj instance (which is stored in the ServletContext) with the jsp:useBean standard action. Then the c:set JSTL core tag stores this object in application scope, which is an alias for the ServletContext. The ContextObj class stores information with a Map type that it contains. This code in Example 16-4 stores data in the ServletContext attribute:

```
<c:set target=
   "${applicationScope[\"com.jspservletcookbook.ContextObject\"].map}"
       value="${date}" property="${pageContext.request.remoteAddr}"/>
```

The value of the target attribute has the effect of calling getMap( ) on the ContextObj object. The code then creates a new key-value pair in the Map, consisting of the remote IP address of the client making the request (the key) and the current date (the value). I chose this information at random to demonstrate how to store pieces of data in a ServletContext attribute using the JSTL and JSPs. Your own code may store data of practical value to your application such as a customer's unique ID and the item that he is purchasing.

Example 16-4. The contextBind.jsp file

```
<%@ taglib uri="http://java.sun.com/jstl/core" prefix="c" %>

<html>
<head><title>Context binding JSP</title></head>
<body>
<h2>Here is the bound ContextObject</h2>

//create an instance of ContextObject; store it as a Page scoped attribute
<jsp:useBean id="contextObj" class=
    "com.jspservletcookbook.ContextObject" />

//create an instance of Date; store it as a Page scoped attribute
<jsp:useBean id="date" class="java.util.Date" />

//bind the object to the ServletContext represented by the
//'application' implicit object
<c:set var=
    "com.jspservletcookbook.ContextObject" value="${contextObj}" scope=
        "application" />
```

Example 16-4. The contextBind.jsp file (continued)

```
//create a new key/value pair in the bound object's Map
<c:set target=
    "${applicationScope[\"com.jspservletcookbook.ContextObject\"].map}"
        value="${date}" property="${pageContext.request.remoteAddr}"/>

</body>
</html>
```

After looking at this code, you may wonder why the `ContextObject` variable is effectively named twice, once by `jsp:useBean` when it creates the object (giving the object an `id` or name `contextObj`) and again by `c:set` when it binds the object to the `ServletContext` (and creating the name `com.jspservletcookbook.ContextObject`).

By convention, you should name the attribute after its fully qualified class name. However, you cannot use this format with `jsp:useBean`, because this action creates a Java variable in the underlying servlet. The Java variable is named `contextObj`.

 The JSP container creates a servlet behind the scenes to implement each JSP page.

You cannot include period (.) characters when naming Java variables, so the code renames the object in `c:set`'s `var` attribute when the object is bound to the `ServletContext`.

See Also

Chapter 23 on using the JSTL; Recipe 16.1 on setting `ServletContext` attributes in servlets; Recipe 16.4 on accessing or removing a `ServletContext` attribute in a JSP; Recipes 16.5–16.8 on handling session attributes in servlets and JSPs; Recipes 16.9–16.12 on handling request attributes in servlets and JSPs; Recipe 14.5 on using a `ServletContext` event listener; the Javadoc for `javax.servlet.ServletContextAttributeListener`: *http://java.sun.com/j2ee/1.4/docs/api/javax/servlet/ServletContextAttributeListener.html*.

16.3   Accessing or Removing ServletContext Attributes in Servlets

Problem

You want to access a `ServletContext` attribute to work with it in code, or completely remove it.

Solution

Use the ServletContext.getAttribute(String attributeName) method to access the attribute. Use the ServletContext.removeAttribute(String attributeName) method to remove the attribute from the ServletContext.

Discussion

The code in Example 16-5 gets the ServletContext attribute and stores it in a local variable. Then the code adds a new key/value to the attribute (which contains a java.util.Map type for storing the keys and values). Later, the servlet prints out a list of the attribute's keys, which are IP addresses associated with requests to the servlet.

Example 16-5. Accessing a ServletContext attribute in a servlet

```java
package com.jspservletcookbook;

import javax.servlet.*;
import javax.servlet.http.*;

public class ContextAccessor extends HttpServlet {

  public void doGet(HttpServletRequest request,
    HttpServletResponse response) throws ServletException,
    java.io.IOException {

    //get a ServletContext attribute
    ContextObject contextObj = (ContextObject)
        getServletContext( ).getAttribute(
        "com.jspservletcookbook.ContextObject");

    if (contextObj != null)
        contextObj.put(request.getRemoteAddr( ),""+
            new java.util.Date( ));

    //display the context attribute values
      response.setContentType("text/html");
      java.io.PrintWriter out = response.getWriter( );
      out.println(
          "<html><head><title>Context Attribute</title></head><body>");

      if (contextObj != null){
          out.println("<h2>ServletContext Attribute Values</h2>");
          out.println(contextObj.getValues( ));
      } else {
          out.println("<h2>ServletContext Attribute is Null</h2>");
      }
      out.println("</body></html>");
  } //end doGet
}
```

Example 16-1 in Recipe 16.1 shows the ContextObject source code. Here, the ContextObject put( ) method passes its key and value parameters to the Map method of the same name, except that the ContextObject put( ) method does not allow null values for either its keys or values.

If you want to remove the same attribute that was bound by this recipe, call the ServletContext.removeAttribute( ) method with the attribute name as a parameter:

```
getServletContext( ).removeAttribute(
    "com.jspservletcookbook.ContextObject");
```

After the attribute removal code executes, any further calls to ServletContext. getAttribute( ) using the same attribute name will return null.

See Also

Recipes 16.1 and 16.2 on setting ServletContext attributes in servlets and JSPs; Recipes 16.5–16.8 on handling session attributes in servlets and JSPs; Recipes 16.9– 16.12 on handling request attributes in servlets and JSPs; Recipe 14.5 on using a ServletContext event listener; the Javadoc for javax.servlet. ServletContextAttributeListener: *http://java.sun.com/j2ee/1.4/docs/api/javax/servlet/ ServletContextAttributeListener.html.*

16.4   Accessing or Removing ServletContext Attributes in JSPs

Problem

You want to access or remove a ServletContext attribute in a JSP.

Solution

Use the c:out JSTL core tag to display the value of an attribute and the c:remove tag to remove the attribute from the ServletContext.

Discussion

By now you are probably familiar with the object attribute that the previous recipes stored in the ServletContext under the name com.jspservletcookbook.ContextObject. If you are not, Recipes 16.1 and 16.2 show the source code for this class and how it is bound as an attribute to a servlet and a JSP. This recipe shows the JSTL tags that you can use in JSP code to access this attribute and optionally remove or unbind it.

Example 16-6 includes the taglib directive that is required for using JSTL 1.0 tags in a JSP. The c:out tag then accesses the ServletContext attribute in the tag's value attribute. The tag gets the value of the ServletContext attribute by using the applicationScope JSTL implicit object, which is a java.util.Map type.

Example 16-6. Accessing an application attribute in a JSP

```
<%@ taglib uri="http://java.sun.com/jstl/core" prefix="c" %>
//HTML or other presentation code here...
<c:out value=
    "${applicationScope[\"com.jspservletcookbook.ContextObject\"].values}"
        escapeXml="false" />
```

 An implicit object is an object that the JSTL automatically makes available to the developer. You use the term applicationScope within ${...} characters, and this term evaluates to a java.util.Map of any object attributes that are bound to the ServletContext.

The code:

```
${applicationScope[\"com.jspservletcookbook.ContextObject\"].values}
```

uses EL syntax to access the ServletContext attribute named com.jspservletcookbook.ContextObject and get its values property, which effectively calls the getValues() method on the ContextObject object. This method displays all the keys of the Map contained by ContextObject, separated by an HTML line break (<br>). The attribute escapeXml="false" prevents the < and > characters in <br> from being escaped (and being replaced by < and >, respectively), which would prevent its proper display in a web browser.

 If I wanted to make the ContextObject more universal, I could include a JavaBean property allowing the user of the class to set the line separator, so that the output of the getValues() method could be used in different contexts, not just HTML.

Figure 16-1 shows the result of accessing a JSP that uses this code in a browser.

To remove the attribute from the ServletContext, use the c:remove JSTL tag. This tag removes the named variable from the specified scope:

```
<c:remove var=
    "com.jspservletcookbook.ContextObject" scope="application" />
```

application is an alias for the ServletContext. After a JSP that contains this tag is executed, any further attempts to access a ServletContext attribute of the same name will return null.

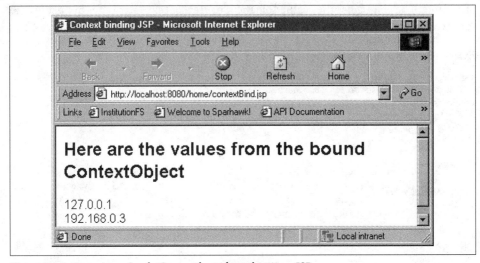

Figure 16-1. Accessing a ServletContext bound attribute in a JSP

See Also

Chapter 23 on using the JSTL; Recipes 16.1 and 16.2 on setting ServletContext attributes in servlets and JSPs; Recipe 16.3 on accessing or removing ServletContext attributes in servlets; Recipes 16.5–16.8 on handling session attributes in servlets and JSPs; Recipes 16.9–16.12 on handling request attributes in servlets and JSPs; Recipe 14.5 on using a ServletContext event listener; the Javadoc for javax.servlet. ServletContextAttributeListener: *http://java.sun.com/j2ee/1.4/docs/api/javax/servlet/ ServletContextAttributeListener.html.*

16.5   Setting Session Attributes in Servlets

Problem

You want to store an object attribute in a session.

Solution

Use the javax.servlet.http.HttpSession class's setAttribute( ) method.

Discussion

The mechanism for placing object attributes in sessions is very similar to storing objects in the ServletContext, which Recipe 16.1 described. The difference lies in the scope of the objects; in other words, which users and how many concurrent users can access the bound objects.

A *session* represents the interaction of a user with a web site. The sequence of web pages or components that a single user requests from a web site represents a single session (detailed in Chapter 11). Therefore, when you store an object instance in a session attribute, every user who participates in sessions interacts with his own instance of that object attribute. With ServletContext attributes, however, all of the application's users interact with the same attribute instance, since each web application has only one ServletContext and each context is associated with one attribute instance.

 A distributed web application has one ServletContext instance per Java virtual machine (JVM). Instead of using the ServletContext to store information globally for the application, the ServletContext Javadoc makes brief mention of using a database instead, to ensure that servlets in a distributed application are accessing the same data. See the ServletContext Javadoc at: *http://java.sun.com/j2ee/1.4/docs/api/javax/servlet/ServletContext.html*.

A shopping cart storing a user's item choices is an example of an object that web developers typically store as a session attribute. Example 16-7 shows a fragment of servlet code for storing an object in a session.

Example 16-7. Storing an object attribute in a session

```
<!-- this code appears in the servlet's doGet or doPost method, whichever is appropriate -
->

//Create a session if one does not exist yet
HttpSession session = request.getSession();

//bind an object attribute in the session
if (session != null)
session.setAttribute(
    "com.jspservletcookbook.ContextObject", new ContextObject());
```

Gain access to a session in a servlet by using the javax.servlet.http. HttpServletRequest object's getSession() method. Then call HttpSession. setAttribute(), passing in the name of the attribute and an instance of the object attribute. The code in Example 16-7 uses the same ContextObject that Example 16-1 showed (Recipe 16.1). The ContextObject uses a synchronized java.util.Map type to handle multiple threads that might be using the attribute concurrently.

 Pay attention to the possibility of multiple threads accessing a session object attribute. According to the servlet specification v2.4 (Chapter SRV.7.7.1), "Multiple servlets executing request threads may have active access to a single session object at the same time. The developer has the responsibility for synchronizing access to session resources as appropriate."

See Also

Recipes 16.1–16.4 on handling `ServletContext` attributes in servlets and JSPs; Recipe 16.7 on accessing or removing session attributes in servlets; Recipes 16.6 and 16.8 on handling session attributes in JSPs; Recipes 16.9–16.12 on handling request attributes in servlets and JSPs; Recipe 14.6 on using a session event listener; the Javadoc for javax.servlet.http.HttpSessionAttributeListener: *http://java.sun.com/ j2ee/1.4/docs/api/javax/servlet/http/HttpSessionAttributeListener.html*.

16.6   Setting Session Attributes in JSPs

Problem

You want to bind an object to a session in a JSP.

Solution

Use the `jsp:useBean` and `c:set` tags to create an instance of an object and assign it as an attribute to the session.

Discussion

The JSTL core tags and the `jsp:useBean` standard action can be used to manage session attributes in JSPs. Example 16-8 binds an object attribute to a session, displays a value from the object, and then shows the session ID of the client who requested the JSP. The bound object is the `ContextObject` that I have used throughout this chapter as the stored attribute. It contains a `java.util.Map` type for storing the IP addresses of users who request the JSP (see Example 16-1 and the accompanying description of the code).

Example 16-8. Setting a session attribute in a JSP

```
<%@ taglib uri="http://java.sun.com/jstl/core" prefix="c" %>
<html>
<head><title>Context binding JSP</title></head>
<body>
<h2>Here are the values from the bound ContextObject</h2>
<%-- Create instances of the ContextObject and Date classes --%>
<jsp:useBean id="contextObj" class=
    "com.jspservletcookbook.ContextObject" />

<jsp:useBean id="date" class="java.util.Date" />

<%-- Bind the object attribute to the session scope--%>
<c:set var=
    "com.jspservletcookbook.ContextObject" value="${contextObj}" scope=
        "session" />
```

Example 16-8. Setting a session attribute in a JSP (continued)

```
<%-- Put a value in the object, then display the value--%>
<c:set target=
    "${sessionScope[\"com.jspservletcookbook.ContextObject\"].map}" value=
        "${date}" property="${pageContext.request.remoteAddr}"/>

<c:out value="${sessionScope[\"com.jspservletcookbook.ContextObject\"].
    values}" escapeXml="false" />

<h2>Here is the session ID</h2>
<c:out value="${pageContext.session.id}" />
</body>
</html>
```

This code from Example 16-8 binds the object to the session:

```
<c:set var=
    "com.jspservletcookbook.ContextObject" value="${contextObj}" scope=
        "session" />
```

The only difference between Example 16-8 and the JSP of Recipe 16.2, which binds the object to the ServletContext, is the value of the scope attribute in the c:set tag (session in this case). In similar fashion, the c:set tag sets a value in the session attribute by referring to the sessionScope implicit variable:

```
<c:set target=
    "${sessionScope[\"com.jspservletcookbook.ContextObject\"].map}" value=
        "${date}" property="${pageContext.request.remoteAddr}"/>
```

The EL mechanism automatically makes available the sessionScope implicit variable, which represents a java.util.Map type that stores any object variables in session scope.

> If you have an attribute name that does not include period characters in it, you can provide the attribute name without any further context, and the EL will search the page, request, session, and application scopes for an attribute of that name. For example, the following EL syntax returns a session object attribute named contextObj without using an implicit variable (or null if that session attribute does not exist) to further qualify the name:
>
> ```
> ${contextObj}
> ```

See Also

Chapter 23 on using the JSTL; Recipes 16.1–16.4 on handling ServletContext attributes in servlets and JSPs; Recipe 16.7 on accessing or removing session attributes in servlets; Recipe 16.8 on accessing or removing session attributes in JSPs; Recipes 16.9–16.12 on handling request attributes in servlets and JSPs; Recipe 14.6 on using a session event listener; the Javadoc for javax.servlet.http. HttpSessionAttributeListener: *http://java.sun.com/j2ee/1.4/docs/api/javax/servlet/http/HttpSessionAttributeListener.html*.

16.7 Accessing or Removing Session Attributes in Servlets

Problem

You want to access or remove a session attribute in a servlet.

Solution

Use the javax.servlet.http.HttpSession.getAttribute(*String attributeName*) method to access the attribute. Use the removeAttribute(*String attributeName*) method to remove the attribute from the session.

Discussion

To access a session attribute, you must first bind the attribute to a session, as in Recipe 16.5. The object attribute is now available to the user associated with that session. Example 16-9 accesses an attribute named com.jspservletcookbook. ContextObject. The example just shows the code relating to accessing an attribute from the session. Example 16-5 in Recipe 16.3 shows the entire servlet and doGet() method for accessing an object attribute.

 The HttpSession.getAttribute() method returns an Object type, so the return value has to be cast to the appropriate type before calling any methods on it.

Example 16-9. Gaining access to the session attribute in a servlet

```
package com.jspservletcookbook;
...
<!-- this code appears in the servlet's doGet or doPost method, whichever is appropriate.
The ContextObject class is stored in WEB-INF/classes/com/jspservletcookbook/ -->

//Create a session if one does not exist yet
HttpSession session = request.getSession();

//This local variable will hold the object attribute
ContextObject contextObj = null;

//get access to an object attribute in the session
if (session != null)
    contextObj = (ContextObject) session.getAttribute(
        "com.jspservletcookbook.ContextObject");

//ensure the contextObj is not null before calling any methods
if (contextObj != null)
    out.println( contextObj.getValues() );

<!-- rest of servlet class and doGet or doPost method goes here -->
```

You must take these steps before accessing a session attribute:

1. Compile the class of the object that will be stored in the session.
2. Place this class in *WEB-INF/classes* or in *WEB-INF/lib* if it's stored in a JAR file.
3. Make sure a servlet, JSP, or other web component sets the attribute to the session with the `HttpSession.setAttribute( )` method.

Removing the session attribute from a servlet

To remove an attribute, call `HttpSession.removeAttribute( )` with the name of the attribute. Use the following code in a servlet to remove the attribute this chapter has been working with:

```
HttpSession session = request.getSession( );
<!-- HttpSession.removeAttribute will have no effect if an attribute of that name
does not exist -->

if (session != null)
    session.removeAttribute("com.jspservletcookbook.ContextObject");
```

Now the attribute is no longer available in the session associated with the user that requested the servlet. The session attribute *is* still available in other sessions where it may be stored (albeit in the form of a different instance). Each user is associated with a specific session, and each session can carry its own instance of the object attribute.

 When you remove the attribute from the `ServletContext`, on the other hand, it is no longer available to any users, because there is only one `ServletContext` for each nondistributed web application.

See Also

Recipes 16.1–16.4 on handling `ServletContext` attributes in servlets and JSPs; Recipe 16.5 on setting session attributes in servlets; Recipe 16.6 on setting session attributes in JSPs; Recipe 16.8 on accessing or removing session attributes in JSPs; Recipes 16.9–16.12 on handling request attributes in servlets and JSPs; Recipe 14.6 on using a session event listener; the Javadoc for javax.servlet.http. `HttpSessionAttributeListener`: *http://java.sun.com/j2ee/1.4/docs/api/javax/servlet/ http/HttpSessionAttributeListener.html*.

16.8 Accessing or Removing Session Attributes in JSPs

Problem

You want to access or remove a session attribute in a JSP.

Solution

Use the c:out JSTL core tag to display the value of an attribute and the c:remove tag to remove the attribute from the session.

Discussion

Here are the steps to access or remove a session-scoped variable with the JSTL and a JSP:

1. Make sure that your web application is able to use the JSTL (i.e., you have the proper JAR files such as *jstl.jar* and *standard.jar* in your *WEB-INF/lib* directory; see Chapter 23 for instructions).

2. Include the taglib directive, which makes the JSTL core tags available to the JSP (see the upcoming code).

3. Make sure the object attribute is bound to the session in the first place, either by the same JSP that accesses the attribute, or by another web component (such as a servlet).

The code in this recipe shows how to reference a session-scoped variable, as opposed to a ServletContext attribute (shown in Recipe 16.4). This code uses the sessionScope implicit object of the EL, which is an automatically available variable in EL format that contains any session-scoped object attributes. This code represents a portion of a JSP that displays the values contained in an attribute named com.jspservletcookbook.ContextObject.

Example 16-4 in Recipe 16.2 shows a complete JSP that accesses object attributes. Recipe 16.2 accesses a ServletContext attribute in a JSP, rather than a session-scoped attribute.

```
<%@ taglib uri="http://java.sun.com/jstl/core" prefix="c" %>
//HTML or other presentation code here...
<c:out value=
    "${sessionScope[\"com.jspservletcookbook.ContextObject\"].values}"
        escapeXml="false" />
```

The escapeXml="false" part of the c:out tag tells the tag to leave characters that are part of the tag's output such as < and > unescaped (in other words, do not convert them to character entities such as < and >).

This JSP code removes a session-scoped variable using the c:remove core tag:

```
<c:remove var=
    "com.jspservletcookbook.ContextObject" scope="session" />
```

The object attribute is no longer available for the individual session associated with the user that requested this JSP. In other words, the c:remove tag does not remove all session attributes of the specified name, just the session attribute(s) associated with any user who requests the JSP containing the c:remove tag.

See Also

Chapter 23 on using the JSTL; Recipes 16.1–16.4 on handling ServletContext attributes in servlets and JSPs; Recipe 16.5 on setting session attributes in servlets; Recipe 16.6 on setting session attributes in JSPs; Recipe 16.7 on accessing or removing session attributes in servlets; Recipes 16.9–16.12 on handling request attributes in servlets and JSPs; Recipe 14.6 on using a session event listener; the Javadoc for javax.servlet.http.HttpSessionAttributeListener: *http://java.sun.com/j2ee/1.4/docs/ api/javax/servlet/http/HttpSessionAttributeListener.html*.

16.9 Setting Request Attributes in Servlets

Problem

You want to use a servlet to store an attribute in a request.

Solution

Use the javax.servlet.ServletRequest.setAttribute( ) method.

Discussion

The ServletRequest.setAttribute( ) method is often used in code that dynamically forwards requests or includes content with a javax.servlet.RequestDispatcher.

Web applications that use RequestDispatchers to share requests between web components can communicate between these components using request attributes. Both the recipient of the RequestDispatcher.forward( ) method and the included file or page involved with the RequestDispatcher.include( ) method have access to the original or enclosing request. Therefore, these web components can also access any object attributes that are stored in those requests.

The servlet in Example 16-10 creates an instance of a ContextObject, stores some information in the object by calling its put( ) method, and then places the object in the HttpServletRequest under the name "com.jspservletcookbook.ContextObject." The servlet then uses a RequestDispatcher to forward the request (including the attribute) and response to the servlet path */displayAttr*. The web component mapped to that servlet path now has access to the previously created request attribute.

Example 16-10. Binding an object to a request

```
package com.jspservletcookbook;

import javax.servlet.*;
import javax.servlet.http.*;

public class RequestBinder extends HttpServlet {

  public void doGet(HttpServletRequest request,
    HttpServletResponse response) throws ServletException,
      java.io.IOException {

      //bind an object to the request
      ContextObject contextObj = new ContextObject();

      contextObj.put( request.getRemoteAddr(), ""+new java.util.Date());

      request.setAttribute(
        "com.jspservletcookbook.ContextObject",contextObj );

      //use RequestDispatcher to forward request to another servlet
      // mapped to the servlet path '/displayAttr'
      RequestDispatcher dispatcher = request.getRequestDispatcher(
        "/displayAttr");

      dispatcher.forward(request,response);

  } //doGet

}
```

Example 16-11 shows the servlet that receives the forwarded request. The RequestDisplay servlet is mapped in *web.xml* to the */displayAttr* servlet path. This servlet gets the request attribute from the HttpServletRequest object by calling getAttribute( ) with the attribute name: com.jspservletcookbook.ContextObject. Since the return value of getAttribute( ) is typed to Object, the code must cast the result to ContextObject.

Example 16-11. The target of RequestDispatcher.forward has access to the request attribute

```
package com.jspservletcookbook;

import javax.servlet.*;
import javax.servlet.http.*;

public class RequestDisplay extends HttpServlet {

public void doGet(HttpServletRequest request, HttpServletResponse response) throws
ServletException, java.io.IOException {

    ContextObject obj = (ContextObject) request.getAttribute(
        "com.jspservletcookbook.RequestObject");
```

Example 16-11. The target of RequestDispatcher.forward has access to the request attribute

```
response.setContentType("text/html");
java.io.PrintWriter out = response.getWriter();
out.println(
    "<html><head><title>Request Attribute</title></head><body>");
out.println("<h2>Request attribute values</h2>");

//display the keys of the java.util.Map stored in the request object
//attribute
if (obj != null)
    out.println( obj.getValues() );

out.println("</body></html>");

} //end doGet

}
```

Make sure to check whether the ServletRequest.getAttribute( ) return value is null before calling any of the object attribute's methods. The getAttribute( ) method returns null if the request does not contain an attribute of the specified name.

See Also

Recipes 16.1–16.4 on handling ServletContext attributes in servlets and JSPs; Recipes 16.5–16.8 on handling session attributes in servlets and JSPs; Recipe 16.10 on setting request attributes in JSPs; Recipes 16.11 and 16.12 on accessing or removing request attributes in servlets and JSPs; the Javadoc for javax.servlet. ServletRequestAttributeListener: *http://java.sun.com/j2ee/1.4/docs/api/javax/servlet/ ServletRequestAttributeListener.html.*

16.10 Setting Request Attributes in JSPs

Problem

You want to set a request attribute using a JSP.

Solution

Use the JSTL core tags and the jsp:useBean standard action to create an instance of an object and bind it to the request.

Discussion

The JSP in Example 16-12 stores a com.jspservletcookbook.ContextObject in the request scope by first creating an instance of that object with jsp:useBean. As in

Recipes 16.2 and 16.6, the code uses the c:set tag to bind the object to the request, but this time gives its scope attribute a value of request.

 You should store the classes for the objects that JSPs use as request attributes in *WEB-INF/classes,* or in *WEB-INF/lib* if the class is part of a JAR file.

The JSP in Example 16-12 is exactly like the JSP code shown in Recipes 16.2 and 16.6, except this time the code uses the requestScope implicit object to fetch the request attribute and give it a new property and value. The requestScope is used in EL syntax (see Chapter 23) to access request attributes.

Example 16-12. Setting a request attribute and forwarding the request in a JSP

```
<%@ taglib uri="http://java.sun.com/jstl/core" prefix="c" %>

<jsp:useBean id="contextObj" class=
    "com.jspservletcookbook.ContextObject" />

<jsp:useBean id="date" class="java.util.Date" />
<c:set var="com.jspservletcookbook.ContextObject" value=
    "${contextObj}" scope="request" />

<c:set target=
    "${requestScope[\"com.jspservletcookbook.ContextObject\"].map}" value=
        "${date}" property="${pageContext.request.remoteAddr}"/>

<jsp:forward page="/displayAttr" />
```

After setting the request attribute and giving it some values, the JSP forwards the request to the servlet path */displayAttr.* The servlet or JSP mapped to that path has access to the new request attribute.

See Also

Chapter 23 on using the JSTL; Recipes 16.1–16.4 on handling ServletContext attributes in servlets and JSPs; Recipes 16.5–16.8 on handling session attributes in servlets and JSPs; Recipes 16.11 and 16.12 on accessing or removing request attributes in servlets and JSPs; the Javadoc for javax.servlet. ServletRequestAttributeListener: *http://java.sun.com/j2ee/1.4/docs/api/javax/servlet/ ServletRequestAttributeListener.html.*

16.11 Accessing or Removing Request Attributes in Servlets

Problem

You want a servlet to access or remove a request attribute.

Solution

Use the `javax.servlet.ServletRequest.getAttribute( )` and `javax.servlet.ServletRequest.removeAttribute( )` methods, including the name of the attribute as the method parameter.

Discussion

Example 16-13 is derived from the doGet( ) method of Example 16-11 in Recipe 16.9 (refer to that class if you need to review the complete code of a servlet handling request attributes). Example 16-13 gets an object attribute from the HttpServletRequest object, which is the doGet( ) method's first parameter.

 The servlet container creates an HttpServletRequest object and passes it as the first parameter to all of the HttpServlet's service methods, including doGet( ) and doPost( ).

Example 16-13 calls one of the attribute's methods, then removes the request attribute.

Example 16-13. A servlet accesses and removes a request attribute

```
public void doGet(HttpServletRequest request, HttpServletResponse response)
    throws ServletException, java.io.IOException {

    ContextObject obj = (ContextObject) request.getAttribute(
        "com.jspservletcookbook.ContextObject");

    response.setContentType("text/html");
    java.io.PrintWriter out = response.getWriter( );
    out.println(
        "<html><head><title>Request Attribute</title></head><body>");

    //display the attribute's Map keys
    out.println("<h2>Request attribute values</h2>");

    if (obj != null)
        out.println( obj.getValues( ) );

    //This method call may not be necessary as request attributes
```

```
    //persist only as long as the request is being handled,
    //according to the ServletRequest API documentation.
    request.removeAttribute("com.jspservletcookbook.ContextObject");

    out.println("</body></html>");

} //doGet
```

If the attribute does not exist in the request (because it was not bound to the request in the first place), ServletRequest.getAttribute( ) returns null. Make sure the servlet code checks for a null value before it calls the object's methods. In addition, the ServletRequest.getAttribute( ) method returns an Object type, so ensure that the servlet code casts the return value to the proper type before calling the expected type's methods.

See Also

Recipes 16.1–16.4 on handling ServletContext attributes in servlets and JSPs; Recipes 16.5–16.8 on handling session attributes in servlets and JSPs; Recipe 16.12 on accessing or removing request attributes in JSPs; Chapter 6 on including content in servlets and JSPs; the Javadoc for javax.servlet. ServletRequestAttributeListener: *http://java.sun.com/j2ee/1.4/docs/api/javax/servlet/ ServletRequestAttributeListener.html*.

16.12 Accessing or Removing Request Attributes in JSPs

Problem

You want to use a JSP to access or remove a request attribute.

Solution

Use the JSTL core tags c:out and c:remove to access and optionally remove the attribute.

Discussion

Example 16-14 accesses an object attribute that is bound to the HttpServletRequest. The JSP accesses this attribute by using EL syntax inside the c:out JSTL tag.

Example 16-12 in Recipe 16.10 forwards a request attribute to a servlet using the jsp:forward standard action. The JSP in that example can forward its request attribute to the JSP in Example 16-14 by using the code:

```
<jsp:forward page="/requestDisplay.jsp" />
```

The code:

```
"${requestScope[\"com.jspservletcookbook.ContextObject\"].
    values}"
```

uses the requestScope JSTL implicit object. This variable, which the JSTL automatically makes available to EL-related code, is a java.util.Map type containing any attributes bound to the request scope. The code then displays the values the attribute contains by accessing the object attribute's values property (see Recipe 16.1 for a discussion of the object used for storing an attribute in various scopes throughout this chapter).

Example 16-14. Accessing and removing a request attribute with the JSTL

```
<%@ taglib uri="http://java.sun.com/jstl/core" prefix="c" %>

<html>
<head><title>Request reading JSP</title></head>
<body>
<h2>Here are the values from the bound RequestObject</h2>

<c:out value=
    "${requestScope[\"com.jspservletcookbook.ContextObject\"].
        values}" escapeXml="false" />

<%-- c:remove may not be necessary as request attributes persist only as long as the
request is being handled --%>
<br>Removing request attribute with c:remove ... <c:remove var=
    "com.jspservletcookbook.ContextObject" scope="request" />

</body>
</html>
```

The c:remove tag removes the attribute named in its var attribute from the specified scope. Use scope="request" because you are removing this attribute from the JSP's request scope. Figure 16-2 shows the output of the *displayRequest.jsp* page in a web browser.

The JSP that appears in the browser's address field, *requestBind.jsp*, actually set the attribute and forwarded the request (see Recipe 16.10). When code uses jsp:forward, the original JSP remains in the browser's address field, even though the browser displays the output of the JSP targeted by the forward action.

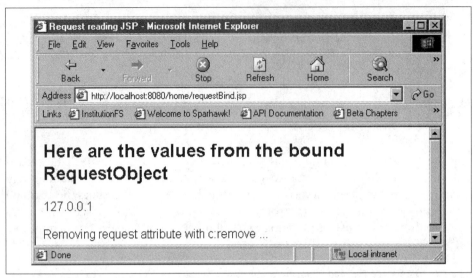

Figure 16-2. The browser display after accessing and removing a request attribute in a JSP

See Also

Chapter 23 on using the JSTL; Recipes 16.1–16.4 on handling `ServletContext` attributes in servlets and JSPs; Recipes 16.5–16.8 on handling session attributes in servlets and JSPs; Recipe 16.11 on accessing or removing request attributes in servlets; the Javadoc for `javax.servlet. ServletRequestAttributeListener`: *http://java. sun.com/j2ee/1.4/docs/api/javax/servlet/ServletRequestAttributeListener.html*.

CHAPTER 17

Embedding Multimedia in JSPs

17.0 Introduction

Most web sites include some type of multimedia and interactive programs, such as digital videos, digital audio files, Macromedia Flash movies, and Java applets. Therefore, Java web sites often integrate this type of content with servlets and JavaServer Pages (JSPs). This chapter explains the basics of embedding multimedia in Java web components. This process involves including the object and embed tags in your component's HTML output.

A JSP is the preferred choice for combining multimedia with dynamic content, because you can make the tags that you use to embed the multimedia a part of the JSP's HTML template text. However, Recipe 17.5 also shows how to include multimedia as part of a servlet's output.

 If the page containing the multimedia content does not have to include any other type of dynamic output, just use a static HTML page instead of executing JSPs and servlets. A static page typically requires fewer server resources to respond to HTML page requests.

17.1 Embedding an Applet in a JSP Using jsp:plugin

Problem

You want to use the jsp:plugin standard action to execute a Java applet with the Java Plug-in software.

Solution

Use the jsp:plugin action positioned in the area of a JSP where you want the applet to appear.

Discussion

The JSP specification provides a standard action, jsp:plugin, which produces the object and embed tags that are designed to allow browsers to load a Java applet. The action will run the applet using Sun Microsystems's Java Plug-in or initiate the download of the Plug-in if the user has not yet installed the Plug-in.

 The Java Plug-in is designed to execute an applet using Sun Microsystems's Java 2 Runtime Environment, rather than any Java runtime provided by the browser. The installation of the Java JRE or Software Development Kit automatically installs the Java Plug-in.

Use nested jsp:param elements to provide the applet with any necessary parameter and value pairs. The jsp:param elements must be nested within a single jsp:params element.

Example 17-1 shows a JSP file that uses jsp:plugin to embed an applet named *Clock.class*. In this case, the *Clock.class* file is located in the same directory as the JSP in Example 17-1.

 This applet originates from Sun Microsystems's sample applets: *http://java.sun.com/products/plugin/1.4.1/demos/plugin/applets/Clock/example1.html*

Example 17-1. Embedding a Java applet with jsp:plugin

```
<%@ taglib uri="http://java.sun.com/jstl/core" prefix="c" %>

<jsp:useBean id="date" class="java.util.Date" />

<html>
<head><title>A Clock in a JSP</title></head>
<body>
<h2>The time...</h2>

<jsp:plugin type="applet" code="Clock.class" codebase=
    "http://localhost:8080/home/applets" jreversion="1.4.1">

<jsp:params>
    <jsp:param name="scriptable" value="false"/>
</jsp:params>

<jsp:fallback>
Sorry, we are unable to start the Java plugin <br />
</jsp:fallback>

</jsp:plugin>

<br /><c:out value="${date}"/>
</body>
</html>
```

Users who have installed Internet Explorer for Windows depend on an HTML object tag to provide the direction for loading the applet. In browsers that support the Netscape-style plug-in, the HTML uses it's embed tag. The `jsp:plugin` standard action generates HTML that should work with both browser types (but you still should test the resulting JSP, of course).

Example 17-2 shows the HTML tags generated by the `jsp:plugin` action when the Internet Explorer 5.5 and the Netscape browsers request the JSP in Example 17-1.

Example 17-2. HTML tags generated by the jsp:plugin action for loading a Java applet

```
<OBJECT classid=
    clsid:8AD9C840-044E-11D1-B3E9-00805F499D93 codebase=
    "http://java.sun.com/products/plugin/1.2.2/jinstall-1_2_2-win.cab#
    Version=1,2,2,0">

<PARAM name="java_code" value="Clock.class">

<PARAM name="java_codebase" value="http://localhost:8080/home/applets">

<PARAM name="type" value="application/x-java-applet;version=1.4.1">

<PARAM name="scriptable" value="false">

<COMMENT>

<EMBED type="application/x-java-applet;version=1.4.1" pluginspage=
    "http://java.sun.com/products/plugin/" java_code=
    "Clock.class" java_codebase=
    "http://localhost:8080/home/applets" scriptable="false"/>

<NOEMBED>
Sorry, we are unable to start the Java plugin <br />
</NOEMBED>

</COMMENT>
</OBJECT>
```

Figure 17-1 shows the JSP with the embedded applet.

See Also

The Java Plug-in technology page: *http://java.sun.com/products/plugin/*; Recipe 17.2 on embedding an applet using the Sun Microsystems HTML Converter.

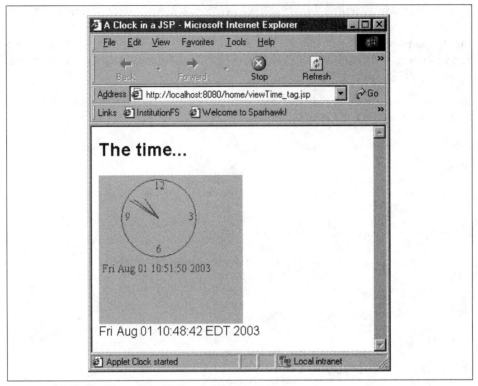

Figure 17-1. A JSP with an embedded applet

17.2 Embedding an Applet in a JSP Using the HTML Converter

Problem

You want to use the Java Plug-in HTML Converter tool to generate the tags for embedding an applet.

Solution

Use the HTML Converter tool within *htmlconverter.jar*, which is located in the *lib* directory of the directory where you have the Java SDK installed.

Discussion

A busy developer can let the Java Plug-in HTML Converter tool produce the HTML tags that are responsible for loading Java applets. The Java Plug-in is a Java-based tool that allows applets to be run in the Sun Microsystems Java 2 runtime environment, rather than within the web browser's Java runtime environment. The Java Plug-in is installed on your machine when you install the JRE, including the installation of the SDK.

The HTML Converter tool will convert a specified JSP file that contains an `applet` HTML tag, replacing the applet tag with a more complex tag collection that allows most browsers to load the Java applet. The Converter leaves the rest of your JSP code untouched; it only replaces the JSP's applet tag.

Here is how to use the HTML Converter tool:

1. Write the JSP file, adding an applet tag. Example 17-3 shows a JSP that embeds a *Clock.class* applet reference. This JSP, rather redundantly, dynamically writes a time string beneath the applet. I included this code to show that the Converter does not change the JSP code; it just alters the applet tag template text included with the JSP.

   Example 17-3. A JSP with an applet tag

   ```
   <%@ taglib uri="http://java.sun.com/jstl/core" prefix="c" %>

   <jsp:useBean id="date" class="java.util.Date" />

   <html>
   <head><title>A Clock in a JSP</title></head>
   <body>
   <h2>The time...</h2>
   <applet code="Clock.class" codebase="http://localhost:8080/home/applets">
   </applet>

   <br /><c:out value="${date}"/>

   </body>
   </html>
   ```

2. Open a command-line window to the *lib* directory of your SDK installation, such as *H:\j2sdk1.4.1_01\lib*.

3. Type `java -jar htmlconverter.jar -gui`. This command launches the Swing version of the HTML Converter tool. Figure 17-2 shows what the tool looks like.

    The HTML Converter can also be run from the command line. See the Java Plug-in Developer Guide for supported options: *http://java.sun.com/j2se/1.4.1/docs/guide/plugin/*.

4. If you want to choose a back-up folder where the tool saves the old JSP file (with the applet tag), use the HTML Converter GUI window to choose this folder.

5. Click the "Convert…" button with the JSP file specified in the top text field, and the Converter will overwrite the original file with additional `object` and `embed` tags.

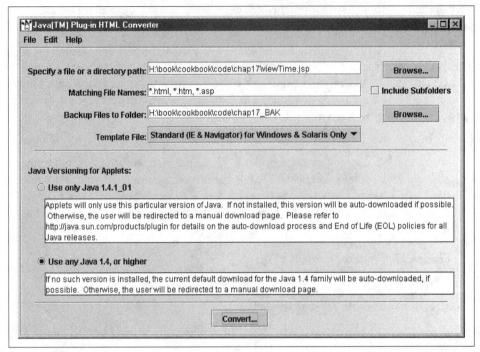

Figure 17-2. The HTML Converter (GUI version)

Example 17-4 shows the code that replaced the applet tag in Example 17-3 (in bold font), as well as the code that the converter tool did not modify.

Example 17-4. The object and embed tags produced by the HTML Converter

```
<%@ taglib uri="http://java.sun.com/jstl/core" prefix="c" %>

<jsp:useBean id="date" class="java.util.Date" />

<html>
<head><title>A Clock in a JSP</title></head>
<body>
<h2>The time...</h2>

<!--"CONVERTED_APPLET"-->
<!-- HTML CONVERTER -->
<OBJECT
    classid =
    "clsid:8AD9C840-044E-11D1-B3E9-00805F499D93"

    codebase =
    "http://java.sun.com/products/plugin/autodl/jinstall-1_4-windows-
    i586.cab#Version=1,4,0,0"
    >
```

Example 17-4. The object and embed tags produced by the HTML Converter (continued)

```
    <PARAM NAME = CODE VALUE = "Clock.class" >
    <PARAM NAME = CODEBASE VALUE = "http://localhost:8080/home/applets" >
    <PARAM NAME = "type" VALUE = "application/x-java-applet;version=1.4">
    <PARAM NAME = "scriptable" VALUE = "false">

    <COMMENT>
    <EMBED
            type = "application/x-java-applet;version=1.4"
            CODE = "Clock.class"
            JAVA_CODEBASE = "http://localhost:8080/home/applets"
        scriptable = false
        pluginspage =
       "http://java.sun.com/products/plugin/index.html#download">
        <NOEMBED>

        </NOEMBED>
    </EMBED>
    </COMMENT>
</OBJECT>

<!--
<APPLET CODE = "Clock.class" JAVA_CODEBASE =
    "http://localhost:8080/home/applets">
</APPLET>
-->


<!--"END_CONVERTED_APPLET"-->


<br /><c:out value="${date}"/>

</body>
</html>
```

 Users may have trouble loading the applet in their browsers if they have several installed versions of the Java Plug-in. This occurs when users steadily upgrade their JRE or Java SDK versions, which install the corresponding version of the Java Plug-in. The simplest solution in these cases is to uninstall the old Java Plug-ins.

See Also

The Java Plug-in technology page: *http://java.sun.com/products/plugin/*; Recipe 17.1 on embedding a Java applet using the jsp:plugin standard JSP action.

17.3 Automatically Creating HTML Template for Including Flash Files

Problem

You want to automatically generate the required HTML for embedding a Flash file in a web component.

Solution

From within Macromedia Flash 6, use the "File → Publish" menu command to output an HTML file that includes the object and embed tags.

Discussion

With an *.swf* file open in Macromedia Flash 6, use the "File → Publish" menu command to create an HTML file. This file includes the necessary tags to embed the Flash movie you are working on in a web component. Then cut and paste these tags and attributes into your JSP. Example 17-5 shows the output from using this menu command with an *.swf* file named *example.swf*.

Example 17-5. Automatically generated template text from within the Flash application

```
<HTML>
<HEAD>
<meta http-equiv=Content-Type content="text/html;  charset=ISO-8859-1">
<TITLE>example</TITLE>
</HEAD>
<BODY bgcolor="#FFFFFF">

<!-- URL's used in the movie-->
<!-- text used in the movie-->
<!--DeductionsPaycheckSDIAnnual SalaryMedicareSocial
securityESPP401k$#%FederalStateMarriedSingleactions-->

<OBJECT classid="clsid:D27CDB6E-AE6D-11cf-96B8-444553540000"
  codebase=
  "http://download.macromedia.com/pub/shockwave/cabs/flash/swflash.
  cab#version=6,0,0,0"WIDTH="550" HEIGHT="400" id="example" ALIGN=""
>

 <PARAM NAME=movie VALUE="example.swf">
 <PARAM NAME=quality VALUE=high> <PARAM NAME=bgcolor VALUE=#FFFFFF>

 <EMBED src="example.swf" quality=high bgcolor=#FFFFFF  WIDTH="550" HEIGHT=
   "400" NAME="example" ALIGN=""
   TYPE="application/x-shockwave-flash" PLUGINSPAGE=
   "http://www.macromedia.com/go/getflashplayer">
```

```
    </EMBED>
</OBJECT>

</BODY>
</HTML>
```

Your JSP probably already includes the boilerplate HTML such as the body tag; therefore, you only have to cut and paste the noncommented, emphasized code in Example 17-5.

The *example.swf* file resides in the same directory as the HTML file in this example.

Example 17-6 in the next recipe shows a JSP file with the same type of Flash-related object and embed tags as those illustrated in this recipe. Figure 17-3 shows the automatically generated HTML file from Example 17-5.

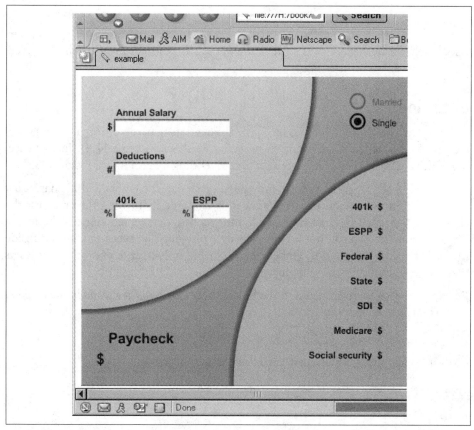

Figure 17-3. HTML template text with an embedded Flash file

The displayed Flash movie is derived from one of the Flash samples that accompanies the Flash 6 application: *Paycheck_calculator.swf*.

See Also

Macromedia technical notes page: *http://www.macromedia.com/support/flash/technotes.html*; an article about alternative techniques to using the embed tag: *http://www.macromedia.com/devnet/mx/dreamweaver/articles/flash_satay.html*.

17.4 Writing HTML Template to Embed a Flash File

Problem

You want to write the HTML template text to embed a Flash file in your JSP.

Solution

Use the object and embed tags so that the HTML is read correctly by the browsers that support either of these tags.

Discussion

You may not have the Macromedia Flash application that can automatically generate the HTML which is necessary to embed a Flash file (Recipe 17.4). In this case, write the required HTML template text for embedding a Flash movie inside a JSP.

Example 17-6 shows a JSP with an embedded Flash file (the embedded file has a *.swf* extension). The same concept applies to this example as to the other recipes: the object tag is for the Internet Explorer Windows browser, which embeds the media file as an ActiveX control, not a Netscape-style plug-in. The embed tag, nested inside the object tag, is designed to embed the Flash file in Netscape and other browsers that support Netscape-style plug-ins.

Example 17-6 is derived from a technical note at *http://www.macromedia.com/support/flash/technotes.html*.

Example 17-6. A JSP contains an embedded file

```
<%@ taglib uri="http://java.sun.com/jstl/core" prefix="c" %>

<jsp:useBean id="date" class="java.util.Date" />

<html>
```

Example 17-6. A JSP contains an embedded file

```
<head><title>Flash in a JSP</title></head>
<body>
<h2>Enjoy the Flash Movie</h2>

<OBJECT CLASSID=
    "clsid:D27CDB6E-AE6D-11cf-96B8-444553540000" CODEBASE=
    "http://download.macromedia.com/pub/shockwave/cabs/flash/swflash.cab#
     version=6,040,0" width="293" height="423"
>

<PARAM name="movie" VALUE="coolFlashMov.swf">

<PARAM name="quality" VALUE="high">

<PARAM name="bgcolor" VALUE="#FFFFFF">

<EMBED SRC=
    "coolFlashMov.swf" quality="high" width="293" height="423"
    bgcolor="#FFFFFF" type="application/x-shockwave-flash" PLUGINSPAGE=
    "http://www.macromedia.com/go/getflashplayer"
>

</EMBED>

</OBJECT>

<br /><c:out value="${date}"/>

</body>
</html>
```

Both the embed and object tags are designed to prompt the end user to download the required version of the Flash plug-in or ActiveX control if they do not already have it installed.

See Also

Macromedia technical notes page: *http://www.macromedia.com/support/flash/technotes.html*; an article about alternative techniques to using the embed tag: *http://www.macromedia.com/devnet/mx/dreamweaver/articles/flash_satay.html*.

17.5   Embedding Flash in a Servlet

Problem

You want to embed a Flash file in a servlet's output.

Solution

Use the `javax.servlet.RequestDispatcher.include(request,response)` method in the `doGet()` method of the servlet that includes the necessary HTML template text.

Discussion

The servlet can include the HTML fragment that loads the Flash movie into the page by using a `RequestDispatcher`. This process is similar to server-side includes in traditional Common Gateway Interface (CGI) programs. When the servlet receives a request, it includes the text fragment containing the Flash-related tags in its HTML output. This design separates the servlet itself from the tags and parameters that load the Flash movie, so that each of these entities evolves independently. For example, you can change the filename of the Flash movie or some of the `object` or `embed` parameters without recompiling the servlet code.

Example 17-7 is a servlet that uses a `RequestDispatcher` to include the text shown in Example 17-8. The text appears in a *flash.txt* file that is stored at the top level of the web application.

 RequestDispatchers typically include the output of servlets and JSPs, not just text fragments. See Chapter 6 for more detailed RequestDispatcher-related recipes.

Example 17-7. A servlet uses a RequestDispatcher to include object and embed tags

```
package com.jspservletcookbook;
import javax.servlet.*;
import javax.servlet.http.*;

public class FlashServlet extends HttpServlet {

  public void doGet(HttpServletRequest request,
    HttpServletResponse response) throws ServletException,
    java.io.IOException {


      response.setContentType("text/html");
      java.io.PrintWriter out = response.getWriter();
      out.println(
      "<html><head><title>Embedded Flash content</title></head><body>");
```

Example 17-7. A servlet uses a RequestDispatcher to include object and embed tags (continued)

```
    RequestDispatcher dispatcher = request.getRequestDispatcher(
    "/flash.txt");

    dispatcher.include(request, response);

    out.println("</body></html>");
  } //doGet

  public void doPost(HttpServletRequest request,
    HttpServletResponse response) throws ServletException,
    java.io.IOException {

    doGet(request,response);

  }//doPost
}
```

Example 17-8 shows the text fragment included by the servlet in Example 17-7.

Example 17-8. An included text fragment (flash.txt) that a servlet uses to embed Flash

```
<OBJECT classid="clsid:D27CDB6E-AE6D-11cf-96B8-444553540000" codebase=
  "http://download.macromedia.com/pub/shockwave/cabs/flash/swflash.cab#
  version=6,0,0,0" WIDTH="550" HEIGHT="400" id="example" ALIGN=""
>

  <PARAM NAME=movie VALUE="/home/example.swf">
  <PARAM NAME=quality VALUE=high>
  <PARAM NAME=bgcolor VALUE=#FFFFFF>

  <EMBED src="/home/example.swf" quality=high bgcolor=#FFFFFF  WIDTH=
    "550" HEIGHT="400" NAME="example" ALIGN="" TYPE=
    "application/x-shockwave-flash" PLUGINSPAGE=
    "http://www.macromedia.com/go/getflashplayer">
  </EMBED>

</OBJECT>
```

The result in a web browser looks exactly like Figure 17-3.

See Also

Chapter 6 on dynamically including content into servlets; Macromedia technical notes page: *http://www.macromedia.com/support/flash/technotes.html*; an article about alternative techniques to using the embed tag: *http://www.macromedia.com/dev-net/mx/dreamweaver/articles/flash_satay.html*.

17.6 Embedding a QuickTime Movie in a JSP

Problem

You want to embed a QuickTime movie in your JSP.

Solution

Use the embed tag nested inside the object tag. The object tag has to contain the CLASSID attribute with the proper value.

Discussion

Similar to using the Java Plug-in, a JSP uses the embed tag inside of an HTML object tag to properly load one of Apple Computer's QuickTime movies. You must include the CLASSID attribute value exactly as Example 17-9 specifies. You also must include the same CODEBASE attribute value. If the user has an Internet Explorer Windows browser, but has not yet installed the QuickTime ActiveX control, the CODEBASE attribute value specifies where the user can download it.

Example 17-9. Embedding a QuickTime movie in a JSP

```
<%@ taglib uri="http://java.sun.com/jstl/core" prefix="c" %>

<jsp:useBean id="date" class="java.util.Date" />

<html>
<head><title>QuickTime in a JSP</title></head>
<body>
<h2>Ladies and Gentlemen, The Who</h2>

<OBJECT CLASSID=
    "clsid:02BF25D5-8C17-4B23-BC80-D3488ABDDC6B" WIDTH="320"
    HEIGHT="256" CODEBASE="http://www.apple.com/qtactivex/qtplugin.cab">

<PARAM name="SRC" VALUE="http://www.parkerriver.com/films/who_bene2.mov">

<PARAM name="AUTOPLAY" VALUE="true">

<PARAM name="CONTROLLER" VALUE="true">

<EMBED SRC=
    "http://www.parkerriver.com/films/who_bene2.mov"
    WIDTH="240" HEIGHT="196"
    AUTOPLAY="true" CONTROLLER=
    "true" PLUGINSPAGE="http://www.apple.com/quicktime/download/">

</EMBED>

</OBJECT>
```

Example 17-9. Embedding a QuickTime movie in a JSP (continued)

```
<br /><c:out value="${date}"/>

</body>
</html>
```

If the browser uses Netscape-style plug-ins, then the embed tag will initiate the loading of the QuickTime movie. The JSP in Example 17-6 properly loaded the movie into the Safari web browser on my Macintosh laptop, for instance. One of the advantages of the embed tag is that you can use a number of proprietary attributes that the embedded object, such as QuickTime, understands. Example 17-9 specifies that the movie should start playing as soon as the browser has loaded enough data (AUTOPLAY="true") as well as that the browser should show the movie controls, which lets the user stop or start the movie (CONTROLLER="true").

Figure 17-4 shows the QuickTime movie embedded in the JSP of Example 17-9.

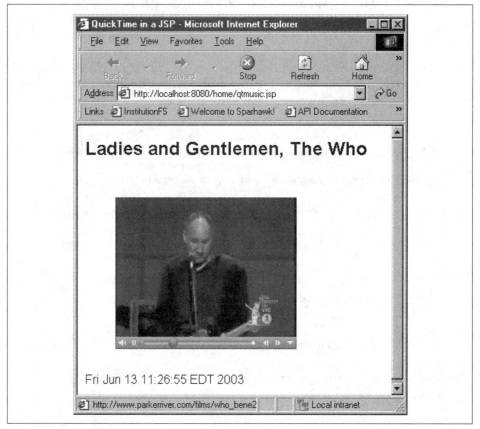

Figure 17-4. A QuickTime movie embedded in a JSP

See Also

Apple Computer's guide on embedding QuickTime in Web pages: *http://www.apple.com/quicktime/authoring/embed.html*; Recipes 17.3–17.5 on embedding a Flash file; Recipe 17.7 on embedding an SVG file in a JSP; Recipe 17.8 on embedding a background soundtrack.

17.7   Embedding an SVG File in a JSP

Problem

You want to display a Scalable Vector Graphics (SVG) image inside a JSP.

Solution

Use the embed HTML element to position the SVG in the JSP.

Discussion

Developers typically use the embed tag to place an SVG file in an HTML file or JSP. SVG is an XML-based graphics technology that provides developers and designers leverage in producing and displaying interactive graphics.

Browsers use special SVG viewer applications to handle the embedded SVG files. Adobe System's SVG Viewer application can be downloaded from *http://www.adobe.com/svg/viewer/install/*. Corel's SVG Viewer can be downloaded from *http://www.corel.com/svgviewer/*.

Example 17-10 embeds an SVG file named *testLogo.svg* and points the user to the Adobe SVG Viewer download site if they have not installed an SVG Viewer application.

SVG files have extensions of either *.svg* or (in compressed form) *.svgz*, even though they are XML files.

Example 17-10. An SVG graphics file embedded in a JSP

```
<%@ taglib uri="http://java.sun.com/jstl/core" prefix="c" %>
<jsp:useBean id="date" class="java.util.Date" />

<html>
<head><title>SVG in a JSP</title></head>
<body>
<h2>A Scalable Vector Graphics example</h2>
```

Example 17-10. An SVG graphics file embedded in a JSP

```
<embed src=
    '<c:out value="${param.svg_source}"/>.svg' width=
    "200" height="200" type="image/svg-xml" pluginspage=
    "http://www.adobe.com/svg/viewer/install/"
>

<br /><c:out value="${date}"/>

</body>
</html>
```

Example 17-10 shows how to place an SVG within other JSP code elements, such as the taglib directive and the jsp:useBean standard action. Example 17-10 also dynamically loads an SVG based on the request parameter named svg_source. The code uses the JSTL c:out tag and the EL's param implicit object to output the parameter value (see Chapter 23 on the JSTL).

Figure 17-5 shows the result of requesting the JSP in Example 17-10, including the name of the SVG file as a request parameter. The request URL looks like:

```
http://localhost:8080/home/svg.jsp?svg_source=testLogo
```

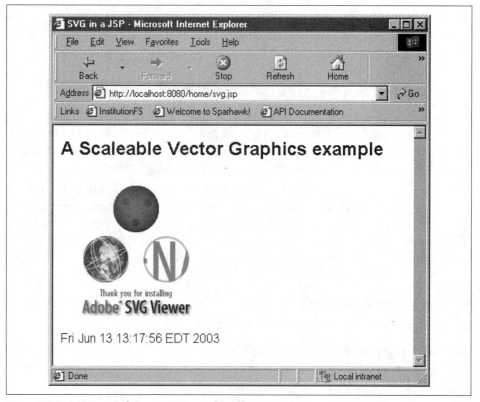

Figure 17-5. A JSP page shows an SVG graphics file

The SVG shown in Figure 17-5 is derived from Adobe Systems Inc., which creates the Adobe SVG Viewer and an SVG-enabled graphics application, Adobe Illustrator.

See Also

SVG specifications at the W3 Consortium: *http://www.w3.org/Graphics/SVG/Overview.htm8*; Adobe's SVG Viewer install page: *http://www.adobe.com/svg/viewer/install/*; Recipes 17-3-5 on embedding a Flash file in servlets and JSPs; Recipe 17.6 on embedding a QuickTime movie in a JSP.

17.8 Embedding a Background Soundtrack in a JSP

Problem

You want to embed an audio file in your JSP.

Solution

Use the embed tag in the JSP. Use the `hidden` attribute if you want to hide the audio controls; otherwise, specify a `width` and `height` attribute for showing the audio controls.

Discussion

The embed tag is used to include an audio file with a JSP, so that when a user requests the JSP, the browser plays music. Specifically, the browser is designed to detect the MIME type of the embedded file, then activate a helper application such as QuickTime or RealAudio to handle the embedded file and play the music.

Example 17-11 shows a JSP that embeds an MPEG, audio layer 3 (MP3) file. The JSP displays some information about the artist based on a request parameter; this random information is included to show how to combine JSP code with the embed tag. The embed tag includes width and height attributes to show the audio controls in the web page. The controls allow the user to turn the volume off or down if they do not want to be serenaded while surfing.

Example 17-11. A JSP with an embedded audio file

```
<%@ taglib uri="http://java.sun.com/jstl/core" prefix="c" %>

<c:set var="artist" value="${param.artist}" />

<html>
<head><title>Choose Your Tunes</title></head>
<body>
```

Example 17-11. A JSP with an embedded audio file (continued)

```
<h2>You chose music from the artist <c:out value="${artist}" /></h2>

<embed src="ConstantCraving.mp3" width="240" height="160">
</embed>

</body>
</html>
```

Figure 17-6 shows the output from the JSP in Example 17-11.

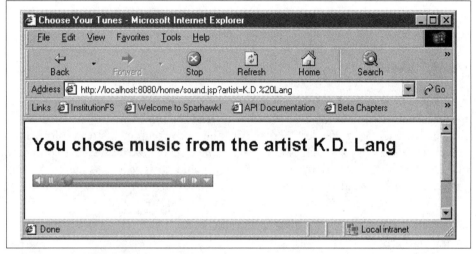

Figure 17-6. Embedded song file controls in a JSP

See Also

Recipes 17.1 and 17.2 on embedding a Java applet in a JSP; Recipes 17.3–17.5 on embedding a Flash file in a JSP; Recipe 17.6 on embedding a QuickTime movie; Recipe 17.7 on embedding an SVG file.

CHAPTER 18

Working With the Client Request

18.0 Introduction

A number of web applications must examine the client request before sending a response. An example is a servlet that has to read (or *sniff*) the browser type (often through the User-Agent header). Servlets or other web components read information about the request by examining HTTP *request headers*. These headers are composed of header names followed by colon characters and their values, such as Accept-Language: en. The headers precede any message body that the client is sending to the server, such as text that has been posted from an HTML form.

Here is an example of a group of request headers sent with a request for a JSP named *contextBind.jsp*:

```
GET /home/contextBind.jsp HTTP/1.1
User-Agent: Opera/5.02 (Windows NT 4.0; U) [en]
Host: localhost:9000
Accept: text/html, image/png, image/jpeg, image/gif, image/x-xbitmap, */*
Accept-Language: en
Accept-Encoding: deflate, gzip, x-gzip, identity, *;q=0
Cookie: mycookie=1051567248639; JSESSIONID=1D51575F3F0B17D26537338B5A29DB1D
Connection: Keep-Alive
```

The recipes in this chapter show how to examine request headers with servlet and JSPs, use filters to alter requests, automatically refresh servlets and JSPs, and count the number of application requests.

18.1 Examining HTTP Request Headers in a Servlet

Problem

You want to examine the HTTP request headers in a servlet.

Solution

Use the `javax.servlet.http.HttpServletRequest.getHeaderNames()` and `getHeader()` methods to access the names and values of various request headers.

Discussion

The `HttpServletRequest.getHeaderNames()` method returns all of the request header names for an incoming request. You can then obtain the value of a specific header by providing the header name to the method `HttpServletRequest.getHeader()` method. Example 18-1 gets an `Enumeration` of header names in the servlet's `doGet()` method, and then displays each header and value on its own line in the resulting HTML page.

Example 18-1. A servlet displays request headers and values

```
package com.jspservletcookbook;

import java.util.Enumeration;

import javax.servlet.*;
import javax.servlet.http.*;

public class RequestHeaderView extends HttpServlet {

  public void doGet(HttpServletRequest request,
    HttpServletResponse response) throws ServletException,
      java.io.IOException {

      //get an Enumeration of all the request header names
      Enumeration enum = request.getHeaderNames();

      response.setContentType("text/html");
      java.io.PrintWriter out = response.getWriter();
      out.println(
          "<html><head><title>Request Header View</title></head><body>");
      out.println("<h2>Request Headers</h2>");

      String header = null;

      //display each request header name and value
      while (enum.hasMoreElements()){
          header = (String) enum.nextElement();

      //getHeader returns null if a request header of that name does not
      //exist in the request
      out.println("<strong>"+header+"</strong>"+": "+
          request.getHeader(header)+"<br>" );
      }

      out.println("</body></html>");
  } //doGet
}
```

Figure 18-1 shows the RequestHeaderView servlet's output.

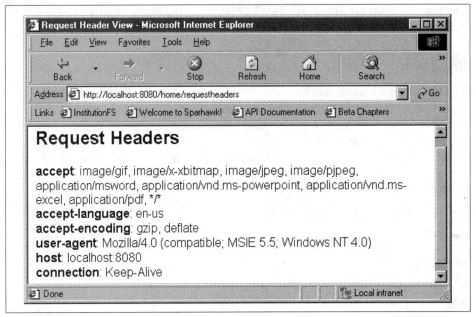

Figure 18-1. A servlet shows the request header names and values

See Also

Recipe 18.2 on examining request headers in a JSP; Recipe 18.3 on using a filter to wrap the request and forward it along the filter chain; Recipe 18.6 on using a listener to track requests; Chapter 7 on handling request parameters and JavaBean properties with servlets, JSPs, and filters.

18.2   Examining HTTP Request Headers in a JSP

Problem

You want to use a JSP to display the request headers and values.

Solution

Use the c:forEach and c:out JSTL tags to view the header names and values.

Discussion

The JSTL v1.0 makes all existing request headers available via the header implicit object. The JSTL automatically makes this variable available to JSPs; the header object evaluates to a java.util.Map type.

In Example 18-2, the c:forEach tag iterates over this Map and stores each header name and value in the loop variable named by c:forEach's var attribute (in Example 18-2 it's called req). The c:forEach var attribute is implemented as a java.util.Map.Entry type, which is a data type that stores keys and their values. The c:out tag displays each header name by using EL format: ${req.key}. Consequently c:out displays the value with ${req.value}.

Example 18-2. Viewing the request header names and values in a JSP

```jsp
<%@ taglib uri="http://java.sun.com/jstl/core" prefix="c" %>

<html>
<head><title>Request Headers</title></head>
<body>
<h2>Here are the Request Header names and values</h2>

<c:forEach var="req" items="${header}">

    <strong><c:out value=
        "${req.key}"/></strong>: <c:out value="${req.value}"/><br>

</c:forEach>

</body>
</html>
```

Figure 18-2 shows the result in a browser of requesting the *displayHeaders.jsp* page.

Figure 18-2. A JSP page shows request headers using JSTL tags

See Also

Chapter 23 on using the JSTL; Recipe 18.2 on examining request headers in a servlet; Recipe 18.3 on using a filter to wrap the request and forward it along the filter chain; Recipe 18.6 on using a listener to track requests; Chapter 7 on handling request parameters and JavaBean properties with servlets, JSPs, and filters.

18.3   Using a Filter to Alter Request Headers

Problem

You want to use a filter to change the request headers before a servlet or JSP receives the request.

Solution

Wrap the request in your own custom request class. Pass the request wrapper or decorator class to the `FilterChain.doFilter( )` method, instead of the original request destination.

Discussion

The `javax.servlet.http.HttpServletRequestWrapper` is a convenience class that you can extend to provide additional functionality for an HTTP request. Here is how to alter and forward a request using a filter:

1. Create a class that extends `HttpServletRequestWrapper`.
2. Place this class in the web application's *WEB-INF/classes* (including package-related directories) directory or *WEB-INF/lib* if the class is part of a JAR file.
3. Create a class that implements `javax.servlet.Filter`, such as Example 18-3. This class uses your custom request wrapper class to enclose the `ServletRequest` parameter of the `Filter.doFilter( )` method.
4. Store the filter class in *WEB-INF/classes* or *WEB-INF/lib* (if it's in a JAR).
5. Register the filter in *web.xml*. In this recipe, the filter is mapped to all of the requests in the web application with the URL mapping /*.

Example 18-3 shows the filter class that passes the request-wrapper class along the filter chain. The file is named `RequestFilter`; the wrapper class is named `ReqWrapper`.

Example 18-3. A filter that wraps the HttpServletRequest

```
package com.jspservletcookbook;

import javax.servlet.*;
import javax.servlet.http.*;
```

Example 18-3. A filter that wraps the HttpServletRequest (continued)

```java
public class RequestFilter implements Filter {

    private FilterConfig config;

    /** Creates new RequestFilter */
    public RequestFilter( ) {}

    public void  init(FilterConfig filterConfig)  throws ServletException{

        this.config = filterConfig;
    }

public void  doFilter(ServletRequest request,
    ServletResponse response, FilterChain chain) throws java.io.IOException,
    ServletException {

    ReqWrapper wrapper = null;
    ServletContext context = null;

    //create the request wrapper object, an instance of the
    //ReqWrapper class. The client request is passed into
    //ReqWrapper's constructor

    if (request instanceof HttpServletRequest)
        wrapper = new ReqWrapper((HttpServletRequest)request);

    //use the ServletContext.log method to log param names/values

    if (wrapper != null){
        context = config.getServletContext( );

    context.log("Query: " + wrapper.getQueryString( ));}


    //continue the request, response to next filter or servlet
    //destination

    if (wrapper != null)
        chain.doFilter(wrapper,response);
    else
        chain.doFilter(request,response);

}//doFilter

public void destroy( ){

/*called before the Filter instance is removed
    from service by the web container*/
}//destroy
}
```

Example 18-3 uses the servlet context to log the ReqWrapper's query string. The ReqWrapper class adds a parameter to the query string, but you could make this class implement whatever behavior you need in your own application. Example 18-4 shows the filter-mapping entries in the deployment descriptor (*web.xml*), which ensures that every application request passes through this filter.

Example 18-4. The filter mapping in web.xml

```
<filter>

    <filter-name>RequestFilter</filter-name>
    <filter-class>com.jspservletcookbook.RequestFilter</filter-class>

</filter>

<filter-mapping>

    <filter-name>RequestFilter</filter-name>
    <url-pattern>/*</url-pattern>

</filter-mapping>
```

The ReqWrapper is a simple example of an HttpServletRequestWrapper subclass that encapsulates the original request. This class overrides the getQueryString( )method in order to add a parameter to the request's query string.

 To access the new filter parameter, you must call getQueryString( ) on the request once it reaches its destination servlet, then parse the getQueryString( ) return value for individual parameters. Using the EL will not work with request wrappers that override getQueryString( ):

```
//does not return the new parameter value
//added by the overridden getQueryString
//method
${param.filter}
```

The request that passes through the filter is the parameter to ReqWrapper's constructor, so the filter (in Example 18-3) wraps the request with this code:

```
wrapper = new ReqWrapper((HttpServletRequest)request);
```

A URL sent to the application containing the query string name=Bruce displays the following text in the server log (as a result of the ServletContext.log method):

```
Query: name=Bruce&filter=com.jspservletcookbook.ReqWrapper.
```

Example 18-5 is the code for the ReqWrapper object.

Example 18-5. The ReqWrapper class for encapsulating the HttpServletRequest

```
package com.jspservletcookbook;

import javax.servlet.*;
import javax.servlet.http.HttpServletRequestWrapper;
import javax.servlet.http.HttpServletRequest;
```

Example 18-5. The ReqWrapper class for encapsulating the HttpServletRequest (continued)

```java
public class ReqWrapper extends HttpServletRequestWrapper{

    private static final String AMP = "&";

  public ReqWrapper(HttpServletRequest request){

      super(request);
  }

  public String getQueryString( ){

      String query = null;

      //get the query string from the wrapped request object
      query = ((HttpServletRequest)getRequest()).getQueryString( );

      //add a 'filter' parameter to this query string with the class
      //name as the value
      if (query != null)
          return query +AMP+"filter="+getClass().getName( );
      else
          return "filter="+getClass().getName( );

  }//getQueryString
}
```

The method call `chain.doFilter(wrapper,response)` at the end of Example 18-3 passes the request (wrapped in our own custom class) and response to the next filter, or to the destination servlet or JSP if no other filters are registered.

See Also

Recipes 18.1 and 18.2 on examining request headers in a servlet and a JSP respectively; Recipe 18.3 on using a filter to wrap the request and forward it along the filter chain; Recipe 18.6 on using a listener to track requests; Chapter 7 on handling request parameters and JavaBean properties with servlets, JSPs, and filters.

18.4   Automatically Refreshing a Servlet

Problem

You want to automatically refresh a servlet-generated page at a specified interval.

Solution

Add a `Refresh` response header, using the `javax.servlet.http.HttpServletResponse` object.

Discussion

Suppose that your servlet is monitoring a Red Sox versus Yankees baseball game. You want to be able to allow a user to follow the game almost pitch by pitch, and have your web application constantly update the status of the game. If you add a Refresh response header to your client response, the browser will continually refresh the page according to the specified interval.

Example 18-6 adds a response header that the web container will send to the client in the format Refresh: 60, which means "request this page again in 60 seconds."

Example 18-6. Refreshing a servlet every 60 seconds

```
package com.jspservletcookbook;

import javax.servlet.*;
import javax.servlet.http.*;

public class AutoServlet extends HttpServlet {

  public void doGet(HttpServletRequest request,
    HttpServletResponse response) throws ServletException,
      java.io.IOException {

      //client browser will request the page every 60 seconds
      response.addHeader("Refresh","60");

      response.setContentType("text/html");
      java.io.PrintWriter out = response.getWriter();
      out.println(
          "<html><head><title>Client Refresh</title></head><body>");

      out.println("<h2>Welcome to the Red Sox - Yankees series...</h2>");

      //More HTML or dynamic content
      out.println("</body></html>");

  } //doGet
}
```

There are some caveats to this approach—if the end user walks away from her desk, her browser will blithely continue to request the page. If your servlet doesn't impose some control over this, you could add a lot of unnecessary load to your application. One example of a solution to this problem is to keep track of how many times the servlet has been refreshed with a session attribute (detailed in Chapter 16). If the number of times exceeds a certain limit, you could stop adding the header to the response. Example 18-7 shows part of a doPost() method body for keeping track of a user's refresh count.

Example 18-7. Tracking a user's refresh count

```
//inside doPost (or doGet) method
HttpSession session = request.getSession( );

Long times = (Long) session.getAttribute("times");

//create session attribute if it doesn't exist
if (times == null)
    session.setAttribute("times",new Long(0));

//local variable 'temp' will hold the session attribute value
long temp = 1;

//increment the attribute value to account for this request
if (times != null)
    temp = times.longValue( ) + 1;

if (temp < 60) //only allow 60 refreshes; about an hour's worth
    response.addHeader("Refresh","60");

//update the session attribute value
session.setAttribute("times",new Long(temp));
```

 This code works equally well inside of a doGet( ) method.

See Also

Recipe 18.5 on automatically refreshing a JSP; Recipes 18.1 and 18.2 on examining request headers in a servlet and a JSP; Recipe 18.3 on using a filter to wrap the request and forward it along the filter chain; Recipe 18.6 on using a listener to track requests.

18.5   Automatically Refreshing a JSP

Problem

You want to refresh a JSP request at a specified interval.

Solution

Use a JSP scriptlet that adds a Refresh response header to the response.

Discussion

The following scriptlet code adds a Refresh header that specifies a 60-second interval for refreshing the JSP. Place this code at the top of the JSP before any content appears:

```
<% response.addHeader("Refresh","60"); %>
```

 If you want to refresh the JSP to another web component or page, use this syntax:

```
<% response.addHeader("Refresh","10;
    http://localhost:8080/home/thanks.jsp"); %>
```

See Also

Example 18-6 in Recipe 18.4 on refreshing a servlet; Example 18-7 in Recipe 18.4 on limiting the number of automatic refreshes of a servlet; Recipes 18.1 and 18.2 on examining request headers in a servlet and a JSP, respectively; Recipe 18.3 on using a filter to wrap the request and forward it along the filter chain; Recipe 18.6 on using a listener to track requests.

18.6 Counting the Number of Web Application Requests

Problem

You want to count the number of requests handled by a web application.

Solution

Use a javax.servlet.ServletRequestListener to be notified whenever an HTTP request is initialized.

Discussion

A request listener is a good candidate for tracking requests, because the web container notifies the listener of new requests by calling its requestInitialized() method. Example 18-8 keeps track of the request count with a static class variable named reqCount. The program increments this variable in a synchronized block within the requestInitialized() method.

The ServletContext is used to log a message about the request so that you can observe the listener behavior. However, a busy production application that logs information about every request typically represents an inefficient use of web container resources. This type of logging activity should be reserved for development applications.

Example 18-8. A request listener class for counting application requests

```
package com.jspservletcookbook;

import javax.servlet.*;
import javax.servlet.http.*;

public class ReqListener implements ServletRequestListener {

    private static long reqCount;

  public void requestInitialized(ServletRequestEvent sre){

      //used for logging purposes
      ServletContext context = sre.getServletContext();

      //Used to get information about a new request
      ServletRequest request = sre.getServletRequest();

      //The static class variable reqCount is incremented in this block;
      //the incrementing of the variable is synchronized so that one
      // thread is not reading the variable while another increments it

      synchronized (context){

          context.log(
            "Request for "+
              (request instanceof HttpServletRequest ?
              ((HttpServletRequest) request).getRequestURI() :
              "Unknown")+ "; Count="+ ++reqCount);

      }//synchronized

}

    public void requestDestroyed(ServletRequestEvent sre){

      //Called when the servlet request is going oout of scope.

    }//requestDestroyed

}
```

 You can access the new ServletRequest in the two ServletRequestListener methods by calling ServletRequestEvent. getServletRequest( ). You must cast the ServletRequest return value to an HttpServletRequest to call the latter class's methods. Example 18-8 accesses the new HttpServletRequests in order to call those object's getRequestURI( ) method, which provides part of the information the code includes in a logging message.

You must register the ServletRequestListener in *web.xml*:

```
<listener>
    <listener-class>com.jspservletcookbook.ReqListener</listener-class>
</listener>
```

The web container then creates an instance of the listener when it starts up. Here is an example of a server-log entry when a request is made to the application within which the request listener is registered:

```
2003-05-30 07:22:21 Request for /home/servlet/com.jspservletcookbook.SessionDisplay;
Count=2
```

 For Tomcat, this line would be displayed in the log file found in *<Tomcat-installation-directory>/logs*.

See Also

Recipes 18.1 and 18.2 on examining request headers in a servlet and a JSP; Recipe 18.3 on using a filter to wrap the request and forward it along the filter chain; Chapter 7 on handling request parameters and JavaBean properties with servlets, JSPs, and filters.

CHAPTER 19

Filtering Requests and Responses

19.0 Introduction

Servlet filtering was introduced with the servlet API v2.3 in 2001. Filtering is a powerful technology for servlet developers, who can use it to generate chains of Java classes that execute in sequence in response to client requests.

Developers begin by creating one or more Java classes that implement the javax. servlet.Filter interface. These classes can undertake a number of actions prior to a servlet's request handling, creating a chain of actions before the request is delivered to its destination (including blocking the request altogether). These actions include, according to the Filter API documentation:

- Authentication of requests
- Data encryption
- Data compression
- Logging
- Extensible Stylesheet Language Transformation (XSLT) filtering
- Image conversion

 Access the Javadoc for the Filter interface at: *http://java.sun.com/j2ee/ 1.4/docs/api/javax/servlet/Filter.html*.

Register a filter in the deployment descriptor, and then map the registered filter to either servlet names or URL patterns in your application's deployment descriptor. When the web container starts up your web application, it creates an instance of each filter that you have declared in the deployment descriptor. The filters execute in the order that they are declared in the deployment descriptor.

19.1   Mapping a Filter to a Servlet

Problem

You want to map or apply a filter to an individual servlet.

Solution

Use the filter and filter-mapping elements in *web.xml* to associate the filter with the servlet.

Discussion

The web container finds out about the filters that you want to apply to a servlet by using information in the deployment descriptor. The filter element associates a filter name with a Java class that implements the javax.servlet.Filter interface. The filter-mapping element then associates individual filters with URL mappings or paths, similar to the servlet-mapping element that you have probably used before in *web.xml*. Example 19-1 shows a deployment descriptor from the servlet API v2.3 that includes the mapping of a filter named LogFilter to the servlet path */requestheaders*.

Example 19-1. Mapping a filter to a servlet

```
<?xml version="1.0" encoding="ISO-8859-1"?>
<!DOCTYPE web-app
    PUBLIC "-//Sun Microsystems, Inc.//DTD Web Application 2.3//EN"
           "http://java.sun.com/dtd/web-application_2_3.dtd"
>

<web-app>

<!-- register the filter -->

<filter>
    <filter-name>LogFilter</filter-name>
    <filter-class>com.jspservletcookbook.LogFilter</filter-class>
</filter>

<filter-mapping>
    <filter-name>LogFilter</filter-name>
    <url-pattern>/requestheaders</url-pattern>
</filter-mapping>

<!-- register the servlet to which the filter is mapped -->

<servlet>
    <servlet-name>requestheaders</servlet-name>
    <servlet-class>com.jspservletcookbook.RequestHeaderView</servlet-class>
</servlet>
```

Example 19-1. Mapping a filter to a servlet (continued)

```
<!-- Here is the URL mapping for the requestheaders servlet -->

<servlet-mapping>
    <servlet-name>requestheaders</servlet-name>
    <url-pattern>/requestheaders</url-pattern>
</servlet-mapping>

</web-app>
```

When a client sends a request to the servlet path */requestheaders*, the web container applies the LogFilter filter to the request. This servlet path, as in:

```
http://localhost:8080/home/requestheaders
```

is the only servlet path to which this filter is applied. As you might have guessed, the LogFilter logs some information about the request before the request continues along to its servlet destination. Example 19-2 shows the filter class for the LogFilter in Example 19-1.

> This filter class provides the additional benefit of showing you how to log a message inside of a filter!

Make sure to:

- Create the filter with a constructor that does not take any parameters
- Give the filter class a package name
- Store the filter in the *WEB-INF/classes* directory of the web application, including its package-related directories
- Map the filter to the servlet in *web.xml*, as in Example 19-1

Example 19-2. A filter that logs some information

```
package com.jspservletcookbook;

import javax.servlet.*;
import javax.servlet.http.*;

import org.apache.log4j.Logger;
import org.apache.log4j.PropertyConfigurator;

public class LogFilter implements Filter {

    private FilterConfig config;
    private Logger log;

    // Creates new LogFilter
    public LogFilter() {}
```

Example 19-2. A filter that logs some information (continued)

```java
    public void  init(FilterConfig filterConfig) throws ServletException{

        this.config = filterConfig;

        //load the configuration for this application's loggers using the
        // servletLog.properties file
        PropertyConfigurator.configure(config.getServletContext( ).
          getRealPath("/") +
              "WEB-INF/classes/servletLog.properties");

        log = Logger.getLogger(LogFilter.class);

        log.info("Logger instantiated in "+ getClass().getName( ));

    }//init

    public void  doFilter(ServletRequest request, ServletResponse response,
          FilterChain chain) throws java.io.IOException, ServletException {

        HttpServletRequest req = null;

        if (log != null && (request instanceof HttpServletRequest)){

            req = (HttpServletRequest) request;
            log.info(
              "Request received from: " + req.getRemoteHost( ) + " for: " +
                  req.getRequestURL( )); }

        //pass request back down the filter chain
        chain.doFilter(request,response);
    }// doFilter

    public void destroy( ){

        /*called before the Filter instance is removed
          from service by the web container*/
        log = null;
    }
}
```

This filter logs the remote host of the client request and the URL that the client
requested. Here is an example of the logged information:

```
    INFO - Request received from: localhost for: http://localhost:8080/home/
    requestheaders
```

The filter uses the *log4j* library (see Chapter 14) from the Apache Software
Foundation.

Since the first parameter to the filter's dofilter( ) method is a javax. servlet.ServletRequest type, this parameter must be cast to an HttpServletRequest to call methods such as HttpServletRequest. getRemoteHost( ).

See Also

Recipe 7.9 on using a filter to read request parameter values; Recipe 11.11 on using a filter to monitor session attributes; Recipe 18.3 on using a filter to alter the request; Recipes 19.2–19.4 on mapping filters to web components; Recipe 19.5 on configuring filter initialization parameters; Recipe 19.6 on blocking requests; Recipe 19.7 on filtering the HttpServletResponse; Recipe 19.8 on using filters with RequestDispatchers; Recipe 19.9 on using filters to check request parameters; Recipe 19.10 on using filters to disallow requests from certain IP addresses.

19.2   Mapping a Filter to a JSP

Problem

You want to have the web container apply a filter to requests for a certain JSP page.

Solution

Use the url-pattern child element of the filter-mapping element in the deployment descriptor to map the filter to the JSP.

Discussion

Map a filter to a JSP by specifying the path to the JSP page using the filter-mapping element's url-pattern subelement. Example 19-3 shows a *web.xml* configuration that maps the filter in Example 19-2 to the *requestHeaders.jsp*.

Example 19-3. Mapping a filter to a JSP

```
<!-- top of web.xml deployment descriptor -->

<filter>
    <filter-name>LogFilter</filter-name>
    <filter-class>com.jspservletcookbook.LogFilter</filter-class>
</filter>

<filter-mapping>
    <filter-name>LogFilter</filter-name>
    <url-pattern>/displayHeaders.jsp</url-pattern>
</filter-mapping>

<!-- rest of deployment descriptor -->
```

You can create a number of filter mappings for a single filter, each with their own type of URL pattern.

With the configuration of Example 19-3, any requests for *displayHeaders.jsp* will pass through the filter named `LogFilter`. Example 19-2 shows the source code for the `LogFilter` class. The code logs a message about the request, before the request is passed along the filter chain to the JSP. The logged message looks like:

```
INFO - Request received from: localhost for: http://localhost:8080/home/
displayHeaders.jsp
```

The JSP itself does not have to be configured in a special way for the filter to be applied to it. You can apply the filter to all JSPs with this configuration:

```
<filter-mapping>
    <filter-name>LogFilter</filter-name>
    <url-pattern>*.jsp</url-pattern>
</filter-mapping>
```

The URL pattern *.jsp* is an extension mapping that associates the `LogFilter` with any of the web application's components that end with *.jsp*.

See Also

Recipe 7.9 on using a filter to read request parameter values; Recipe 11.11 on using a filter to monitor session attributes; Recipe 18.3 on using a filter to alter then forward the request; Recipe 19.3 on mapping more than one filter to a servlet; Recipe 19.4 on changing the order filters are applied to a servlet; Recipe 19.5 on configuring filter initialization parameters; Recipe 19.6 on blocking requests; Recipe 19.7 on filtering the `HttpServletResponse`; Recipe 19.8 on using filters with `RequestDispatchers`; Recipe 19.9 on using filters to check request parameters; Recipe 19.10 on using filters to disallow requests from certain IP addresses.

19.3   Mapping More Than One Filter to a Servlet

Problem

You want requests for a servlet or JSP to pass through more than one filter.

Solution

Map each filter to the servlet or JSP using `filter-mapping` elements in the deployment descriptor. The filters are applied to the servlet in the order they appear in the deployment descriptor.

Discussion

Your web application may define several different filters with a specific purpose. For instance, one filter might log messages, while another filter authenticates users. It is straightforward to create a filter chain that applies each filter in a specified order to a servlet. You use the `filter-mapping` element to map each filter to the target servlet (or JSP). The web container then applies the filters to the target in the order that the `filter-mapping` elements are defined in the deployment descriptor.

Example 19-4 configures two filters: `AuthenFilter` and `LogFilter`. The `filter-mapping` elements for these filters then map the servlet name `requestheaders` to each of these filters. The order of the `filter-mapping` elements in Example 19-4 specifies that the authentication filter (`AuthenFilter`) must be applied to the servlet named `requestheaders` first, followed by the `LogFilter`.

To map a filter to a servlet name, the servlet has to be registered in *web.xml*. Example 19-4 registers the `requestheaders` servlet beneath the `filter` and `filter-mapping` elements.

Example 19-4. Mapping more than one filter to a servlet

```
<!-- top of web.xml deployment descriptor -->

<filter>
    <filter-name>AuthenFilter</filter-name>
    <filter-class>com.jspservletcookbook.AuthenticateFilter</filter-class>
</filter>

 <filter>
    <filter-name>LogFilter</filter-name>
    <filter-class>com.jspservletcookbook.LogFilter</filter-class>
</filter>

<filter-mapping>
    <filter-name>AuthenFilter</filter-name>
    <servlet-name>requestheaders</servlet-name>
</filter-mapping>

<filter-mapping>
    <filter-name>LogFilter</filter-name>
    <servlet-name>requestheaders</servlet-name>
</filter-mapping>

<!-- servlet definitions -->

<servlet>
    <servlet-name>requestheaders</servlet-name>
    <servlet-class>com.jspservletcookbook.RequestHeaderView</servlet-class>
</servlet>

<!-- servlet-mapping section of web.xml -->
```

Example 19-4. Mapping more than one filter to a servlet (continued)

```
<servlet-mapping>
    <servlet-name>requestheaders</servlet-name>
    <url-pattern>/requestheaders</url-pattern>
</servlet-mapping>

<!-- rest of deployment descriptor -->
```

When a user requests the requestheaders servlet using the servlet path */requestheaders*, as specified in the servlet-mapping element, the request passes through the AuthenFilter and LogFilter before it reaches its servlet destination.

 The same process applies to a filter-mapping that uses a url-pattern element instead of a servlet-name element. The order of the filter-mapping elements in the deployment descriptor determines the order of the filters applied to the web components that match the url-pattern.

See Also

Recipe 7.9 on using a filter to read request parameter values; Recipe 11.11 on using a filter to monitor session attributes; Recipe 18.3 on using a filter to alter then forward the request; Recipe 19.4 on changing the order filters are applied to a servlet; Recipe 19.5 on configuring filter init parameters; Recipe 19.6 on blocking requests; Recipe 19.7 on filtering the HttpServletResponse; Recipe 19.8 on using filters with RequestDispatchers; Recipe 19.9 on using filters to check request parameters; Recipe 19.10 on using filters to disallow requests from certain IP addresses.

19.4   Changing the Order in Which Filters are Applied to Servlets

Problem

You want to change the order in which filters are applied to web components.

Solution

Change the order of filter-mapping elements in the deployment descriptor.

Discussion

The order of filter-mapping elements in *web.xml* determines the order in which the web container applies the filter to the servlet. Example 19-5 reverses the order of the filter-mapping elements that map two filters to the servlet named *requestheaders*, compared with Recipe 19.3. The LogFilter is thus applied to the servlet before the

AuthenFilter. Any requests for the servlet pass through a chain: LogFilter →
AuthenFilter → *requestheaders* servlet.

Example 19-5. Reversing the order of filter-mapping elements

```
<!-- LogFilter applies to the requestheaders servlet
before AuthenFilter -->

<filter-mapping>
    <filter-name>LogFilter</filter-name>
    <servlet-name>requestheaders</servlet-name>
</filter-mapping>

<filter-mapping>
    <filter-name>AuthenFilter</filter-name>
    <servlet-name>requestheaders</servlet-name>
</filter-mapping>
```

See Also

Recipe 7.9 on using a filter to read request parameter values; Recipe 11.11 on using a
filter to monitor session attributes; Recipe 18.3 on using a filter to alter then forward
the request; Recipes 19.1-3 on mapping filters to web components; Recipe 19.5 on
configuring filter init parameters; Recipe 19.6 on blocking requests; Recipe 19.7 on
filtering the HttpServletResponse; Recipe 19.8 on using filters with
RequestDispatchers; Recipe 19.9 on using filters to check request parameters;
Recipe 19.10 on using filters to disallow requests from certain IP addresses.

19.5   Configuring Initialization Parameters
for a Filter

Problem

You want to make an initialization (init) parameter available to a filter .

Solution

Use the init-param child element of the filter element to declare the initialization
parameter and its value. Inside the filter, access the init parameter by calling the
FilerConfig object's getInitParameter method.

Discussion

Example 19-6 shows a filter declared in the deployment descriptor. The filter
includes an init parameter named log-id.

Example 19-6. A filter declared in the deployment descriptor with an init parameter

```
<filter>
    <filter-name>LogFilter</filter-name>
    <filter-class>com.jspservletcookbook.LogFilter</filter-class>
    <init-param>
        <param-name>log-id</param-name>
        <param-value>A102003</param-value>
    </init-param>
</filter>
```

Example 19-7 shows the code you would use inside the filter to access the init parameter and its value. The code initializes the `FilterConfig` object in its `init` method, which is called once when the web container creates an instance of the filter. The code then gets the value of the filter's init parameter by calling:

```
String id = config.getInitParameter("log-id");
```

Make sure that the code checks whether the return value from `getInitParameter` is null before the code does something with that object.

Example 19-7. Accessing an init param value in a filter

```
package com.jspservletcookbook;

import javax.servlet.*;
import javax.servlet.http.*;

import org.apache.log4j.Logger;
import org.apache.log4j.PropertyConfigurator;

public class LogFilter implements Filter {

    private FilterConfig config;
    private Logger log;

    // Creates new LogFilter
    public LogFilter() {}

    public void  init(FilterConfig filterConfig) throws ServletException{

    this.config = filterConfig;

    //load the configuration for this application's loggers
    //using the servletLog.properties file
    PropertyConfigurator.configure(config.getServletContext().
       getRealPath("/") +
           "WEB-INF/classes/servletLog.properties");

      log = Logger.getLogger(LogFilter.class);

      log.info("Logger instantiated in "+ getClass().getName());
    }
```

Example 19-7. Accessing an init param value in a filter (continued)

```
public void  doFilter(ServletRequest request, ServletResponse response,
    FilterChain chain) throws java.io.IOException, ServletException {

HttpServletRequest req = null;

String id = config.getInitParameter("log-id");

if (id == null)
    id = "unknown";

if (log != null && (request instanceof HttpServletRequest)){

    req = (HttpServletRequest) request;
    log.info("Log id:" + id + ": Request received from: " +
        req.getRemoteHost() + " for " + req.getRequestURL()); }

    chain.doFilter(request,response);

}// doFilter

public void destroy(){
    /*called before the Filter instance is removed
    from service by the web container*/
    log = null;
}
}
```

Here is how the log output appears:

```
INFO - Log id:A102003: Request received from: localhost for http://localhost:8080/
home/requestheaders
```

> You can also use the FilterConfig object's getInitParameterNames
> method to get all of the init parameter names in a java.util.
> Enumeration object.

See Also

Recipe 7.9 on using a filter to read request parameter values; Recipe 11.11 on using a filter to monitor session attributes; Recipe 18.3 on using a filter to alter then forward the request; Recipes 19.1–19.4 on mapping filters to web components; Recipe 19.6 on blocking a request; Recipe 19.7 on filtering the HttpServletResponse; Recipe 19.8 on using filters with RequestDispatchers; Recipe 19.9 on using filters to check request parameters; Recipe 19.10 on using filters to disallow requests from certain IP addresses.

19.6   Optionally Blocking a Request with a Filter

Problem

You want the option to block a request with a filter.

Solution

Do not call the FilterChain object's doFilter( ) method inside of the filter. Output the response to the client inside of the filter's doFilter( ) method instead.

Discussion

A filter blocks a request from getting to a web component, such as a servlet, JSP, or HTML page, by never calling FilterChain.doFilter( ) inside the filter's own doFilter( ) method.

The BlockFilter class in Example 19-8 attempts to authenticate the user based on a request parameter. If the authentication fails, the filter uses the response object to output a response to the client, and the request is effectively blocked from reaching the requested servlet. A filter can output the final response to the client, not just initiate its filtering tasks.

Example 19-8. A filter optionally blocks the request and issues a response itself

```
package com.jspservletcookbook;

import java.io.PrintWriter;
import java.io.IOException;

import javax.servlet.*;
import javax.servlet.http.*;

public class BlockFilter implements Filter {

    private FilterConfig config;

    /** Creates new BlockFilter */
    public BlockFilter( ) {}

    public void  init(FilterConfig filterConfig)  throws ServletException{

        this.config = filterConfig;
    }

   public void  doFilter(ServletRequest request, ServletResponse response,
        FilterChain chain) throws IOException, ServletException {

    HttpServletRequest req = null;
    boolean authenticated = false;
```

```
        PrintWriter out = null;

    if (request instanceof HttpServletRequest){

        req = (HttpServletRequest) request;

        String user = req.getParameter("user");//get the user name

        authenticated = authenticateUser(user);//authenticate the user
    }

    if (authenticated){

        //they are authenticated, so pass along the request

        chain.doFilter(request,response);

        else {
        //have the filter send back the response

        response.setContentType("text/html");

        out = response.getWriter();

        out.println(
            "<html><head><title>Authentication Response</title>");
        out.println("</head><body>");
        out.println("<h2>Sorry your authentication attempt failed</h2>");

        out.println("</body></html>");

    }
    }// doFilter

public void destroy(){
    /*called before the Filter instance is removed
    from service by the web container*/
}

private boolean authenticateUser(String userName){

    //authenticate the user using JNDI and a database, for instance
    //return false for demonstration purposes
    return false;

    }// authenticateUser
}
```

The code authenticates the user by getting the hypothetical username as a request parameter. The name is the parameter for the filter's authenticateUser( ) method, which returns false to demonstrate the filter's response to the client. The filter uses the `PrintWriter` from the `javax.servlet.ServletResponse` object, which is a parameter to the `doFilter( )` method. The `PrintWriter` sends HTML back to the client. Figure 19-1 shows the response output in a web browser.

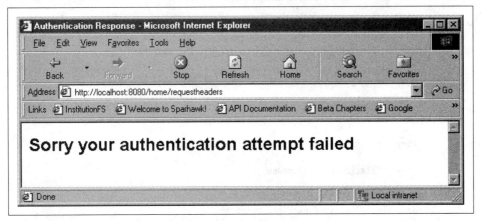

Figure 19-1. The HTML page returned by a blocking filter

 If you regularly use filters to send responses to a client, consider creating a JavaBean to customize the response. Store the bean class in its package beneath *WEB-INF/classes*, and use the bean inside the filter.

See Also

Recipe 7.9 on using a filter to read request parameter values; Recipe 11.11 on using a filter to monitor session attributes; Recipe 18.3 on using a filter to alter then forward the request; Recipes 19.1–19.4 on mapping filters to web components; Recipe 19.5 on configuring init parameters for a filter; Recipe 19.7 on filtering the HTTP response; Recipe 19.8 on using filters with `RequestDispatchers`; Recipe 19.9 on using filters to check request parameters; Recipe 19.10 on using filters to disallow requests from certain IP addresses.

19.7   Filtering the HTTP Response

Problem

You want to change the response with a filter while the client request is en route to the servlet.

Solution

Change the `javax.servlet.ServletResponse` inside the filter's `doFilter( )` method by wrapping the response with your own object. Then pass the wrapped response as a parameter into the `FilterChain.doFilter( )` method.

Discussion

Here are the steps for changing a response with a filter and a wrapper class:

1. Create a Java class that extends `javax.servlet.http. HttpServletResponseWrapper`.
2. Place this class, including its package-related directories, in *WEB-INF/classes*.
3. Use the wrapper class in the filter to wrap the response object, which is a parameter to the filter's `doFilter( )` method.
4. Call the `chain.doFilter( )` method with the wrapped response as a parameter.

Example 19-9 shows the Java class that we will use to wrap the response object.

 If you are just making a simple response change, you do not *have* to go to the trouble of using an `HttpServletResponseWrapper` class. This code inside of a filter's method adds a header to the response, then calls the `chain.doFilter( )` method with the altered response:

```
if(response instanceof HttpServletResponse){
    //cast to HttpServletResponse  to call
    //addHeader
    myHttpResponse =
        ((HttpServletResponse)response);

    myHttpResponse.addHeader("WWW-Authenticate",
            "BASIC realm=\"Admin\"");

    chain.doFilter(request,response); }
```

The `ResponseWrapper` class contains the skeleton of a new method named `getWebResource`. I want to show the mechanics of wrapping the response in a filter, so have kept this wrapper class very simple.

All the other `HttpServletResponse`-derived method calls are delegated to the wrapped response object, which is the convenience of extending `HttpServletResponseWrapper`.

Example 19-9. An HttpServletResponseWrapper class for use in a filter

```
package com.jspservletcookbook;

import javax.servlet.*;
import javax.servlet.http.HttpServletResponseWrapper;
import javax.servlet.http.HttpServletResponse;

public class ResponseWrapper extends HttpServletResponseWrapper{
```

Example 19-9. An HttpServletResponseWrapper class for use in a filter (continued)

```
public ResponseWrapper(HttpServletResponse response){

    super(response);
}

public String getWebResource(String resourceName){

    //Implement a method to return a String representing
    //the output of  a web resource
    //See Recipe 13.5
    return "resource"; //for the compiler...

}// getWebResource
}
```

Example 19-10 shows the doFilter() method inside the filter that uses this ResponseWrapper class.

 The class extending HttpServletResponseWrapper must be placed beneath *WEB-INF/classes*, with a directory structure that matches its package name.

Example 19-10. The doFilter() method of a filter that uses a HttpServletResponseWrapper class

```
public void doFilter(ServletRequest request, ServletResponse response,
    FilterChain chain) throws java.io.IOException, ServletException {

    if(response instanceof HttpServletResponse){

        chain.doFilter(request,
            new ResponseWrapper((HttpServletResponse)response));

    } else {

        chain.doFilter(request,response);

    }
}//doFilter
```

The code calls the chain.doFilter() method and passes in the wrapped response as a parameter. The web resource at the end of the chain has access to the customized response object and can call the additional method the response wrapper class has defined. All the other method calls on the HttpServletResponse object, such as getWriter() or getOutputStream(), are passed through to the wrapped response object.

See Also

Recipe 7.9 on using a filter to read request parameter values; Recipe 11.11 on using a filter to monitor session attributes; Recipe 18.3 on using a filter to alter the request; Recipes 19.1–19.4 on mapping filters to web components; Recipe 19.5 on configuring init parameters for a filter; Recipe 19.6 on blocking a request; Recipe 19.8 on using filters with RequestDispatchers; Recipe 19.9 on using filters to check request parameters; Recipe 19.10 on using filters to disallow requests from certain IP addresses.

19.8 Using Filters with RequestDispatcher Objects

Problem

You want to apply a filter to a servlet whose output is included in another servlet.

Solution

Use the javax.servlet.RequestDispatcher object to include the servlet's output. Configure the filter in *web.xml* with a dispatcher element containing the content "INCLUDE" (servlet API v2.4 and above only!).

Discussion

The servlet API v2.4 introduced a new twist for working with RequestDispatchers. Using the filter-mapping element in the deployment descriptor, you can specify that the filter applies to a servlet that is part of a RequestDispatcher include or forward action.

Example 19-11 shows a *web.xml* configuration for a filter.

Example 19-11. Applying a filter to a servlet using a RequestDispatcher

```
<?xml version="1.0" encoding="ISO-8859-1"?>

<web-app xmlns="http://java.sun.com/xml/ns/j2ee"
  xmlns:xsi="http://www.w3.org/2001/XMLSchema-instance" xsi:schemaLocation=
    "http://java.sun.com/xml/ns/j2ee
      http://java.sun.com/xml/ns/j2ee/web-app_2_4.xsd" version="2.4">


<filter>
    <filter-name>LogFilter</filter-name>
    <filter-class>com.jspservletcookbook.LogFilter</filter-class>
</filter>
```

Example 19-11. Applying a filter to a servlet using a RequestDispatcher (continued)

```
<filter-mapping>
    <filter-name>LogFilter</filter-name>
    <url-pattern>/requestheaders</url-pattern>
    <dispatcher>REQUEST</dispatcher>
    <dispatcher>INCLUDE</dispatcher>
</filter-mapping>
```

The dispatcher elements in the example configuration specify that the LogFilter applies to requests for the servlet path */requestheaders*, as well as to any RequestDispatchers that include the output of the servlet path */requestheaders*.

Similarly, if you want to initiate a filter when you are using a RequestDispatcher to *forward* a request to another component, use the FORWARD value with the dispatcher element, as in:

```
<filter-mapping>
    <filter-name>LogFilter</filter-name>
    <url-pattern>/requestheaders</url-pattern>
    <dispatcher>REQUEST</dispatcher>
    <dispatcher>FORWARD</dispatcher>
</filter-mapping>
```

Example 19-12 shows a servlet's doGet method that creates a RequestDispatcher specifying the path */requestheaders*. This code includes the servlet output represented by that path. Because of Example 19-11's configuration in *web.xml*, however, the web container applies the LogFilter before the servlet mapped to the */requestheaders* path is executed.

Example 19-12. A servlet includes another servlet's output, triggering a filter

```
public void doGet(HttpServletRequest request, HttpServletResponse response)
    throws ServletException, java.io.IOException {

    /* The output of the servlet at path "/requestheaders" will
       be included in this servlet's output, but first the request
       will pass through the LogFilter before it is sent to the
       "/requestheaders" servlet */
    RequestDispatcher dispatch = request.getRequestDispatcher(
        "/requestheaders");

    dispatch.include(request,response);

}
```

Figure 19-2 illustrates the process of filters and RequestDispatchers.

In Figure 19-2, a web client requests the servlet at path */home/servlet1*, with */home* representing the context path. The servlet1 component uses a RequestDispatcher to include the output of servlet2. Based on a filter-mapping element in *web.xml*, any requests for servlet2 involving a RequestDispatcher include action must first pass

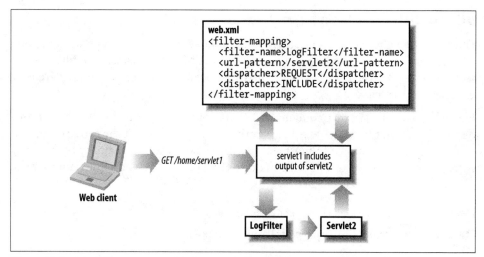

```
web.xml
<filter-mapping>
    <filter-name>LogFilter</filter-name>
    <url-pattern>/servlet2</url-pattern>
    <dispatcher>REQUEST</dispatcher>
    <dispatcher>INCLUDE</dispatcher>
</filter-mapping>
```

GET /home/servlet1

servlet1 includes
output of servlet2

Web client

LogFilter   Servlet2

Figure 19-2. A log filter intervenes between a servlet, including another servlet's output

through the log filter. This filter is configured with a `filter` element in *web.xml* with the name "LogFilter" (Figure 19-2 does not show this configuration; see Example 19-11).

 This type of `RequestDispatcher` set-up is only supported by Servlet API v2.4 and above.

See Also

Chapter 6 on including content using `RequestDispatchers`; Recipe 7.9 on using a filter to read request parameter values; Recipe 11.11 on using a filter to monitor session attributes; Recipe 18.3 on using a filter to alter then forward the request; Recipes 19.1–19.4 on mapping filters to web components; Recipe 19.5 on configuring init parameters for a filter; Recipe 19.6 on blocking a request; Recipe 19.7 on filtering the HTTP response; Recipe 19.9 on using filters to check request parameters; Recipe 19.10 on using filters to disallow requests from certain IP addresses.

19.9   Checking Form Parameters with a Filter

Problem

You want to use a filter to check the values that a user has entered into a form.

Solution

Use the deployment descriptor to map the filter to the servlet or JSP that is the target of the form.

Discussion

Filters offer an alternative to JavaScript and other server-side languages for checking whether the user has entered valid values into HTML form fields. The filter in this recipe initiates a basic check of the request parameters to determine if they are null or the empty String.

Example 19-13 is a JSP that contains an HTML form. The JSP includes some embedded JSTL tags that fill in the text fields with any correct values if the form is returned to the user for corrections. In most cases, a user fills in the vast majority of the fields correctly, but might make a mistake in one or two of them. You do not want to make him fill out all of the fields again.

Example 19-13. A JSP containing a form for users to fill out

```
<%@ taglib uri="http://java.sun.com/jstl/core" prefix="c" %>

<!DOCTYPE HTML PUBLIC "-//W3C//DTD HTML 4.0 Transitional//EN">
<html>
<head>
    <title>Personal Information</title>
</head>
<body bgcolor="#ffffff">

<c:if test="${! (empty errorMsg)}">

<font color="red"> <c:out value="${errorMsg}"/> </font>

</c:if>

<h2>Please enter your name and email address</h2>
<table>

<form action="/home/thanks.jsp">

<tr><td valign="top">First name: </td>
<td valign="top">

    <input type="text" name="first" size="15" value=
    '<c:out value="${first}" />'>

</td>
<td valign="top">Middle initial: </td>
<td valign="top">

    <input type="text" name="middle" size="2" value=
        '<c:out value="${middle}"/>'>

</td>
</tr>
<tr>
<td valign="top">Last name: </td>
```

Example 19-13. A JSP containing a form for users to fill out (continued)

```
<td valign="top">

    <input type="text" name="last" size="20" value=
    '<c:out value="${last}"/>'>

</td></tr>
<tr>
<td valign="top">Your email: </td>
<td valign="top">

    <input type="text" name="email" size="20" value=
        '<c:out value="${email}"/>'>

</td></tr>

<tr><td valign="top"><input type="submit" value="Submit"> </td>
<td></td></tr>
</form>
</table>

</body>
</html>
```

When the user submits Example 19-13, the browser sends the form information to the URL specified in the form tag's action attribute: a JSP page named *thanks.jsp*. The deployment descriptor maps the filter in Example 19-14 to the URL *thanks.jsp*. The filter is designed to check the fields' values to determine if the user left any of them blank and, if so, return the user to the form (named *form.jsp*).

 Make sure to develop all filters with a constructor that does not take any arguments.

Example 19-14. The filter that checks parameters values

```
package com.jspservletcookbook;

import java.io.IOException;
import java.util.Enumeration;

import javax.servlet.*;
import javax.servlet.http.*;

public class CheckFilter implements Filter {

    private FilterConfig config;

  public CheckFilter( ) {}

  public void  init(FilterConfig filterConfig)  throws ServletException {
```

Example 19-14. The filter that checks parameters values (continued)

```
    this.config = filterConfig;

}

public void doFilter(ServletRequest request, ServletResponse response,
    FilterChain chain) throws IOException, ServletException {

    //Get all the parameter names associated with the form fields
    Enumeration params = request.getParameterNames();
    boolean rejected = false;

    //Cycle through each one of the parameters; if any of them
    //are empty, call the 'reject' method
    while (params.hasMoreElements()){

        if (isEmpty( request.getParameter( (String) params.
            nextElement()) ) ){

            rejected = true;

            reject(request,response);

        }//if

    }//while

    //Pass the request to its intended destination, if everything
    //is okay
    if (! rejected)
        chain.doFilter(request,response);

}// doFilter

private boolean isEmpty(String param){

    if (param == null || param.length() < 1){
        return true;
    }

    return false;
}

private void reject(ServletRequest request, ServletResponse response)
    throws IOException, ServletException {

    //Create an error message; store it in a request attribute
    request.setAttribute("errorMsg",
        "Please make sure to provide a valid value for all of the text "+
        "fields.");

    Enumeration params = request.getParameterNames();
```

Example 19-14. The filter that checks parameters values (continued)

```
    String paramN = null;

    //Create request attributes that the form-related JSP will
    //use to fill in the form fields that have already been
    //filled out correctly. Then the user does not have to fill
    //in the entire form all over again.
    while (params.hasMoreElements()){

        paramN = (String) params.nextElement();

        request.setAttribute(
          paramN, request.getParameter(paramN));

    }

    //Use a RequestDispatcher to return the user to the form in
    //order to fill in the missing values

    RequestDispatcher dispatcher = request.
     getRequestDispatcher("/form.jsp");

    dispatcher.forward(request,response);

 }//reject

public void destroy(){
     /*called before the Filter instance is removed
     from service by the web container*/
 }

}
```

The Java comments in Example 19-14 explain what is going on in this filter. Basically, the user is returned to the form, which displays an error message if any of the request parameters are empty. Example 19-15 shows how the `CheckFilter` is mapped in *web.xml*. If the user fills in the form correctly, his request is sent to the *thanks.jsp* page without interuption by the filter.

Example 19-15. The CheckFilter is registered and mapped in web.xml

```
<!-- start of web.xml... -->

<filter>
    <filter-name>CheckFilter</filter-name>
    <filter-class>com.jspservletcookbook.CheckFilter</filter-class>
</filter>

<filter-mapping>
    <filter-name>CheckFilter</filter-name>
    <url-pattern>/thanks.jsp</url-pattern>
</filter-mapping>

<!-- rest of web.xml... -->
```

Figure 19-3 shows an HTML form that was partially filled out and submitted. The filter sent the form back to the user with a message (in a red font).

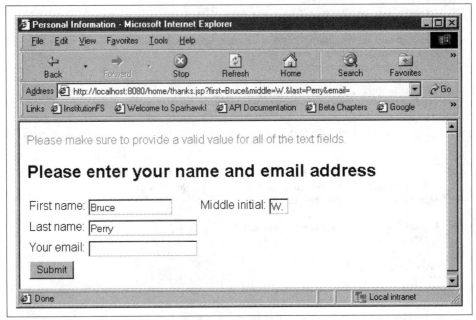

Figure 19-3. A filter forwards an error message to a JSP

See Also

Chapter 6 on including content using RequestDispatchers; Recipe 19.8 on using filters with RequestDispatchers; Recipe 7.9 on using a filter to read request parameter values; Recipe 18.3 on using a filter to alter then forward the request; Recipes 19.1–19.4 on mapping filters to web components; Recipe 19.5 on configuring init parameters for a filter; Recipe 19.6 on blocking a request; Recipe 19.7 on filtering the HTTP response.

19.10 Blocking IP Addresses with a Filter

Problem

You want to use a filter that checks the IP address associated with the request.

Solution

Use a filter that calls the HttpServletRequest's getRemoteAddr( ) method inside the doFilter( ) method and blocks the request by *not* calling chain.doFilter( ).

Discussion

A typical use of a filter in a web application is to check the request to make sure it's acceptable. Let's say your security division has discovered that a certain range of IP addresses represent nasty clients—you want to rebuff those folks with a "403 Forbidden" HTTP response.

Example 19-16 blocks any client IP address beginning with "192.168."

Example 19-16. A filter for blocking a certain range of IP addresses

```java
package com.jspservletcookbook;

import java.io.IOException;
import java.util.StringTokenizer;

import javax.servlet.*;
import javax.servlet.http.*;

public class IPFilter implements Filter {

    private FilterConfig config;
    public final static String IP_RANGE = "192.168";

    public IPFilter( ) {}

    public void  init(FilterConfig filterConfig) throws ServletException {

      this.config = filterConfig;

    }

    public void  doFilter(ServletRequest request,
      ServletResponse response,
        FilterChain chain) throws IOException, ServletException {

        String ip = request.getRemoteAddr( );

        HttpServletResponse httpResp = null;

        if (response instanceof HttpServletResponse)
            httpResp = (HttpServletResponse) response;

        //Break up the IP address into chunks representing each byte
        StringTokenizer toke = new StringTokenizer(ip,".");

        int dots = 0;

        String byte1 = "";

        String byte2 = "";

        String client = "";
```

Example 19-16. A filter for blocking a certain range of IP addresses (continued)

```
    //
    while (toke.hasMoreTokens()){

        ++dots;

        //This token is the first number series or byte
        if (dots == 1){

            byte1 = toke.nextToken();

        } else {

            //This token is the second number series or byte
            byte2 = toke.nextToken();

            break;//only interested in first two bytes
        }

    }//while

    //Piece together half of the client IP address so it can be
    // compared with the forbidden range represented by
    //IPFilter.IP_RANGE

    client = byte1+"."+byte2;

    //if the client IP fits the forbidden range...
    if (IP_RANGE.equals(client)){

        httpResp.sendError(HttpServletResponse.SC_FORBIDDEN,
            "That means goodbye forever!" );

    } else {

        //Client is okay; send them on their merry way
        chain.doFilter(request,response);
    }

}// doFilter

public void destroy(){
    /*called before the Filter instance is removed
    from service by the web container*/
}

}
```

The filter obtains the client's IP address with the ServletRequest's getRemoteAddr() method. The filter than parses the return value to determine if the IP address falls into the "192.168" range. If the IP address does fall into this range, then the code calls the HttpServletResponse sendError() method with the "403 Forbidden" type HTTP status code, as in:

```
httpResp.sendError(HttpServletResponse.SC_FORBIDDEN,
    "That means goodbye forever!" );
```

This method call effectively short circuits the request by preventing the user from reaching their original destination. If the IP address is acceptable, the code calls chain.doFilter(), which passes the request and response objects along the filter chain. In this case, the application does not map any other filters to *thanks.jsp*, so the web container invokes that JSP page.

Example 19-17 shows the mapping for this filter in *web.xml*. The filter is mapped to *all* requests with the URL mapping "/*."

Example 19-17. The mapping of the IP-blocking filter

```
<filter>
    <filter-name>IPFilter</filter-name>
    <filter-class>com.jspservletcookbook.IPFilter</filter-class>
</filter>

<filter-mapping>
    <filter-name>IPFilter</filter-name>
    <url-pattern>/*</url-pattern>
</filter-mapping>
```

Figure 19-4 shows the page the web browser will display if the client IP address is blocked.

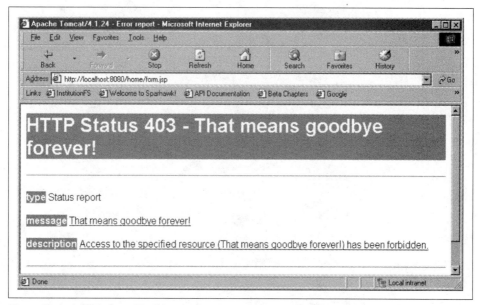

Figure 19-4. A filtered out IP address receives an HTTP Status 403 message

See Also

Chapter 9 on handling errors in web applications; Recipe 19.8 on using filters with RequestDispatchers; Recipe 18.3 on using a filter to alter then forward the request; Recipes 19.1–19.4 on mapping filters to web components; Recipe 19.5 on configuring init parameters for a filter; Recipe 19.7 on filtering the HTTP response; Recipe 19.9 on checking form parameters with a filter.

CHAPTER 20

Managing Email in Servlets and JSPs

20.0 Introduction

This chapter describes how to manage email in your servlets using the JavaMail and JavaBeans Activation Framework (JAF) APIs. JavaMail provides Java classes for dealing with most aspects of creating, sending, and accessing email. The JAF is a separate API for handling the datatypes and Multipurpose Internet Mail Extension (MIME) types you may encounter when generating email, such as the many different kinds of file attachments. Both of these APIs are a part of the Java 2 Enterprise Edition (J2EE) platform.

JavaMail models an email system with classes that represent mail sessions (the `javax.mail.Session` class), message stores (the `javax.mail.Store` class), folders (the `javax.mail.Folder` class, such as the INBOX folder), email messages (`javax.mail.Message`), and email addresses (the `javax.mail.internet.InternetAddress` class). For example, an email message is similar to a JavaBean, with setter methods to build the various message components (e.g., `setFrom( )`, `setRecipients( )`, `setSubject( )`, etc.).

The following recipes show how to manage basic email messaging using a single servlet, as well as methods for separating the responsibility for emailing and handling HTTP requests into JavaBeans and servlets.

20.1 Placing the Email-Related Classes on your Classpath

Problem

You want to use the `javax.mail` and related Java packages to handle email in a servlet.

Solution

Download the ZIP files containing the *mail.jar* and *activation.jar* archives. Add these JAR files to a shared directory for JAR files whose contents are loaded by the web container. If this directory type is not available, add the *mail.jar* and *activation.jar* files to the *WEB-INF/lib* directory of your web application.

Discussion

If your classpath for compiling servlets already includes the JAR files made available by your web container (such as the JAR files in Tomcat's *common/lib* directory), test if an email-related servlet such as Example 20-1 compiles successfully. If the compiler reports that the packages javax.mail and javax.mail.internet do not exist, you must add the proper JAR files to your classpath.

 See Recipe 4.3 on using Ant to include Tomcat's JAR files in your classpath.

Download the *mail.jar* component from *http://java.sun.com/products/javamail/*. The downloaded file is a ZIP archive containing the *mail.jar* archive. This file includes the required packages for handling email in a servlet, such as javax.mail and javax.mail. internet.

Then download the JAF from *http://java.sun.com/products/javabeans/glasgow/jaf. html*. Servlets can use these classes, as part of the *javax.activation* package, to handle the different data types that can be transferred with email messages, such as file attachments.

 You can handle basic file attachments using the JavaMail API alone (without JAF), as in Recipes 20.5 and 20.6. See Recipe 20.7 for examples of how to use some of the javax.activation classes to add file attachments to emails.

Add the *mail.jar* and *activation.jar* archives to the *WEB-INF/lib* directory of your web application to make the JavaMail and JAF packages available to a servlet.

See Also

The Sun Microsystems JavaMail API page: *http://java.sun.com/products/javamail/*; the JAF web page: *http://java.sun.com/products/javabeans/glasgow/jaf.html*; Recipe 20.2 on sending email from a servlet; Recipe 20.3 on sending email using a JavaBean; Recipe 20.4 covering how to access email in a servlet; Recipe 20.5 on accessing email with a JavaBean; Recipe 20.6 on handling attachments in a servlet; Recipe 20.7 on adding attachments to an email message; Recipe 20.8 on reading an email's headers.

20.2 Sending Email from a Servlet

Problem

You want to send emails from a servlet.

Solution

Import the javax.mail and javax.mail.internet packages at the top of the servlet source code. Create a sendMessage() method (or a method with a different name) that can be called from the servlet methods doGet() or doPost().

Discussion

The sendMessage() method in Example 20-1 uses the JavaMail API to connect with a mail server, construct an email message, and then send that message to one or more recipients. The servlet obtains the various components of an email—the target email address, the sender's address, the subject field, and the email's body content—from request parameters. The servlet can handle a form submitted by a client using a web browser.

 The form tag might look like this:

```
<form method="POST" action=
"/home/servlet/com.jspservletcookbook.EmailServlet">
```

Example 20-1 calls the sendMessage() method from the service method doPost(). The sendMessage() method parameters comprise the parts of an email: the SMTP server, the recipient of the email (the variable to), the "from" address of the sender, the email subject, and the email's content.

Example 20-1. A servlet sends email based on request parameter values

```
package com.jspservletcookbook;

import java.io.IOException;
import java.io.PrintWriter;
import java.util.Properties;

import javax.mail.*;
import javax.mail.internet.*;

import javax.servlet.*;
import javax.servlet.http.*;

public class EmailServlet extends HttpServlet {

    //default value for mail server address, in case the user
    //doesn't provide one
```

Example 20-1. A servlet sends email based on request parameter values (continued)

```
    private final static String DEFAULT_SERVER = "mail.attbi.com";

  public void doPost(HttpServletRequest request,
    HttpServletResponse response) throws ServletException,
      java.io.IOException {

      //obtain the values for email components from
      //request parameters
      String smtpServ = request.getParameter("smtp");
      if (smtpServ == null || smtpServ.equals(""))
          smtpServ = DEFAULT_SERVER;

      String from = request.getParameter("from");
      String to = request.getParameter("to");
      String subject = request.getParameter("subject");
      String emailContent = request.getParameter("emailContent");

      response.setContentType("text/html");
      java.io.PrintWriter out = response.getWriter();

      out.println(
        "<html><head><title>Email message sender</title></head><body>");

      try {

          sendMessage(smtpServ, to, from, subject, emailContent);

      } catch (Exception e) {

          throw new ServletException(e.getMessage());

      }

      out.println(
          "<h2>The message was sent successfully</h2>");

      out.println("</body></html>");

  } //doPost

  private void sendMessage(String smtpServer, String to, String from,
    String subject,String emailContent) throws Exception {

      Properties properties = System.getProperties();
      //populate the 'Properties' object with the mail
      //server address, so that the default 'Session'
      //instance can use it.
      properties.put("mail.smtp.host", smtpServer);

      Session session = Session.getDefaultInstance(properties);
      Message mailMsg = new MimeMessage(session);//a new email message
      InternetAddress[] addresses = null;
```

```
    try {

        if (to != null) {

            //throws 'AddressException' if the 'to' email address
            //violates RFC822 syntax
            addresses = InternetAddress.parse(to, false);
            mailMsg.setRecipients(Message.RecipientType.TO, addresses);

        } else {

            throw new MessagingException(
                "The mail message requires a 'To' address.");

        }

        if (from != null) {

            mailMsg.setFrom(new InternetAddress(from));

        } else {

            throw new MessagingException(
                "The mail message requires a valid 'From' address.");

        }

        if (subject != null)
            mailMsg.setSubject(subject);

        if (emailContent != null)
            mailMsg.setText(emailContent);

        //Finally, send the mail message; throws a 'SendFailedException'
        //if any of the message's recipients have an invalid address
        Transport.send(mailMsg);

    } catch (Exception exc) {

        throw exc;

    }

}//sendMessage

public void doGet(HttpServletRequest request,
    HttpServletResponse response) throws ServletException,
        java.io.IOException {

    //doGet() calls doPost()...
```

Example 20-1. A servlet sends email based on request parameter values (continued)

```
        doPost(request, response);

    }//doGet

}//EmailServlet
```

The servlet interacts with a mail server in the following manner:

1. The code creates a `javax.mail.Session` object, which contains various defaults and property values (such as `mail.smtp.host`) that the other JavaMail objects will use. You can share a single `Session` object in an application.

2. The code creates a `MimeMessage` object (passing in the `Session` as a constructor parameter).

3. The servlet then populates the `MimeMessage` with an email's various components, such as the "to" and "from" email addresses, the email subject, as well as the message content.

4. The code sends the email using the `javax.mail:Transport` static `send( )` method.

See Also

The Sun Microsystems JavaMail API page: *http://java.sun.com/products/javamail/*; Recipe 20.1 on adding JavaMail-related JARs to your web application; Recipe 20.3 on sending email using a JavaBean; Recipe 20.4 covering how to access email in a servlet; Recipe 20.5 on accessing email with a JavaBean; Recipe 20.6 on handling attachments in a servlet; Recipe 20.7 on adding attachments to an email message; Recipe 20.8 on reading an email's headers.

20.3 Sending Email from a Servlet Using a JavaBean

Problem

You want to use a JavaBean or helper class to send email from a servlet.

Solution

Develop a Java class that implements a `sendMessage( )` method (just a name I gave it) to construct an email and send it. Store the new class in the *WEB-INF/classes* folder of the web application, including the class's package-related folders.

Discussion

You may choose to separate the responsibilities of handling HTTP requests and managing email by encapsulating these tasks in separate classes. A JavaBean that provides the essential function of sending email fits the bill here.

Recipes 20.5 and 20.6 show JavaBeans that are used to *access* email and handle attachments. A bean that does *everything* email-related grows fairly large in size, so developers must make a design decision about whether to separate these tasks into different JavaBeans (or utility classes) that can be used from servlets.

Create the bean and store it in the *WEB-INF/classes* folder. Example 20-3 shows the doGet( ) method of an HttpServlet using a JavaBean to send an email. Example 20-2 shows the bean class itself. The difference between the sendMessage( ) method of Example 20-1 and the one in Example 20-2 is in the way the bean receives the various email parts, such as the recipient's email address. The bean stores these parts as properties and uses setter methods to provide the property values.

On the other hand, Example 20-1 uses request parameters and method arguments to provide these values.

Example 20-2. A JavaBean used to send email

```
package com.jspservletcookbook;

import java.io.IOException;
import java.io.PrintWriter;
import java.util.Properties;

import javax.mail.*;
import javax.mail.internet.*;

public class EmailBean  {

  public EmailBean( ){}

     //set defaults
     private final static String DEFAULT_CONTENT = "Unknown content";
     private final static String DEFAULT_SUBJECT= "Unknown subject";
     private static String DEFAULT_SERVER = null;
     private static String DEFAULT_TO = null;
     private static String DEFAULT_FROM = null;
     static{
         //set Mail defaults based on a properties file
         java.util.ResourceBundle bundle =
           java.util.ResourceBundle.
           getBundle("com.jspservletcookbook.mailDefaults");
```

Example 20-2. A JavaBean used to send email (continued)

```
            DEFAULT_SERVER = bundle.getString("DEFAULT_SERVER");
            DEFAULT_TO = bundle.getString("DEFAULT_TO");
            DEFAULT_FROM = bundle.getString("DEFAULT_FROM");

    }//static


    //JavaBean properties
    private String smtpHost;
    private String to;
    private String from;
    private String content;
    private String subject;

public void sendMessage() throws Exception {

    Properties properties = System.getProperties();

    //populate the 'Properties' object with the mail
    //server address, so that the default 'Session'
    //instance can use it.
    properties.put("mail.smtp.host", smtpHost);
    Session session = Session.getDefaultInstance(properties);
    Message mailMsg = new MimeMessage(session);//a new email message
    InternetAddress[] addresses = null;

    try {


        if (to != null) {

            //throws 'AddressException' if the 'to' email address
            //violates RFC822 syntax
            addresses = InternetAddress.parse(to, false);
            mailMsg.setRecipients(Message.RecipientType.TO, addresses);

        } else {

            throw new MessagingException(
              "The mail message requires a 'To' address.");

        }

        if (from != null) {

            mailMsg.setFrom(new InternetAddress(from));

        } else {

            throw new MessagingException(
              "The mail message requires a valid 'From' address.");

        }
```

Example 20-2. A JavaBean used to send email (continued)

```
            if (subject != null)
                mailMsg.setSubject(subject);

            if (content != null)
                mailMsg.setText(content);

            //Finally, send the mail message; throws a 'SendFailedException'
            //if any of the message's recipients have an invalid address
            Transport.send(mailMsg);

        } catch (Exception exc) {

            throw exc;

        }

    }//sendMessage

    //The setter methods are all the same structure,
    //so we're just showing two

    public void setSmtpHost(String host){

        if (check(host)){
            this.smtpHost = host;
        } else {
            this.smtpHost = DEFAULT_SERVER;
        }

    }//setSmtpHost

    public void setTo(String to){

        if (check(to)){
            this.to = to;
        } else {
            this.to = DEFAULT_TO;
        }

    }//setTo

    /* -- Not shown: 'setter' methods continue with exactly the same structure for
'from', 'subject', and 'content' -- */

    private boolean check(String value){

        if(value == null || value.equals(""))
            return false;

        return true;
    }//check

}
```

Example 20-3 uses the java.util.ResourceBundle class to set default property values for variables such as the name of the server. The *mailDefaults.properties* file is stored in *WEB-INF/classes/com/jspservletcookbook*. Here is an example of the properties file's contents:

```
DEFAULT_SERVER=smtp.comcast.net
DEFAULT_TO=author@jspservletcookbook.com
DEFAULT_FROM=author@jspservletcookbook.com
```

The bean allows the setting of the various email parts with the following methods (Example 20-3 does not show all of them): setSmtpHost( ), setTo( ), setFrom( ), setSubject( ), and setContent( ).

The servlet in Example 20-3 creates an instance of an EmailBean, sets the various parts of the email message, then calls the sendMessage( ) method. Example 20-3 shows only the doGet( ) method. The servlet's doPost( ) method could call doGet( ) as in: doGet(request, response).

Example 20-3. A servlet uses the JavaBean to send email

```
public void doGet(HttpServletRequest request,
  HttpServletResponse response)
  throws ServletException, java.io.IOException {

    response.setContentType("text/html");
    java.io.PrintWriter out = response.getWriter();
    out.println(
    "<html><head><title>Email message sender</title></head><body>");

    EmailBean emailer = new EmailBean();
    emailer.setSmtpHost("mail.attbi.com");
    emailer.setTo("myfriend@yahoo.com");
    emailer.setFrom("author@jspservletcookbook.com");
    emailer.setSubject("This is not spam!");
    emailer.setContent("Please call ASAP.");

    try{
        emailer.sendMessage();
    } catch (Exception e) {throw new ServletException(e);}

    out.println("</body></html>");

} //doGet
```

The bean itself throws MessagingExceptions if, for instance, the "to" email address that the user provides is in an invalid format. The bean rethrows any exceptions that it catches while building and sending the email.

See Also

Recipe 20.4 covering how to access email in a servlet; Recipe 20.5 on accessing email with a JavaBean; Recipe 20.6 on handling attachments in a servlet; Recipe 20.7 on adding attachments to an email message; Recipe 20.8 on reading an email's headers.

20.4 Accessing Email from a Servlet

Problem

You want to access and display the content of email in a servlet.

Solution

Use the JavaMail API and a method inside the servlet to handle and display the values of email messages.

Discussion

Fetching email messages using JavaMail and a servlet is a straightforward process:

1. Import the `javax.mail` and `javax.mail.internet` packages at the top of the servlet source code.

2. Inside the servlet's mail-fetching method, create a `javax.mail.Session` object to handle this mail session.

3. Get a message store object (a `javax.mail.Store`) from the session to represent the POP3 mail account.

4. Connect to the `Store` using the `connect(String host, String user, String password)` method of the `Store` object (there are overloaded versions of this method). The `Store` is designed to authenticate a user and connect with a mail server.

5. Access the INBOX folder from the message store.

6. Obtain any messages that folder contains as a `Message[]` type, then do whatever you want with each message, iterating through the array.

Example 20-4 fetches email messages by calling its `handleMessages()` method in the `doGet()` service method.

Example 20-4. A servlet that fetches email messages

```
package com.jspservletcookbook;

import java.io.IOException;
import java.io.PrintWriter;

import java.util.Properties;
```

Example 20-4. A servlet that fetches email messages (continued)

```java
import javax.mail.*;
import javax.mail.internet.*;
import javax.servlet.*;
import javax.servlet.http.*;

public class MailAccessor extends HttpServlet {

    private final static String DEFAULT_SERVER = "mail.attbi.com";

    public void doGet(HttpServletRequest request,
        HttpServletResponse response) throws ServletException,
          java.io.IOException {

        response.setContentType("text/html");
        java.io.PrintWriter out = response.getWriter();
        out.println("<html><head><title>Email Reader</title></head><body>");

        //This method accesses any email and displays the contents
        handleMessages(request, out);

        out.println("</body></html>");

    }//doGet

    private void handleMessages(HttpServletRequest request,
        PrintWriter out) throws IOException, ServletException {

        //Obtain user authentication information for a POP server,
        //used to access email. This information is stored in a
        //HttpSession object
        HttpSession httpSession = request.getSession();
        String user = (String) httpSession.getAttribute("user");
        String password = (String) httpSession.getAttribute("pass");
        String popAddr = (String) httpSession.getAttribute("pop");

        Store popStore = null;
        Folder folder = null;

        if (! check(popAddr))
            popAddr = MailAccessor.DEFAULT_SERVER;

        try {

            //basic check for null or empty user and password
            if ((! check(user)) || (! check(password)))
              throw new ServletException(
                "A valid username and password is required.");

            Properties properties = System.getProperties();
            //Obtain default 'Session' for this interaction with
            //a mail server
            Session session = Session.getDefaultInstance(properties);
```

Example 20-4. A servlet that fetches email messages (continued)

```
        //Obtain a message store (i.e., a POP3 email account, from
        //the Session object
        popStore = session.getStore("pop3");

        //connect to the store with authentication information
        popStore.connect(popAddr, user, password);
        //Get the INBOX folder, open it, and retireve any emails
        folder = popStore.getFolder("INBOX");

        if (! folder.exists())
          throw new ServletException(
            "An 'INBOX' folder does not exist for the user.");

        folder.open(Folder.READ_ONLY);
        Message[] messages = folder.getMessages();
        int msgLen = messages.length;

        if (msgLen == 0){
        out.println(
          "<h2>The INBOX folder doesn't contain any email "+
          "messages.</h2>");}

        //for each retrieved message, use displayMessage method to
        //display the mail message
        for (int i = 0; i < msgLen; i++){

            displayMessage(messages[i], out);

            out.println("<br /><br />");
        }

    } catch (Exception exc) {

        out.println(
          "<h2>Sorry, an error occurred while accessing the email" +
          " messages.</h2>");

        out.println(exc.toString());

    } finally {

        try{

            //close the folder and the store in the finally block
            //if 'true' parameter, any deleted messages will be expunged
            //from the Folder
            if (folder != null)
                folder.close(false);

    if (popStore != null)
            popStore.close();
```

Example 20-4. A servlet that fetches email messages (continued)

```
            } catch (Exception e) { }
        }
}//printMessages

    private void displayMessage(Message msg, PrintWriter out)
        throws MessagingException, IOException{

        if (msg != null && msg.getContent() instanceof String){
            if (msg.getFrom()[0] instanceof InternetAddress){
                out.println(
                  "Message received from: " +
                  ((InternetAddress)msg.getFrom()[0]).getAddress() +
                  "<br />");
            }

            out.println("Message content type: " + msg.getContentType() +
              "<br />");
            out.println("Message body content: " +
              (String) msg.getContent());

        } else{

            out.println(
              "<h2>The received email message was not of a text " +
                "content type.</h2>");

        }//outer if

    }//displayMessage

    private boolean check(String value){

        if(value == null || value.equals(""))
            return false;

        return true;

    }//check


}
```

The displayMessage( ) method displays each message's "from" address, the message's content type (i.e., the MIME type as in *text/plain*), and the email's content. You can get the String from a typical email message that contains just headers and the text message by calling Message.getContent( ). Getting the "from" address is a little trickier:

```
out.println("Message received from: " +
    ((InternetAddress)msg.getFrom()[0]).getAddress() +"<br />");
```

The Message.getFrom( ) method returns an array of javax.mail.Address objects. This code is designed to access the first email address, since an email is typically sent by one party to its recipient (not including those malicious spammers, of course).

The code accesses the first array member, casts the return value to a javax.mail.InternetAddress, then calls getAddress( ) on that object, which returns the String email address.

Figure 20-1 shows the servlet's return value in a browser window. Since the servlet receives its email authentication information from session attributes, the first request targets a JSP, which sets the session attributes. Then the JSP forwards the request to the MailAccessor servlet. The servlet displays each received email separated by two line breaks. In other words, the information the servlet displays about each email includes who sent the email, the mail's content type, and the content of the message itself.

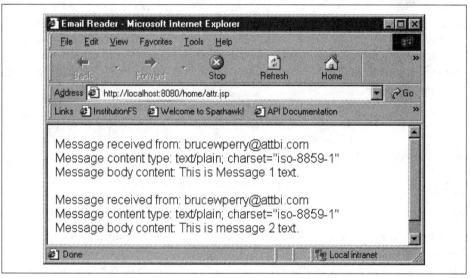

Figure 20-1. A servlet fetches and displays two email messages

See Also

Chapter 16 on setting session attributes; Chapter 25 on accessing a javax.mail. Session JNDI object on BEA WebLogic; Sun Microsystem's JavaMail API page: *http:/ /java.sun.com/products/javamail/*; Recipe 20.1 on adding JavaMail-related JARs to your web application; Recipe 20.2 on sending email using a servlet; Recipe 20.3 on sending email using a JavaBean; Recipe 20.5 on accessing email with a JavaBean; Recipe 20.6 on handling attachments in a servlet; Recipe 20.7 on adding attachments to an email message; Recipe 20.8 on reading an email's headers.

20.5 Accessing Email from a Servlet Using a JavaBean

Problem

You want to use a JavaBean or helper class to access and display email messages.

Solution

Add the `handleMessages( )` and `displayMessage( )` methods from Example 20-4 to the JavaBean class defined in Example 20-2. Then use the JavaBean from a servlet's `doGet( )` or `doPost( )` method.

Discussion

When we last encountered the `EmailBean` in Example 20-2 it contained a `sendMessage( )` method, along with several property "setter" methods (such as `setSmtpHost(String host)`). If you add the `handleMessages( )` and `displayMessage( )` methods from Example 20-4 to this same class, you can use the JavaBean to both send and access email.

 This code in `handleMessages( )` from Example 20-4 needs to be changed to include the `EmailBean` class name:

```
//static reference to a constant value
if (! check(popAddr))
    popAddr = EmailBean.DEFAULT_SERVER;
```

However, the `EmailBean` class will have grown quite large as a result of adding the two methods, so you might create two JavaBeans—one for sending mail and another for accessing it. Example 20-5 creates and uses an instance of a special email Java-Bean. You must store the bean class in the *WEB-INF/classes* directory or in a JAR file in *WEB-INF/lib*.

 Example 20-6 also shows a JavaBean that defines `handleMessages( )` and `displayMessage( )` for dealing with email attachments.

Example 20-5. A servlet uses a JavaBean to access email messages

```
public void doGet(HttpServletRequest request, HttpServletResponse response)
    throws ServletException, java.io.IOException {

    response.setContentType("text/html");
    java.io.PrintWriter out = response.getWriter( );
```

Example 20-5. A servlet uses a JavaBean to access email messages (continued)

```
out.println(
"<html><head><title>Email message sender</title></head><body>");

EmailBean emailer = new EmailBean( );
emailer.setSmtpHost("mail.attbi.com");
emailer.handleMessages(request,out);

  out.println("</body></html>");

}//doGet
```

See Also

Sun Microsystem's JavaMail API page: *http://java.sun.com/products/javamail/*;
Recipe 20.1 on adding JavaMail-related JARs to your web application; Recipe 20.2
on sending email from a servlet; Recipe 20.3 on sending email using a JavaBean;
Recipe 20.4 covering how to access email in a servlet; Recipe 20.6 on handling
attachments in a servlet; Recipe 20.7 on adding attachments to an email message;
Recipe 20.8 on reading an email's headers.

20.6 Handling Attachments from an Email Received in a Servlet

Problem

You want to read an email message and save any attachments from a servlet.

Solution

Use the JavaMail API and a special JavaBean to save the InputStreams from attached
files to a specified folder.

Discussion

Accessing email usually involves authenticating a user with a POP account, then connecting with the mail server and downloading any email messages. Example 20-6
uses the Session, Store, Folder, and Message classes from the JavaMail API to download an array of Messages from a particular user's email account. However, the servlet in Recipe 20.4 was designed to deal only with Messages whose content was of type
String (the return value of the Message.getContent( ) method).

If the Message's content is of type Multipart, then the process of handling attachments mirrors the peeling of an onion—more code is involved. Example 20-6 separates the email-related code into a JavaBean that can be used from a servlet. The

bean's displayMessage( ) method tests the content of each Message. If the content is of type Multipart, then the code examines each contained BodyPart.

Picture a Multipart message type as a container. The container's headers are like any other email message's headers (but with different values). The container encloses BodyParts, which are like messages inside of messages. Some BodyParts represent the text message accompanying a Multipart email message. Other BodyParts represent the attached files, such as a Microsoft Word file or JPEG image.

If the BodyPart's content is a String, then the bean displays the text message. Otherwise, the bean assumes the BodyPart is an attached file; it saves the file to a special *attachments* folder. You're probably already familiar with the handleMessages( ) code, so you can skip to the displayMessage( ) method, which deals with saving any file attachments.

Example 20-6. A JavaBean that handles attachments and delivers a browser message

```
package com.jspservletcookbook;

import java.io.*;
import java.util.Properties;

import javax.mail.*;
import javax.mail.internet.*;
import javax.servlet.*;
import javax.servlet.http.*;

public class AttachBean  {

    /* NOT SHOWN: private bean fields (or, properties); default variables;
       and the sendMessage method
       See Example 20-2 */

    public AttachBean( ){}

    private void handleMessages(HttpServletRequest request,
        PrintWriter out) throws IOException, ServletException {

        /* get the user and password information for a POP
           account from an HttpSession object */

        HttpSession httpSession =  request.getSession( );
        String user = (String) httpSession.getAttribute("user");
        String password = (String) httpSession.getAttribute("pass");
        String popAddr = (String) httpSession.getAttribute("pop");

        Store popStore = null;
        Folder folder = null;

        if (! check(popAddr))
```

```java
            popAddr = AttachBean.DEFAULT_SERVER;

    try {

            if ((! check(user)) || (! check(password)))
             throw new ServletException(
             "A valid username and password is required to check email.");

            Properties properties = System.getProperties( );
            Session session = Session.getDefaultInstance(properties);
            popStore = session.getStore("pop3");
            popStore.connect(popAddr, user, password);
            folder = popStore.getFolder("INBOX");
            if (! folder.exists( ))
                throw new ServletException(
                    "An 'INBOX' folder does not exist for the user.");

            folder.open(Folder.READ_ONLY);
            Message[] messages = folder.getMessages( );

            int msgLen = messages.length;
            if (msgLen == 0)
                out.println(
                    "<h2>The INBOX folder does not yet contain any " +
                    " email messages.</h2>");

            for (int i = 0; i < msgLen; i++){

                displayMessage(messages[i], out);
                out.println("<br /><br />");

            }//for

    } catch (Exception exc) {

        out.println(
        "<h2>Sorry, an error occurred while accessing " +
        "the email messages.</h2>");

        out.println(exc.toString( ));

    } finally {

        try{

            if (folder != null)
                folder.close(false);

            if (popStore != null)
                popStore.close( );

        } catch (Exception e) { }
```

```
        }
    }//handleMessages

    private void displayMessage(Message msg, PrintWriter out)
        throws MessagingException, IOException{

        if (msg != null){

            /* get the content of the message; the message could
               be an email without attachments, or an email
               with attachments. The method getContent() will return an
               instance of 'Multipart' if the msg has attachments */

            Object o = msg.getContent();

            if ( o instanceof String){

                //just display some info about the message content
                handleStringMessage(msg,(String) o, out);

            } else if ( o instanceof Multipart ) {

                //save the attachment(s) to a folder
                Multipart mpart = (Multipart) o;
                Part part = null;
                File file = null;
                FileOutputStream stream = null;
                InputStream input = null;
                String fileName = "";

                //each Multipart is made up of 'BodyParts' that
                //are of type 'Part'
                for (int i = 0; i < mpart.getCount(); i++){

                    part = mpart.getBodyPart(i);
                    Object partContent = part.getContent();

                    if (partContent instanceof String){
                        handleStringMessage(msg,(String) partContent,
                            out);

                    } else {//handle as a file attachment

                        fileName = part.getFileName();

                        if (! check(fileName)){//default file name
                            fileName = "file"+
                                new java.util.Date().getTime();}

                        //write the attachment's InputStream to a file
                        file = new File( attachFolder +
                        System.getProperty("file.separator") + fileName);
                        stream = new FileOutputstream(file);
```

```
                        input = part.getInputStream( );
                        int ch;

                        while ( (ch = input.read( )) != -1){
                           stream.write(ch);}

                     input.close( );
                     out.println(
                        "Handled attachment named: "+
                             fileName+"<br /><br />");
                  }// if
               }//for

            }//else if instanceof multipart

         } else{

            out.println(
               "<h2>The received email message returned null.</h2>");

         }// if msg != null

   }//displayMessage

   private void handleStringMessage(Part part, String emailContent,
       PrintWriter out)  throws MessagingException {

      if (part instanceof Message){
         Message msg = (Message) part;
         if (msg.getFrom( )[0] instanceof InternetAddress){

            out.println("Message received from: " +
            ((InternetAddress) msg.getFrom()[0]).getAddress( ) +
               "<br />");
         }

            out.println(
               "Message content type: " + msg.getContentType( ) +
                  "<br />");
            out.println("Message content: " + emailContent +"<br />");
      }

   }

   private boolean check(String value){

      if(value == null || value.equals(""))
         return false;

      return true;

   }//check
```

Example 20-6. A JavaBean that handles attachments and delivers a browser message (continued)

```
/* NOT SHOWN: various 'setter' methods for the bean's properties
     See Example 20-2 */

}// AttachBean
```

Once the displayMessage( ) code identifies a BodyPart as an attached file, it receives the bytes that represent the file as an InputStream. A BodyPart implements the Part interface, which defines the method getInputStream( ). The code saves the file using the InputStream and the java.io.FileOutputStream class.

Example 20-7 shows the doGet( ) method of a servlet using com.jspservletcookbook. AttachBean.

Example 20-7. A servlet's doGet() method uses a JavaBean to deal with email attachments

```
public void doGet(HttpServletRequest request,
  HttpServletResponse response)
  throws ServletException, java.io.IOException {

    response.setContentType("text/html");
    java.io.PrintWriter out = response.getWriter( );

    out.println(
    "<html><head><title>Email message sender</title></head><body>");

    AttachBean emailer = new AttachBean( );
    emailer.setSmtpHost("mail.attbi.com");
    emailer.setAttachFolder(getServletContext().getRealPath("/") + "attachments");
    emailer.handleMessages(request,out);

    out.println("</body></html>");

}//doGet
```

Figure 20-2 shows the messages that the servlet (using the JavaBean) displays in a browser. The first email is a simple text message without attachments. The second email contains two attachments; its MIME type is *multipart/mixed*.

See Also

Sun Microsystem's JavaMail API page: *http://java.sun.com/products/javamail/*; Recipe 20.1 on adding JavaMail-related JARs to your web application; Recipe 20.2 on sending email from a servlet; Recipe 20.3 on sending email using a JavaBean; Recipe 20.4 covering how to access email in a servlet; Recipe 20.5 on accessing email with a JavaBean; Recipe 20.7 on adding attachments to an email message; Recipe 20.8 on reading an email's headers.

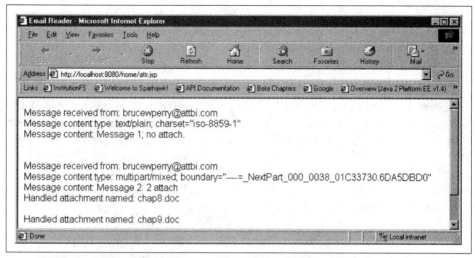

Figure 20-2. A servlet displays information about received attachments and messages

20.7 Adding Attachments to an Email in a Servlet

Problem

You want to build an email message with attachments in a servlet.

Solution

Use the JavaMail API for basic email messaging, and the the JavaBeans Activation Framework (JAF) to generate the file attachments.

Discussion

The JAF classes provide fine-grained control over setting up a file attachment for an email message.

 If you are using both the JavaMail API and the JAF, make sure to import the packages in your servlet class:

```
import javax.activation.*;
import javax.mail.*;
import javax.mail.internet.*;

//class definition continues
```

The sendMessage( ) method in Example 20-8 creates a new email message (specifically, a new javax.mail.internet.MimeMessage), adds its text message, and inserts a file attachment inside the message. The method then sends the message using the code you may have seen in Recipes 20.2 and 20.3:

```
Transport.send(mailMsg);
```

To accomplish this, the code creates a container (a javax.mail.Multipart object) and two javax.mail.BodyParts that make up the the container. The first BodyPart is a text message (used usually to describe the file attachment to the user), while the second BodyPart is the file attachment (in this case, a Microsoft Word file). Then the code sets the content of the MimeMessage to the Multipart. In a nutshell, the MimeMessage (an email message) contains a Multipart, which itself is composed of two BodyParts: the email's text message and an attached file.

 If you want to look at the headers of a MimeMessage that contains attachments, call the getAllHeaders( ) method on the MimeMessage. See Recipe 20.8 for details.

Example 20-8. Making email attachment in a servlets

```
package com.jspservletcookbook;

import java.io.*;
import java.util.Properties;

import javax.activation.*;
import javax.mail.*;
import javax.mail.internet.*;

import javax.servlet.*;
import javax.servlet.http.*;

public class EmailAttachServlet extends HttpServlet {

    //default value for mail server address, in case the user
    //doesn't provide one
    private final static String DEFAULT_SERVER = "mail.attbi.com";

    public void doPost(HttpServletRequest request,
      HttpServletResponse response) throws ServletException,
        java.io.IOException {

        response.setContentType("text/html");
        java.io.PrintWriter out = response.getWriter( );
        out.println(
          "<html><head><title>Email message sender</title></head><body>");

        String smtpServ = request.getParameter("smtp");
        if (smtpServ == null || smtpServ.equals(""))
          smtpServ = DEFAULT_SERVER;
```

Example 20-8. Making email attachment in a servlets (continued)

```
        String from = request.getParameter("from");
        String to = request.getParameter("to");
        String subject = request.getParameter("subject");

        try {
            sendMessage(smtpServ, to, from, subject);
        } catch (Exception e) {
            throw new ServletException(e.getMessage( ));
        }
        out.println(
            "<H2>Your attachment has been sent.</H2>");
        out.println("</body></html>");

}//doPost

public void doGet(HttpServletRequest request,
    HttpServletResponse response) throws ServletException,
        java.io.IOException {

    doPost(request,response);

}//doGet

private void sendMessage(String smtpServ, String to, String from,
    String subject) throws Exception {

    Multipart multipart = null;
    BodyPart bpart1 = null;
    BodyPart bpart2 = null;

    Properties properties = System.getProperties( );

    //populate the 'Properties' object with the mail
    //server address, so that the default 'Session'
    //instance can use it.
    properties.put("mail.smtp.host", smtpServ);

    Session session = Session.getDefaultInstance(properties);
    Message mailMsg = new MimeMessage(session);//a new email message
    InternetAddress[] addresses = null;

    try {

        if (to != null) {

            //throws 'AddressException' if the 'to' email address
            //violates RFC822 syntax
            addresses = InternetAddress.parse(to, false);

            mailMsg.setRecipients(Message.RecipientType.TO, addresses);

        } else {
```

Example 20-8. Making email attachment in a servlets (continued)

```
        throw new MessagingException(
            "The mail message requires a 'To' address.");
    }

    if (from != null) {
        mailMsg.setFrom(new InternetAddress(from));
    } else {

        throw new MessagingException(
            "The mail message requires a valid 'From' address.");
    }

    if (subject != null)
      mailMsg.setSubject(subject);

    //This email message's content is a 'Multipart' type
    //The MIME type for the message's content is 'multipart/mixed'
    multipart = new MimeMultipart( );

    //The text part of this multipart email message
    bpart1 = new MimeBodyPart( );

    String textPart =
    "Hello, just thought you'd be interested in this Word file.";

    // create the DataHandler object for the text part
    DataHandler data = new DataHandler(textPart, "text/plain");

    //set the text BodyPart's DataHandler
    bpart1.setDataHandler(data);

    //add the text BodyPart to the Multipart container
    multipart.addBodyPart( bpart1);

    //create the BodyPart that represents the attached Word file
    bpart2 = new MimeBodyPart( );

    //create the DataHandler that points to a File
    FileDataSource fds = new FileDataSource( new File(
    "h:/book/chapters/chap1/chap1.doc") );

    //Make sure that the attached file is handled as
    //the appropriate MIME type: application/msword here
    MimetypesFileTypeMap ftm = new MimetypesFileTypeMap( );

    //the syntax here is the MIME type followed by
    //space separated extensions
    ftm.addMimeTypes("application/msword doc DOC" );

    fds.setFileTypeMap(ftm);
    //The DataHandler is instantiated with the
    //FileDataSource we just created
```

Example 20-8. Making email attachment in a servlets (continued)

```
            DataHandler fileData = new DataHandler( fds );

            //the BodyPart will contain the word processing file
            bpart2.setDataHandler(fileData);

            //add the second BodyPart, the one containing the attachment, to
            //the Multipart object
            multipart.addBodyPart( bpart2 );

            //finally, set the content of the MimeMessage to the
            //Multipart object
            mailMsg.setContent( multipart );

            // send the mail message; throws a 'SendFailedException'
            //if any of the message's recipients have an invalid adress
            Transport.send(mailMsg);


        } catch (Exception exc) {

            throw exc;

        }//try

    }//sendMessage

}//EmailAttachServlet
```

The comments in Example 20-8 explain what happens when you use the javax. activation classes to create a file attachment of the intended MIME type. The most confusing part is creating a javax.activation.FileDataSource that points to the file that you want to attach to the email message. The code uses the FileDataSource to instantiate the javax.activation.DataHandler, which is responsible for the content of the file attachment.

```
//create the DataHandler that points to a File
FileDataSource fds = new FileDataSource( new File(
  "h:/book/chapters/chap1/chap1.doc") );
```

Make sure that the MimeMessage identifies the attached file as a MIME type of *application/msword*, so that the user's email application can try to handle the attachment as a Microsoft Word file. Set the FileTypeMap of the FileDataSource with the following code:

```
//Make sure that the attached file is handled as
//the appropriate MIME type: application/msword here
MimetypesFileTypeMap ftm = new MimetypesFileTypeMap( );

//the syntax here is the MIME type followed by
//space separated extensions
ftm.addMimeTypes("application/msword doc DOC" );

fds.setFileTypeMap(ftm);
```

A `MimetypesFileTypeMap` is a class that associates MIME types (like *application/ msword*) with file extensions such as *.doc*.

 Make sure you associate the correct MIME type with the file that you are sending as an attachment, since you explicitly make this association in the code. See *http://java.sun.com/j2ee/1.4/docs/api/javax/ activation/MimetypesFileTypeMap.html* for further details.

Then the code performs the following steps:

1. Creates a `DataHandler` by passing this `FileDataSource` in as a constructor parameter.

2. Sets the content of the `BodyPart` with that `DataHandler`.

3. Adds the `BodyPart` to the `Multipart` object (which in turn represents the content of the email message).

See Also

Sun Microsystem's JavaMail API page: *http://java.sun.com/products/javamail/*; the JAF web page: *http://java.sun.com/products/javabeans/glasgow/jaf.html*; Recipe 20.1 on adding JavaMail-related JARs to your web application; Recipe 20.2 on sending email from a servlet; Recipe 20.3 on sending email using a JavaBean; Recipe 20.4 covering how to access email in a servlet; Recipe 20.5 on accessing email with a JavaBean; Recipe 20.6 on handling attachments in a servlet; Recipe 20.8 on reading an email's headers.

20.8   Reading a Received Email's Headers from a Servlet

Problem

You want to read the headers from an email in a servlet.

Solution

Use the JavaMail API to access each email message. Call the `getAllHeaders()` method of the `Part` interface, then iterate through the `Enumeration` return value to get the name and value of each header.

Discussion

An advanced email program, such as a spam filter, is designed to examine an email's headers, not just its message and file attachments.

A header is composed of a name, a colon character (:), and a value. The headers provide details about the email message, such as who sent the message and the mail server(s) that handled the message during its network travels. An example header is:

```
To: <bwperry@parkerriver.com>
```

The JavaMail API makes it easy to list an email's headers. The `Message` object has a `getAllHeaders( )` method (via the `Part` interface that the `Message` class implements). This method returns a `java.util.Enumeration`, holding a collection of `javax.mail.Header` objects. To get the header name and value from these `Header` objects, just call their `getName( )` and `getValue( )` methods.

The `Part` interface also has a `getHeader(String headerName)` method that you can use to obtain the value for a particular header. This method returns a `String` array containing the value(s) for the header of that name.

Example 20-9 shows the same servlet from Recipe 20.4, revised to list both the message contents and the header values. The header-related code appears in the `displayMessage( )` method.

Example 20-9. A servlet displays email header names and values

```java
package com.jspservletcookbook;

import java.io.IOException;
import java.io.PrintWriter;

import java.util.Properties;
import java.util.Enumeration;

import javax.mail.*;
import javax.mail.internet.*;
import javax.servlet.*;
import javax.servlet.http.*;

public class HeaderAccessor extends HttpServlet {

    private final static String DEFAULT_SERVER = "mail.attbi.com";

    public void doGet(HttpServletRequest request,
        HttpServletResponse response) throws ServletException,
        java.io.IOException {

        response.setContentType("text/html");
        java.io.PrintWriter out = response.getWriter();
        out.println("<html><head><title>Email Reader</title></head><body>");

        handleMessages(request, out);
```

Example 20-9. A servlet displays email header names and values (continued)

```
    out.println("</body></html>");
} //doGet

private void handleMessages(HttpServletRequest request,
    PrintWriter out) throws IOException, ServletException {

    HttpSession httpSession =  request.getSession( );
    String user = (String) httpSession.getAttribute("user");
    String password = (String) httpSession.getAttribute("pass");
    String popAddr = (String) httpSession.getAttribute("pop");
    Store popStore = null;
    Folder folder = null;

    if (! check(popAddr))
        popAddr = HeaderAccessor.DEFAULT_SERVER;

    try {

        if ((! check(user)) || (! check(password)))
            throw new ServletException(
            "A valid username and password is required to check email.");

        Properties properties = System.getProperties( );
        Session session = Session.getDefaultInstance(properties);
        popStore = session.getStore("pop3");
        popStore.connect(popAddr, user, password);
        folder = popStore.getFolder("INBOX");
        if (! folder.exists( ))
            throw new ServletException(
            "An 'INBOX' folder does not exist for the user.");

        folder.open(Folder.READ_ONLY);
        Message[] messages = folder.getMessages( );
        int msgLen = messages.length;

        if (msgLen == 0)
            out.println(
            "<h2>The INBOX folder does not yet contain any " +
            "email messages.</h2>");

        for (int i = 0; i < msgLen; i++){

            displayMessage(messages[i], out);
            out.println("<br /><br />");

        }//for

    } catch (Exception exc) {

        out.println(
          "<h2>Sorry, an error occurred while accessing the " +
          "email messages.</h2>");
```

Example 20-9. A servlet displays email header names and values (continued)

```
        out.println(exc.toString( ));

    } finally {

        try{

            if (folder != null)
                folder.close(false);

    if (popStore != null)
            popStore.close( );

        } catch (Exception e) { }
    }
}//handleMessages

    private void displayMessage(Message msg, PrintWriter out)
        throws MessagingException, IOException{

        if (msg != null && msg.getContent( ) instanceof String){

            if (msg.getFrom( )[0] instanceof InternetAddress){

                out.println(
                "Message received from: " +
                ((InternetAddress)msg.getFrom()[0]).getAddress( ) +"<br />");
            }
            out.println("Message content type: " + msg.getContentType( ) +
              "<br />");
            out.println(
              "Message body content: " + (String) msg.getContent( ));

            //List each of the email headers using a ul tag
            out.println("<ul>");
            Header head = null;
            Enumeration headers = msg.getAllHeaders( );

            while ( headers.hasMoreElements( ) ){
                head = (Header) headers.nextElement( );
                out.println(
                  "<li>" + head.getName() + ": " + head.getValue( )+ "</li>");
            }//while

            out.println("</ul>");

        } else{

            out.println(
              "<h2>The received email message was not " +
              "a text content type.</h2>");
        }
```

Example 20-9. A servlet displays email header names and values (continued)

```
    }//displayMessage

    private boolean check(String value){

        if(value == null || value.equals(""))
        return false;

        return true;
    }
}
```

Figure 20-3 shows the browser display of the servlet in Example 20-9. Each of the headers is preceded by a bullet character, followed by the header name, a colon, and the header value.

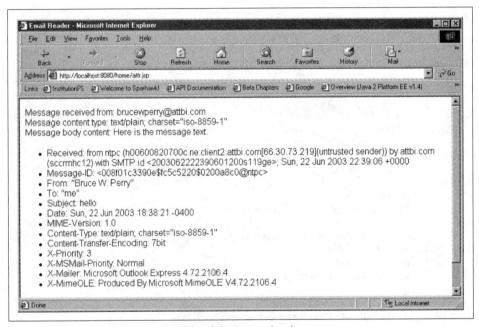

Figure 20-3. A servlet accesses an email and displays its headers

See Also

Sun Microsystem's JavaMail API page: *http://java.sun.com/products/javamail/*; Recipe 20.1 on adding JavaMail-related JARs to your web application; Recipe 20.2 on sending email from a servlet; Recipe 20.3 on sending email using a JavaBean; Recipe 20.4 covering how to access email in a servlet; Recipe 20.5 on accessing email with a JavaBean; Recipe 20.6 on handling attachments in a servlet; Recipe 20.7 on adding attachments to an email message.

CHAPTER 21

Accessing Databases

21.0 Introduction

If you are a Java web developer who has never written database-related code, I have some advice for you: don't hold your breath until you receive this type of assignment!

These recipes show you how to access a database resource by using a Java Naming and Directory Interface (JNDI) lookup, which is the most efficient (and probably the most common) method of accessing database resources in a portable manner. JNDI is a Java API that is designed to store objects in a hierarchical tree structure, similar to a filesystem composed of directories, subdirectories, and files. Servlets and JSPs can then use the methods of the JNDI API (shown by several examples in this chapter) to obtain references from Java objects, such as JavaBeans, and use them in their programs.

For database code, this usually means javax.sql.DataSource objects, which are factories for database connections. The DataSources provide "connection pools," another very important web database tool. Connection pools are groups of database connections shared by servlets, JSPs, and other classes. Application servers such as WebLogic usually allow you to determine how many connections are stored in the pool, which database table can be used by the server to automatically test a connection to determine if it is fit to be returned to the shared pool, and other pool properties.

These recipes explain the basics of setting up a connection pool on both Tomcat and WebLogic.

The recipes also cover some other practical database topics, such as how to call stored procedures in servlets and JSPs, as well as how to include more than one Structured Query Language (SQL) statement in a transaction.

21.1 Accessing a Database from a Servlet Without DataSource

Problem

You want to access a database from a servlet without a DataSource configuration for the database.

Solution

Use the Java Database Connectivity (JDBC) API to access a java.sql.Connection object that connects the servlet with the database.

Discussion

On occasion, developers require a quick, less elegant solution to accessing a database. This recipe explains how to use the java.sql.DriverManager class to obtain a connection to a datasource in a servlet. The DriverManager class communicates with a database driver, which is software that allows Java code to interact with a particular database, such as MySQL or Oracle.

 The preferred design is to use a javax.sql.Datasource to get a database connection from a connection pool, as described in Recipes 21.2–21.6

Example 21-1 accomplishes this task in its doGet( ) service method.

Example 21-1. A servlet accesses a database using the JDBC API

```
package com.jspservletcookbook;

import java.sql.*;

import javax.servlet.*;
import javax.servlet.http.*;

public class DatabaseServlet extends HttpServlet {

  public void doGet(HttpServletRequest request,
     HttpServletResponse response) throws ServletException,
       java.io.IOException {

       String sql = "select * from athlete";

       Connection conn = null;

       Statement stmt = null;
```

```java
ResultSet rs = null;

ResultSetMetaData rsm = null;

response.setContentType("text/html");
java.io.PrintWriter out = response.getWriter( );

out.println(
    "<html><head><title>Servlet Database Access</title></head><body>");

out.println("<h2>Database info</h2>");
out.println("<table border='1'><tr>");

try{

    //load the database driver
    Class.forName ("oracle.jdbc.driver.OracleDriver");

    //The JDBC URL for this Oracle database
    String url = "jdbc:oracle:thin:@192.168.0.2:1521:ORCL";

    //Create the java.sql.Connection to the database, using the
    //correct username and password
    conn = DriverManager.getConnection(url,"scott", "tiger");

    //Create a statement for executing some SQL
    stmt = conn.createStatement( );

    //Execute the SQL statement
    rs = stmt.executeQuery(sql);

    //Get info about the return value in the form of
    //a ResultSetMetaData object
    rsm = rs.getMetaData( );

    int colCount =  rsm.getColumnCount( );

    //print column names in table header cells
    for (int i = 1; i <=colCount; ++i){

        out.println("<th>" + rsm.getColumnName(i) + "</th>");

    }

    out.println("</tr>");

    while( rs.next( )){

        out.println("<tr>");

        //print the values for each column
```

```
              for (int i = 1;  i <=colCount; ++i)
                  out.println("<td>" + rs.getString(i) + "</td>");

              out.println("</tr>");

          }

      } catch (Exception e){

          throw new ServletException(e.getMessage( ));

      } finally {

          try{

              //this will close any associated ResultSets
              if(stmt != null)
                  stmt.close( );

              if (conn != null)
                  conn.close( );

          } catch (SQLException sqle){ }

      }//finally

      out.println("</table><br><br>");

      out.println("</body>");
      out.println("</html>");


  } //doGet
}
```

Here are the steps needed to run a servlet, as shown in Example 21-1:

1. Take the JAR file that contains your database driver, and store it either in a common server directory, such as Tomcat's *<Tomcat-root>/common/lib* directory or in the *WEB-INF/lib* directory of your web application.

> Change the extension of the Oracle JDBC driver (such as *classes12.zip*) to *.jar*, so that the Java classes that it contains can be loaded properly into the JVM.

2. Derive the database URL from vendor literature, and the username and password for the database from a database administrator (that might be you!) or other appropriate means. The code will not be able to access the database without a valid username and password.

The downside of this approach is that you are mixing up sensitive database security information with servlet code. It makes more sense to adopt the strategies that the upcoming five recipes describe, beginning with Recipe 21.2, "Configuring a DataSource in Tomcat."

Figure 21-1 shows the result of running this servlet.

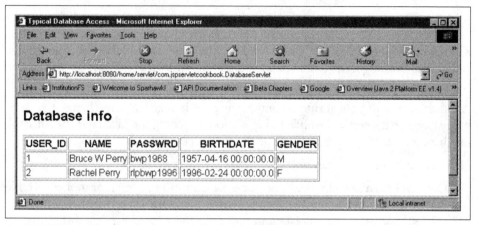

Figure 21-1. A servlet that displays some database information

 Chapter 23 on the JSTL shows how to use a JSP to access a database without a DataSource configuration.

See Also

The JDBC specification: *http://java.sun.com/products/jdbc/download.html*; Recipes 21.2–21.6 on configuring and using DataSources on Tomcat and WebLogic; Recipes 21.7 and 21.8 on calling stored procedures from servlets and JSPs; Recipe 21.9 on converting a java.sql.ResultSet object to a javax.servlet.jsp.jstl.sql Result; Recipes 21.10 and 21.11 on using transactions in servlets and JSPs; Recipe 21.12 on finding out information about a ResultSet.

21.2   Configuring a DataSource in Tomcat

Problem

You want to configure a javax.sql.DataSource for use in a servlet with the Tomcat web container.

Solution

Create a resource element in Tomcat's *server.xml* file and an associated `resource-ref` element in the *web.xml* deployment descriptor.

Discussion

Tomcat makes it easy to set up a connection pool so that servlets and JSPs can efficiently share database connections. In web sites that have many simultaneous users, a connection pool improves efficiency by sharing existing database connections, rather than creating a new connection and tearing it down every time an application has to use the database.

Another benefit of configuring a connection pool is that you can change the database system that a servlet or JSP is using without touching the Java code, because the database resource is configured outside of the servlet or JSP.

Here are the steps for configuring a `DataSource` with Tomcat:

1. Create a `Resource` and a `ResourceParams` element in *server.xml*, or in the XML file that you have placed in Tomcat's *webapps* directory. These elements describe the JNDI object you are creating in order to provide your servlets or JSPs with a `DataSource`.

2. Add a `resource-ref` element to *web.xml*, which allows the components in the associated web application to access the configured `DataSource`.

Example 21-2 shows the `Resource` and a `ResourceParams` elements in *server.xml*. This example describes a `DataSource` that connects with an Oracle 8*i* database.

Example 21-2. The resource element in server.xml

```
<Resource name="jdbc/oracle-8i-athletes" scope=
  "Shareable" type="javax.sql.DataSource" auth=
    "Container" description="Home Oracle 8i Personal Edition"/>

  <ResourceParams name="jdbc/oracle-8i-athletes">

    <parameter>
        <name>driverClassName</name>
        <value>oracle.jdbc.driver.OracleDriver</value>
    </parameter>

    <parameter>
        <name>url</name>
        <value>jdbc:oracle:thin:@192.168.0.2:1521:ORCL</value>
    </parameter>

    <parameter>
        <name>username</name>
        <value>scott</value>
```

Example 21-2. The resource element in server.xml (continued)

```
        </parameter>

        <parameter>
            <name>password</name>
            <value>tiger</value>
        </parameter>

</ResourceParams>
```

Create a `Resource` and `ResourceParams` element for each database that your application uses. Example 21-3 shows the `resource-ref` element associated with the Resource specified by Example 21-2.

Example 21-3. A resource-ref element specifies a DataSource in web.xml

```
<!-- top of web.xml file -->
<resource-ref>

    <res-ref-name>jdbc/oracle-8i-athletes</res-ref-name>

    <res-type>javax.sql.DataSource</res-type>

    <res-auth>Container</res-auth>

</resource-ref>
<!-- rest of web.xml file -->
```

The JNDI path to this `DataSource`, which you use in a JNDI lookup (see the next recipe), is *jdbc/oracle-8i-athletes*.

 The servlet 2.4 API does not require the *web.xml* elements such as resource-ref to appear in a specific order. The servlet 2.3 API specifies the order these elements must appear in with a Document Type Definition (DTD). See Chapter 1.

See Also

The JDBC specification: *http://java.sun.com/products/jdbc/download.html*; Recipe 21.3 on using a DataSource in a servlet with Tomcat; Recipes 21.4–21.6 on configuring and using DataSources with servlets and JSPs on WebLogic; Recipes 21.7 and 21.8 on calling stored procedures from servlets and JSPs; Recipe 21.9 on converting a `java.sql.ResultSet` object to a `javax.servlet.jsp.jstl.sql` `Result`; Recipes 21.10 and 21.11 on using transactions in servlets and JSPs; Recipe 21.12 on finding out information about a `ResultSet`.

21.3 Using a DataSource in a Servlet with Tomcat

Problem

You want to use a DataSource that you have configured with Tomcat.

Solution

Use the JNDI API classes to obtain the DataSource, then access a database connection from that DataSource.

Discussion

Use classes from the javax.naming package to access the configured DataSource. For example, use a javax.naming.InitialContext object to look up a DataSource that has been bound as a JNDI object.

 The javax.naming package is a part of the Java Platform Standard Edition 1.3 and 1.4.

Example 21-4 instantiates a javax.sql.DataSource instance variable in its init( ) method, which the servlet container calls when it creates a servlet instance. In Tomcat, JNDI objects are stored under the root level specified by the "java:comp/env" string.

Example 21-4. Using a DataSource in a servlet

```java
package com.jspservletcookbook;

import java.sql.*;

import javax.naming.Context;
import javax.naming.InitialContext;
import javax.naming.NamingException;
import javax.sql.*;

import javax.servlet.*;
import javax.servlet.http.*;

public class DbServlet extends HttpServlet {

    DataSource pool;


    public void init( ) throws ServletException {
```

Example 21-4. Using a DataSource in a servlet (continued)

```java
        Context env = null;

        try{

            env = (Context) new InitialContext( ).lookup("java:comp/env");

            //Look up a DataSource, which represents a connection pool
            pool = (DataSource) env.lookup("jdbc/oracle-8i-athletes");

            if (pool == null)
                throw new ServletException(
                "'oracle-8i-athletes' is an unknown DataSource");

        } catch (NamingException ne) {

            throw new ServletException(ne.getMessage( ));

        }//try


    }

    public void doGet(HttpServletRequest request,
      HttpServletResponse response)
      throws ServletException, java.io.IOException {

        String sql = "select * from athlete";

        Connection conn = null;

        Statement stmt = null;

        ResultSet rs = null;

        ResultSetMetaData rsm = null;

        //Start building the HTML page
        response.setContentType("text/html");
        java.io.PrintWriter out = response.getWriter( );
        out.println(
        "<html><head><title>Typical Database Access</title></head><body>");

        out.println("<h2>Database info</h2>");
        out.println("<table border='1'><tr>");

        try{

            //Get a Connection from the connection pool
            conn = pool.getConnection( );

            //Create a Statement object that can be used to execute
```

Example 21-4. Using a DataSource in a servlet (continued)

```
        //a SQL query
        stmt = conn.createStatement();

        //execute a simple SELECT query
        rs = stmt.executeQuery(sql);

        //Get the ResultSetMetaData object so we can dynamically
        //display the column names in the ResultSet
        rsm = rs.getMetaData();

        int colCount = rsm.getColumnCount();

        //print column names in table header cells
        for (int i = 1; i <=colCount; ++i){

            out.println("<th>" + rsm.getColumnName(i) + "</th>");
        }

        out.println("</tr>");

        //while the ResultSet has more rows...

        while( rs.next()){

            out.println("<tr>");

            //Print each column value for each row with the
            //ResultSet.getString() method
            for (int i = 1;  i <=colCount; ++i)
                out.println("<td>" + rs.getString(i) + "</td>");

            out.println("</tr>");

        }//while

} catch (Exception e){

    throw new ServletException(e.getMessage());

} finally {

    try{

        //When a Statement object is closed, any associated
        //ResultSet is closed
        if (stmt != null)
            stmt.close();

        //VERY IMPORTANT! This code returns the Connection to the
        //pool
        if (conn != null)
            conn.close();
```

Example 21-4. Using a DataSource in a servlet (continued)

```
        } catch (SQLException sqle){ }

    }
        out.println("</table></body></html>");

    }//doGet
}
```

Example 21-4 gets a DataSource by using the address configured in Tomcat (Recipe 21.2; *jdbc/oracle-8i-athletes*) in a JNDI lookup. This code looks like this:

```
env = (Context) new InitialContext( ).lookup("java:comp/env");

//Look up a DataSource, which represents a connection pool
pool = (DataSource) env.lookup("jdbc/oracle-8i-athletes");
```

The code then obtains a database connection from the connection pool by calling the DataSource object's getConnection( ) method. It is very important to call the Connection object's close( ) method when the servlet is finished with it, because this method call returns the shared Connection to the pool.

Requesting the servlet of Example 21-4 in a browser creates output that looks just like Figure 21-1.

Chapter 23 on the JSTL shows how to use a JSP to access a database with a DataSource configuration.

See Also

The JDBC specification: *http://java.sun.com/products/jdbc/download.html*; Recipe 21.1 on accessing a database from a servlet without a connection pool; Recipe 21.2 on configuring a DataSource on Tomcat; Recipes 21.4–21.6 on configuring and using DataSource with servlets and JSPs on WebLogic; Recipes 21.7 and 21.8 on calling stored procedures from servlets and JSPs; Recipe 21.9 on converting a java.sql. ResultSet object to a javax.servlet.jsp.jstl.sql Result; Recipes 21.10 and 21.11 on using transactions in servlets and JSPs; Recipe 21.12 on finding out information about a ResultSet.

21.4 Creating a DataSource on WebLogic

Problem

You want to create a javax.sql.DataSource on BEA WebLogic for use in your servlets.

Solution

Use the WebLogic console to configure a new connection pool, then configure a new `DataSource` associated with that pool.

Discussion

Configuring a WebLogic `DataSource` involves the following steps:

1. Login to the WebLogic console, which allows you to manage the WebLogic server from a browser. The URL for the console is typically *http://<localhost:7001>/console* (substitute your host name for "localhost" and the port number that matches your own WebLogic configuration).

2. Click on *Your-domain-name* → Services → JDBC → Connnection Pools on the menu tree in the console's lefthand column. Then click on "Configure a new JDBC Connection Pool...".

3. In the resulting window, enter a name for the connection pool, the JDBC URL (e.g., *jdbc:oracle:thin:@192.168.0.2:1521:ORCL*), the `Driver` class name (e.g., `oracle.jdbc.driver.OracleDriver`), as well as the username and password in the "Properties" text field. Figure 21-2 shows a configured connection pool named "OraclePool." Remember this name—you'll need it to configure a `DataSource` further along in the process.

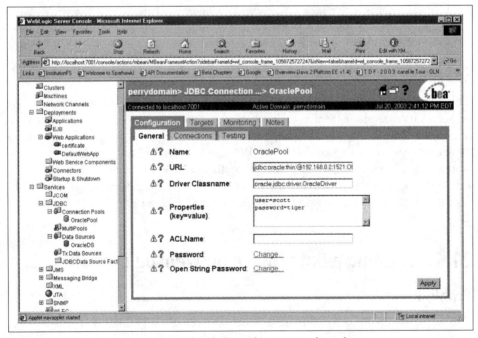

Figure 21-2. Creating a connection pool with the WebLogic console application

4. Click on the "Create" button in this window to create the connection pool, then choose the "Targets" tab. The resulting screen allows you to choose a server to which the connection pool will apply. After you have chosen the server, click on the "Apply" button in the Targets screen. The name of the new pool should appear in the lefthand menu frame.

5. Click on *Your-domain-name* → Services → JDBC → Data Sources and click on the URL "Configure a New JDBC Data Source...". Figure 21-3 shows a DataSource configuration window that includes the DataSource name ("oracle-8i-athletes") under which WebLogic will bind the DataSource as a JNDI object. The window also has a text field where you must enter the name of the connection pool that you just configured: "OraclePool." Click the "Create" button to create the new DataSource. Figure 21-3 shows the JDBC Data Sources window.

6. Take the same steps as in step 4 with the "Targets" screen to apply this DataSource to the appropriate server. Painless, right?

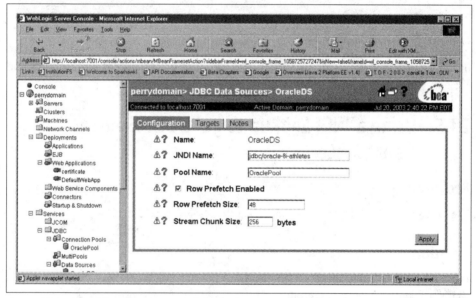

Figure 21-3. Creating a DataSource with the WebLogic console application

Figure 21-4 shows the WebLogic JNDI tree where the DataSource that you have just created is bound.

See Also

The JDBC specification: *http://java.sun.com/products/jdbc/download.html*; Chapter 2 on deploying servlets and JSPs on WebLogic; Recipes 21.2 and 21.3 on using a

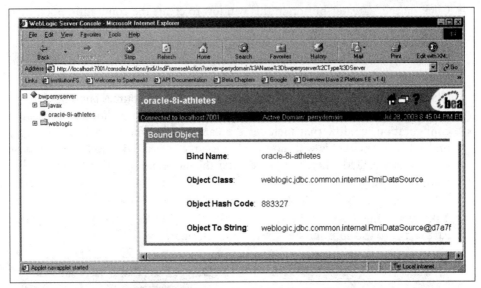

Figure 21-4. A view of the WebLogic JNDI tree containing the DataSource

DataSource on Tomcat; Recipes 21.5 and 21.6 on using DataSources with servlets and JSPs on WebLogic.

21.5 Using a JNDI Lookup to get a DataSource from WebLogic

Problem

You want to use a JNDI lookup to access a WebLogic DataSource.

Solution

Use the JNDI API and the classes in the javax.naming package to get the JNDI object that you have bound on WebLogic.

Discussion

Accessing a Connection from a WebLogic DataSource and connection pool uses similar Java code compared with Tomcat.

1. Set up the connection pool and DataSource by following Recipe 21.4's instructions.

2. In the servlet code, get the DataSource by using a JNDI lookup. This involves creating an instance of a javax.naming.InitialContext and then calling its lookup( )
method with the name that you gave your DataSource (Recipe 21.4).

3. Get a Connection from the DataSource by calling the DataSource's
getConnection( ) method.

Example 21-5 creates an instance of an InitialContext by passing in a Hashtable that
contains some property values.

Example 21-5. A servlet that uses a WebLogic connection pool

```
package com.jspservletcookbook;

import java.util.Hashtable;

import java.sql.*;

import javax.naming.Context;
import javax.naming.InitialContext;
import javax.naming.NamingException;
import javax.sql.*;

import javax.servlet.*;
import javax.servlet.http.*;

public class WeblogicDbServlet extends HttpServlet {

 DataSource pool;


  public void init( ) throws ServletException {

        Context env = null;

        Hashtable ht = new Hashtable( );

        //Create property names/values that will be passed to
        //the InitialContext constructor

        ht.put(Context.INITIAL_CONTEXT_FACTORY,
          "weblogic.jndi.WLInitialContextFactory");

        // t3://localhost:7001 is the default value
        //Add your own value if necessary:
        // ht.put(Context.PROVIDER_URL,"t3://localhost:7001");

      try {

         env = new InitialContext(ht);

         pool = (javax.sql.DataSource) env.lookup (
           "oracle-8i-athletes");
```

Example 21-5. A servlet that uses a WebLogic connection pool (continued)

```
        if (pool == null)
            throw new ServletException(
                "'oracle-8i-athletes' is an unknown DataSource");

    } catch (NamingException ne) {

        throw new ServletException(ne);

    }

  }

  public void doGet(HttpServletRequest request,
    HttpServletResponse response)
      throws ServletException, java.io.IOException {

      String sql = "select * from athlete";

      Connection conn = null;
      Statement stmt = null;
      ResultSet rs = null;
      ResultSetMetaData rsm = null;

      response.setContentType("text/html");

      java.io.PrintWriter out = response.getWriter( );

      out.println(
      "<html><head><title>Weblogic Database Access</title></head><body>");

      out.println("<h2>Database info</h2>");
      out.println("<table border='1'><tr>");

      try{

          conn = pool.getConnection( );

          stmt = conn.createStatement( );

          rs = stmt.executeQuery(sql);

          rsm = rs.getMetaData( );

          int colCount =  rsm.getColumnCount( );

          //print column names
          for (int i = 1; i <=colCount; ++i){

              out.println("<th>" + rsm.getColumnName(i) + "</th>");
          }
```

Example 21-5. A servlet that uses a WebLogic connection pool (continued)

```
        out.println("</tr>");

        while( rs.next( )){

            out.println("<tr>");

            for (int i = 1;  i <=colCount; ++i)
                out.println("<td>" + rs.getString(i) + "</td>");

            out.println("</tr>");
            }

    } catch (Exception e){

        throw new ServletException(e.getMessage( ));

    } finally {

        try{

            if (stmt != null)
                stmt.close( );

            //RETURN THE CONNECTION TO THE POOL!
            if (conn != null)
                conn.close( );

        } catch (SQLException sqle){ }

        }
    out.println("</table></body></html>");

    } //doGet

}
```

Once you have accessed a Connection from the WebLogic connection pool, the code can execute various SQL statements in order to interact with the associated database. Always call the Connection's close( ) method when you are finished with the Connection, because this method call returns the shared Connection to the pool.

 Example 21-5 cannot work without a properly configured connection pool and DataSource, which is very easy to do with the WebLogic console (as explained in Recipe 21.4).

The servlet output looks just like Figure 21-1, except for the different URL in the web browser's address field (*http://localhost:7001/dbServlet*).

See Also

The JDBC specification: *http://java.sun.com/products/jdbc/download.html*; Recipe 21.1 on accessing a database from a servlet without a connection pool; Recipes 21.2 and 21.3 on using a DataSource on Tomcat; Recipe 21.6 on using a DataSource with a JSP on WebLogic; Recipes 21.7 and 21.8 on calling stored procedures from servlets and JSPs; Recipe 21.9 on converting a java.sql.ResultSet object to a javax.servlet.jsp. jstl.sql Result; Recipes 21.10 and 21.11 on using transactions in servlets and JSPs; Recipe 21.12 on finding out information about a ResultSet.

21.6   Using a DataSource from WebLogic in a JSP

Problem

You want to use the javax.sql.DataSource that you set up on WebLogic in a JSP.

Solution

Use JSP scriptlets to access the DataSource with a JNDI lookup, then use the JDBC API in the scriptlets to access the database.

Discussion

The JSP in Example 21-6 transplants code from a servlet inside of HTML template text. The JSP uses *scriptlets*, which contain Java code within "<% %>" characters.

 JSTL SQL tags are preferable to scriptlets in a JSP; however, the JSTL implementation I use for this book's examples cannot access a DataSource from WebLogic's JNDI implementation. See Recipe 23.6 for an example that uses the JSTL SQL tags with a Tomcat DataSource.

Example 21-6 imports the necessary classes at the top of the code using the page directive and its import attribute. Otherwise, this JSP accomplishes everything that the servlet of the prior recipe does, including the display of nearly identical output in the web browser (see Figure 21-1 in Recipe 21.1).

Example 21-6. Using a JSP scriptlet to access a WebLogic DataSource

```
<%@ page import="java.util.Hashtable,java.sql.*,javax.naming.*,javax.sql.*" %>

<html>
<head><title>Database Query in WebLogic</title></head>
<body>
<h2>Querying a database with a JSP in WebLogic</h2>

<%
```

Example 21-6. Using a JSP scriptlet to access a WebLogic DataSource (continued)

```
    Context env = null;

    DataSource pool = null;

    Hashtable ht = new Hashtable( );

    ht.put(Context.INITIAL_CONTEXT_FACTORY,
      "weblogic.jndi.WLInitialContextFactory");

    ht.put(Context.PROVIDER_URL,"t3://localhost:7001");

    env = new InitialContext(ht);

    //Lookup this DataSouce at the top level of the WebLogic JNDI tree
    pool = (DataSource) env.lookup ("oracle-8i-athletes");

    String sql = "select * from athlete";

    Connection conn = null;
    Statement stmt = null;
    ResultSet rs = null;
    ResultSetMetaData rsm = null; %>

<table border='1'><tr>

  <%
    try{
            //get a java.sql.Connection from the pool
            conn = pool.getConnection( );

            stmt = conn.createStatement( );//create a java.sql.Statement

            //execute a SQL statement,generating  a ResultSet
            rs = stmt.executeQuery(sql);

            rsm = rs.getMetaData( );

            int colCount =  rsm.getColumnCount( );

            //print column names
            for (int i = 1; i <=colCount; ++i) { %>

              <th><%=rsm.getColumnName(i)%> </th>

        <% } %>

        </tr>

        <% while( rs.next( )){ %>

            <tr>
```

```
<%      for (int i = 1;  i <=colCount; ++i) { %>
    <td>     <%= rs.getString(i) %> </td>
<%}//for %>
        </tr>
<%} //while

} catch (Exception e) {

    throw new JspException(e.getMessage( ));

} finally {

  try{

    stmt.close( );
    conn.close( );

  } catch (SQLException sqle){ }

}                 %>

</body>
</html>
```

After making sure that you have properly configured the connection pool and DataSource in the WebLogic console, view this JSP's output by copying it to WebLogic's default web application, then request a URL in your browser that looks like this one: *http://localhost:7001/sqlWeblogic.jsp*.

See Also

The JDBC specification: *http://java.sun.com/products/jdbc/download.html*; Chapter 2 on deploying servlets and JSPs on WebLogic; Recipe 21.1 on accessing a database from a servlet without a connection pool; Recipes 21.2 and 21.3 on using a DataSource on Tomcat; Recipes 21.4 and 21.5 on using DataSources with servlets on WebLogic; Recipes 21.7 and 21.8 on calling stored procedures from servlets and JSPs; Recipe 21.9 on converting a java.sql.ResultSet object to a javax.servlet.jsp. jstl.sql Result; Recipes 21.10 and 21.11 on using transactions in servlets and JSPs; Recipe 21.12 on finding out information about a ResultSet.

21.7 Calling a Stored Procedure from a Servlet

Problem

You want to call a stored procedure from a servlet.

Solution

Use the `java.sql.CallableStatement` class inside a servlet service method, such as `doGet( )` or `doPost( )`.

Discussion

Database developers create stored procedures typically for SQL code that they want to execute on a regular basis, similar to a Java developer's reason for creating a method. A stored procedure is a piece of SQL that the database system pre-compiles under a specific name. The stored procedure that I use in this recipe is named addEvent.

Naturally, a web developer who is using a database will want to call these stored procedures. The `java.sql.CallableStatement` class encapsulates a particular stored procedure, so that you can use these tools within JDBC code.

Table 21-1 shows the table schema for the table that addEvent uses. The table has four columns: EVENT_ID, NAME, LOCATION, and RACEDATE.

Table 21-1. The RACEEVENT database table schema

Name	Null?	Type
EVENT_ID	NOT NULL	NUMBER
NAME	NOT NULL	VARCHAR2(30)
LOCATION	NOT NULL	VARCHAR2(30)
RACEDATE		DATE

Example 21-7 shows the addEvent definition using Oracle 8*i*'s syntax. This stored procedure takes an event name, location, and date as arguments. It then inserts these values into a new row in the RACEEVENT table.

 A piece of code called a *sequence* named log_seq provides the value for the new row's EVENT_ID column. In Oracle's database system, a sequence can keep track of a long sequence of numbers. The database developer creates the sequence, just as they would create a stored procedure.

Example 21-7. A SQL stored procedure designed to add a row to the EVENT table

```
create or replace procedure addEvent(eventname in varchar2,
    location_ in varchar2,date_ in date)

as -- need to do inserts in raceevent

begin
    insert into raceevent values(log_seq.nextval,
```

Example 21-7. A SQL stored procedure designed to add a row to the EVENT table (continued)

```
        eventname,location_,date_);
end;
/
```

If you're using a database tool such as SQL PLUS from the command line, call the addEvent procedure in the following manner:

```
    exec addEvent('Falmouth Triathlon','Falmouth MA','26-Jul-2003');
```

Example 21-8 shows how you can call addEvent in a servlet. The following servlet calls the stored procedure from doGet( ) in its own addRaceEvent method. This method has a java.util.List as an argument. The List contains the values that the code uses as arguments to call the addEvent stored procedure.

Example 21-8. A servlet uses CallableStatement to call the stored procedure

```java
package com.jspservletcookbook;

import java.sql.*;
import java.util.ArrayList;
import java.util.List;
import java.util.Iterator;

import javax.naming.Context;
import javax.naming.InitialContext;
import javax.naming.NamingException;
import javax.sql.*;

import javax.servlet.*;
import javax.servlet.http.*;

public class StoredProcServlet extends HttpServlet {

    DataSource pool;


    public void init( ) throws ServletException {

        Context env = null;

        try{

            env = (Context) new InitialContext( ).lookup("java:comp/env");

            pool = (DataSource) env.lookup("jdbc/oracle-8i-athletes");

            if (pool == null)
                throw new ServletException(
                    "'oracle-8i-athletes' is an unknown DataSource");

        } catch (NamingException ne) {
```

```
          throw new ServletException(ne);

     }
}

public void doGet(HttpServletRequest request,
   HttpServletResponse response)
     throws ServletException, java.io.IOException {

     String eventName = request.getParameter("eName");
     String location = request.getParameter("eLocation");
     String date = request.getParameter("eDate");

     List paramList = new ArrayList( );
     paramList.add(eventName);
     paramList.add(location);
     paramList.add(date);

     try{

         addRaceEvent(paramList);

     } catch (SQLException sqle){

         throw new ServletException(sqle.getMessage( ));

     }//try

     response.setContentType("text/html");
     java.io.PrintWriter out = response.getWriter( );
     out.println("<html><head><title>Add an Event</title></head><body>");

     out.println(
        "<h2>The Event named "+ eventName +
          " has been added to the database</h2>");

     out.println("</body>");
     out.println("</html>");


} //doGet

public Connection getConnection( ){

   Connection  conn = null;

   try{

        conn = pool.getConnection( );

   } catch (SQLException sqle){
```

Example 21-8. A servlet uses CallableStatement to call the stored procedure (continued)

```
        throw new ServletException(sqle.getMessage( ));

    } finally {

    return conn;

    }

}

public void addRaceEvent(List values) throws SQLException{

    if (values == null)
        throw new SQLException(
        "Invalid parameter in addRaceEvent method.");

    Connection conn = null;

    conn = getConnection( );

    if (conn == null )
      throw new SQLException(
      "Invalid Connection in addRaceEvent method");

    Iterator it = values.iterator( );

    CallableStatement cs = null;

    //Create an instance of the CallableStatement
    cs = conn.prepareCall( "{call addEvent (?,?,?)}" );

    for (int i = 1; i <= values.size( ); i++)
        cs.setString(i,(String) it.next( ));

    //Call the inherited PreparedStatement.executeUpdate( ) method
    cs.executeUpdate( );

    // return the connection to the pool
    conn.close( );

  }//addRaceEvent
}
```

Example 21-8 gets a Connection from a connection pool using the techniques explained in the prior recipes. The code uses the Connection to create a CallableStatement that the example can use to call the underlying stored procedure:

```
    cs = conn.prepareCall( "{call addEvent (?,?,?)}" );
```

The String argument to the Connection's prepareCall method contains question marks (?) as placeholders for the stored procedure's parameters. The code then calls the CallableStatement's setString( ) method to give these placeholders values.

Finally, the code calls the `CallableStatement`'s `executeUpdate( )` method to execute addEvent.

 If calling the stored procedure causes a database error, the addRaceEvent method throws a `SQLException`.

The servlet receives values for the new row from request parameters. The following URL calls the servlet with three parameters: eName, eLocation, and eDate:

```
http://localhost:8080/home/servlet/com.jspservletcookbook.
   StoredProcServlet?eName=
   Falmouth%20Triathlon&eLocation=Falmouth%20MA&eDate=26-July-2003
```

Figure 21-5 shows the servlet's output in a web browser.

Figure 21-5. The browser output of the StoredProcServlet

See Also

The JDBC specification: *http://java.sun.com/products/jdbc/download.html*; Recipe 21.1 on accessing a database from a servlet without a connection pool; Recipes 21.2 and 21.3 on using a DataSource on Tomcat; Recipes 21.4–21.6 on using DataSources with servlets and JSPs on WebLogic; Recipe 21.8 on calling a stored procedure from a JSP; Recipe 21.9 on converting a java.sql.ResultSet object to a javax.servlet.jsp.jstl. sql Result; Recipes 21.10 and 21.11 on using transactions in servlets and JSPs; Recipe 21.12 on finding out information about a ResultSet.

21.8 Calling a Stored Procedure from a JSP

Problem

You want to call a stored procedure from a JSP.

Solution

Using a JSP 2.0 container, develop an Expression Language (EL) function that will call the stored procedure for you.

Discussion

JSP 2.0 introduced *functions*, which are static methods that you can call inside EL statements.

 See Chapter 23 if you need to familiarize yourself with the EL.

This recipe explains the steps for developing a function that calls a stored procedure:

1. Create the stored procedure in your database system.
2. Write the Java class that implements the function as a `static` or class method.
3. Define the function in a Tag Library Descriptor (TLD), which is an XML configuration file that you incude with the web application.
4. In the JSP itself, use the `taglib` directive to declare the tag library that contains the function.
5. Call the function in the JSP, using the proper prefix for your tag library. The function I use in this recipe looks like this:

   ```
   <cbck:addRaceEvent("My Race", "Anytown USA", "11-Dec-2003") />
   ```

Example 21-9 shows the Java class that implements this function.

Example 21-9. The Java class that implements an EL function

```
package com.jspservletcookbook;

import java.sql.*;

import javax.naming.Context;
import javax.naming.InitialContext;
import javax.naming.NamingException;
import javax.sql.*;


public class StoredProcUtil {

  private static DataSource pool;
  private static Context env;

  static { //static initialization of the Context and DataSource

    try{
```

Example 21-9. The Java class that implements an EL function (continued)

```
        env = (Context) new InitialContext( ).lookup("java:comp/env");

        pool  = (DataSource) env.lookup("jdbc/oracle-8i-athletes");

        if (pool == null)
            throw new Exception(
                "'oracle-8i-athletes' is an unknown DataSource");

    } catch (Exception e) {

        System.out.println(e);

    }

}//static

/* This static method will be configured in a TLD file and provide the
implementation for an EL function. An example use of the function is:
<cbck:addRaceEvent("My Race","Anytown USA","11-Dec-2003") /> */

public static void addRaceEvent(String name,String location,String date) {

    if( (! check(name)) || (! check(location)) || (! check(date)))
        throw new IllegalArgumentException(
            "Invalid param values passed to addRaceEvent( )");

    Connection conn = null;

    try{

        conn = pool.getConnection( );

      if (conn == null )
          throw new SQLException(
          "Invalid Connection in addRaceEvent method");

    CallableStatement cs = null;

    //Create an instance of the CallableStatement
    cs = conn.prepareCall( "{call addEvent (?,?,?)}" );

    cs.setString(1,name);
    cs.setString(2,location);
    cs.setString(3,date);

    //Call the inherited PreparedStatement.executeUpdate( ) method
    cs.executeUpdate( );

    // return the connection to the pool
    conn.close( );
```

Example 21-9. The Java class that implements an EL function (continued)

```
    } catch (SQLException sqle) { }


}//addRaceEvent

private static boolean check(String value){

    if(value == null || value.equals(""))
        return false;

    return true;
  }
}
```

The addRaceEvent( ) method creates a java.sql.CallableStatement, which calls the underlying stored procedure (addEvent). Recipe 21.7 explains this process.

> The Java method that implements the function for a JSP must be defined as static.

This Java class must be stored in your web application beneath the *WEB-INF/classes* directory (with a subdirectory structure matching its package name) or in a JAR file stored in *WEB-INF/lib*. For example, the Java class of Example 21-9 should be stored in *WEB-INF/classes/com/jspservletcookbook/StoredProcUtil.class*.

Example 21-10 shows the TLD file that defines the EL function.

> The TLD file has a *.tld* extension and lives in a *WEB-INF* subdirectory of your web application, such as *WEB-INF/tlds*.

Example 21-10. The TLD file for configuring the EL function

```
<taglib xmlns="http://java.sun.com/xml/ns/j2ee" xmlns:xsi=
  "http://www.w3.org/2001/XMLSchema-instance" xsi:schemaLocation=
  "http://java.sun.com/xml/ns/j2ee http://java.sun.com/xml/ns/j2ee/
  web-jsptaglibrary_2_0.xsd"
  version="2.0"
>

    <tlib-version>1.0</tlib-version>
    <jsp-version>2.0</jsp-version>
    <short-name>cbck</short-name>
    <uri>jspservletcookbook.com.tags</uri>
    <description>Cookbook custom tags</description>

    <function>
```

Example 21-10. The TLD file for configuring the EL function (continued)

```
<name>addRaceEvent</name>

<function-class>
    com.jspservletcookbook.StoredProcUtil
</function-class>

<function-signature>
    void addRaceEvent(java.lang.String,
    java.lang.String,java.lang.String)
</function-signature>

</function>

<tag>
    <!-- define a custom tag here if you have to -->
</tag>

</taglib>
```

Example 21-10 defines the function with the function tag and its `name`, `function-class`, and `function-signature` attributes. Make sure to include the fully qualified class name under `function-class`. The JSP container knows how to call the function by inspecting the `function-signature`. This signature includes the return type ("void" in this case), the function name, and all of its parameters specified by their fully qualified class names.

Example 21-11 is a JSP that calls our defined function. First, the `taglib` directive declares the tag library and prefix ("cbck") that the function uses.

Example 21-11. A JSP uses an EL function to call a stored procedure

```
<%@ taglib uri="jspservletcookbook.com.tags" prefix="cbck" %>

<html>
<head><title>Calling a Stored procedure</title></head>
<body>
<h2>This JSP calls a stored procedure with a JSP 2.0 function</h2>

${cbck:addRaceEvent("Falmouth Triathlon","Falmouth MA","26-Jul-2003")}

</body>
</html>
```

Since this is a feature of the EL, the syntax encapsulates the function call within the "${ }" character string. Next comes the prefix (cbck), a colon, and the function call itself:

```
${cbck:addRaceEvent("Falmouth Triathlon","Falmouth MA","26-Jul-2003")}
```

This process appears complicated the first time around, but once you create your first JSP 2.0 function, the rest of them will be much easier! This feature does not involve much more than creating a static Java method, configuring the function with the proper values in an XML file, then calling the function in a JSP. This is a nifty way to call stored procedures!

See Also

The JDBC specification: *http://java.sun.com/products/jdbc/download.html*; Chapter 23 on the JSTL; Chapter 22 on creating custom tag libraries; Recipe 21.1 on accessing a database from a servlet without a connection pool; Recipes 21.2 and 21.3 on using a DataSource on Tomcat; Recipes 21.5 and 21.6 on using DataSources with servlets and JSPs on WebLogic; Recipe 21.7 on calling a stored procedure from a servlet; Recipe 21.9 on converting a java.sql.ResultSet object to a javax.servlet.jsp.jstl. sql.Result; Recipes 21.10 and 21.11 on using transactions in servlets and JSPs; Recipe 21.12 on finding out information about a ResultSet.

21.9   Converting a ResultSet to a Result Object

Problem

You want to convert a java.sql.ResultSet to a javax.servlet.jsp.jstl.sql.Result object so that the object can be used with the JSTL.

Solution

Use the javax.servlet.jsp.jstl.sql.ResultSupport.toResult( ) method.

Discussion

The Result interface allows code to work with ResultSets in the form of Java arrays or java.util.Maps. The JSTL tags often use arrays or Maps to iterate through values (which is why they included the Result interface in the JSTL specification). Therefore, you might want to convert a ResultSet to a Result, then hand the Result to a JSP that uses the JSTL tags.

Example 21-12 is a servlet that:

1. Creates a ResultSet by querying a database.
2. Converts the ResultSet to a Result.
3. Forwards the Result to a JSP by storing the Result as a session attribute.

Example 21-12. A servlet converts a ResultSet to a Result

```
package com.jspservletcookbook;

import java.sql.*;
```

Example 21-12. A servlet converts a ResultSet to a Result (continued)

```
import javax.naming.Context;
import javax.naming.InitialContext;
import javax.naming.NamingException;
import javax.sql.*;

import javax.servlet.jsp.jstl.sql.Result;
import javax.servlet.jsp.jstl.sql.ResultSupport;

import javax.servlet.*;
import javax.servlet.http.*;

public class DbServletResult extends HttpServlet {

    DataSource pool;


    public void init( ) throws ServletException {

        Context env = null;

        try{

            env = (Context) new InitialContext( ).lookup("java:comp/env");

            pool  = (DataSource) env.lookup("jdbc/oracle-8i-athletes");

            if (pool == null)
                throw new ServletException(
                    "'oracle-8i-athletes' is an unknown DataSource");

        } catch (NamingException ne) {

            throw new ServletException(ne);

        }

    }//init

    public void doGet(HttpServletRequest request,
        HttpServletResponse response) throws ServletException,
        java.io.IOException {

        String sql = "select * from athlete";

        try{

            //Get a Result object that represents the return value of the SQL
            //statement 'select * from athlete'
            Result jspResult = select(sql);

            HttpSession session = request.getSession( );
```

Example 21-12. A servlet converts a ResultSet to a Result (continued)

```
              //store the Result in a session attribute,
              //where it can be passed to
              //a JSP and used with the JSTL tags
              session.setAttribute(
                "javax.servlet.jsp.jstl.sql.Result",jspResult);

              RequestDispatcher dispatcher = request.getRequestDispatcher(
                "/useResult.jsp");

              dispatcher.forward(request,response);

          } catch (SQLException sqle){
              throw new ServletException(sqle.getMessage());}

    } //doGet

    private Result select(String sql) throws SQLException{

        if (sql == null || sql.equals(""))
            throw new SQLException("Invalid  parameter in select method");

        ResultSet rs = null;

        Connection conn = null;

        Result res = null;

        //Get a Connection from the pool
        conn = pool.getConnection();

        if (conn == null )
            throw new SQLException("Invalid Connection in select method");

        PreparedStatement stmt = conn.prepareStatement(sql);

        //Create the ResultSet
        rs = stmt.executeQuery();

        //Convert the ResultSet to a
        //Result object that can be used with JSTL tags
        res=ResultSupport.toResult(rs);

        stmt.close();//this will close any associated ResultSets

        conn.close();//return Connection to pool

        return res;//return Result object

    }//select
}
```

Example 21-12 imports the necessary Java classes including the Result and ResultSupport classes:

```
import javax.servlet.jsp.jstl.sql.Result;
import javax.servlet.jsp.jstl.sql.ResultSupport;
```

The select( ) method does the important work: creating the ResultSet, converting this object to a Result, and returning the Result. Here is the code that performs the conversion:

```
res=ResultSupport.toResult(rs);
```

The ResultSupport class's static toResult( ) method takes a ResultSet as an argument and returns a Result.

The servlet's doGet( ) method then creates a session attribute from the Result and uses a RequestDispatcher to forward the request to a JSP. The JSP is named *useResult.jsp*.

 The user initially requests the servlet in his browser, and the servlet passes the request to the JSP. The user then sees the JSP's output in their browser.

The RequestDispatcher code looks like this:

```
RequestDispatcher dispatcher = request.getRequestDispatcher(
        "/useResult.jsp");
dispatcher.forward(request,response);
```

Example 21-13 uses the JSTL core tags (with the "c" prefix). The c:set tag gains access to the session attribute and stores the attribute's value in a resultObj variable. The c:forEach and c:out tags then display the database values in the JSP.

Example 21-13. The JSP that uses a Result object stored as a session attribute

```
<%@ taglib uri="http://java.sun.com/jstl/core" prefix="c" %>
<%@ taglib uri="http://java.sun.com/jstl/sql" prefix="sql" %>

<html>
<HEAD>
      <TITLE>Using a Result object</TITLE>
    </HEAD>
<body bgcolor="white">
<h2>View Database Data</h2>

<%--store a session attribute (the Result object) in a variable named 'resultObj'--%>
<c:set var="resultObj" value=
  "${sessionScope[\"javax.servlet.jsp.jstl.sql.Result\"]}" />

<table border="1" cellspacing="2">
<%-- for every row in the Result ...--%>
<c:forEach items="${resultObj.rows}" var="row">
```

```
<%-- for every column in the row ...--%>
<c:forEach items="${row}" var="column">

   <tr>
    <td align="right">
      <b> <c:out value="${column.key}" /> </b>
      </td>
      <td>
        <c:out value="${column.value}" />
        </td></tr>
   </c:forEach>

</c:forEach>
      </table>
</body>
</html>
```

The syntax "${sessionScope[\"javax.servlet.jsp.jstl.sql.Result\"]}" is necessary, because the session attribute name contains periods (.). Otherwise, the EL can acccess a scoped attribute, if the attribute is named myAttribute, using this simpler syntax:

> ${myAttribute}

Figure 21-6 shows how a web browser displays the JSP's output.

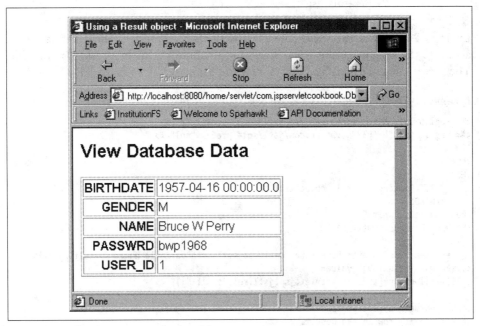

Figure 21-6. The JSP page output in a web browser

See Also

The JDBC specification: *http://java.sun.com/products/jdbc/download.html*; Chapter 23 on the JSTL; Chapter 16 on using session attributes; Recipe 21.1 on accessing a database from a servlet without a connection pool; Recipes 21.2 and 21.3 on using a DataSource on Tomcat; Recipes 21.5 and 21.6 on using DataSources with servlets and JSPs on WebLogic; Recipes 21.7 and 21.8 on calling stored procedures from servlets and JSPs; Recipes 21.10 and 21.11 on using transactions in servlets and JSPs; Recipe 21.12 on finding out information about a ResultSet.

21.10 Executing Several SQL Statements Within a Single Transaction

Problem

You want to execute more than one SQL statement within a single transaction.

Solution

Use the java.sql.Connection API and the setAutoCommit( ), commit( ), and rollback( ) methods to create a transaction.

Discussion

Some SQL statements, such as those that update customer information in two different database tables, are meant to be executed only as a group. If one of them does not succeed, the database is returned to its previous state. This is the purpose of using a transaction in your Java code. A transaction is a logical unit of database operations that can be "rolled back" or canceled as a group if something goes wrong with one of the operations.

Once you have a database connection (an instance of java.sql.Connection), you can call various Connection methods to create a transaction. Here are the steps for executing a transaction:

1. Call the Connection object's setAutoCommit( ) method with false as the parameter. This turns off the default behavior for JDBC code, which is to commit each separate SQL statement instead of automatically grouping sequential statements as a single transaction.

2. Follow the setAutoCommit( ) method call with the database code that you want to treat as a single transaction.

3. Call the `Connection`'s `commit( )` method to commit the SQL statements, which writes any database changes associated with the SQL (such as a DELETE or UPDATE statement) to the underlying database file.

4. In the area of Java code reserved for dealing with errors or unexpected conditions, such as a catch block, call the `Connection`'s `rollback( )` method, which rolls back the SQL that was included in the transaction.

Example 21-14 is a servlet that illustrates this process.

Example 21-14. A servlet that uses a SQL transaction

```java
package com.jspservletcookbook;

import java.sql.*;

import javax.naming.Context;
import javax.naming.InitialContext;
import javax.naming.NamingException;
import javax.sql.*;

import javax.servlet.*;
import javax.servlet.http.*;

public class DbServletTrans extends HttpServlet {

  DataSource pool;

  /*Initialize the DataSource in the servlet's init( ) method
    which the servlet container calls once when it creates an instance of
    the servlet */
  public void init( ) throws ServletException {

    Context env = null;

    try{

        env = (Context) new InitialContext( ).lookup("java:comp/env");

        pool = (DataSource) env.lookup("jdbc/oracle-8i-athletes");

        if (pool == null)
            throw new ServletException(
                "'oracle-8i-athletes' is an unknown DataSource");

    } catch (NamingException ne) {

        throw new ServletException(ne);

    }

  }//init
```

Example 21-14. A servlet that uses a SQL transaction (continued)

```java
public void doGet(HttpServletRequest request,
  HttpServletResponse response) throws ServletException,
  java.io.IOException {

    Connection conn = null;

    Statement stmt = null;

    response.setContentType("text/html");
    java.io.PrintWriter out = response.getWriter();

    out.println(
    "<html><head><title>Using transactions</title></head><body>");

    out.println(
    "<h2>These SQL statements are part of a transaction</h2>");

    out.println("CallableStatement.executeUpdate( )");
    out.println("<br><br>");
    out.println("Statement.executeUpdate( )");
    out.println("<br><br>");

    try{

        //Get a connection from the pool
        conn = pool.getConnection( );

        //Display the default values for setAutoCommit( )
        //and the isolation level

        out.println("AutoCommit before setAutoCommit( ): " +
          conn.getAutoCommit( ) + "<br><br>");

        out.println("Transaction isolation level: ");

        //just out of curiosity, display the existing transaction
        // isolation level
         witch(conn.getTransactionIsolation( )){

            case 0 : out.println("TRANSACTION_NONE<br><br>"); break;

            case 1 : out.println(
            "TRANSACTION_READ_UNCOMMITTED<br><br>"); break;

            case 2 : out.println(
            "TRANSACTION_READ_COMMITTED<br><br>"); break;

            case 4 : out.println(
            "TRANSACTION_REPEATABLE_READ<br><br>"); break;

            case 8 : out.println(
            "TRANSACTION_SERIALIZABLE<br><br>"); break;
```

Example 21-14. A servlet that uses a SQL transaction (continued)

```
        default: out.println("UNKNOWN<br><br>");

    }//switch

//set Autocommit to false so that individual SQL statements will
//not be committed until Connection.commit() is called
conn.setAutoCommit(false);

//Transaction-related SQL begins...
CallableStatement cs = null;

//Create an instance of the CallableStatement
cs = conn.prepareCall( "{call addEvent (?,?,?)}" );

 cs.setString(1,"Salisbury Beach 5-Miler");
 cs.setString(2,"Salisbury MA");
 cs.setString(3,"14-Aug-2003");

//Call the inherited PreparedStatement.executeUpdate( ) method
cs.executeUpdate( );

String sql = "update raceevent set racedate='13-Aug-2003' "+
    "where name='Salisbury Beach 5-Miler'";

int res = 0;

stmt = conn.createStatement( );

res = stmt.executeUpdate(sql);

//commit the two SQL statements
conn.commit( );

} catch (Exception e){

    try{

        //rollback the transaction in case of a problem
        conn.rollback( );

    } catch (SQLException sqle){ }

        throw new ServletException(e.getMessage( ));

} finally {

    try{

        if (stmt != null)
            stmt.close( );
```

Example 21-14. A servlet that uses a SQL transaction (continued)

```
                if (conn != null)
                    conn.close( );

            } catch (SQLException sqle){ }

    }
        out.println("</table></body></html>");

    } //doGet

}
```

The doGet( ) method in Example 21-14 displays the default values for "auto committing" SQL statements and the transaction isolation level (the level of database-locking that occurs as the transactions within your Java code are initiated). For example, if your SQL statements include the updating of database fields, can other users of the database view the new column values before your transaction is committed? If allowed, this type of behavior is called a *dirty read*.

Table 21-2 shows the different types of transaction isolation levels, from the least to most restrictive level. Two other terms need addressing before you inspect this table:

- A *non-repeatable read* occurs when one transaction reads a row, another transaction changes the same row, and the first transaction reads the same row and receives the different value.

- A *phantom read* happens when one transaction obtains a result set based on a WHERE condition and a second transaction inserts a new row that satisfies this WHERE condition. The first transaction then evaluates the same database table again with the same WHERE condition and retrieves the new "phantom" row.

Table 21-2. Transaction isolation levels

Transaction isolation level	Return value of java.sql.Connection. getTransactionIsolation( )	Definition
TRANSACTION_NONE	0	The database driver does not support transactions.
TRANSACTION_READ_ UNCOMMITTED	1	Another transaction can see uncommitted changes; "dirty reads" are allowed.
TRANSACTION_READ_ COMMITTED	2	Uncommitted changes are not visible to other transactions.
TRANSACTION_ REPEATABLE_READ	4	Uncommitted changes are not visible to other transactions; nonrepeatable reads are also disallowed.
TRANSACTION_ SERIALIZABLE	8	Uncommitted changes are not visible to other transactions; nonrepeatable reads and phantom reads are also disallowed.

Check your database vendor's specifications or literature for how the database system you use handles transaction isolation. Use the Connection object's getTransactionIsolation( ) method to find out the value associated with a particular database driver that JDBC-related code is using. This method returns an int. For example, a "2" return value means that the Connection is associated with a TRANSACTION_ READ_COMMITTED transaction isolation level.

Example 21-14 runs two SQL statements within a transaction: it executes a stored procedure and initiates an UPDATE statement. Then the code calls commit( ) on the Connection object to commit any database changes to the underlying data store. If this SQL code throws an exception, the transaction is rolled back with a call to Connection's rollback( ) method. This method call prevents the prior SQL statements from having any effect on the underlying database.

Figure 21-7 shows the output of the servlet in Example 21-14, as it would appear in a web browser.

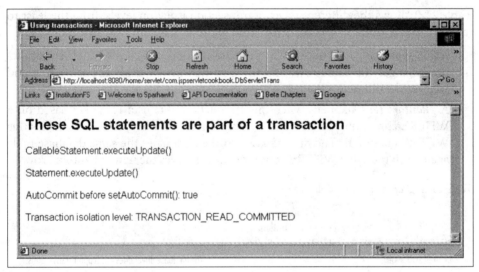

Figure 21-7. A servlet with a database transaction provides browser output

See Also

The JDBC specification: *http://java.sun.com/products/jdbc/download.html*; Recipe 21.1 on accessing a database from a servlet without a connection pool; Recipes 21.2 and 21.3 on using a DataSource on Tomcat; Recipes 21.4–21.6 on using DataSources with servlets and JSPs on WebLogic; Recipes 21.7 and 21.8 on calling stored procedures from servlets and JSPs; Recipe 21.11 on using transactions in JSPs; Recipe 21.12 on finding out information about a ResultSet.

21.11 Using Transactions with JSPs

Problem

You want to run SQL statements within.a transaction in a JSP.

Solution

Use the `sql:transaction` JSTL tag.

Discussion

The JSTL has a `sql:transaction` tag that executes any nested SQL actions (such as `sql:update`) in a transaction.

 The `sql:transaction` tag uses the same `java.sql.Connection` methods that you would use in a transaction-related servlet (Recipe 21.10): `setAutoCommit(false)`, `commit( )`, and `rollback( )`.

Example 21-15 uses a `DataSource` that is configured in *web.xml*, so that none of the database-related information appears in the JSP. See Recipe 23.6 for how to configure a `DataSource` in the deployment descriptor. The INSERT and SELECT SQL statements that are nested inside the `sql:transaction` tag will both be rolled back if any problems arise within the transaction.

Example 21-15. A JSP executes INSERT and SELECT SQL statements in a transaction

```
<%@ taglib uri="http://java.sun.com/jstl/core" prefix="c" %>
<%@ taglib uri="http://java.sun.com/jstl/sql" prefix="sql" %>
<html>
<HEAD>
      <TITLE>Using a Transaction with a JSP</TITLE>
</HEAD>
<body bgcolor="white">
        <h2>View Athlete Data</h2>

<sql:transaction>

   <sql:update>
   insert into athlete values(2, 'Rachel Perry','rlpbwp1996',
   '24-Feb-1996','F')
   </sql:update>

   <sql:query var="resultObj">
   select * from athlete
   </sql:query>

</sql:transaction>
```

```
<table>
<c:forEach items="${resultObj.rows}" var="row">
  <c:forEach items="${row}" var="column">
    <tr>
    <td align="right">
      <b><c:out value="${column.key}" /></b>
    </td>
    <td>
        <c:out value="${column.value}" />
    </td></tr>
  </c:forEach>
 </c:forEach>

</table>
</body>
</html>
```

After executing SQL within a transaction, the JSP displays the database table's updated values. The content of the sql:update and sql:query tags are traditional SQL statements.

> Make sure to include the proper taglib directive to ue the JSTL 1.0 sql tag library:
>
> ```
> <%@ taglib uri=
> "http://java.sun.com/jstl/sql" prefix="sql" %>
> ```

The sql:transaction tag also has an isolation attribute in which you can specify an isolation level for the transaction (see Recipe 21.10). Here is an example:

```
<sql:transaction isolation="TRANSACTION_READ_COMMITTED">

<%-- SQL statements and tags here... --%>

</sql:transaction>
```

Figure 21-8 shows the output of the *sqlTrans.jsp* file.

See Also

The JDBC specification: *http://java.sun.com/products/jdbc/download.html*; Chapter 23 on the JSTL and its sql tag library; Recipe 21.1 on accessing a database from a servlet without a connection pool; Recipes 21.2 and 21.3 on using a DataSource on Tomcat; Recipes 21.4–21.6 on using DataSources with servlets and JSPs on WebLogic; Recipes 21.7 and 21.8 on calling stored procedures from servlets and JSPs; Recipe 21.10 on using transactions in servlets; Recipe 21.12 on finding out information about a ResultSet.

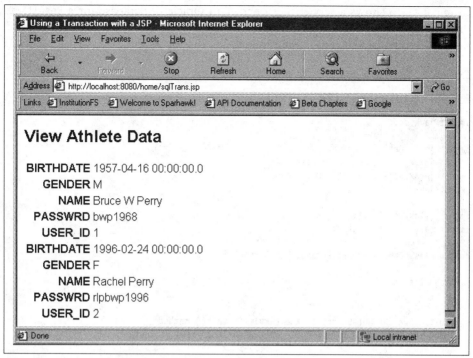

Figure 21-8. A JSP displays an updated database table

21.12 Finding Information about a ResultSet

Problem

You want to dynamically discover details about the rows and columns in a `java.sql.ResultSet`.

Solution

Use the `ResultSetMetaData` class obtained by calling the `java.sql.ResultSet`'s `getMetaData( )` method.

Discussion

Web developers sometimes need to work with database tables that have unknown column names and types. The `java.sql` package contains a very useful `ResultSetMetaData` interface that defines methods designed to provide information about a `java.sql.ResultSet`. A `ResultSet` encapsulates the rows returned by a SELECT SQL statement.

Example 21-16 shows a servlet that queries an Oracle 8*i* database for a `ResultSet`, then displays the column names, the column index, the SQL type of the column, and the number of characters the column requires to display its values.

Example 21-16. A servlet uses the ResultSetMetaData class

```java
package com.jspservletcookbook;

import java.sql.*;

import javax.naming.Context;
import javax.naming.InitialContext;
import javax.naming.NamingException;
import javax.sql.*;

import javax.servlet.*;
import javax.servlet.http.*;

public class DbMetaServlet extends HttpServlet {

  DataSource pool;


  /*Initialize the DataSource in the servlet's init( ) method
    which the servlet container calls once when it creates an instance of
    the servlet */
  public void init( ) throws ServletException {

    Context env = null;

    try{

        env = (Context) new InitialContext( ).lookup("java:comp/env");

        pool  = (DataSource) env.lookup("jdbc/oracle-8i-athletes");

        if (pool == null)
            throw new ServletException(
              "'oracle-8i-athletes' is an unknown DataSource");

    } catch (NamingException ne) {

        throw new ServletException(ne);

    }

  }//init

  public void doGet(HttpServletRequest request,
    HttpServletResponse response)
    throws ServletException, java.io.IOException {

      String sql = "select * from athlete";
```

Example 21-16. A servlet uses the ResultSetMetaData class (continued)

```
Connection conn = null;
Statement stmt = null;
ResultSet rs = null;
ResultSetMetaData rsm = null;

response.setContentType("text/html");
java.io.PrintWriter out = response.getWriter( );

out.println(
"<html><head><title>Discover a ResultSet</title></head><body>");

out.println("<h2>Here is Info about the returned ResultSet</h2>");
out.println("<table border='1'><tr>");

try{

    //Get a connection from the pool
    conn = pool.getConnection( );

    //Create a Statement with which to run some SQL
    stmt = conn.createStatement( );

    //Execute the SQL
    rs = stmt.executeQuery(sql);

    //Get a ResultSetMetaData object from the ResultSet
    rsm = rs.getMetaData( );


    int colCount =  rsm.getColumnCount( );


    //print column names
    printMeta(rsm,"name",out,colCount);

    //print column index
    printMeta(rsm,"index",out,colCount);

    //print column type
    printMeta(rsm,"column type",out,colCount);

    //print column display size
    printMeta(rsm,"column display",out,colCount);


} catch (Exception e){

    throw new ServletException(e.getMessage( ));

} finally {

    try{
```

Example 21-16. A servlet uses the ResultSetMetaData class (continued)

```
                    stmt.close( );
                    conn.close( );

                } catch (SQLException sqle){ }

    }
        out.println("</table></body></html>");

} //doGet

private void printMeta(ResultSetMetaData metaData, String type,
    java.io.PrintWriter out, int colCount) throws SQLException {

    if (metaData == null || type == null || out == null)
        throw new IllegalArgumentException(
        "Illegal args passed to printMeta( )");

    out.println("<tr>");

    if (type.equals("table")){

        out.println("<td><strong>Table name</strong></td>");

        for (int i = 1; i <=colCount; ++i){

            out.println("<td>" + metaData.getTableName(i) + "</td>");
        }

    } else if (type.equals("name")){

        out.println("<td><strong>Column name</strong></td>");

        for (int i = 1; i <=colCount; ++i){

            out.println("<td>" + metaData.getColumnName(i) + "</td>");
         }

    } else if (type.equals("index")){

        out.println("<td><strong>Column index</strong></td>");

        for (int i = 1; i <=colCount; ++i){

            out.println("<td>" + i + "</td>");
         }

    } else if (type.equals("column type")){

        out.println("<td><strong>Column type</strong></td>");

        for (int i = 1; i <=colCount; ++i){
```

Example 21-16. A servlet uses the ResultSetMetaData class (continued)

```
            out.println("<td>" + metaData.getColumnTypeName(i) +
            "</td>");
        }


    } else if (type.equals("column display")){

        out.println("<td><strong>Column display size</strong></td>");

        for (int i = 1; i <=colCount; ++i){

            out.println("<td>" + metaData.getColumnDisplaySize(i) +
            "</td>");
        }
    }

    out.println("</tr>");

  }//printMeta

}
```

Example 21-16 uses ResultSetMetaData methods to obtain information about each of the columns in the ResultSet. The code calls these methods inside its printMeta( ) method. For example, the code:

```
    metaData.getColumnName(1)
```

returns the name of the first column the table schema specifies, such as "USER_ID." Figure 21-9 shows the servlet's HTML output in a web browser.

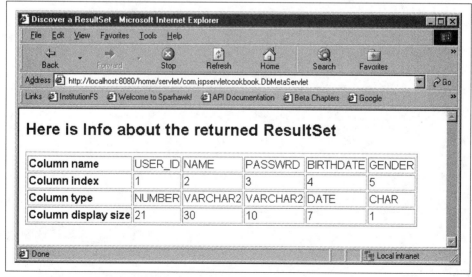

Figure 21-9. A servlet displays meta information about a ResultSet

Use the java.sql.DatabaseMetaData interface to get a large amount of information about the database system associated with the java.sql. Connection the code is using. The Connection method getMetaData( ) returns an object that implements the DatabaseMetaData interface.

See Also

The JDBC specification: *http://java.sun.com/products/jdbc/download.html*; The ResultSetMetaData class: *http://java.sun.com/j2se/1.4.1/docs/api/java/sql/ResultSetMetaData.html*; Recipe 21.1 on accessing a database from a servlet without a connection pool; Recipes 21.2 and 21.3 on using a DataSource on Tomcat; Recipes 21.4–21.6 on using DataSources with servlets and JSPs on WebLogic; Recipes 21.7 and 21.8 on calling stored procedures from servlets and JSPs; Recipes 21.10 and 21.11 on using transactions in servlets and JSPs.

CHAPTER 22

Using Custom Tag Libraries

22.0 Introduction

A very powerful feature of JavaServer Pages technology is the ability to create your own XML tags for use in JSPs. Custom tags have been a part of the JSP specification since Version 1.1. JSP 2.0 is dedicated to making custom tag development less complex than prior versions. JSP 2.0's introduction of simple tag handlers and *tag files*, which we cover in Recipes 22.8–22.14, are a big part of this strategy.

Let's familiarize ourselves with a few terms before we move on to custom tag recipes. A *tag* is an instance of an XML element and a member of a specified namespace. For example, the prefix for all tags associated with this cookbook is cbck. The JSP refers to an individual tag associated with the cbck namespace (say, the myTag tag) as follows:

```
<cbck:myTag>whatever this tag does...</cbck:myTag>
```

Tags are XML elements; therefore, their names and attributes are case sensitive. A collection of tags that provide similar functionality or that logically collaborate with each other is called a *tag library*. Developers can install one or more tag libraries in a web application.

A Java class called the *tag handler* provides the tag's functionality in a JSP. A *custom action* is a tag that you invent for use in JSPs and that is powered behind the scenes by a tag-handler object that the web container keeps in memory.

A *classic tag handler* uses the tag extension API that evolved from JSP v1.1 to 1.2. A *simple tag handler* is a Java class that implements the SimpleTag interface, which JSP 2.0 introduced.

A *tag file* defines a custom tag in JSP syntax. It is designed to make life easier for tag developers. The web container generates from the tag file a Java class that implements the SimpleTag interface, and then creates an object from that class to interpret the tag's use in JSPs.

Finally, a *tag library descriptor* (TLD) is an XML file that provides a mapping between references to tag libraries in JSPs (with the `taglib` directive) and the tag-library classes that you install in the web application. A TLD is a configuration file, similar to a web application's deployment descriptor. The recipes in this chapter provide examples of how to create classic tag handlers, simple tag handlers, and tag files. The recipes also show how to package these components in web applications.

22.1   Creating a Classic Tag Handler

Problem

You want to create a classic JSP 1.2-style tag handler for a custom action.

Solution

Create a Java class that extends one of the Tag support classes in the `javax.servlet.jsp.tagext` package, such as `BodyTagSupport`.

Discussion

There are numerous types of custom tags you can create for JSPs, such as actions that ignore their bodies (empty tags), actions that are nested within other custom actions, and custom tags that use their body content. In fact, entire books have been dedicated solely to JSP custom tag development! Instead of being exhaustive in this book, I show how to create a fairly simple classic tag that adds an image logo to a JSP page with a text message. You can then infer details for your own programming tasks from this example.

The sample tag is designed to allow a page designer to specify an logo's image, its width and height, and a text message to sit alongside the image.

Example 22-1 shows the classic tag handler for this custom action. This Java class extends `BodyTagSupport`, since it uses the tag's nested content for the logo's text message.

Example 22-1. A classic tag handler for inserting an image and markup

```
package com.jspservletcookbook;

import javax.servlet.*;
import javax.servlet.http.*;
import javax.servlet.jsp.*;
import javax.servlet.jsp.tagext.*;

/** This tag generates a thumbnail image using the HTML img tag, next to  a text message.
The user specifies the content of the message and the Heading level (i.e., <H1>-<H6>) */
```

Example 22-1. A classic tag handler for inserting an image and markup (continued)

```java
public class LogoTag extends BodyTagSupport {

    //These variable represent the custom tag's attributes
    private String heading = null;
    private String image =null;
    private String width =null;
    private String height =null;

    //this method assumes that attribute properties have been set.
    public int doStartTag() throws JspException{

        try {

        int h = new Integer(heading).intValue();

        if(! (h > 0 && h < 7))
            throw new JspException(
            "The 'heading' attribute value must between 1 and 6 inclusive.");

        } catch (Exception e) { throw new JspException(e.getMessage()); }

        return EVAL_BODY_BUFFERED;

    }

    public int doEndTag() throws JspException {

        JspWriter out = pageContext.getOut();

        //the 'images' directory is located in the web app's
        //root directory
        String imgDir = ((HttpServletRequest) pageContext.
        getRequest()).getContextPath() + "/images/";

        //get the text provided between the custom action's
        // start and end tags
        String message = getBodyContent().getString().trim();

        try{

            //build the HTML img tag
            out.println("<img src=\""+ imgDir + image + "\" width=\"" + width +
            "\" height=\"" + height + "\" align=\"left\">" + "<H" + heading + ">" +
            message + "</H" + heading+ ">");

        } catch (java.io.IOException io) {}


        return EVAL_PAGE;

    } //doEndTag
```

Example 22-1. A classic tag handler for inserting an image and markup (continued)

```
//methods designed to set attribute values
public void setHeading(String level){

  this.heading= level;

}

public void setImage(String name){

  this.image = name;

}

public void setWidth(String width){

  this.width = width;

}

public void setHeight(String height){

  this.height = height;

}

//the JSP container may cache and reuse tag handler objects.
//this method releases instance variables so that the tag handler
//can be reused afresh
public void release( ){

    heading = null;
    image =null;
    width =null;
    height =null;

}// release
}
```

Classic tag handlers are like JavaBeans. You declare the custom tag's attributes as instance variables, or *properties*, and define setter methods for each attribute. If you just want to manipulate the custom tag's body, define the doEndTag( ) method. When the JSP container invokes doEndTag( ), developers can use this method to evaluate the body content that the tag user has placed between the action's start and end tags. Example 22-1 also defines the doStartTag( ) method to check that the tag user has included a valid value for the header attribute (a number between one and six, inclusive, for this example code).

 When the doStartTag( ) method is invoked, any attribute values that the user has set are available, but the tag's body content is not.

The doEndTag( ) method uses the various tag attribute values to build an img and H tag that results in the display of a simple logo in the JSP page where the tag is used. Here's an example of how a JSP would use the action defined by this tag handler:

```
<%-- import the tag library with 'taglib' directive --%>
<%@ taglib uri="jspservletcookbook.com.tags" prefix="cbck" %>

<%-- JSP page continues... --%>

<%-- Use the 'logo' tag --%>
<cbck:logo heading="1" image="stamp.gif" width="42" height="54">Thanks for visiting</
cbck:logo>
```

Figure 22-1 shows a JSP that uses the tag defined by Example 22-1.

Figure 22-1. A JSP page uses a custom tag that displays an image and a heading

The JSP using this tag outputs HTML that looks like this:

```
<img src="/home/images/stamp.gif" width="42" height="54" align="left">
    <H1> Thanks for visiting</H1>
```

You might respond by exclaiming, "The designer can just enter these HTML tags manually, and they don't have to deal with the custom tag's syntax!" This is absolutely true; however, the tag takes care of the default location for the images directory, positions and aligns the image, and checks whether the attribute level is correct. In other words, it performs a lot of routine work and removes the possibility of silly typographical mistakes.

Also consider that this is a simple example; what if the image was a Flash file instead? A custom tag could take care of all of the complex details for embedding the Flash in the HTML page and generating proprietary attribute values, leaving the graphical positioning of the media file up to the tag user.

A nice rule of thumb with custom tags is this: leave automated, complex, or tedious work to the tag handler, and reserve configurable details for the tag's attributes.

See Also

The JSP 2.0 specification web page: *http://jcp.org/en/jsr/detail?id=152*; Recipes 22.2 and 22.3 on creating TLD files for tag libraries; Recipes 22.4 and 22.5 on packaging tag libraries in a web application; Recipe 22.6 on using the custom tag in a JSP; Recipe 22.7 on handling exceptions in tags; Recipes 22.8 and 22.9 on creating a simple tag handler; Recipe 22.10 on using the simple tag handler in a JSP; Recipes 22.11–22.14 on using a JSP tag file; Recipe 22.15 on adding a listener class to a tag library; the custom-tag sections of Hans Bergsten's *JavaServer Pages*, Third Edition (O'Reilly).

22.2 Creating a JSP 1.2 TLD for a Classic Tag Handler

Problem

You want to create a JSP 1.2 TLD file for one or more custom tags.

Solution

Create the XML file using the proper DOCTYPE declaration for a JSP 1.2 TLD.

Discussion

A TLD is an XML file that describes your custom tags, the tag's attributes (if any), as well as the Java classes that provide the tag's functionality. The JSP container uses this configuration file when it interprets custom tags that appear in JSP pages. If you are using a JSP v1.2 container, your tag library's TLD has the DOCTYPE declaration shown in Example 22-2. This TLD describes the tag handler of the previous recipe.

Example 22-2. The TLD file for a classic JSP 1.2 tag handler

```
<?xml version="1.0" encoding="ISO-8859-1" ?>

<!DOCTYPE taglib
        PUBLIC "-//Sun Microsystems, Inc.//DTD JSP Tag Library 1.2//EN"
        "http://java.sun.com/dtd/web-jsptaglibrary_1_2.dtd">

<taglib>

    <tlib-version>1.0</tlib-version>
    <jsp-version>1.2</jsp-version>
    <short-name>cbck</short-name>
```

Example 22-2. The TLD file for a classic JSP 1.2 tag handler (continued)

```
<!-- Here is the URI you use with the 'taglib' directive in the JSP -->
<uri>com.jspservletcookbook.tags</uri>

<description>Cookbook custom tags</description>

<tag>

    <name>logo</name>

    <!-- make sure to use the fully qualifed class name -->
    <tag-class>com.jspservletcookbook.LogoTag</tag-class>

    <body-content>JSP</body-content>

    <description>This tag writes a logo inside the JSP.</description>

    <attribute>
        <name>heading</name>
        <!-- The logo tag requires this attribute -->
        <required>true</required>
        <!-- The attribute can take a JSP expression as a value -->
        <rtexprvalue>true</rtexprvalue>
        <description>The heading level for the logo; 1 through 6.
        </description>
    </attribute>

    <attribute>
        <name>image</name>
        <required>true</required>
        <rtexprvalue>true</rtexprvalue>
        <description>The image name for the logo.</description>
    </attribute>

    <attribute>
        <name>width</name>
        <required>true</required>
        <rtexprvalue>true</rtexprvalue>
        <description>The image width for the logo.</description>
    </attribute>

    <attribute>
        <name>height</name>
        <required>true</required>
        <rtexprvalue>true</rtexprvalue>
        <description>The image height for the logo.</description>
    </attribute>

</tag>

</taglib>
```

In JSP 1.2 and 2.0, a JSP container automatically searches *WEB-INF*, as well as the *META-INF* directory of your application's JAR files, for any file that ends with the extension *.tld*.

 Because *.tld* is a fixed extension, it is mandatory to give your tag library descriptor filenames that end in *.tld*.

The container then uses the information it finds in the TLD to interpret custom tags that the web application may use. For example, the container maps the uri elements it finds in the TLD to the URIs specified by any taglib directives in JSP files. Example 22-2 specifies a uri of *com.jspservletcookbook.tags* for the tag library that contains the logo tag. A taglib directive that uses this tag library in a JSP looks like this:

```
<%@ taglib uri="com.jspservletcookbook.tags" prefix="cbck" %>
```

When the logo tag appears later on in the JSP, the JSP container knows that the tag belongs in the tag library with the *com.jspservletcookbook.tags* uri value, and the container can evaluate the JSP's tag use based on the TLD's specification of the tag class and the tag's various attributes. Based on the TLD, the JSP container knows that the logo tag's attributes are all required, so a JSP that uses the logo tag and omits an attribute fails to compile.

See Also

The JSP 2.0 specification web page: *http://jcp.org/en/jsr/detail?id=152*; Recipe 22.3 on creating a JSP 2.0 TLD file for tag libraries; Recipes 22.4 and 22.5 on packaging tag libraries in a web application; Recipe 22.6 on using the custom tag in a JSP; Recipe 22.7 on handling exceptions in tags; Recipes 22.8 and 22.9 on creating a simple tag handler; Recipe 22.10 on using the simple tag handler in a JSP; Recipes 22.11–22.14 on using a JSP tag file; Recipe 22.15 on adding a listener class to a tag library; the custom tag sections of Hans Bergsten's *JavaServer Pages*, Third Edition (O'Reilly).

22.3   Creating a JSP 2.0 TLD for a Classic Tag Handler

Problem

You want to create a JSP 2.0 TLD file for a tag library.

Solution

Create a tag library descriptor with the proper taglib root element, including the taglib's various xmlns attributes and values.

Discussion

If you are using any JSP 2.0 features with your tag library and TLD, such as a function or tag-file element, then you must use the JSP 2.0-style TLD, as shown in Example 22-3.

The JSP 2.0 TLD is backward compatible with elements defined in the JSP 1.2 DTD. Therefore you can use the taglib and tag elements as they are specified in any existing JSP 1.2 TLDs when you upgrade your TLD file to JSP 2.0. For example, the only difference between the TLD in Example 22-3 and the JSP 1.2 TLD in Example 22-2 is the taglib start tag, which must have exactly the same content as shown here.

Example 22-3. The JSP 2.0 TLD file for our classic tag handler

```
<taglib xmlns="http://java.sun.com/xml/ns/j2ee"
 xmlns:xsi="http://www.w3.org/2001/XMLSchema-instance"
 xsi:schemaLocation=
    "http://java.sun.com/xml/ns/j2ee
    http://java.sun.com/xml/ns/j2ee/web-jsptaglibrary_2_0.xsd"
 version="2.0"
>

<!-- THE REST OF THE XML CONTENT IS ALMOST EXACTLY THE SAME AS THE JSP 1.2 TLD VERSION
EXCEPT FOR <jsp-version>2.0</jsp-version> AND <body-content>scriptless</body-content>. The
"scriptless" value means that the content of the tag can only be template text (such as
HTML content), Expression Language code, or JSP action elements, but not "scripting"
elements such as the JSP code delineated by <% %> -->

    <tlib-version>1.0</tlib-version>
    <jsp-version>2.0</jsp-version>
    <short-name>cbck</short-name>
    <uri>com.jspservletcookbook.tags</uri>
    <description>Cookbook custom tags</description>

    <tag>

        <name>logo</name>

        <tag-class>com.jspservletcookbook.LogoTag</tag-class>

        <body-content>scriptless</body-content>

        <description>This tag writes a logo inside the JSP.</description>

        <attribute>
            <name>heading</name>
```

```
                <required>true</required>
                <rtexprvalue>true</rtexprvalue>
                <description>
                    The heading level for the logo; 1 through 6.
                </description>
            </attribute>

            <attribute>
                <name>image</name>
                <required>true</required>
                <rtexprvalue>true</rtexprvalue>
                <description>The image name for the logo.</description>
            </attribute>

            <attribute>
                <name>width</name>
                <required>true</required>
                <rtexprvalue>true</rtexprvalue>
                <description>The image width for the logo.</description>
            </attribute>

            <attribute>
                <name>height</name>
                <required>true</required>
                <rtexprvalue>true</rtexprvalue>
                <description>The image height for the logo.</description>
            </attribute>

        </tag>

</taglib>
```

The JSP 2.0 TLD is based on an XML Schema file, rather than a DTD (the XML Schema file: *http://java.sun.com/xml/ns/j2ee/web-jsptaglibrary_2_0.xsd*).

> XML Schemas allow the definers of XML documents to create more complex elements and attributes than those allowed in DTDs. XML Schemas are also designed to be valid XML documents themselves, which makes it easier to integrate them with XML-based applications.

The taglib element in Example 22-3 has four attributes. The xmlns attribute specifies that the TLD has the same default namespace as all J2EE deployment descriptors: *http://java.sun.com/xml/ns/j2ee*.

A namespace is a unique identifier that helps avoid the collision of two XML elements of the same name. For example, the taglib element that is part of the *http://java.sun.com/xml/ns/j2ee* namespace is different from a taglib element that might be defined as part of the *http://acme.com* namespace. A namespace has to be unique only within its domain (such as an Internet URL); it does not necessarily represent an actual web document.

The xmlns:xsi attribute specifies the namespace for a set of XML elements related to XML Schema *instances*. The xsi:schemaLocation attribute specifies the location of the XML Schema on which the current XML document is based.

An XML Schema describes a related set of elements and attributes. An XML Schema *instance* is an XML document that uses the previously defined XML elements and attributes. This concept is similar to a Java class and its object instances.

Finally, the taglib element's version attribute specifies the JSP-specification version on which the tag library is based, as in JSP 2.0.

See Also

The XML schema file for the JSP 2.0 TLD: *http://java.sun.com/xml/ns/j2ee/web-jsptaglibrary_2_0.xsd*; Recipe 22.2 on creating a JSP 1.2 TLD file for tag libraries; Recipes 22.4 and 22.5 on packaging tag libraries in a web application; Recipe 22.6 on using the custom tag in a JSP; Recipe 22.7 on handling exceptions in tags; Recipes 22.8 and 22.9 on creating a simple tag handler; Recipe 22.10 on using the simple tag handler in a JSP; Recipes 22.11–22.14 on using a JSP *tag file*; Recipe 22.15 on adding a listener class to a tag library; the custom tag sections of Hans Bergsten's *JavaServer Pages*, Third Edition (O'Reilly).

22.4   Packaging a Tag Library in a Web Application

Problem

You want to make your tag library available in a web application.

Solution

Place your TLD file in *WEB-INF* or a *WEB-INF* subdirectory (with the exception of *WEB-INF/lib* and *WEB-INF/classes*). Place the tag handler class or classes in *WEB-INF/classes*.

Discussion

Packaging your tag library outside of a JAR file is typically a two-step process:

1. Store the TLD file in the *WEB-INF* directory or a *WEB-INF* subdirectory, and a JSP container (compliant with Versions 1.2 and 2.0) automatically configures your tag library. The TLD file must have a *.tld* extension. For example, if you store a *mytags.tld* in *WEB-INF/tlds*, then the JSP container automatically finds your TLD file and configure your tag library.

 The JSP 2.0 specification states that TLDs should not be placed in *WEB-INF/lib* or *WEB-INF/classes*. The JSP container will *not* look for the TLDs in these locations.

2. Make sure the tag handler classes for your tag library have a package name (such as com.jspservletcookbook) and are stored in *WEB-INF/classes* or in a JAR file in *WEB-INF/lib*.

The next recipe shows how to package your tag library, including the TLD, in a JAR file.

See Also

The XML schema file for the JSP 2.0 TLD: *http://java.sun.com/xml/ns/j2ee/web-jsptaglibrary_2_0.xsd*; Recipes 22.2 and 22.3 on creating TLD files for tag libraries; Recipe 22.5 on packaging tag libraries in a JAR file; Recipe 22.6 on using the custom tag in a JSP; Recipe 22.7 on handling exceptions in tags; Recipes 22.8 and 22.9 on creating a simple tag handler; Recipe 22.10 on using the simple tag handler in a JSP; Recipes 22.11–22.14 on using a JSP *tag file*; Recipe 22.15 on adding a listener class to a tag library; the custom-tag sections of Hans Bergsten's *JavaServer Pages*, Third Edition (O'Reilly).

22.5   Packaging the Tag Library in a JAR File

Problem

You want to make your tag library available in a JAR file.

Solution

Create a JAR file that contains your tag handler class or classes in the correct directory structure (with subdirectory names matching the package names). Place the tag library descriptor file in the JAR's *META-INF* directory. Then put the JAR in the *WEB-INF/lib* directory of your web application.

Discussion

To make your tag library portable, store all of your tag handler classes and tag files in a JAR file.

 In a JAR, store any tag files in *META-INF/tags* or a subdirectory of *META-INF/tags*. If you don't, the JSP container will not recognize them as legitimate tag files. See Recipe 22.11 for details.

You can generate this JAR file from a directory that contains your tag library classes, including their package-related subdirectories. For example, the `logo` tag I developed in this chapter has a package name of `com.jspservletcookbook`, so the relative path to this file is *com/jspservletcookbook/LogoTag.class*. Include a *META-INF* directory at the top level of the directory where the classes are stored (e.g., in the same directory as the one containing *com*). Place your tag library descriptor file in the *META-INF* directory or a *META-INF* subdirectory.

If your library includes any tag files, place them in *META-INF/tags* or a subdirectory of *META-INF/tags*. Change to the directory containing all these subdirectories and type the following command line, substituting your own JAR filename for *cookbook-tags.jar*:

```
jar cvf cookbooktags.jar .
```

Don't forget that period (.) character at the end. This tells the `jar` tool to include all of the files and directories that the current directory contains in the archive.

 Make sure your computer's PATH environment variable includes the path to the *bin* directory of your Java SDK installation, as in *h:\j2sdk1.4.1_01\bin*. This allows you to type jar at the command line to launch the Java jar tool.

To install the tag library, just take the resulting JAR file and move it into your web application's *WEB-INF/lib* directory.

The JSP container (in JSP 1.2 and 2.0) automatically looks in the JAR's *META-INF* directory for the TLD file—you do not have to include a `taglib` element in the *web.xml* deployment descriptor.

See Also

The JSP 2.0 specification web page: *http://jcp.org/en/jsr/detail?id=152*; Recipes 22.2 and 22.3 on creating TLD files for tag libraries; Recipe 22.4 on packaging a tag library in a web application without using a JAR file; Recipe 22.6 on using the custom tag in a JSP; Recipe 22.7 on handling exceptions in tags; Recipes 22.8 and 22.9 on creating a simple tag handler; Recipe 22.10 on using the simple tag handler in a

JSP; Recipes 22.11 and 22.14 on using a JSP tag file; Recipe 22.15 on adding a listener class to a tag library; the custom tag sections of Hans Bergsten's *JavaServer Pages*, Third Edition (O'Reilly).

22.6   Using the Custom Tag in a JSP

Problem

You want to use a custom tag that you have developed and installed.

Solution

Include a `taglib` directive at the top of the JSP. The `taglib` directive must identify the uri for your tag library, as that uri is specified in your TLD file.

Discussion

To use the custom tags from your tag library, the JSP has to have a `taglib` directive, as in Example 22-4. The uri attribute matches the uri your TLD file specifies (see Recipe 22.5). The `prefix` attribute specifies the namespace for your tags. Example 22-4 specifies the prefix cbck; therefore, the JSP uses the logo tag from that tag library in the manner of `<cbck:logo>...</cbck:logo>`.

 If the tag encloses body content (it's not an *empty* tag), make sure to close the tag properly, as in `</cbck:logo>` as opposed to `</logo>`.

If the JSP does not use the tag as specified in the TLD (for example, if it leaves out a mandatory attribute), the JSP will fail to compile the first time it is requested.

Example 22-4. The Logo tag used in a JSP

```
<%@ taglib uri="jspservletcookbook.com.tags" prefix="cbck" %>

<html>
<head><title>Mi casa es su casa</title></head>
<body>

<cbck:logo heading="<%=request.getParameter("level") %>" image="stamp.gif" width="42"
height="54">Thanks for visiting</cbck:logo>

Here's all the other stuff this page contains...
</body>
</html>
```

In Example 22-4, the `logo` tag's heading attribute takes a runtime expression value so that the user can dynamically set the attribute value, as in the following URL: *http://localhost:8080/home/logoTest.jsp?level=1*.

Figure 22-2 shows the web browser display for this JSP.

Figure 22-2. The web browser display of a custom tag output

See Also

The JSP 2.0 specification web page: *http://jcp.org/en/jsr/detail?id=152*; Recipes 22.2 and 22.3 on creating TLD files for tag libraries; Recipes 22.4 and 22.5 on packaging a tag library in a web application; Recipe 22.7 on handling exceptions in tags; Recipes 22.8 and 22.9 on creating a simple tag handler; Recipe 22.10 on using the simple tag handler in a JSP; Recipes 22.11–22.14 on using a JSP *tag file*; Recipe 22.15 on adding a listener class to a tag library; the custom tag sections of Hans Bergsten's *JavaServer Pages*, Third Edition (O'Reilly).

22.7 Handling Exceptions in a Custom Tag Class

Problem

You want your custom tag handler to deal with any exceptions thrown inside the tag.

Solution

Implement the `TryCatchFinally` interface in your tag handler.

Discussion

The tag extension API provides the TryCatchFinally interface, which you can implement in your tag handler class to write code dealing with any exceptions the tag handler might throw. If the class implements TryCatchFinally, it must include the methods doCatch( ) and doFinally( ). In doCatch( ), the code has access to any Throwable object thrown by doStartTag( ) or doEndTag( ), for instance. In doFinally( ), the code closes any resources the tag uses, such as a database connection.

In general, this interface allows the tag handler itself to catch and handle any exceptions that do not affect the output of the JSP enclosing the tag. Example 22-5 uses the same code as Example 22-1, but additional methods are added by implementing the TryCatchFinally interface.

Example 22-5. A logo tag handler that catches any exceptions

```
package com.jspservletcookbook;

import javax.servlet.*;
import javax.servlet.http.*;
import javax.servlet.jsp.*;
import javax.servlet.jsp.tagext.*;

/** This tag generates a thumbnail image using the HTML img tag, next to a text message.
The user specifies the content of the message and the Heading level (i.e., <H1>-<H6>) */

public class LogoTag extends BodyTagSupport implements TryCatchFinally{

    private String heading = null;
    private String image =null;
    private String width =null;
    private String height =null;

    //this method assumes that attribute properties have been set.
    public int doStartTag( ) throws JspException{

        try {

            int h = new Integer(heading).intValue( );

            if(! (h > 0 && h < 7))

                throw new JspException(
                "The 'heading' attribute value must between 1 and 6"+
                " inclusive.");

        } catch (Exception e) {
            throw new JspException(e.getMessage( ));
        }

        return EVAL_BODY_BUFFERED;
```

Example 22-5. A logo tag handler that catches any exceptions (continued)

```
    }

    public int doEndTag( ) throws JspException {

        JspWriter out = pageContext.getOut( );

        String imgDir = ((HttpServletRequest) pageContext.getRequest( )).
        getContextPath( ) + "/images/";

        String message = getBodyContent().getString().trim( );

        try{

            out.println("<img src=\""+ imgDir + image + "\" width=\"" +
            width + "\" height=\"" + height + "\" align=\"left\">" + "<H" +
            heading + ">" + message + "</H" + heading+ ">");

        } catch (java.io.IOException io) {}


        return EVAL_PAGE;

    } //doEndTag

    /* The next two methods have to be implemented in this class since the class implements
    TryCatchFinally */

    public void doCatch(Throwable t){

        try{

            //print the exception message inside the JSP where the tag
            //appears
            pageContext.getOut().println(t.getMessage( )+"<br />");

        } catch (java.io.IOException io) {}
    }

    public void doFinally( ){

        //do nothing here, since we don't have any resources open
        //like database connections

    }

    public void setHeading(String level){

      this.heading= level;

    }

    /* THE REST OF THE SOURCE CODE FROM EXAMPLE 22-1 CONTINUES... */
}
```

If the tag throws an exception, then the web container invokes the doCatch( ) method and the tag handler prints the exception message where the JSP would otherwise output the image produced by the tag. Our doFinally( ) method does not do anything, because this code does not have any open resources such as a FileInputStream.

See Also

The JSP 2.0 specification web page: *http://jcp.org/en/jsr/detail?id=152*; Recipes 22.2 and 22.3 on creating TLD files for tag libraries; Recipes 22.4 and 22.5 on packaging a tag library in a web application; Recipe 22.6 on using the custom tag in a JSP; Recipes 22.8 and 22.9 on creating a simple tag handler; Recipe 22.10 on using the simple tag handler in a JSP; Recipes 22.11–22.14 on using a JSP *tag file*; Recipe 22.15 on adding a listener class to a tag library; the custom tag sections of Hans Bergsten's *JavaServer Pages*, Third Edition (O'Reilly).

22.8   Creating a Simple Tag Handler

Problem

You want to create a JSP 2.0 simple tag handler.

Solution

Create a Java class that either implements the SimpleTag interface or extends the SimpleTagSupport class.

Discussion

In an effort to simplify custom tag development, the JSP 2.0 specification added the javax.servlet.jsp.tagext.SimpleTag interface and the SimpleTagSupport class. The SimpleTagSupport class is designed to be the base class for tag handlers that implement SimpleTag. These tag handlers have to implement just one method, doTag( ).

 The JSP 2.0 specification states that vendors should not cache simple tag handlers, so developers do not have to worry about the reuse of tag handler objects and releasing object state in their code.

Example 22-6 mimics the logo tag handler created in earlier recipes, but uses the SimpleTagSupport class from the JSP 2.0 API instead.

Example 22-6. A simple tag handler displaying a logo

```
package com.jspservletcookbook;

import java.io.IOException;

import javax.servlet.*;
import javax.servlet.http.*;
import javax.servlet.jsp.*;
import javax.servlet.jsp.tagext.*;

/** This tag generates a thumbnail image using an HTML img tag, aligned next to a text
message. The user specifies the content of the message and the Heading level (i.e., <H1>-
<H6>) */

public class SimpleLogoTag extends SimpleTagSupport{

    private String heading = null;
    private String image =null;
    private String width =null;
    private String height =null;

  public void doTag() throws JspException, IOException{

        //JspContext provides access to the JspWriter for generating
        //text from the tag. You can also get any stored attribute values
        //using JspContext
        JspContext jspContext = getJspContext();

        //this method assumes that attribute properties have been set.
        try {

            int h = new Integer(heading).intValue();

            if(! (h > 0 && h < 7))
                throw new JspException(
                  "The 'heading' attribute value must between 1 and 6"+
                  " inclusive.");

        } catch (Exception e) { throw new JspException(e.getMessage()); }

        //Get a JspWriter to produce the tag's output
        JspWriter out = jspContext.getOut();

        //the value of the 'imgDir' attribute is the web app's /images
        //directory; the directory path is stored in a session attribute
        String imgDir = (String) jspContext.findAttribute("imgDir");

        if (imgDir == null || "".equals(imgDir))
            throw new JspException(
              "No attribute provided specifying the application's " +
              "image directory.");
```

Example 22-6. A simple tag handler displaying a logo (continued)

```
        //display the img and H HTML tags
        out.println(new StringBuffer("<img src=\"").append(imgDir).
         append(image).append("\" width=\"").append(width).
         append("\" height=\"").append(height).append("\" align=\"left\">").
         append("<H").append(heading).append(">").toString( ));

        // getJspBody() returns a 'JspFragment' object; calling 'invoke( )'
        //on this object with a 'null' parameter will use the JSP page's
        //JspWriter to output the tag's nested content in the JSP
        getJspBody( ).invoke(null);

        out.println(new StringBuffer("</H").append(heading).
         append(">").toString( ));


    }//doTag

    //Attribute-related setter methods

    public void setHeading(String level){

        this.heading= level;

    }

    public void setImage(String name){

        this.image = name;

    }

    public void setWidth(String width){

        this.width = width;

    }

    public void setHeight(String height){

        this.height = height;

    }

}// SimpleLogoTag
```

This simple tag handler accesses a JspContext object by calling the SimpleTagSupport's getJspContext( ) method. The code uses the JspContext to obtain the value of an attribute stored in the session, as well as to access a `JspWriter` to generate the tag's output:

```
JspContext jspContext = getJspContext();

//further along in the code...

JspWriter out = jspContext.getOut();

//the value of the 'imgDir' attribute is the web app's images
//directory; it is stored in a session attribute
String imgDir = (String) jspContext.findAttribute("imgDir");
//code continues...
```

Calling the `SimpleTagSupport`'s `getJspBody()` method returns a `JspFragment` object, which represents a chunk of JSP code as an object. Calling this object's `invoke()` method with `null` as the parameter directs the output of the fragment to the `JspWriter` available to the tag handler:

```
//Get the tag's body content and output it using the JspWriter
//that is available by calling JspContext.getOut()
getJspBody().invoke(null);
```

This code displays the content or text that the JSP developer included within the custom action's start and end tags. The tag handler uses the tag's body content as the textual logo message. Figure 22-1 in Recipe 22.1 shows what the JSP page looks like in a web browser.

See Also

The JSP 2.0 specification web page: *http://jcp.org/en/jsr/detail?id=152*; Recipes 22.2 and 22.3 on creating TLD files for tag libraries; Recipes 22.4 and 22.5 on packaging a tag library in a web application; Recipe 22.6 on using the custom tag in a JSP; Recipe 22.7 on handling exceptions in tags; Recipe 22.9 on creating a TLD for a simple tag handler; Recipe 22.10 on using the simple tag handler in a JSP; Recipes 22.11–22.14 on using a JSP *tag file*; Recipe 22.15 on adding a listener class to a tag library; the custom tag sections of Hans Bergsten's *JavaServer Pages*, Third Edition (O'Reilly).

22.9   Creating a TLD for a Simple Tag Handler

Problem

You want to create a TLD for a simple tag handler.

Solution

Use the JSP 2.0-style TLD for the simple tag handler.

Discussion

The simple tag handler derives from the JSP 2.0 API, so you can use the TLD version from JSP 2.0 as well. Example 22-7 shows the taglib start tag and the various xmlns attributes that your TLD must reproduce exactly. Then, unless you are using JSP 2.0 TLD features such as the tag-file element, you can specify the tag element and its nested elements with the same XML syntax that you used for the prior TLD version.

Example 22-7. A JSP 2.0 TLD file for a simple tag handler

```
<taglib xmlns="http://java.sun.com/xml/ns/j2ee"
    xmlns:xsi="http://www.w3.org/2001/XMLSchema-instance"
    xsi:schemaLocation=
      "http://java.sun.com/xml/ns/j2ee
      http://java.sun.com/xml/ns/j2ee/web-jsptaglibrary_2_0.xsd"
    version="2.0"
>

<!-- THE REST OF THE XML CONTENT IS THE SAME AS THE JSP 1.2 TLD VERSION EXCEPT FOR <jsp-
version>2.0</jsp-version> -->

    <tlib-version>1.0</tlib-version>
    <jsp-version>2.0</jsp-version>
    <short-name>cbck</short-name>
    <uri>com.jspservletcookbook.tags</uri>
    <description>Cookbook custom tags</description>

    <tag>

        <name>simplelogo</name>

        <tag-class>com.jspservletcookbook.SimpleLogoTag</tag-class>

        <body-content>JSP</body-content>

        <description>This tag writes a logo inside the JSP.</description>

        <attribute>
            <name>heading</name>
            <required>true</required>
            <rtexprvalue>true</rtexprvalue>
            <description>
              The heading level for the logo; 1 through 6.
            </description>
        </attribute>

        <attribute>
            <name>image</name>
            <required>true</required>
            <rtexprvalue>true</rtexprvalue>
            <description>The image name for the logo.</description>
        </attribute>
```

Example 22-7. A JSP 2.0 TLD file for a simple tag handler (continued)

```
    <attribute>
        <name>width</name>
        <required>true</required>
        <rtexprvalue>true</rtexprvalue>
        <description>The image width for the logo.</description>
    </attribute>

    <attribute>
        <name>height</name>
        <required>true</required>
        <rtexprvalue>true</rtexprvalue>
        <description>The image height for the logo.</description>
    </attribute>

</tag>

</taglib>
```

 To use the simple tag handler in a web application, place the TLD in a subdirectory of *WEB-INF* like *WEB-INF/tlds*. Or, store the TLD in a JAR file's *META-INF* directory or a subdirectory thereof. Then put the JAR in the *WEB-INF/lib* directory.

See Also

The JSP 2.0 specification web page: *http://jcp.org/en/jsr/detail?id=152*; Recipes 22.2–22.3 on creating TLD files for tag libraries; Recipes 22.4–22.5 on packaging a tag library in a web application; Recipe 22.6 on using the custom tag in a JSP; Recipe 22.7 on handling exceptions in tags; Recipe 22.8 on creating a simple tag handler; Recipe 22.10 on using the simple tag handler in a JSP; Recipes 22.11–22.14 on using a JSP *tag file*; Recipe 22.15 on adding a listener class to a tag library; the custom tag sections of Hans Bergsten's *JavaServer Pages*, Third Edition (O'Reilly).

22.10 Using a Simple Tag Handler in a JSP

Problem

You want to use a custom tag based on a simple tag handler.

Solution

Use the taglib directive in the JSP, specifying the proper uri attribute for the tag library.

Discussion

Make sure to package the tag library, the simple tag handler, and its associated TLD, as described by Recipes 22.4 and 22.5 and the note in Recipe 22.9. Example 22-8 shows the rest of the setup needed to use the tag in a JSP.

 Simple tag handlers are designed to be easier to develop (by having only one method that you need to implement: void doTag( )). Use the associated tags in a JSP the same way you use the tags associated with classic tag handlers.

Example 22-8. A JSP uses a tag defined by a simple tag handler

```
<%@ taglib uri="jspservletcookbook.com.tags" prefix="cbck" %>
<html>
<head><title>Me Casa Su Casa</title></head>
<body>

<% session.setAttribute("imgDir",(request.getContextPath( ) +
 "/images/")); %>

<cbck:simplelogo heading=
  "<%=request.getParameter(\"level\") %>" image=
   "stamp.gif" width="42" height="54">
      Thanks for visiting here</cbck:simplelogo>

Here's all the other stuff this page contains...
</body>
</html>
```

The JSP in Example 22-8 obtains the value for the logo tag's heading attribute with a JSP expression. The JSP page user provides the value in the URL as in:

```
http://localhost:8080/home/logoTest.jsp?level=1
```

The JSP's output looks the same as the output shown in Figure 22-1 of Recipe 22.1.

See Also

The JSP 2.0 specification web page: *http://jcp.org/en/jsr/detail?id=152*; Recipes 22.2 and 22.3 on creating TLD files for tag libraries; Recipes 22.4 and 22.5 on packaging a tag library in a web application; Recipe 22.6 on using the custom tag in a JSP; Recipe 22.7 on handling exceptions in tags; Recipes 22.8 and 22.9 on creating a simple tag handler; Recipes 22.11–22.14 on using a JSP *tag file*; Recipe 22.15 on adding a listener class to a tag library; the customtag sections of Hans Bergsten's *JavaServer Pages*, Third Edition (O'Reilly).

22.11 Creating a JSP Tag File

Problem

You want to create a custom tag in the form of a tag file.

Solution

Create the tag file using JSP syntax and with an extension of *.tag* or *.tagx*. Place the tag file in *WEB-INF/tags* or in *META-INF/tags* inside a JAR file, or in a subdirectory of either of these directories.

Discussion

JSP 2.0 introduced tag files, which are custom tags that you write using JSP syntax. Tag files are designed to allow developers with little or no Java experience to create simple tags using only JSP and XML elements. In addition, tag files do not require a TLD, although you can describe a tag file in a TLD (see Recipe 22.12). If you create the tag file, then drop it in the *WEB-INF/tags* directory, the JSP container compiles the file into a tag handler class the first time its associated tag is used in a JSP.

> The JSP container converts the tag file into a class that extends javax.servlet.jsp.tagext.SimpleTagSupport. See Recipe 22.8 for more details on that class.

Tag files have introduced a few more directives and standard actions, such as the tag and attribute directives, as well as the jsp:doBody action. Example 22-9 shows these new syntax elements. The example creates the same logo tag we have worked on throughout this chapter, but uses tag file format.

> Recipe 22.14 shows how the resulting custom tag can be used in a JSP.

Example 22-9 uses a tag directive to specify that the tag's body content (the text that appears between the start and end tags) is *scriptless*. This means that the body content contains only template text, EL code, and JSP action elements.

> If you are defining an empty tag, the body-content value is "empty." If the tag accepts JSP code in its body, use "JSP" for this value. The fourth body-content option is "tagdependent," meaning that the tag itself interprets the code in its body (such as SQL statements).

Since a tag *file* can use normal JSP syntax, Example 22-9 uses a `taglib` directive to use the JSTL (see Chapter 23). Then the example defines each one of the tag's attributes.

 Remember that tag and attribute are *directives*, so their code starts with "<%@."

Example 22-9. A tag file generates a custom tag that inserts a logo in a JSP

```
<%@ tag body-content="scriptless" description="Writes the HTML code for inserting a logo."
%>

<%@ taglib prefix="c" uri="http://java.sun.com/jstl/core" %>

<%@ attribute name="heading" required="true" rtexprvalue=
  "true" description="The heading level for the logo."%>

<%@ attribute name="image" required="true" rtexprvalue=
  "true" description="The image name for the logo."%>

<%@ attribute name="width" required="true" rtexprvalue=
  "true" description="The image width for the logo."%>

<%@ attribute name="height" required="true" rtexprvalue=
  "true" description="The image height for the logo."%>

<img src="<c:out value="${imgDir}${image}"/>" width=
  "<c:out value="${width}"/>" height="<c:out value=
    "${height}"/>" align="left">

<H<c:out value="${heading}"/>><jsp:doBody/></H<c:out value="${heading}"/>>
```

The attributes for the attribute directive are the same as the attributes that you use for a JSP 1.2-style TLD file (see Recipe 22.2). Since a tag file accepts plain template text, this is how we have set up the HTML `img` tag that the tag file is designed to generate.

The `img` tag gets the values for its own attributes using the `c:out` JSTL tag and the EL (see Chapter 23). For example, the expression "${imgDir}" returns the value for a stored object attribute of the same name, which specifies a directory that contains the image used in the logo. The expression "${image}" returns the value of the tag's `image` attribute which, by this line of the code, has already been set by the user.

The `jsp:doBody` standard action is a nifty way to output the text between the custom action's start tag and end tag.

The jsp:doBody action, as well as the tag, attribute, and variable (not shown in this recipe) directives, can be used only in *tag files*.

See Also

The JSP 2.0 specification web page: *http://jcp.org/en/jsr/detail?id=152*; Recipes 22.2 and 22.3 on creating TLD files for tag libraries; Recipes 22.4 and 22.5 on packaging a tag library in a web application; Recipe 22.6 on using the custom tag in a JSP; Recipe 22.7 on handling exceptions in tags; Recipes 22.8 and 22.9 on creating a simple tag handler; Recipe 22.10 on using the simple tag handler in a JSP; Recipes 22. 12–22.14 on using a JSP *tag file*; Recipe 22.15 on adding a listener class to a tag library; the custom tag sections of Hans Bergsten's *JavaServer Pages*, Third Edition (O'Reilly).

22.12 Packaging the JSP Tag File in a Web Application

Problem

You want to store the tag file for use in a web application.

Solution

Place the tag file in *WEB-INF/tags* or in *META-INF/tags* inside a JAR file or in a subdirectory of either of these directories. If you do this you do not need to describe the tag in a TLD file.

Discussion

The JSP container finds the tag file by using the `tagDir` attribute of the `taglib` directive. In other words, the `tagDir` attribute provides the path to the web application directory where you stored the tag file. Here's an example:

```
<%@ taglib prefix="cbck" tagdir="/WEB-INF/tags" %>
```

As long as you place the tag file, which has a *.tag* extension (or *.tagx* extension if the tag file is in XML syntax) in */WEB-INF/tags*, JSPs can to use the tag associated with the tag file.

The JSP has to position the `taglib` directive in the code before the JSP uses the associated custom tag.

The JSP 2.0 TLD can also specify the tag file in the following manner:

```
<tag-file>
    <name>dbSelect</name>
    <path>/WEB-INF/tags/dbtags</path>
</tag-file>
```

This TLD entry specifies a tag file named *dbSelect.tag*, which resides in the */WEB-INF/tags/dbtags* directory. The path attribute must begin with "/META-INF/tags" if the *tag file* resides in a JAR, and "/WEB-INF/tags" if the tag file is located in a Web Archive (WAR) file or in a nonarchived web application.

See Also

The JSP 2.0 specification web page: *http://jcp.org/en/jsr/detail?id=152*; Recipes 22.2 and 22.3 on creating TLD files for tag libraries; Recipes 22.4 and 22.5 on packaging a tag library in a web application; Recipe 22.6 on using the custom tag in a JSP; Recipe 22.7 on handling exceptions in tags; Recipes 22.8 and 22.9 on creating a simple tag handler; Recipe 22.10 on using the simple tag handler in a JSP; Recipes 22.13 and 22.14 on packaging a *tag file* and using it in a JSP; Recipe 22.15 on adding a listener class to a tag library; the custom tag sections of Hans Bergsten's *JavaServer Pages*, Third Edition (O'Reilly).

22.13 Packaging the JSP Tag File in a JAR

Problem

You want to store the tag file in a JAR file.

Solution

Place the tag file in the JAR's *META-INF/tags* directory or a subdirectory thereof.

Discussion

Developers commonly distribute tag libraries as JAR files, particularly if they have designed the tag library to be portable. For JSP 2.0-style tag libraries that are using tag files, place the tag file in *META-INF/tags* or a subdirectory of *META-INF/tags*. The tag file must have a *.tag* extension, or a *.tagx* extension if it's a tag file in XML syntax.

Then place the JAR file in *WEB-INF/lib* of any web application containing JSPs that will use the tag.

See Also

The JSP 2.0 specification web page: *http://jcp.org/en/jsr/detail?id=152*; Recipes 22.2 and 22.3 on creating TLD files for tag libraries; Recipes 22.4 and 22.5 on packaging a tag library in a web application; Recipe 22.6 on using the custom tag in a JSP; Recipe 22.7 on handling exceptions in tags; Recipes 22.8 and 22.9 on creating a simple tag handler; Recipe 22.10 on using the simple tag handler in a JSP; Recipe 22.14 on using a tag tag file based on a tag file; Recipe 22.15 on adding a listener class to a tag library; the custom tag sections of Hans Bergsten's *JavaServer Pages*, Third Edition (O'Reilly).

22.14 Using a Custom Tag Associated with a Tag File

Problem

You want to use a custom tag associated with a tag file.

Solution

Use the `taglib` directive in the JSP, before the code that uses the tag file related tag.

Discussion

The `taglib` directive identifies the tag with its `tagdir` attribute, which is the web application path to the *tags* directory. Example 22-10 uses the tag from a tag file stored at */WEB-INF/tags/logo.tag*.

The tag name in the JSP is the same as the tag filename, without the *.tag* extension. The `prefix` attribute represents the custom tag's namespace, so the entire tag is used in the JSP as "<cbck:logo heading=...> ...tag content...</cbck:logo>."

Example 22-10. A JSP uses a tag defined in a tag file

```
<%@ taglib prefix="cbck" tagdir="/WEB-INF/tags" %>

<html>
<head><title>Me Casa Su Casa</title></head>
<body>

<% session.setAttribute("imgDir",(request.getContextPath( ) + "/images/")); %>

<cbck:logo heading="<%=request.getParameter(\"level\") %>" image=
  "stamp.gif" width="42" height="54">
Thanks for visiting here ...
</cbck:logo>
```

Example 22-10. A JSP uses a tag defined in a tag file (continued)

```
Here's all the other stuff this page contains...
</body>
</html>
```

 I use the same basic logo tag throughout this chapter to illustrate the various custom-tag syntax differences. See Recipe 22.2 for details on the logo tag itself.

See Also

The JSP 2.0 specification web page: *http://jcp.org/en/jsr/detail?id=152*; Recipes 22.2 and 22.3 on creating TLD files for tag libraries; Recipes 22.4 and 22.5 on packaging a tag library in a web application; Recipe 22.6 on using the custom tag in a JSP; Recipe 22.7 on handling exceptions in tags; Recipes 22.8 and 22.9 on creating a simple tag handler; Recipe 22.10 on using the simple tag handler in a JSP; Recipes 22.11–22.13 on setting up a JSP tag file; Recipe 22.15 on adding a listener class to a tag library; the custom tag sections of Hans Bergsten's *JavaServer Pages*, Third Edition (O'Reilly).

22.15 Adding a Listener Class to a Tag Library

Problem

You want to include a listener class with your tag library.

Solution

Add a listener element to your TLD file.

Discussion

The servlet API includes "application event listeners," which are special Java classes that are notified by the web container when certain events occur, such as the creation of a new user session (see Chapter 11). You can include listener classes with your tag libraries. For example, you might have a session-related tag that needs to know when sessions are created or destroyed.

The listener element has exactly the same syntax as it may appear in the *web.xml* deployment descriptor. Example 22-11 shows a listener element included in a JSP Version 2.0 TLD.

Example 22-11. Adding a listener element to a JSP 2.0 TLD

```
<!-- beginning of the TLD file. The listener element is nested in the taglib element. SEE
CHAPTER 11 OR 14 FOR LISTENER CODE EXAMPLES -->

<taglib xmlns="http://java.sun.com/xml/ns/j2ee"
 xmlns:xsi="http://www.w3.org/2001/XMLSchema-instance"
 xsi:schemaLocation=
    "http://java.sun.com/xml/ns/j2ee
    http://java.sun.com/xml/ns/j2ee/web-jsptaglibrary_2_0.xsd"
    version="2.0"
>

    <tlib-version>1.0</tlib-version>
    <jsp-version>2.0</jsp-version>
    <short-name>cbck</short-name>
    <uri>com.jspservletcookbook.tags</uri>
    <description>Cookbook custom tags</description>

    <listener>
        <listener-class>
        com.jspservletcookbook.ReqListener
        </listener-class>
    </listener>


    <tag>

    <!-- declare a tag here. See Examples 22-2 (Recipe 22.2), 22-3 (recipe
    22.3), or 22-7 (Recipe 22.9) -->

    </tag>

</taglib>
```

The JSP specification requires the JSP container to automatically instantiate and register the listeners that are associated with tag libraries. A listener can be used with a tag library to track the number of requests the web application is receiving, as shown in the ServletRequestListener in Example 18-8 (Recipe 18.6).

JSP 1.2's TLD file uses an XML DTD. Therefore, the TLD elements must appear in a specific sequence. The listener element is nested inside the taglib element; listener appears after all of the other nested elements except for tag. You can precede your tag elements with the listener element. In the JSP 2.0 TLD, on the other hand, you can position the listener right after the taglib root element.

Store any listener classes in the same JAR file as the one containing any tag handler classes.

Make sure to specify the listener class in the listener-class element as a fully qualified class name, or the JSP container will probably have trouble finding the class.

See Also

Example 18-8 in Recipe 18.6 for an example of a class that implements the javax. servlet.ServletRequestListener; Chapter 11 and Chapter 14 for several listener-related recipes; Recipe 22.2 on creating a JSP 1.2 TLD file; Recipe 22.3 on creating a JSP 2.0 TLD; Recipe 22.9 on creating a TLD for a simple tag handler; the custom tag sections of Hans Bergsten's *JavaServer Pages*, Third Edition (O'Reilly).

CHAPTER 23

Using the JSTL

23.0 Introduction

JavaServer Page's custom tags and tag handlers are designed to help you invent your own tags. While this is a powerful tool for Java web developers, developing custom tags entails a steep learning curve and can be time consuming. Luckily, some hard-working volunteer software developers have developed a bunch of highly useful tags for you. This tag collection is called the JavaServer Pages Standard Tag Library (JSTL). The JSTL specification arises from the Java Community Process (JSR-052) and the Apache Jakarta Project has developed a JSTL implementation, the Standard 1.0 taglib.

The JSTL has very broad functionality. It includes tags that:

1. Set object attributes for web applications (c:set).

2. Output text to web pages (c:out and x:out).

3. Iterate over collections of data (c:forEach and x:forEach).

4. Format numbers, dates, and currencies using different international styles (e.g., fmt:formatDate, fmt:formatNumber).

5. Transform XML (x:transform).

6. Interact with databases using SQL (e.g., sql:query, sql:update).

7. Allow you to embed function calls in JSP code and template text (e.g., fn:substring( )). This functionality is available only with JSP 2.0 and JSTL 1.1 (see Recipe 23.14).

The JSTL originated a very important new JSP technology, the Expression Language (EL). This is a scripting language based generally on JavaScript and other scripting tools that, with JSP 2.0, can be embedded in HTML template text.

The EL was once part of JSTL 1.0 but has now migrated to the JSP specification. The EL must be implemented with JSP 2.0 containers such as Tomcat 5.

This chapter is designed to start you quickly with the JSTL, which commonly has to be downloaded and installed in a web application. Many web containers eventually integrate or have already integrated a JSTL implementation with their servlet and JSP engines.

23.1 Downloading the JSTL 1.0 and Using the JSTL Tags in JSPs

Problem

You want to download and use the JSTL.

Solution

Download the JSTL distribution, in a ZIP or TAR file, from the Apache Jakarta Project.

Discussion

The Apache Jakarta Project hosts the reference implementation (RI) for the JSTL. An RI is software that is designed to implement a particular Java technology specification in order to demonstrate how the software is intended to function. RIs are freely available for use by software vendors and developers. You can download the binary or source distribution of the JSTL from *http://jakarta.apache.org/taglibs/doc/standard-doc/intro.html*.

Unpack the ZIP or TAR file into the directory of your choice. This creates a *jakarta-taglibs* directory.

> This recipe uses the Standard Taglib Version 1.0.3, an implementation of the JSTL 1.0. However, by the time you read this, the Jakarta Taglibs site will have introduced Standard Taglib Version 1.1, which is an implementation of the JSTL 1.1. The new version includes some new features such as functions, which are described in Recipe 23.14.

Inside the *standard-1.0.3* directory is a *lib* subdirectory. This directory contains a number of JAR files, including *jstl.jar* and *standard.jar*. The *jstl.jar* contains the JSTL 1.0 API classes; *standard.jar* is a collection of JSTL 1.0 implementation classes. Add *all* of the JAR files found in your JSTL distribution's *lib* directory (*jakarta-taglibs/standard-1.0.3/lib* in the example) to *WEB-INF/lib*.

> JSTL 1.1 only requires the installation of *jstl.jar* and *standard.jar* in */WEB-INF/lib* if you are using J2SE 1.4.2 or higher (as well as Servlet 2.4 and JSP 2.0).

Table 23-1 describes each of the JAR files found in the distribution's *lib* directory (courtesy of the Standard Taglib 1.0 documentation).

Table 23-1. Contents of the JSTL 1.0 reference implementation lib directory

File name	Purpose
jstl.jar	JSTL1.0 API classes
standard .jar	JSTL1.0 implementation classes
jaxen_full.jar	Xpath engine classes
jdbc2_0-stdext.jar	Java Database Connectivity (JDBC) implementation classes (also included with J2SE 1.4)
saxpath.jar	Simple API for Xpath parsing
xalan.jar	Apache Xalan Extensible StyleSheet Transformations (XSLT) processor
dom.jar, jaxp-api.jar, sax.jar, xercesImpl.jar	Java API for XML Processing (JAXP) 1.2 API libraries

In the JSP where you want to use the JSTL tags, use the proper `taglib` directive shown in Table 23-2. For example, if you use all of the different JSTL functions (core, XML, formatting, and SQL), your JSP contains *all* of the following `taglib` directives, preferably at the top of the JSP page (they must appear before the tags are used).

Table 23-2. The taglib directives for different JSTL functions, version 1.0

JSTL library	taglib directive
Core	<%@ taglib uri="java.sun.com/jstl/core" prefix="c" %>
XML processing	<%@ taglib uri="java.sun.com/jstl/xml" prefix="x" %>
Formatting data (such as dates and currencies) for international users	<%@ taglib uri="java.sun.com/jstl/fmt" prefix="fmt" %>
SQL and Database access	<%@ taglib uri="java.sun.com/jstl/sql" prefix="sql" %>

 The Java community is now working on the JSTL Version 1.1, which will require a JSP-2.0 compatible JSP container. JSTL 1.1 will use these different uri values in the `taglib` directive:

- *http://java.sun.com/jsp/jstl/core*, so the entire taglib directive would look like: <%@ taglib uri="java.sun.com/jsp/jstl/core" prefix="c" %>
- *http://java.sun.com/jsp/jstl/xml*, creating a taglib directive of: <%@ taglib uri="java.sun.com/jsp/jstl/xml" prefix="x" %>
- *http://java.sun.com/jsp/jstl/fmt*, as used in the taglib directive: <%@ taglib uri="java.sun.com/jsp/jstl/fmt" prefix="fmt" %>
- *http://java.sun.com/jsp/jstl/sql*, creating a taglib directive of: <%@ taglib uri="java.sun.com/jsp/jstl/sql" prefix="sql" %>

See Also

The Jakarta Project's Taglibs site: *http://jakarta.apache.org/taglibs/index.html*; Sun Microsystem's JSTL information page: *http://java.sun.com/products/jsp/jstl/*; Recipe 23.3 on using the core tags; Recipes 23.4 and 23.5 on using XML-related tags; Recipe 23.6 on using the formatting tags; Recipes 23.7 and 23.8 on the JSTL's SQL features; Recipes 23.9–23.14 on using the EL to access scoped variables, cookies, and JavaBean properties.

23.2 Downloading the Java Web Services Developer Pack

Problem

You want to download the Java Web Services Developer Pack (WSDP) so that you can use a JSTL 1.1 reference implementation.

Solution

Visit the Sun Microsystems Java WSDP download site at *http://java.sun.com/webservices/jwsdp*.

Discussion

The Java WSDP Version 1.2 contains reference implementations of the JSTL 1.1, as well as several other web tier technologies, including the Servlet API 2.4 and JSP 2.0. The WSDP is bundled with Tomcat 5, so once you install the WSDP you can experiment with the various technologies, including JavaServer Faces, Java Architecture for XML Binding (JAXB), Java API for XML Processing, and Java API for XML-based RPC (Jax-RPC).

The Java WSDP 1.2 installs on both Windows and various Unix systems, such as Solaris and Linux. Recipe 23.15 shows how to use JSTL 1.1 functions; I use the WSDP for this recipe.

 Using Tomcat 5 and the new JSTL 1.1 features such as functions and the embedding of EL code in template text requires you to use the servlet API 2.4 version of *web.xml*. See Recipe 23.15 for more details on this issue.

See Also

The Sun Microsystems Java WSDP download site at: *http://java.sun.com/webservices/jwsdp*; Recipe 23.15 on using JSTL 1.1 *functions*; Sun's JSTL information page: *http://java.sun.com/products/jsp/jstl/*; Recipe 23.3 on using the core tags; Recipes 23.4 and 23.5 on using XML-related tags; Recipe 23.6 on using the formatting tags; Recipes 23.7 and 23.8 on the JSTL's SQL features; Recipes 23.9–23.14 on using the EL to access scoped variables, cookies, and JavaBean properties.

23.3 Using the Core JSTL Tags

Problem

You want to use the core JSTL tags in a JSP.

Solution

Use the `taglib` directive with the core `uri` attribute value to make the tags available in the JSP.

Discussion

This recipe demonstrates several JSTL tags that you use all the time: `c:set`, `c:out`, `c:forEach`, and `c:if`. Here are the tag summaries:

- The `c:set` tag sets object attributes to `page`, `request`, `session`, or `application` scopes.
- The `c:out` tag displays text literals or the values of variables or bean properties in your JSPs.
- The `c:forEach` tag iterates over `Maps`, `Collections`, and `arrays`.
- The `c:if` tag tests expressions for `true` or `false` values, then conditionally executes the code nested in the `c:if` body.

 Remember to use the prefix for the certain functional area of the JSTL, such as c, followed by a colon, and the tag name, as in "c:forEach."

Example 23-1 is a helper class that I find necessary to properly return a `String` array of TimeZone IDs to the JSP in Example 23-2.

Example 23-1. A helper class to help display TimeZone IDs

```
package com.jspservletcookbook;

import java.util.TimeZone;

public class ZoneWrapper  {

    public ZoneWrapper( ){}

    public String[] getAvailableIDs( ){

        return TimeZone.getAvailableIDs( );

    }

}
```

Example 23-2 shows how to use a number of the core JSTL tags. The code uses the jsp:useBean standard action to create ZoneWrapper (Example 23-1) and java.util. Date objects for use by the tags.

Example 23-2. Using core JSTL 1.0 tags in a JSP

```
<%@ taglib uri="http://java.sun.com/jstl/core" prefix="c" %>

<jsp:useBean id="zone" class="com.jspservletcookbook.ZoneWrapper" />

<jsp:useBean id="date" class="java.util.Date" />

<html>
<head><title>Using the Core JSTL tags</title></head>
<body>
<h2>Here are the available Time Zone IDs on your system</h2>

<c:if test="${date.time != 0}" >

    <c:out value=
      "Phew, time has not stopped yet...<br /><br />" escapeXml="false"/>

</c:if>

<%-- The variable 'zones' contains a String array of TimeZone IDs; it is stored as a
'session' object attribute. The '${zone.availableIDs}' expression is the equivalent of
calling the ZoneWrapper.getAvailableIDs( ) method --%>

<c:set var="zones" value="${zone.availableIDs}" scope="session" />

<c:forEach var="id" items="${zones}">

        <c:out value="${id}<br />" escapeXml="false" />
```

Example 23-2. Using core JSTL 1.0 tags in a JSP (continued)
```
</c:forEach>

</body>
</html>
```
The c:if tag uses an EL phrase to test whether the Date object's getTime() method returns a value that is not zero (of course it does! I'm just demonstrating how to use the c:if tag).
```
${date.time != 0}
```
The prior code represents a boolean expression that returns true if Date.getTime() is greater than zero. If true, then the code executes the nested c:out tag, which writes a message that the client's browser displays.

 The escapeXml="false" code displays the characters

 correctly in the HTML output by the c:out tag. See Table 23-3.

Example 23-2 sets an object attribute to session scope. This object is a String[] type containing time zone IDs, such as "Pacific/Tahiti." The c:forEach tag then iterates over all of these array members, displaying each ID with the c:out tag:
```
<c:forEach var="id" items="${zones}">
    <c:out value="${id}<br />" escapeXml="false" />
</c:forEach>
```
The var attribute of the c:forEach tag stores the current array member as c:forEach cycles over the collection. The c:out tag uses an EL expression to access the value of the current array member:
```
<c:out value="${id}<br />" escapeXml="false" />
```
If you do not give the escapeXml attribute a false value when using c:out, the character entity codes shown in Table 23-3 will display instead of the escaped characters.

Table 23-3. The c:out tag's escaped characters

c:out value attribute character	Character entity code
<	&lt;
>	&gt;
&	&amp;
'	&#039;
"	&#034;

Figure 23-1 shows a part of the JSP using the code in Example 23-2.

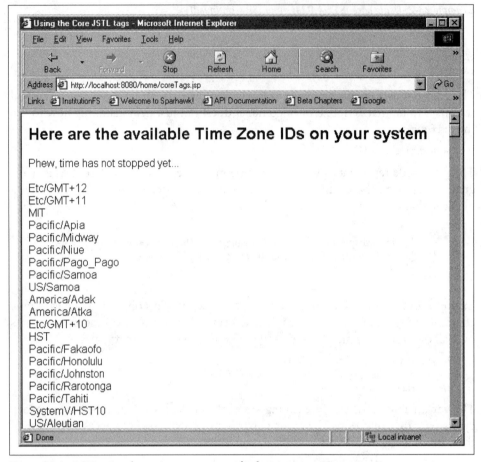

Figure 23-1. A JSP using the various core tags to display time zone IDs

See Also

Recipe 6.8 on including content in a JSP with the c:url tag; the Jakarta Project's Taglibs site: *http://jakarta.apache.org/taglibs/index.html*; the Sun Microsystems JSTL information page: *http://java.sun.com/products/jsp/jstl/*; Recipes 23.4 and 23.5 on using XML-related tags; Recipe 23.6 on using the formatting tags; Recipes 23.7 and 23.8 on the JSTL's SQL features; Recipes 23.9–23.14 on using the EL to access scoped variables, cookies, and JavaBean properties.

23.4   Using the XML Core JSTL Tags

Problem

You want to use the JSTL's XML tags in a JSP.

Solution

Use the various XML tags after declaring the tag library with the proper taglib directive (uri attribute of *http://java.sun.com/jstl/xml* for JSTL 1.0 or *http://java.sun.com/
jsp/jstl/xml* for JSTL 1.1).

Discussion

Many web developers have to write programs that parse or read XML to find information, or they have to write code that displays the encapsulated XML information
in a readable format. The JSTL XML tags are a nice tool for these tasks.
Example 23-3 displays some information from an Ant *build.xml* file. (See Chapter 4
on the Ant tool if you are new to Ant.) I'm using this XML file just for an example of
how to use the XML-related JSTL tags. Notice that the taglib directives at the top of
the page allow the use of the XML and core JSTL tags further along in the code.

Example 23-3. A JSP parses an ant build file

```
<%@ taglib uri="http://java.sun.com/jstl/xml" prefix="x" %>
<%@ taglib uri="http://java.sun.com/jstl/core" prefix="c" %>
<html>
<head><title>Using the Core XML tags</title></head>
<body>
<h2>Here are the target and property values from the XML file</h2>

<c:import url="http://localhost:8080/home/build.xml" var="buildXml" />

<x:parse xml="${buildXml}" var="antDoc" />

<h3>First the target names...</h3>

<x:forEach select="$antDoc/project/target" >

    <x:out select="@name"/>
    <x:if select="@depends"> : depends=<x:out select="@depends"/></x:if><br />

</x:forEach>

 <h3>Then property names and values...</h3>

<x:forEach select="$antDoc/project/target/property" >

    <x:out select="@name"/>: value= <x:out select="@value"/><br />

</x:forEach>

</body>
</html>
```

Example 23-3 uses the c:import tag to import a build file and store it in a variable called buildXml. The the x:parse tag then parses the imported document into a form or object that the other XML tags can work with. The code stores the parsing result in another variable named antDoc.

The XML JSTL tags use some of the same tag names as the core library, but a different prefix ("x"). The x:forEach tag in Example 23-3 uses an XPath expression as the value of the x:forEach select attribute.

> XPath is an XML technology that is designed to search for and select portions or "node sets" of the hierarchical tree represented by an XML document. While an XPath tutorial is well beyond the scope of this recipe (it is like a little programming language in itself), there are plenty of online tutorials and books on the subject. You can start at the Sun Microsystems web services tutorial, which includes a discussion of XPath: *http://java.sun.com/webservices/docs/1.3/tutorial/doc/*.

The x:forEach tag makes nested elements such as x:out available to any nodes grabbed by the XPath expression. The code in Example 23-3 displays the name of each Ant target in the *build.xml* file by first collecting a set of all of the target elements with this expression:

```
<%-- this XPath expression is the equivalent of "begin at the root 'project' element
and get all of its nested 'target' elements" --%>

<x:forEach select="$antDoc/project/target" >
```

Example 23-3 outputs the name of each target with this code:

```
<x:out select="@name"/>
```

> The enclosing x:forEach tag establishes the context of the XPath expression in this x:out tag.

The following code states "return true if the current node has a valid depends attribute."

```
<x:if select="@depends">
```

If that expression returns true, the nested x:out tag outputs the value of the depends attribute. Figure 23-2 shows the result of requesting the JSP of Example 23-3 in a browser. I've converted the XML information into a more readable format for a browser. XML mavens (meaning those who can sift through all of these crazy acronyms!) declare that you can also use Extensible Stylesheet Language Transformations (XSLT) for converting XML information to HTML or other readable forms. This is the next recipe's topic.

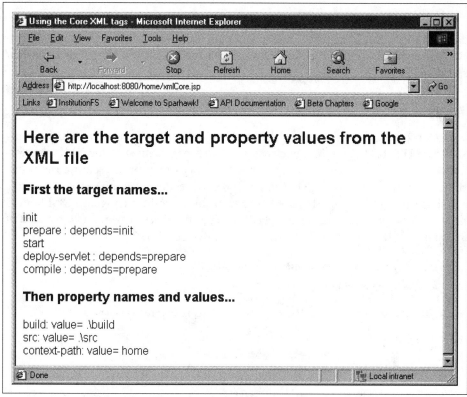

Figure 23-2. A JSP shows the output of a parsed XML file

See Also

The Jakarta Project's Taglibs site: *http://jakarta.apache.org/taglibs/index.html*; Sun Microsystem's JSTL information page: *http://java.sun.com/products/jsp/jstl/*; Recipe 23.3 on using the core tags; Recipes 23.5 on using the XML Transform tags; Recipe 23.6 on using the formatting tags; Recipes 23.7 and 23.8 on the JSTL's SQL features; Recipes 23.9–23.14 on using the EL to access scoped variables, cookies, and JavaBean properties.

23.5   Using the XML Transform Tags

Problem

You want to use the JSTL's XML and XSLT-related tags.

Solution

Use the various XML tags after declaring the tag library with the proper `taglib` directive (uri attribute of *http://java.sun.com/jstl/xml* for JSTL 1.0 or *http://java.sun.com/jsp/jstl/xml* for JSTL 1.1).

Discussion

A number of web site teams may already have devised stylesheets for transforming XML into HTML. In addition, you may want to separate most of the XML transformation responsibilities from JSPs, so that JSPs focus only on presenting the transformed information. The JSTL provides XML-related tags to easily integrate stylesheets into JSPs. Example 23-4 is an Extensible Stylesheet Language (XSL) document that converts an XML file into HTML. The stylesheet provides a conversion of an Ant build file similar to the one described in Recipe 23-3.

Example 23-4. The stylesheet for transforming an XML file

```
<?xml version="1.0" encoding="ISO-8859-1"?>

<xsl:stylesheet xmlns:xsl="http://www.w3.org/1999/XSL/Transform" version="1.0">

<xsl:output method="html"/>

<xsl:template match="/">

    <html><head><title>List of build.xml targets
    </title></head><body bgcolor="white"><h2>Build.xml targets</h2>

    <xsl:apply-templates />

    </body></html>

</xsl:template>

<xsl:template match="/project">

<dl>
    <xsl:for-each select="./target">

      <dt><b>
      <xsl:value-of select="@name" /></b> </dt>

      <xsl:if test="@depends">
      <dd>depends=<xsl:value-of select="@depends" /> </dd>

      </xsl:if>

    </xsl:for-each><!--end for-each -->
</dl>

</xsl:template>
```

Example 23-4. The stylesheet for transforming an XML file (continued)

```
<xsl:template match="text( )">
    <xsl:value-of select="normalize-space( )" />
</xsl:template>

 </xsl:stylesheet>
```

How do you apply this XSL file to the *build.xml* file to produce a readable format? Example 23-5 uses the x:transform tag to associate a stylesheet with an XML file. First, the JSP has to import both the stylesheet of the prior example and the XML file this stylesheet transforms by using the c:import tag. The c:import tag imports the resource specified by its url attribute and stores it in a variable (e.g., buildXml) that the x:transform tag can access.

Example 23-5. A JSP displays the result of an XSL transformation

```
<%@ taglib uri="http://java.sun.com/jstl/xml" prefix="x" %>
<%@ taglib uri="http://java.sun.com/jstl/core" prefix="c" %>

<c:import url="http://localhost:8080/home/build.xml" var="buildXml" />

<c:import url="/WEB-INF/xslt/chap23.xsl" var="xslt" />

<x:transform xml="${buildXml}" xslt="${xslt}" />
```

The x:transform tag makes the transformation process very easy, once you've put together a valid stylesheet file. The x:transform tag's xml attribute specifies the XML file that the x:transform tag handler transforms by applying a stylesheet. The code specifies the stylesheet to use in the transformation with the x:transform tag's xslt attribute.

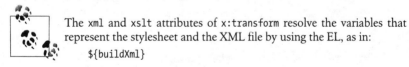

> The xml and xslt attributes of x:transform resolve the variables that represent the stylesheet and the XML file by using the EL, as in:
> ${buildXml}

Figure 23-3 shows the result of running the JSP of Example 23-5. In short, x:transform provides your very own XSLT processor for use in the JSP.

See Also

The Jakarta Project's Taglibs site: *http://jakarta.apache.org/taglibs/index.html*; the Sun Microsystems JSTL information page: *http://java.sun.com/products/jsp/jstl/*; Recipe 23.2 on using the core tags; Recipes 23.3 on using the various XML-related tags; Recipe 23.5 on using the formatting tags; Recipes 23.6 and 23.7 on the JSTL's SQL features; Recipes 23.9–23.14 on using the EL to access scoped variables, request headers and parameters, cookies, and JavaBean properties.

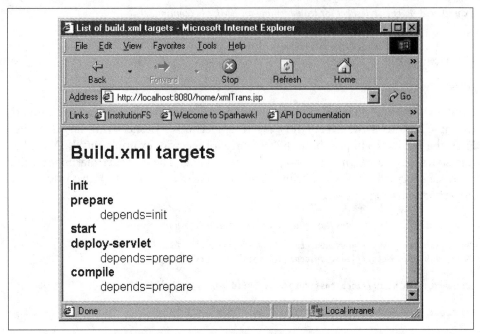

Figure 23-3. A JSP shows transformed XML content

23.6   Using the Formatting JSTL Tags

Problem

You want to format a date or a number using the JSTL.

Solution

Use the `fmt:formatDate` and `fmt:formatNumber` actions.

Discussion

Internationalization or "i18n" is the process by which web developers design their web sites to accommodate visitors who use different languages.

> The term "i18n" means internationalization begins with "i," is followed by 18 letters, and ends with "n." It is designed to relieve the tedium of spelling out the word several times.

Localization means adding specific resources to a web site to enable messages such as web page greetings to be translated into the visitor's language. For example, you might localize a site for Japanese visitors by adding resources that contain Japanese translations of text that appears on web pages (I cover more i18n-related Java code in Chapter 24). Example 23-6 uses the JSTL formatting tag library to display the current date and a large number in Swiss and U.S. styles.

Example 23-6. showing a date and a number for U.S. and Swiss audiences

```
<%@ taglib uri="http://java.sun.com/jstl/core" prefix="c" %>

<%--include this taglib for i18n related actions --%>
<%@ taglib uri="http://java.sun.com/jstl/fmt" prefix="fmt" %>

<html>
<head><title>Formatting numbers and dates</title></head>
<body>
<h2>Dates and numbers in Swiss and US style formats</h2>

<%-- create an object representing the current date --%>
<jsp:useBean id="now" class="java.util.Date"/>

<%-- set the locale to German language, Swiss country code --%>
<fmt:setLocale value="de_CH"/>

<strong>Swiss-style date:</strong>

<%-- output the date --%>
<fmt:formatDate type=
   "both" value="${now}" dateStyle="full" timeStyle="short" />

<br />

<strong>Swiss-style number:</strong>

<%-- output the equivalent of java.util.Date.getTime( ) to show how numbers are formatted
--%>
<fmt:formatNumber value="${now.time}" />

<br /><br />

<%-- reset the locale to English language, US country code --%>
<fmt:setLocale value="en_US"/>

<strong>US-style date:</strong>

<%-- output the date --%>
<fmt:formatDate type="both" value="${now}" dateStyle=
   "full" timeStyle="short" />

<br />

<strong>US-style number:</strong>

<fmt:formatNumber value="${now.time}" />
```

```
<br /><br />

</body>
</html>
```

Example 23-6 uses `fmt:setLocale` to set the context for formatting dates and numbers first to Swiss-German ("de_CH"), then back to U.S. English ("en_US").

 A "locale" represents a particular cultural, geographic, or political region. Locales are typically specified by a `String` showing a language code followed by an underscore "_" and the country code. See Chapter 24 for an expanded discussion of i18n topics.

Both `fmt:formateDate` and `fmt:formatNumber` use the current locale to format their information. The `fmt:formateDate` tag has several attributes that are designed to configure the date format. The both attribute specifies whether to output only the date, the time, or both the date and time, as in Example 23-6. The `dateStyle` and `timeStyle` attributes have settings that derive from the `java.text.DateFormat` class. Example 23-6 specifies a "full" date display that includes the day of week, the month, and the year. The code also specifies a "short" time display (such as "8:07").

Figure 23-4 shows the JSP that formats dates and numbers for Swiss-German and U.S. English speakers. There are several other formatting related JSTL tags, which the recipes of Chapter 24 cover in more detail.

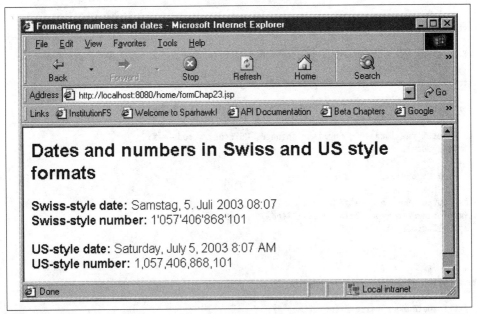

Figure 23-4. The fmt:formatDate and fmt:formateNumber tags perform translation magic in a JSP

See Also

Chapter 24 on using the JSTL's several i18n-related tags; the Jakarta Project's Taglibs site: *http://jakarta.apache.org/taglibs/index.html*; the Sun Microsystems JSTL information page: *http://java.sun.com/products/jsp/jstl/*; Recipe 23.3 on using the core tags; Recipes 23.5 on using the XML Transform tags; 23.7 and 23.8 on the JSTL's SQL features; 23.9–23.14 on using the EL to access scoped variables, cookies, and JavaBean properties.

23.7 Using A SQL JSTL Tag with a DataSource Configuration

Problem

You want to interact with a relational database by configuring the javax.sql. DataSource in the deployment descriptor.

Solution

Add a context-param element to *web.xml*, creating a parameter named javax. servlet.jsp.jstl.sql.dataSource that connects with a particular database.

Discussion

The JSTL SQL tag library allows a JSP to interact with a database using custom tags. Java Database Connectivity (JDBC) and the classes in the javax.sql package allow this technology to work. The first step in this recipe is to configure the DataSource that the tags will use to connect with a database.

 A DataSource is a factory for java.sql.Connection objects, which represent a socket connection with a particular database server such as MySQL or Oracle.

Example 23-7 creates a context-param element in *web.xml*. For the JSTL's SQL tags to automatically receive their Connections from this setting, the param name must be javax.servlet.jsp.jstl.sql.dataSource. The param value comprises comma-separated phrases:

```
[JDBC URL],[Driver name],[user],[password]
```

Developers commonly derive the JDBC URL and driver name from database vendor documentation (and often from mailing lists, because debugging backend database connections with JDBC can be tricky!). The code I show here contains an example of a JDBC URL for Oracle8*i* Personal Edition.

Example 23-7. An example web.xml configuration for a javax.sql.Datasource

```
<!-- top of web.xml file -->

<context-param>

    <param-name>javax.servlet.jsp.jstl.sql.dataSource</param-name>

    <param-value>jdbc:oracle:thin:@192.168.0.2:1521:ORCL,
      oracle.jdbc.driver.OracleDriver,scott,tiger</param-value>

</context-param>

<!-- rest of web.xml file -->
```

The JSTL software uses these values to generate a DataSource for its SQL tags. The advantage of using an external setting for the DataSource is that to switch databases, you can change the value of the context-param to the configuration representing the new database without touching the JSP code. The JSP deals transparently with the SQL tags and DataSource object.

Now on to the JSP. Remember that the SQL tags (the ones using the "sql" prefix) use the DataSource that we just set with the context-param element in *web.xml*.

Web applications always have a *web.xml* file in the *WEB-INF* directory. See Chapter 1 if you need a further explanation.

The taglib directives at the top of Example 23-8 are required if you want to use the JSTL 1.0 core and SQL libraries.

Example 23-8. A JSP uses JSTL sql tags to display database information

```
<%@ taglib uri="http://java.sun.com/jstl/core" prefix="c" %>
<%@ taglib uri="http://java.sun.com/jstl/sql" prefix="sql" %>

<html>
<head><title>Database Query</title></head>
<body>
<h2>Querying a database from a JSTL tag</h2>

<sql:query var="athletes">
SELECT * FROM athlete
</sql:query>

<table border="1">

<c:forEach var="row" items="${athletes.rows}">

<tr>
<th>user_id</th>
<th>name</th>
```

```
<th>birthdate</th>
<th>passwrd</th>
<th>gender</th></tr>

<tr>
<td><c:out value="${row.user_id}"/></td>
<td><c:out value="${row.name}"/></td>
<td><c:out value="${row.birthdate}"/></td>
<td><c:out value="${row.passwrd}"/></td>
<td><c:out value="${row.gender}"/></td>
</tr>

</c:forEach>
</table>

</body>
</html>
```

The `sql:query` tag uses its nested content to send the SQL SELECT statement "select * from athlete" to a database. The database connection derives from the `DataSource` you have already configured. The statement is designed to "select all rows from the table named 'athlete.'" The `sql:query` tag saves the result set in a `javax.servlet.jsp.jstl.sql.Result` object, in a variable named `athletes`.

 Result objects are converted from `java.sql.ResultSet` objects. Result objects have methods (such as `getRows()`) that are designed to interact with the JSTL SQL tags.

The code:

```
${athletes.rows}
```

is an EL phrase that calls the `Result` object's `getRows()` method. This method returns a `java.util.SortedMap[]` type or an array of `SortedMaps`. Example 23-8 uses the `c:forEach` tag to iterate over this array and create an HTML table row out of each of the returned database rows.

 You can use this form of code to display the *column names* of a result set ('athletes' is the variable storing the result set):

```
<c:forEach var="col" items=
    "${athletes.columnNames}">

    <c:out value="${col}"/>

</c:forEach>
```

The next recipe shows how a JSP accomplishes this same task without a context-param configuring the `DataSource`.

Try to stick with the strategy of setting the DataSource in *web.xml*, because it represents a better software design than cluttering up a JSP with a DataSource configuration.

Figure 23-5 shows the JSP displaying the database row information in a web browser.

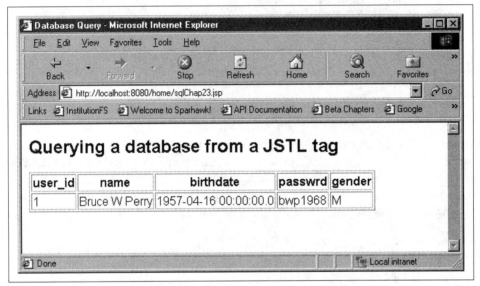

Figure 23-5. Displaying database information in a JSP

See Also

Chapter 21 on working with databases; the Jakarta Project's Taglibs site: *http://jakarta.apache.org/taglibs/index.html*; the Sun Microsystems JSTL information page: *http://java.sun.com/products/jsp/jstl/*; Recipe 23.3 on using the core tags; Recipes 23.5 on using the XML Transform tags; Recipe 23.6 on using the formatting tags; Recipes 23.8 on using a SQL JSTL tag without a DataSource configuration; Recipes 23.9–23.14 on using the EL to access scoped variables, cookies, and Java-Bean properties.

23.8   Using A SQL JSTL Tag Without a DataSource Configuration

Problem

You want to specify the DataSource for the JSTL SQL tags inside a JSP.

Solution

Use the `sql:setDataSource` tag to establish a `DataSource` for the other SQL tags, such as `sql:query`.

Discussion

You can explicitly set the `DataSource` for the JSTL SQL tags in a JSP using `sql: setDataSource` and its `dataSource` attribute. Example 23-9 creates the same `DataSource` as Recipe 23.6 and stores it in a variable named dSource. The `sql:query` tag then specifies this `DataSource` with its own `dataSource` attribute. The code otherwise accomplishes the same task as Example 23-8: the JSP sends a SELECT SQL statement to the database system, then displays the results.

Example 23-9. Using the sql:setDataSource tag

```
<%@ taglib uri="http://java.sun.com/jstl/core" prefix="c" %>
<%@ taglib uri="http://java.sun.com/jstl/sql" prefix="sql" %>

<html>
<head><title>Database Query</title></head>
<body>
<h2>Querying a database from a JSTL tag</h2>

<sql:setDataSource dataSource=
"jdbc:oracle:thin:@192.168.0.2:1521:ORCL,oracle.jdbc.driver.OracleDriver,scott,tiger"
var="dSource" scope="application"/>

<sql:query var="athletes" dataSource="dSource">
SELECT * FROM athlete
</sql:query>

<table border="1">

<c:forEach var="row" items="${athletes.rows}">

<tr>
<th>user_id</th>
<th>name</th>
<th>birthdate</th>
<th>passwrd</th>
<th>gender</th></tr>

<tr>
<td><c:out value="${row.user_id}"/></td>
<td><c:out value="${row.name}"/></td>
<td><c:out value="${row.birthdate}"/></td>
<td><c:out value="${row.passwrd}"/></td>
<td><c:out value="${row.gender}"/></td>
</tr>
```

Example 23-9. Using the sql:setDataSource tag (continued)

```
</c:forEach>
</table>

</body>
</html>
```

The code stores the DataSource in an application-scoped variable, so that another JSP can access the DataSource this way:

```
<sql:query var="athletes" dataSource="${dSource}">
SELECT * FROM athlete
</sql:query>
```

The only difference between this sql:query usage and Example 23-9 is that the value of the dataSource attribute has to be resolved using the EL; the tag has to find and get the value of an application-scoped variable (a servlet context attribute) named "dSource."

 You can also specify a DataSource in the JSTL SQL tags as a Java Naming and Directory Interface (JNDI) string, but we will reserve discussion of that topic for Chapter 21, which covers using databases with servlets and JSPs.

See Also

Chapter 21 on working with databases; the Jakarta Project's Taglibs site: *http://jakarta.apache.org/taglibs/index.html*; the Sun Microsystems JSTL information page: *http://java.sun.com/products/jsp/jstl/*; Recipe 23.3 on using the core tags; Recipes 23.4 and 23.5 on using the XML tags; Recipe 23.6 on using the formatting tags; Recipes 23.7 and 23.8 on using the SQL JSTL tags; Recipes 23.9–23.14 on using the EL to access scoped variables, cookies, and JavaBean properties.

23.9   Accessing Scoped Variables with the EL

Problem

You want to grab and display the value of an object attribute using a JSTL custom tag.

Solution

Use the EL and the c:out tag to get the value of an attribute that has been stored in a certain scope.

Discussion

An object such as a `java.util.Date`, a `java.lang.Integer`, or an object that you design, can be stored in four different scopes:

- page, so that it's only available in the servlet or JSP where it is created
- request scope, which makes the object available to any pages that interact with the JSP using a `RequestDispatcher`, such as a request that is forwarded from one JSP to another
- session scope stores object attributes for any servlets or JSPs that participate in the same session (see Chapter 11)
- application scope, which represents the entire servlet context for one web application

Example 23-10 uses the `c:set` JSTL tag to set a variable named `com.jspservletcookbook.SessionObject` to session scope. Then `c:out` accesses and displays the value of the variable.

Example 23-10. Accessing the value of an object stored in session scope

```
<%@ taglib uri="http://java.sun.com/jstl/core" prefix="c" %>

<html>
<head><title>Accessing a Scoped Value</title></head>
<body>
<h2>Here is the value of the Session-Scoped Attribute</h2>

<c:set var=
  "com.jspservletcookbook.SessionObject" value=
    "My object attribute.<br />" scope="session" />

<c:out value=
  "${sessionScope[\"com.jspservletcookbook.SessionObject\"]}" escapeXml="false" />

</body>
</html>
```

By convention, object attributes are named after fully qualified Java classes (usually, after the Java type of the stored object). Therefore, the attribute name has period characters (.) in it. This is the purpose of the syntax `${sessionScope[\"com.jspservletcookbook.SessionObject\"]}`. If the attribute name does not contain periods, then you can use an EL expression consisting of just the variable name, without the `sessionScope` JSTL implicit object, in order to access the object attribute:

```
<c:out value=
  "${SessionObject}" escapeXml="false" />
```

If you just include the scoped object's name, as in the prior code fragment, then the JSTL will search the page, request, session, and application scopes for an attribute of that name, returning null if the JSTL does not find one.

You must use the required characters of an EL expression (the dollar sign and curly braces surrounding the expression: "${ ... }"). Otherwise the c:out tag will just output a String literal such as "SessionObject."

See Also

The Jakarta Project's Taglibs site: *http://jakarta.apache.org/taglibs/index.html*; Sun Microsystem's JSTL information page: *http://java.sun.com/products/jsp/jstl/*; Recipe 23.3 on using the core tags; Recipes 23.4 and 23.5 on using the XML tags; Recipe 23.6 on using the formatting tags; Recipes 23.7 and 23.8 on using the SQL JSTL tags; Recipes 23.10–23.14 on using the EL to access request parameters, cookies, and JavaBean properties.

23.10 Accessing Request Parameters with the EL

Problem

You want to access a request parameter using the EL in a JSP.

Solution

Use the param implicit object in your JSP code.

Discussion

The JSTL provides an implicit object named param that you can use to get a request parameter. Simply follow the term "param" with a period and the parameter name. Use this terminology with the EL to output the value of a request parameter with the c:out tag. Example 23-11 displays a greeting with the visitor's name. The request might look like:

```
http://localhost:8080/home/welcome.jsp?name=Bruce%20Perry
```

If the URL does not include the "name" parameter, the JSP displays the message "Hello Esteemed Visitor."

Example 23-11. Using the JSTL in a JSP to display the result of a request parameter

```
<%@ taglib uri="http://java.sun.com/jstl/core" prefix="c" %>

<html>
<head><title>Accessing a Scoped Value</title></head>
<body>
<h2>Hello

<c:choose>

<c:when test="${empty param.name}">
 Esteemed Visitor
 </c:when>

<c:otherwise>

<c:out value="${param.name}" />

</c:otherwise>

</c:choose>

</h2>

</body>
</html>
```

The code tests whether the request contains a value for name by using the empty EL keyword:

```
<c:when test="${empty param.name}">
```

The c:choose, c:when, and c:otherwise tags are like if/then/else statements in Java code. If the request parameter name does not have a value, the browser will display "Esteemed Visitor". Otherwise, it displays the value of name.

Figure 23-6 shows a JSP displaying the message, including the parameter value.

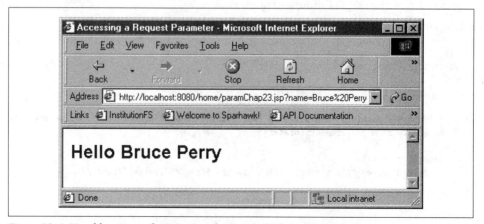

Figure 23-6. Humble output of a JSP using the param JSTL implicit object

See Also

Chapter 18 on working with the client request; the Jakarta Project's Taglibs site: *http://jakarta.apache.org/taglibs/index.html*; Sun Microsystem's JSTL information page: *http://java.sun.com/products/jsp/jstl/*; Recipe 23.3 on using the core tags; Recipes 23.4 and 23.5 on using the XML tags; Recipe 23.6 on using the formatting tags; 23.7 and 23.8 on using the SQL JSTL tags; Recipes 23.11–23.14 on using the EL to access request headers, cookies, and JavaBean properties.

23.11 Using the EL to Access Request Headers

Problem

You want to use the EL to access the value of various HTTP request headers.

Solution

Use the header implicit object that the EL makes available for custom tags.

Discussion

The header implicit object is a java.util.Map type that contains a request header value mapped to each header key (which is the header name, such as "accept" or "user-agent"). Web clients (usually browsers) send these headers or name/value pairs along with the web address of the page they are interested in.

Example 23-12 uses the c:forEach iteration tag to cycle through each of the Map's stored request headers. The variable reqHead stores the current header/value pair. The code uses the EL to display the header name ("${reqHead.key}") and header value ("${reqHead.value}").

Example 23-12. Using the JSTL to display request headers

```
<%@ taglib uri="http://java.sun.com/jstl/core" prefix="c" %>

<html>
<head><title>Request header display</title></head>
<body>
<h2>Here are all the Request Headers</h2>

<%-- 'header' represents a java.util.Map type holding request-header names and values --%>
<c:forEach var="reqHead" items="${header}">

    <strong><c:out value=
        "${reqHead.key}"/></strong>: <c:out value="${reqHead.value}"/><br />
```

Example 23-12. Using the JSTL to display request headers (continued)

```
</c:forEach>
```

```
</body>
</html>
```

Figure 23-7 shows the result of requesting this JSP in a web browser.

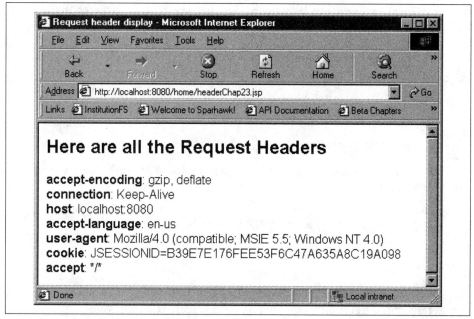

Figure 23-7. Displaying request headers in a JSP

See Also

Chapter 18 on working with the client request; the Jakarta Project's Taglibs site: *http://jakarta.apache.org/taglibs/index.html*; Sun Microsystem's JSTL information page: *http://java.sun.com/products/jsp/jstl/*; Recipe 23.3 on using the core tags; Recipes 23.4 and 23.5 on using the XML tags; Recipe 23.6 on using the formatting tags; Recipes 23.4 and 23.5 on using the SQL JSTL tags; Recipes 23.12–23.14 on using the EL to access one request header, cookies, and JavaBean properties.

23.12 Using the EL to Access One Request Header

Problem

You want to use the EL to access the value of one particular HTTP request header.

Solution

Use the headerValues implicit object that the EL makes available for custom tags.

Discussion

The headerValues implicit object is a java.util.Map type that contains a String array (a String[] type) for every header name. Example 23-13 displays only the value of the "user-agent" request header, which identifies the type of browser the client is using.

Example 23-13. Using the JSTL to display request headers

```
<%@ taglib uri="http://java.sun.com/jstl/core" prefix="c" %>

<html>
<head><title>User Agent</title></head>
<body>
<h2>Here is your user agent</h2>

<%-- 'headerValues' represents a java.util.Map type holding a String[] type for every
request header--%>

    <strong><c:out value=
        "${headerValues[\"user-agent\"][0]}"/> </strong>

</body>
</html>
```

The code accesses only the first member of the String array (it is highly likely that the user-agent request header only involves one value). The expression:

```
${headerValues[\"user-agent\"]}
```

returns the array, and the entire expression, including the "[0]" array operator, which returns the name of the user agent, such as "Mozilla/4.0 (compatible; MSIE 5.5; Windows NT 4.0)."

See Also

Chapter 18 on working with the client request; Recipe 23.11 on how to use the EL to access all the available request headers; the Jakarta Project's Taglibs site: *http:// jakarta.apache.org/taglibs/index.html*; the Sun Microsystems JSTL information page: *http://java.sun.com/products/jsp/jstl/*; Recipe 23.3 on using the core tags; Recipes 23.4 and 23.5 on using the XML tags; Recipe 23.6 on using the formatting tags; Recipes 23.7 and 23.8 on using the SQL JSTL tags; Recipe 23-10 on using the EL to access request parameters; Recipes 23.13 and 23.14 on using the EL to access cookies and JavaBean properties.

23.13 Accessing Cookies with the EL

Problem

You want to take a look at all of the cookie names and values using EL code.

Solution

Use the cookie EL implicit object in the JSP to display any cookie names and values.

Discussion

The cookie EL implicit object is a `java.util.Map` type that maps cookie names (like "JSESSIONID") to `javax.servlet.Cookie` objects. Since the cookies are stored in a Map, you can use the `c:forEach` tag to cycle through the map and display each cookie name and value using `c:out` (see Example 23-14).

 Make sure to include the taglib directive at the top of the JSP so the page can use the core JSTL tags.

Example 23-14. using the EL to display each cookie name and value in a JSP

```
<%@ taglib uri="http://java.sun.com/jstl/core" prefix="c" %>

<html>
<head><title>Cookie display</title></head>
<body>
<h2>Here are all the Available Cookies</h2>

<%-- ${cookies.key}equals the cookie name; ${cookies.value} equals the Cookie object;
${cookies.value.value} returns the cookie value --%>

<c:forEach var="cookies" items="${cookie}">

    <strong>
    <c:out value="${cookies.key}"/>
    </strong>: Object=
    <c:out value="${cookies.value}"/>, value=
    <c:out value="${cookies.value.value}"/><br />

</c:forEach>


</body>
</html>
```

The c:forEach tag stores the entry in the Map for each cookie in a variable named cookies. The code uses the EL phrase "${cookies.key}" to access the name of each cookie. You would think "${cookies.value}" returns the value for each cookie; however, this syntax returns the Cookie object itself. The weird syntax "${cookies.value.value}" returns the value of the cookie. Figure 23-8 shows how the JSP displays this information.

Figure 23-8. Displaying a cookie object and value with the JSTL

See Also

Chapter 10 on reading and setting cookies; the Jakarta Project's Taglibs site: *http://jakarta.apache.org/taglibs/index.html*; the Sun Microsystems JSTL information page: *http://java.sun.com/products/jsp/jstl/*; Recipe 23.3 on using the core tags; Recipes 23.4 and 23.5 on using the XML tags; Recipe 23.6 on using the formatting tags; Recipes 23.7 and 23.8 on using the SQL JSTL tags; Recipes 23.9–23.12 on using the EL to access scoped variables, request parameters, and request headers; Recipe 23.14 on using the EL to access JavaBean properties.

23.14 Using the EL to Access JavaBean Properties

Problem

You want to use the EL to access the properties of a JavaBean in a JSP.

Solution

Use the jsp:useBean standard action to create or access an instance of the bean, then use the EL to access the bean properties.

Discussion

You can use the c:out JSTL core tag and the EL to display the values of JavaBean properties in a JSP. Example 23-15 shows the skeleton of a JavaBean that is designed to handle email. I used this bean in Chapter 20, which contains details about all of its email-sending and -accessing methods.

Example 23-15. A JavaBean that a JSP will instantiate and access

```
package com.jspservletcookbook;

import java.io.IOException;
import java.io.PrintWriter;
import java.util.Properties;

import javax.mail.*;
import javax.mail.internet.*;
import javax.servlet.*;
import javax.servlet.http.*;

public class EmailBean {

    //defaults
    private final static String DEFAULT_SERVER = "smtp.comcast.net";
    private final static String DEFAULT_TO =
    "author@jspservletcookbook.com";

    private final static String DEFAULT_FROM =
       "author@jspservletcookbook.com";

    private final static String DEFAULT_CONTENT = "Unknown content";
    private final static String DEFAULT_SUBJECT= "Unknown subject";


    //JavaBean properties
     private String smtpHost;
     private String to;
     private String from;
     private String content;
     private String subject;

    //no-args constructor for the bean
    public EmailBean(){}

     //configure an email message with request params and send the email
     public void sendMessage(HttpServletRequest request,
            PrintWriter out) throws IOException {

        //SEE RECIPE 20.3 AND 20.6 FOR MORE DETAILS ON THIS EMAIL BEAN
        //METHOD

}//sendMessage
```

```
    //get email messages using a POP account
    private void handleMessages(HttpServletRequest request,
        PrintWriter out) throws IOException, ServletException {

        //SEE RECIPE 20.3 AND 20.6 FOR MORE DETAILS ON THIS EMAIL BEAN
        //METHOD

    }//handleMessages

  //display info about received email messages
  private void displayMessage(Message msg, PrintWriter out)
    throws MessagingException, IOException{

//SEE RECIPE 20.3 AND 20.6 FOR MORE DETAILS ON THIS EMAIL BEAN

  }//displayMessage

  //getter or accessor methods

  public String getSmtpHost( ){

      return (smtpHost == null || smtpHost.equals("")) ?
        EmailBean.DEFAULT_SERVER : smtpHost;

  }//getSmtpHost

  public String getTo( ){

    return to;

  }//getTo

  public String getFrom( ){

    return from;

  }//getFrom

  public String getContent( ){

    return content;

  }//getContent

  public String getSubject( ){

    return subject;

  }//getSubject

  //setter or mutator methods
```

Example 23-15. A JavaBean that a JSP will instantiate and access (continued)

```
public void setSmtpHost(String host){
    if (check(host)){
        this.smtpHost = host;
    } else {
   this.smtpHost = EmailBean.DEFAULT_SERVER;
    }
}//setSmtpHost

public void setTo(String to){
    if (check(to)){
        this.to = to;
    } else {
   this.to = EmailBean.DEFAULT_TO;
    }
}//setTo

public void setFrom(String from){
    if (check(from)){
        this.from = from;
    } else {
   this.from = EmailBean.DEFAULT_FROM;
    }
}//setFrom

public void setContent(String content){
    if (check(content)){
        this.content = content;
    } else {
   this.content = EmailBean.DEFAULT_CONTENT;
    }
}//setContent

public void setSubject(String subject){
    if (check(subject)){
        this.subject = subject;
    } else {
   this.subject = EmailBean.DEFAULT_SUBJECT;
    }
}//setSubject

private boolean check(String value){

    if(value == null || value.equals(""))
        return false;

    return true;
    }
}
```

Example 23-16 shows the JSP that creates an instance of this bean using the jsp: useBean standard action. The id attribute of jsp:useBean specifies "emailer" as the bean name. This is the name the code uses to access the bean instance's property values using the EL.

Example 23-16. Creating a JavaBean and using the JSTL to display its property values

```
<%@ taglib uri="http://java.sun.com/jstl/core" prefix="c" %>

<jsp:useBean id="emailer" class="com.jspservletcookbook.EmailBean"/>

<jsp:setProperty name="emailer" property="*" />

<html>
<head><title>Bean property display</title></head>
<body>
<h2>Here are the EmailBean properties</h2>

<strong>SMTP host: </strong> <c:out value="${emailer.smtpHost}" /><br />

<strong>Email recipient: </strong> <c:out value="${emailer.to}" /><br />

<strong>Email sender: </strong> <c:out value="${emailer.from}" /><br />

<strong>Email subject: </strong> <c:out value="${emailer.subject}" /><br />

<strong>Email content: </strong> <c:out value="${emailer.content}" /><br />

</body>
</html>
```

When the code uses an expression such as "${emailer.smtpHost}," it calls the getSmtpHost( ) method of the EmailBean (the SMTP server from which you receive email, such as "smtp.comcast.net"). The variable emailer refers to the instance of the EmailBean.

 Example 23-16 set all of the EmailBean's settable properties from request parameters of the same name. This is the purpose of the code:
```
<jsp:setProperty name=
    "emailer" property="*" />
```

Providing the c:out value attribute with this expression outputs the value of the bean's property. Figure 23-9 shows the JSP of Example 23-16 in a web browser.

See Also

Chapter 20 on using JavaBeans to handle email; the Jakarta Project's Taglibs site: *http://jakarta.apache.org/taglibs/index.html*; the Sun Microsystems JSTL information page: *http://java.sun.com/products/jsp/jstl/*; Recipe 23.3 on using the core tags; Recipes 23.4 and 23.5 on using the XML tags; Recipe 23.6 on using the formatting

Figure 23-9. Displaying a JavaBean's properties using JSTL c:out tags

tags; Recipes 23.7 and 23.8 on using the SQL JSTL tags; Recipes 23.9–23.13 on using the EL to access scoped variables, request parameters, request headers, and cookies.

23.15 Using JSTL Functions

Problem

You want to use the built-in functions included with JSTL 1.1.

Solution

Use the proper `taglib` directive (with the `uri` value of "http://java.sun.com/jsp/jstl/functions") and prefix (e.g., the `fn:` in `fn:contains`) in your JSP.

Discussion

The JSTL 1.1 and its EL includes a nifty new *functions* library. These tags allow JSP developers to call built-in functions to handle and return values from `Strings`, arrays, `Maps`, and `Collections`. The nature of these functions will be familiar to anyone who has worked with `java.lang.String` and its numerous methods (see Table 23-4). Functions represent an evolution of JSTL from involving a collection of custom tags to giving you the ability to make function calls embedded inside template text.

Here is the setup that you need to use JSTL functions in your JSPs:

1. A JSP 2.0 JSP container

2. An implementation of JSTL 1.1 (I use the Java Web Services Developer Pack 1.2 in this recipe)

3. A conversion of your *web.xml* file to the servlet API Version 2.4 (see later on in this recipe)

Example 23-17 shows the new taglib uri and prefix values to use with the *functions* library. This JSP uses the String "I am a test String" as input to four of the available functions: fn:length( ), fn:contains( ), fn:toUpperCase( ), and fn:split( ).

Example 23-17. A JSP that uses JSTL 1.1 functions

```
<%@ taglib uri="http://java.sun.com/jsp/jstl/functions" prefix="fn" %>

<%@ taglib uri="http://java.sun.com/jsp/jstl/core" prefix="c" %>

<html>
<head><title>Using the JSTL functions</title></head>
<body>
<h2>Using various JSTL 1.1 functions</h2>

<c:set var="tempStr" value="I am a test String"/>

The length of the test String: ${fn:length(tempStr)}<br />

Does the test String contain "test"? ${fn:contains(tempStr,"test")}<br />

Putting the String into upper case using fn:toUpperCase( ): ${fn:toUpperCase(tempStr)}<br
/>

Splitting the String into a String array using fn:split( ), and returning the array
length: ${fn:length(fn:split(tempStr," "))}

</body>
</html>
```

JSTL 1.1 function calls can be intermingled with template text, as in Example 23-17. Surround the function calls with the EL delimiters ("${...}"), and make sure to use the fn: prefix, as in ${fn:toUpperCase(tempStr)}.

Example 23-18 shows how you can change *web.xml* to the servlet API 2.4 version, so that the JSP 2.0 container interprets the EL functions in your code.

 The major difference between JSTL 1.0 and 1.1 is that the JSP 2.0 specification has taken over the EL responsibility. Therefore, the JSP 2.0 container, not the JSTL libraries, now evaluates the EL syntax.

If you stick with the servlet API 2.3 deployment descriptor, then the JSP 2.0 container will not evaluate the EL expressions and function calls. Using the old servlet 2.3 deployment descriptor "turns off" EL evaluation by the JSP container; consequently, you cannot use the functions library or include EL syntax in template text. This automatic disabling of EL expressions by the JSP container is designed as a way of easing the migration of existing JSP pages to JSP 2.0. In short, a JSP that includes the JSTL 1.0 usages and is associated with a servlet 2.3 deployment descriptor works the same under a JSP 2.0 container.

However, you may want to use the new functions! Therefore, Example 23-18 shows how to migrate to the servlet 2.4 version of *web.xml*.

Example 23-18. Change web.xml to servlet API 2.4 to use JSTL 1.1 features

```
<?xml version="1.0" encoding="ISO-8859-1"?>

<web-app xmlns="http://java.sun.com/xml/ns/j2ee"
  xmlns:xsi="http://www.w3.org/2001/XMLSchema-instance"
    xsi:schemaLocation=
    "http://java.sun.com/xml/ns/j2ee
      http://java.sun.com/xml/ns/j2ee/web-app_2_4.xsd"
        version="2.4"
>

<!-- REST OF DEPLOYMENT DESCRIPTOR ELEMENTS -->

</web-app>
```

Example 23-18 alters the web-app element to include the required attributes of the servlet 2.4 deployment descriptor (See Chapter 1). The rest of *web.xml* can remain as it appeared using the servlet 2.3 DTD.

Table 23-4 describes the purpose of each *function* that the JSTL 1.1 includes in its *function* library.

Table 23-4. JSTL 1.1 functions

Function name	Arguments	Return type	Purpose
fn:contains	String, String	boolean	Finds out whether a String (first argument) contains a certain substring (second argument)
fn:containsIgnoreCase	String, String	boolean	Finds out whether a String contains a substring (second argument) in a case-insensitive manner
fn:endsWith	String, String	boolean	Finds out whether a String (first argument) ends with another String (second argument)
fn:escapeXML	String	String	Escapes characters that could be interpreted as XML markup, such as ">"

Table 23-4. JSTL 1.1 functions (continued)

Function name	Arguments	Return type	Purpose
fn:indexOf	String, String	int	Returns the index or position of one String (second argument) inside another (first argument)
fn:join	String[], String	String	Joins all String[] array elements into a String, using the specified separator (second argument) as the character between each array element.
fn:length	Map, array, Collection, Iterator, Enumeration, or String	int	Finds out the length of the array, collection, or String.
fn:replace	String, String, String	String	Replaces all instances of a String (second argument) in an input String (first argument) with another String (third)
fn:split	String, String	String[]	Splits a String into an array, using the specified delimiter(s) (second argument)
fn:startsWith	String, String	boolean	Finds out whether a String (first argument) starts with another String.
fn:substring	String, int, int	String	Returns a substring from the input String (first argument), from the index second argument (inclusive) to the index third argument (exclusive)
fn:substringAfter	String, String	String	Returns the part of the String *after* the specified substring (second argument)
fn:substringBefore	String, String	String	Returns the part of the String *before* the specified substring (second argument), begining with the first character of the first String argument.
fn:toLowerCase	String	String	Returns the specified String in all lower case.
fn:toUpperCase	String	String	Returns the specified String in all upper case.
fn:trim	String	String	Removes white space from each end of the specified String.

Figure 23-10 shows the web browser output of a JSP that uses various members of the JSTL 1.1 functions library.

See Also

Sun Microsystem's JSTL information page: *http://java.sun.com/products/jsp/jstl/*; Recipe 23.2 on using the core tags; Recipes 23.3 and 23.4 on using XML-related tags;

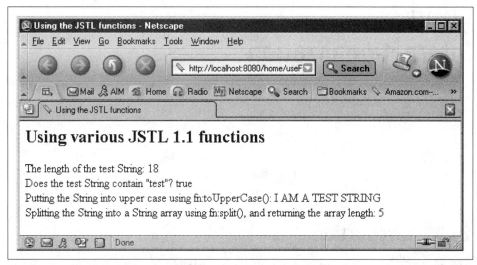

Figure 23-10. A JSP displays the results of using some JSTL 1.1 functions

Recipe 23.5 on formatting dates and numbers; Recipes 23.6 and 23.7 on the JSTL's SQL features; Recipe 23.8 on accessing scoped variables; Recipe 23.9 on using the EL with request parameters; Recipes 23.10 and 23.11 on using the EL with request headers; Recipe 23.12 on finding out information about cookies; Recipe 23.13 on using the EL to access JavaBean properties.

CHAPTER 24

Internationalization

24.0 Introduction

The audience for almost all web sites is global. Many sites have at least a subset of content that must be adapted to the language and nationality of their visitors, so that the visitor's browser formats numbers and dates properly and translates text into the proper language. An obvious example is a product documentation or help web site. What if most of your customers or viewers for this product speak a language other than English? Java provides tools that allow web developers to internationalize their sites.

Before I show these tools, let's first explain a few terms that always appear in discussions of web site translation.

1. Internationalization, or *i18n* in its abbreviated version, means enabling a web site or other Java program to provide different versions of content translated into the visitor's language or nationality. This term basically means making your site global.

2. Localization, or *l10n*, means adding resources to a web site to adapt it to a particular geographical or cultural region. An example of l10n is adding Korean language translations to a web site. The web developers who have this responsibility are often referred to as *localizers*.

3. A *locale* is a particular cultural or geographical region. It is usually referred to as a language symbol followed by a country symbol (separated by an underscore character), as in "en_US" for the English locale, "de_DE" for German speakers in Germany, or "de_CH" for Swiss-German speakers, or "fr_CH" for people in Switzerland who speak French. A locale can also represent just the language, as in "ja" for Japanese or "it" for Italian. Finally, locales can have a third segment or "variant" that reflects a certain browser-type or vendor, such as "MAC" for Macintosh. An example of a locale for English with a Windows variant is "en_US_WIN."

The language element is represented by an International Standards Organization (ISO) language code (*http://www.ics.uci.edu/pub/ietf/http/ related/iso639.txt*); the country is encoded under ISO-3166 (*http:// www.chemie.fu-berlin.de/diverse/doc/ISO_3166.html*).

So how do you internationalize or localize a Java web site? This is a big subject and the topic of several books. The following recipes provide the basics of how to create properties files (called *ResourceBundles*). These files (they can also be implemented as Java classes) provide language translations for phrases that your web pages use. A servlet can then access these resources and provide different text versions according to the requester's locale.

The recipes in this chapter also cover how to adapt JSP pages to visitors who speak different languages by using the JSTL tags. I begin by describing how to detect the locale of a request using a servlet or JSP.

24.1   Detecting the Client Locale in a Servlet

Problem

You want to detect the client locale in a servlet.

Solution

Use the ServletRequest.getLocale( ) method.

Discussion

The locale is represented by a class in Java: java.util.Locale. The ServletRequest object can access the client's "preferred" locale with its getLocale( ) method, which returns a Locale object.

The preferred locale is the user's top preference. For example, a user may configure their browser with a Spanish language locale ("es_ES") as the preferred one.

Java code can access the list of locales that a user configures a browser with by calling ServletRequest's getLocales( ) method, which returns an Enumeration object. This object contains the preferred and less-preferred locales.

To set the language preference(s) in Netscape 7.1, go to "Edit → Preferences → Netscape → Languages." In the Macintosh Safari browser, open System Preferences and drag your language preference(s) to the top of the list (then restart Safari). In Internet Explorer 5.5, go to "Tools → Internet Options → Languages."

Example 24-1 accesses the client's preferred locale by calling `request.getLocale( )`. The servlet then displays information about the locale by calling some `Locale` methods. Example 24-1 also displays infomation about the less-preferred locales by using the method `request.getLocales( )`.

Example 24-1. Accessing the Locale object in a servlet

```
package com.jspservletcookbook;

import java.util.Enumeration;
import java.util.Locale;

import javax.servlet.*;
import javax.servlet.http.*;

public class LocaleDisplay extends HttpServlet {

    public void doGet(HttpServletRequest request,
      HttpServletResponse response)
      throws ServletException, java.io.IOException {

        //Get the client's Locales
        Enumeration enum = request.getLocales( );
        //Get the preferred Locale
        Locale preferred = request.getLocale( );
        String prefDisplay = "";
        if (preferred != null)
            prefDisplay = preferred.getDisplayName( );

        //Display the preferred and any other locales
        response.setContentType("text/html");
        java.io.PrintWriter out = response.getWriter( );
        out.println(
          "<html><head><title>Locale Display</title></head><body>");

        out.println("<h2>Here is your Locale info...</h2>");
        out.println("<b>Preferred Locale:</b> ");
        out.println( prefDisplay );
        out.println("<br />");
        out.println("Locale country: ");
        if (preferred != null)
          out.println( preferred.getDisplayCountry( ) );

        out.println("<br />");
        out.println("Locale language: ");
        if (preferred != null)
            out.println( preferred.getDisplayLanguage( ) );
        out.println("<br /><br />");
        out.println("<h3>Lower priority Locales...</h3>");
        Locale loc = null;
        while (enum.hasMoreElements( )){
            loc = (Locale)enum.nextElement( );
            if (! (loc.getDisplayName( ).equals( prefDisplay ))){
                out.println("Locale: ");
```

Example 24-1. Accessing the Locale object in a servlet (continued)

```
            out.println( loc.getDisplayName() );
            out.println("<br />");
            out.println("Locale country: ");
            out.println( loc.getDisplayCountry() );
            out.println("<br />");
            out.println("Locale language: ");
            out.println( loc.getDisplayLanguage() );
            out.println("<br /><br />");
        }//if
    }//while
    out.println("</body></html>");

  } //doGet

}
```

Figure 24-1 shows the web browser output when a visitor with a preferred locale of "en_US" requests the servlet.

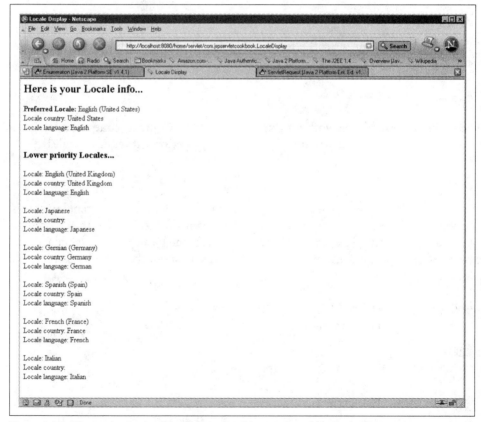

Figure 24-1. The servlet displays the preferred and less-preferred locales

This user has configured their browser with several other locales. As you can see, the method `locale.getDisplayName( )` is designed to return a more readable name (compared with "de_CH") for the locale.

 The `com.oreilly.servlet` library includes the `LocaleNegotiator` class, which uses the client request to figure out the best charset, locale, and resource bundle to use with the response. See Recipe 8.4 for tips on using the `com.oreilly.servlet` library. I don't cover `LocaleNegotiator` in particular here, but the Javadoc explains this class. See *http://www. servlets.com/cos/javadoc/com/oreilly/servlet/LocaleNegotiator.html*.

See Also

The Javadoc describing the `Locale` class: *http://java.sun.com/j2se/1.4.1/docs/api/java/ util/Locale.html*; Recipe 24.2 on detecting the locale using a JSP.

24.2   Detecting the Client's Locales in a JSP

Problem

You want to find out what the request's preferred locale and less-preferred locales are and display this information in a JSP.

Solution

Grab the preferred locale with the expression "${pageContext.request.locale}." Get access to all of the locales with the expression "${pageContext.request.locales}."

Discussion

The JSTL tags make it easy to adapt a JSP for visitors who speak different languages. Example 24-2 uses the EL to create a variable named `clientLocale` that represents the request's preferred locale. Then the JSP displays the locale's name, language, and country. Example 24-2 also displays any information about the client's less-preferred locales.

Example 24-2. Accessing the request's locale in a JSP

```
<%@ taglib uri="http://java.sun.com/jsp/jstl/core" prefix="c" %>

<html>
<head><title>Locale Display</title></head>
<body>
<h2>Here is your preferred locale info...</h2>

<c:set var="clientLocale" value="${pageContext.request.locale}" />
```

Example 24-2. Accessing the request's locale in a JSP (continued)

```
<c:set var="clientLocales" value="${pageContext.request.locales}" />

Preferred locale: ${clientLocale.displayName}
 <br />
Preferred locale country: ${clientLocale.displayCountry}
<br />
Preferred locale language: ${clientLocale.displayLanguage}
<h3>Lower priority locales...</h3>
<c:forEach var="loc" items="${clientLocales}" begin="1">
    Locale: ${loc.displayName}
    <br />
     Locale country: ${loc.displayCountry}
     <br />
    Locale language: ${loc.displayLanguage}
    <br /><br />
</c:forEach>

</body>
</html>
```

The expression "${pageContext.request.locale}" gets the request object from the pageContext implicit object, then accesses the Locale object, representing the client's preferred locale, from the request. Fairly efficient, huh? Then an expression such as "${clientLocale.displayName}" represents the equivalent of calling the Locale object's getDisplayName( ) method.

The EL phrase "${pageContext.request.locales}" represents the equivalent of calling the ServletRequest object's getLocales() method, which returns a java.util. Enumeration type. The Enumeration contains all of the client's configured locales, begining with their preferred locale.

Example 24-2 uses an implmentation of JSTL 1.1 and JSP 2.0. Make sure to include the proper taglib directive at the top of the JSP file, so that the JSP can use the EL and core tags. If all this terminology is new and strange to you, read Chapter 23 on the JSTL.

Example 24-2 iterates through each of the locales using the c:forEach tag, as in:

```
<c:forEach var="loc" items="${clientLocales}" begin="1">
```

The begin="1" attribute begins the c:forEach iteration with the second locale object, since the first locale is the client's preferred one, and the JSP has already displayed information on that one. The begin attribute uses "0" as the index for the first item in the Enumeration.

Figure 24-2 shows the JSP's web browser output. This output results from a visitor whose browser specifies the locale "es_ES" as preferred.

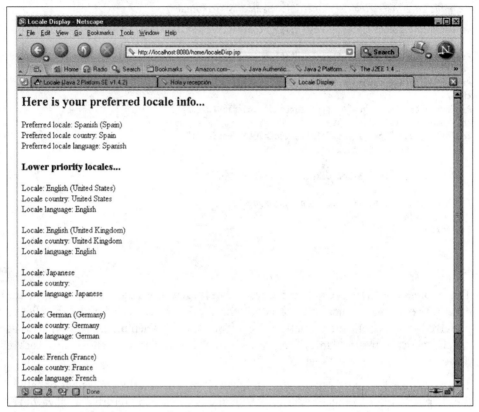

Figure 24-2. A browser requests a locale-sensitive JSP

See Also

Chapter 23 on the JSTL; the Javadoc describing the Locale class: *http://java.sun.com/ j2se/1.4.1/docs/api/java/util/Locale.html*.

24.3 Creating a ResourceBundle as a Properties File

Problem

You want to store your i18n resources in your web application.

Solution

Create a text file with name/value pairs representing your i18n resources. Name the file with your global resource name and store it beneath *WEB-INF*.

Discussion

Adding i18n-related resources to your web application involves creating properties files or ResourceBundle classes (Recipe 24.4). A ResourceBundle that takes the form of a properties file is simply a list of keys and values, produced in any text editor. The keys represents the words that you want to be translated, and the values are the translations. These files are the resources that the web application uses to dynamically translate text into the appropriate language.

Imagine that you are creating some resources with a global name, or basename, of "WelcomeBundle." Example 24-3 shows the subclass of this resource for the visitors from the locale "es_ES," or people from Spain who speak Spanish.

For example, the key "Welcome" is associated with its Spanish equivalent "Hola y recepción." Recipe 24.5 shows how a servlet would use a ResourceBundle like this to dynamically translate "Welcome" to the visitor's language.

Example 24-3. The contents of a ResourceBundle file named WelcomeBundle_es_ES.properties

```
#Spanish language resources
Welcome = Hola y recepción
```

These are just keys and values separated by newline characters. Comments are delineated by a hash (#) character.

This text file has to be stored in a place where other web components can find it, similar to installing a Java class in your web application. This is the path to the properties file, which has a fully qualified name of *i18n.WelcomeBundle_es_ES.properties*. The *.properties* extension is an essential detail!

```
WEB-INF/i18n/WelcomeBundle_es_ES.properties
```

 Centralizing the i18n resources in their own *WEB-INF* subdirectory in a web application is a sensible way to organize this information and avoid clutter.

See Also

Recipe 24.4 on creating ResourceBundle as a Java class; the PropertyResourceBundle Javadoc: *http://java.sun.com/j2se/1.4.1/docs/api/java/util/PropertyResourceBundle.html.*

24.4   Creating a ResourceBundle as a Java Class

Problem

You want to create a ResourceBundle as a Java class.

Solution

Create a class that extends `java.util.ListResourceBundle`.

Discussion

If your application requires more functionality than a static properties file can provide (Recipe 24.3), you can create your ResourceBundles as Java classes: `java.util.ListResourceBundle` types. For instance, a particular resource might need to select its translation information from a database.

Example 24-4 includes the same information as the properties file in the prior recipe. However, its key/value pairs are stored in the form of a two-dimensional `Object` array. This class is stored in the same place as the *.properties* files in *WEB-INF/i18n*.

Example 24-4. Storing language information in a ListResourceBundle

```
package com.jspservletcookbook;

import java.util.ListResourceBundle;

public class WelcomeBundle_es_ES extends ListResourceBundle {

    static final Object[][] contents = {

        {"Welcome", "Hola y recepción"}
    };

    public Object[][] getContents() {
        return contents;
    }

}
```

This code snippet from a servlet shows how you could use this class.

Example 24-5. Calling a ListResourceBundle method from a ResourceBundle created as a Java class

```
<!-- inside servlet goGet() or doPost() method, for instance -->

ResourceBundle bundle = ResourceBundle.getBundle(
    "i18n.WelcomeBundle_es_ES");

//Call inherited ListResourceBundle getKeys() method
java.util.Enumeration enum = bundle.getKeys();

while (enum.hasMoreElements()){

    //Prints out key: "Welcome"
    out.println((String) enum.nextElement());
    out.println("<br /><br />");

}//while
```

The ResourceBundle.getBundle( ) static method tries to find a Java class with the fully qualified name "i18n.WelcomeBundle_es_ES" (in this example). Failing that, it looks for a properties file of the same name (minus the *.properties* extension): *i18n.WelcomeBundle_es_ES.properties*.

See Also

The Javadoc for ListResourceBundle: *http://java.sun.com/j2se/1.4.1/docs/api/java/util/ListResourceBundle.html*; Recipe 24.3 on creating a ResourceBundle as a properties file.

24.5   Using the ResourceBundle in a Servlet

Problem

You want a servlet to dynamically display a "Welcome" message to visitors depending on their locale.

Solution

Use the servlet to access the translated text dynamically from a ResourceBundle.

Discussion

Once you have added ResourceBundles to the web application, then servlets can use them to dynamically display text based on the user's locale.

Remember, the web application stores ResourceBundles as *.properties* files (text) or Java classes.

Example 24-6 uses a ResourceBundle with a basename of "WelcomeBundle." It is stored in *WEB-INF/i18n*, so its fully qualified name is *i18n.WelcomeBundle*.

Example 24-6. A servlet uses a to dynamically display translated text

```
package com.jspservletcookbook;

import java.util.Locale;
import java.util.ResourceBundle;

import javax.servlet.*;
import javax.servlet.http.*;

public class WelcomeServlet extends HttpServlet {
```

Example 24-6. A servlet uses a to dynamically display translated text (continued)

```
public void doGet(HttpServletRequest request,
  HttpServletResponse response) throws ServletException,
  java.io.IOException {

    //Get the client's Locale
    Locale locale = request.getLocale( );

    ResourceBundle bundle = ResourceBundle.getBundle(
      "i18n.WelcomeBundle",locale);

    String welcome =  bundle.getString("Welcome");


    //Display the locale
    response.setContentType("text/html");
    java.io.PrintWriter out = response.getWriter( );

    out.println("<html><head><title>"+welcome+"</title></head><body>");

    out.println("<h2>"+welcome+"</h2>");

    out.println("Locale: ");
    out.println( locale.getLanguage()+"_"+locale.getCountry( ) );

    out.println("</body></html>");

  } //end doGet

// doPost method ...

}//WelcomeServlet
```

Here is how the application uses this resource in response to a visitor from a Spanish locale ("es_ES"):

1. The servlet accesses the locale as a `java.util.Locale` object.
2. It passes the locale into the `ResourceBundle.getBundle( )` method, which uses the locale to search for a `ResourceBundle` named *i18n.WelcomeBundle_es_ES*. The method forms this search term by attaching the current request's locale name to the end of the `ResourceBundle` basename. In this case, the bundle is stored as a Java class (Recipe 24.4).
3. The bundle then displays the message by accessing the "Welcome" key, which is specified by the `ResourceBundle` (Example 24-4 or Example 24-5).

Sometimes the browser sends the locale information as a language code only, as in "es" for Spanish (instead of "es_ES" with language code *and* country code). If the application has only installed a resource named *WelcomeBundle_es_ES,* but not *WelcomeBundle_es,* then the getBundle( ) method defaults to a resource named *WelcomeBundle* (which might not be the optimal outcome), and therefore may not display the translated text. Make sure to include a *WelcomeBundle_es* resource to cover these cases.

Figure 24-3 shows the servlet's output in response to a request from a Spanish locale.

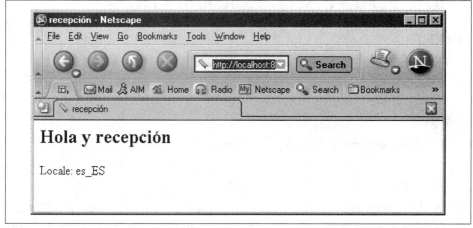

Figure 24-3. A Spanish client requests the LocaleServlet

Figure 24-4 shows the servlet's response when it deals with a locale for which the application has not provided a resource. In this case, the browser is set for the Japanese language, but the application has not yet provided a resource for this locale.

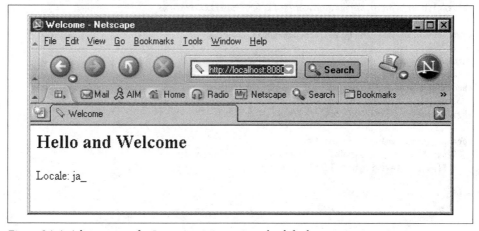

Figure 24-4. A browser set for Japanese visits receives the default message

The text that the browser displays derives from the default properties file: *WelcomeBundle.properties* (notice the absence of any locale-related suffix in the filename).

See Also

Recipe 24.6 on using the ResourceBundle in a JSP; The Javadoc for ResourceBundle: *http://java.sun.com/j2se/1.4.1/docs/api/java/util/ResourceBundle.html*.

24.6 Using the ResourceBundle in a JSP

Problem

You want to dynamically display text in the JSP according to the locale of the request.

Solution

Use the JSTL tags from the formatting library.

Discussion

The JSTL's formatting tags make it easy to dynamically display text based on the browser's language setting. Example 24-7 makes available the formatting and core JSTL tags with the taglib directive. Then it uses the fmt:setBundle tag to specify the i18n resources that will be used by the page (the localization context).

Example 24-7. Using the formatting tags to display a locale-sensitive message in a JSP

```
<%@ taglib uri="http://java.sun.com/jstl/core" prefix="c" %>
<%@ taglib uri="http://java.sun.com/jstl/fmt" prefix="fmt" %>

<fmt:setBundle basename="i18n.WelcomeBundle" />

<html>
<head><title> <fmt:message key="Welcome" /></title></head>
<body>

<h2><fmt:message key="Welcome" /></h2>

Locale: <c:out value=
  "${pageContext.request.locale.language}" />_<c:out value=
    "${pageContext.request.locale.country}" />

</body>
</html>
```

Just like the servlet code in the prior recipe, the tag dynamically uses the `WelcomeBundle` resource based on the request's locale. In other words, if the browser's locale is "es_ES," a Spanish locale, then the `fmt:message` tags uses the keys and values from the *WelcomeBundle_es_ES* properties file or Java class (however it is implemented).

 If you set the localization context as a `context-param` element in the deployment descriptor, the JSP does not have to use the `fmt:setBundle` tag. See Recipe 24.13.

In the JSP, the code:

```
<fmt:message key="Welcome" />
```

is replaced by the value of the "Welcome" key in the chosen `ResourceBundle` file ("Hola y recepción"). The result of requesting this JSP looks just like Figure 24-3 in Recipe 24.5.

See Also

Recipe 24.5 on using the `ResourceBundle` in a servlet; Chapter 23 on the JSTL; the Javadoc for `ResourceBundle`: *http://java.sun.com/j2se/1.4.1/docs/api/java/util/ResourceBundle.html*.

24.7   Formatting Dates in a Servlet

Problem

You want to format a date for display in a servlet based on the request's locale.

Solution

Use the `java.text.DateFormat` class.

Discussion

Different countries have their own ways of displaying the date and time. The `DateFormat` class, like many of the classes in the `java.text` package, is "locale sensitive." Your code displays the date depending on the browser's language setting. All you have to do is pass the `Locale` object to the static `DateFormat.getDateTimeInstance( )` method, as in the servlet of Example 24-8.

Example 24-8. Displaying a date String in a locale-sensitive manner

```java
package com.jspservletcookbook;

import java.text.DateFormat;

import java.util.Date;
import java.util.Locale;
import java.util.ResourceBundle;

import javax.servlet.*;
import javax.servlet.http.*;

public class DateLocaleServlet extends HttpServlet {

  public void doGet(HttpServletRequest request,
  HttpServletResponse response) throws ServletException,
  java.io.IOException {

      //Get the client's Locale
      Locale locale = request.getLocale( );

      ResourceBundle bundle = ResourceBundle.getBundle(
        "i18n.WelcomeBundle",locale);

      String welcome =  bundle.getString("Welcome");

      String date = DateFormat.getDateTimeInstance(DateFormat.FULL,
        DateFormat.SHORT, locale).format(new Date( ));


      //Display the locale
      response.setContentType("text/html");
      java.io.PrintWriter out = response.getWriter( );

      out.println("<html><head><title>"+welcome+"</title></head><body>");

      out.println("<h2>"+bundle.getString("Hello") + " " +
        bundle.getString("and") + " " +
          welcome+"</h2>");

      out.println(date+  "<br /><br />");

      out.println("Locale: ");
      out.println( locale.getLanguage()+"_"+locale.getCountry( ) );

      out.println("</body></html>");

    } //doGet

  //implement doPost and call doGet(request, response);

}
```

The `DateFormat.getDateTimeInstance()` method includes parameters in the form of constants (e.g., `DateFormat.FULL`) that allow your code to customize the date format. Example 24-8 displays the date in a way that includes the name of the day of the week and a short form for the time. You can experiment with these constants in order to determine how browsers display the servlet's output. Figure 24-5 shows how the date is displayed in response to a German-language locale of "de_DE."

Figure 24-5. Displaying the date in a servlet according to the request's locale

See Also

The Javadoc for the `DateFormat` class: *http://java.sun.com/j2se/1.4.1/docs/api/java/text/DateFormat.html*; Recipe 24.8 on formatting dates in a JSP.

24.8   Formatting Dates in a JSP

Problem

You want to display a date in a JSP that is customized for the user's locale.

Solution

Use the `fmt:formatDate` JSTL tag.

Discussion

The JSTL includes the "formatting" library, which allows JSP code to display dates in a locale-sensitive manner. Example 24-9 uses the `fmt:formatDate` tag. The code uses the standard action `jsp:useBean` to create a `java.util.Date` object representing the current date and time. The code passes the date object to `fmt:formatDate`'s `value` attribute. When a user requests the JSP, the `fmt:formatDate` tag is replaced by text displaying the formatted date.

Example 24-9. Formatting a date using fmt:formatDate

```
<%@ taglib uri="http://java.sun.com/jstl/core" prefix="c" %>
<%@ taglib uri="http://java.sun.com/jstl/fmt" prefix="fmt" %>

<jsp:useBean id="date" class="java.util.Date" />

<html>
<head><title> <fmt:message key="Welcome" /> </title></head>
<body>

<h2> <fmt:message key="Hello" /> <fmt:message key="and" />
  <fmt:message key="Welcome" /> </h2>

<fmt:formatDate value="${date}" type="both" dateStyle=
  "full" timeStyle="short" /> <br />

Locale: <c:out value=
  "${pageContext.request.locale.language}" />_<c:out value=
  "${pageContext.request.locale.country}" />

</body>
</html>
```

The `fmt:message` tags here depend on a configuration parameter, or context-param element, in the deployment descriptor. The context-param element specifies the i18n-related resources . See Recipe 24.13.

The element has attributes named `dateStyle` and `timeStyle` that allow the code to customize the format of the date and time Strings.

See the Javadoc for the `DateFormat` class for more details: *http://java. sun.com/j2se/1.4.1/docs/api/java/text/DateFormat.html*.

The output of the JSP in Example 24-9 looks just like Figure 24-5 in the prior recipe.

See Also

The Javadoc for the `DateFormat` class: *http://java.sun.com/j2se/1.4.1/docs/api/java/text/ DateFormat.html*; Chapter 23 on the JSTL; Recipe 24.7 on formatting dates in a servlet.

24.9   Formatting Currencies in a Servlet

Problem

You want to format a currency value according to the request's locale.

Solution

Use the java.text.NumberFormat class.

Discussion

The NumberFormat class can format a number, such as a long or double type, as a percentage. This class has a static getCurrencyInstance( ) method. This method can take a java.util.Locale object as a parameter, to display the currency according to the user's language setting.

Example 24-10 is a servlet that demonstrates the locale-sensitive display of a currency, by showing both the currency amount and the locale language and country code.

Example 24-10. Formatting a number as a percentage in a servlet

```
package com.jspservletcookbook;

import java.text.NumberFormat;

import java.util.Locale;
import java.util.ResourceBundle;

import javax.servlet.*;
import javax.servlet.http.*;

public class CurrLocaleServlet extends HttpServlet {

  public void doGet(HttpServletRequest request,
    HttpServletResponse response)
    throws ServletException, java.io.IOException {

      //Get the client's Locale
      Locale locale = request.getLocale( );

      ResourceBundle bundle = ResourceBundle.getBundle(
        "i18n.WelcomeBundle",locale);

      String welcome =  bundle.getString("Welcome");

      NumberFormat nft = NumberFormat.getCurrencyInstance(locale);

      String formattedCurr = nft.format(1000000);
```

```
        //Display the locale
        response.setContentType("text/html");
        java.io.PrintWriter out = response.getWriter();
        out.println("<html><head><title>"+welcome+"</title></head><body>");

        out.println("<h2>"+bundle.getString("Hello") + " " +
          bundle.getString("and") + " " +
            welcome+"</h2>");


        out.println("Locale: ");
        out.println( locale.getLanguage()+"_"+locale.getCountry() );

        out.println("<br /><br />");

        out.println(formattedCurr);

        out.println("</body></html>");

    } //doGet

//implement doPost() to call doGet()...

}
```

The NumberFormat class' format( ) method returns a String that represents the formatted currency. Figure 24-6 shows the servlet's output when requested by a browser where the user has set the language setting to the locale "en_GB" (English language, Great Britain).

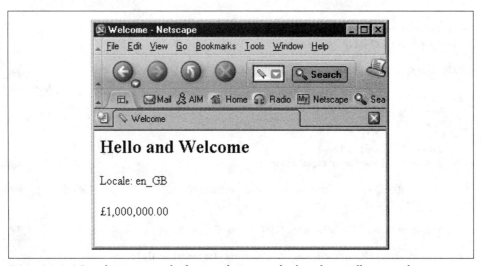

Figure 24-6. A British visitor sees the formatted currency display of one million pounds

See Also

The Javadoc for the `NumberFormat` class: *http://java.sun.com/j2se/1.4.1/docs/api/java/text/NumberFormat.html*; Recipe 24.10 on formatting currencies in a JSP.

24.10 Formatting Currencies in a JSP

Problem

You want to format currency values in a JSP.

Solution

Use the JSTL tag `fmt:formatNumber`.

Discussion

The `fmt:formatNumber` tag is designed to display a currency value based on the visitor's locale. Example 24-11 first uses the `taglib` directive to make the JSTL 1.0 formatting library available to the JSP.

Example 24-11. formatting a number using the JSTL 1.0 tags

```
<%@ taglib uri="http://java.sun.com/jstl/core" prefix="c" %>

<%-- the formatting library includes fmt:formatNumber --%>
<%@ taglib uri="http://java.sun.com/jstl/fmt" prefix="fmt" %>

<html>
<head><title> <fmt:message key="Welcome" /></title></head>
<body>
<h2> <fmt:message key="Hello" /> <fmt:message key="and" /> <fmt:message key="Welcome" /></
h2>


Locale: <c:out value="${pageContext.request.locale.language}" />_<c:out
value="${pageContext.request.locale.country}" />

<br /><br />

<fmt:formatNumber value="1000000" type="currency" />

</body>
</html>
```

The `fmt:formatNumber` tag is quite straightforward. The value attribute takes the number you want to format as a currency, and the value of the type attribute must be "currency." The text representing the formatted number then replaces the tag when a browser displays the JSP's output. The JSP in Example 24-11 displays the same browser information as shown in Figure 24-6 of the prior recipe.

See Also

Chapter 23 on the JSTL; the Javadoc for the NumberFormat class: *http://java.sun.com/ j2se/1.4.1/docs/api/java/text/NumberFormat.html*; Recipe 24.9 on formatting currencies in a servlet.

24.11 Formatting Percentages in a Servlet

Problem

You want to format numbers as percentages and display them in a servlet.

Solution

Use the java.txt.NumberFormat class and its static getPercentInstance( ) method.

Discussion

Example 24-12 uses the NumberFormat.getPercentInstance( ) method, with the user's locale as an argument, to get a NumberFormat type for displaying a number as a percentage. The code in Example 24-12 calls the NumberFormat's format( ) method, with a number as an argument.

 The format( ) method displays the number 51 as "5100%"; a double type including the decimal point, such as 0.51 produces the intended result (51%).

Example 24-12. Using NumberFormat to display a percentage in a servlet

```
package com.jspservletcookbook;

import java.text.NumberFormat;

import java.util.Locale;
import java.util.ResourceBundle;

import javax.servlet.*;
import javax.servlet.http.*;

public class PerLocaleServlet extends HttpServlet {

    public void doGet(HttpServletRequest request,
    HttpServletResponse response)
    throws ServletException, java.io.IOException {
```

Example 24-12. Using NumberFormat to display a percentage in a servlet (continued)

```java
        //Get the client's Locale
        Locale locale = request.getLocale( );

        ResourceBundle bundle = ResourceBundle.getBundle(
        "i18n.WelcomeBundle",locale);

        String welcome =  bundle.getString("Welcome");

        NumberFormat nft = NumberFormat.getPercentInstance(locale);

        String formatted = nft.format(0.51);

        //Display the locale
        response.setContentType("text/html");
        java.io.PrintWriter out = response.getWriter( );

        out.println("<html><head><title>"+welcome+"</title></head><body>");

        out.println("<h2>"+bundle.getString("Hello") + " " +
          bundle.getString("and") + " " +
            welcome+"</h2>");


        out.println("Locale: ");
        out.println( locale.getLanguage()+"_"+locale.getCountry( ) );

        out.println("<br /><br />");

        out.println("NumberFormat.getPercentInstance( ): "+formatted);

        out.println("</body></html>");

    } //doGet

//implement doPost() to call doGet( )...

}
```

Figure 24-7 shows the servlet's output in a browser.

See Also

The Javadoc for the NumberFormat class: *http://java.sun.com/j2se/1.4.1/docs/api/java/text/NumberFormat.html*; Recipe 24.12 on formatting percentages in a JSP.

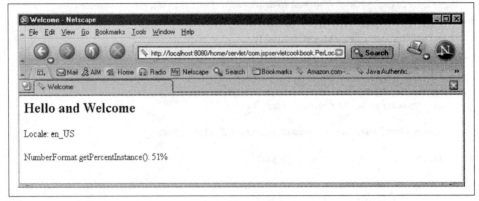

Figure 24-7. The browser displays a percentage for a certain locale

24.12 Formatting Percentages in a JSP

Problem

You want to display a number as a percentage in a JSP.

Solution

Use the `fmt:formatNumber` tag.

Discussion

The JSTL's `fmt:formatNumber` tag can display a number the code provides in the tag's value attribute as a percentage. The value of the type attribute must be "percent" (not "percentage"). Example 24-13 passes the String ".51" to the value attribute. This code displays the text "51%" in the browser.

Example 24-13. Using the fmt:formatNumber tag in a JSP to display a percentage

```
<%@ taglib uri="http://java.sun.com/jstl/core" prefix="c" %>
<%@ taglib uri="http://java.sun.com/jstl/fmt" prefix="fmt" %>

<html>
<head><title><fmt:message key="Welcome" /></title></head>
<body>
<h2><fmt:message key="Hello" /> <fmt:message key="and" /> <fmt:message key="Welcome" /></
h2>


Locale: <c:out value="${pageContext.request.locale.language}" />_<c:out
value="${pageContext.request.locale.country}" />

<br /><br />
```

Example 24-13. Using the fmt:formatNumber tag in a JSP to display a percentage (continued)

```
<fmt:formatNumber value=".51" type="percent" />

</body>
</html>
```

Figure 24-8 shows the JSP's output.

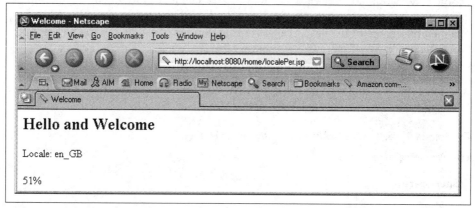

Figure 24-8. A JSP displays a number formatted as a percentage

See Also

The Javadoc for the NumberFormat class: *http://java.sun.com/j2se/1.4.1/docs/api/java/text/NumberFormat.html*; Chapter 23 on the JSTL; Recipe 24.12 on formatting percentages in a servlet.

24.13 Setting the Localization Context in the Deployment Descriptor

Problem

You want to configure the localization context for the JSTL tags used by a web application.

Solution

Use a context-param element in the application's deployment descriptor.

Discussion

A localization context is a set of resources such as `ResourceBundles` that your web application's use to provide locale information for a JSP. If the JSP is displaying translated text, it can use JSTL tags (such as `fmt:fmtMessage`) that detect the user's locale, and then searches within the localization context for the proper text to display.

Set the localization context with a `context-param` element in *web.xml*. The parameter name must be `javax.servlet.jsp.jstl.fmt.localizationContext`. Its value is the fully qualified basename of the `ResourceBundle` that you have installed in the web application. Example 24-14 shows a `context-param` element that points to the `ResourceBundle` we have used throughout this chapter.

Add this type of element to your deployment descriptor as an alternative to using the JSTL tag `fmt:setBundle` inside JSPs to specify a `ResourceBundle`.

Example 24-14. Setting the localization context for JSTL tags

```
<!-- Beginning of web.xml -->

<context-param>

    <param-name>
        javax.servlet.jsp.jstl.fmt.localizationContext
    </param-name>

    <param-value>i18n.WelcomeBundle</param-value>

</context-param>

<!-- Rest of web.xml -->
```

See Also

Chapter 23 on the JSTL; Recipe 24.2 on detecting the client locale in a JSP; Recipe 24.6 on using a `ResourceBundle` in a JSP; Recipe 24.8 on formatting dates; Recipe 24.10 on formatting currencies; Recipe 24.12 on formatting percentages.

CHAPTER 25

Using JNDI and Enterprise JavaBeans

25.0 Introduction

The Java Naming and Directory Interface (JNDI) is an API that Java developers use to access naming and directory services. These services are technologies that Java programs use to store or *bind* objects for later use, as well as search for or "look up" object references. The purpose of JNDI is to separate the responsibility of maintaining a repository of commonly used objects from the wide variety of Java classes that use those objects, including servlets and JSPs.

Examples of JNDI services are the Remote Method Invocation registry and the Lightweight Directory Access Protocol (LDAP). The JNDI API, represented by the javax. naming package, provides a common implementation for accessing objects that are bound to these services.

 The javax.naming package is part of the Java 2 1.3 and 1.4 Software Development Kits (SDKs).

Each of these technologies has a naming scheme with which "JNDI objects" can be found. The structure of these schemes is often hierarchical; you start at the top of the JNDI tree, then work your way down to each of the branches to find what you are looking for. Using JNDI, Java programs begin with an "initial context," similar to the forward slash (/) from which Unix begins to describe the location of a file. The / represents the root of a storage medium or hard disk; you can find the *Users* folder at the top level of the disk by entering */Users*.

In Tomcat, the initial context of its built-in JNDI implementation is the address *java: comp/env*—all lookups start from there. Chapter 21 describes how to access a javax. sql.Datasource from a JNDI implementation by starting at the initial context *java: comp/env*, and then looking up the DataSource at the address *jdbc/MyDataSource*. All DataSources are stored under *jdbc*, so this is how Java code accesses a DataSource named "MyDataSource." Using a filesystem analogy, the "root" folder in Tomcat's JNDI structure is "java:comp/env" and specific DataSources are stored under the *jdbc* subdirectory.

You can use JNDI to get access to any Java object, not just DataSources. This chapter describes how to store a JavaBean using Tomcat's JNDI implementation, and then look up the bean using a servlet or JSP. The chapter also describes how to configure a mail session (with a javax.mail.Session object) using BEA WebLogic's JNDI implementation, and then to gain access to that mail session by enabling a servlet or JSP to send email.

A servlet can also access Enterprise JavaBeans (EJBs) using JNDI.

> An EJB is a Java class that resides in the "business tier" of the Java 2 Enterprise Editon (J2EE) multi-tier architecture. The J2EE includes a web tier containing our familiar servlets and JSPs, and an Enterprise Information System (EIS) tier involving database systems. See the "See Also" section of Recipe 25.8.

The servlets or JSPs may represent the presentation logic of a system that uses EJBs to access databases and implement tasks that are specific to a business or organization. The last recipe shows how to access an EJB from a servlet using BEA WebLogic as the application server.

25.1 Configuring a JNDI Object in Tomcat

Problem

You want to configure a JavaBean as a JNDI object using Tomcat 4.

Solution

Create Resource and ResourceParam elements in *server.xml* or in the XML file that represents your web application (located in Tomcat's *webapps* folder). Then add a resource-env-ref element to *web.xml*.

Discussion

The JNDI object for Tomcat is set up in *conf/server.xml*. If you have configured a web application as a separate XML file in Tomcat's *webapps* folder, then configure the JNDI resource in this XML file instead. Example 25-1 shows the set up for binding a JavaBean as a JNDI object. The bean is named com.jspservletcookbook. StockPriceBean.

Example 25-1. The server.xml element for configuring a JNDI object

```
<Resource name="bean/pricebean" type=
  "com.jspservletcookbook.StockPriceBean" auth="Container" description=
  "A web harvesting bean"/>

<ResourceParams name="bean/pricebean">

    <parameter>
        <name>factory</name>
        <value>org.apache.naming.factory.BeanFactory</value>
    </parameter>

</ResourceParams>
```

Example 25-1 includes a `Resource` element and a `ResourceParams` element that refer-ences the `Resource` by name ("bean/pricebean"). This name is the address by which Java code accesses a bean instance using the JNDI API.

Example 25-2 shows the `resource-env-ref` element that must appear in the deploy-ment descriptor (*web.xml*) in order for web application code to access the JNDI object. Store the `com.jspservletcookbook.StockPriceBean` class in *WEB-INF/classes* or in a JAR file placed in *WEB-INF/lib*.

Example 25-2. Place this element in the deployment descriptor web.xml

```
<!-- start of deployment descriptor -->

<resource-env-ref>

    <description>
     A factory for StockPriceBean
    </description>

    <resource-env-ref-name>
    bean/pricebean
    </resource-env-ref-name>

    <resource-env-ref-type>
    com.jspservletcookbook.StockPriceBean
    </resource-env-ref-type>

</resource-env-ref>

<!-- rest of deployment descriptor -->
```

Example 25-3 shows a snippet of code that uses the JNDI API, just to start you on how the configuration fits in with JNDI-related code.

Example 25-3. Code snippet for accessing a Tomcat JNDI resource

```java
import javax.naming.Context;
import javax.naming.InitialContext;
import javax.naming.NamingException;

//This code may appear in a servlet's init( ) method or perhaps
//in doGet() or doPost( )

Context env = null;

StockPriceBean spbean = null;

 try{

     env = (Context) new InitialContext( ).lookup("java:comp/env");

     spbean = (StockPriceBean) env.lookup("bean/pricebean");

     if (spbean == null)
         throw new ServletException(
         "bean/pricebean is an unknown JNDI object");

     //close the InitialContext
     env.close( );

 } catch (NamingException ne) {

     //close the Context if you're not using it again
     try{ env.close( ); } catch(NamingException nex) {}

     throw new ServletException(ne);
}
```

Example 25-3 imports the necessary classes from the javax.naming package. Then two lookups take place to get a reference to a JavaBean that has been bound to a JNDI implementation. The first lookup provides the initial context:

```java
env = (Context) new InitialContext( ).lookup("java:comp/env");
```

The second lookup attempts to return a StockPriceBean object:

```java
spbean = (StockPriceBean) env.lookup("bean/pricebean");
```

The code closes the InitialContext to release the object's resources, if the code is not going to use the context again for another lookup. The next recipe uses code like this from servlets and JSPs.

See Also

Recipe 25.2 on accessing the Tomcat JNDI object from a servlet; Recipe 25.3 on accessing the Tomcat JNDI object from a JSP; Chapter 21 on accessing DataSources with JNDI.

25.2 Accessing the Tomcat JNDI Resource from a Servlet

Problem

You want to access a JNDI object with a servlet using Tomcat's JNDI implementation.

Solution

Use the `javax.naming` classes in the servlet's `init( )` method to look up a JNDI object. Then use the object in a service method like `doGet( )`.

Discussion

A servlet can access a JavaBean as a JNDI registered resource after you have:

1. Developed the JavaBean class and stored it in *WEB-INF/classes* or in a JAR in *WEB-INF/lib*.

2. Changed the server configuration file and *web.xml* as described in Recipe 25.1, in order to bind the object to the Tomcat JNDI tree.

Example 25-4 creates a `javax.naming.InitialContext` in its `init( )` method, then looks up a JavaBean: `com.jspservletcookbook.StockPriceBean`. This bean is bound to the JNDI implementation under the name "bean/pricebean." The `init( )` method is called only when the servlet container creates a servlet instance, so the servlet has access to one instance of `StockPriceBean`.

Example 25-4. Using a Tomcat JNDI object from a servlet

```
package com.jspservletcookbook;

import java.io.IOException;
import java.io.PrintWriter;

import javax.naming.Context;
import javax.naming.InitialContext;
import javax.naming.NamingException;

import javax.servlet.*;
import javax.servlet.http.*;

public class BeanServlet extends HttpServlet {

    private StockPriceBean spbean;

    public void init( ) throws ServletException {
```

Example 25-4. Using a Tomcat JNDI object from a servlet (continued)

```
    Context env = null;

    try{

        env = (Context) new InitialContext( ).lookup("java:comp/env");

        spbean = (StockPriceBean) env.lookup("bean/pricebean");

        //close the InitialContext, unless the code will use it for
        //another look up
        env.close( );

        if (spbean == null)
            throw new ServletException(
            "bean/pricebean is an unknown JNDI object");

    } catch (NamingException ne) {

        try{ env.close( );} catch (NamingException nex) { }

        throw new ServletException(ne);

    }//try


}//init

public void doGet(HttpServletRequest request,
  HttpServletResponse response)
  throws ServletException, java.io.IOException {

    //set the MIME type of the response, "text/html"
    response.setContentType("text/html");

    //use a PrintWriter to send text data to the client
    java.io.PrintWriter out = response.getWriter( );

    //Begin assembling the HTML content
    out.println("<html><head>");

    out.println("<title>Stock Price Fetcher</title></head><body>");
    out.println("<h2>Please submit a valid stock symbol</h2>");

    //make sure method="POST" so that the servlet service method
    //calls doPost in the response to this form submit
    out.println(
      "<form method=\"POST\" action =\"" + request.getContextPath( ) +
        "/namingbean\" >");

    out.println("<table border=\"0\"><tr><td valign=\"top\">");
    out.println("Stock symbol: </td>  <td valign=\"top\">");
    out.println("<input type=\"text\" name=\"symbol\" size=\"10\">");
    out.println("</td></tr><tr><td valign=\"top\">");
```

Example 25-4. Using a Tomcat JNDI object from a servlet (continued)

```
            out.println(
            "<input type=\"submit\" value=\"Submit Info\"></td></tr>");

            out.println("</table></form>");
            out.println("</body></html>");

    } //doGet

    public void doPost(HttpServletRequest request,
        HttpServletResponse response)
        throws java.io.IOException{

        String symbol;//this will hold the stock symbol

        float price = 0f;

        symbol = request.getParameter("symbol");

        boolean isValid = (symbol == null || symbol.length() < 1) ?
        false : true;

        //set the MIME type of the response, "text/html"
        response.setContentType("text/html");

        //use a PrintWriter send text data to the client
        java.io.PrintWriter out = response.getWriter();

        //Begin assembling the HTML content
        out.println("<html><head>");
        out.println("<title>Latest stock value</title></head><body>");

        if ((! isValid) || spbean == null){
            out.println(
            "<h2>Sorry, the stock symbol parameter was either "+
            "empty or null</h2>");

        } else {

            out.println("<h2>Here is the latest value of "+ symbol +"</h2>");
            spbean.setSymbol(symbol);
            price = spbean.getLatestPrice();
            out.println( (price==0?
              "The symbol is probably invalid." : ""+price) );
        }
        out.println("</body></html>");
    }//doPost
}//BeanServlet
```

Example 25-4 calls close() on the InitialContext to free up any resources this object is using, since the code does not use it again to initiate a lookup. Then the servlet uses the bean object to access a live stock quote in its doGet() method. The servlet first calls the bean's setter method setSymbol( ) to notify the bean about which stock symbol it is looking up.

Example 25-5 shows the bean that Tomcat has stored as a JNDI object (it's the same bean used in Example 25-4). Chapter 26 explains this bean, which "scrapes" a stock price off of a web page. Chapter 26 covers the bean's details; the methods this chapter's servlet uses are setSymbol( ) and getLatestPrice( ). The bean handles all the details of downloading the stock price.

Example 25-5. The bean that is stored as a JNDI object

```
package com.jspservletcookbook;

import java.io.BufferedReader;
import java.io.IOException;
import java.io.InputStreamReader;
import java.net.URL;
import java.net.MalformedURLException;

import javax.swing.text.html.HTMLEditorKit.ParserCallback;
import javax.swing.text.MutableAttributeSet;
import javax.swing.text.html.parser.ParserDelegator;

public class StockPriceBean {

    private static final String urlBase =
      "http://finance.yahoo.com/q?d=t&s=";
    private BufferedReader webPageStream = null;
    private URL stockSite = null;
    private ParserDelegator htmlParser = null;
    private MyParserCallback callback = null;
    private String htmlText = "";
    private String symbol = "";
    private float stockVal = 0f;

  public StockPriceBean( ) {}//no-arguments constructor for the bean

  public void setSymbol(String symbol){
      this.symbol = symbol;
  }

  public String getSymbol( ){
      return symbol;
    }

//Inner class provides the callback
class MyParserCallback extends ParserCallback {

    private boolean lastTradeFlag = false;
    private boolean boldFlag = false;
  public MyParserCallback( ){
      if (stockVal != 0)
          stockVal = 0f;
  }
```

Example 25-5. The bean that is stored as a JNDI object (continued)

```
    public void handleStartTag(javax.swing.text.html.HTML.Tag t,
      MutableAttributeSet a,int pos) {
          if (lastTradeFlag && (t == javax.swing.text.html.HTML.Tag.B )){
              boldFlag = true;
          }
    }//handleStartTag

    public void handleText(char[] data,int pos){
        htmlText  = new String(data);
        if (htmlText.indexOf("No such ticker symbol.") != -1){
            throw new IllegalStateException(
                "Invalid ticker symbol in handleText( ) method.");
        } else if (htmlText.equals("Last Trade:")){
            lastTradeFlag = true;
          } else if (boldFlag){

            try{
                stockVal = new Float(htmlText).floatValue( );
            } catch (NumberFormatException ne) {

                try{
                    //tease out any commas in the number using NumberFormat
                    java.text.NumberFormat nf = java.text.NumberFormat.
                    getInstance( );
                    Double f = (Double) nf.parse(htmlText);
                    stockVal =  (float) f.doubleValue( );
                } catch (java.text.ParseException pe){
                    throw new IllegalStateException(
                      "The extracted text " + htmlText +
                        " cannot be parsed as a number!");
                }//inner try

            }//outer try
            lastTradeFlag = false;
            boldFlag = false;

        }//if
    } //handleText
}//MyParserCallback

  public float getLatestPrice( ) throws IOException,MalformedURLException {

      stockSite = new URL(urlBase + symbol);
      webPageStream = new BufferedReader(new InputStreamReader(stockSite.
        openStream( )));
      htmlParser = new ParserDelegator( );
      callback = new MyParserCallback( );//ParserCallback

      synchronized(htmlParser){
          htmlParser.parse(webPageStream,callback,true);
      }//sychronized
```

Example 25-5. The bean that is stored as a JNDI object (continued)

```
        //reset symbol
        setSymbol("");
        return stockVal;

    }//getLatestPrice
}//StockPriceBean
```

 The ParserDelegator.parse( ) method is synchronized and therefore designed to only allow one thread at a time to parse the web page and pull out the stock quote.

Figure 25-1 shows the web page form generated by the servlet's doGet( ) method. The user enters a stock symbol into this form, then submits the form to the servlet's doPost( ) method.

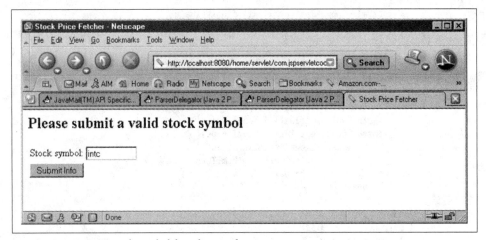

Figure 25-1. Enter a stock symbol for a live stock price

Figure 25-2 shows the stock information that the JNDI object found for the servlet.

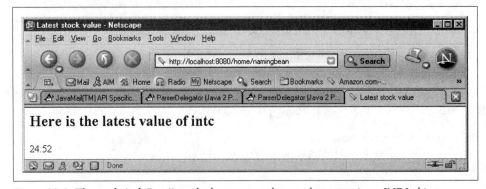

Figure 25-2. The servlet's doPost( ) method generates a live stock quote using a JNDI object

---

See Also

Recipe 25.1 on configuring a JNDI object with Tomcat; Recipe 25.3 on accessing the Tomcat JNDI object from a JSP; Chapter 21 on accessing DataSources with JNDI; Chapter 26 on harvesting web information.

25.3   Accessing the Tomcat JNDI Resource from a JSP

Problem

You want to access a JNDI resource from a JSP.

Solution

Use a filter to place the object in request or session scope. Access the object in the JSP with the c:set and c:out JSTL tags.

Discussion

A nice job for a filter is accessing a JNDI object, then placing a reference to that object in a session for a JSP to use. See Chapter 19 for more information on filters.

Here are the steps needed to use a filter with JNDI and a JSP:

1. Develop and compile the filter, including a no-arguments constructor.
2. Use the JNDI API and javax.naming package in the filter to set a session attribute using the JNDI object.
3. Place the filter in *WEB-INF/classes* or in a JAR in *WEB-INF/lib*.
4. Add filter and filter-mapping elements to *web.xml*; map the filter to the JSP that will use the JNDI object (Example 25-7).
5. Create a JSP that uses the session attribute.

Example 25-6 shows the filter. The filter initializes a javax.naming.Context type in its init( ) method (when the servlet container creates the filter instance). The doFilter( ) method grabs a JNDI object and stores the object as a session attribute. The filter chain ends at the JSP to which the filter is mapped; therefore, the JSP has access to the session attribute (i.e., the JNDI object).

Example 25-6. A Filter accesses a JNDI object and sets the object as a session attribute

```
package com.jspservletcookbook;

import java.io.IOException;
```

```java
import javax.naming.Context;
import javax.naming.InitialContext;
import javax.naming.NamingException;

import javax.servlet.*;
import javax.servlet.http.*;

public class JndiTFilter implements Filter {

    private FilterConfig config;
    private Context env;

    //No-arguments constructor required for a filter; we've made it
    //explicit here, even though the compiler would have created one
    //in the absence of this or any other constructor
    public JndiTFilter( ) {}

    public void  init(FilterConfig filterConfig)  throws ServletException {

        this.config = filterConfig;
        try {
            env = (Context) new InitialContext( ).lookup("java:comp/env");
            env.close( );
        } catch (NamingException ne) {
            try{ env.close( ); } catch (NamingException nex) {}
            throw new ServletException(ne);
        }
    }

    public void doFilter(ServletRequest request,
      ServletResponse response, FilterChain chain) throws IOException,
        ServletException {

        StockPriceBean spbean = null;

        try {
            spbean = (StockPriceBean) env.lookup("bean/pricebean");
        } catch (NamingException ne) { }

        HttpServletRequest hRequest = null;
        if (request instanceof HttpServletRequest)
            hRequest = (HttpServletRequest) request;

        HttpSession hSession = hRequest.getSession( );
        if (hSession != null)
            hSession.setAttribute("MyBean",spbean);


        chain.doFilter(request,response);
    }// doFilter

    public void destroy( ){
```

Example 25-6. A Filter accesses a JNDI object and sets the object as a session attribute (continued)

```
        /*called before the Filter instance is removed
        from service by the web container*/
    }
}//Filter
```

The filter's doFilter( ) method is called each time a client requests the JSP, so each client is associated with a different bean instance. In other words, each session stores its own bean instance.

 The JSP could then remove the session attribute (if it was not going to be used again) to conserve server resources. See Chapter 16 for recipes on setting and removing session attributes.

Example 25-7 shows the filter and filter-mapping elements that you can add to the deployment descriptor. This causes the servlet container to create an instance of the filter (calling the filter's init( ) method). Then the container calls the filter's doFilter( ) method whenever it receives a request matching the URL(s) associated with the filter-mapping element.

Example 25-7. The filter and elements for a JNDI-related filter

```
<!-- start of web.xml -->

<filter>

    <filter-name>JndiTFilter</filter-name>
    <filter-class>com.jspservletcookbook.JndiTFilter</filter-class>

</filter>

<filter-mapping>

    <filter-name>JndiTFilter</filter-name>
    <url-pattern>/jndiJsp.jsp</url-pattern>

 </filter-mapping>

<!-- rest of web.xml -->
```

Example 25-7 maps the JndiTFilter to the web component at the URL */jndiJsp.jsp*. Example 25-8 shows the JSP that uses the session attribute, called "MyBean" to display a stock quote.

Example 25-8. A JSP uses a session attribute originating as a JNDI object

```
<%@ taglib uri="http://java.sun.com/jstl/core" prefix="c" %>

<html>
<head><title>Jndi Bean</title></head>
```

```
<body>
<h2>Getting a StockPriceBean object via JNDI...</h2>

<c:set var="priceBean" value="${MyBean}"/>

<%-- set the 'symbol' property to the stock symbol --%>
<c:set target="${priceBean}" property="symbol" value="${param.symbol}"/>

<%-- get the latest price by calling getLatestPrice( ) on the bean object --%>
The latest price: <c:out value="${priceBean.latestPrice}" />

</body>
</html>
```

Figure 25-3 shows this JSP's output. Example 25-5 in Recipe 25.2 shows the code for the JavaBean that this JSP uses.

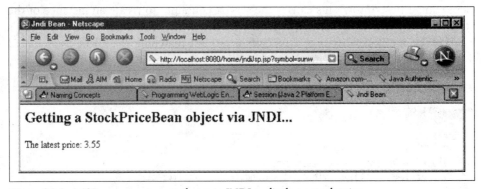

Figure 25-3. A JSP uses a session attribute via JNDI to display a stock price

See Also

Recipe 25.1 on configuring a JNDI object with Tomcat; Recipe 25.2 on accessing the Tomcat JNDI object from a servlet; Chapter 21 on accessing DataSources with JNDI.

25.4   Configuring a JNDI Resource in WebLogic

Problem

You want to bind an object to BEA WebLogic's JNDI implementation.

Solution

Use the WebLogic Administration console.

Discussion

Here are the steps needed to bind a `javax.mail.Session` object (which I use as an example for this recipe) to WebLogic's JNDI implementation. The advantage of this approach is that the available `Session` is already configured with elements such as its SMTP host (see Table 25-1). The `Session` is "ready to go" for the code that will eventually look up and use the object.

1. Log in to the WebLogic Administration console, which involves using a browser URL such as *http://localhost:7001/console*.

2. Go to *Your-domain-name* → Services → Mail in the lefthand column menu.

3. Click on "Configure a new Mail Session…" This produces the window shown in Figure 25-4.

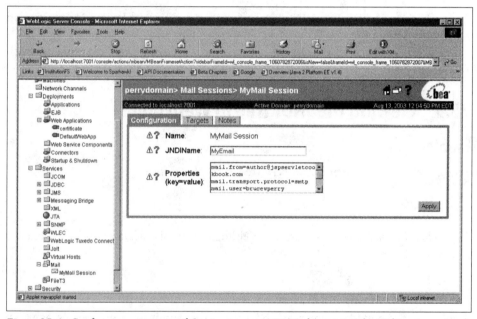

Figure 25-4. Configuring a javax.mail.Session type as a JNDI object using the WebLogic Administration console

4. Fill in the text fields in the resulting window. Give the `Session` object a JNDI name (under "JndiName"), which is the name that the code uses to look up the object.

5. Enter any properties for the `Session` by typing in the property name, an equals sign (=), and the property value. See Table 25-1.

6. Click the "Apply" button, then choose the "Targets" tab. The resulting screen allows you to associate the JNDI object with one or more servers.

Now the JNDI object is available to Java programs using the JNDI API and the name you bound the object under. Recipe 25.5 shows how to view the JNDI tree graphically to verify that the object has been bound properly.

Table 25-1. JavaMail properties set for this recipe's Session JNDI object

Property name	Description	Example
mail.host	The default mail server	mail.comcast.net
mail.smtp.host	Protocol-specific mail host; defaults to mail.host value	mail.comcast.net
mail.user	The username for connecting to the mail server	bruceperry
mail.from	The return address to use when sending mail.	author@jspservletcookbook.com

See Also

Recipe 25.6 on accessing a JNDI object with a servlet on WebLogic; Recipe 25.7 on accessing a JNDI object with a JSP on WebLogic; Chapter 2 on on accessing a JNDI object with a JSP on WebLogic; Chapter 2 on deploying web components with WebLogic.

25.5   Viewing the JNDI Tree in WebLogic

Problem

You want to view the WebLogic JNDI tree in graphical form.

Solution

Right click on the server name in the WebLogic Administration console and choose "View JNDI Tree."

Discussion

After you have bound an object to JNDI using the Administration console, you can then view the JNDI tree to see if WebLogic has bound your object as intended. Right-click on "*My-domain-name* → Servers → *Server-name*" in the lefthand menu and choose "View JNDI Tree." This generates a new browser window that looks like the one in Figure 25-5.

The new object ("MyEmail") is represented at the top of the tree as a purple dot. This is a nice graphical way of viewing the hierarchical structure of the JNDI tree, including its subdirectories and various objects, that are available to a WebLogic server.

Figure 25-5 shows the "MyEmail" bound object selected in the JNDI tree. Information about the object is displayed in the righthand frame of the browser window.

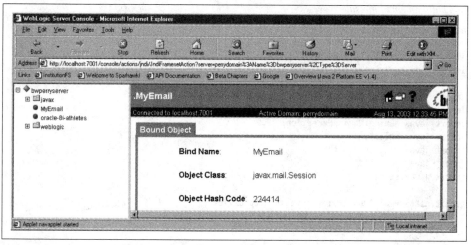

Figure 25-5. A graphical display of the WebLogic JNDI tree

See Also

Recipe 25.4 on configuring a JNDI object on WebLogic; Recipe 25.6 on accessing a JNDI object with a servlet on WebLogic; Recipe 25.7 on accessing a JNDI object with a JSP on WebLogic; Chapter 2 on deploying web components with WebLogic.

25.6   Accessing the WebLogic JNDI Resource from a Servlet

Problem

You want to access the JNDI object created and bound on WebLogic.

Solution

Use the JNDI API in the servlet to access a reference to the bound object.

Discussion

Example 25-9 is an HttpServlet that obtains a javax.mail.Session object from WebLogic's JNDI implementation. The servlet uses this object to build an email message. The servlet initiates the JNDI lookup in its init( ) method for an object bound under the name "MyEmail" (Recipe 25.4). The servlet container calls the init( ) once when the container creates the servlet instance.

Example 25-9. Servlet to obtain a javax.mail.Session object from WebLogic's JNDI implementation and build an email message

```java
package com.jspservletcookbook;

import java.io.IOException;
import java.io.PrintWriter;

import javax.naming.Context;
import javax.naming.InitialContext;
import javax.naming.NamingException;
import javax.mail.*;
import javax.mail.internet.*;
import javax.servlet.*;
import javax.servlet.http.*;

public class EmailJndiServlet extends HttpServlet {

    private Session mailSession;

    public void init( ) throws ServletException {

        Context env = null;

        try{

            env = (Context) new InitialContext( );
            mailSession = (Session) env.lookup("MyEmail");
            if (mailSession == null)
                throw new ServletException(
                    "MyEmail is an unknown JNDI object");

            //close the InitialContext
            env.close( );

        } catch (NamingException ne) {
            try{ env.close( );} catch (NamingException nex) { }
            throw new ServletException(ne);
        }
    }//init

    public void doPost(HttpServletRequest request,
        HttpServletResponse response) throws ServletException,
            java.io.IOException {

        response.setContentType("text/html");
        java.io.PrintWriter out = response.getWriter( );

        out.println(
        "<html><head><title>Email message sender</title></head><body>");
```

```
    String to = request.getParameter("to");
    String from = request.getParameter("from");
    String subject = request.getParameter("subject");
    String emailContent = request.getParameter("emailContent");
    try{
        sendMessage(to,from,subject,emailContent);
    } catch(Exception exc){
        throw new ServletException(exc.getMessage( ));
    }


    out.println(
    "<h2>The message was sent successfully</h2></body></html>");

    out.println("</body></html>");

} //doPost

public void doGet(HttpServletRequest request,
    HttpServletResponse response) throws ServletException,
        java.io.IOException {

    //doGet() calls doPost( )
    doPost(request,response);

}

private void sendMessage(String to, String from, String subject,
    String bodyContent) throws Exception {

    Message mailMsg = null;

    mailMsg = new MimeMessage(mailSession);//a new email message
    InternetAddress[] addresses = null;

    try {
        if (to != null) {

            //throws 'AddressException' if the 'to' email address
            //violates RFC822 syntax
            addresses = InternetAddress.parse(to, false);
            mailMsg.setRecipients(Message.RecipientType.TO, addresses);

        } else {
            throw new MessagingException(
                "The mail message requires a 'To' address.");
        }

        if (from != null)
            mailMsg.setFrom(from);

        if (subject != null)
```

```
        mailMsg.setSubject(subject);

    if (bodyContent != null)
        mailMsg.setText(bodyContent);

    //Finally, send the mail message; throws a 'SendFailedException'
    //if any of the message's recipients have an invalid adress
    Transport.send(mailMsg);

    } catch (Exception exc) {
        throw exc;

    }//sendMessage
}//EmailJndiServlet
```

The doPost( ) method calls the servlet's sendMessage( ) method, passing in the email message parts such as the recipient and the email's content. The servlet derives this information from request parameters that the user submits. A typical request for the servlet looks like:

```
http://localhost:7001/email?to=author@jspservletcookbook.com&
    from=bwperry@parkerriver.com&subject=hello&
    emailContent=A web message
```

A user can also POST information to the servlet with an HTML form.

The servlet's sendMessage( ) method uses the JNDI object in the javax.mail. internet.MimeMessage constructor when the method creates a new email message.

Figure 25-6 shows the servlet's simple return message in a browser window.

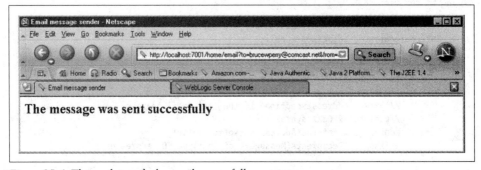

Figure 25-6. The servlet sends the email successfully

See Also

Recipe 25.4 on configuring a JNDI object on WebLogic; Recipe 25.5 on viewing the WebLogic JNDI tree with the Administration console; Recipe 25.7 on accessing a JNDI object with a JSP on WebLogic; Chapter 2 on deploying web components with WebLogic.

25.7 Accessing the WebLogic JNDI Resource from a JSP

Problem

You want to use a WebLogic JNDI object in a JSP.

Solution

Create a filter that accesses the JNDI object and sets the object as a session attribute.

Discussion

Any sense of dejá vu comes from a few recipes ago, when you used a filter to pass a JNDI object to a JSP on Tomcat. The only difference in this recipe is that the application server used is WebLogic and the JNDI object is a JavaMail Session, not a JavaBean.

The filter accesses the object using the JNDI API on WebLogic. Then the filter sets the object as a session attribute, so that the JSP can access the javax.mail.Session. Example 25-10 shows the code for the filter that recipe uses on the WebLogic server.

Example 25-10. A filter stores a WebLogic JNDI object in a session attribute

```
package com.jspservletcookbook;

import java.io.IOException;

import javax.naming.Context;
import javax.naming.InitialContext;
import javax.naming.NamingException;

import javax.servlet.*;
import javax.servlet.http.*;

public class JndiFilter implements Filter {

    private FilterConfig config;
    private Context env;

  public JndiFilter( ) {}

  public void  init(FilterConfig filterConfig)  throws ServletException {
    this.config = filterConfig;
    try {
       env = (Context) new InitialContext( );
     } catch (NamingException ne) {
        throw new ServletException(ne);
    }
```

Example 25-10. A filter stores a WebLogic JNDI object in a session attribute (continued)

```
}//init

public void  doFilter(ServletRequest request, ServletResponse response,
   FilterChain chain) throws IOException, ServletException {

    javax.mail.Session mailSession = null;
     try {
         mailSession = (javax.mail.Session) env.lookup("MyEmail");
     } catch (NamingException ne) { }

    HttpServletRequest hRequest = null;
    if (request instanceof HttpServletRequest){
       hRequest = (HttpServletRequest) request;
       HttpSession hSession = hRequest.getSession( );
       if (hSession != null)
            hSession.setAttribute("MyEmail",mailSession);

    }//if
    chain.doFilter(request,response);

  }// doFilter

public void destroy( ){
     /*called before the Filter instance is removed
     from service by the web container*/
 }
}
```

Example 25-11 shows the filter configuration inside the deployment descriptor. This deployment descriptor must accompany a web application that you or another deployer has installed on WebLogic server.

Example 25-11. A filter that accesses a JNDI object on Weblogic

```
<!-- start of web.xml -->

<filter>

    <filter-name>JndiFilter</filter-name>
    <filter-class>com.jspservletcookbook.JndiFilter</filter-class>

</filter>

<filter-mapping>

    <filter-name>JndiFilter</filter-name>
    <url-pattern>/jndiJsp.jsp</url-pattern>

</filter-mapping>

<!-- rest of web.xml -->
```

Example 25-12 shows a JSP that accesses the JNDI object. This code displays the class name of the object, a javax.mail.Session type that Recipe 25.4 bound as a JNDI object on WebLogic. The filter in Recipe 25.11 then set the object as a session attribute (not to be confused with the Session type of the object). This attribute is available to all web components that participate in the same session. Therefore, the c:set tag in this JSP uses the following EL code to get access to the attribute.

```
${MyEmail}
```

Then the c:out tag displays the class name of the session attribute, in order to verify that the object is a javax.mail.Session. Recipe 25.6 gives the complete JavaMail code for sending an email.

Example 25-12. The JSP accesses the JavaMail object as a session attribute

```
<%@ taglib uri="http://java.sun.com/jstl/core" prefix="c" %>

<html>
<head><title>Jndi Email</title></head>
<body>
<h2>Getting a javax.mail.Session object via JNDI...</h2>

<c:set var="mSession" value="${MyEmail}" />

<c:out value="${mSession.class.name}" />

</body>
</html>
```

Figure 25-7 shows a web browser window after a user has requested the JSP.

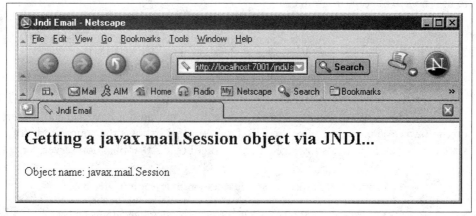

Figure 25-7. A JSP accesses a JNDI object via a servlet filter

See Also

Chapter 19 on filters; Chapter 23 on the JSTL; Recipe 25.4 on configuring a JNDI object with WebLogic; Recipe 25.6 on accessing a JNDI object with a servlet on WebLogic; Chapter 2 on deploying web components with WebLogic.

25.8 Accessing an EJB Using the WebLogic JNDI Tree

Problem

You want to access an Enterprise JavaBean (EJB) from a servlet on WebLogic.

Solution

Find out the EJB's JNDI name and use the javax.naming package to get a reference to the EJBObject or remote interface so that you can call the EJB's methods.

Discussion

A servlet accesses an EJB by using a specified JNDI name. The process is therefore transparent to the servlet developer. Any EJBs an application uses comprise the *business tier* of an application. The servlets and JSPs represent the *web tier* within the multi-tiered distributed architecture of a typical Java 2 Enterprise Edition (J2EE) application. All you need to know is the JNDI name associated with the EJB in order to use the EJB in your programs.

> Enterprise JavaBeans is a comprehensive topic; however, this recipe is devoted to showing how a servlet can connect to an EJB. The "See Also" segment of this recipe includes several links to EJB and J2EE information and books.

You should be aware of the EJB's business methods, but do not have to be an expert on the javax.ejb package to use the EJB. Example 25-13 shows the source code for a stateless session EJB that is managed by BEA WebLogic 7.0 application server.

> A certain type of EJB, a stateless session bean encapsulates business logic that does not require persistence or the saving of the object's state between method calls. On the other hand, a *stateful* session bean (such as a shopping cart object), must remember the object's state (such as the value of various instance variables) between method calls, as part of a conversation with the EJB client.

Example 25-13 provides a java.util.Map that links U.S. state names with their postal abbreviations. The session bean includes one business method, getAbbreviation( ), which receives a state name as a parameter and returns its postal abbreviation.

Example 25-13. The stateless session EJB

```
package com.jspservletcookbook;

import javax.ejb.*;

import java.util.Map;
import java.util.HashMap;

public class AbbrevBean implements SessionBean{

    private SessionContext context;
    private Map abbrevMap;


  public AbbrevBean( ){ //the bean's no-arguments constructor

    //A Map containing the names of states and abbreviations
    abbrevMap = new HashMap( );

    abbrevMap.put("ALABAMA","AL");
    abbrevMap.put("ALASKA","AK");
    abbrevMap.put("AMERICAN SAMOA","AS");
    abbrevMap.put("ARIZONA","AZ");
    abbrevMap.put("ARKANSAS","AR");
    abbrevMap.put("CALIFORNIA","CA");
    abbrevMap.put("COLORADO","CO");
    abbrevMap.put("CONNECTICUTT","CT");

    abbrevMap.put("DELAWARE","DE");
    abbrevMap.put("DISTRICT OF COLUMBIA","DC");
    abbrevMap.put("FEDERATED STATES OF MICRONESIA","FM");
    abbrevMap.put("FLORIDA","FL");
    abbrevMap.put("GEORGIA","GA");
    abbrevMap.put("GUAM","GU");
    abbrevMap.put("HAWAII","HI");
    abbrevMap.put("IDAHO","ID");

    abbrevMap.put("ILLINOIS","IL");
    abbrevMap.put("INDIANA","IN");
    abbrevMap.put("IOWA","IA");
    abbrevMap.put("KANSAS","KS");
    abbrevMap.put("KENTUCKY","KY");
    abbrevMap.put("LOUISIANA","LA");

    abbrevMap.put("MAINE","ME");
    abbrevMap.put("MARSHALL ISLANDS","MH");
    abbrevMap.put("MARYLAND","MD");
    abbrevMap.put("MASSACHUSETTS","MA");
```

Example 25-13. The stateless session EJB (continued)

```
        abbrevMap.put("MICHIGAN","MI");
        abbrevMap.put("MINNESOTA","MN");

        abbrevMap.put("MISSISSIPPI","MS");
        abbrevMap.put("MISSOURI","MO");
        abbrevMap.put("MONTANA","MT");
        abbrevMap.put("NEBRASKA","NE");
        abbrevMap.put("NEVADA","NV");
        abbrevMap.put("NEW HAMPSHIRE","NH");

        abbrevMap.put("NEW JERSEY","NJ");
        abbrevMap.put("NEW MEXICO","NM");
        abbrevMap.put("NEW YORK","NY");
        abbrevMap.put("NORTH CAROLINA","NC");
        abbrevMap.put("NORTH DAKOTA","ND");
        abbrevMap.put("NORTHERN MARIANA ISLANDS","MP");

        abbrevMap.put("OKLAHOMA","OK");
        abbrevMap.put("OREGON","OR");
        abbrevMap.put("PALAU","PW");
        abbrevMap.put("PENNSYLVANIA","PA");
        abbrevMap.put("PUERTO RICO","PR");
        abbrevMap.put("RHODE ISLAND","RI");
        abbrevMap.put("SOUTH CAROLINA","SC");
        abbrevMap.put("SOUTH DAKOTA","SD");

        abbrevMap.put("TENNESSEE","TN");
        abbrevMap.put("TEXAS","TX");
        abbrevMap.put("UTAH","UT");
        abbrevMap.put("VERMONT","VT");
        abbrevMap.put("VIRGIN ISLANDS","VI");
        abbrevMap.put("VIRGINIA","VA");
        abbrevMap.put("WASHINGTON","WA");
        abbrevMap.put("WEST VIRGINIA","WV");
        abbrevMap.put("WISCONSIN","WI");
        abbrevMap.put("WYOMING","WY");

    }//constructor

    public void setSessionContext(SessionContext ctx) throws
      EJBException {
        context = ctx;
    }//setSessionContext

    public Map getAbbrevMap(){
        return abbrevMap;
    }

    //The bean's business method
    public String getAbbreviation(String state){
        return (String) abbrevMap.get(state);
    }
```

Example 25-13. The stateless session EJB (continued)

```
//javax.ejb.SessionBean method; it has to be implemented in a session
//bean, but is not relevant to Stateless session beans.
public void ejbActivate( ){}

//javax.ejb.SessionBean method; it has to be implemented in a Session
//bean, but is not relevant to stateless session beans.
public void ejbPassivate( ){}

//javax.ejb.SessionBean method;
public void ejbRemove( ) {}

}
```

Example 25-13 could easily be implemented as an ordinary Java helper or utility class. However, I show a simple example of an EJB so that the recipe can focus on how a servlet connects to these objects.

EJBs have a deployment descriptor, similar to the *web.xml* file that web applications use. The EJB deployment descriptor must be named *ejb-jar.xml*. When you package the EJB(s) before they are deployed on an application server, include this deployment descriptor as part of the archive. The *ejb-jar.xml* file describes the related EJB component(s); the application server uses this descriptive information in order to properly deploy the EJB.

For example, the *ejb-jar.xml* file in Example 25-14 specifies the type of EJB (e.g., stateless session bean) and the fully qualified class names of its related Java classes, such as its remote interface.

Example 25-14. The ejb-jar.xml file

```
<?xml version="1.0"?>

  <!DOCTYPE ejb-jar PUBLIC "-//Sun Microsystems, Inc.
  //DTD Enterprise JavaBeans 2.0//EN"
  "http://java.sun.com/dtd/ejb-jar_2_0.dtd"
   >

<ejb-jar>
  <enterprise-beans>
    <session>
      <ejb-name>AbbreviationEjb</ejb-name>
      <home>com.jspservletcookbook.AbbrevHome</home>
      <remote>com.jspservletcookbook.Abbrev</remote>
      <local-home>com.jspservletcookbook.AbbrevLocalHome</local-home>
      <local>com.jspservletcookbook.AbbrevLocal</local>
      <ejb-class>com.jspservletcookbook.AbbrevBean</ejb-class>
      <session-type>Stateless</session-type>
      <transaction-type>Container</transaction-type>
    </session>
  </enterprise-beans>
</ejb-jar>
```

The package that contains this EJB, and with which the EJB is deployed on the application server, is a JAR file named *myejb.jar* (just a name I concocted; you do not have to use the same name).

Since this stateless session bean is deployed on BEA WebLogic Server, the JAR file must include a vendor-specific deployment descriptor named *weblogic-ejb-jar.xml*. This deployment descriptor gives the deployer the opportunity to configure several aspects of how the EJB is deployed on WebLogic, such as the JNDI names of its home and local home interfaces.

 The "home" object is an implementation of the "home" interface, and the "local home" object is an implmentation of the local home interface. These objects are "factories" for EJB objects, which delegate the business-method calls to the EJB deployed in the server. A factory is a Java class that generates objects of a different kind of Java class. In this recipe's case, the client uses JNDI to get a reference to the home object, which creates an EJB object. The servlet (client) then calls the *EJB object's* getAbbreviation( ) method; the EJB object is a remote object or "stub" that delegates this method call to the original EJB stored on the server.

You will encounter the home object's JNDI name in the servlet depicted later on in this recipe.

 When you deploy an EJB on WebLogic using the Administration Console, WebLogic automatically binds the home and local home objects within the WebLogic JNDI tree, using the names specified by the *weblogic-ejb-jar.xml* deployment descriptor.

Example 25-15 shows the *weblogic-ejb-jar.xml* deployment descriptor for our stateless session bean.

Example 25-15. The weblogic-ejb-jar.xml file

```
<!DOCTYPE weblogic-ejb-jar PUBLIC
  '-//BEA Systems, Inc.//DTD WebLogic 7.0.0 EJB//EN'
  'http://www.bea.com/servers/wls700/dtd/weblogic-ejb-jar.dtd'>

<weblogic-ejb-jar>
  <weblogic-enterprise-bean>
    <ejb-name>AbbreviationEjb</ejb-name>
    <stateless-session-descriptor>
        <pool>
            <initial-beans-in-free-pool>1</initial-beans-in-free-pool>
        </pool>
    </stateless-session-descriptor>
    <jndi-name>AbbrevHome</jndi-name>
    <local-jndi-name>AbbrevLocalHome</local-jndi-name>
  </weblogic-enterprise-bean>
</weblogic-ejb-jar>
```

An EJB module is a complicated package that includes bean classes, remote interfaces, and two different deployment descriptors. Example 25-16 shows the contents of the *myejb.jar* file. I use the jar tvf myejb.jar. command in a command-line window to display the contents of the specified JAR file (it works in both Unix and Windows).

Example 25-16. The contents of the ejb-jar.xml file

H:\book\cookbook\code\chap27\src\ejbs\ejbjar>jar tvf myejb.jar

```
META-INF/
META-INF/MANIFEST.MF
com/
com/jspservletcookbook/
com/jspservletcookbook/Abbrev.class
com/jspservletcookbook/AbbrevBean.class
com/jspservletcookbook/AbbrevHome.class
com/jspservletcookbook/AbbrevLocal.class
com/jspservletcookbook/AbbrevLocalHome.class

META-INF/ejb-jar.xml
META-INF/weblogic-ejb-jar.xml
```

In Example 25-16, the session bean is *AbbrevBean.class*, the remote interface is *Abbrev.class*, and the home object (the factory for EJB objects that implement the Abbrev interface) is *AbbrevHome.class*.

Finally, Example 25-17 shows the servlet that uses the session bean from Example 25-13. The code is self-explanatory. The important thing to remember is that the servlet receivese a reference to the AbbrevHome object from the WebLogic JNDI tree. Then the servlet, in its doGet( ) method, calls the AbbrevHome object's create( ) method to get an instance of the session bean's remote interface (in this example, it's an Abbrev type).

Example 25-17. A servlet that accesses the EJB on WebLogic using JNDI

```
package com.jspservletcookbook;

import java.io.IOException;
import java.io.PrintWriter;

import javax.naming.Context;
import javax.naming.InitialContext;
import javax.naming.NamingException;

import javax.rmi.PortableRemoteObject;

import javax.servlet.*;
import javax.servlet.http.*;

public class WebJndiServlet extends HttpServlet {
```

Example 25-17. A servlet that accesses the EJB on WebLogic using JNDI (continued)

```java
public void doGet(HttpServletRequest request,
  HttpServletResponse response)
  throws ServletException, java.io.IOException {

    //The request parameter looks like 'state=Massachusetts'
    String state = request.getParameter("state");
    Context env = null;
    Abbrev abbrev = null;
    AbbrevHome home = null;

    try{

        env = (Context) new InitialContext();

        //Look up the home or factory object on the WebLogic JNDI tree
        Object localH  = env.lookup("AbbrevHome");

        //This method call is necessary for EJB code that uses a
        //technology called RMI-IIOP
        home = (AbbrevHome) PortableRemoteObject.narrow(localH,
            AbbrevHome.class);

        //close the InitialContext
        env.close();

        if (home == null)
            throw new ServletException(
            "AbbrevHome is an unknown JNDI object");

        //Get the remote interface by calling the home object's create()
        //method
        abbrev = (Abbrev) PortableRemoteObject.narrow(home.create(),
            Abbrev.class);

    } catch (NamingException ne) {
        try{ env.close();} catch (NamingException nex) { }
        throw new ServletException(ne);
    } catch (javax.ejb.CreateException ce) {
            throw new ServletException(ce);
    }


    //set the MIME type of the response, "text/html"
    response.setContentType("text/html");

    java.io.PrintWriter out = response.getWriter();

    out.println("<html><head>");

    out.println("<title>State abbreviations</title></head><body>");
    out.println("<h2>Here is the state's abbreviation</h2>");

    //Call the EJBObject's getAbbreviation() method; the EJBObject
    //delegates this method call to the session bean. Put the request
```

```
        //parameter in all upper-case, because this is how the session bean's
        //java.util.Map stores the state names, which are the Map's keys

        if (state != null)
            out.println( abbrev.getAbbreviation(state.toUpperCase()) );

        try{
            //The servlet is through with the EJBObject; call its remove()
            //method
            abbrev.remove();
        } catch (javax.ejb.RemoveException re){}

        out.println("</body></html>");

    }//doGet

public void doPost(HttpServletRequest request,
    HttpServletResponse response)
    throws ServletException, java.io.IOException {

        doGet(request, response);

    }//doPost

}//WebJndiServlet
```

The value of the abbreviation for a state such as "Oregon" is ultimately retrieved on the server side by calling the session bean's getAbbreviation( ) method. Figure 25-8 shows a web browser window after a user has requested the servlet. The URL looks something like *http://localhost:7001/webjndi?state=Oregon*. The URL pattern */webjndi* is mapped in *web.xml* to the servlet of Example 25-17.

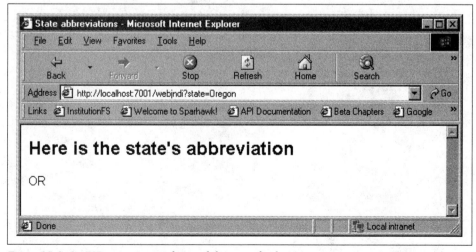

Figure 25-8. An EJB-accessing servlet's web browser display

See Also

Recipe 25.4 on configuring a JNDI object with WebLogic; Recipe 25.6 on accessing a JNDI object with a servlet on WebLogic; Chapter 2 on deploying web components with WebLogic; a web link for the javax.ejb API: *http://java.sun.com/j2ee/1.4/docs/api/javax/ejb/package-summary.html*; the documentation page for WebLogic Server 7.0: *http://edocs.bea.com/wls/docs70/index.html*; a link to J2EE tutorials, including an Enterprise JavaBean tutorial: *http://java.sun.com/j2ee/tutorial/index.html*; *Enterprise JavaBeans*, Third Edition (O'Reilly); *J2EE Design Patterns* (O'Reilly).

CHAPTER 26

Harvesting Web Information

26.0 Introduction

The Web contains information galore. Much of this information is freely available by simply surfing over to an organization's web site and reading their pages or search results. However, it can be difficult separating the dross from the gems. The vast majority of a web page's visual components are typically dedicated to menus, logos, advertising banners, and fancy applets or Flash movies. What if all you are interested in is a tiny nugget of data awash in an ocean of HTML?

The answer lies in using Java to parse a web page to extract only certain pieces of information from it. The web terms for this task are *harvesting* or *scraping* information from a web page. Perhaps web services (Chapter 27) will eventually replace the need to harvest web data. But until most major sites have their web services APIs up and running, you can use Java and certain `javax.swing.text` subpackages to pull specified text from web pages.

How does it work? Basically, your Java program uses HTTP to connect with a web page and pull in its HTML text.

 Parsing the HTML from web sites still involves transferring the entire web page over the network, even if you are only interested in a fraction of its information. This is why using web services is a much more efficient manner of sharing specific data from a web site.

Then use Java code to parse the HTML page in order to pull from it only the piece of data you are interested in, such as weather data or a stock quote. The following recipes show the Java classes that you can use to harvest web information. Then the recipes show a servlet and a JSP using a JavaBean to grab and display, as an example, a live stock quote.

26.1 Parsing an HTML Page Using the javax.swing.text Subpackages

Problem

You want to use the classes the Java 2 Standard Edition (J2SE) makes available for parsing HTML.

Solution

Use the various subpackages of the javax.swing.text package to create a parser for HTML.

Discussion

The J2SE 1.3 and 1.4 versions include the necessary classes for sifting through web pages in search of information. The Java programs these recipes use import the following classes:

```
javax.swing.text.html.HTMLEditorKit.ParserCallback;
javax.swing.text.MutableAttributeSet;
javax.swing.text.html.parser.ParserDelegator;
```

The design pattern that these classes use to read web pages involves three main elements:

1. A java.net.URL object that opens up a socket or InputStream to the web page using HTTP. The code then uses this object to read the web page.

2. A ParserDelegator object with which the code sifts through the web page by calling this object's parse( ) method.

3. A ParserCallback object that the ParserDelegator uses to take certain actions while it is parsing the web page's HTML text. A *callback* in general is an object that Java code typically passes into another object's constructor. The enclosing object then *drives* the callback by invoking the callback's methods, which the Java programmer implements according to what they want to accomplish by parsing the HTML. The role of the callback will become clearer as you read through these recipes.

The servlet and JavaBean defined in this chapter use an inner class to implement the callback. Example 26-1 shows the callback that extends javax.swing.text.html. HTMLEditorKit.ParserCallback.

Example 26-1. A callback class for sifting through web pages

```
class MyParserCallback extends ParserCallback {

    //bread crumbs that lead us to the stock price
    private boolean lastTradeFlag = false;
    private boolean boldFlag = false;

  public MyParserCallback(){
    //Reset the enclosing class' stock-price instance variable
    if (stockVal != 0)
      stockVal = 0f;
}

  //A method that the parser calls each time it confronts a start tag
  public void handleStartTag(javax.swing.text.html.HTML.Tag t,
    MutableAttributeSet a,int pos) {
      if (lastTradeFlag && (t == javax.swing.text.html.HTML.Tag.B )){
          boldFlag = true;
      }

  }//handleStartTag

  //A method that the parser calls each time it reaches nested text content
  public void handleText(char[] data,int pos){

    htmlText  = new String(data);
    if (htmlText.indexOf("No such ticker symbol.") != -1){
        throw new IllegalStateException(
      "Invalid ticker symbol in handleText( ) method.");

    } else if (htmlText.equals("Last Trade:")){
        lastTradeFlag = true;
    } else if (boldFlag){
        try{
            stockVal = new Float(htmlText).floatValue( );
        } catch (NumberFormatException ne) {
            try{
                // tease out any commas in the number using NumberFormat
                java.text.NumberFormat nf = java.text.NumberFormat.
                  getInstance( );
                Double f = (Double) nf.parse(htmlText);
                stockVal =  (float) f.doubleValue( );
            } catch (java.text.ParseException pe){
                throw new IllegalStateException(
                "The extracted text " + htmlText +
                    " cannot be parsed as a number!");

            }//try
        }//try

        //Reset the inner class's instance variables
        lastTradeFlag = false;
```

Example 26-1. A callback class for sifting through web pages (continued)

```
        boldFlag = false;
    }//if

    } //handleText
}//MyParserCallback
```

A callback includes methods that represent the attainment of a certain element of a web page during the parsing process. For example, the parser (the object that encloses the callback object) calls handleStartTag( ) whenever it runs into an opening tag as it traverses the web page. Examples of opening tags are <html>, <title>, or <body>. Therefore, when you implement the handleStartTag( ) method in the code, you can control what your program does when it finds an opening tag, such as "prepare to grab the text that appears within the opening and closing title tag."

Example 26-1 uses a particular algorithm to search a web page for an updated stock quote, and this is what the two methods (handleStartTag( ) and handleText( )) accomplish in the MyParserCallback class:

1. It looks for the text "Last Trade" in the handleText( ) callback method; if it's found, the lastTradeFlag boolean variable is set to true. This is like "dropping a bread crumb" as the program travels through the vast HTML of the web page.

2. If handleStartTag( ) finds a b tag right after "Last Trade" is found (the lastTradeFlag flag is true), it grabs the nested content of that b tag, because this content represents the stock quote.

 The big negative of web harvesting, which web services is partly designed to solve, is that when the web page you are parsing is changed, your program throws exceptions and no longer pulls out the information, because its algorithms are based on the old page structure.

Example 26-2 shows a snippet of code that uses the ParserDelegator and MyParserCallback objects, just to give you an idea of how they fit together before we move on to the servlet and JSP.

Example 26-2. A code snippet shows the parser and callback classes at work

```
//Instance variables
private ParserDelegator htmlParser = null;
private MyParserCallback callback = null;

//Initialize a BufferedReader and a URL inside of a method for connecting
//to and reading a web page
BufferedReader webPageStream = null;
URL stockSite = new URL(BASE_URL + symbol);
```

Example 26-2. A code snippet shows the parser and callback classes at work (continued)

```
//Connect inside of a method
webPageStream = new BufferedReader(
  new InputStreamReader(stockSite.openStream( )));

//Create the parser and callback
htmlParser = new ParserDelegator( );

callback = new MyParserCallback( );//ParserCallback

//Call parse( ), passing in the BufferedReader and callback objects
htmlParser.parse(webPageStream,callback,true);
```

The parse( ) method of ParserDelegator is what triggers the calling of the callback's methods, with the callback passed in as an argument to parse( ).

Now let's see how these classes work in a servlet, JavaBean, and JSP.

See Also

A Javadoc link for ParserDelegator: *http://java.sun.com/j2se/1.4.1/docs/api/javax/swing/text/html/parser/ParserDelegator.html*; Chapter 27 on using web services APIs to grab information from web servers.

26.2   Using a Servlet to Harvest Web Data

Problem

You want to use a servlet to harvest web information.

Solution

Use the HTML parsing API classes of the Java 2 Software Development Kit (SDK).

Discussion

The last recipe introduced the relevant subpackages of the javax.swing.text package; this is where I show how to use them in a servlet. Example 26-3 imports the necessary classes to parse an HTML page. The servlet's doGet( ) method displays a form in which the user enters a stock symbol (such as "INTC," case insensitive).

Then the doPost( ) method attempts to get a live stock quote for that symbol by parsing a web page from *finance.yahoo.com*.

Example 26-3. Harvesting web data from a servlet

```java
package com.jspservletcookbook;

import java.io.IOException;
import java.io.PrintWriter;
import java.io.BufferedReader;
import java.io.InputStreamReader;
import java.net.URL;
import java.net.MalformedURLException;
import javax.servlet.*;
import javax.servlet.http.*;
import javax.swing.text.html.HTMLEditorKit.ParserCallback;
import javax.swing.text.MutableAttributeSet;
import javax.swing.text.html.parser.ParserDelegator;

public class HtmlParseServlet extends HttpServlet {

    private static final String BASE_URL = "http://finance.yahoo.com"+
        "/q?d=t&s=";
    private ParserDelegator htmlParser = null;
    private MyParserCallback callback = null;
    private String htmlText = "";
    private boolean lastTradeFlag = false;
    private boolean boldFlag = false;
    private float stockVal = 0f;

    public void doGet(HttpServletRequest request,
      HttpServletResponse response) throws ServletException,
        java.io.IOException {

        //set the MIME type of the response, "text/html"
        response.setContentType("text/html");

         //use a PrintWriter to send text
        java.io.PrintWriter out = response.getWriter( );

         //Begin assembling the HTML content
        out.println("<html><head>");

        out.println("<title>Stock Price Fetcher</title></head><body>");
        out.println("<h2>Please submit a valid stock symbol</h2>");

        //make sure method="post" so that the servlet service method
        //calls doPost in the response to this form submit
        out.println(
          "<form method=\"post\" action =\"" + request.getContextPath( ) +
              "/stockservlet\" >");

        out.println("<table border=\"0\"><tr><td valign=\"top\">");
        out.println("Stock symbol: </td>  <td valign=\"top\">");
        out.println("<input type=\"text\" name=\"symbol\" size=\"10\">");
        out.println("</td></tr><tr><td valign=\"top\">");
```

Example 26-3. Harvesting web data from a servlet (continued)

```
        out.println(
        "<input type=\"submit\" value=\"Submit Info\"></td></tr>");

        out.println("</table></form>");
        out.println("</body></html>");


} //doGet

public void doPost(HttpServletRequest request,
    HttpServletResponse response)
        throws java.io.IOException{
        String symbol;//this will hold the stock symbol
        float price;//The stock's latest price
        symbol = request.getParameter("symbol");
        boolean isValid = (symbol == null || symbol.length() < 1) ?
        false : true;

        //set the MIME type of the response, "text/html"
        response.setContentType("text/html");
        java.io.PrintWriter out = response.getWriter();

        //Begin assembling the HTML content
        out.println("<html><head>");
        out.println("<title>Latest stock value</title></head><body>");
        if (! isValid){
        out.println(
          "<h2>Sorry, the stock symbol parameter was either empty "+
          "or null</h2>");
        } else {
          out.println("<h2>Here is the latest value of "+ symbol +"</h2>");
          price = getLatestPrice(symbol);
          out.println( (price==0? "The symbol is probably invalid." :
            ""+price) );
        }
    out.println("</body></html>");


}// doPost

private float getLatestPrice(String symbol) throws IOException,
    MalformedURLException {

        BufferedReader webPageStream = null;
        URL stockSite = new URL(BASE_URL + symbol);
        webPageStream = new BufferedReader(new InputStreamReader(stockSite.
          openStream()));
        htmlParser = new ParserDelegator();
        callback = new MyParserCallback();
        //the code is designed to make calling parse() thread-safe
        synchronized(htmlParser){
            htmlParser.parse(webPageStream,callback,true);
```

Example 26-3. Harvesting web data from a servlet (continued)

```java
      }//synchronized
      return stockVal;
}//getLatestPrice

class MyParserCallback extends ParserCallback {

    //bread crumbs that lead us to the stock price
    private boolean lastTradeFlag = false;
    private boolean boldFlag = false;

  public MyParserCallback(){
    //Reset the enclosing class' instance variable
    if (stockVal != 0)
        stockVal = 0f;
  }

    public void handleStartTag(javax.swing.text.html.HTML.Tag t,
      MutableAttributeSet a,int pos) {
        if (lastTradeFlag && (t == javax.swing.text.html.HTML.Tag.B )){
            boldFlag = true;
        }
    }//handleStartTag

    public void handleText(char[] data,int pos){

        htmlText  = new String(data);
        if (htmlText.indexOf("No such ticker symbol.") != -1){
            throw new IllegalStateException(
            "Invalid ticker symbol in handleText() method.");
        } else if (htmlText.equals("Last Trade:")){
            lastTradeFlag = true;
        } else if (boldFlag){
            try{

                stockVal = new Float(htmlText).floatValue();
            } catch (NumberFormatException ne) {
                try{
                    // tease out any commas in the number using
                    //NumberFormat
                    java.text.NumberFormat nf = java.text.NumberFormat.
                      getInstance();
                    Double f = (Double) nf.parse(htmlText);
                    stockVal =  (float) f.doubleValue();
                } catch (java.text.ParseException pe){
                    throw new IllegalStateException(
                    "The extracted text " + htmlText +
                        " cannot be parsed as a number!");
                }//try
            }//try
```

Example 26-3. Harvesting web data from a servlet (continued)

```
                lastTradeFlag = false;
                boldFlag = false;
            }//if
        } //handleText
    }//MyParserCallback
}//HttpServlet
```

The MyParserCallback inner class defines the parsing algorithm for the servlet, which is explained in Recipe 26.1. The getLatestPrice() method uses this callback class and an HTML parser to return a stock quote as a float type.

 The ParserDelegator object is synchronized as it calls parse(), so that only one thread is parsing the web page and setting the value of stockVal (an instance variable representing the stock value) at one time.

This servlet is a little too complicated for one class, as it uses servlet API and HTML parsing API classes. A better design would separate these responsibilities into different Java classes. The upcoming recipes create a JavaBean whose responsibility is to parse HTML for a live stock quote.

Figure 26-1 shows the output of the servlet's doGet() method.

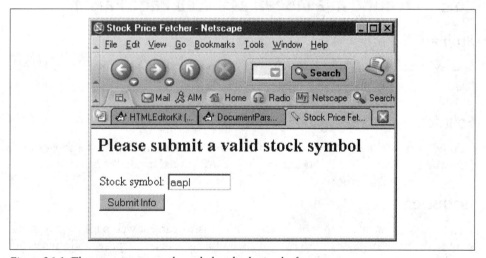

Figure 26-1. The user enters a stock symbol and submits the form

Figure 26-2 shows the servlet's doPost( ) method output in a Netscape browser.

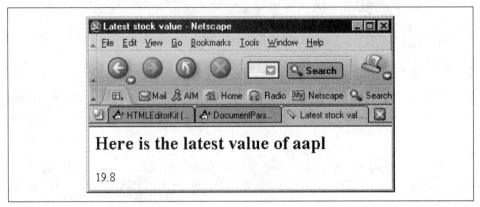

Figure 26-2. The servlet returns the latest stock price for the symbol

See Also

Recipe 26.3 on creating a JavaBean as a web-page parser; Recipes 26.4 and 26.5 on using the bean with a servlet and a JSP, respectively.

26.3   Creating a JavaBean as a Web Page Parser

Problem

You want to create a JavaBean that web components can use to parse an HTML page.

Solution

Use the Java API classes for parsing HTML from the `javax.swing.text` subpackages. Store the JavaBean in *WEB-INF/classes* or in a JAR placed inside *WEB-INF/lib*.

Discussion

Example 26-4 is a JavaBean whose sole purpose is to parse a web page for live stock quotes. A servlet or JSP can use this JavaBean for its special purpose, and thus avoid the clutter of taking on the parsing responsibility itself. All of the code, including the inner class representing a `ParserCallback`, is reproduced from this chapter's earlier recipes. What's new is the setter or mutator method for the bean's stock symbol: `setSymbol(String symbol)`.

Example 26-4. A JavaBean for use with servlets and JSPs

```java
package com.jspservletcookbook;

import java.io.BufferedReader;
import java.io.IOException;
import java.io.InputStreamReader;
import java.net.URL;
import java.net.MalformedURLException;

import javax.swing.text.html.HTMLEditorKit.ParserCallback;
import javax.swing.text.MutableAttributeSet;
import javax.swing.text.html.parser.ParserDelegator;

public class StockPriceBean {

    private static final String urlBase =  "http://finance.yahoo.com/"+
    "q?d=t&s=";

    private BufferedReader webPageStream = null;

    private URL stockSite = null;

    private ParserDelegator htmlParser = null;

    private MyParserCallback callback = null;

    private String htmlText = "";
    private String symbol = "";
    private float stockVal = 0f;

    public StockPriceBean() {}

    //Setter or mutator method for the stock symbol
    public void setSymbol(String symbol){
        this.symbol = symbol;
    }

    class MyParserCallback extends ParserCallback {

        //bread crumbs that lead us to the stock price
        private boolean lastTradeFlag = false;
        private boolean boldFlag = false;

        public MyParserCallback(){
        //Reset the enclosing class' instance variable
        if (stockVal != 0)
            stockVal = 0f;
        }

        public void handleStartTag(javax.swing.text.html.HTML.Tag t,
          MutableAttributeSet a,int pos) {
            if (lastTradeFlag && (t == javax.swing.text.html.HTML.Tag.B )){
                boldFlag = true;
```

Example 26-4. A JavaBean for use with servlets and JSPs (continued)

```
        }

    }//handleStartTag

    public void handleText(char[] data,int pos){
        htmlText = new String(data);
        if (htmlText.indexOf("No such ticker symbol.") != -1){
            throw new IllegalStateException(
            "Invalid ticker symbol in handleText() method.");
        } else if (htmlText.equals("Last Trade:")){
            lastTradeFlag = true;
        } else if (boldFlag){
            try{

                stockVal = new Float(htmlText).floatValue();
            } catch (NumberFormatException ne) {
                try{
                    // tease out any commas in the number using
                    //NumberFormat
                    java.text.NumberFormat nf = java.text.NumberFormat.
                      getInstance();
                    Double f = (Double) nf.parse(htmlText);
                    stockVal =  (float) f.doubleValue();
                } catch (java.text.ParseException pe){
                    throw new IllegalStateException(
                    "The extracted text " + htmlText +
                        " cannot be parsed as a number!");
                }//try
            }//try

            lastTradeFlag = false;
            boldFlag = false;

        }//if
    } //handleText

}//MyParserCallback

public float getLatestPrice() throws IOException,MalformedURLException {
    stockSite = new URL(urlBase + symbol);
    webPageStream = new BufferedReader(new InputStreamReader(stockSite.
      openStream()));
    htmlParser = new ParserDelegator();
    callback = new MyParserCallback();//ParserCallback
    synchronized(htmlParser){
        htmlParser.parse(webPageStream,callback,true);
     }//synchronized
     //reset symbol
     symbol = "";
    return stockVal;
}//getLatestPrice

}//StockPriceBean
```

This bean resets the symbol instance variable to the empty String when it's finished fetching the stock quote. The MyParserCallback class resets the stockVal instance variable to 0, so that the previously attained stock price does not linger between different thread's calls to getLatestPrice( ).

Now let's see how a servlet and JSP use the bean.

See Also

Recipe 26.4 on using this JavaBean in a servlet; Recipe 26.5 on using the bean in a JSP.

26.4   Using the Web Page Parsing JavaBean in a Servlet

Problem

You want to use the JavaBean for parsing HTML in a servlet.

Solution

Create an instance of the bean in the appropriate service method (e.g., doGet( ) or doPost( )) and call its methods.

Discussion

The JavaBean has to be available to the servlet, and therefore stored in *WEB-INF/ classes*, including subdirectories that match the bean's package name. The JavaBean can also be stored in a JAR inside of *WEB-INF/lib*.

Since the JavaBean in Example 26-5 shares the servlet's package (com. jspservletcookbook), the servlet class does not have to import the bean class.

 If the JavaBean resides in a different package in the web application, then the servlet has to include an import statement such as the following example:

```
import com.parkerriver.beans.BeanParserServlet;
```

The doGet( ) method provides an HTML form for entering a stock symbol (such as "intc"). The doPost( ) method then creates an instance of the StockPriceBean, calls the bean's setSymbol( ) method, and finally displays the stock price by calling the bean's getLatestPrice( ) method.

Example 26-5. A servlet uses a specially designed JavaBean to get a live stock quote

```
package com.jspservletcookbook;

import java.io.IOException;
import java.io.PrintWriter;

import javax.servlet.*;
import javax.servlet.http.*;

public class BeanParserServlet extends HttpServlet {

  public void doGet(HttpServletRequest request,
    HttpServletResponse response)
      throws ServletException, java.io.IOException {

      //set the MIME type of the response, "text/html"
      response.setContentType("text/html");

       //use a PrintWriter send text data to the client
      java.io.PrintWriter out = response.getWriter();

       //Begin assembling the HTML content
      out.println("<html><head>");
      out.println("<title>Stock Price Fetcher</title></head><body>");
      out.println("<h2>Please submit a valid stock symbol</h2>");

      //make sure method="POST" so that the servlet service method
      //calls doPost in the response to this form submit
      out.println(
        "<form method=\" POST \" action =\"" + request.getContextPath() +
          "/stockbean\" >");

      out.println("<table border=\"0\"><tr><td valign=\"top\">");
      out.println("Stock symbol: </td>  <td valign=\"top\">");
      out.println("<input type=\"text\" name=\"symbol\" size=\"10\">");
      out.println("</td></tr><tr><td valign=\"top\">");
      out.println("<input type=\"submit\" value=\"Submit Info\"></td></tr>");
      out.println("</table></form>");
      out.println("</body></html>");


  } //doGet

  public void doPost(HttpServletRequest request,
    HttpServletResponse response)
      throws ServletException, java.io.IOException {


      String symbol;//this will hold the stock symbol

      float price = 0f;

      symbol = request.getParameter("symbol");
```

```
                boolean isValid = (symbol == null || symbol.length() < 1) ?
                false : true;

                //set the MIME type of the response, "text/html"
                response.setContentType("text/html");

                //use a PrintWriter send text data to the client
                java.io.PrintWriter out = response.getWriter();

                //Begin assembling the HTML content
                out.println("<html><head>");
                out.println("<title>Latest stock value</title></head><body>");

            if (! isValid){
                out.println(
                "<h2>Sorry, the stock symbol parameter was either empty "+
                "or null</h2>");
            } else {
                out.println("<h2>Here is the latest value of "+ symbol +"</h2>");
                StockPriceBean spbean = new StockPriceBean();
                spbean.setSymbol(symbol);
                price = spbean.getLatestPrice();
                out.println( (price==0? "The symbol is probably invalid." :
                ""+price) );
            }//if
            out.println("</body></html>");
            }// doPost
}//HttpServlet
```

The servlet's HTML form (generated by the doGet( ) method) and the stock price display (generated by doPost( )) has the same web browser display as the one shown in Figures 26-1 and 26-2.

See Also

Recipe 26.3 on creating a JavaBean as a web page parser; Recipe 26.5 on using a web page parsing JavaBean in a JSP.

26.5 Using the Web Page Parsing JavaBean in a JSP

Problem

You want to use a JavaBean and JSP to harvest information from a web page.

Solution

Use the jsp:useBean standard action to create an instance of the bean.

Discussion

The same JavaBean that prior recipes created and stored in the web application in *WEB-INF/classes* can be used by a JSP. The JSP in Example 26-6 uses `jsp:useBean` to create an instance of the bean named `priceFetcher`. If the request does not contain a symbol parameter, the JSP displays the HTML form shown in Figure 26-1.

The JSP uses the JSTL core tags to generate this conditional behavior. These tags include `c:choose`, `c:when`, and `c:otherwise`.

If the request to the JSP contains a symbol parameter, the JSP sets the `priceFetcher`'s `symbol` property to the value of this request parameter. This code is the equivalent of calling the bean's `setSymbol( )` method; it passes the name of the stock symbol to the bean so that it can grab a live stock quote from the web page.

Example 26-6. A JSP uses jsp:useBean to employ a web-harvesting JavaBean

```jsp
<%@ taglib uri="http://java.sun.com/jstl/core" prefix="c" %>

<jsp:useBean id="priceFetcher" class=
  "com.jspservletcookbook.StockPriceBean" />

<html>
<head><title>Price Fetch</title></head>
<body>

<c:choose>

  <c:when test="${empty param.symbol}">

    <h2>Please submit a valid stock symbol</h2>

    <form method="POST" action =
     '<c:out value="${pageContext.request.contextPath}" />/priceFetch.jsp'>

    <table border="0"><tr><td valign="top">Stock symbol: </td>
    <td valign="top">
    <input type="text" name="symbol" size="10"></td></tr>
    <tr><td valign="top">
    <input type="submit" value="Submit Info"></td></tr>
    </table></form>

  </c:when>

  <c:otherwise>

    <h2>Here is the latest value of <c:out value="${param.symbol}" /></h2>

    <jsp:setProperty name="priceFetcher" property="symbol" value=
      "<%= request.getParameter(\"symbol\") %>" />

    <jsp:getProperty name="priceFetcher" property="latestPrice"/>
```

Example 26-6. A JSP uses jsp:useBean to employ a web-harvesting JavaBean (continued)

```
    </c:otherwise>

  </c:choose>

</body>
</html>
```

Now that the JSP has seeded the bean with the stock symbol, this code will call the bean's getLatestPrice( ) method:

```
    <jsp:getProperty name="priceFetcher" property="latestPrice"/>
```

The JSP's output replaces the jsp:getProperty standard action with the stock price, as long as the stock symbol sent to the bean with jsp:setProperty was valid.

The output of the JSP in Example 26-6 looks just like the output shown in Figures 26-1 and 26-2.

See Also

Chapter 23 on the JSTL; Recipe 26.4 on using a web page parsing JavaBean in a servlet.

CHAPTER 27

Using the Google and Amazon Web APIs

27.0 Introduction

Google and Amazon.com are both early adopters in the emerging field of web services.

Google is a giant web search engine and directory. Amazon.com is a e-commerce web site that began as an online bookstore and has since branched out into numerous products such as software and electronics. Both sites separately offer software developers web services Application Programming Interfaces (APIs) that give you the ability to manage Google searches using Java objects and access Amazon's comprehensive product catalogs with your Java code.

For us Java developers, web services means making requests and receiving responses using a special XML format. In other words, you make a request using XML elements and attributes in text form, and receive a response in the same format. Web services typically use an XML-based protocol named Simple Object Access Protocol (SOAP) to transfer information.

In a nutshell, SOAP represents the abstraction of an envelope, that in turn contains optional headers and the message body. The message, composed of its outer envelope, as well as the headers and body, is made up of XML elements that are associated with specified namespaces. The technologies this chapter describes use HTTP to carry these XML-based SOAP messages.

I never really understood SOAP messages until I looked at some samples. Example 27-1 is part of a SOAP response to an Amazon Web Services keyword-search request using the query "Lance Armstrong."

The response is an XML file composed of a `ProductInfo` root element, which contains one or more `Details` elements. Each one of these `Details` represents a book from Amazon's catalog (I omitted all but one of the `Details` elements, just to make the sample easier to view). Only one of the returned books is shown.

Example 27-1. A SOAP response from Amazon Web Services based on a search for the terms "Lance Armstrong"

```xml
<?xml version="1.0" encoding="UTF-8"?>

<!DOCTYPE ProductInfo PUBLIC "-//Amazon.com //DTD  Amazon Product Info//EN"
 "http://xml.amazon.com/schemas/dev-lite.dtd">

<ProductInfo xmlns:xsi="http://www.w3.org/2001/XMLSchema-instance"
  xsi:noNamespaceSchemaLocation=
  "http://xml.amazon.com/schemas/dev-lite.xsd">

  <Details url=
   "http://www.amazon.com/exec/obidos/ASIN/0399146113/webservices-20?
    dev-t=DCJEAVXSDVPUD%26camp=2025%26link_code=xm2">

        <Asin>0399146113</Asin>
        <ProductName>It's Not About the Bike: My Journey Back to Life
        </ProductName>
        <Catalog>Book</Catalog>
        <Authors>
           <Author>Lance Armstrong</Author>
           <Author>Sally Jenkins</Author>
        </Authors>
        <ReleaseDate>June, 2000</ReleaseDate>
        <Manufacturer>Putnam Pub Group</Manufacturer>

        <ImageUrlSmall>
        http://images.amazon.com/images/P/0399146113.01.THUMBZZZ.jpg
        </ImageUrlSmall>

        <ImageUrlMedium>
        http://images.amazon.com/images/P/0399146113.01.MZZZZZZZ.jpg
        </ImageUrlMedium>

        <ImageUrlLarge>
        http://images.amazon.com/images/P/0399146113.01.LZZZZZZZ.jpg
        </ImageUrlLarge>

        <ListPrice>$24.95</ListPrice>
        <OurPrice>$17.47</OurPrice>
        <UsedPrice>$9.99</UsedPrice>

  </Details>

</ProductInfo>
```

Three principal reasons for adopting SOAP-based web services are:

1. SOAP is standards-based, so you can use any technology that has developed a SOAP API or toolkit, including Java, .NET, Perl, and Python. Object-oriented technologies (like Java) allow you to build and read SOAP messages using

objects, instead of having to deal with raw XML, which can make web services gratifying to work with.

2. Web services represent interoperability between technologies. A server that is using J2EE technologies such as servlets and JSPs can easily exchange messages with a server running .NET, because they speak the same language: SOAP and XML.

3. SOAP messages can easily be exchanged between web servers without running afoul of the limitations of firewalls, because the messages are made of up XML text and carried by HTTP (in a very general way, just like an HTML page). Developers are embracing SOAP as an easier form of distributed computing: it allows an object residing in the memory of one server to call methods on one or more objects residing on distant computers by exchanging SOAP messages.

A recipe introduction cannot do justice to a complicated topic such as SOAP, but there are plenty of books and free tutorials on this topic (see this chapter's "See Also" sections for some suggestions).

Mostly in a beta stage of development, the Amazon and Google web services APIs allow a Java program to create very useful and complex systems that interact with Amazon and Google. The Amazon and Google web services programs are designed to familiarize developers with these new ways of handling requests and responses to the two popular web destinations.

The programs generally involve creating a developer's account and recieving a key, or token, that will accompany each one of your requests to these sites. This chapter describes how to get set up with using Amazon and Google web services, then shows you how to integrate these APIs with a servlet and JSP.

27.1   Getting Set Up with Google's Web API

Problem

You want to use Google's Web API to make Java-enabled searches of Google's vast web index.

Solution

Download the Google Web APIs SDK. Create a Google account and get a license key that allows the use of Google's Web API.

Discussion

The Google Web APIs SDK includes an archive named *google.jar*. This file contains the classes that your program will use to connect with Google during searches. Here are the specific steps you take to prepare the web application for connecting with Google:

1. Download the zipped SDK from *http://www.google.com/apis/download.html*. Unpack this file into a directory (named *googleapi* in Beta Version 3.0 of the Google Web APIs). This directory contains *google.jar*, along with a lot of code samples and documentation.

2. Create a Google account and get a license key, which is encoded text that looks like "5W1ABCyzPSyI3rIa5Pt3DtXMatsdzaSGB." Your Java code uses this key when it queries Google's index. The query will fail if it is not accompanied by a valid key.

3. Place the *google.jar* file in the *WEB-INF/lib* directory of the web application.

4. Develop your Java classes for connecting with Google, using the `com.google. soap.search` package from the *google.jar* file.

See Also

The home for the Google Web APIs: *http://www.google.com/apis/*; the Google web APIs SDK: *http://www.google.com/apis/download.html*.

27.2 Creating a JavaBean to Connect with Google

Problem

You want to use Google's Web APIs to make Java-enabled searches to Google's site.

Solution

Create a JavaBean so that you can use the bean in both a servlet and JSP.

Discussion

The first thing to do is get set up with a Google Web Services account, as described in Recipe 27-1. Now create a JavaBean that will make keyword searches of Google and return the results.

Example 27-2 first imports the package contained in *googleapi.jar*: `com.google.soap. search`. Remember, you stored that JAR file in *WEB-INF/lib*. This means that the web application can find the Java classes in that package and the `GoogleBean` in Example 27-2 can use it.

Example 27-2. A JavaBean that searches Google's web database

```java
package com.jspservletcookbook;

import com.google.soap.search.*;

public class GoogleBean {

    private GoogleSearch search;
    private GoogleSearchResult googleRes;
    private final static String GOOGLE_KEY =
        "5W1BWPyzPSyI3rIa5Pt3DtXMatsniSGB";

    private String lineSep = "\n";

    //Settable bean properties
    private String query;
    private boolean filter;
    private int maxResults;
    private int startRes;
    private boolean safeSearch;
    private String restrict;
    private String langRestrict;

    public GoogleBean(){ //No-arguments constructor for the bean
        query = "";
        restrict = "";
        langRestrict = "";
    }

    public String structureResult(GoogleSearchResult res){
        //Each GoogleSearchResultElement
        GoogleSearchResultElement[] elements = res.getResultElements();
        String url ="";
        String results = "Estimated total results count: " +
            res.getEstimatedTotalResultsCount() + lineSep + lineSep;

        for (int i = 0; i < elements.length; i++){
          url = elements[i].getURL();
          results += ("Title: " + elements[i].getTitle() + lineSep +
              "URL: <a href=\"" + url + "\">" + url + "</a>"+ lineSep +
              "Summary: " + elements[i].getSummary() + lineSep +
              "Snippet: " + elements[i].getSnippet() + lineSep + lineSep);
        }
        return results;
    }

    public String getSearchResults() throws GoogleSearchFault {

        search = new GoogleSearch();
        search.setKey(GOOGLE_KEY);
        search.setFilter(filter);
        if(restrict.length() > 0)
            search.setRestrict(restrict);
```

Example 27-2. A JavaBean that searches Google's web database (continued)

```
        search.setQueryString(query);
        googleRes = search.doSearch( );
        return structureResult(googleRes);
    }

    public void setLineSep(String lineSep){
        this.lineSep=lineSep;
    }
    public String getLineSep( ){
        return lineSep;
    }
    public void setQuery(String query){
        this.query = query;
    }

    public String getQuery( ){
        return query;
    }

    public void setRestrict(String query){
        this.restrict = restrict;
    }

    public String getRestrict( ){
        return restrict;
    }

    public void setLangRestrict(String langRestrict){

        this.langRestrict = langRestrict;
    }

    public String getLangRestrict( ){
        return langRestrict;
    }

    public void setFilter(boolean filter){
        this.filter = filter;
    }

    public boolean getFilter( ){
        return filter;
    }

    public void setSafeSearch(boolean safeSearch){
        this.safeSearch = safeSearch;
    }

    public boolean getSafeSearch( ){
        return safeSearch;
    }
```

Example 27-2. A JavaBean that searches Google's web database (continued)

```
    public void setMaxResults(int maxResults){
        this.maxResults = maxResults;
    }

    public int getMaxResults(){
        return maxResults;
    }

    public void setStartRes(int startRes){
        this.startRes = startRes;
    }

    public int getStartRes(){
        return startRes;
    }
}//GoogleBean
```

The interesting action in Example 27-2 occurs in the methods getSearchResults( ) and structureResults( ).

In getSearchResults( ), the code creates a GoogleSearch object, which is then customized with Google search options before the GoogleSearch doSearch( ) method is called. The GoogleSearch object uses setter methods to design a specific *google.com* search. For example, the setQueryString( ) method provides the user's search terms. The Java objects that are using the bean provides the search terms by calling the bean's setQuery( ) method.

> You can set the various options for Google searches by calling the GoogleSearch setter methods. For example, calling setFilter(true) filters out all the results that derive from the same web host. And you can restrict the search to specific Google subsites by calling setRestrict("mac"). See *http://www.google.com/apis/reference.html*.

Every SOAP-related search of Google must call the GoogleSearch setKey( ) method with the proper license key, or the search is rejected.

The structureResults( ) method formats the search results. Google search results are encapsulated by a GoogleSearchResult object. This object contains an array of GoogleSearchResultElement objects, which represent each URL that the Google search has returned. The GoogleSearchResult getResultElements( ) method returns the GoogleSearchResultElement array.

The code then iterates through the array. Each returned element (the GoogleSearchResultElement object) has getter or accessor methods that provides information about the web-page search result:

- getURL( ) returns the URL of the found item
- getTitle( ) returns the title of the found HTML page

- getSnippet( ) returns a snippet (a small, possibly ambiguous, piece of text from the web page)
- getSummary( ) returns a text summary of the found web page

The bean uses these methods to display the URL, title, snippet, and summary of each web page the search returns. Figure 27-2 shows how these results are displayed.

See Also

The home for Google Web Service: *http://www.google.com/apis/*; the Google Web APIs SDK: *http://www.google.com/apis/download.html*; Recipe 27.1 on setting up your programming environment for use with the Google Web APIs.

27.3   Using a Servlet to Connect with Google

Problem

You want to connect to Google with a servlet and initiate a search.

Solution

Use the JavaBean described in Recipe 27.2 as a Google search utility class.

Discussion

The servlet in Example 27-3 uses the GoogleBean from Recipe 27.2 to initiate *google. com* searches and display the results.

The servlet displays an HTML form in its doGet( ) method. The client uses this form to input Google search parameters, and then POST the form parameters back to the same servlet. Finally, the servlet's doPost( ) method creates an instance of the GoogleBean to initiate the search. In this case, use the deployment descriptor to map any requests of the form "/googleservlet" to Example 27-3.

Example 27-3. A servlet uses a special JavaBean to search Google and display any results

```
package com.jspservletcookbook;

import java.io.IOException;
import java.io.PrintWriter;

import javax.servlet.*;
import javax.servlet.http.*;

public class GoogleServlet extends HttpServlet {

  public void doGet(HttpServletRequest request,
```

Example 27-3. A servlet uses a special JavaBean to search Google and display any results (continued)

```
    HttpServletResponse response)
    throws ServletException, java.io.IOException {

        response.setContentType("text/html");

        java.io.PrintWriter out = response.getWriter( );

        out.println("<html><head>");
        out.println("<title>Initiate a Google Search</title></head><body>");
        out.println("<h2>Please enter your search terms</h2>");

        //Make sure method="POST" so that the servlet service method
        //calls doPost in the response to this form submit
        out.println(
          "<form method=\"POST\" action =\"" + request.getContextPath( ) +
              "/googleservlet\" >");

        out.println("<table border=\"0\"><tr><td valign=\"top\">");
        out.println("Search terms: </td>  <td valign=\"top\">");
        out.println("<input type=\"text\" name=\"query\" size=\"15\">");
        out.println("</td></tr><tr><td valign=\"top\">");
        out.println(
        "Restrict to Google sub-site... </td>  <td valign=\"top\">");
        out.println(
          "<select name=\"restrict\"><option>unclesam</option>"+
          "<option>linux</option>option>mac</option><option>bsd</option>"+
          "</select>");
        out.println("</td></tr><tr><td valign=\"top\">");
        out.println(
        "<input type=\"submit\" value=\"Submit Info\"></td></tr>");
        out.println("</table></form>");
        out.println("</body></html>");
    } //doGet

  public void doPost(HttpServletRequest request,
     HttpServletResponse response)
     throws ServletException,java.io.IOException{

        String query = request.getParameter("query");
        String restrict = request.getParameter("restrict");
        boolean isValid = (query == null || query.length( ) < 1) ?
            false : true;

        //set the MIME type of the response, "text/html"
        response.setContentType("text/html");

        java.io.PrintWriter out = response.getWriter( );

        out.println("<html><head>");
        out.println("<title>Google results</title></head><body>");

        if (! isValid){
```

```
                out.println(
                "<h2>Sorry, the query parameter was either empty or null</h2>");
            } else {
                out.println("<h2>Here are your search results</h2>");
                GoogleBean gb = new GoogleBean( );
                gb.setFilter(true);
                //Configure for web display
                gb.setLineSep("<br />");
                if (restrict != null && restrict.length( ) > 0)
                    gb.setRestrict(restrict);
                gb.setQuery(query);
                try {
                    out.println( gb.getSearchResults( ) );
                } catch (Exception e){
                throw new ServletException( e.getMessage( ) );
                }
        }//if
        out.println("</body></html>");

    }// doPost
}//GoogleServlet
```

Using the GoogleBean class in doPost( ) is straightforward. The code sets a few search options (such as setFilter(true)), then calls the bean's getSearchResults( ) method. This method returns a String of formatted search results, which the servlet's PrintWriter sends to the browser for display.

Figure 27-1 shows the simple HTML form displayed in the servlet's doGet( ) method.

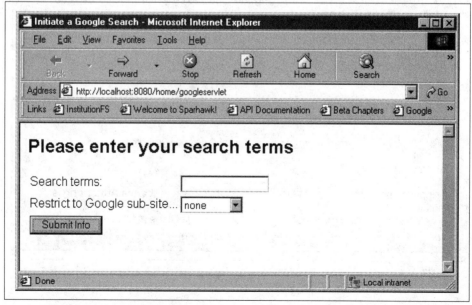

Figure 27-1. Enter keywords to search Google with a servlet

The "Restrict to Google sub-site..." part allows the user to choose one of none, unclesam, linux, mac, or bsd. The user enters the search term "Lance Armstrong" in the HTML form's text field, then presses the "Submit Info" button. Figure 27-2 shows the search results dispalyed by the servlet's doPost( ) method.

 The Google Web APIs display a maximum of 10 results per search

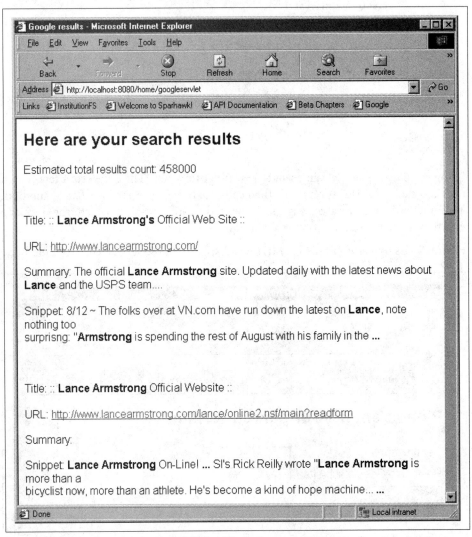

Figure 27-2. A servlet using the Google Web APIs displays some search results

See Also

The home for Google Web Service: *http://www.google.com/apis/*; the Google Web APIs SDK: *http://www.google.com/apis/download.html*; Recipe 3.1 on mapping a servlet to a name in *web.xml*; Recipe 27.1 on setting up your programming environment for use with the Google Web APIs; Recipe 27.4 on using a JSP to connect with Google web services.

27.4   Using a JSP to Connect with Google

Problem

You want to search Google using the Google Web APIs and a JSP.

Solution

Use the `jsp:useBean` standard action to get access to the `GoogleBean` from Example 27.2, then use this bean instance to connect with Google's web tools.

Discussion

The JSP in Example 27-4 uses the JSTL core tags to determine if the user has sent a search query along with their request. If the query request parameter is empty, then the JSP displays a form (see Figure 27-1). See Chapter 23 for details on the JSTL core tags.

If the request parameter is filled by a search query, the JSP uses the `GoogleBean` to search *google.com* and display the results. The JSP uses the `jsp:useBean` standard action to create an instance of the bean, which is stored in the *WEB-INF/lib* directory.

Example 27-4. A JSP uses a JavaBean to search google.com

```
<%@ taglib uri="http://java.sun.com/jstl/core" prefix="c" %>

<html>
<head><title>Search Google from a JSP</title></head>
<body>

<c:choose>

    <c:when test="${empty param.query}">

    <h2>Please enter your search terms...</h2>

    <%-- Display the HTML form... --%>

    <form method="POST" action ='<c:out value=
    "${pageContext.request.contextPath}" />/google.jsp'>
```

Example 27-4. A JSP uses a JavaBean to search google.com (continued)

```
    <table border="0">

    <tr><td valign="top">

    Search terms: </td>  <td valign="top">
    <input type="text" name="query" size="15">
    </td></tr>

    <tr><td valign="top">
    Restrict to Google sub-site... </td>  <td valign="top">

    <select name="restrict">
    <option selected>none</option><option>unclesam</option>
    <option>linux</option>
    <option>mac</option><option>bsd</option></select>
    </td></tr>

    <tr><td valign="top">
    <input type="submit" value="Submit Info"></td></tr>
    </table></form>

<%-- End of the HTML form... --%>

    </c:when>

    <c:otherwise>

    <%-- Create an instance of the GoogleBean --%>
    <jsp:useBean id="gBean" class="com.jspservletcookbook.GoogleBean" />

    <h2>Here are your search results</h2>

    <%-- Set the query, restrict, and lineSep properties of the GoogleBean --%>

    <jsp:setProperty name="gBean" property="query" param="query"/>
    <jsp:setProperty name="gBean" property="restrict" param="restrict"/>
    <jsp:setProperty name="gBean" property="lineSep" value="<br /><br />"/>

    <%-- Now display any results of the search --%>

    <jsp:getProperty name="gBean" property="searchResults" />

    </c:otherwise>

</c:choose>

</body>
</html>
```

The JSP uses the jsp:setProperty standard action to the bean instance's query, restrict, and lineSep properties. The query represents the search terms; restrict can have values of mac, linux, bsd, or unclesam, representing various Google sub-sites, and the lineSep property determines the line-separation characters to use when formatting the results (
 in this example).

Finally, the code uses jsp:getProperty to effectively call the GoogleBean's getSearchResults( ) method, which sends a SOAP message to Google and formats the response.

See Also

The home for Google Web Service: *http://www.google.com/apis/*; the Google web APIs SDK: *http://www.google.com/apis/download.html*; Recipe 27.1 on setting up your programming environment for use with the Google Web APIs; Recipe 27.3 on using a servlet to connect with Google web services.

27.5 Getting Set Up with Amazon's Web Services API

Problem

You want to connect to Amazon Web Services (AWS) with a servlet or JSP.

Solution

Download the Amazon Web Services SDK, acquire an Amazon developer's token, and create a Java-SOAP package for interacting with AWS.

Discussion

The process for setting up AWS goes like this:

1. Download the AWS SDK at *http://www.amazon.com/gp/aws/download_sdk.html/ 002-2688331-0628046*. This *kit.zip* file includes several code samples and web services API documentation in HTML format.

2. Acquire a developer's token from: *http://associates.amazon.com/exec/panama/ associates/join/developer/application.html/002-2688331-0628046*. Similar to the license key you use with Google's Web APIs, the free-of-charge token comprises a series of encoded characters that must accompany each interaction between your Java code and AWS.

3. Develop the Java API for making SOAP requests to AWS. The end result is a JAR file containing the classes that your servlets or JSPs use to make SOAP requests. The rest of this recipe describes how to generate this JAR file, because it is a multistep process.

Interacting with AWS using SOAP messages is one option that Amazon makes available to developers. Another one involves encoding the web services requests in URLs, and thereby making AWS requests via HTTP (called "XML over HTTP"). Recipe 27-7 shows an example of this URL search (they are useful for debugging your SOAP applications). If you store an XSLT file on the Web, AWS uses this file to format the response to XML-over-HTTP requests. See the SDK documentation for more details.

SOAP with Apache Axis

The creation of a Java-SOAP API for using AWS begins with downloading an open source SOAP toolkit named Apache Axis (*http://ws.apache.org/axis/*). Here are the steps involved in creating the API:

1. Download Axis and extract the Axis ZIP file to the directory of your choice (this creates a directory named *axis-1_1*).

2. Inside the *axis-1_1/lib* directory are several JAR files. Place these JAR files on your classpath and then run a program named `org.apache.axis.wsdl.WSDL2Java` to generate Java source files. These Java source files comprise the Java API you will use with AWS when you compile the files.

3. Download the Web Services Description Language (WSDL) file associated with the Amazon Web Services. At this writing, the file can be found at: *http://soap.amazon.com/schemas3/AmazonWebServices.wsdl*.

4. The following command line generates the `com.amazon.soap.axis` package for your Java API. The command lines in this recipe work on both Windows- and Unix-based machines. The command line is designed to refer to the *Amazon-WebServices.wsdl* file in the current directory. The `WSDL2Java` program generates Java classes based on the XML elements described by the WSDL XML file (XML-to-Java conversion). This allows you to work with AWS using only Java objects, which is very nice—it's why you are enduring the initial pain of creating these Java classes! Break up this command line into separate lines to make it more readable, but when you actually run it, the commands must all be combined on one line:

```
java -cp .;lib/axis.jar;lib/commons-discovery.jar;lib/commons-
    logging.jar;lib/jaxrpc.jar;lib/saaj.jar;lib/wsdl4j.jar
        org.apache.axis.wsdl.WSDL2Java AmazonWebServices.wsdl --verbose
            --package com.amazon.soap.axis
```

5. This command line generates Java source files in a directory tree that matches the specified package name (`com.amazon.soap.axis`). Now you have to compile these classes with the *javac* tool, as in the following command line (the current directory contains the *com* directory). Once again, we break up this single-line

command into separate lines just for the sake of readability (you have to run the command line unbroken by any newline characters):

```
javac -classpath .;lib/axis.jar;lib/commons-discovery.jar;lib/commons-
logging.jar;lib/jaxrpc.jar;lib/saaj.jar;lib/wsdl4j.jar
com/amazon/soap/axis/*.java
```

6. Now JAR up all these files. In the same directory containing the top-level *com* directory, this command creates a JAR file named *amazonapi.jar*, which is just a name I created for it:

```
jar cvf amazonapi.jar ./com
```

7. Take the *amazonapi.jar* (or whatever you've named the JAR file) and place it in *WEB-INF/lib*. There's one more step left.

8. Make sure that the JAR files or libraries that the com.amazon.soap.axis package depends on are also available to the web application. The *amazonapi.jar* file depends on the same Axis libraries that you added to the class path in the prior *java* and *javac* command-line sequences. You have to add these JARs to *WEB-INF/lib* as well (unless your application server makes all of these libraries generally available to web applications).

Okay, now for the fun part, where your Java code gets to explore books and other stuff at Amazon using servlets. Your servlets should use the com.amazon.soap.axis package for this purpose.

See Also

The AWS SDK *http://www.amazon.com/gp/aws/download_sdk.html/002-2688331-0628046*; Apache Axis: *http://ws.apache.org/axis/*; the Amazon Web Services WSDL file: *http://soap.amazon.com/schemas3/AmazonWebServices.wsdl*.

27.6 Creating a JavaBean to Connect with Amazon

Problem

You want to create a JavaBean as a type of Amazon search utility class.

Solution

Set up your Amazon API as described in Recipe 27.5, then code a JavaBean that uses the com.amazon.soap.axis package from this API.

Discussion

The JavaBean in Example 27-5, named AmazonBean, imports the com.amazon.soap. axis package. This package is stored in *amazonapi.jar*, which (generated by Recipe 27.5). Store the JAR in the web application's *WEB-INF/lib* directory and the AmazonBean in *WEB-INF/classes* (or also in a JAR in *WEB-INF/*lib).

Example 27-5 connects with Amazon in its getSearchResults( ) method. The AmazonBean formats and displays the search results in structureResults( ). The code comments describe what's going on in detail.

Example 27-5. A JavaBean class that searches Amazon

```
package com.jspservletcookbook;

import java.net.URL;

import com.amazon.soap.axis.*;

public class AmazonBean {

    //The developer's token
    private final static String AMAZON_KEY = "DCJEAVDSXVPUD";

    //NOTE: AWS Version 3 uses "http://xml.amazon.com/xml3"
    private final static String END_POINT =
      "http://soap.amazon.com/onca/soap";

    private final static String AMAZON_TAG = "webservices-20";

    private URL endpointUrl;

    private String lineSep = "\n";
    private String totalResults;
    private String keyword;
    private String page;
    private String type;
    private String mode;


    public AmazonBean( ){}//no-arguments constructor required for a bean

    //an easy way to test the bean outside of a servlet
    public static void main(String[] args) throws Exception{

        AmazonBean bean = new AmazonBean( );
        bean.setKeyword("Lance%20Armstrong");
        bean.setType("heavy");
        bean.setMode("books");
        bean.setPage("1");

        System.out.println( bean.getSearchResults( ) );
    }
```

Example 27-5. A JavaBean class that searches Amazon (continued)

```java
//Structure the search result as a String
public String structureResult(ProductInfo info){

    //Amazon searches return ProductInfo objects, which
    //contains array of Details object. A Details object
    //represents an individual search result
    Details[] details = info.getDetails();

    String results = "";

    //each found book includes an array of authors in its Details
    String[] authors = null;

    String usedP = null;//UsedPrice object

    String rank = null;//SalesRank object

    //for each returned search item...
    for (int i = 0; i < details.length; i++){

        if(mode != null && mode.equals("books")){
            authors = details[i].getAuthors(); }

        //Include the product name
        results +=
          "<strong>"+(i+1)+". Product name:</strong> " +
          details[i].getProductName() + lineSep;

        //If they are books include each author's name
          if(mode != null && mode.equals("books")){

              for (int j = 0; j < authors.length; j++){
                  results += "Author name "+(j+1)+": " + authors[j] +
                  lineSep;

              }//for
          }//if

        usedP = details[i].getUsedPrice();//get the used price

        rank = details[i].getSalesRank();//get the sales rank

        results += "Sales rank: " + (rank == null ? "N/A" : rank) +
         lineSep +"List price: " + details[i].getListPrice() + lineSep +
           "Our price: " + details[i].getOurPrice() + lineSep +
            "Used price: " + (usedP == null ? "N/A" : usedP) + lineSep +
              lineSep;

    }

    return results;
```

Example 27-5. A JavaBean class that searches Amazon (continued)

```java
}//structureResult

//Connect with Amazon Web Services then call structureResult()
public String getSearchResults() throws Exception{

    endpointUrl = new URL(END_POINT);
    AmazonSearchService webService = new AmazonSearchServiceLocator();
    //Connect to the AWS endpoint
    AmazonSearchPort port = webService.getAmazonSearchPort(endpointUrl);
    KeywordRequest request = getKeywordRequest();
    //Return results of the search
    ProductInfo prodInfo = port.keywordSearchRequest(request);
    //Set totalResults with any provided results total
    setTotalResults( prodInfo.getTotalResults() );
    //Make sure the book-search results are structured and displayed
    return structureResult(prodInfo);

}//getSearchResults

//Setter and getter methods...

public void setLineSep(String lineSep){
    this.lineSep=lineSep;
}

 public String getLineSep(){
    return lineSep;
}

//A KeywordRequest object initialized with search terms, the mode, the
//number of pages to be returned, the type ('lite' or 'heavy'), and the
//developer's token.
public KeywordRequest getKeywordRequest(){
    KeywordRequest request = new KeywordRequest();
    request.setKeyword(keyword);//the search terms
    request.setMode(mode);//the mode, as in 'books'
    request.setPage(page);//the number of pages to return
    request.setType(type);//the type, 'lite' or 'heavy'
    request.setDevtag(AMAZON_KEY);//developer's token
    request.setTag(AMAZON_TAG);//the tag, 'webservices-20'
    return request;

}

public void setKeyword(String keyword){
    this.keyword = keyword;
}

public String getKeyword(){
    return keyword;
}
```

Example 27-5. A JavaBean class that searches Amazon (continued)

```java
public void setMode(String mode){
    this.mode = mode;
}

public String getMode( ){
    return mode;
}

public void setPage(String page){
    this.page = page;
}

public String getPage( ){
    return page;
}

 public void setType(String type){
    this.type = type;
}

public String getType( ){
    return type;
}

public void setTotalResults(String results){
    totalResults = results;
}

public String getTotalResults( ){
    return totalResults;
}
}//AmazonBean
```

The bean has a main( ) method that allows you to test the bean from the command line. Here is code from that method that creates a bean instance, searches for a book using the search terms "Lance Armstrong," and displays some results:

```java
AmazonBean bean = new AmazonBean( );
bean.setKeyword("Lance%20Armstrong");
bean.setType("heavy");
bean.setMode("books");
bean.setPage("1");
System.out.println( bean.getSearchResults( ) );
```

To run the bean from a command line, make sure include all of the necessary Axis-related libraries on your classpath (see Recipe 27.5). The following command line runs the bean to test it. Note that this command line includes the *amazonapi.jar* file generated by Recipe 27.5:

```
java -cp .;jaxrpc.jar;axis.jar;amazonapi.jar;commons-logging.jar;commons-discovery.
jar;saaj.jar com.jspservletcookbook.AmazonBean
```

If you set the type option to heavy (as opposed to lite), then the search returns the book's sales rank at Amazon. The lite SOAP responses do not include a value for sales rank.

See Also

The AWS SDK *http://www.amazon.com/gp/aws/download_sdk.html/002-2688331-0628046*; Recipe 27.7 on using a servlet and a JavaBean to connect with AWS.

27.7   Using a Servlet to Connect with Amazon

Problem

You want to connect with AWS using a servlet.

Solution

Use a specially designed JavaBean to peform the AWS-related tasks.

Discussion

Example 27-6 uses the same design that the Google recipes used, so you should find this servlet code very familiar if you have worked through those examples before. The servlet generates an HTML form in response to a GET HTTP request, which sends the Amazon search terms back to the same servlet. The interesting action takes place in the doPost( ) method, where the servlet uses an AmazonBean class (from Recipe 27.6) to connect with AWS and display any search results.

Example 27-6. A servlet uses a JavaBean to connect with AWS

```
package com.jspservletcookbook;

import java.io.IOException;
import java.io.PrintWriter;

import javax.servlet.*;
import javax.servlet.http.*;

public class AmazonServlet extends HttpServlet {

  public void doGet(HttpServletRequest request,
    HttpServletResponse response)
    throws ServletException, java.io.IOException {

      //set the MIME type of the response, "text/html"
      response.setContentType("text/html");

      java.io.PrintWriter out = response.getWriter( );
```

Example 27-6. A servlet uses a JavaBean to connect with AWS (continued)

```
    //Begin assembling the HTML content
    out.println("<html><head>");

    out.println(
    "<title>Initiate an Amazon Book Search</title></head><body>");

    out.println("<h2>Please enter your Amazon search terms</h2>");

    //Display an HTML form that sends the request back to this
    //'/amazonservlet' which will cause the calling of doPost()

    //make sure method="POST" so that the servlet service method
    //calls doPost in the response to this form submit
    out.println(
      "<form method=\"POST\" action =\"" + request.getContextPath() +
        "/amazonservlet\" >");

    out.println("<table border=\"0\"><tr><td valign=\"top\">");
    out.println("Search terms: </td>  <td valign=\"top\">");
    out.println("<input type=\"text\" name=\"query\" size=\"15\">");
    out.println("</td></tr>");
    out.println("<tr><td valign=\"top\">");
    out.println(
    "<input type=\"submit\" value=\"Submit Info\"></td></tr>");
    out.println("</table></form>");
    out.println("</body></html>");

  } //doGet

public void doPost(HttpServletRequest request,
  HttpServletResponse response)
    throws ServletException,java.io.IOException{

    String query = request.getParameter("query");

    boolean isValid = (query == null || query.length() < 1) ?
    false : true;

    response.setContentType("text/html");

    java.io.PrintWriter out = response.getWriter();

    out.println("<html><head>");
    out.println("<title>Amazon book results</title></head><body>");

    if (! isValid){
        out.println(
        "<h2>Sorry, the query parameter was either empty or null</h2>");
    } else {
        AmazonBean amBean = new AmazonBean();
        amBean.setKeyword(query);
        amBean.setType("lite");
        amBean.setMode("books");
```

Example 27-6. A servlet uses a JavaBean to connect with AWS (continued)

```
        amBean.setPage("1");
        amBean.setLineSep("<br />");
        out.println("<h2>Here are your search results</h2>");
        try {
            out.println( amBean.getSearchResults() );
        } catch (Exception e){
          out.println(
          "The search terms either returned zero results "+
          "or were invalid.");
      }
    }

    out.println("</body></html>");

  }//doPost
}//AmazonServlet
```

To keep the code simple, limit the keyword search to books. AWS offers a comprehensive method of searching its several catalogs, however, with the API not limited to keyword searches of books. For example, the product modes include DVD, electronics, music, hardware, software, and toys. You can also initiate several different search types (in addition to keywords), such as Amazon Standard Item Number (ASIN) searches.

Figure 27-3 shows the return value of the servlet's doGet( ) method.

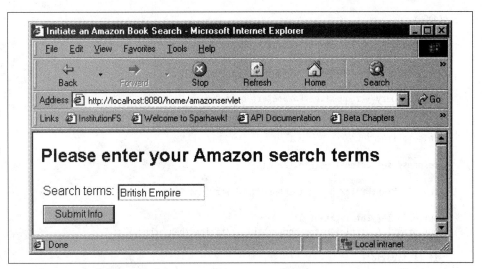

Figure 27-3. A servlet's HTML form accepts Amazon search terms

Figure 27-4 shows parts of the servlet's displayed results that are handled by the servlet's doPost( ) method.

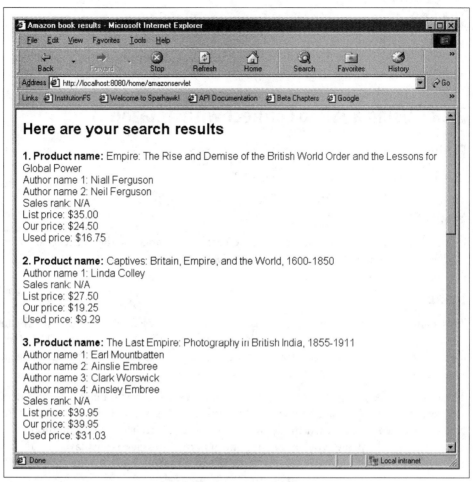

Figure 27-4. The results of an Amazon book search

 Once you have downloaded and unpacked the AWS SDK, the software documentation is located at: *AmazonWebServices/API Guide/index.html*.

To help debug your AWS searches and servlets, you can initiate an AWS search using a Uniform Resource Locator (URL) in your browser. The following URL initiates a keyword seach for a book using the terms "British Empire."

```
http://xml.amazon.com/onca/xml?v=1.0&t=webservices-20&
    dev-t=DCJEAVXSDVPUD&KeywordSearch=British%20Empire&mode=books&
      type=lite&page=1&f=xml
```

An request for this URL returns an XML file that looks similar to Example 27-1. The sales rank reads "N/A" because the search option `type=lite` returns a `null` value for this ranking. Use `type=heavy` to get a value for the Amazon sales rank.

See Also

The AWS SDK *http://www.amazon.com/gp/aws/download_sdk.html/002-2688331-0628046*; *Web Services Essentials* (O'Reilly); Recipe 3.1 on mapping a servlet to a name in *web.xml*; Recipe 27.8 on using a JSP and a JavaBean to connect with AWS.

27.8   Using a JSP to Connect with Amazon

Problem

You want to connect with AWS using a JSP.

Solution

Use the `jsp:useBean` standard action to create an instance of the `AmazonBean` from Recipe 27.6. Use this instance to manage the AWS search and results.

Discussion

This recipe uses the same strategy as the JSP in Recipe 27.4: create a JavaBean instance that handles the AWS search and displays the search results. The `jsp:useBean` standard action creates an instance of `com.jspservletcookbook.AmazonBean`, which is located in *WEB-INF/classes*.

Then the code uses `jsp:setProperty` to set some search options, before the JSP uses `jsp:getProperty` to launch the seach. Example 27-7 uses the JSTL tag `c:catch` to catch any exceptions thrown by the `AmazonBean`'s `getSearchResults()` method. The variable except is of the type `Throwable`, and its error message is displayed by the `c:out` tag if the search query is invalid. The JSP in Example 27-7 displays the HTML form and search results shown in Figures 27-3 and 27-4.

This `jsp:getProperty` code is the equivalent of calling the `AmazonBean`'s `getSearchResults()` method, which returns a `String` of formatted search results.

Example 27-7. A JSP launches an AWS book search

```
<%@ taglib uri="http://java.sun.com/jstl/core" prefix="c" %>

<html>
<head><title>Search Amazon.com for a Book</title></head>
<body>

<c:choose>

  <c:when test="${empty param.keyword}">

  <h2>Please enter your Amazon search terms...</h2>

  <%-- Display the HTML form... --%>
```

Example 27-7. A JSP launches an AWS book search (continued)

```
<form method="POST" action =
'<c:out value="${pageContext.request.contextPath}" />/amazon.jsp'>

<%-- form and table tags... --%>
<table border="0"><tr><td valign="top">
Search terms: </td>  <td valign="top">
<input type="text" name="keyword" size="15">
</td></tr><tr><td valign="top">

<tr><td valign="top">

<input type="submit" value="Submit Info"></td></tr>
</table></form>
</body></html>

   </c:when>

   <c:otherwise>

   <jsp:useBean id="aBean" class="com.jspservletcookbook.AmazonBean" />
   <jsp:setProperty name="aBean" property="keyword" param="keyword"/>
   <jsp:setProperty name="aBean" property="mode" value="books"/>
   <jsp:setProperty name="aBean" property="page" value="1"/>
   <jsp:setProperty name="aBean" property="type" value="lite"/>
   <jsp:setProperty name="aBean" property="lineSep" value="<br />"/>

   <h2>Here are your search results</h2>

   <c:catch var="excep">

     <%-- Now display any results of the search --%>
     <jsp:getProperty name="aBean" property="searchResults" />

   </c:catch >

   <%-- Print any error messages, such as 'Bad Request' if the search
   terms are meaningless --%>

   <c:out value="${excep.message}"/>

</c:choose>

</body>
</html>
```

See Also

The AWS SDK: *http://www.amazon.com/gp/aws/download_sdk.html/002-2688331-0628046*; *Web Services Essentials* (O'Reilly); Recipe 27.7 on using a servlet and a JavaBean to connect with AWS; Chapter 23 on using the JSTL.

Index

Numbers

401 Unauthorized HTTP status code, 330
403 Forbidden HTTP status code, 437
404 Not Found HTTP status code, 193
500 Internal Server Error HTTP status
        code, 193

Symbols

${ } EL expression delimiters, 574
    dereferencing variable and property
        values, 241
    encapsulating function call within, 499
<%-- --%> in JSP comments, 10
<!-- -->, in Tomcat server.xml file
        comments, 327
* (asterisk)
    ** pattern in Ant elements, for zero or
        more directories, 82, 91
    wildcard character in URL patterns, 53
. (dot)
    in attribute names, 573
    specifying current directory, 12
. (dot) operator, 241
/ (forward slash)
    /* in URL patterns, 53
        for controller servlet, 59, 63
        for invoker servlet, 58
        overriden by controller servlet, 61
    in URL patterns, 51, 55
        excluding from extension mapping, 55
% in conversion patterns, 308
<% %>, in JSP scriptlets, 488
<%@ syntax, JSP directives, 8, 108

A

abort( ) (LoginModule), 342
actions in JSPs created as XML files, 106
activation.jar archive, 440
ActiveX control, Flash file embedded in JSP
        by Internet Explorer, 388
addCookie( ) (HttpServletResponse), 211
addresses, email, 439, 453
Administration console (WebLogic), xv
    configuring JNDI resource, 628
    viewing JNDI tree, 630
Adobe System's SVG Viewer
        application, 394
aliases to servlets, creating in web.xml
        file, 50–52
already.deployed property (Ant, build.xml
        file), 35
Amazon Web Services, 666
    connecting to with a JSP, 688
    connecting to with a servlet, 684–688
    creating JavaBean to connect
        with, 679–684
    setting up, 677–679
    SOAP response to keyword search
        request, 664
Ant tool, 74–97
    build.xml file, 21
    compiling and creating WAR files
        with, 13
    compiling servlet classes, 10
    compiling servlet with build file, 83–86
    creating JAR files, 89–92

We'd like to hear your suggestions for improving our indexes. Send email to *index@oreilly.com*.

Ant tool (*continued*)
  deploying servlet on WebLogic Server
    7.0, 26–29
  deploying single servlet on
    Tomcat, 18–22
  deploying web application on
    Tomcat, 31–36
    build.properties file (example), 33
    build.xml file (example), 33–36
    steps in process, 32
  deploying web application on WebLogic
    Server 7.0, 37
  global.properties file, 20
  obtaining and setting up, 74
    downloading binary or source
      distribution, 75
    JAXP-compliant XML parser, 75
  online manual for, 21
  starting Tomcat application with, 92–95
  stopping Tomcat application with, 95–97
  targets, using, 76–79
    build.xml file, executing, 77
    executing several targets in specified
      sequence, 78
  Tomcat JAR files, including in Ant
    classpath, 80–83
  WAR files, creating, 86–89
antcall element, 22
antcall task, 36
ANT_HOME environment variable, 75
Apache
  Ant (see Ant tool)
  Xerces2 XML parser, 75
Apache Jakarta Project
  log4j distribution, downloading
    from, 300
  reference implementation (RI) for the
    JSTL, 552
  Standard 1.0 taglib, 551
Apache Software Foundation, Log4j
  library, 414
Apache Software License, 300
appBase directory (Tomcat, server.xml
  file), 37
appenders, 297
  adding to root logger, 303–306
  ConsoleAppender, 302
  inheritance of, 319
    layout specification, 322
  rolling file appender, 307
  using a pattern with, 306–310
Apple Computer's QuickTime movies, 392

applet tags (HTML), 383
applets
  embedding in JSPs with HTML Converter
    tool, 382–385
  embedding in JSPs with
    jsp:plugin, 379–381
  example (Sun Microsystems), 380
application event listeners, 316
application implicit object, 133, 357
application name (web applications), 13
application scope, 367, 573
  binding an object to, 357
application servers, xiv
  BEA WebLogic, recipes in this book
    for, xv
applicationScope JSTL implicit object, 363
ArithmeticException class, 198
array of cookies, 214, 220
arrays
  GoogleSearchResultElement array, 670
  iterating over with c:forEach tag, 557
  of SortedMaps, iterating over, 569
attachments, email
  adding to an email in a servlet, 461–466
  handling for email received in a
    servlet, 455–460
attribute directive, 544, 545
attributeAdded( )
  (HttpSessionAttributeListener),
  254
attributeRemoved( )
  (HttpSessionAttributeListener),
  254
attributeReplaced( )
  (HttpSessionAttributeListener),
  254
attributes, 354–378
  cookies, 210
  custom logging tag, 313
  definition of, 354
  JSP scoped attribute, setting to value of
    form parameter, 158–161
  object, naming convention for, 573
  ServletContext, setting in JSPs, 357–360
  ServletContext, setting in
    servlets, 354–357
    object that servlet binds to
      ServletContext, 355
    servlet that binds object to
      ServletContext, 356
attribution for use of code examples, xviii

audio files
    embedding in JSPs, 396–397
    sending as MP3 files, 289–292
auth-constraint element (web.xml), 68
    roles in, 329
authentication, 68, 324–353
    authorization vs., 338
    BASIC authentication, use with web
        applications on Tomcat, 328–330
    creating usernames and passwords with
        Tomcat, 324
    form-based, 331
        logging out user, 335–337
    JAAS configuration file,
        creating, 344–346
    JAAS, using in a JSP, 349–353
    JAAS, using in a servlet, 346–349
    LoginModule, creating with
        JAAS, 337–344
    SSL, setting up on Tomcat, 325
auth-method element (web.xml), 328
    form-based authentication, 332
    values for, 69
authorization
    authentication vs., 338
    (see also JAAS)
available task (Ant, build.xml file), 35

B

background soundtrack, embedding in a
    JSP, 396–397
Base64 content-encoding mechanism, 328
basedir attribute
    Ant jar task, 91
    Ant project element, 77
BASIC authentication, 69
    form-based authentication, using
        with, 331
    using with web applications on
        Tomcat, 328–330
    web.xml elements for initiation of, 329
BasicConfigurator class, 301
batch file, for precompiling JSPs with
    Tomcat, 101
BEA WebLogic (see WebLogic)
binary data, 279
    PDF file, sending as, 280–284
    word processing file, sending as, 284–286
    XML file, sending as, 286–289

binding objects
    listening for binding or unbinding of
        session objects, 255
    Session object, to WebLogic JNDI
        implementation, 629
    to the ServletContext
        with a JSP, 357–360
        with a servlet, 355–357
blocking filters
    IP addresses, blocking requests
        from, 434–438
    requests, optionally blocking, 422–424
body tags (HTML), 387
BodyPart class, 456, 460, 462
BodyTagSupport class, 313, 520
boundary pattern separating files in HTTP
    upload requests, 174
browser windows, creating with
    JavaScript, 265
    in a JSP, 272–273
    in a servlet, 269–271
browsers
    cookies supported by, 210
    detecting MIME type for embedded MP3
        file and activating helper
        application to play music, 396
    displaying XML files in readable
        format, 293
    embedding Flash file in a JSP, 388
    JavaScript in, 263
    viewer applications for SVG files, 394
BufferedInputStream class, 283
build directory, 11
    inclusion of nested directories in WAR file
        with Ant war task, 35
build files (Ant), 18
    command-line sequence for executing, 77
    compiling servlet with, 83–86
    deploying web application
        (example), 33–36
    edited to deploy on WebLogic 7.0, 38
    executing several targets in specified
        sequence, 78
    functions of, 21
    importing build.properties file into, 33
    JSP parsing, using JSTL XML tags, 559
    names other than build.xml, 78
    Tomcat Manager application, using
        from, 92
    transforming into HTML, using XSL
        stylesheet, 562
    wl.properties for WebLogic Ant file, 28

Builder (WebLogic), xv
build.properties file (Ant), 33
    deploying web application on WebLogic
        Server 7.0, 38
build.xml file (see build files)

C

C language, printf function, 308
CallableStatement class, 491–495
    executeUpdate( ), 495
    servlet using to call stored
        procedure, 492–495
CallbackHandler class, 338, 342, 347
callbacks
    class for sifting through web
        pages, 648–650
    definition of, 648
    ParserDelegator, using with, 650
case sensitivity
    url pattern in servlet-mapping
        elements, 52
    usernames and passwords in
        tomcat-users.xml file, 328
casting
    request parameters, 260
    ServletRequest type to
        HttpServletRequest, 415
Caucho Resin (servlet engine), xv
cbck:log (custom JSP tag), 311, 314
c:choose tag, 575
CDATA sections in XML files, using to pass
        well-formed test, 143
c:forEach tag, 153, 551
    interations performed by, 555
    iterating over map values, 223
    iterating through a Map's stored request
        headers, 576
CGI (Common Gateway Interface), 2
character entity codes, 245, 247
    escaped characters in c:out tag, 557
    listing of, 247
CheckEmail function, JavaScript, 265
c:if tag
    testing expressions for conditional code
        execution, 555
    use in a JSP (example), 557
c:import tag, 144
    importing Ant build file into JSP, 560
    including JavaScript module in a JSP, 267

JavaScript module, importing into a
    JSP, 268
use by JSP to access forbidden
    resource, 146
classes
    JavaServer Page implementation class, 98
    servlet, 1, 10
        servlet-class element in web.xml, 50
classes directory, 12, 30
    log4j.properties file, 304–305
    specifying classes with Ant war task, 35
    TLDs and, 530
    WebLogic 7.0 server, pasting servlet class
        into, 24
classes element (Ant), 88
classic tag handlers, 519
    creating for a custom action, 520–524
    creating JSP 1.2 TLD for, 524–526
    creating JSP 2.0 TLD for, 526–529
classpath element (Ant), 81
    nested inside the javac task, 82
CLASSPATH environment variable,
        precompiling JSPs and, 101
classpaths
    Ant classpath that includes Tomcat JAR
        files, 80–83
    email-related classes, placing on, 439
    in build.xml file, for JAR files in Tomcat
        directories, 21
    user, represented by CLASSPATH
        environment variable, 75
    WLCLASSPATH environment
        variable, 102
client authentication (see authentication)
client requests, 398–410
    counting for web application, 408
    examining HTTP request headers in a
        JSP, 400
    examining HTTP request headers in a
        servlet, 398–400
    filter, using to alter request
        headers, 402–405
    refreshing a JSP automatically, 407
    refreshing a servlet automatically, 405
client state, 209
Clock class (example applet), 380
    reference to, embedded by JSP, 383
close( )
    InitialContext class, 621
    PrintWriter class, 129

closing database connections, 481, 487
code examples in this book, use of, xviii
Collections class, synchronizedMap( ), 356
comment attribute (cookies), 210
comments
    JSP, 10
    uncommenting Connector element in
        Tomcat server.xml, 327
commercial servlet engines, xv
commit( )
    Connection class, 506, 510
    LoginModule class, 342
Common Gateway Interface (CGI), 2
com.oreilly.servlet library
    classes for file uploads, 177
    LocaleNegotiator class, 594
    MultipartFilter class, 187
com.oreilly.servlet.multipart package, 185
compiling servlets, 10
    Ant tool, using, 10
    PATH environment variable for javac, 11
    with Ant build file, 83–86
    (see also precompiling JSPs)
configure( ) (BasicConfigurator), 302
configure( ) (PropertyConfigurator)
    specifying name of log4j.properties
        file, 316
Connection class
    commit( ), 506, 510
    getMetaData( ), 518
    getTransactionIsolation( ), 510
        listing of isolation levels, 509
    rollback( ), 506, 510
    setAutoCommit( ), 505
connections, database, 471
    creating connection pool with WebLogic
        Console, 482
    DataSource as factory for, 567
    opening and closing, 481
    servlet using WebLogic connection
        pool, 484–488
Connector element (server.xml), 327
ConsoleAppender class, 304
container-managed security, 66
content
    non-HTML, sending, 279–295
        audio files, 289–292
        PDF files, 280–284
        viewing internal resources in a
            servlet, 292–295
        word processing files, 284–286

        XML files, 286–289
    (see also dynamically including content;
        static content)
content types
    email, 452, 455
        Multipart, 455
    multipart/form-data, 174
Content-Disposition header, 175, 283
Content-Length header, 283
contentType attribute (jsp
    directive.page element), 111
Content-Type header, 175
    application/msword, 284
    MIME types, 280
context
    default, for servlets, 51
    including JSP file, importing content from
        outside, 144–147
Context element (Tomcat server.xml
    file), 22, 36
context path for web application, 13
    path attribute of Context element
        (Tomcat), 37
contextDestroyed( )
    (ServletContextListener), 318
contextInitialized
    (ServletContextListener), 318
ContextObject class (example), 355
context-param element (web.xml)
    cookie age, values for, 213
    dataSource parameter that connects with
        a database, 567
    internationalization resources, 606
    JSP that opens pop-up window, 273
    localization context, setting, 603, 613
    providing path for an included file in a
        JSP, 140
context-relative path, 130
controller servlet, 59–61
    exclusive access to certain servlets, setting
        up, 71–73
    mapping all requests to while preserving
        all servlet mappings, 61
conversion of a JSP into a servlet, 8
conversion patterns, layout of logged
    messages, 298
conversion specifiers in pattern
    language, 308
Cookie class, 211
    getName( ) and getValue( ), 215, 220
    getPath( ), 221

Cookie class (*continued*)
  getter and setter methods for
      attributes, 221
  setMaxAge( ), 213, 217
      argument value of zero, 225
  setValue( ), 217
cookie implicit object (JSTL), 222, 579
Cookie request header, 221
cookies, 209–226, 321
  accessing with EL, 579
  definition of, 209
  deletion by users, 213
  disabled by users, 210
  name/value pair, 209
  optional attribute/value pairs, 210
  overwriting or removing existing
      cookies, 225
  reading values with a JSP, 222–224
  reading values with a servlet, 220–222
  session tracking, use in, 227
      disabled cookies, 244
  setting
      with a JSP, 215–219
      with a servlet, 211–215
  storing request cookies in an array, 214
copy task (Ant), 77
Copyright servlet (example), 121
Core J2EE Blueprints web page, 59
Corel's SVG Viewer, 394
cos.jar file, 178
c:otherwise tag, 575
country codes (ISO), 601, 607
c:out tag, 10, 139, 551
  displaying a JavaBean's properties, 584
  displaying form input via a JavaBean, 156
  displaying individual parameter
      values, 154
  escaped characters, 557
  exception information, displaying for
      JSP, 206
  passing value of request_uri attribute
      to, 204
  summary of functions, 555
  use in a JSP (example), 557
c:param tags, including parameter values in
      JSP, 146
create-jar target (Ant), 90
create-war target (Ant, build.xml file), 35
CreateWindow function, JavaScript, 265
  creating new browser window in a
      servlet, 269–271
creation time for sessions
  tracking with JSPs, 240–244

tracking with servlets, 237–239
c:set tag, 551
  binding an object to application
      scope, 357
  setting variable to session scope, 573
  summary of functions, 555
currencies, formatting for locales
  in a JSP, 609–610
  in a servlet, 607–609
custom actions, 519
  JSP using to access log4j, 314
  (see also custom tags)
custom tags, 7, 310, 519–550
  associated with a tag file, using, 547
  cbck:log tag
      logging level, 314
  configuration file, including your
      own, 315
  creating classic tag handler for, 520–524
  creating JSP 1.2 TLD for classic tag
      handler, 524–526
  creating JSP 2.0 TLD for classic tag
      handler, 526–529
  creating TLD for a simple tag
      handler, 539
  function calls embedded in template
      text, 585
  handling exceptions in custom tag
      class, 533–536
  JSP tag file, creating, 543–545
  listener class, adding to tag library, 548
  packaging a tag library in a web
      application, 529
  packaging JSP tag file in a JAR, 546
  packaging tag library in a JAR file, 530
  simple tag handler, creating, 536–539
  simple tag handler, using in a JSP, 541
  tag file, packaging in web
      application, 545
  tag that uses log4j, 311–313
  TLD for custom logger tag, 313
  using in a JSP, 532
c:when tag, 575

D

DatabaseMetaData interface, 518
databases, 471–517
  accessing from servlet without DataSource
      configuration, 472–475
  calling stored procedure from a
      JSP, 495–500
  configuring DataSource in Tomcat, 475

converting ResultSet to Result
    object, 500–505
creating DataSource on
    WebLogic, 481–484
DataSource, using in servlet with
    Tomcat, 478–481
executing several SQL statements in one
    transaction, 505–510
interacting with by configuring
    DataSource in web.xml, 567–570
JNDI lookup, using to access a WebLogic
    DataSource, 484
JSTL tags that interact with, 551
ResultSet information, finding
    out, 513–518
stored procedure, calling from a
    servlet, 490–495
transactions, using with JSPs, 511–513
WebLogic DataSource, using in a
    JSP, 488–490
DataHandler class, 465
DataSource
    configuration in web.xml, 511
    configuring for servlet in Tomcat, 475
    configuring in web.xml for SQL JSTL
        tags, 567–568
    creating DataSource object on
        WebLogic, 481–484
        configuration, steps in, 482
    explicitly setting for JSTL SQL tags in a
        JSP, 570–572
    getConnection( ), 481, 485
    JNDI, accessing with, 615
    using in servlet with Tomcat, 478–481
    WebLogic DataSource, using in a
        JSP, 488–490
DataSourceLoginModule, 342, 348
Date class, getTime( ), 557
DateFormat class, 566, 603
    format( ), 239
    getDateTimeInstance( ), 605
dates and times
    creation and last-accessed time for
        sessions
        tracking with JSPs, 240–244
        tracking with servlets, 237–239
    expiration for cookies, 210
    formatting dates according to request
        locale
        in a JSP, 605
        in a servlet, 603

formatting with JSTL tags
    current date in Swiss and U.S.
        style, 565
    fmt:formatDate tag, attributes of, 566
    JSP that displays current, 8
    log4j date formatter, 308
    of logging activity, 299
dateStyle and timeStyle attributes
    (fmt:formatDate), 566
Davidson, James Duncan, 74
DEBUG level logging, 297, 303
    in root logger, 304
declarative security, 66
default attribute (Ant project element), 77
DefaultFileRenamePolicy class, 185
    file-uploading JavaBean, use in, 189
deleting a cookie, 225
depends attribute (Ant target elements), 78
deploy-application target (Ant, build.xml
    file), 35
    edited to deploy on WebLogic 7.0, 38
Deployer utility (WebLogic), 46–48
deploying servlets and JSPs, 17–48
    deploying as part of Tomcat's Context
        element in server.xml file, 22
    individual JSP, deploying on Tomcat, 29
    individual JSP, deploying on
        WebLogic, 30
    individual servlet, deploying on
        Tomcat, 17–22
        Ant tool, using, 18–22
        steps in process, 18
    individual servlet, deploying on WebLogic
        Server 7.0, 24–29
        Ant file, using, 26–29
        editing web.xml file to register
        servlet, 24
        redeploying web application, 26
    web application, deploying on
        Tomcat, 31–37
        Ant build file, using, 31–36
    web application, deploying on WebLogic
        using Ant tool, 37
        using WebLogic Administration
        Console, 39–42
        using WebLogic Builder, 43–45
        using weblogic.Deployer
        command-line utility, 46–48

deployment descriptors
    creating, 14–16
        for servlet API 2.3, 15
        servlet API 2.4, 16
        web.xml file contents, 14
    EJB, 641
        vendor-specific
            (weblogic-ejb-jar.xml), 642–643
    J2EE, namespace of, 528
    opening and editing in WebLogic
        Builder, 44
    security-related elements in versions other
        than servlet v2.4, 67
    storage in WEB-INF directory, 12
    taglib element, 112
    web.xml file in WEB-INF directory, 30
    (see also web.xml file)
deploy-servlet target (Ant, build.xml
    file), 21, 28
description attribute (Ant target
    elements), 77
destfile attribute
    Ant jar task, 91
    Ant war task, 88
digital certificate, creating for Tomcat
    server, 325
dir attributes
    Ant classes element, 88
    Ant fileset elements, 81
directives, JSP, 8
    in well-formed XML file, 108
    XML equivalents for, 107
directories
    ** pattern in Ant elements (zero or more
        directories), 82, 91
    local, saving file uploads to, 180
    URLs that specify a directory only, 65
directory structure of web applications, 12
    for application deployed by Ant tool, 32
    example of, 13
    exploded directory format, 44
    JSP files in, 29
dirty read, 509
dispatcher elements (web.xml), 427, 428
displayMessage( )
    AttachBean class (example), 456
    EmailBean class (example), 454
    HeaderAccessor class (example), 467
    MailAccessor class (example), 452
distributed computing, SOAP as easier form
    of, 666

doCatch( ) (TryCatchFinally), 534
docBase attribute (Context element,
    Tomcat), 37
Document Type Definition (DTD), 15
    in JSP 1.2 TLD file, 549
    JSP 1.2, 527
    order for elements in web.xml (servlet 2.3
        API), 477
    XML Schema vs., 528
doEndTag( ), 522, 534
doFilter( ), 258
    blocking requests, 422
    casting request parameter, 260
    changing servlet response, 425
    filter using HttpServletResponseWrapper
        class, 426
    FilterChain class, 402
doFinally( ) (TryCatchFinally), 534
doGet( )
    encodeRedirectURL, using in, 249
    FirstServlet class (example), 3
        output displayed in browser, 6
    HttpServlet class, 3
        including content in, 120
        JavaBean, using to send email, 445
    PrivacyServlet class (example), including
        resource specified by init
        parameter, 123
    servlet accessing database using
        JDBC, 472
    servlet method to which filter is
        mapped, 261
    servlet using a JavaBean to handle email
        attachments, 460
    servlet using JavaBean to send email, 448
domain attribute (cookies), 210
doPost( )
    FirstServlet class (example), 3
        output displayed in browser, 7
    HttpServlet class, 3
        including content in, 120
    POST HTTP requests, responding to, 149
    tracking a user's refresh count, 406
doStartTag( ), 522, 534
doTag( ), 536
    simple tag handlers, 542
download progress, showing to user, 283
DriverManager class, 472
DTD (see Document Type Definition)
dynamic content, combining multimedia
    in JSPs, 379

dynamically including content, 119–147
  configuring included resource in external file, 122
  external configuration file, using to include resource in a JSP, 137–140
  importing a resource each time servlet handles a request, 120–122
  including content from outside a context in JSP, 144–147
  including content in a JSP for each request, 133–136
  including XML fragment in JSP document, 141–144
  resources nested at multiple levels in servlet, 125–130
    exception information, displaying, 129
    first inner included servlet, 127
    outer including servlet, 126
    request attributes, access by included resources, 128
    second included servlet, 129
  resources that seldom change, including in JSP, 130–133
  server performance and, 122

E

EAR (Enterprise Application Archive) file, 40
echo task (Ant), 77
EIS (Enterprise Information Systems), xiv
ejb-jar.xml file, 641
  contents of, displaying, 643
EJBs (Enterprise JavaBeans), 616
  accessing an EJB on WebLogic from a servlet, using JNDI, 638–646
    deployment descriptor (ejb-jar.xml), 641
    deployment descriptor, vendor-specific, 642–643
    servlet (example), 643–646
    stateless session bean (example), 639–641
EL (see Expression Language)
elements, XML
  Ant tasks, 76
  build.xml file (Ant), 21
  Context element (Tomcat server.xml file), 22
  in web.xml file for servlet API 2.3, 15
  in web.xml file for servlet API 2.4, 16
  order in valid XML file, 65

email, 439–470
  accessing from a servlet, 449–453
  accessing from a servlet using a JavaBean, 454
  adding attachments to an email in a servlet, 461–466
  JavaBeans Activation Framework (JAF), 439
  JavaMail API, 439
  placing classes related to on classpath, 439
  reading received email headers from a servlet, 466–470
  received in a servlet, handling attachments from, 455–460
  sending from a servlet, 441–444
    servlet interaction with mail server, 444
  sending from a servlet using a JavaBean, 444–449
    EmailBean (example), 445–448
    servlet using JavaBean to send email, 448
    setting email parts with bean methods, 448
email addresses, validating in form input with JavaScript, 265
embed tags (HTML), 380, 381
  automatic HTML file generation by Flash, 386
  produced by HTML Converter, 384
encodeRedirectURL (HttpServletResponse), 249
encodeURL( ) (HttpServletResponse), 248
Enterprise Application Archive (EAR) file, 40
Enterprise Information Systems (EIS), xiv
Enterprise JavaBeans (see EJBs)
entity codes for special characters, 245, 247
  c:out tag, escaped characters, 557
  listing of, 247
entrySet( ) (Map), 152, 172
Enumeration type, 595
ERROR level logging, 297
ErrorData class, 207
errorPage attribute (page directive), 205
error-page configuration, 15
  authentication failure page (/loginError.html), 332
  element in web.xml for IOExceptions, 178

error-page configuration (*continued*)
    in web.xml, example of, 128
    overridden by page directive
        declaration, 206
error-page element (web.xml), 192, 203
    configuring error pages, 193–195
escaped characters, c:out tag, 557
escapeXml attribute (c:out tag), 557
EventObject class, 257
example code from this book, use of, xviii
exception implicit object, 206
exceptions
    in custom tag class, 533–536
    handling in web applications, 192–208
        creating error-handling JSP, 202–205
        declaring exception handlers in
            web.xml, 192–195
        declaring exception-handling JSP for
            other JSPs, 205–208
        exception-handling servlet, 196–199
        sending error from a JSP, 201
        sending error from a servlet, 199–201
    thrown during include operations, 128
exception-type element (web.xml), 195
exclude element (Ant), 81
executeUpdate( ) (CallableStatement), 495
expiration for cookies
    setting, 213
    setting with jsp:setProperty, 216
expires attribute (cookies), 210
exploded directory format, 44
Expression Language (EL), xvi
    calling LoginBean's
        getLoginSuccess( ), 351
    client locales, preferred and
        less-preferred, 594
    cookie implicit object, 222
    cookies, accessing with, 579
    creating hperlinks in URL rewriting, 246
    creation time for sessions, fetching, 241
    dereferencing of variable and property
        values, 241
    function that calls a stored
        procedure, 496–500
        Java class that implements
            function, 496–498
        JSP, use in, 499
        TLD file for configuring function, 498
    functions, 585
    in JSP error page, 206
    in JSP used as error page, 203

    in template text (JSP 2.0
        specification), 155
    JavaBean properties, accessing
        with, 580–585
    JSP example page, use in, 108
    JSTL and, 551
    map entry key/value pairs, 153
    request headers, accessing with, 576
        value of a particular header, 577
    request parameters, accessing, 246, 574
    scoped attributes, accessing, 504
    scoped variables, accessing with, 572
    template text, using EL expressions
        directly in, 586
    URL for JavaScript window in a JSP,
        getting from a context
        parameter, 272
Extensible Stylesheet Language
    Transformations (XSLT), 287
Extensible Stylesheet Language (XSL), 562
extension mapping URL patterns, 54
    associating filter with any .jsp file, 416
    mapping all references to JSP pages to a
        single servlet, 55
    mapping static content to a servlet, 56
external-include property, 138

F

FATAL level logging, 297
file extensions
    associating MIME types with, 466
file uploads (see uploading files)
FileDataSource class, 465
FilerConfig class
    getInitParameter( ), 419
FileRenamePolicy interface, 185
fileset elements (Ant), 81, 88
    nested within jar task, 91
    nesting multiple in path element, 82
filter elements (web.xml), 412, 627
    init-param child element, 419
Filter interface, 258
    actions that filters can undertake, 411
FilterChain class
    doFilter( ), 402, 422, 425
FilterConfig class
    getInitParameterNames( ), 421
filtering, 411–438
    blocking IP addresses with, 434–438
    changing order in which filters are applied
        to servlets, 418

configuring initialization parameters for a filter, 419

filter configuration in web.xml file (servlet API 2.3), 16

HTTP responses, 424–427

intercepting and reading form input, 171–173

JNDI object, accessing from a JSP, 625–628

   setting object as session attribute, 625–627

mapping a filter to a JSP, 415

mapping a filter to a servlet, 412–415

   filter that logs some information, 413

mapping multiple filters to a servlet, 416–418

monitoring session attributes, 258–262

MultipartFilter class, 187

optionally blocking a request with a filter, 422–424

passing JNDI object to JSP on WebLogic, 635–637

request headers, altering, 402–405

using filters with RequestDispatcher objects, 427–429

validating form input with a filter, 429–434

filter-mapping elements (web.xml), 412, 627

   applying filter to a servlet using a RequestDispatcher, 427

   changing order of, 418

   mapping multiple filters to a servlet, 416

   url-pattern nested element, 415

Flash files

   embedding in a servlet, 390

   HTML template for embedding in a JSP automatically generating, 386

   writing, 388–389

fmt:formatDate tag, 605

   current locale, using to format dates and numbers, 566

fmt:formatNumber tag

   current locale, using to format numbers, 566

   displaying currency value for a locale, 609

   displaying numbers as percentages, 612

fmt:message tags, 606

fmt:setBundle tag, 602

fmt:setLocale tag, 566

fn:contains( ), 586

fn:length( ), 586

fn:split( ), 586

fn:toUpperCase( ), 586

Folder class, 439, 455

footer segment included in JSP with jsp:include action, 136

form tags (HTML), 174

   action attribute, 431

   action, method and enctype attributes for file uploads, 175

format( )

   DateFormat class, 239

   NumberFormat class, 608, 610

formatting tags (JSTL), 564–567

   displaying date in JSP for user locale, 605

   displaying text in JSP for request locale, 602

form-based authentication, 331

   form for use with, 334

   logging out user on system that uses, 335–337

form-login-config element, 332

forward( ) (RequestDispatcher), 168

FORWARD value (dispatcher elements), 428

forwarding requests

   controller servlet forwarding with RequestDispatcher.forward( ), 71

   with forward( ) (RequestDispatcher), 62

   with getNamedDispatcher( ) (ServletContext), 63

   initiating a filter for, 428

   by objects implementing RequestDispatcher interface, without triggering security constraints, 68

fragments, JSP, 539

   included in a servlet by using RequestDispatcher, 124

   now referred to as JSP segments, 132

Front Controller design pattern (Sun Microsystems), 59

fully qualified class names, 12

   invoking registered servlet through, 58

   listener class in listener class element, 550

   object attribute names and, 573

function calls embedded in JSP code with JSTL, 551, 586

function tag, 499

functions

   Expression Language, calling stored procedure, 496–500

   Java class that implements function, 496–498

functions (*continued*)
    JSP, use in, 499
    TLD file for configuring function, 498
  JavaScript, 265
  JSTL
    listing of, with purpose of each, 587
    using in JSPs, 585–589

G

GET requests, 3
  security constraints on, 329
  servlet response to, 149
getAllHeaders( )
  Message class, 467
  Part interface, 466
getAttribute( ) (ServletContext), 355
getBundle( ) (ResourceBundle), 138, 599
getConnection( ) (DataSource), 481, 485
getContent( ) (Message), 452
getContextPath( ) (HttpServletRequest), 211
getCookies( ) (HttpServletRequest), 214, 220
getCurrencyInstance( )
    (NumberFormat), 607
getDateTimeInstance( ) (DateFormat), 605
getDisplayName( ) (Locale), 594
getFilesystemName (MultipartRequest), 180
getFrom( ) (Message), 453
getHeader( )
  HttpServletRequest class, 399
  Part interface, 467
getHeaderNames( )
    (HttpServletRequest), 399
getID( ) (HttpSession), 241
getInitParameter( ) (FilterConfig), 419
getInitParameterNames( ) (FilterConfig), 421
getInputStream( )
  PageData class, 116
  Part interface, 460
getInputStream( ) (PageData), 114
getJspBody( ) (SimpleTagSupport), 539
getJspContext( ) (SimpleTagSupport), 538
getLastAccessedTime( )
    (HttpSession), 237–239
getLocale( ) (ServletRequest), 591
getLocales( ), 592
getLoginSuccess( ), 351
  LoginBean class (example), 352
getMaxInactiveInterval( ) (HttpSession), 229
getMetaData( )
  Connection class, 518
  ResultSet class, 513

getName( )
  Cookie class, 215, 220
  Header class, 467
getNamedDispatcher( ) (ServletContext), 63
getParameter( ) (ServletRequest), 149, 343
  handling posted data, 150
getParameterMap( )
  HttpServletRequest class, 164
  ServletRequest class, 149, 172
    handling posted data, 150
getParameterNames( ) (ServletRequest), 149
getParameterValues( ) (ServletRequest), 149
getPath( ) (Cookie), 221
getPercentInstance( ) (NumberFormat), 610
getQueryString
  HttpServletRequest class, 169
getQueryString( )
  request wrappers that override, 404
getRealPath( ) (ServletContext), 180
getRemoteAddr( ) (HttpServletRequest), 434
getRemoteUser( ) (HttpServletRequest), 336
getRequestDispatcher( )
    (ServletRequest), 121
getRequestURI( ) (HttpServletRequest), 409
getRequestURL( ) (HttpServletRequest), 169
getResultElements( )
    (GoogleSearchResult), 670
getRows( ) (Result), 569
getSearchResults( ), 670, 680
getServletContext( ), 357
getServletRequest( )
    (ServletRequestEvent), 409
getSession( )
  HttpServletRequest class, 233, 234,
    235–237, 238
  HttpSessionBindingEvent class, 256
  HttpSessionEvent class, 253
getSnippet( )
    (GoogleSearchResultElement), 671
getSource( ) (EventObject), 257
getSummary( )
    (GoogleSearchResultElement), 671
getTitle( )
    (GoogleSearchResultElement), 670
getTransactionIsolation( )
    (Connection), 509, 510
getURL( )
    (GoogleSearchResultElement), 670
getValue( )
  Cookie class, 215, 220
  Header class, 467
  HttpSessionBindingEvent class, 257

global.properties file (Ant), 18
    example of, 20, 81
Google Web Services, 666
    connecting to with a JSP, 675–677
    connecting to with a servlet, 671–675
    creating a JavaBean to connect
        with, 667–671
    options for searches, setting, 670
    setting up with, 666
GoogleSearch class (example), 670
GoogleSearchResult class, 670
GoogleSearchResultElement class, 670

H
handleMessages( )
    EmailBean class (example), 454
    MailAccessor class (example), 449
handleStartTag( ), 650
harvesting web information, 647–663
    creating JavaBean as HTML
        parser, 656–659
    JavaBean for HTML parsing
        using in a JSP, 661–663
        using in a servlet, 659–661
    parsing HTML page with javax.swing.text
        subpackages, 648–651
        callback class (example), 648–650
    using a servlet, 651–656
Hashtable class, 485
Header class, 467
header implicit object, 400, 576
header segment included in JSP with
        jsp:include action, 135
headers
    email, reading from a servlet, 466–470
    HTTP (see request headers; response
        headers)
headerValues implicit object, 578
heading attribute (custom tag), 533, 542
home and local home interfaces (EJB on
        WebLogic), 642
Host element (Tomcat server.xml file),
        22, 37
href attribute, 245
HTML
    code for JSP that handles HTTP
        requests, 8
    converting XML file into with XSL
        stylesheet, 562
    error page sent to client, 200

file upload page, preparing, 175–180
    component to receive file and store in
        local directory, 178–180
form tag, 174, 266
    onSubmit event handler, 268
head tag, 266
input tag, 174
JavaBean for parsing
    creating, 656–659
    using in a JSP, 661–663
    using in a servlet, 659–661
parsing API classes, use in
        servlet, 651–655
src attribute of script tag, using to import
        JavaScript module, 267
template for embedding Flash files
    generating automatically, 386
template for including Flash files
    writing, 388–389
HTML Converter (Java Plug-in), 382–385
HTML forms
    adding parameters to query string
        using a JSP, 170
        using a servlet, 168
    intercepting and reading form input with
        a filter, 171–173
    posting submitted data from a
        JSP, 164–167
    servlet, accepting Amazon search
        term, 686
    servlet handling of, 3–7
        FirstServlet class (example), 3
    setting propertes of JavaBean to values
        entered in, 155–158
    setting scoped attribute in a JSP to value
        of a form parameter, 158–161
    submission to server-side program via
        POST method, 148
    validating input with a filter, 429–434
        filter that checks values
            (example), 431–433
        JSP that contains a form
            (example), 430
HTML tags
    applet tag, 383
    embed tag, 380, 381
    generated with Java Plug-in HTML
        Converter for loading applets, 382
    object tag, 380, 381
HTMLEditorKit class, 648

HTTP
    developing JSP for handling of requests, 8
    GET method (see GET requests)
    POST method (see POST requests)
    request headers (see request headers)
    requests for file uploading, 174
    response headers (see response headers)
    secure connections (see Secure Sockets
        Layer)
    security constraints on methods, 68
    XML-based SOAP messages on, 664
HTTP response codes, 192
    403 or 404, handling by web
        container, 195
    500, returned by web container, 195
    int parameter of sendError( ), 199
HttpClient (Jakarta Commons), 105
    automating data posting from servlet to
        other programs, 161
    downloading, 161
    servlet using to post data to a JSP, 162
    use in JavaBean that posts data from JSP
        page, 165
http-method elements, 68
    security constraints for, 329
https://, URLs that start with, 326
HttpServlet class
    init( ), including content in, 120
    service( ), 3
HttpServletRequest class
    checking session existence, 235–237
    getContextPath( ), 211
    getCookies( ), 214, 220
    getHeader( ), 399
    getHeaderNames( ), 399
    getParameterMap( ), 164
    getQueryString( ), 169
    getRemoteAddr( ), 434
    getRemoteUser( ), 336
    getRequestURI( ), 409
    getRequestURL( ), 169
    getSession( ), 233, 234, 238
    isUserInRole( ), 336
HttpServletRequest objects, 3
HttpServletRequestWrapper class, 402
HttpServletResponse class
    addCookie( ), 211
    encodeRedirectURL( ), 249
    encodeURL( ), 248
    Refresh response header, adding, 405
    sendError( ), 199–201, 437
    sendRedirect( ), 236, 249
HttpServletResponse objects, 3

HttpServletResponseWrapper class, for use
        with a filter (example), 425
HttpSession class
    getId( ), 241
    getLastAccessedTime( ), 237–239
    getMaxInactiveInterval( ), 229
    invalidate( ), 335
    removeAttribute( ), 255
    setAttribute( ), 255
    setMaxInactiveInterval( ), 233, 234
HttpSessionActivationListener interface, 251
HttpSessionAttributeListener interface, 254
HttpSessionBindingEvent class
    getSession( ), 256
    getValue( ), 257
HttpSessionBindingListener interface, 251
HttpSessionEvent class, getSession( ), 253
HttpSessionListener interface, 251
    notification of session creation and
        destruction, 253
    sessionCreated( ) and
        sessionDestroyed( ), 321

I

i18n (see internationalization)
if/then/else statements, 575
IllegalStateException, handling in web
        applications, 195
img tag (HTML), 544
implicit objects, 223, 273, 363
implicit objects
    in a JSP, 133
        application, 357
        exception, 206
        pageContext, 241, 595
        response, 202
        session, 134
    in JSTL
        applicationScope, 363
        cookie, 222, 579
        header, 400, 576
        headerValues, 578
        initParam, 272, 273
        param, 153, 246, 395, 574
        requestScope, 374, 377
        sessionScope, 367, 370, 573
import custom action, 133
include( ) (RequestDispatcher), 120, 264
    embedding Flash in a servlet, 390
    including JavaScript CreateWindow
        function in a servlet, 269
    including top-level servlet file, 125

servlet importing JavaScript file, 265
validating JavaScript, including in
    servlet, 274
include directive
    changes made to included page, reflection
        in including page, 137
    in JSP document, expansion by XML
        view, 110
    including seldom changing resource in a
        JSP, 130
    including XML fragment in JSP
        document, 143
    jsp:include action vs., 131, 137
        rule of thumb for using, 144
include element (Ant), 81
include mechanisms for dynamic
        content, 119–147
    configuring included resource in external
        file, 122
    external configuration file, using to
        include resource in a JSP, 137–140
    importing a resource each time servlet
        handles a request, 120–122
    including content from outside a context
        in JSP, 144–147
    including content in a JSP for each
        request, 133–136
    including XML fragment in JSP
        document, 141–144
    resources nested at multiple levels in
        servlet, 125–130
        exception information, displaying, 129
        first inner included servlet, 127
        outer including servlet, 126
        request attributes, access by included
            resources, 128
        second included servlet, 129
    resources that seldom change, including
        in JSP, 130–133
INCLUDE value (dispatcher elements), 427
includes attribute (Ant jar task), 91
IncludeServlet class (example), 120
INFO level logging, 297
inheritance structure in log4j, 306, 319, 322
init target (Ant, build.xml file), 21, 79
initial context, 615
InitialContext class, 478, 619
    close( ), 621
    lookup( ), 481, 485
initialization parameters
    configuring for a filter, 419
    servlet, registered name and, 58

initialize( ) (LoginModule), 342
init-param element (web.xml), 419
    specifying including resource with, 123
    timeout value for servlet, configuring, 229
    URL for loading new window created by
        JavaScript function in a servlet, 270
initParam implicit JSTL object, 272, 273
input tags (HTML), 174
    multiple file uploads, 177
    type, name, and accept attributes, for file
        uploads, 175
InputStream, XML view of JSP page returned
        as, 111, 114
INSERT statement (SQL), executing in JSP in
        a transaction, 511
internal resources from web application,
        viewing, 292–295
internationalization, 564, 590–614
    client locale, detecting in a JSP, 594–596
    client locale, detecting in a
        servlet, 591–593
    creating ResourceBundle as a Java
        class, 597
    definition of, 590
    formatting currencies
        in a JSP, 609–610
        in a servlet, 607–609
    formatting dates
        in a JSP, 605
        in a servlet, 603
    formatting percentages
        in a JSP, 612–613
        in a servlet, 610–611
    localization context, setting in
        web.xml, 613
    ResourceBundle as properties file,
        creating, 596
    ResourceBundle, using in a JSP, 602
    ResourceBundle, using in a
        servlet, 599–602
Internet Explorer
    embedding Flash files in web
        components, 388
    HTML object tag, loading applet
        with, 381
    language preference, setting (v. 5.5), 591
InternetAddress class, 439, 453
invalidate( ) (HttpSession), 335
invoke( ) (JspFragment), 539
invoker servlets, 57
    overriding to direct all requests to
        controller servlet, 60
    registered servlets in web.xml, 58

IOException class, 6, 178
  JSP that throws (example), 205
  web applications, handling in, 195
IP addresses, blocking requests from with a
    filter, 434–438
isErrorPage attribute (page directive), 205
ISO (International Standards Organization)
  country codes, 601, 607
  language codes, 591
isolation levels for transactions, 509
  in sql:transaction tag, 512
isUserInRole( ) (HttpServletRequest), 336
is-xml element, 99
iterating over collections of data, 551
  c:forEach tag, iterating over array, 557
iterating posted data with JSTL, 153
iterator( ) (Set), 172
Iterator class, 152
  next( ), 172

J

J2EE (Java 2 Enterprise Edition), xiv
  Core Blueprints web page, 59
  EJB in business tier, 616
  JavaMail and JavaBeans Activation
    Framework (JAF), 439
J2SE (Java 2 Standard Edition), 648
JAAS (Java Authentication and Authorization
    Service)
  authenticating servlet clients, 346–349
  configuration file, creating, 344–346
    flag values, listing of, 345
    location of file, 346
  LoginModule class, 337–344
    CallbackHandler for, 342
    example code, 338–342
  online documentation, 342
  using in a JSP, 349–353
JAF (JavaBeans Activation Framework), 439,
    461
Jakarta Commons HttpClient (see
    HttpClient)
Jakarta Tomcat (see Tomcat)
JAR (Java ARchive) files
  creating with Ant, 89–92
  for Jakarta Commons HttpClient, 162
  including Tomcat JAR files in Ant
    classpath, 80–83
  log4j.jar, 296
  mail.jar and activation.jar, 440
  packaging JSP tag file in, 546
  packaging tag library in, 530

  Sun Microsystems specification for, 89
  WEB-INF/lib directory, storage in, 12
jar task (Ant), 77, 89–92
  basedir attribute, 91
  destfile attribute, 91
  fileset (nested) element, 91
  includes attribute, 91
  manifest file, creating, 92
jar tool
  placing tag library in a JAR file, 531
jar tool, creating WAR files with, 12
Jasper (Tomcat JSP container), 111
JASPER_HOME environment variable, 100
jasper-runtime.jar, 101
Java 2 Enterprise Edition (see J2EE)
Java API for XML Processing (JAXP), 75,
    116, 554
Java Authentication and Authorization
    Service (see JAAS)
java command-line tool, setting user
    classpath, 75
Java Database Connectivity (see JDBC)
Java Development Kit (JDK), 11
Java Naming and Directory Interface (see
    JNDI)
Java Plug-in, 380
  different installed versions, causing
    problems loading applets, 385
  HTML Converter, embedding applet in a
    JSP, 382–385
Java Runtime Environment (JRE)
  applets, running in, 382
  executing applet with Java Plug-in, 380
Java Virtual Machine (JVM), servlets and, 2
Java Web Services Developer Pack,
    downloading JAXP, 116
Java Web Services Developer Pack
    (WSDP), 554
Java-based web applications, xvi
JavaBeans
  accessing email from a servlet, 454
  configuring as a JNDI object with
    Tomcat, 616–618
  cookies, creating, 216
    CookieBean (example), 217
  creating as web page parser, 656–659
  creating to search Amazon, 679–684
  creating to search Google web
    database, 667–671
  customizing responses sent to clients, 424
  email attachments, handling
    (example), 456–460

file-uploading (example), 187–189
Google search utility class, 671–674
JAAS API, using for
	authentication, 349–352
JSP data, posting dynamically to another
	server-side process, 164–167
JSP using to search google.com, 675–677
properties
	accessing with EL, 580–585
	setting in a JSP, 155–158
sending email from a servlet, 444–449
	EmailBean (example), 445–448
	servlet using JavaBean to send
		email, 448
	setting of email parts with bean
		methods, 448
servlet using to connect to Amazon Web
	Services, 684–686
as Tomcat JNDI resource
	accessing from a servlet, 619–625
web page parser
	using in a JSP, 661–663
	using in a servlet, 659–661
JavaBeans Activation Framework (JAF), 439,
	461
javac compiler, 10
	built-in, with Sun Microsystems JDK, 11
javac task (Ant), 77
	classpath element nested inside of, 82
	compiling application servlets into build
		directory, 36
JAVA_HOME environment variable, 326
	setting in Ant installation, 76
JavaMail, 439
	fetching email messages, 449
	listing email headers, 467
	properties set for Session JNDI
		object, 630
	Session, Store, Folder, and Message
		classes, 455
JavaScript, 263–278
	creating new browser window
		in a JSP, 272–273
		lin a servlet, 269–271
	including JavaScript modules
		in a JSP, 267–269
		in a servlet, 263–267
	validating form values
		in a JSP, 277
		in a servlet, 274–276

JavaServer Pages (see JSPs)
JavaServer Pages Standard Tag Library (see
	JSTL)
javax sub-packages for BEA WebLogic, 10
javax.mail package, 439
javax.mail.internet package, 440
javax.naming package, 478, 615
javax.servlet.jsp.tagext package, 520
javax.sql package, 567
JDBC (Java Database Connectivity), xvi
	accessing database from servlet using
		JDBC, 472–475
	calling stored procedure from a servlet
		with CallableStatement, 491–495
	Connection objects, 472
	database driver and storage location, 474,
		567
	DriverManager class, 472
	javax.sql.DataSource object
		creating on WebLogic, 481–484
		on WebLogic, using in a JSP, 488–490
		SQL JSTL tag, using with, 567
	Oracle classes12.zip driver, 474
	ResultSet, converting to Result
		object, 500–505
	ResultSetMetaData interface, 513–518
	specification, address for
		downloading, 475
	transaction API, 505–510
JDK (Java Development Kit), 11
	version 1.1, Ant support of, 75
JNDI (Java Naming and Directory
	Interface), 471, 615
	configuring JNDI object in
		Tomcat, 616–618
	configuring JNDI resource in
		WebLogic, 628
	lookup, using to access WebLogic
		DataSource, 484
	Tomcat JNDI resource
		accessing from a JSP, 625–628
		accessing from a servlet, 619–624
	using API classes to obtain
		DataSource, 481
	WebLogic JNDI resource
		accessing from a a JSP, 635–638
		accessing from a servlet, 631–634
	WebLogic JNDI tree
		accessing an EJB with, 638–646
		for a DataSource, 483
		viewing, 630

JRE (Java Runtime Environment)
  applets, running in, 382
  executing applet with Java Plug-in, 380
.jsp files, 8
JspC command-line tool (Tomcat), 100
jspc (weblogic.jspc precompilation
     tool), 102–104
JspContext class, 538
jsp:directive.include element, 143
jsp:directive.page element, 108
  added to JSP document by XML
     view, 111
jsp:doBody action, 544, 545
jsp:forward action, 170
JspFragment interface, 539
  .jspf files vs., 132
jsp:getProperty action, 189
jsp:id attribute for XML elements in JSP
     document, 110
jsp:include action, 129
  external configuration file, using to
     include resource in a JSP, 137–140
  immediate reflection of changes to
     included files, 137
  include directive vs., 131, 137
    rule of thumb for using, 144
  including resource in JSP each time it
     receives request, 133–137
  including XML fragment in JSP
     document, 141
jsp:param action, 170
jsp:param elements, providing embedded
     applets with parameter and value
     pairs, 380
jsp:plugin action
  embedding applet in a JSP, 379–381
  HTML tags generated for loading Java
     applet, 381
jsp_precompile parameter, 104
jsp-property-group element, 99, 107
jsp:root element, 99, 107
  added by XML view to JSP
     document, 111
JSPs (JavaServer Pages), xiii
  application servers as software hosts
     for, xiv
  as XML documents, 99
  creating from scratch as JSP
     document, 106–110
  creating JSP-type URL for a servlet, 54
  custom XML tags (see custom tags; tags)

deploying (see deploying servlets
     and JSPs)
fragments, 14
generating XML view from, 110–118
implementation class, 98
packaging in WAR files, 11
precompiled, mapping to page
     implementation class, 105
precompiling, 98
  in Tomcat, 99
  in WebLogic, 102–104
  precompilation protocol, using, 104
request attributes, access by included
     resources, 128
writing, 7–9
  as XML files, 8
  basic steps in, 8
  viewing output in browser, 9
jsp:setProperty action, 155–158
  cookie properties, setting, 216
  cookie value, setting, 217
  setting directory name for saving
     uploaded file, 189
  setting JavaBean property to submitted
     form value, 158
jsp:text element, 109
jsp:useBean action, 8, 10, 108, 155, 243
  cookie-creating bean, using in JSP, 216
  id attribute, 583
  instantiating file-uploading bean in a
     JSP, 189
  use in setting bean property to submitted
     form value, 158
JspWriter class, 539
.jspx files, 8, 99, 107
JSTL (JavaServer Pages Standard Tag
     Library), xv, 551–589
  arrays or Maps, using to iterate through
     values, 500
  c:choose, c:when, and c:otherwise
     tags, 575
  c:forEach tag, 153, 223, 551, 555, 576
    iterating posted data with, 153
  c:if tag, 555, 557
  c:import tag, 144, 146, 267, 268, 560
  cookie implicit object, 222
  cookies, accessing with EL, 579
  core tags, using in a JSP, 555–558
  c:out tag, 10, 139, 154, 204, 551, 584
    escaped characters, 557
    exception information, displaying for a
       JSP, 206

JSTL (JavaServer Pages Standard Tag Library)
  (*continued*)
    summary of functions, 555
    use in a JSP (example), 557
  c:param tag, 146
  c:set tag, 357, 551, 573
    summary of functions, 555
  current session ID, displaying, 241
  custom tags in JSPs created as XML
    files, 106
  downloading and using, 552
    1.0 reference implementation, lib
      directory contents, 553
    JSTL 1.1, 553
    taglib directives for different JSTL 1.0
      libraries, 553
  downloading Java Web Services
    Developer Pack, 554
  Expression Language (EL) (see Expression
    Language)
  fmt:formatDate tag, 605
  fmt:formatNumber tag, 566
    displaying numbers as
      percentages, 612
    formatting currency value for a
      locale, 609
  fmt:message tag, 606
  fmt:setBundle tag, 602
  fmt:setLocale tag, 566
  formatting numbers as percentages, 612
  formatting session creation and
    last-accessed times, 242
  formatting tags, 564–567
    displaying text in JSP for client
      locale, 602
  functionality of, 551
  functions, using in JSPs, 585–589
  header implicit object, 400
  in JSP error page, 203, 206
  JavaBean properties, accessing with
    EL, 580–585
  JSP using Result object stored as session
    attribute, 503
  localization context for tags, setting in
    web.xml, 613
  request headers, accessing with EL, 576
    value of a particular header, 577
  request parameters, accessing with
    EL, 574
  scoped variables, accessing with EL, 572
  session date/times formatted with, 243

  SQL tags, 488
    with DataSource
      configuration, 567–570
    without DataSource
      configuration, 570–572
  sql:query tag, 512, 569
  sql:setDataSource tag, 571–572
  sql:transaction tag, 511
  sql:update tag, 512
  url custom action, 244–247
  XML and XSLT tags, using, 561–563
  XML core tags, using in a JSP, 558–561
  x:out tag, 551
  x:parse tag, 560
  x:transform tag, 551, 563
JVM (Java Virtual Machine), servlets and, 2

K

keystore file, 326
keytool utility, 326
key/value pairs (cookies), 223

L

l10n (see localization)
language codes (ISO), 591
language element, 591
language preference, setting in Netscape
  7.1, 591
last-accessed time for sessions
  tracking with JSPs, 240–244
  tracking with servlets, 237–239
layouts for logged messages, 298
  in inherited appenders, 322
  pattern used for BasicConfigurator, 303
  PatternLayout, 308
  SimpleLayout class, in root logger
    messages, 304
lib directory, 12, 30
  inclusion of nested directories in WAR file
    with Ant war task, 35
  JAR files, storing in, 89
  log4j.jar file, 301
  TLDs and, 530
lib element (Ant), 88
listener element (web.xml), 548
listeners
  adding listener class to a tag library, 548
  application event, 316
  configuration in web.xml file (servlet API
    2.3), 16
  examining HTTP requests with, 64

listeners (*continued*)
    monitoring session attributes, 254–258
    requests, tracking for a web
        application, 408–410
    servlet context event listener, using in
        logging, 316–320
    session event, 316
        using in logging, 320–323
    tracking session lifecycle, 251–254
    validating form input with, 276
ListResourceBundle class, 598
load-on-startup element (web.xml), 319
local home interface (EJB on
        WebLogic), 642
locale
    definition of, 566, 590
    detecting for client in a JSP, 594–596
    detecting for client in a server, 591–593
    displaying message appropriate for using
        JSTL formatting tags, 602
    formatting currency values for
        in a JSP, 609–610
        in a servlet, 607–609
    formatting date for display
        in a JSP, 605
        in a servlet, 603
    preferred, 591
localization, 564
    definition of, 590
localization context
    setting in web.xml, 613
localizers, 590
location element (web.xml), 195
Location header, 250
log( ) (ServletContext), 172, 258, 260,
        298–299, 404
log4j, 296
    Apache Log4j library, 414
    configuration file used by servlet context
        listener, 319
    session event listener that uses, 320–323
    setting up, 300
log4j.properties file, 304–305
    appender configuration, 306
    specifying different name for, 316
LoggerTag class, 311, 313
logging, 296–323
    appenders, 297
        adding to root logger, 303–306
    filter that logs some information
        (example), 413
    layouts, 298

log4j and servlet context event listener,
        using, 316–320
log4j, using in a JSP, 310–316
LogFilter (example), mapped to a
        servlet, 412
loggers, 296
    creating your own and giving it an
        appender, 306–310
    using without configuration file, 301
requests, 408
session event listener, using, 320–323
setting up log4j, 300, 301
with servlet that uses
        ServletContext.log( ), 298–299
logging out users, application with
        form-based
        authentication, 335–337
login( )
    DataSourceLoginModule class, 342, 348
    LoginContext class, 338, 348
    LoginModule, 342
LoginBean class (example), 349–351
    getLoginSuccess( ), 352
login-config elements (web.xml), 67
    auth-method nested element, 328
        values for, 69
    using with security-constraint element, 68
LoginContext class, 348
loginError.html page, 332
loginError.jsp page, 334
login.html page (example), 332
LoginModule class, 337–344
    example code, 338–342
    methods, 342
    validating username and password against
        database information, 342
logout( ) (LoginModule), 342
long datatypes returned by date-related
        HttpSession methods, 239, 242
lookup( ) (InitialContext), 481, 485

M

Macromedia Flash (see Flash files)
mail (see email)
mail server, interaction with email-sending
        servlet, 444
mail sessions, 439, 449
    servlet getting from WebLogic
        JNDI, 631–634
mailDefaults.properties file, 448
mail.jar archive, 440

Manager application (Tomcat), 92
  online documentation for, 93
  StopTask class, 95
manifest file for JAR files, 92
Map objects, 152
  ContextObject class (example), 355, 358
    methods adding keys and values to
      map, 356
  cookie EL implicit object, 579
  Entry subclass, getKey( ) and
      getValue( ), 153
  entrySet( ), 172
  header implicit object, 400, 576
  headerValues implicit object, 578
  JSP parameters passed for posting to
      JavaBean, 164
Message class, 455
  getAllHeaders( ), 467
  getContent( ), 452
  getFrom( ), 453
message stores, 439, 449
MessagingException class, 448
META-INF directory, TLDs in, 530
method attribute (HTML form tag), 175
Method objects, 315
methods (JavaBean), naming conventions
      for, 165
Microsoft Word file
  as email attachment, 465
  sending as binary data, 284–286
MIME types
  application/msword, 465
  application/pdf, 280
  associating file extensions with, 466
  common, listing of, 280
  Microsoft Word document, 284
  MP3 files, 289
  multipart/mixed, 460
MimeMessage class, 444, 462
MimetypesFileTypeMap class, 466
modules, JavaScript
  example of, 264
  organization and storage of, 264
  validating form input (validate.js), 274
MPEG audio layer 3 (MP3)
  embedded file in a JSP, 396
  sending audio file as, 289–292
multimedia, embedding in JSPs, 379–397
  embedding applet with HTML Converter
      tool, 382–385
  embedding applet with
      jsp:plugin, 379–381

embedding background soundtrack in a
      JSP, 396–397
embedding Flash in a servlet, 390
embedding QuickTime movie in a
      JSP, 392
embedding SVG file in a JSP, 394–396
HTML template for embedding Flash files
  generating automatically, 386
  writing, 388–389
Multipart class, 462
Multipart content type, 455
MultipartFilter class, 187
multipart/form-data content type, 174
MultipartParser class, 181–185
MultipartRequest class
  file-uploading JavaBean, use in, 187
  servlet that uses, creating, 178–180
Multipurpose Internet Mail Extensions
      (see MIME types)
MutableAttributeSet class, 648

N

name attribute (Ant project element), 77
namespace, 519
  definition of, 529
  identified by prefix attribute of taglib
      directive, 532
  for XML elements related to XML Schema
      instances, 529
  xmlns attribute of taglib element, 528
naming conventions, log4j, 307
naming servlets, 49–73
  creating multiple mappings to a
      servlet, 52
  creating welcome files for web
      application, 65
  invoking servlet without a web.xml
      mapping, 57
  JSP-type URL for servlets, 54
  mapping all requests from a web
      application to a servlet, 59–61
  mapping all requests to controller while
      preserving all servlet mappings, 61
  mapping servlet to name in
      web.xml, 50–52
  mapping static content to a servlet, 55
  restricting requests for certain
      servlets, 66–71
Netscape
  disabling cookies, 210
  JavaScript, developers' web site, 263
  setting language preference (v. 7.1), 591

next( ) (Iterator), 172
non-repeatable read, 509
nullrole security role, 73
NumberFormat class
    format( ), 608, 610
    getCurrencyInstance( ), 607
    getPercentInstance( ), 610
numbers, formatting with JSTL tags, 565
    fmt:setLocale tag, 566

O

object attributes for web applications, 551
    setting scope with c:set tag, 555
object tags (HTML), 380, 381
    automatic HTML file generation by
        Flash, 386
    produced by HTML Converter
        (example), 384
objects
    EJB, factories for, 642
    scopes of, 573
onSubmit event handler (HTML form
        tag), 266, 268
open source applications, xiv
openConnection( ) (URL), 292
Oracle 8i database
    servlet that queries for a
        ResultSet, 514–517
    stored procedure adding row to
        table, 491
Oracle sequences, 491
org.apache.jasper.runtime package, 101
overwriting a cookie, 225

P

packages
    fully qualified class names and, 12
    for servlet and utility classes, 3
page attribute (jsp:include), 138, 140
page directive
    errorPage attribute, 205
    import attribute, 488
    isErrorPage attribute, 205
    overriding error-page configuration, 206
page implementation object, 8
page relative path, 130
page scope, 367, 573
pageContext implicit object, 241, 595
PageData class, getInputStream( ), 114, 116

pageEncoding attribute (jsp
    directive.page element), 111
PAM (Pluggable Authentication
        Module), 337
param implicit object, 153, 246, 395, 574
param-value element, altering to import
        included resource, 123
parse( ) (ParserDelegator), 624, 651
    synchronization of, 655
ParserCallback, 648
ParserDelegator class, 648
    callbacks, using with, 650
    parse( ), 624, 651
        synchronization of, 655
parsing
    HTML with javax.swing.text
        subpackages, 648–651
    JSPs before conversion to page
        implementation, 99
    XML
        JAXP-compliant parsers, 75
        x:parse tag, 560
Part interface
    getAllHeaders( ), 466
    getHeader( ), 467
    getInputStream( ), 460
passwords
    creating in tomcat-users.xml file, 325
    for keystore file and digital
        certificate, 326
    (see also authentication)
path attribute (Context element,
        Tomcat), 37
path attribute (cookies), 210
    accessing values for, 221
    setting to name of context path, 211
path element (Ant), 21, 28, 80
    nesting three filesets in, 82
PATH environment variable, 35
    Ant /bin directory, adding to, 76
    including path to the bin directory of your
        Java SDK installation, 531
    for Sun JDK javac compiler, 11
path parameter, 246
paths
    context-relative, 130
    cookie, setting with jsp:setProperty, 216
    page-relative, 130
    to save directory, for file upload
        servlet, 178, 180

servlet, 49
    creating for web application users, 51
    differences among servlet engines, 51
pattern language for converting logged
    message layouts, 308
PatternLayout class, 298, 308
PDF (Portable Document Format)
    files, 280–284
percentages
    in a JSP, 612–613
    in a servlet, 610–611
permissions for using code examples, xviii
phantom read, 509
Pluggable Authentication Module
    (PAM), 337
pop-up window, creating with JavaScript
    function in a servlet, 269–271
port numbers, used by secure vs. insecure
    HTTP connections, 327
Portable Document Format files
    (see PDF files)
Portable Document Format (PDF)
    files, 280–284
POST requests, 3
    delivery of HTML form data to server-side
      program via, 148
    file uploads and, 175
    handling in a JSP, 153–155
    handling in a servlet, 149–153
      with ServletRequest.getParameter( )
        and getParameterMap( ), 150–153
    posting data from a JSP, 164–167
    posting data from a servlet to other
      server-side programs, 161–164
      HttpClient, using to post data to a
        JSP, 162
    security constraints on, 329
PRECLASSPATH environmental
    variable, 101
precompiling JSPs, 9, 98
    in Tomcat, 99
    in WebLogic, 102–104
    with precompilation protocol, 104
    servlet mappings, 100
preferred locale, 591
prefix attribute (taglib directive), 532
prepare target (Ant, build.xml file), 21, 28
printf function in C, 308
PrintWriter class, 129
    HTML page returned by blocking
      filter, 424

PrivacyServlet class (example), 123
    doGet( ), including resource specified by
      init parameter, 123
    JSP fragment included by, 124
programmatic security, 67
project element (Ant), 76
    arranging target elements inside, 77
properties
    Ant global.properties file, 20
      loading into build.xml, 21
      making available to build file, 81
    Ant property task, importing
      global.properties file, 96
    build.properties file (Ant), for web
      application deployment, 33
    cookie, setting, 216
    external file (include.properties),
      specifying resource to include in
      JSP, 138
    jar-name property, 91
    JavaBean
      accessing with EL, 580–585
      email parts stored as, 445
      setting in a JSP, 155–158
    log4j.properties file, 304–305
    mailDefaults.properties file, 448
    passing to an Ant file
      command line, using, 94
      property task, using, 94
    properties file for automatically generated
      XML view, 112
    tag attributes as, 522
    wl.properties file for WebLogic Ant
      build, 28
properties file, ResourceBundle as, 596
property task (Ant), 79, 94
PropertyConfigurator class, 316

Q

query strings
    adding parameter to with a servlet, 168
    adding parameters to with a JSP, 170
    request, adding parameter to, 404
QuickTime movie, embedding in a JSP, 392

R

redirecting requests (after checking session
    validity), 236
reference implementation, xiv
    for JSTL, 552

refid attribute (Ant classpath element), 81, 82

reflection, using in logging, 315

Refresh header, 405
JSP that adds to the response, 407

refreshing a JSP automatically, 407

refreshing a servlet automatically, 405

registered names for servlets, 50
filters, mapping to, 261
invoking registered servlets with invoker servlet, 58

reloadable attribute (Context element, Tomcat), 23, 37

Remote Method Invocation registry, 615

removeAttribute( ) (HttpSession), 255

renaming uploaded files, 185–187
with your own Java class, 186

request and response objects, 3
error page access to, 196

request attributes
access by error-handling servlet, 196
access by included resources in JSPs, 128
exception information from, 204

request headers, 398
accessing with EL implicit object, 576
value of one particular header, 577
examining in a JSP, 400
examining in a servlet, 398–400
filter, using to alter, 402–405

request implicit object, 133

request parameters
accessing with EL implicit object, 246, 574
getting for CallbackHandler, 342

request phase (JSPs), 8

request scope, 367, 573

request, ServletRequestListeners, 408–410

RequestDispatcher interface, 62–64, 71
forward( ), 168, 503
forwarding of HTTP requests without triggering security constraints, 68
forwarding requests to servlets under security constraints, 73
include( ), 120, 264
embedding Flash in a servlet, 390
including JavaScript CreateWindow function in a servlet, 269
including top-level servlet file, 125
including validating JavaScript module in a servlet, 274
servlet importing JavaScript file, 265

JSP fragment included in a servlet with, 124

RequestDispatcher objects, using filters with, 427–429

requestInitialized( ), 408

requests
blocking from an IP address with a filter, 434–438
optionally blocking with a filter, 422–424

requestScope implicit JSTL object, 374, 377

Resource elements (server.xml), 476, 616, 617

ResourceBundle objects, 114, 448
creating as a Java class, 597
creating as a property file, 596
getBundle( ), 138, 599
localization context set in web.xml, 614
using in a JSP, 602
using in a servlet, 599–602

resource-env-ref element (web.xml), 616, 617

ResourceParams elements (server.xml), 476, 616, 617

resource-ref element (web.xml), 476

response codes, HTTP
(see HTTP response codes)

response headers
definition of, 227
Refresh, 405
JSPs, adding to, 407

response implicit object (JSP), 202

responses
customizing with a JavaBean, 424
filtering HTTP responses, 424–427

restricting requests for certain servlets, 66–71

Result interface, 500, 503

Result objects, 569
converting ResultSet to, 500–505

ResultSet objects, 569
finding out information about, 513–518

ResultSetMetaData interface, 513
servlet that uses, 514–517

ResultSupport class, 503
toResult( ), 500

roles, 325
checking for users who request servlet, 336
specified in auth-constraint element, 329

rollback( ) (Connection), 506, 510

rolling file appender, 307

RollingFileAppender class, 307

root element (see jsp:root element)
root logger, 306
    adding an appender to, 303–306

S

save-dir element (web.xml), 190
SAX (Simple API for XML), 116
Scalable Vector Graphics (SVG) file,
        embedding in a JSP, 394
scoped attributes
    using EL and c:out tag to get value
        of, 572
scopes
    bound objects, 354
    for stored objects, 573
scraping information from a web page (see
        harvesting web information)
script blocks (JavaScript), 265
scriptlets, 488
SDK (Software Development Kit)
    Google Web APIs SDK, 666
    PATH environment variable, 531
secure attribute (cookies), 210
Secure Sockets Layer (SSL)
    built-in session tracking mechanism, 228
    setting up on Tomcat, 325
security
    configuring web.xml with web application
        security, 66
    elements related to, in deployment
        descriptors not using servlet
        v2.4, 67
    including security-related code in
        servlets, 67
    restricting requests for certain
        servlets, 66–71
    servlet access, restricting to controller
        only, 71–73
security roles, 68
    nullrole, preventing user mapping to in
        tomcat-users.xml, 73
security-constraint elements (web.xml), 61
    auth-constraint nested element, 329
    blocking all requests except from
        RequestDispatcher.forward, 71
    example of, 67
    initiating authentication with a JSP, 329
    login-config element, using with, 68
    restricting requests for certain servlets, 66
    servlet access, restricting to controller
        servlet only, 71

    specifying web resources requiring
        authentication, 328
    web-resource-collection nested
        element, 329
security-role elements (web.xml), 67, 69, 73
segments, JSP, 132
select attribute (x:forEach), 560
SELECT statement (SQL), 513
    executing in JSP in a transaction, 511
    sending to database with sql:query
        tag, 569
self-signed digital certificate, creating for
        Tomcat, 326
send( ) (Transport), 444, 462
sendError( ) (HttpServletResponse),
        199–201, 437
sending non-HTML data, 279–295
    audio files, 289–292
    PDF files, 280–284
    viewing internal resources in a
        servlet, 292–295
    word processing files, 284–286
    XML files, 286–289
sendRedirect( ) (HttpServletResponse),
        236, 249
sequences, Oracle, 491
server response codes
        (see HTTP response codes)
server status code
    403 Forbidden, 437
servers, application, xiv
server.xml file (Tomcat), 22
    Connector element, 327
    Context element, 36
    Resource and ResourceParams
        elements, 476
service( ) (HttpServlet), 3
servlet API 2.3
    deployment descriptor that configures
        error pages, 193–195
    sessions, configuration in web.xml, 16
    web.xml file, 15
        (see also web.xml file)
servlet API 2.4
    filters, using with
        RequestDispatchers, 427
    web.xml file, 15, 586
        (see also web.xml file)
    web.xml, use with Tomcat 5 and JSTL
        1.1, 554
servlet API documentation, 3
servlet containers, 2

servlet elements (web.xml), 50
  associating with multiple servlet-mapping
    elements, 52
  generated by JspC, mapping servlets
    to, 105
  load-on-startup nested element, 319
servlet engines, commercial, xv
Servlet interface, 2
servlet-class element (web.xml), 50
ServletConfig interface, 2
ServletContext attributes
  setting in JSPs, 357–360
  setting in servlets, 354–357
    object that servlet binds to
      ServletContext, 355
    servlet that binds object to
      ServletContext, 356
ServletContext class, 63, 317
  getAttribute( ), 355
  getRealPath( ), 180
  log( ), 172, 258, 260, 298–299, 404
  returning a null dispatcher, 64
  setAttribute( ), 355, 357
ServletContextListener interface, 316–319
  contextInitialized( ) and
    contextDestroyed( ), 318
ServletException class, 6, 195
servlet.jar, inclusion in PRECLASSPATH
  environment variable, 101
servlet-mapping elements (web.xml)
  associating multiple with one servlet
    element, 52
  creating alias to a servlet, 50
  generated by JspC, mapping servlets
    to, 105
  JSP-style URL pattern in, 54
  mapping all requests from web
    application to a servlet, 59
    removing or altering any elements
      allowing requests to bypass
      controller servlet, 60
  mapping static content to a servlet, 56
  removing or altering any that allow
    requests to bypass controller
    servlet, 60
  servlets without, invoking, 57
  url-pattern element, 51
  WebLogic Server 7.0, 24
servlet-name element (web.xml), 50
  * wildcard symbol, not used in, 54
ServletOutputStream class, 284
ServletRequest interface

getLocale( ), 591
getParameter( ), 343
getParameter( ) and
    getParameterMap( ), 150–153
getParameterMap( ), 172
getRequestDispatcher( ), 121
methods, using in servlet's doPost
    method, 149
ServletRequestEvent class,
    getServletRequest( ), 409
ServletRequestListener class, 408–410
ServletResponse class
  changing response with a filter, 425
  setBufferSize( ), 201
servlets, xiii, 10
  application servers as software hosts
    for, xiv
  compiling
    (see compiling servlets)
  conversion of JSPs into, 8
  deploying (see deploying servlets and
    JSPs)
  deployment descriptor, creating
    for servlet API 2.4, 16
  deployment descriptor for servlet API
    2.3, 15
  JavaServer Pages (see JSPs)
  naming (see naming servlets)
  packaging in WAR files, 11
  writing, 1–7
    FirstServlet class (example), 3
    lifecycle, management of, 3
    packages, creating for, 3
Session class, 439, 444, 449, 455
  binding object to WebLogic JNDI, 629
  servlet getting Session object from
    WebLogic JNDI, 631–634
session event listeners, 316
session ID, 228
  displaying with JSTL tag, 241
  URLs that automatically include,
    creating, 244
session implicit object, 133, 134
session scope, 367, 573
  JNDI object placed in, using a
    filter, 625–627
session-config element (web.xml), 15, 228
  session timeout for all Tomcat
    applications, 232
sessionCreated( ) (HttpSessionListener), 251,
    253, 321

sessionDestroyed( )
    (HttpSessionListener), 251, 253,
      321
sessionDidActivate( )
    (HttpSessionActivationListener),
      251
SessionFilter class (example), 259
sessions, 321
    checking existence of in
      HttpServletRequest, 235–237
    configuration in web.xml file for servlet
      API 2.3, 16
    definition of, 227
    invalidating to log out user, 335
    monitoring session attributes with a
      filter, 258–262
    monitoring session attributes with a
      listener, 254–258
    timeout, setting
      in all Tomcat web applications, 231
      in servlet code, 233–235
      in web.xml, 228–231
    tracking lifecycle with a listener, 251–254
    tracking session activity
      in JSPs, 240–244
      in servlets, 237–240
    tracking with URL rewriting
      in a JSP, 244–247
      in a servlet, 247–250
sessionScope implicit JSTL object,
    367, 370, 573
session-timeout element (web.xml), 232
sessionWillActivate( )
    (HttpSessionActicationListener),
      251
Set class, iterator( ), 172
setAttribute( )
    HttpSession class, 255
    ServletContext class, 357
setAutoCommit( ) (Connection), 505
setBufferSize( ) (ServletResponse), 201
setContent( ), 448
Set-Cookie response header, 226, 227
setFrom( ), 448
setKey( ) (GoogleSearch setKey), 670
setMaxAge( ) (Cookie), 217
    calling with argument value of zero, 225
setMaxInactiveInterval( ) (HttpSession), 233,
    234
setQuery( ), 670
setQueryString( ) (GoogleSearch), 670
setValue( ) (Cookie), 217

shell scripts
    for precompiling all JSP pages in
      application (on Unix), 103
    for precompiling JSP files (on Unix), 101
    Tomcat, shutting down, 18
show-props target (Ant), 79
Simple API for XML (SAX), 116
Simple Object Access Protocol (see SOAP)
simple tag handler, 519
    creating a TLD for, 539
    creating (JSP 2.0), 536–539
    using in a JSP, 541
SimpleLayout class, 298
    messages logged by root logger, 304
SimpleTag interface, 519, 536
SimpleTagSupport class, 536
    getJspBody( ), 539
    getJspContext( ), 538
SOAP (Simple Object Access Protocol), 664
    response from Amazon based on keyword
      search (example), 664
    web services based on, reasons to
      use, 665
socket connection with a database
    server, 567
Software Development Kit (SDK)
    Google Web APIs, 666
    PATH environment variable, 531
soundtrack, embedding in a JSP, 396–397
SQL PLUS database, addEvent stored
    procedure (example), 492
SQL (Structured Query Language)
    executing several statements in one
      transaction, 505–510
      servlet using transaction, 506–509
    JSTL SQL tags, 488, 551
      with DataSource
        configuration, 567–570
      SQL JSTL tag without DataSource
        configuration, 570–572
    stored procedures, 490–495
    transactions, using with JSPs, 511–513
sql:query tag, 512
    sending SQL SELECT statement to
      database, 569
sql:setDataSource tag, 571–572
sql:transaction tag, 511
sql:update tag, 512
src attribute (HTML script tag), importing
    JavaScript module into servlet, 267
src directory, 11

SSL (see Secure Sockets Layer)
start and stop tasks (Ant, build.xml file), 21
starting Tomcat from Ant, 93–95
StartTask task, 92
stateless Session bean (EJB), 639–641
   definition of, 638
static content
   mapping to a servlet, 55
   requests for, intercepted by controller
      servlet, 61
   server performance and, 122
static methods, Java method implementing
      EL function for JSP, 498
static page for multimedia content, 379
status codes, HTTP (see HTTP response
      codes)
status_code attribute, 204
stop and start tasks (Ant, build.xml file), 21
stopping a Tomcat application with
      Ant, 95–97
StopTask class, 95
Store class, 439, 449, 455
stored procedures
   calling from a JSP, 495–500
   calling from a servlet, 490–495
structureResults( ), 670, 680
stylesheets (XSL), integrating into JSPs, 562
Sun Microsystems
   Front Controller design pattern, 59
   JAAS documentation, 342
   JAR file specification, 89
   Java Development Kit (JDK), 11
   Java WSDP download site, 554
   online tutorials, 1
   sample applets, 380
   web services tutorial that includes
      XPath, 560
SVG file, embedding in a JSP, 394–396
.swf file extension, 386, 388
synchronizedMap( ) (Collections), 356

T

tag directive, 545
tag files, 519
   creating, 543–545
   custom tag associated with, using, 547
   packaging in a JAR, 546
   packaging in a web application, 545
tag handlers, 519
   classic, 519
      creating, 520–524
      creating JSP 1.2 TLD for, 524–526

package name for classes, 530
simple, 519
   creating, 536–539
   creating TLD for, 539
   using in a JSP, 541
tag library, 519
   listener class, adding to, 548
   packaging in a JAR file, 530
   packaging in a web application, 529
Tag Library Descriptor (TLD) files, 14, 30
   adding listener element to, 548
   configuring an EL function, 498
   creating for simple tag handler, 539
   creating JSP 1.2 TLD for classic tag
      handler, 524–526
   creating JSP 2.0 TLD for classic tag
      handler, 526–529
   custom logger tag, 313
   custom tag information, providing, 311
   definition of, 520
   for XML view custom tag, 113
   placing in tag library JAR's META-INF
      directory, 530
   specifying validator for, 111
   uri for tag library, 532
   XML DTD, use in JSP 1.2, 549
taglib directives, 8, 526
   for custom tag, identifying uri for tag
      library, 532
   for different JSTL 1.0 libraries, 553
   in included JSP segment, for use of c:out
      JSTL 1.0 tags, 139
   JSP segment containing (example), 131
   required for use of JSTL 1.0 core and SQL
      libraries, 568
   specifying core tag library from JSTL, 108
   uri and prefix values to use with functions
      library, 586
   uri attribute values in JSTL 1.1, 553
taglib element
   version attribute, 529
   xmlns attribute, 528
   xmlns:xsi attribute, 529
   xsi:schemaLocation attribute, 529
TagLibraryValidator class, 99
   using XML view to validate custom tags in
      JSP page, 110
tags
   custom
      (see also custom tags)
      custom tags in JSPs, 7
      definition of, 519

including tag libraries as namespace
    attributes in JSP documents, 109
prebuilt for JSPs (JSTL), xv
TagSupport class, 111
target elements (Ant), grouping of tasks
    in, 77
targets (Ant), 76–79
    in build.xml, displaying names of, 560
taskdef element (Ant, build file), 21
    start task, defining, 93
    stop task, defining, 96
tasks (Ant), 76
    filesets, 81
    group of, represented by target
        element, 77
    property task, 79
text files, JSPs written as, 7
thread name in logging messages, 303
Throwable class, 195
Throwable objects
    accessing in JSP error page, 208
    associated with exceptions,
        accessing, 196
thrown exceptions, information about in JSP
    error page, 203, 204
timeout for sessions
    setting in all Tomcat web
        applications, 231
    setting in servlet code, 233–235
    setting in web.xml, 228–231
timeStyle attribute (fmt:formatDate), 566
TimeZone IDs, helper class to display, 555
tld file extension, 526
TLD (see Tag Library Descriptor files)
Tomcat, xiv
    compiling servlet on, 10
    configuring DataSource to use in
        servlet, 475
    context element (conf/server.xml), for JSP
        content imported from outside
        context, 145
    creating usernames and passwords, 324
    DataSource, using in a servlet, 478–481
    deploying individual JSP on, 29
    deploying individual servlet on, 17–22
        Ant tool, using, 18–22
        steps in process, 18
    deploying servlet as part of Context
        element in server.xml, 22
    deploying web application on, 31–37
        Ant build file, using, 31–36

pointing to external directory
    containing web application, 36
error page displayed by error handling
    servlet, 198
implicit mapping to its JSP compiler and
    execution servlet for .jsp
    requests, 55
including JAR files in Ant build file
    classpath, 80–83
initial context of built-in JNDI
    implementation, 615
invoker servlet, 57
    commenting out, 58
Jasper (JSP container), 111
JNDI object, configuring, 616–618
JNDI resource
    accessing from a JSP, 625–628
    accessing from a servlet, 619–624
JSP page implementation class,
    viewing, 98
JSTL 1.1 features, using with Version
    5, 554
log files, 299
precompiling JSPs in, 99
security-constraint element in web.xml,
    using, 67
session timeout, setting for all web
    applications, 231
SSL, setting up, 325
starting web application with Ant, 92–95
stopping web application with
    Ant, 95–97
tomcat-users.xml file, 67
    example of a typical file, 73
    manager role, user mapping to, 93
    nullroll security role, preventing user
        mapping to, 73
    user mapping to security roles, 70
    usernames and passwords, case-sensitivity
        of, 328
    usernames, passwords, and roles for
        authentication, 325
toResult( ) (ResultSupport), 500, 503
ToXmlValidator class, 113
transactions
    creating with Connection methods, 505
    executing several SQL statements in single
        transaction, 505–510
        servlet that uses transaction, 506–509
    isolation levels, 509
    using with JSPs, 511–513

transforming XML, using JSTL XML and
    XSLT-related tags, 561–563
translation phase (for JSPs), 8, 98
    including JSP segment into JSP page, 131
Transport class, send( ), 444, 462
try/catch block, for exceptions thrown during
    include operations, 128
TryCatchFinally interface, 533
t:toxml element, 112
tutorials, online (Sun Microsystems), 1

U

unbinding session objects, listening for, 255
undeploy target (Ant, build.xml file), 35
Unix
    keytool utility, creating digital certificate
        with, 326
    shell script for precompiling all JSP pages
        in application, 103
    shell script for precompiling JSP files, 101
Unix-based Mac OS X 10.2 system, PATH
    variable for javac, 11
UPDATE statement (SQL), 510
uploading files
    com.oreilly.servlet classes for file
        uploads, 177
    JSP, handling with, 187–191
        file uploading JavaBean,
            creating, 187–189
        JSP that uploads and displays
            information about, 189–191
    multiple file uploads, 177, 181–185
    preparing HTML page for, 175–180
        component to receive file upload and
            store in local directory, 178–180
    renaming uploaded files, 185–187
        with your own Java class, 186
uri attribute (taglib directive), 532
    JSTL 1.1, different values in, 553
URIs
    mapping uri elements in TLD as specified
        by taglib directive in JSP files, 526
    request, use by JSP error page, 203
url custom action, 244–247
    adding parameters with, 246
    encodeURL( ) vs., 249
    rewriting URLs with, 245
URL patterns, 50
    aiming all requests at a controller
        servlet, 59
    exact matching requirement for, 53
    *.jsp is an extension mapping, 416

JSP-type, creating for a servlet, 54
restricting any requests from reaching, 71
specified by security-constraint
    elements, 62
/sqlJsp.jsp, initiation of BASIC
    authentication for, 329
URL rewriting, 210, 228
    using in a JSP, 244–247
    using in a servlet, 247–250
URLConnection class, 283
url-pattern element (web.xml), 51
    * wildcard character in, 54
    case sensitivity of, 52
    mapping all requests from web
        application to a servlet, 59
    mapping filter to a JSP, 415
URLs
    connection to, opening, 292
    external importing into JSP with c:import
        tag, 145
    initiating Amazon search with, 687
    invoker-style, for servlets, 57
    specifying a directory only, 65
    for static content, mapping to a
        servlet, 55
user classpath, 75
user roles (see roles)
User-Agent header, 398
users
    manager role (Tomcat), 93
    tomcat-users.xml file, 67
        mapping to security roles, 70
        usernames, passwords, and roles
            in, 325

V

valid partial requests, 65
ValidateHandler class, 116
validating
    custom tags in JSP pages, 111–117
    form input, 152
        filter, using for, 429–434
        JavaBean, using, 158–161
        JavaScript, using in a JSP, 268, 277
        JavaScript, using in a servlet, 265,
            274–276
    XML documents, specifying validator for
        TLD file, 111
var attribute (c:forEach tag), 557
variable directive, 545
variables (scoped), accessing with EL, 367,
    572

variant (in locales), 590
version attribute
    cookies, 210
    taglib element, 529
viewer applications for SVG, 394
viewing internal resources in a
    servlet, 292–295

W

war task (Ant), 77, 86
    classes, lib, and fileset (nested)
        elements, 88
    destfile and webxml attributes, 88
WAR (Web ARchive) files, xiv
    creating with Ant, 86–89
    deploying web application as, using
        WebLogic Administration
        Console, 40
    finding out if already deployed on
        Tomcat, 35
    for servlets and JSPs, 11
    generating with Ant war task, 35
    opeining in WebLogic Builder to edit
        web.xml file, 44
    viewing contents of, 13
WARN level logging, 297
web applications
    configuring log4j mechanism, 322
    counting number of requests for, 408
    creating welcome files for, 65
    definition of, 2
    deploying on Tomcat, 31–37
        Ant build file, using, 31–36
        configuring Tomcat to point to
            application in external
            directory, 36
    deploying on WebLogic
        using Ant tool, 37
        using WebLogic Administration
            Console, 39–42
        using WebLogic Builder, 43–45
        using weblogic.Deployer
            command-line utility, 46–48
    deployment descriptor, creating
        for, 14–16
    directory structure (see directory structure
        of web applications)
    Java-based, xvi
    mapping all requests to controller
        servlet, 59–61
    packaging JSP tag file in, 545
    packaging tag library in, 529

servlet context instance, 317
servlet, writing for, 1–7
    starting on Tomcat using Ant file, 92–95
    stopping on Tomcat using Ant file, 95–97
    WAR files (see WAR files)
web browsers (see browsers)
web components, 2
web containers, 2
    exception handling in, 195
    (see also Tomcat)
web developer tasks, recipes in this book, xiv
    implementation with BEA WebLogic, xv
web directory, inclusion of nested directories
        in WAR file with Ant war task, 35
web page for this book, xix
web services, 664
    Amazon and Google, 666
    Amazon, setting up, 677–679
    Google Web API, setting up, 666
    SOAP, using for information transfer, 664
    SOAP-based, reasons to adopt, 665
    (see also Amazon Web Services; Google
        Web Services)
web-app element (web.xml), 16
    required attributes of servlet 2.4
        deployment descriptor, 587
webapps folder (Tomcat), 32
WEB-INF directory, 3, 12
    contents of, 30
WEB-INF/jspf (optional directory), 14
WEB-INF/tlds (optional directory), 14
WebLogic, xiv
    creating DataSource on, 481–484
        configuration, steps in, 482
    JNDI lookup, using to access
        DataSource, 484
    JNDI resource
        accessing from a JSP, 635–638
        accessing from a servlet, 631–634
        configuring in, 628
    JNDI tree
        accessing an EJB with, 638–646
        viewing, 630
    precompiling JSPs in, 102–104
    recipes for common tasks, xv
    servlet classes and javax subpackages, 10
WebLogic Server 7.0
    deploying individual JSP on, 30
    deploying individual servlet on, 24–29
        Ant file, using, 26–29
        editing web.xml to register servlet, 24
        redeploying web application, 26

WebLogic Server 7.0 (*continued*)
    deploying web application on
        using Ant tool, 37
        using WebLogic Administration
            Console, 39–42
        using WebLogic Builder, 43–45
        using weblogic.Deployer
            command-line utility, 46–48
    security configuration in
        weblogic.xml, 70
weblogic.Deployer command-line
    utility, 46–48
weblogic-ejb-jar.xml file, 642
weblogic.jspc utility, 102–104
weblogic.xml file, security configuration
    in, 70
web-resource-collection elements
    (web.xml), 68
    protected resources in security-constraint
        element, 69
    specifying security restraints, 329
webxml attribute (Ant war task), 88
web.xml file, 30
    BASIC authentication, initiating with JSP
        file, 329
    contents of, 14
    context parameter save-dir element, 190
    context-param element, adding for
        included file in a JSP, 140
    creating multiple mappings to a
        servlet, 52
    creating with JspC utility, 100
    DataSource, configuring in, 511
    declaring exception handlers in, 192–195
    editing for WebLogic to register a
        servlet, 24
    error-page attribute, mapping exception
        types to a JSP, 203
    error-page configuration, 128
    filters
        configuring in, 258
        mapped to the servlet path
            (example), 412
        mapping of, 404
        mapping to a JSP, 415
    form-based authentication, setting
        up, 331
    form-checking filter registered and
        mapped in, 433
    IOExceptions, element for managing, 178
    IP blocking filter, mapping of, 437

jsp-property-group element, 99, 107
JSP-type URL for a servlet, 54
listener element, 548
listeners
    configuration in servlet API 2.3, 16
    for servlet requests, registering, 410
    (see also listeners)
mapping all references to JSP pages to a
    single servlet, 55
mapping servlet to a name, 50–52
preventing requests to non-controller
    servlets, 61
resource-ref element, 476
restricting requests for certain servlets, 66
servlet API 2.3, 15
    converting to 2.4 for JSTL 1.1
        features, 586
servlet API 2.4, 15
    use with Tomcat 5 and JSTL 1.1, 554
servlet element with load-on-startup
    nested element, 319
servlet that creates pop-up window, 271
servlets without a mapping in, 57
session timeout for all Tomcat web
    applications, 232
session timeout, setting, 228–231
viewing with a servlet, 292–295
(see also servlet-mapping elements)
welcome files for a web application, 65
welcome-file-list element (web.xml), 65
wildcards in URL patterns, 53
    overriding with specific mappings, 60
windoid, 269
windows, browser (see browser windows,
    creating with JavaScript)
Windows systems
    launching WebLogic Builder, 44
    local variant for, 590
    PATH environment variable for javac
        compiler (on NT), 11
    precompiling all JSP pages in application
        with weblogic.jspc, 103
    shell script for running JspC, 100
wl.applications property (Ant,
    build.properties file), 38
WLCLASSPATH environment variable, 102
wl.properties file (for WebLogic Ant build
    file), 28
word processing files, sending, 284–286
WSDP (Web Services Developer Pack), 554

X

Xerces2 XML parser, 75
x:forEach tag, 551, 560
x:if tag, 560
XML
    Ant build file, 77
    creating JSP document as XML
        file, 106–110
    including XML fragment in a JSP
        document, 141–144
    JSP document vs. XML view, 110
    JSPs as XML files, 8, 99
        XML equivalents of JSP directives, 106
    JSTL XML and XSLT tags, using in a
        JSP, 561–563
    JSTL XML core tags, using in a
        JSP, 558–561
    sending XML file as binary data, 286–289
    SOAP messages on HTTP, 664
    TLD (Tag Library Descriptor) files, 520
    transforming (x:transform), 551
    web services, 664
XML elements
    Ant tasks, 76
    case-sensitivity in element and attribute
        names, 519
    custom tags used in JSP, 310
    namespace, definition of, 529
    namespace for elements related to XML
        Schema instances, 529
    path element, defining Ant classpath, 80

XML parsers, JAXP-compliant, 75
XML Schema instances, 529
XML Schemas
    for JSP 2.0 TLD, 528
    in servlet API 2.4 web.xml file, 15
XML view, 99
    automatically generating for JSP
        page, 111
    generating from a JSP page, 110–118
    JSP XML document vs., 110
xmlns attribute (taglib element), 528
xmlns:xsi attribute (taglib element), 529
x:out tag, 551
x:parse tag, 560
XPath, 560
xsi:schemaLocation attribute (taglib
    element), 529
XSL (Extensible Stylesheet Language), 562
XSLT, converting XML to readable
    format, 287
x:transform tag, 551
    associating a stylesheet with an XML
        file, 563
    xml attribute, 563
    xslt attribute, 563

About the Author

Bruce W. Perry is an independent software developer and writer. Since 1996, he has developed web applications and databases for various nonprofit organizations, design and marketing firms, and advertising agencies. When not writing or working on software, he loves cycling and hiking in the United States and Switzerland. Perry will finish up a Masters of Software Engineering at Brandeis University in the spring of 2004. He lives in the Newburyport, Massachusetts area with his wife Stacy LeBaron and two children, Rachel and Scott.

Colophon

Our look is the result of reader comments, our own experimentation, and feedback from distribution channels. Distinctive covers complement our distinctive approach to technical topics, breathing personality and life into potentially dry subjects.

The animal on the cover of *Java Servlet and JSP Cookbook* is a fennec fox (*Fennecus zerda*), also known as the desert fox. Fennes foxes live in arid sandy regions of northern Africa, the Sahara, the Sinai Peninsula and Arabia and are one of the tiniest members of the canine family (eight inches at the tallest and usually less than a foot long). Their relatively huge ears and beady black eyes give them a distinctive appearance. The fennec fox's bushy tail is characteristic of most foxes, and a thick creamy coat camouflages them in their sandy habitat.

Fennec foxes live in burrows and are nocturnal hunters, eating plants, small rodents, birds and their eggs, lizards, and insects. Their hearing is so acute that they can hear even the smallest of prey walking across desert sand. These foxes often stalk their prey and pounce upon it; their vertical leap is two feet high and they can jump four feet horizontally from a standing position, astounding feats for an animal of such small stature. They are rapid and prolific diggers, known for "disappearing" into sand while appearing to stand still. Some reports note that this species can dig a 20-foot-long tunnel in one night!

The fennec fox is not listed as endangered, but is now considered rare in some areas where it was once common. They have been hunted extensively and are sometimes taken from the wild for the pet trade.

Philip Dangler was the production editor and copyeditor for *Java Servlet and JSP Cookbook*. Sarah Sherman and Matt Hutchinson were the proofreaders. Reg Aubry and Mary Anne Weeks Mayo provided quality control. Ellen Troutman Zaig wrote the index.

Emma Colby designed the cover of this book, based on a series design by Edie Freedman. The cover image is a 19th-century engraving from *Animate Creations, Volume One*. Emma Colby produced the cover layout with QuarkXPress 4.1 using Adobe's ITC Garamond font.

Melanie Wang designed the interior layout, based on a series design by David Futato. This book was converted Julie Hawks to FrameMaker 5.5.6 with a format conversion tool created by Erik Ray, Jason McIntosh, Neil Walls, and Mike Sierra that uses Perl and XML technologies. The text font is Linotype Birka, the heading font is Adobe Myriad Condensed, and the code font is LucasFont's TheSans Mono Condensed. The illustrations that appear in the book were produced by Robert Romano and Jessamyn Read using Macromedia FreeHand 9 and Adobe Photoshop 6. The tip and warning icons were drawn by Christopher Bing. This colophon was written by Philip Dangler.

Related Titles Available from O'Reilly

Java

Ant: The Definitive Guide
Enterprise JavaBeans, *3rd Edition*
Head First Java
Head First EJB
J2EE Design Patterns
J2ME in a Nutshell
Java and SOAP
Java & XML Data Binding
Java & XML
Java Cookbook
Java Data Objects
Java Database Best Practices
Java Enterprise Best Practices
Java Enterprise in a Nutshell, *2nd Edition*
Java Examples in a Nutshell, *2nd Edition*
Java Extreme Programming Cookbook
Java in a Nutshell, *4th Edition*
Java Management Extensions
Java Message Service
Java Network Programming, *2nd Edition*
Java NIO
Java Performance Tuning, *2nd Edition*
Java RMI
Java Security, *2nd Edition*
Java ServerPages, *2nd Edition*
Java Servlet Programming, *2nd Edition*
Java Swing, *2nd Edition*
Java Web Services in a Nutshell
JXTA in a Nutshell
Learning Java, *2nd Edition*
Mac OS X for Java Geeks
NetBeans: The Definitive Guide
Programming Jakarta Struts
Tomcat: The Definitive Guide

O'REILLY®

Our books are available at most retail and online bookstores.
To order direct: 1-800-998-9938 • *order@oreilly.com* • *www.oreilly.com*
Online editions of most O'Reilly titles are available by subscription at *safari.oreilly.com*

Keep in touch with O'Reilly

1. Download examples from our books

To find example files for a book, go to:

www.oreilly.com/catalog

select the book, and follow the "Examples" link.

2. Register your O'Reilly books

Register your book at *register.oreilly.com*

Why register your books?
Once you've registered your O'Reilly books you can:

- Win O'Reilly books, T-shirts or discount coupons in our monthly drawing.
- Get special offers available only to registered O'Reilly customers.
- Get catalogs announcing new books (US and UK only).
- Get email notification of new editions of the O'Reilly books you own.

3. Join our email lists

Sign up to get topic-specific email announcements of new books and conferences, special offers, and O'Reilly Network technology newsletters at:

elists.oreilly.com

It's easy to customize your free elists subscription so you'll get exactly the O'Reilly news you want.

4. Get the latest news, tips, and tools

www.oreilly.com

- "Top 100 Sites on the Web"—PC Magazine
- CIO Magazine's Web Business 50 Awards

Our web site contains a library of comprehensive product information (including book excerpts and tables of contents), downloadable software, background articles, interviews with technology leaders, links to relevant sites, book cover art, and more.

5. Work for O'Reilly

Check out our web site for current employment opportunities:

jobs.oreilly.com

6. Contact us

O'Reilly & Associates, Inc.
1005 Gravenstein Hwy North
Sebastopol, CA 95472 USA

TEL: 707-827-7000 or 800-998-9938
      (6am to 5pm PST)

FAX: 707-829-0104

order@oreilly.com
For answers to problems regarding your order or our products. To place a book order online, visit:

www.oreilly.com/order_new

catalog@oreilly.com
To request a copy of our latest catalog.

booktech@oreilly.com
For book content technical questions or corrections.

corporate@oreilly.com
For educational, library, government, and corporate sales.

proposals@oreilly.com
To submit new book proposals to our editors and product managers.

international@oreilly.com
For information about our international distributors or translation queries. For a list of our distributors outside of North America check out:

international.oreilly.com/distributors.html

adoption@oreilly.com
For information about academic use of O'Reilly books, visit:

academic.oreilly.com